FREEWAY

MARK KALESNIKO

This book is dedicated to my mother and father, Roberta and Gaston Kalesniko, who encouraged me to draw when I was young and continued to encourage me to dream when I got older. With all my love.

— —

FANTAGRAPHICS BOOKS
7563 Lake City Way NE
Seattle WA 98115

Edited by GARY GROTH
Designed by MARK KALESNIKO
Chinese language translation by JENNIFER YUAN
Production by PAUL BARESH and ALEXA KOENINGS
ERIC REYNOLDS, Associate Publisher
GARY GROTH and KIM THOMPSON, publishers

Photos from the Photo Collection/Los Angeles Public Library used for reference by permission of the Los Angeles Public Library.

"Angels Flight" and the images of the Angels Flight Railway and cars are trademarks of the Angels Flight Railway Company and are used with permission.

Images of California Plaza and the Watercourt are used with permission.

This book is a work of fiction. Characters and institutions are the product of the author's imagination and any resemblance to actual persons, living or dead, or business establishments is entirely coincidental.

To receive a free catalog of comics, including Mark Kalesniko's earlier books *Alex* and *Mail Order Bride*, call 1-800-657-1100 or write us at Fantagraphics Books, 7563 Lake City Way NE, Seattle, WA 98115; you can also visit the Fantagraphics website at www.fantagraphics.com.

Visit www.markkalesniko.com

Distributed in the U.S. by W.W. Norton and Company, Inc.
(800-233-4830)
Distributed in Canada by Canadian Manda Group
(800-452-6642 x862)
Distributed in the United Kingdom by Turnaround Distribution
(44 (0)20 8829-3002)
Distributed to comics shops in the U.S. by Diamond Comic Distributors
(800-452-6642 x215).

First edition: January, 2011

ISBN: 978-1-60699-356-9

Printed in China

CHAPTER 1

SENTIMENTAL JOURNEY

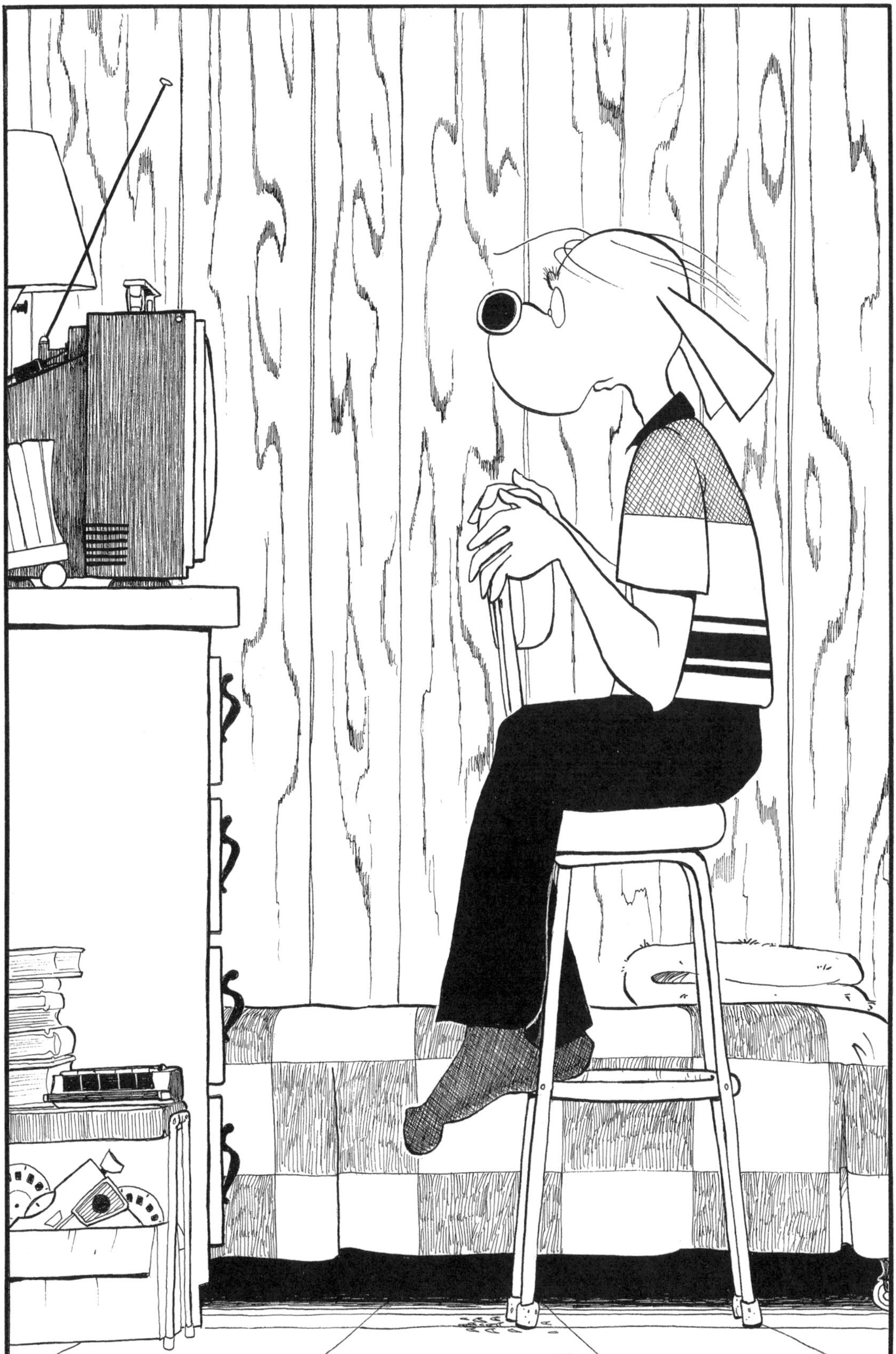

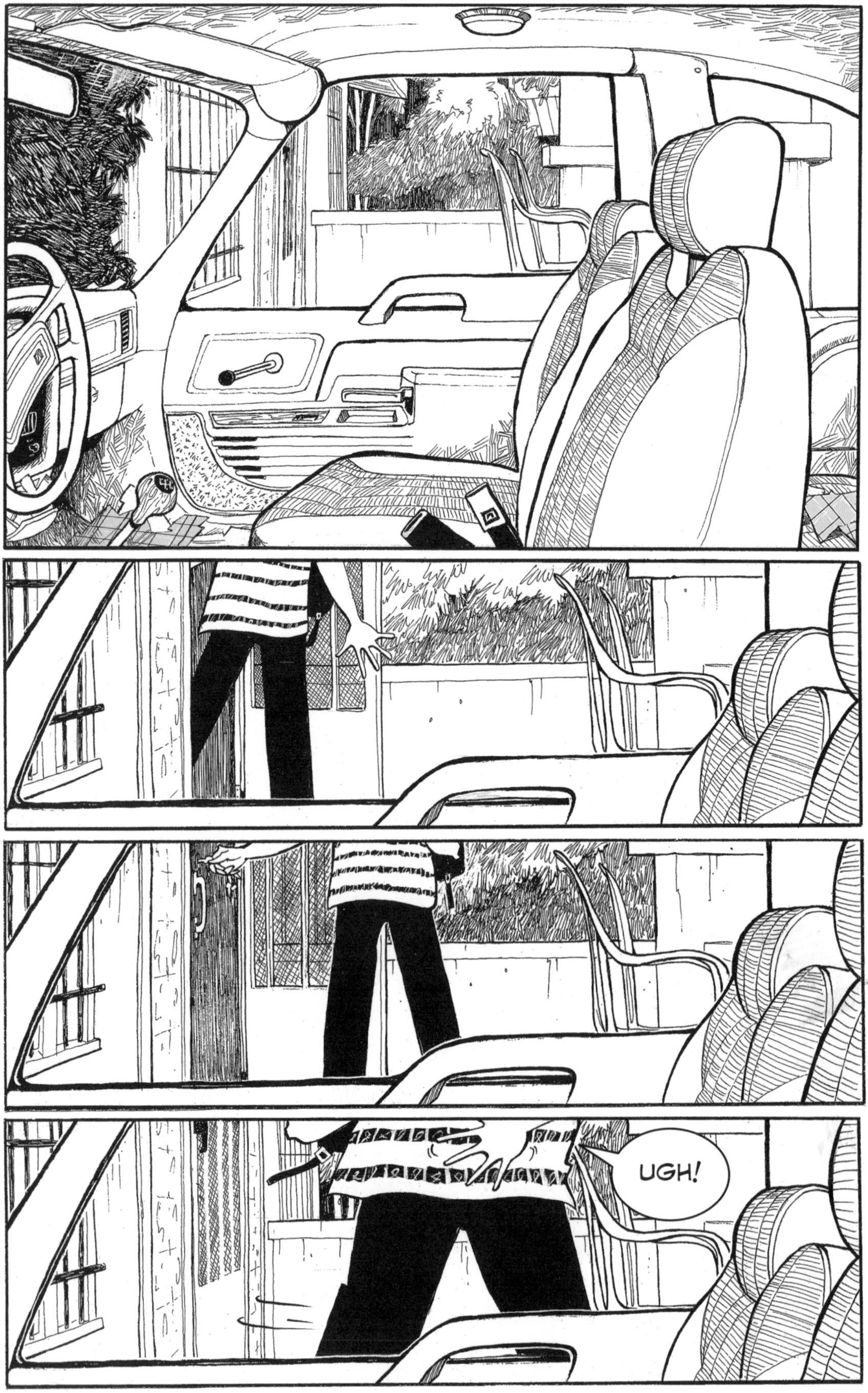
UGH!

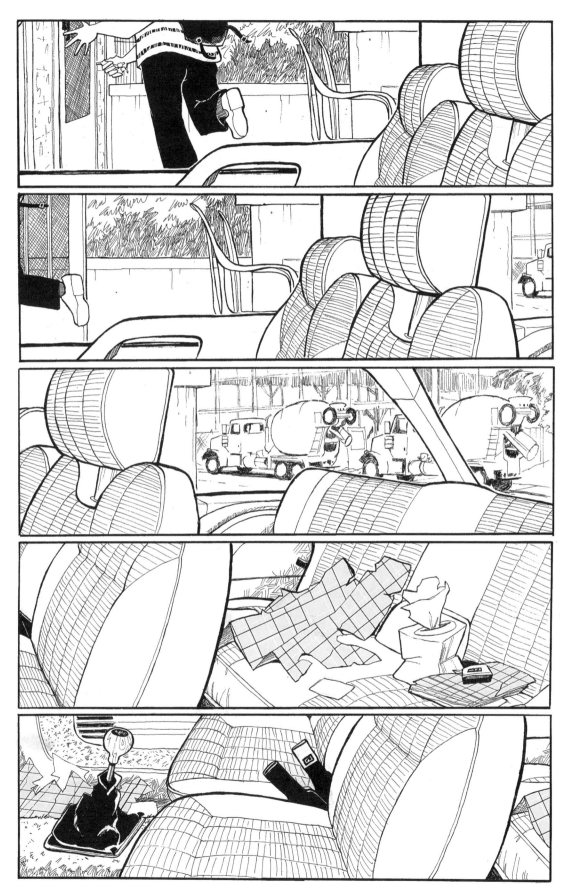

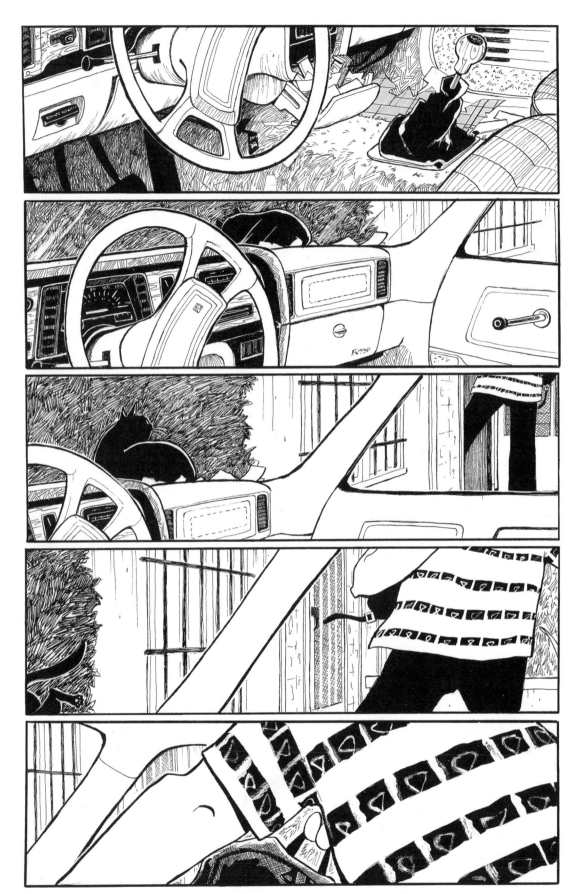

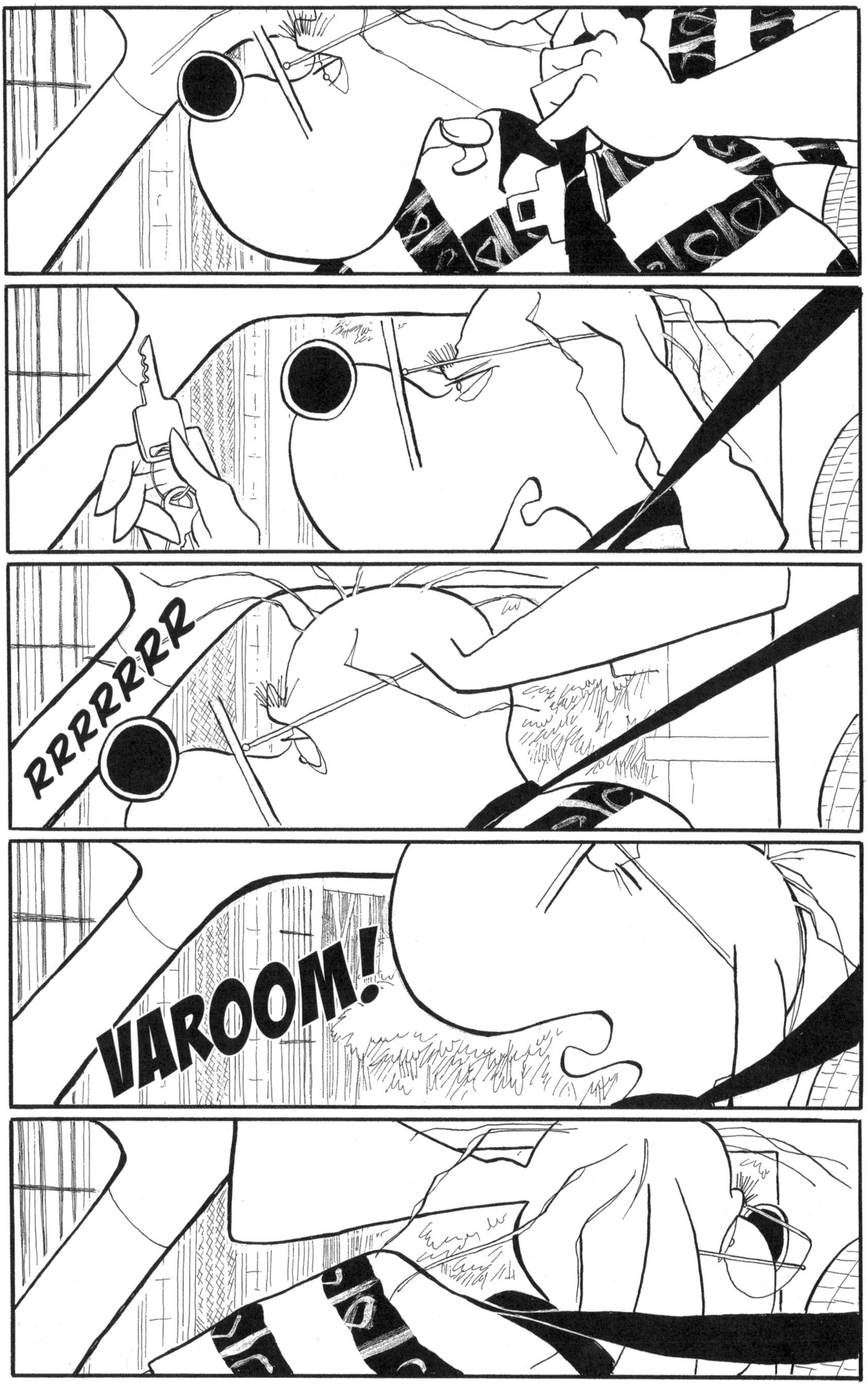
RRRRRRR
VAROOM!

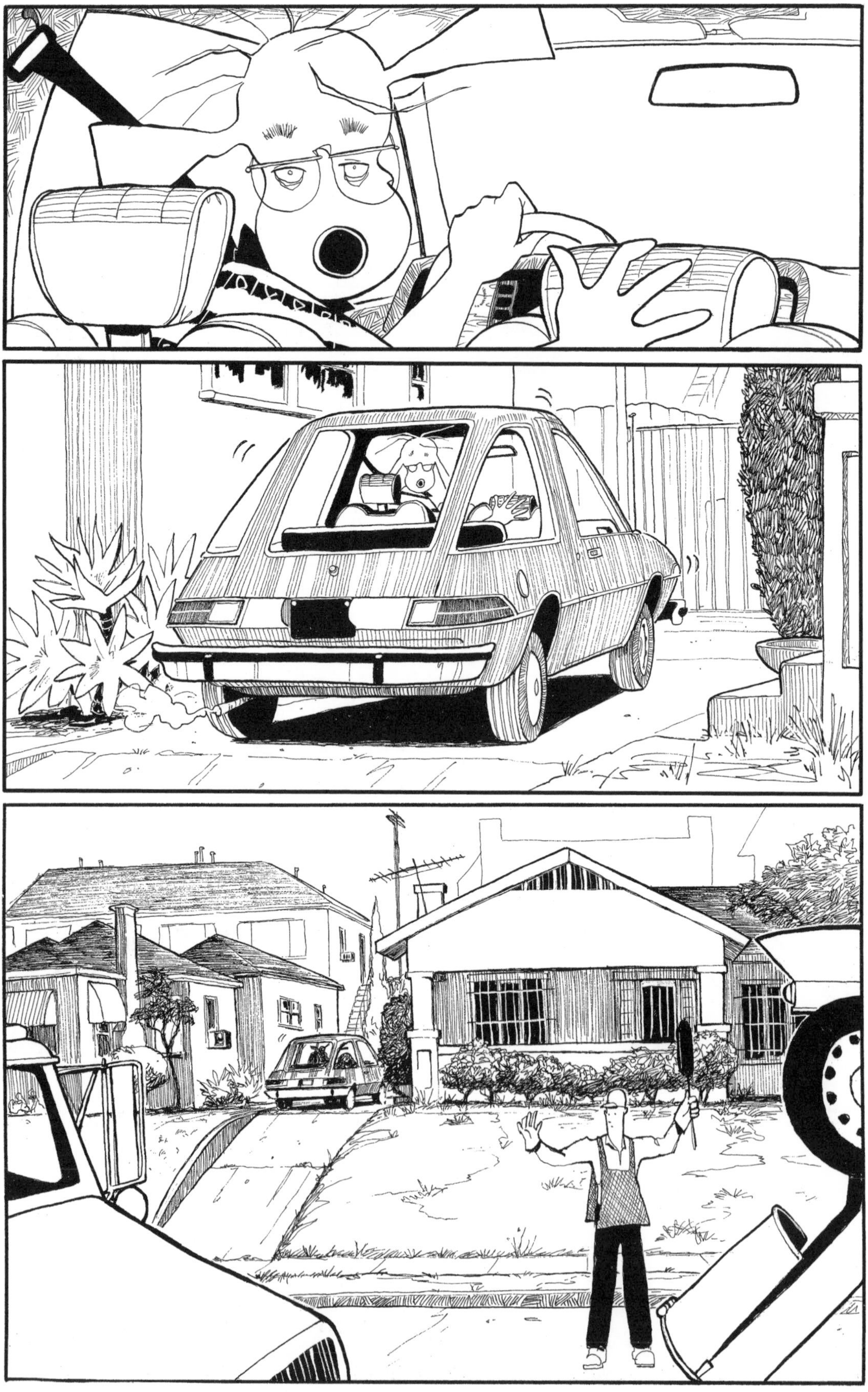

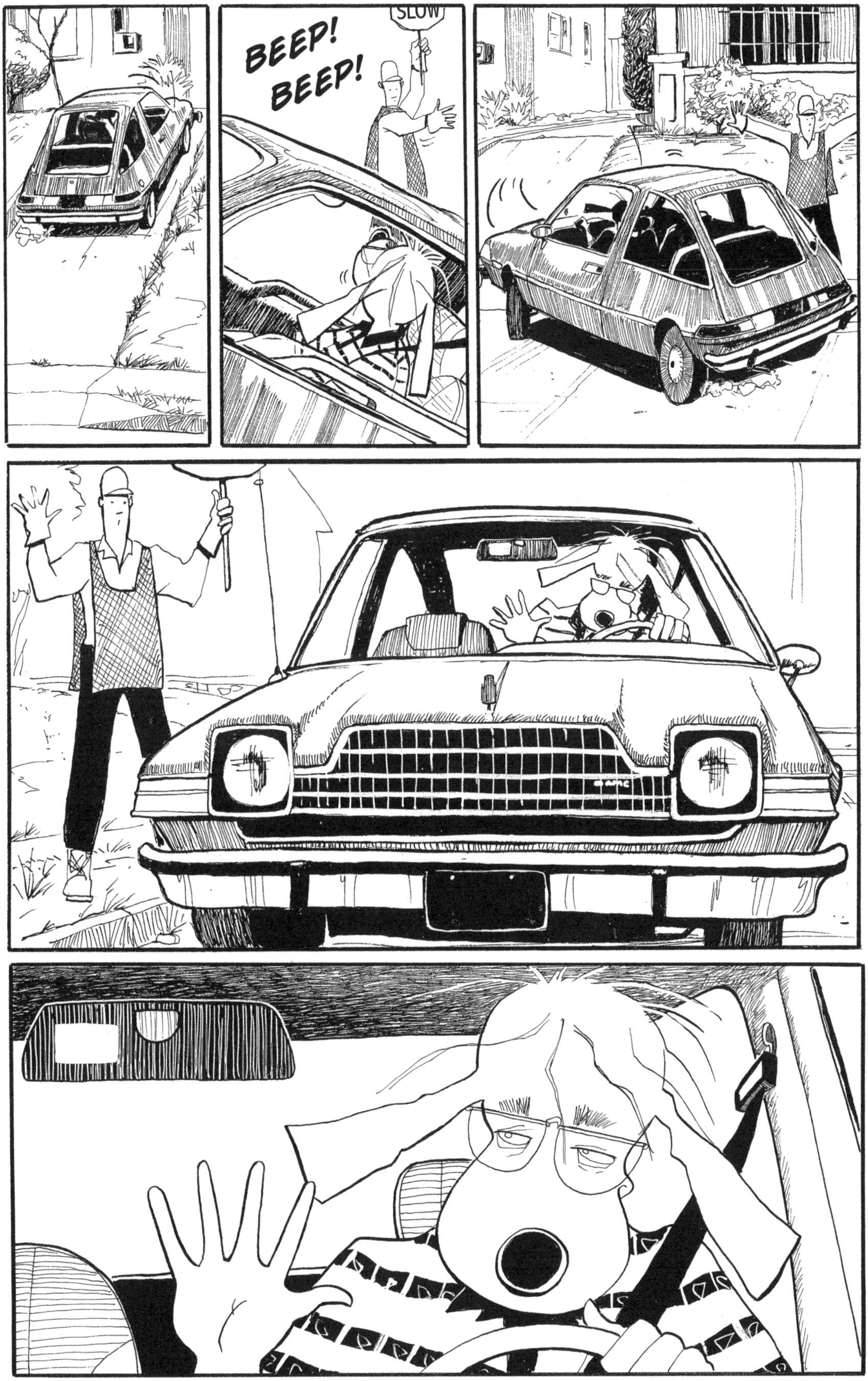
SLOW
BEEP! BEEP!

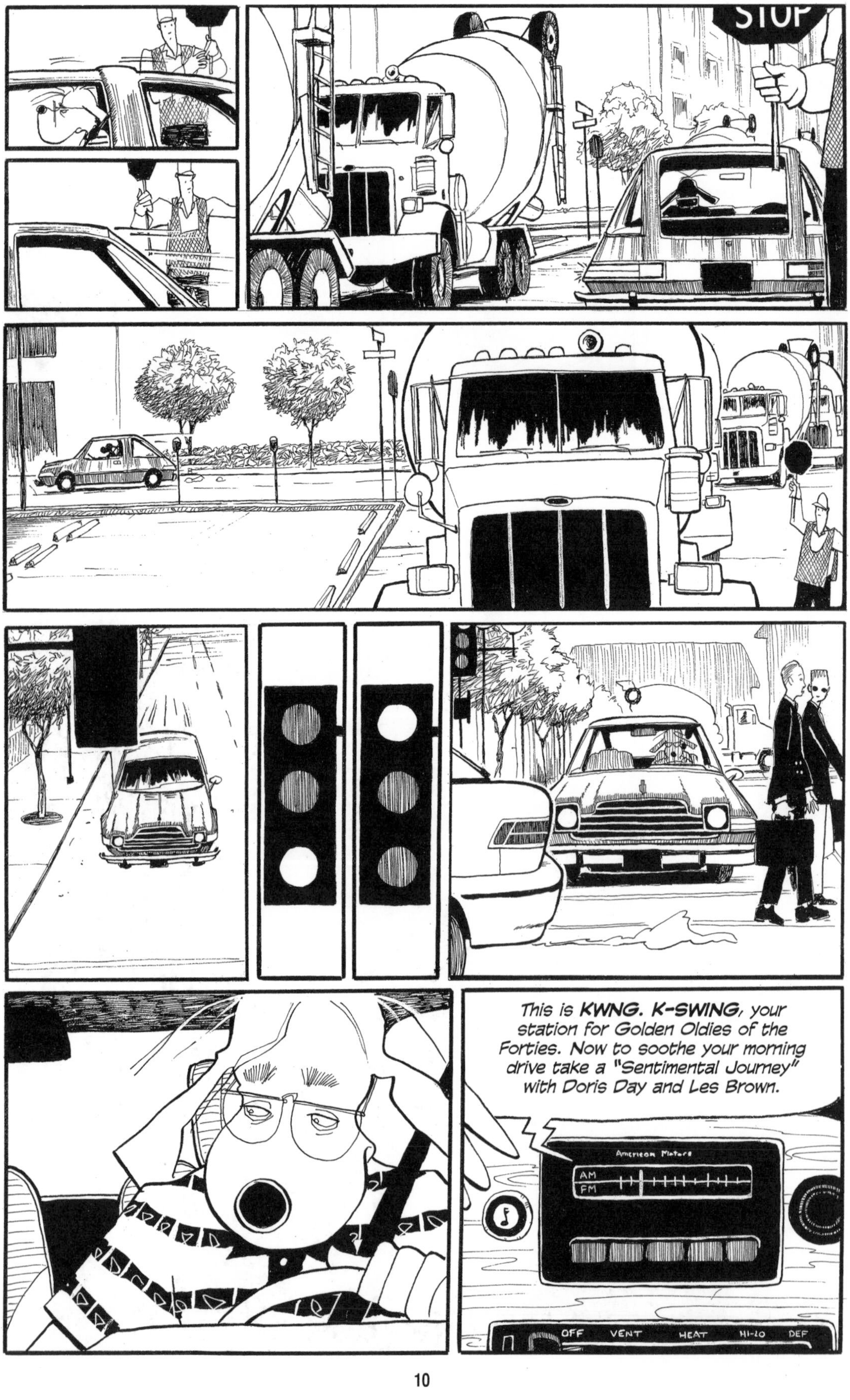
STOP
This is KWNG. K-SWING, your station for Golden Oldies of the Forties. Now to soothe your morning drive take a "Sentimental Journey" with Doris Day and Les Brown.
American Motors
AM
FM
OFF VENT HEAT HI-LO DEF

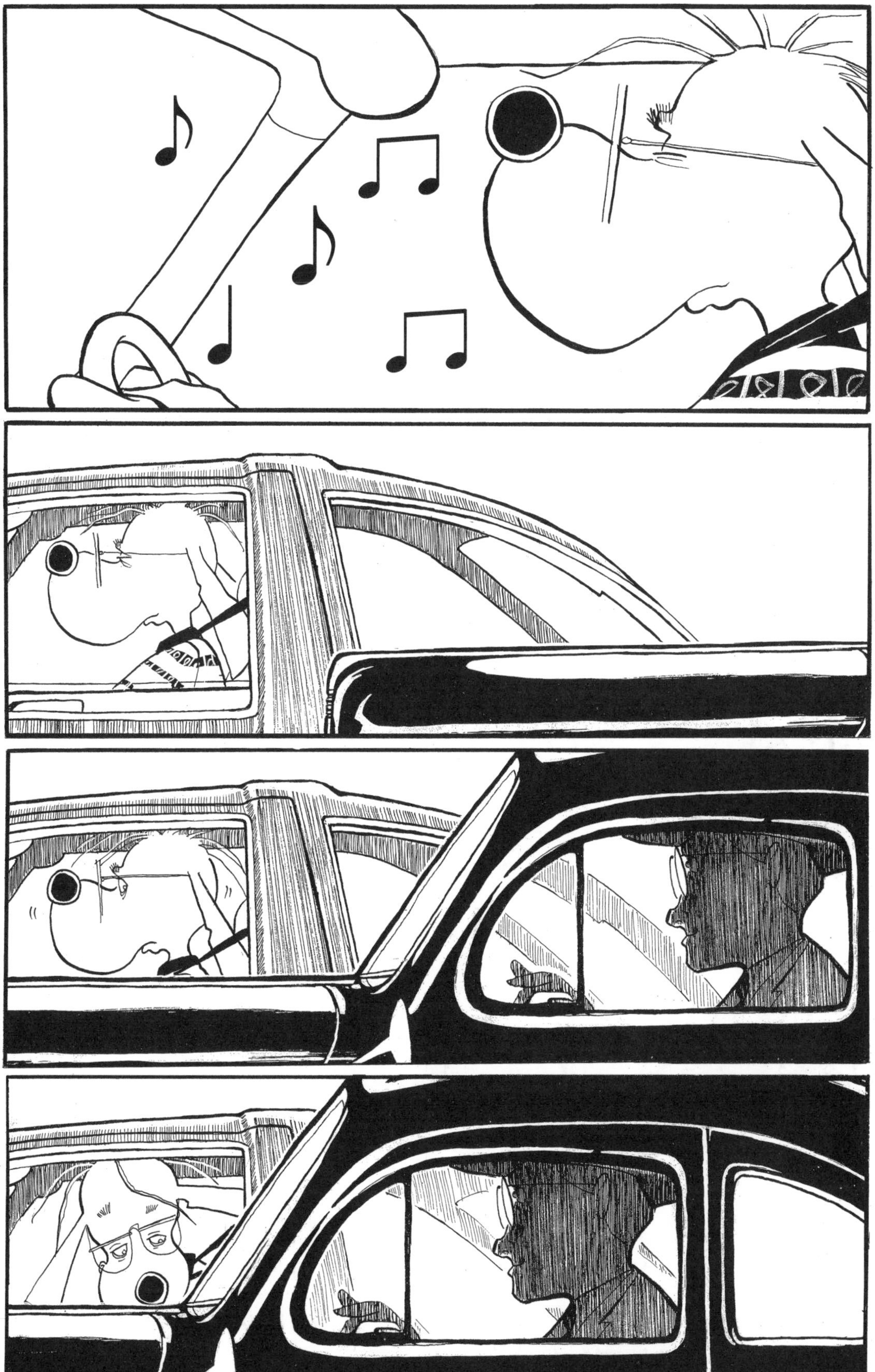

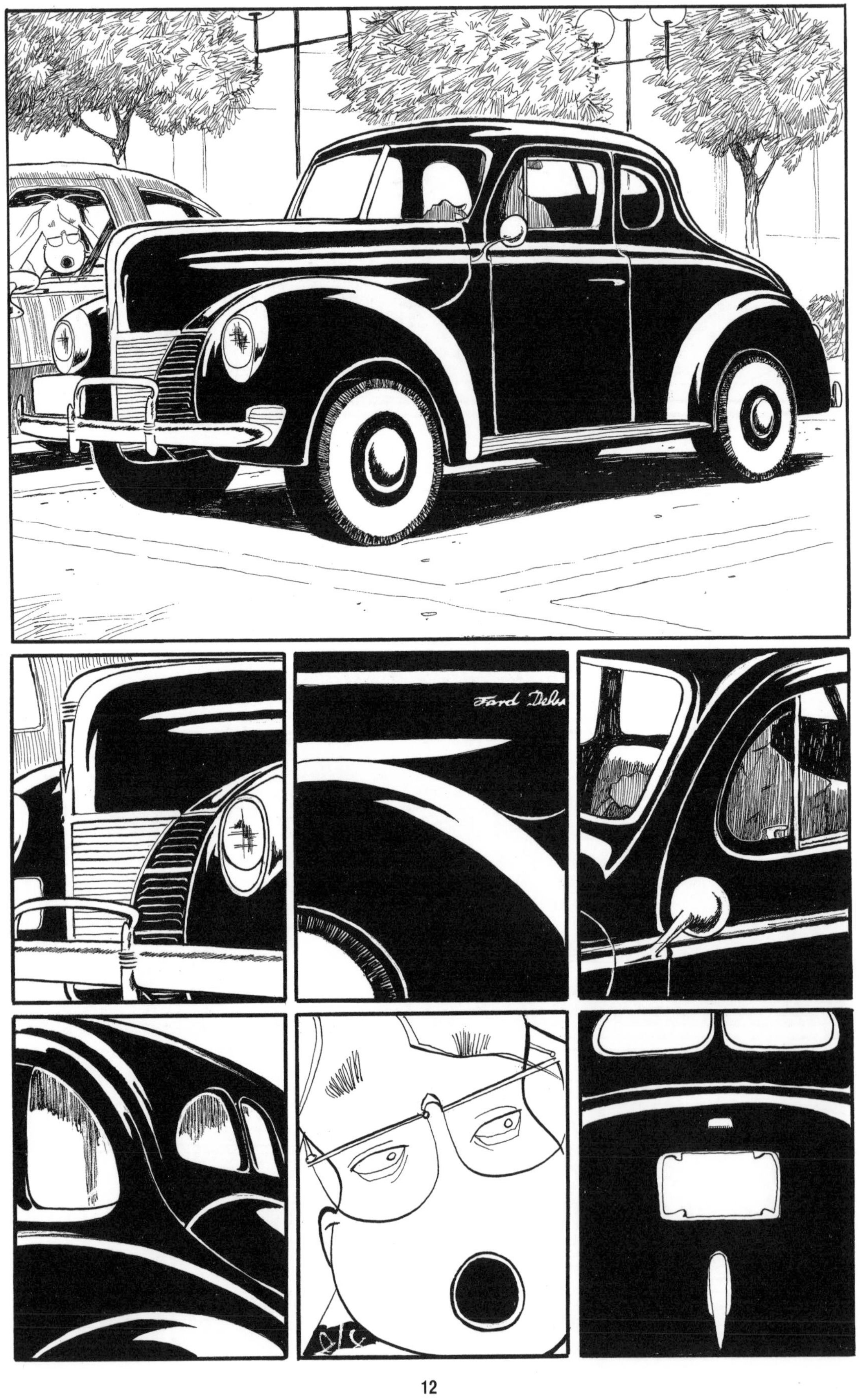

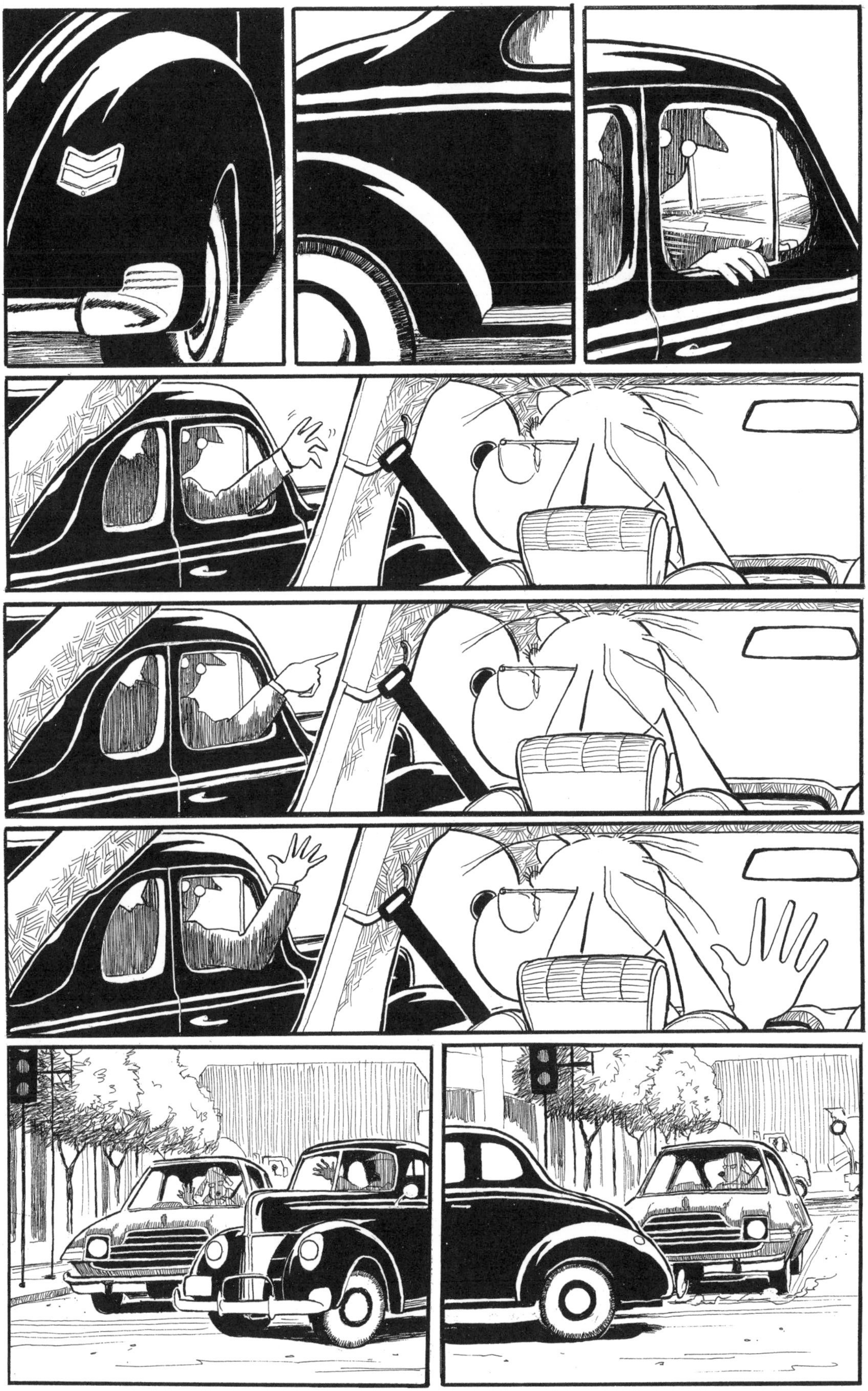

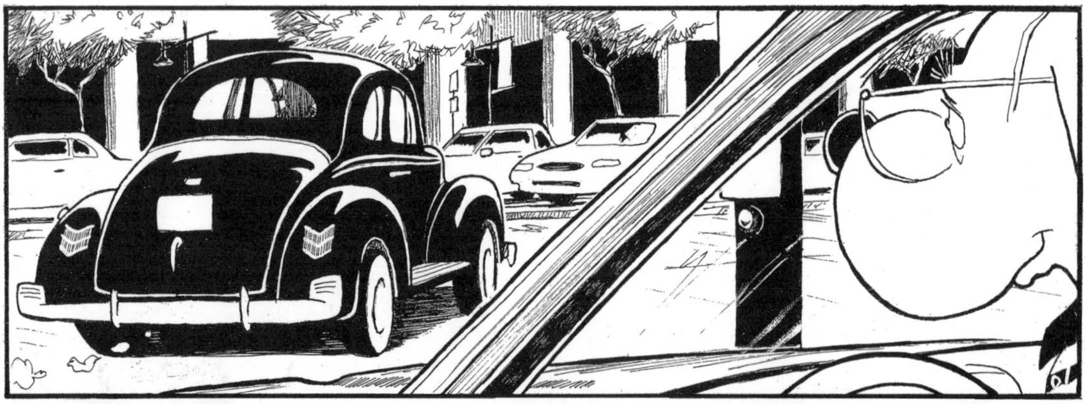

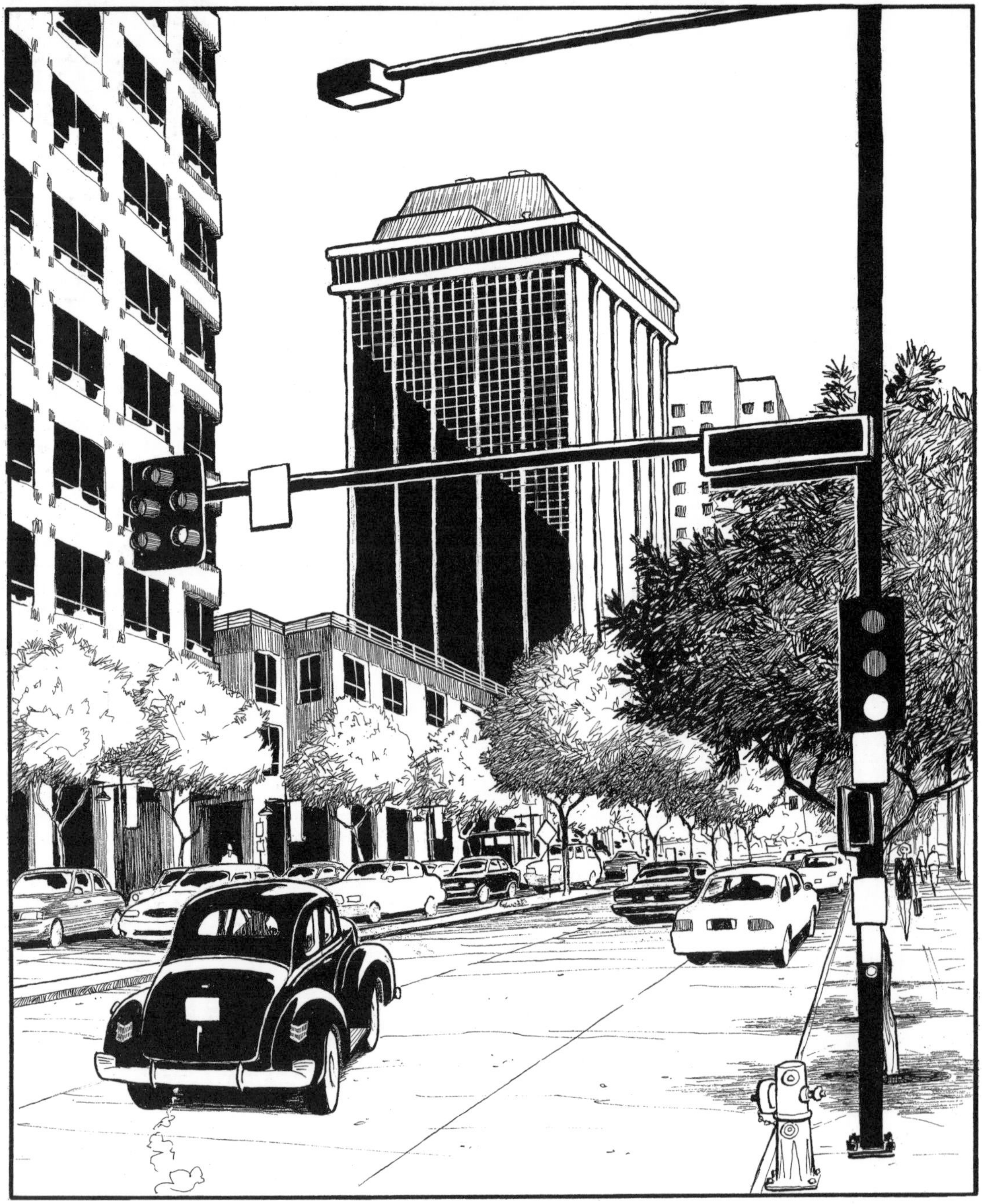

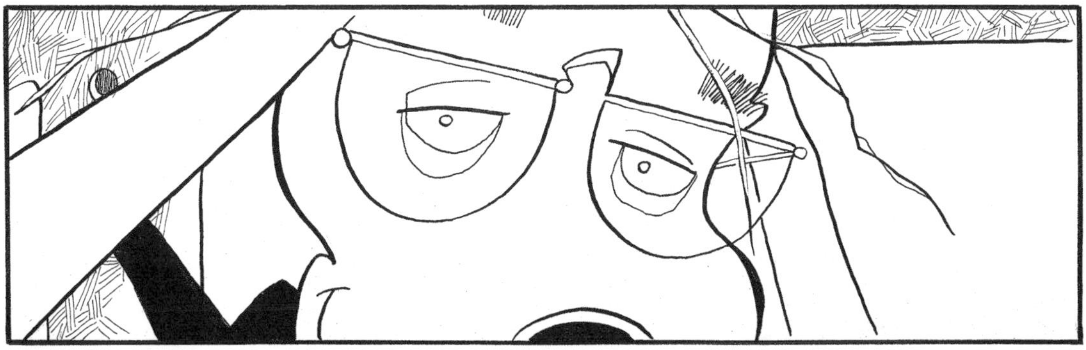

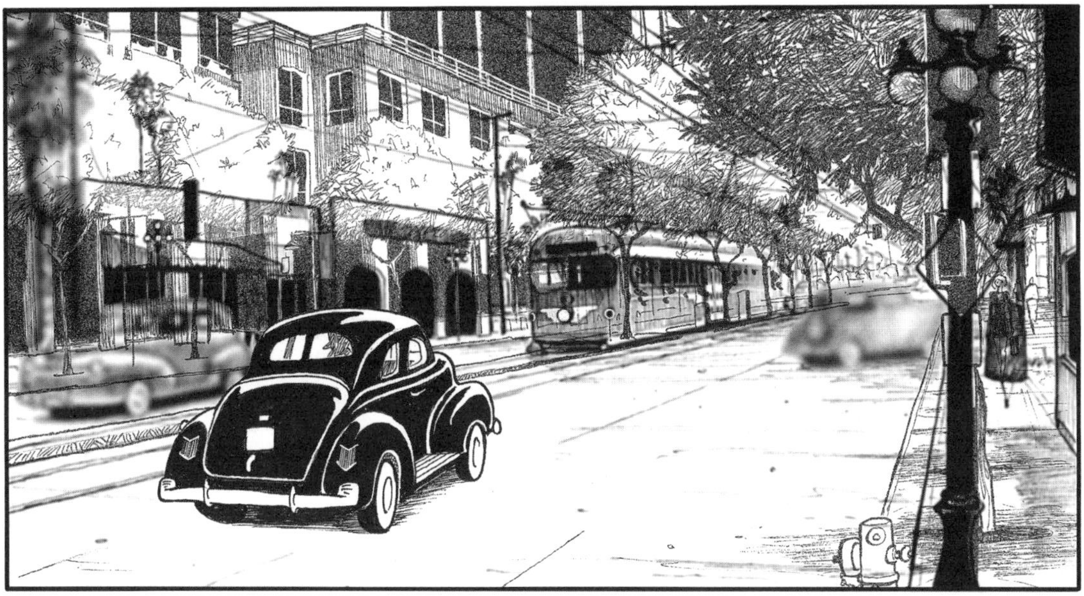

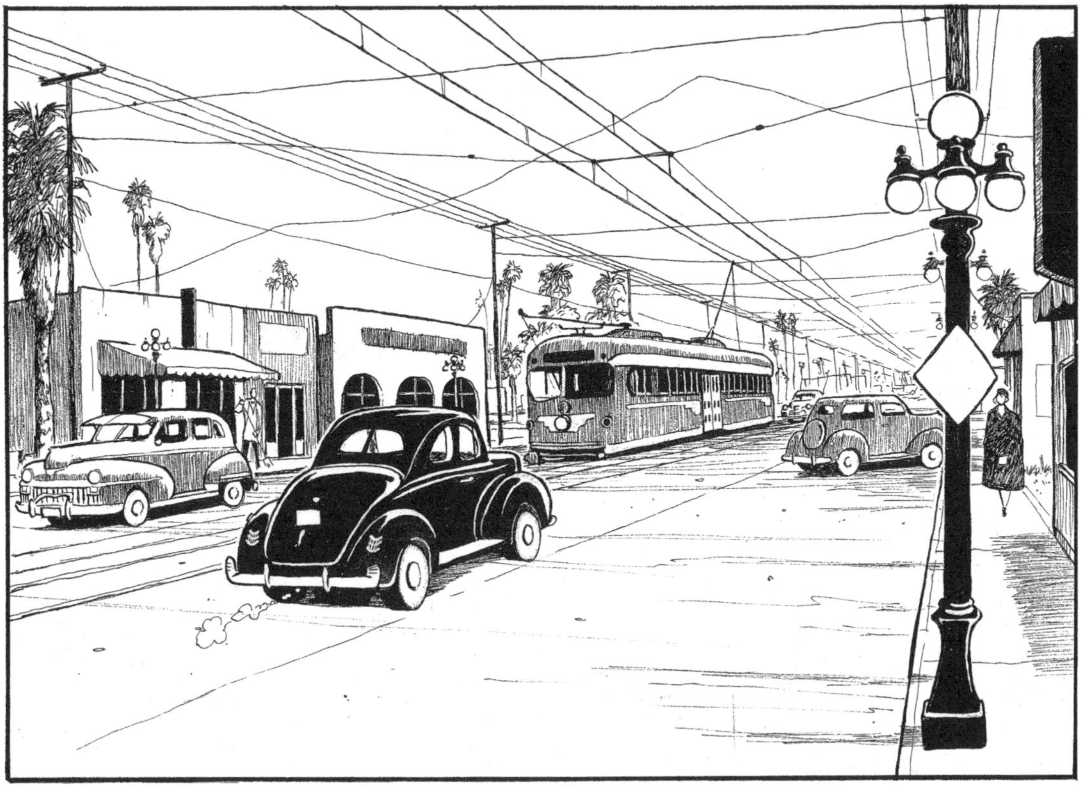

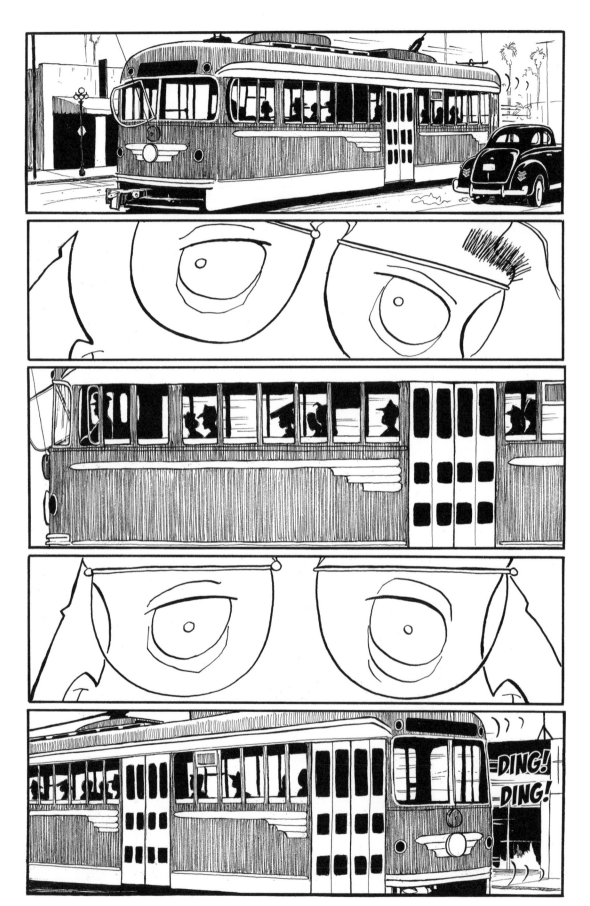

DING!
DING!

16

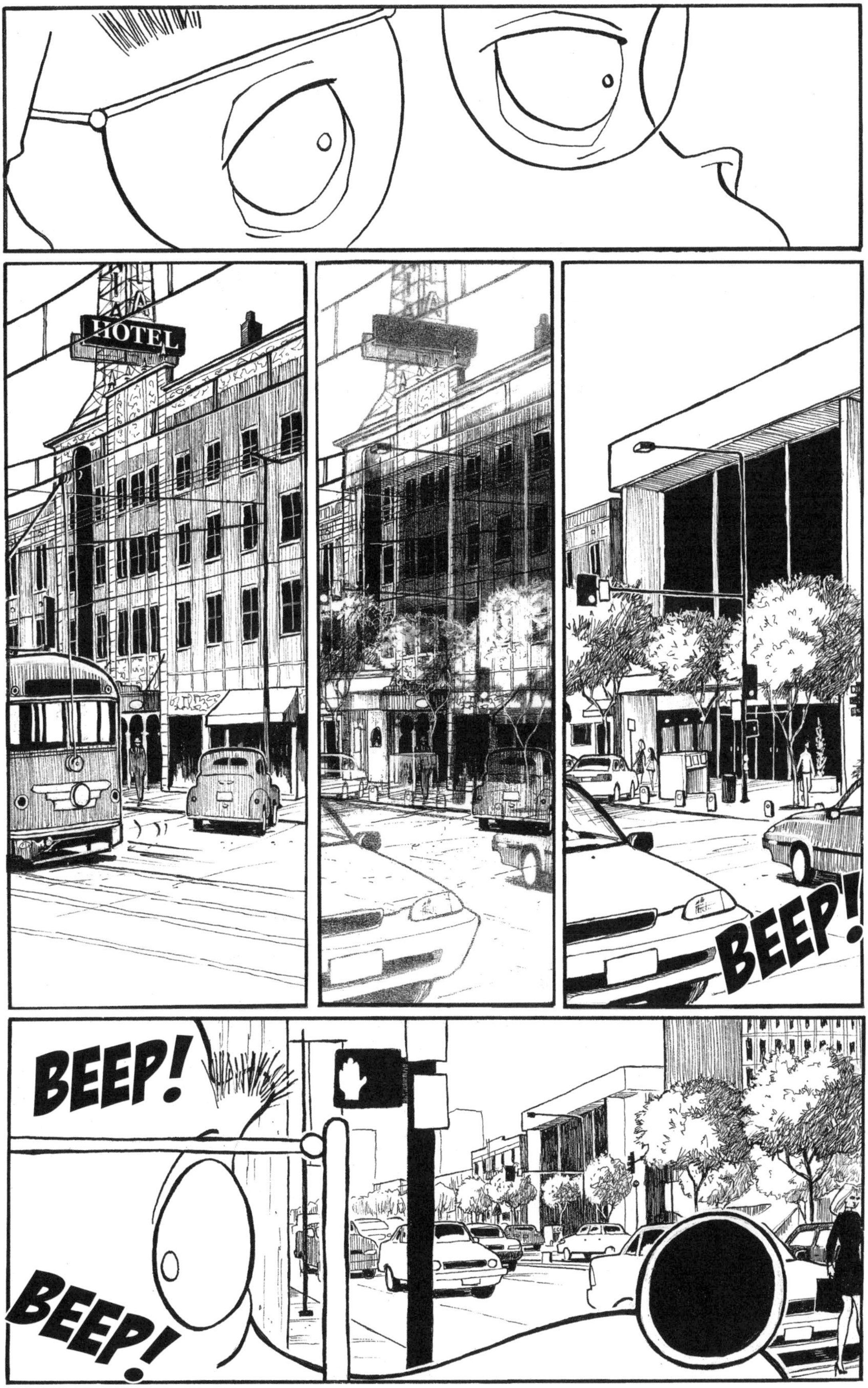
HOTEL
BEEP!
BEEP!
BEEP!

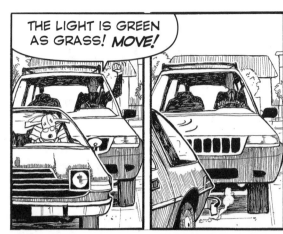

THE LIGHT IS GREEN AS GRASS! *MOVE!*

RATTLE!

CLANK!

RATTLE!
CREAK!

SHAKE!

RATTLE!
CLANK!

CLANK!

CLUNK!

RATTLE!

CLANK!

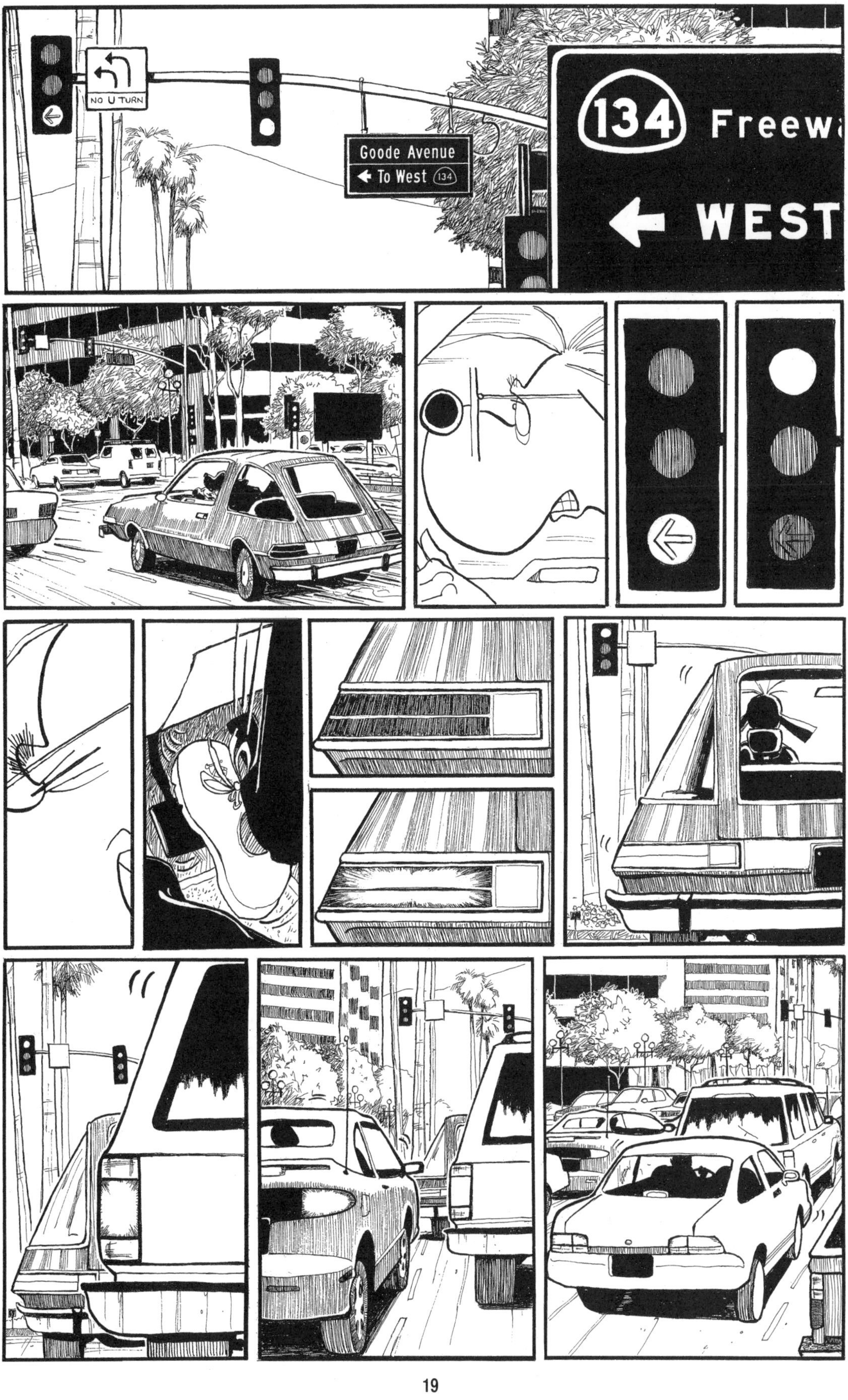
NO U TURN
Goode Avenue
To West 134
134 Freewa
WEST

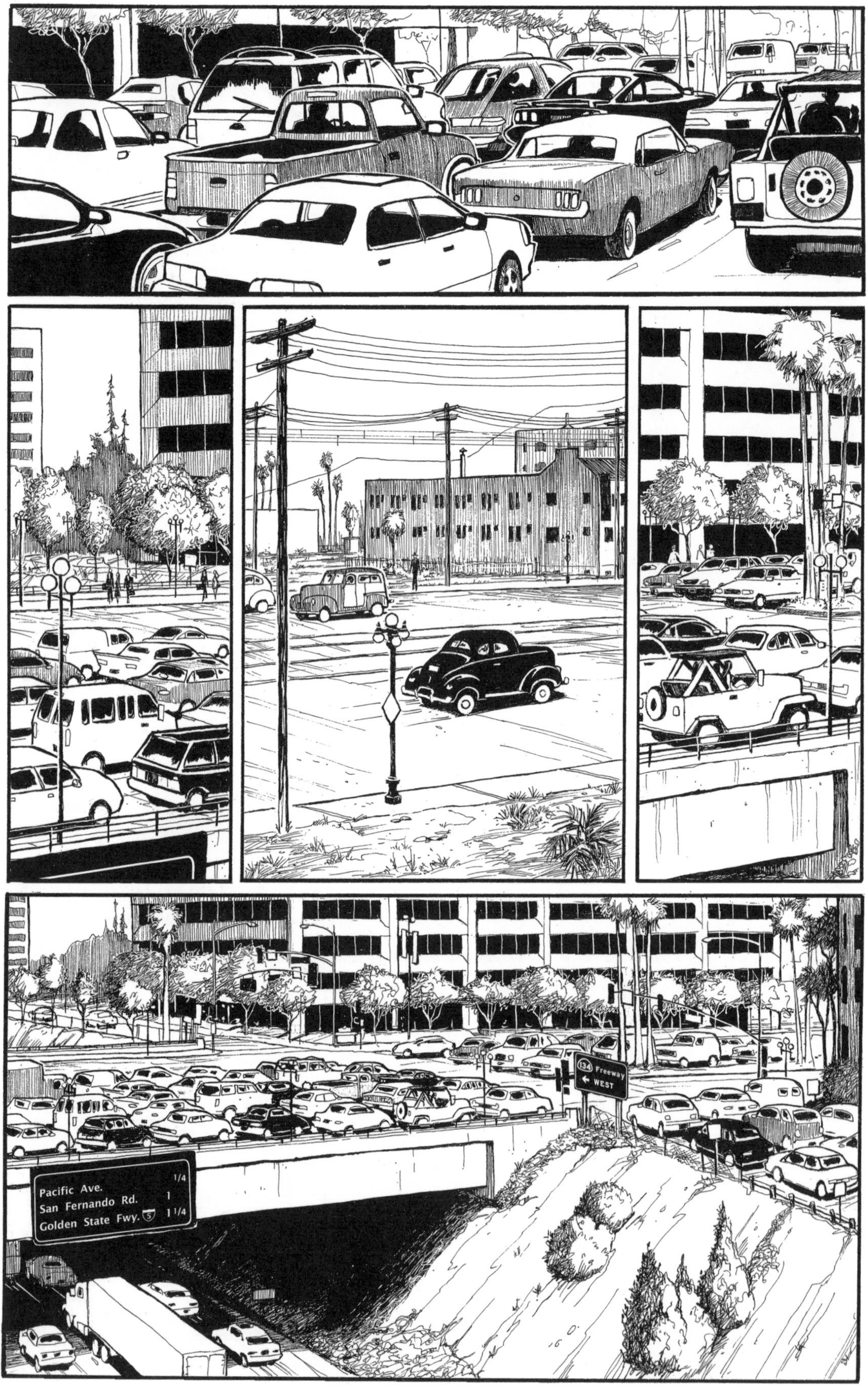
134 Freeway
WEST
Pacific Ave. 1/4
San Fernando Rd. 1
Golden State Fwy. 5 1 1/4

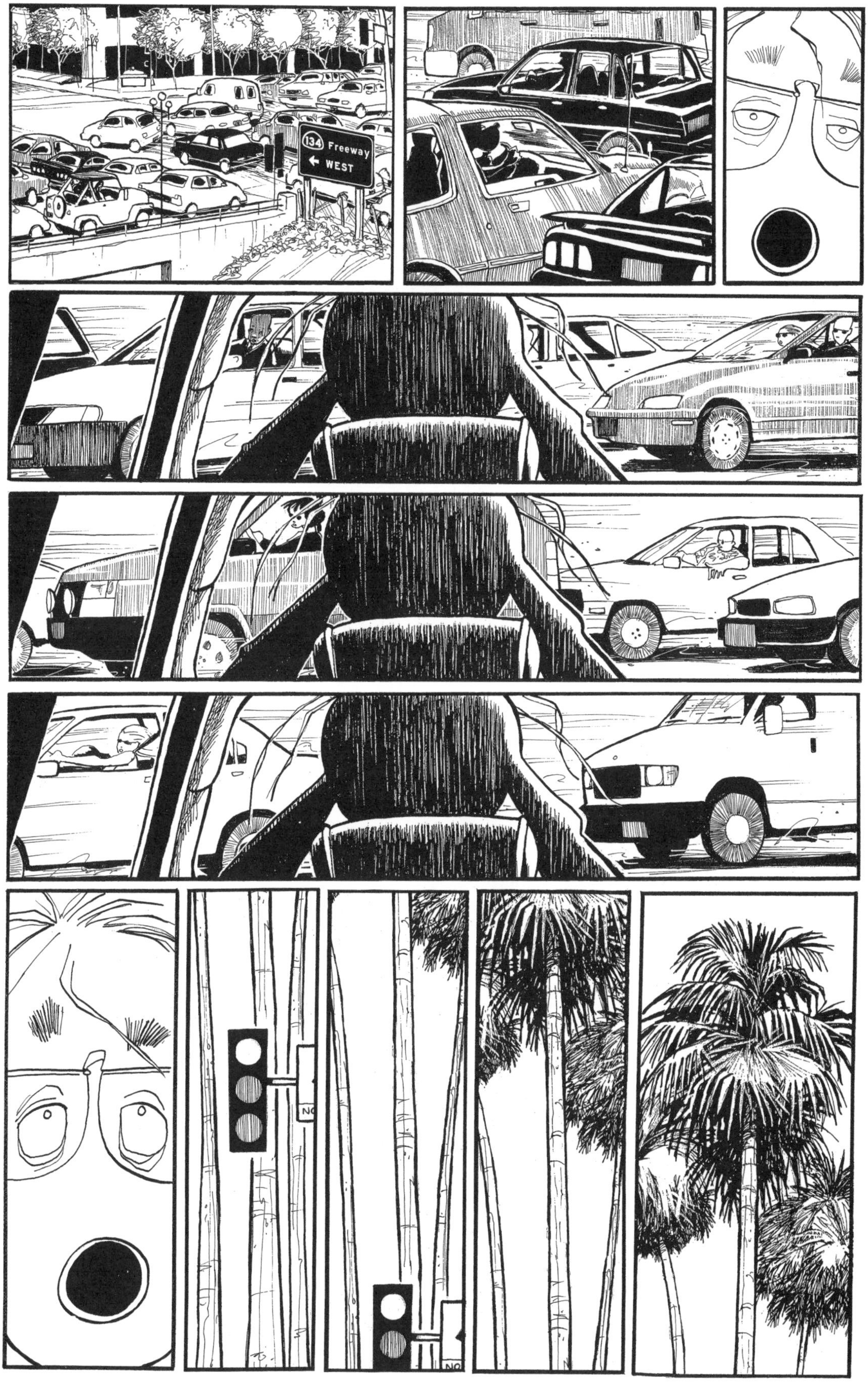
134 Freeway
← WEST
NO
NO

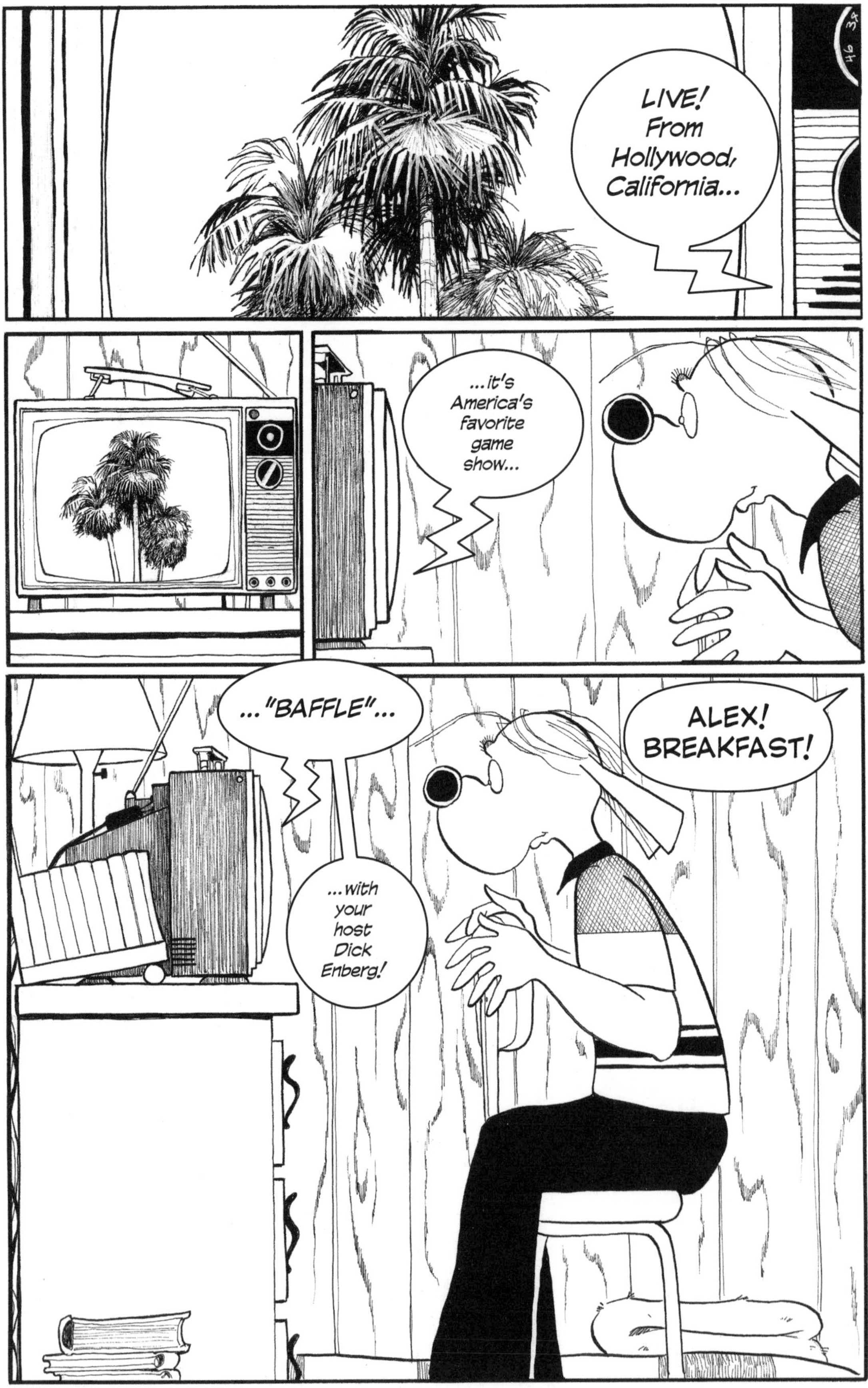
LIVE! From Hollywood, California...
...it's America's favorite game show...
..."BAFFLE"...
...with your host Dick Enberg!
ALEX! BREAKFAST!

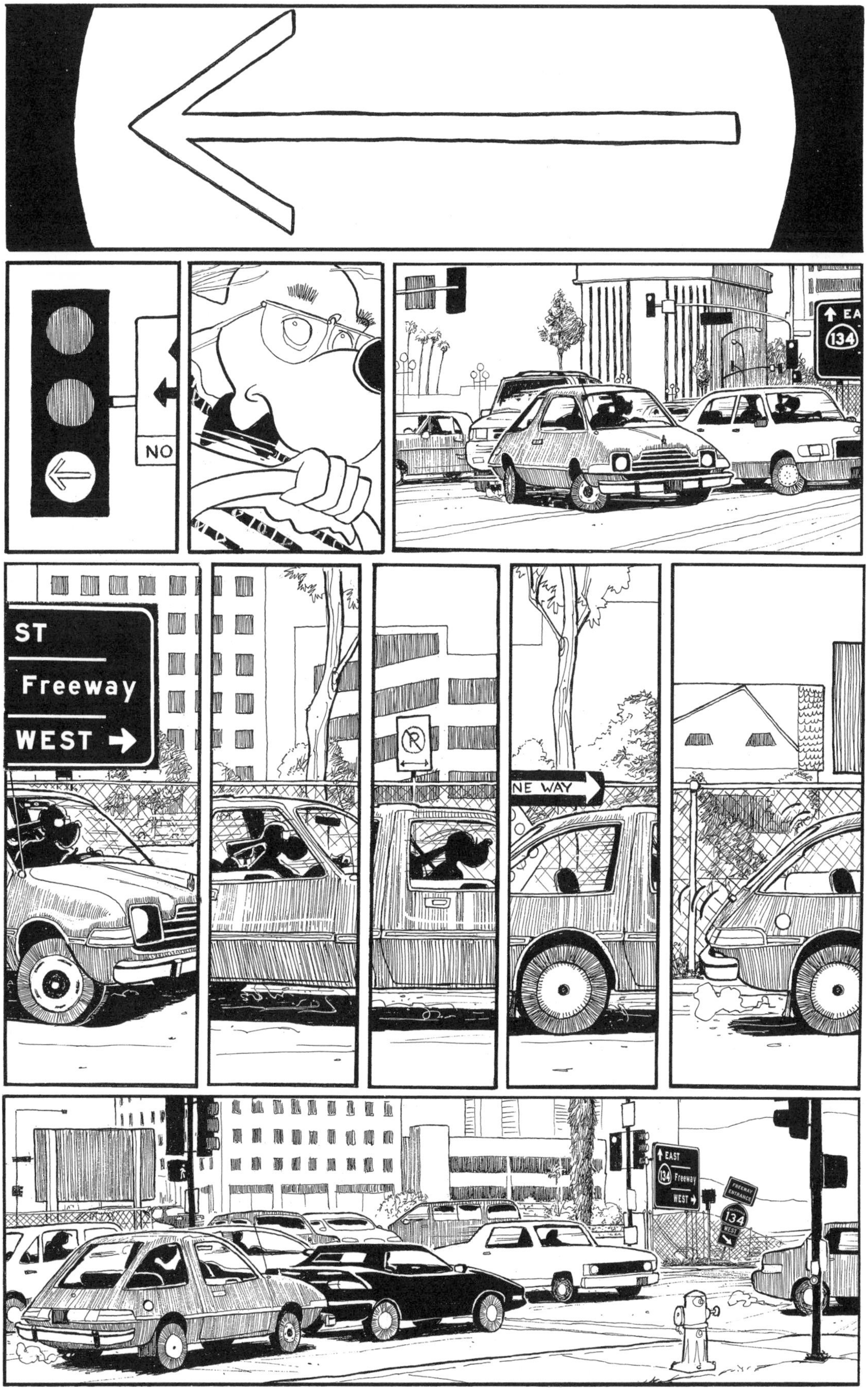
NO
134
ST
Freeway
WEST
NE WAY
EAST
134
Freeway
WEST
134

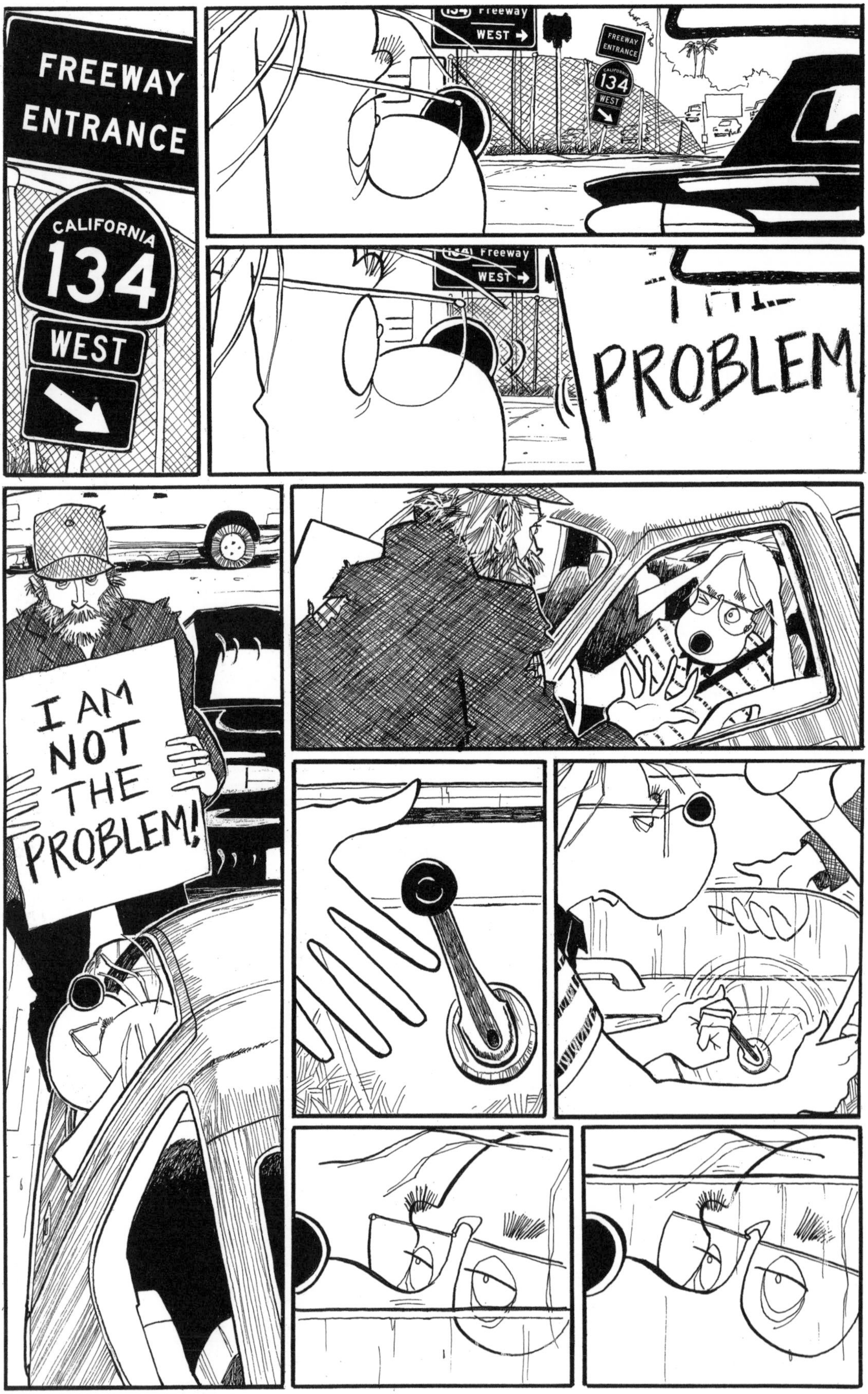

FREEWAY ENTRANCE
CALIFORNIA 134
WEST
134 Freeway WEST
FREEWAY ENTRANCE
CALIFORNIA 134 WEST
PROBLEM
I AM NOT THE PROBLEM!

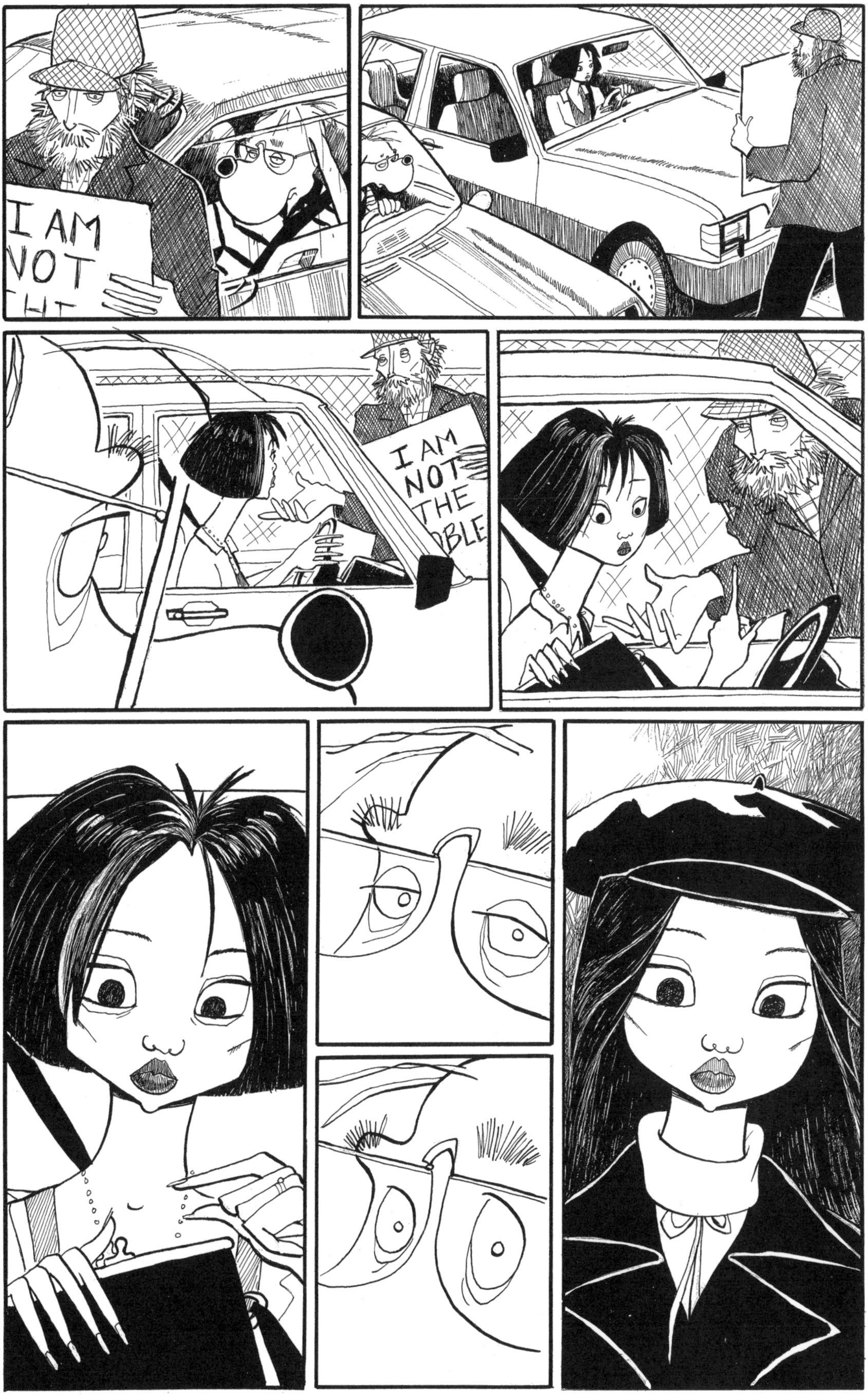
I AM
NOT
I AM
NOT
THE

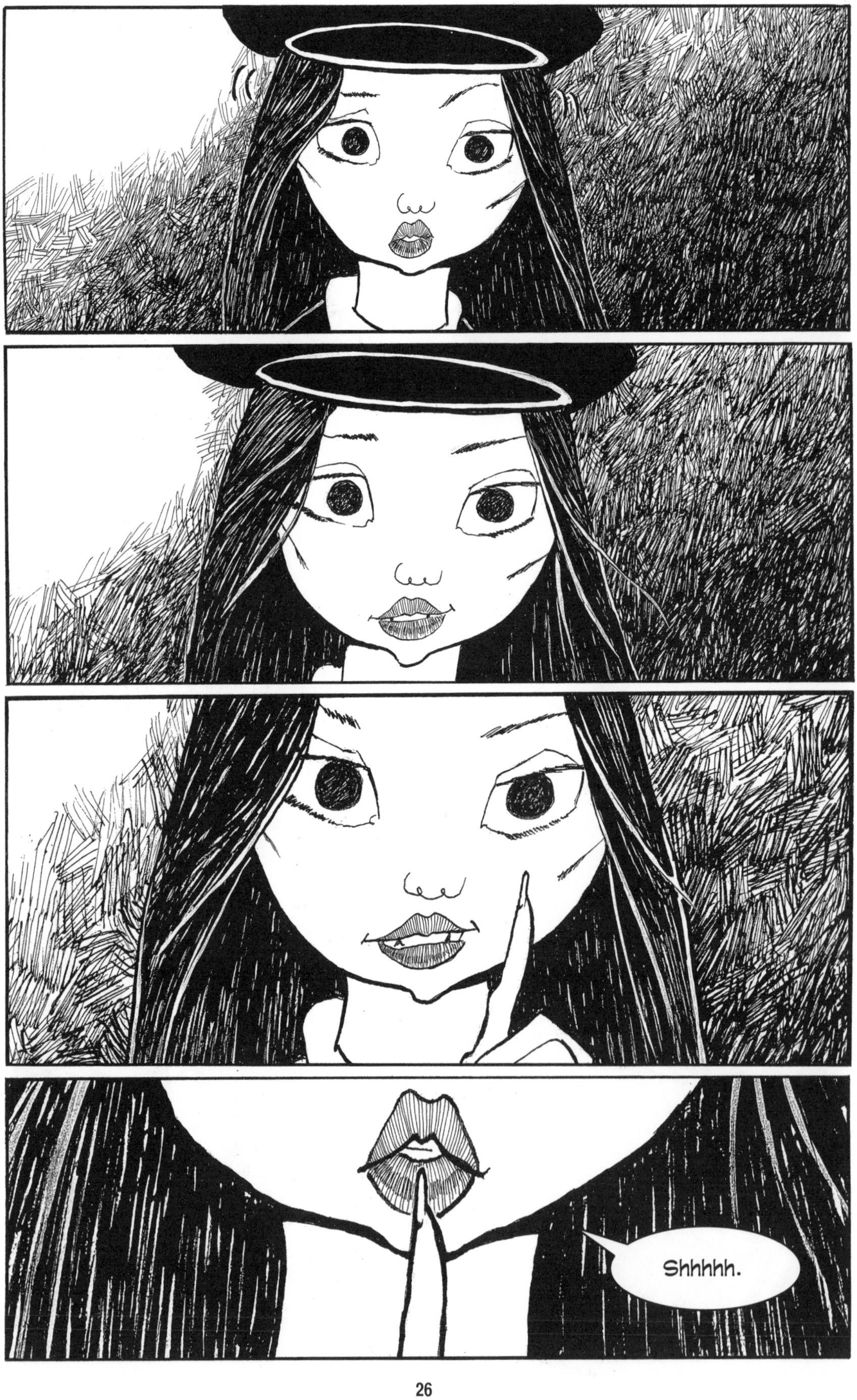
Shhhhh.

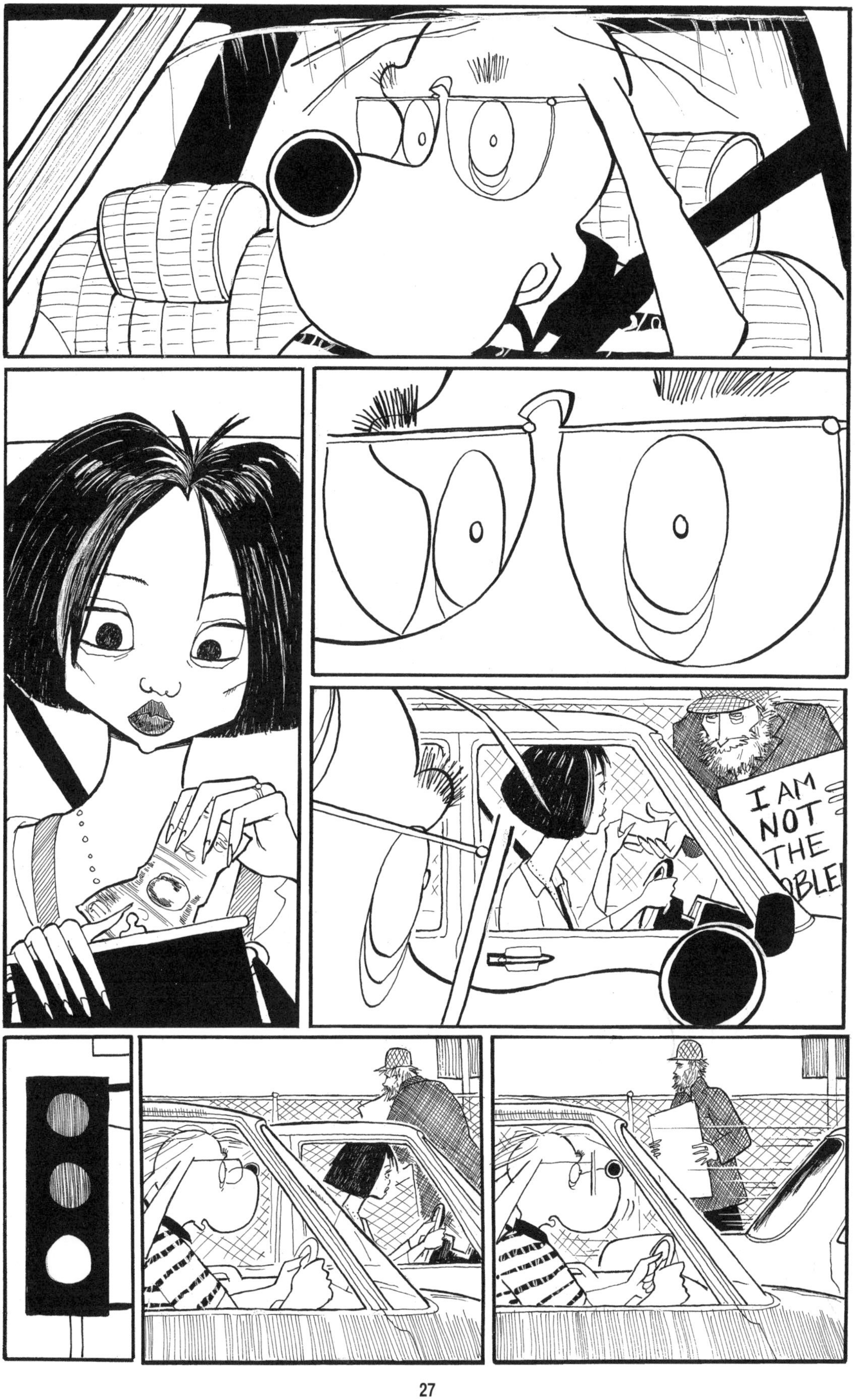
I AM
NOT
THE

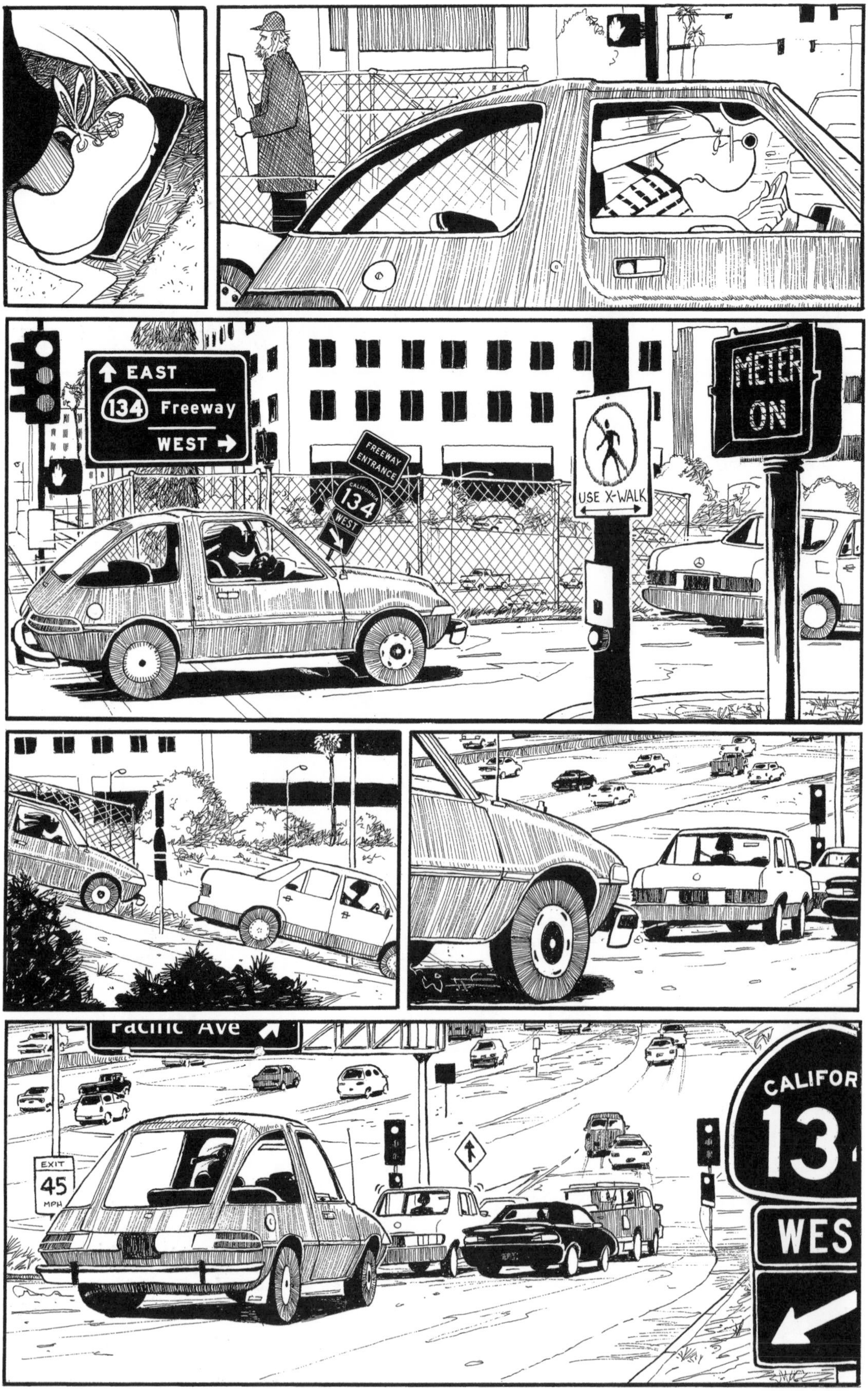
EAST
134 Freeway
WEST
FREEWAY ENTRANCE
CALIFORNIA
134
WEST
USE X-WALK
METER ON
Pacific Ave
EXIT
45
MPH
CALIFOR
13
WES

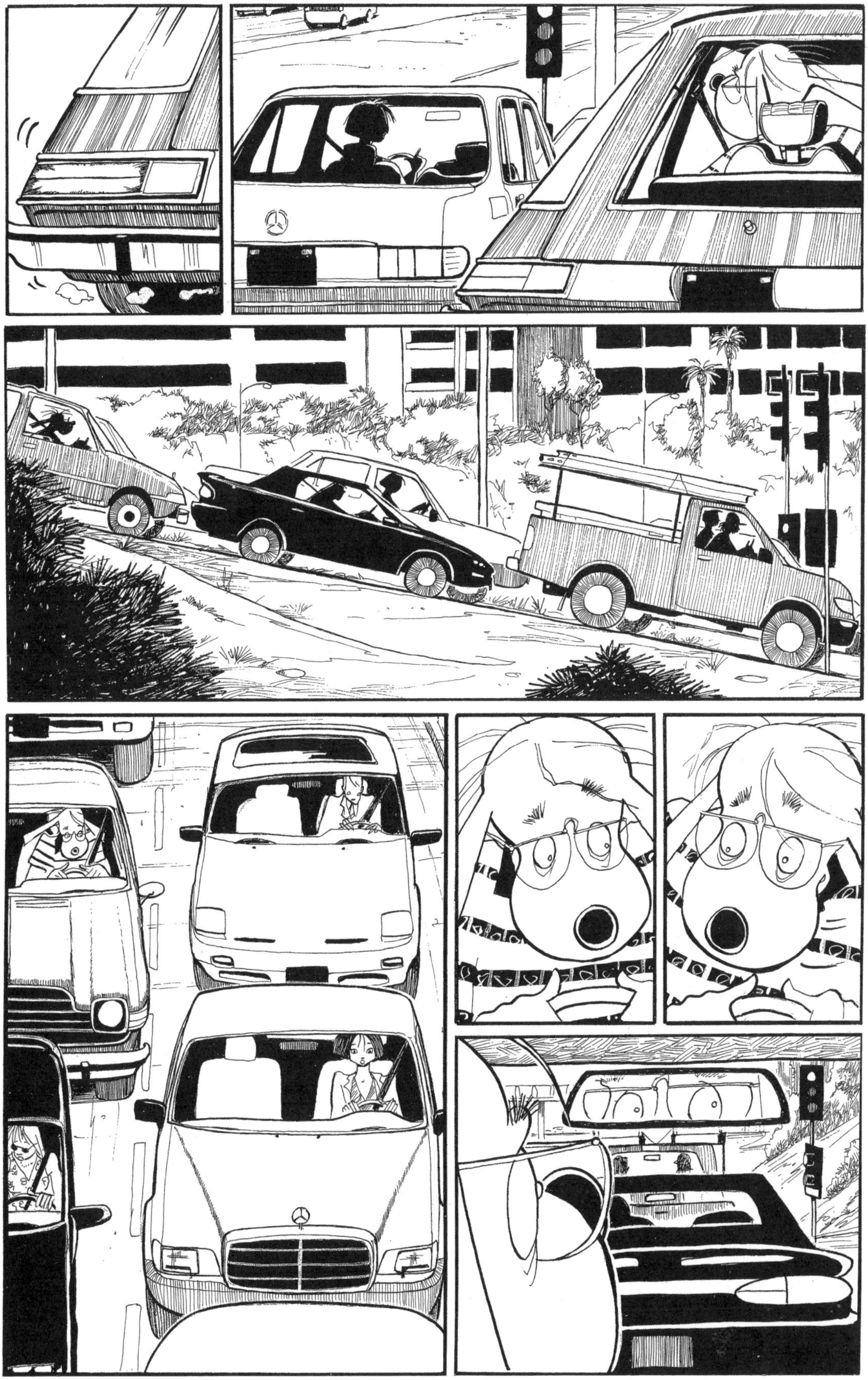

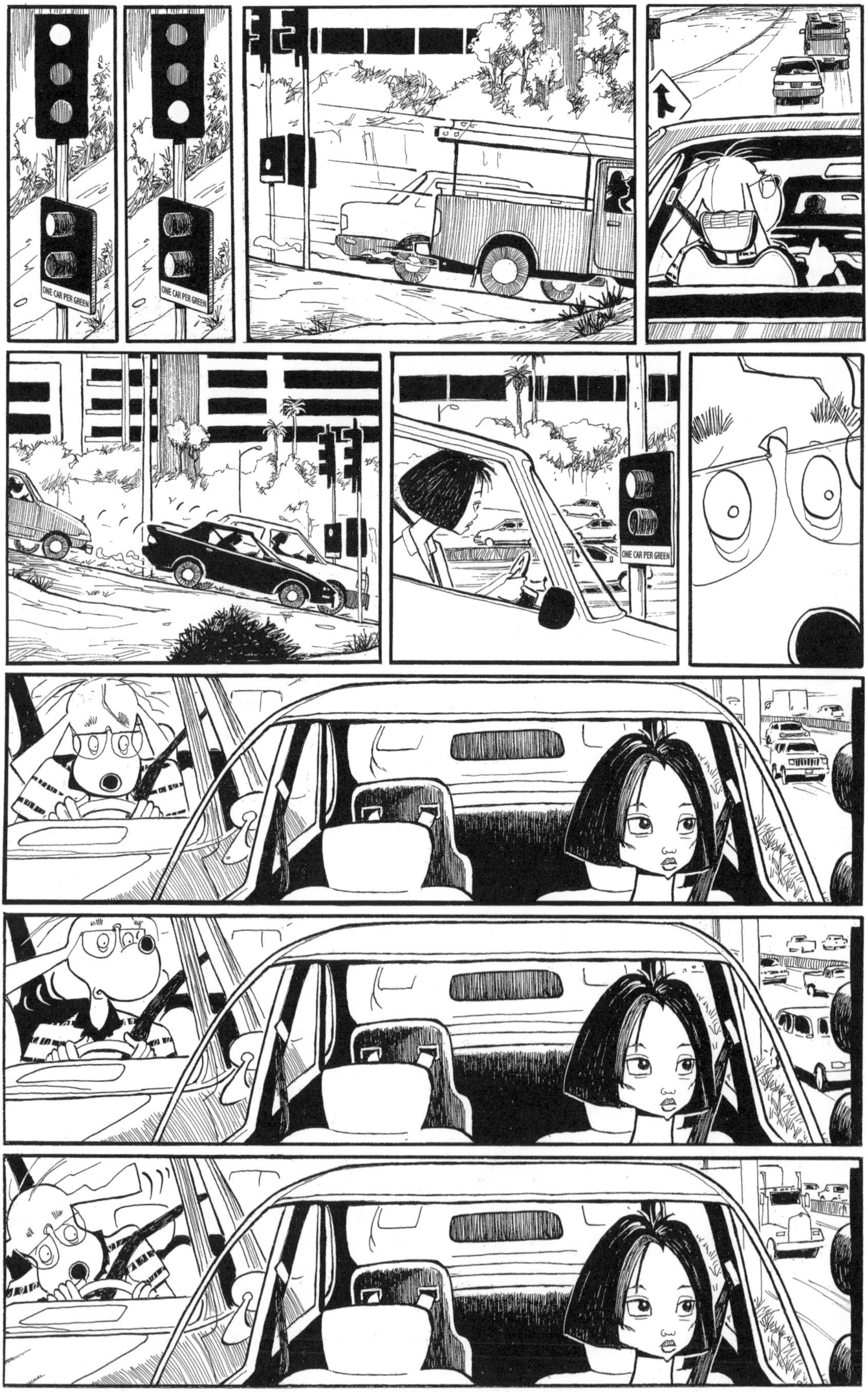
ONE CAR PER GREEN
ONE CAR PER GREEN
ONE CAR PER GREEN

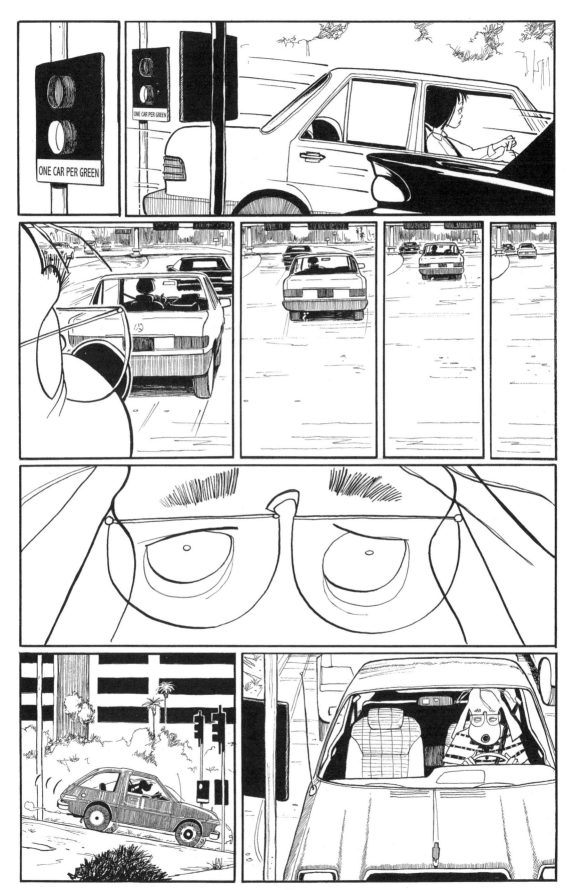

ONE CAR PER GREEN

ONE CAR PER GREEN

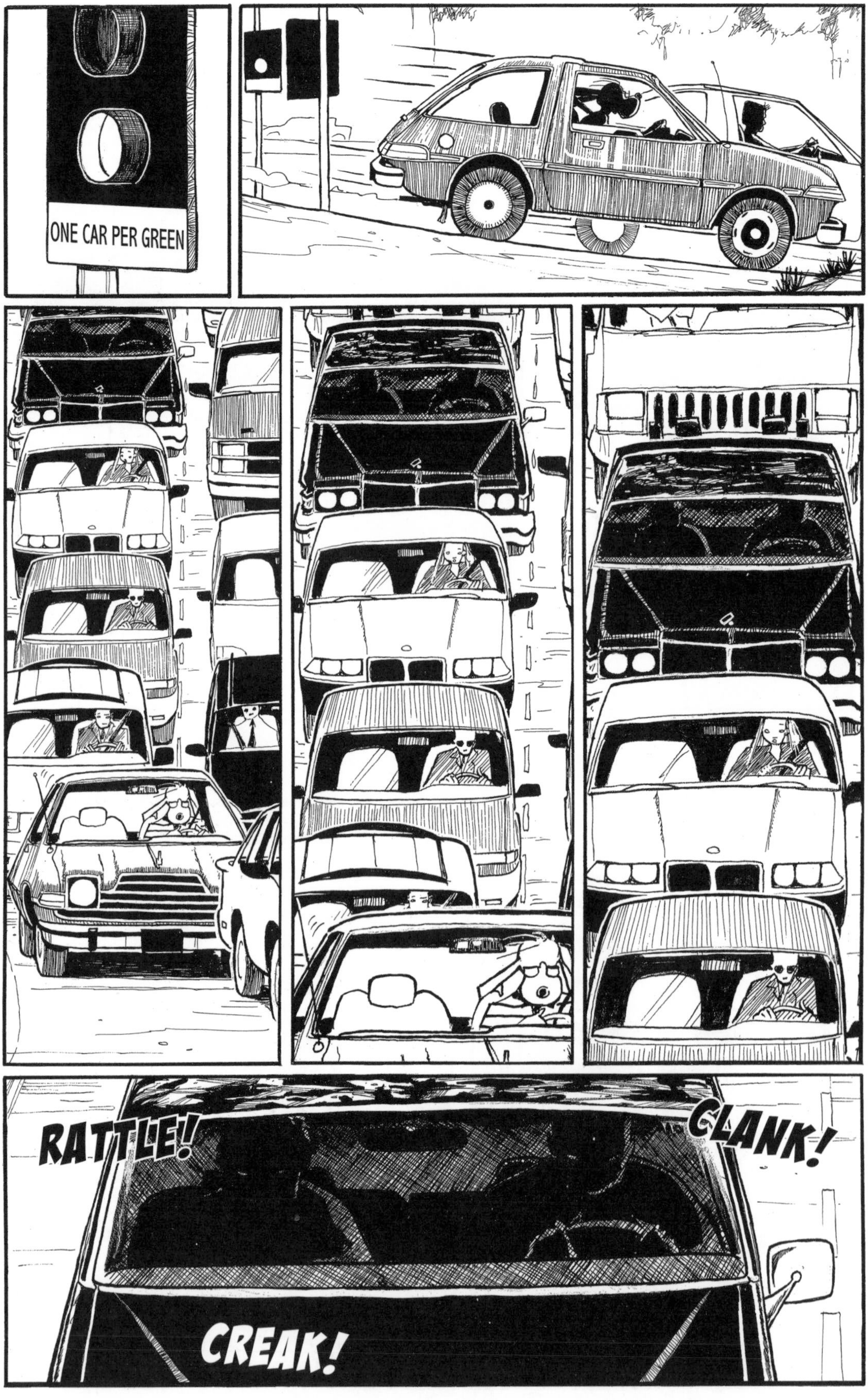
ONE CAR PER GREEN
RATTLE!
CLANK!
CREAK!

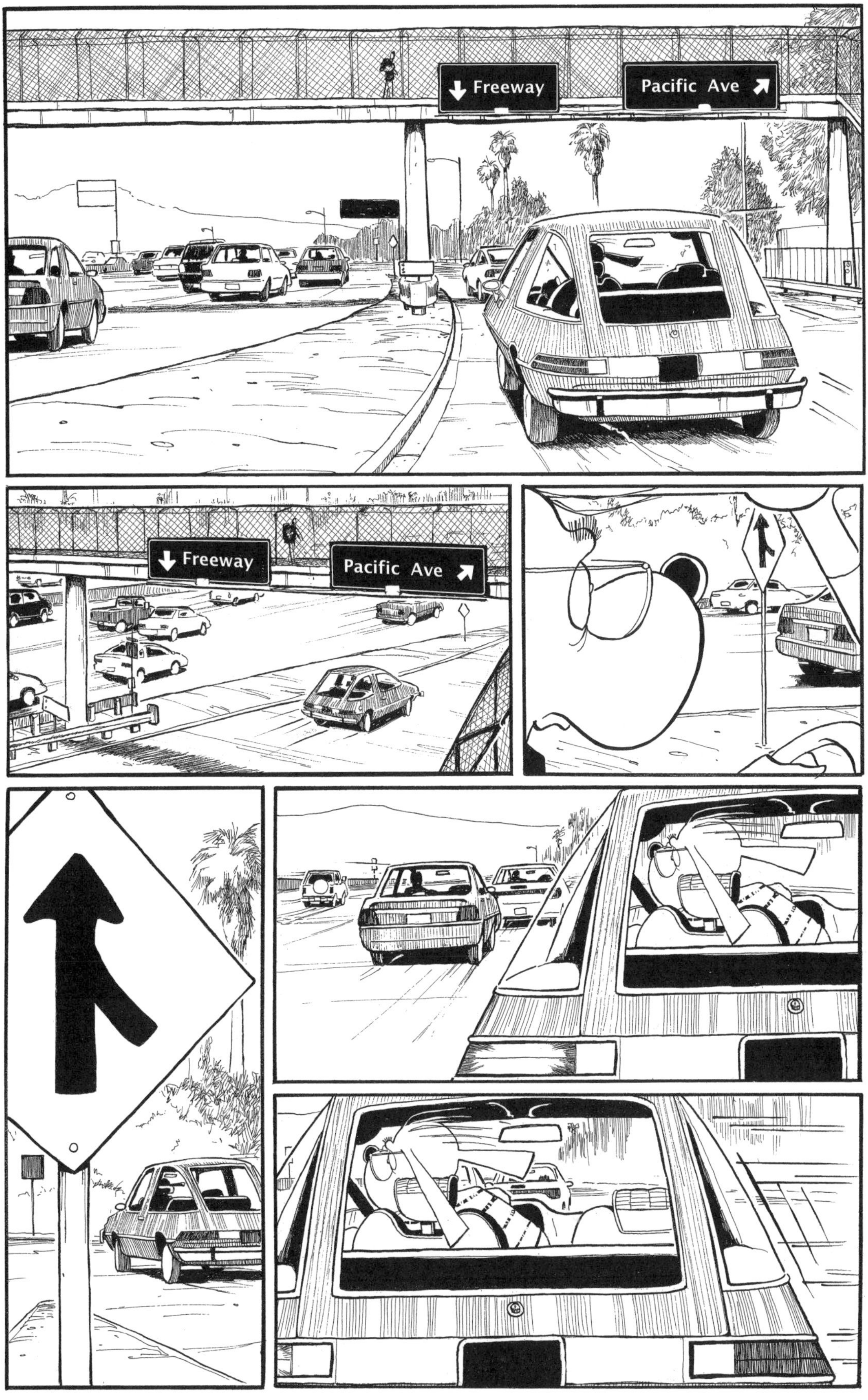
Freeway
Pacific Ave
Freeway
Pacific Ave

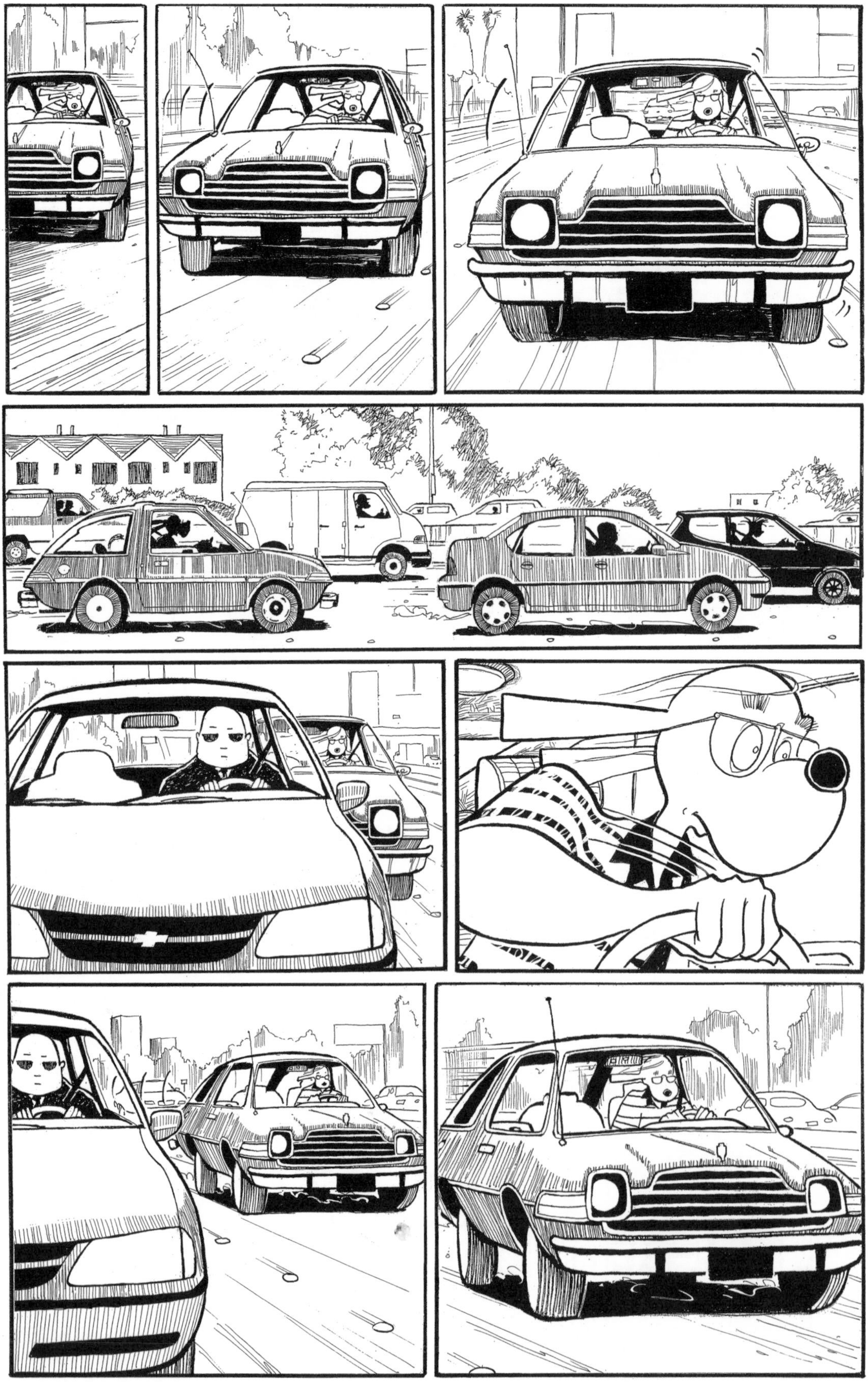

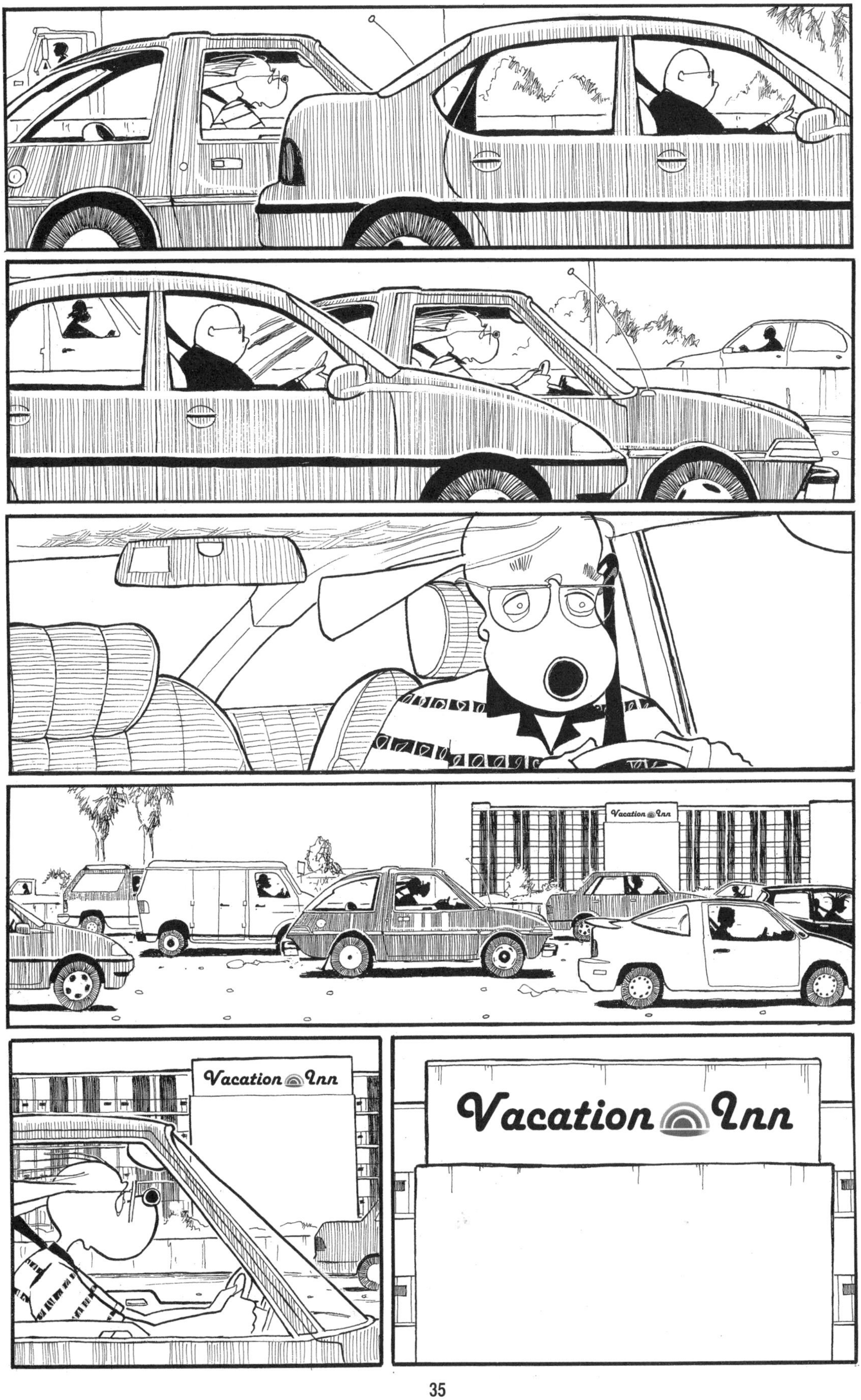
Vacation Inn
Vacation Inn
Vacation Inn

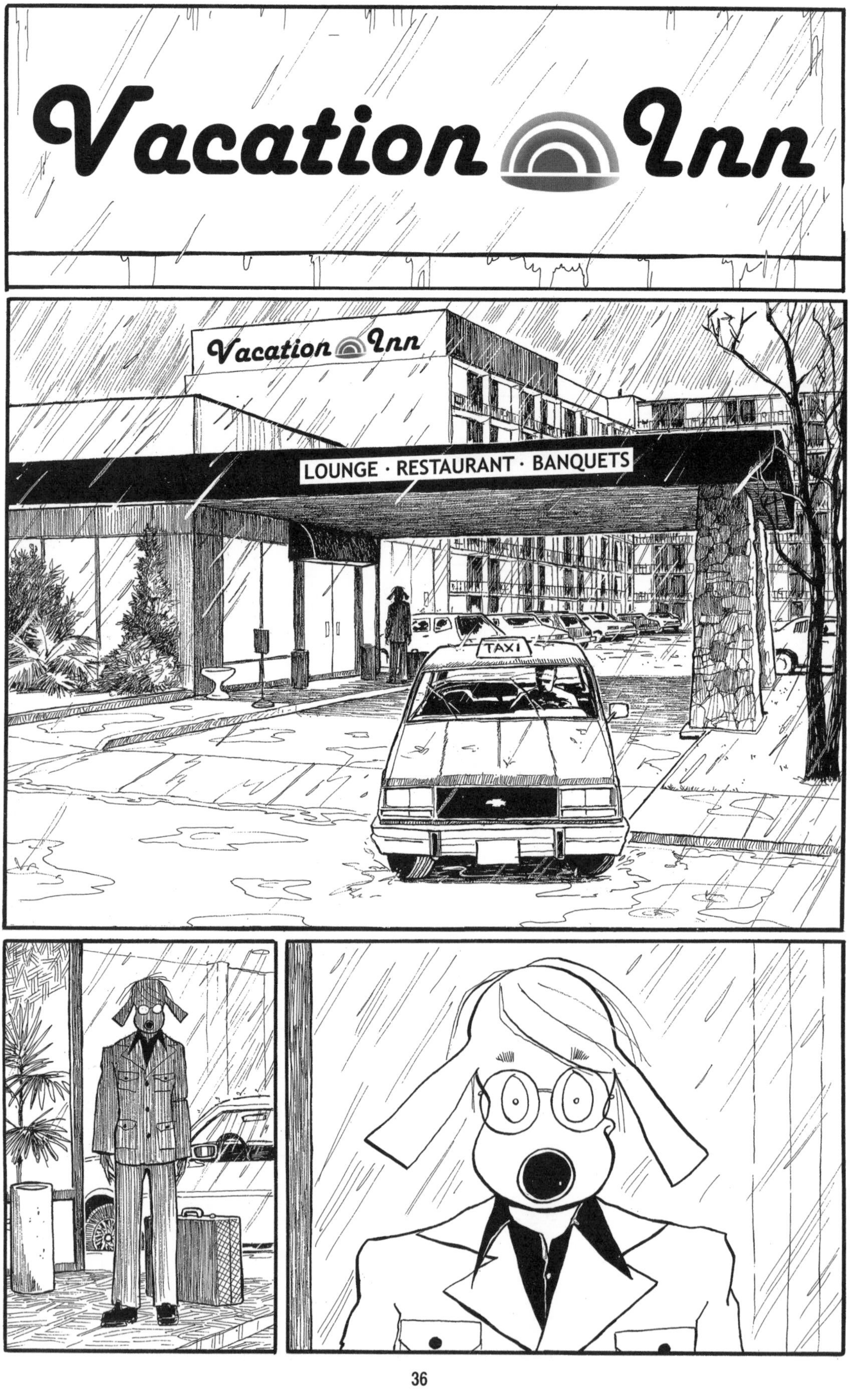
Vacation Inn
Vacation Inn
LOUNGE · RESTAURANT · BANQUETS
TAXI

Excuse me.

Can I help you?

I'm Alex Kalienka. I called from the airport. You said you had rooms.

Yes, we do, Mr. Kalienka.

Would you please fill this out?

ion Inn
RATION CARD
AND OTHER VALUABLES MUST BE PLACED IN THE
NT OFFICE. OTHERWISE THE HOTEL MANAGE-
BE RESPONSIBLE FOR ANY LOSS.
DATE JAN 30, 79
EX KALIEN
825 10TH
BA
RATE   ARRIVED   ORIGIN
CREDIT   EVENT   RKS
SIGNATURE

Here you go.

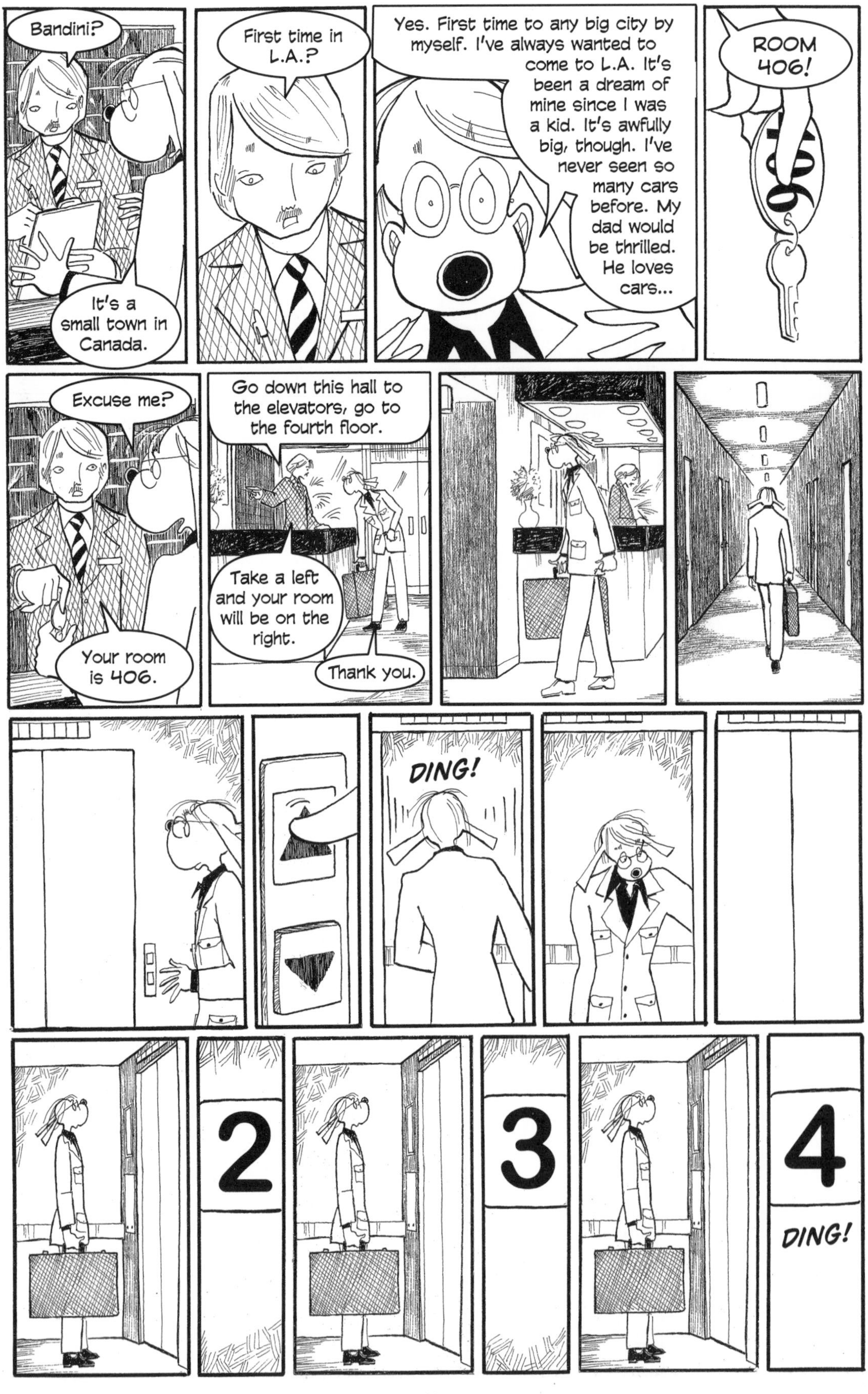
Bandini?
It's a small town in Canada.
First time in L.A.?
Yes. First time to any big city by myself. I've always wanted to come to L.A. It's been a dream of mine since I was a kid. It's awfully big, though. I've never seen so many cars before. My dad would be thrilled. He loves cars...
ROOM 406!
Excuse me?
Your room is 406.
Go down this hall to the elevators, go to the fourth floor.
Take a left and your room will be on the right.
Thank you.
DING!
2
3
4
DING!

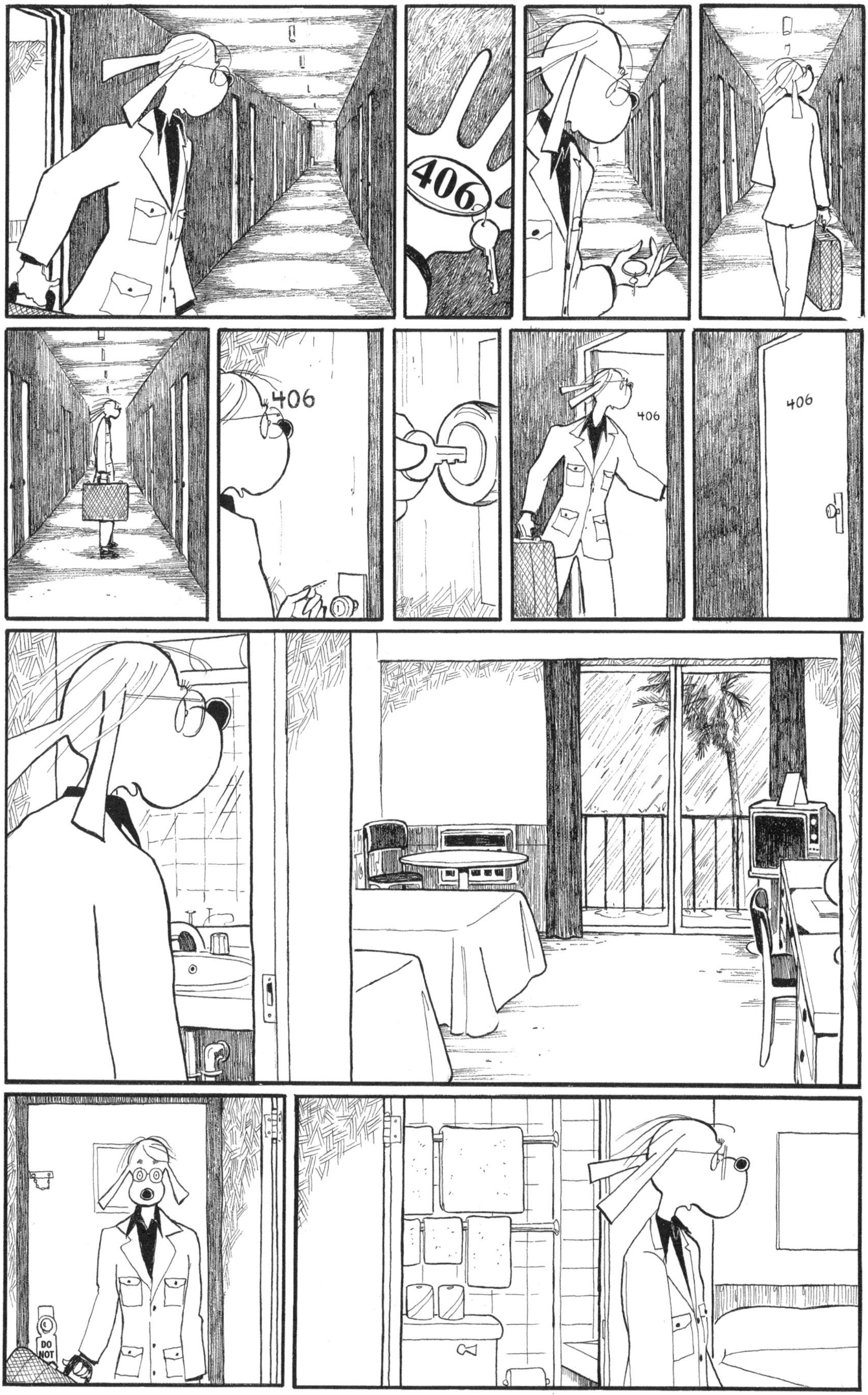
406
406
406
406
DO
NOT

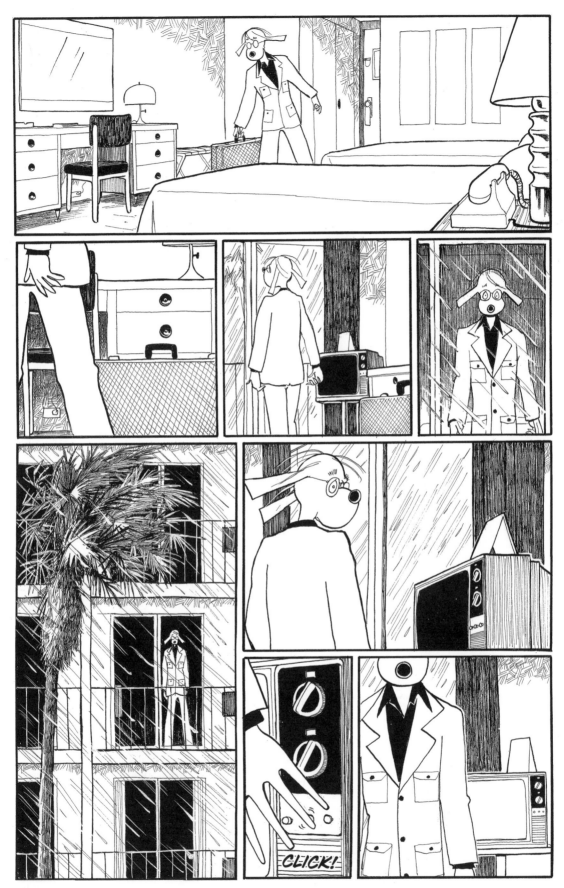

CLICK!

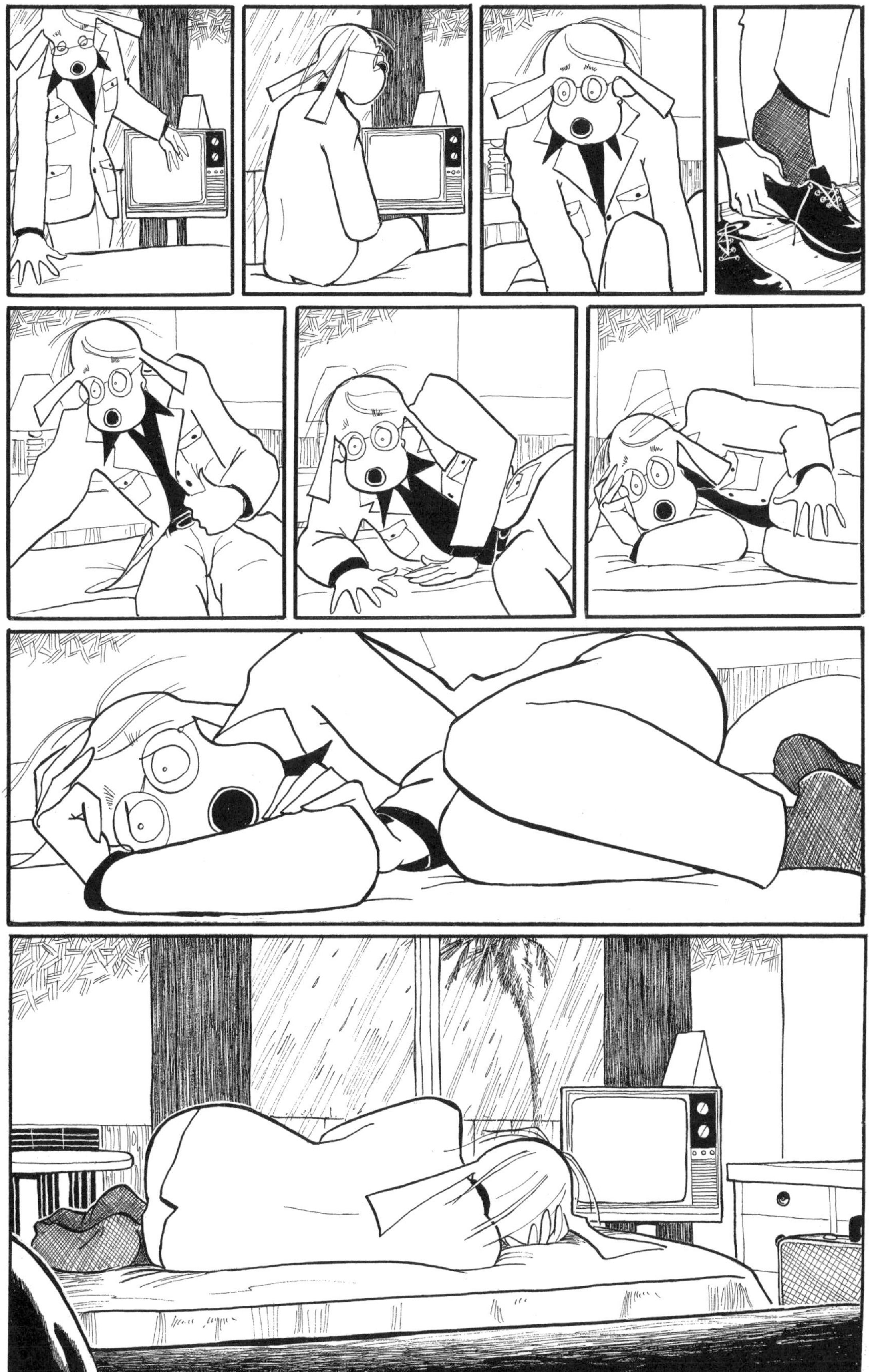

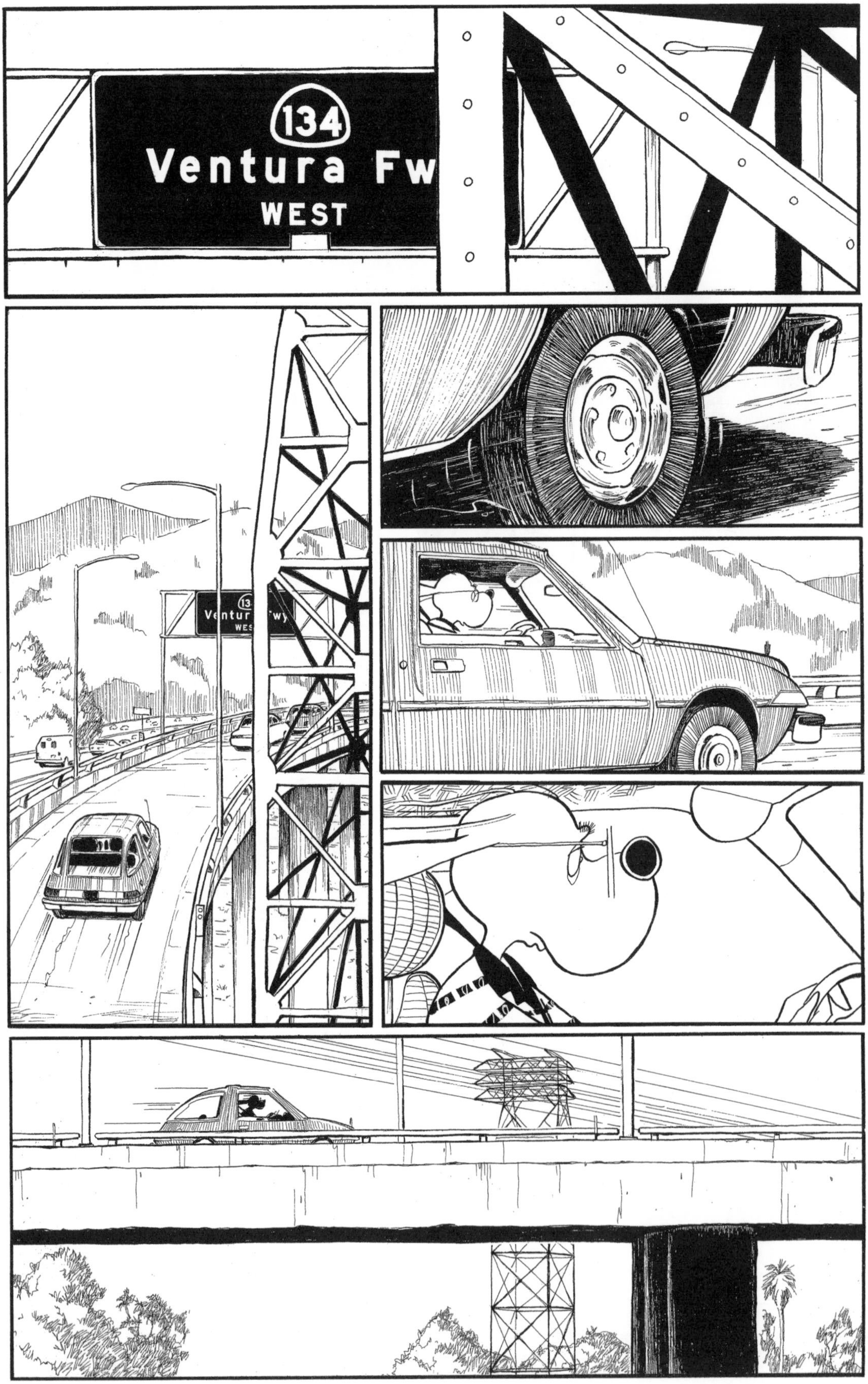
134
Ventura Fw
WEST

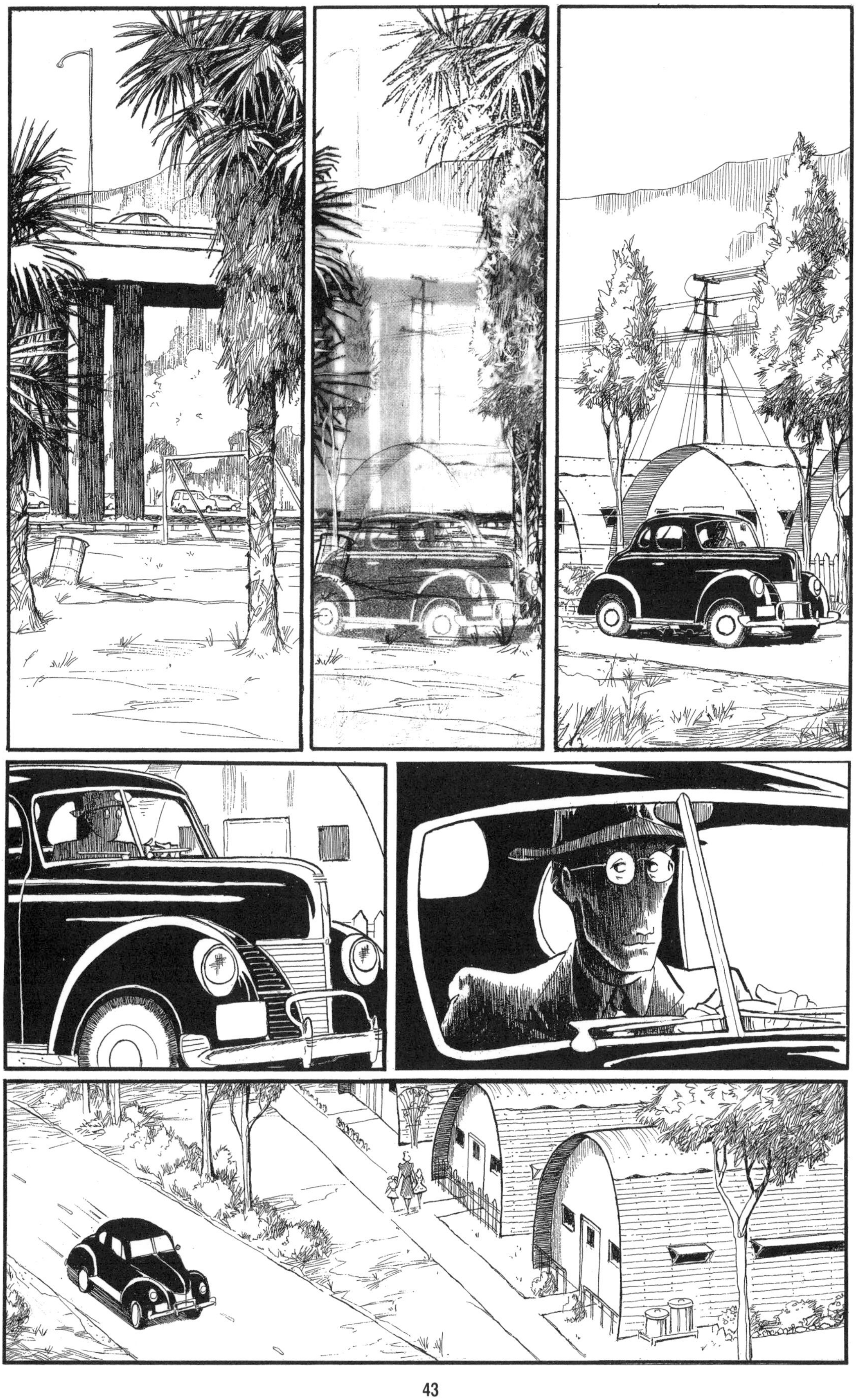

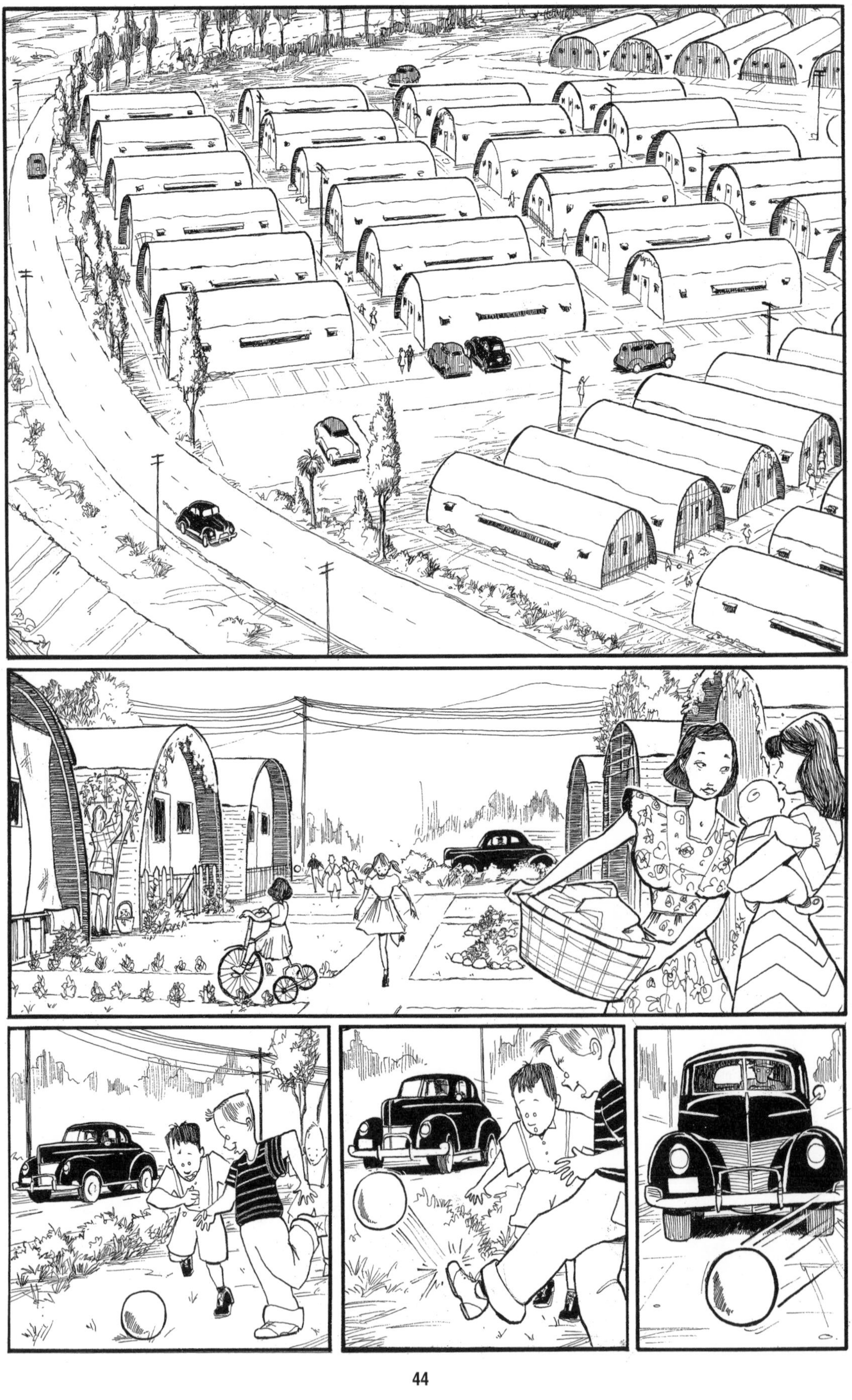

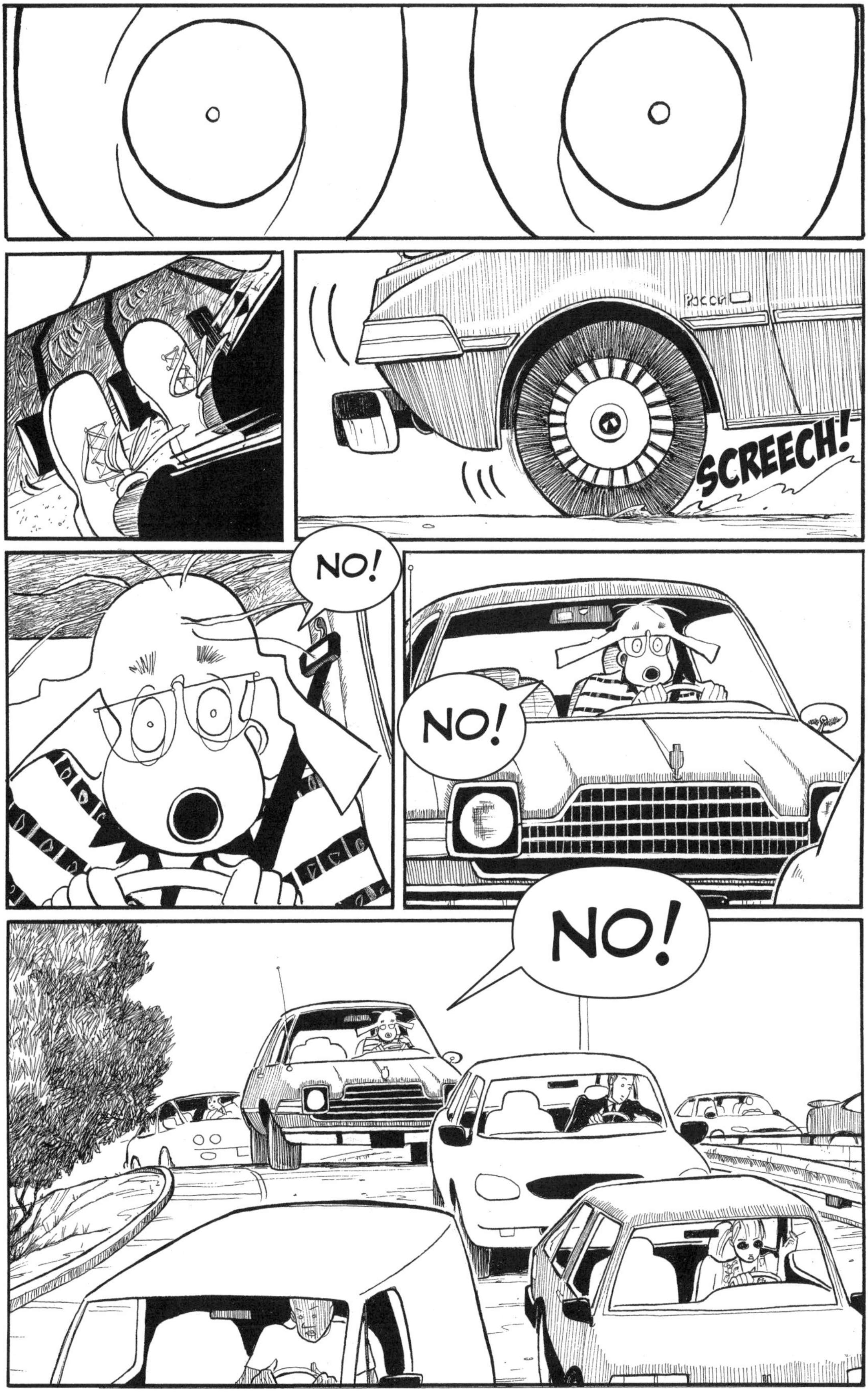
SCREECH!
NO!
NO!
NO!

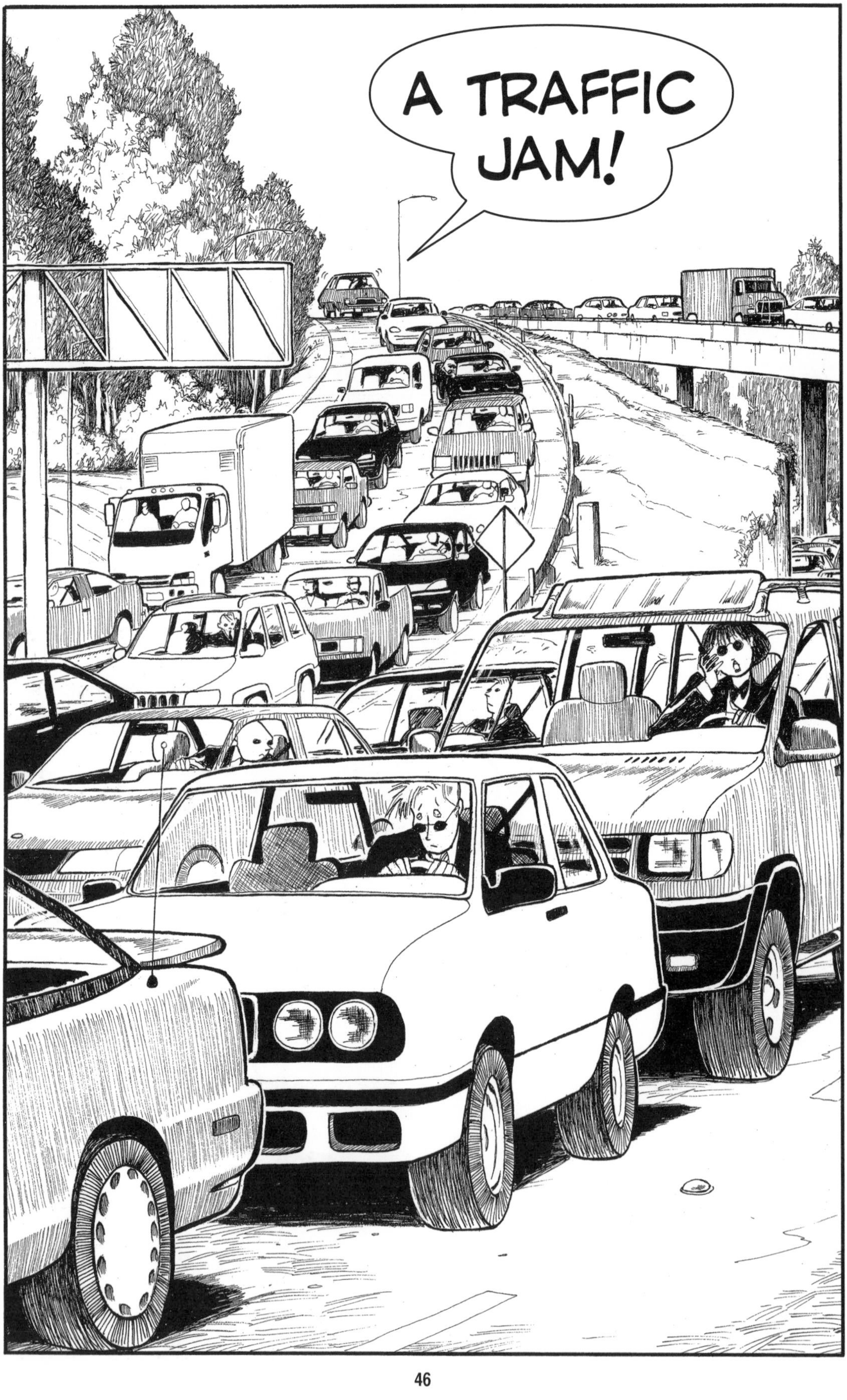
A TRAFFIC JAM!

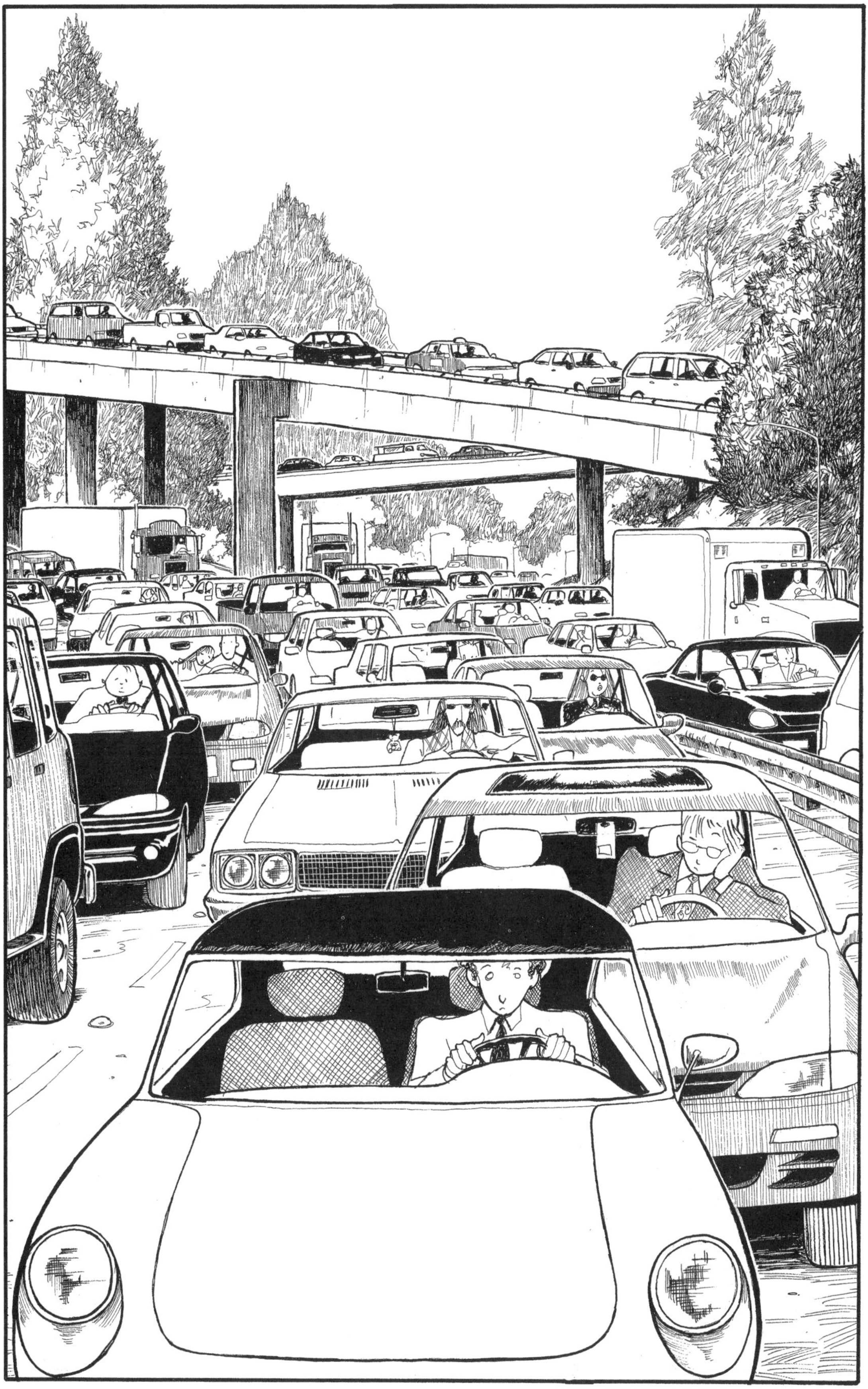

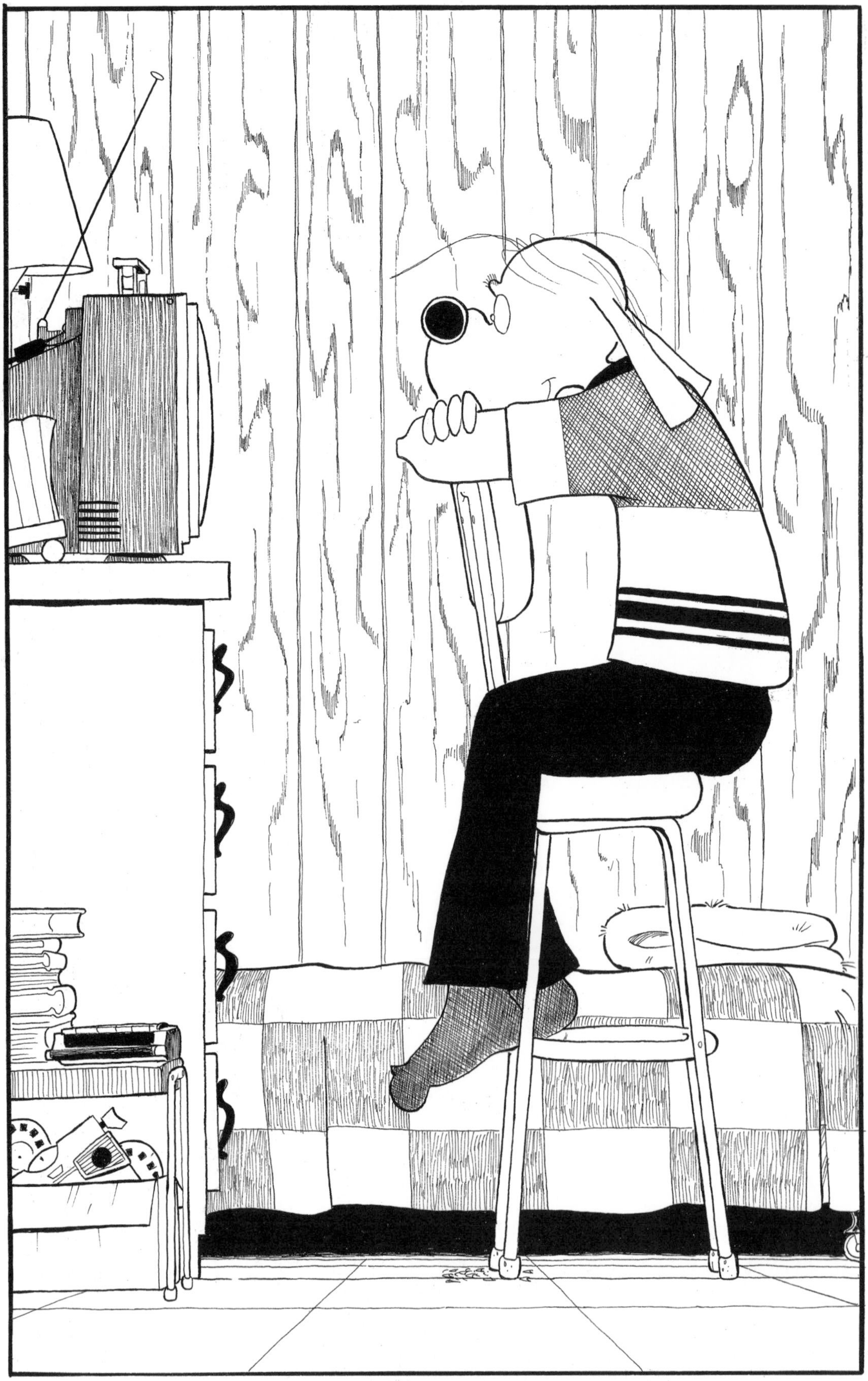

CHAPTER 2

NICE WORK IF YOU CAN GET IT

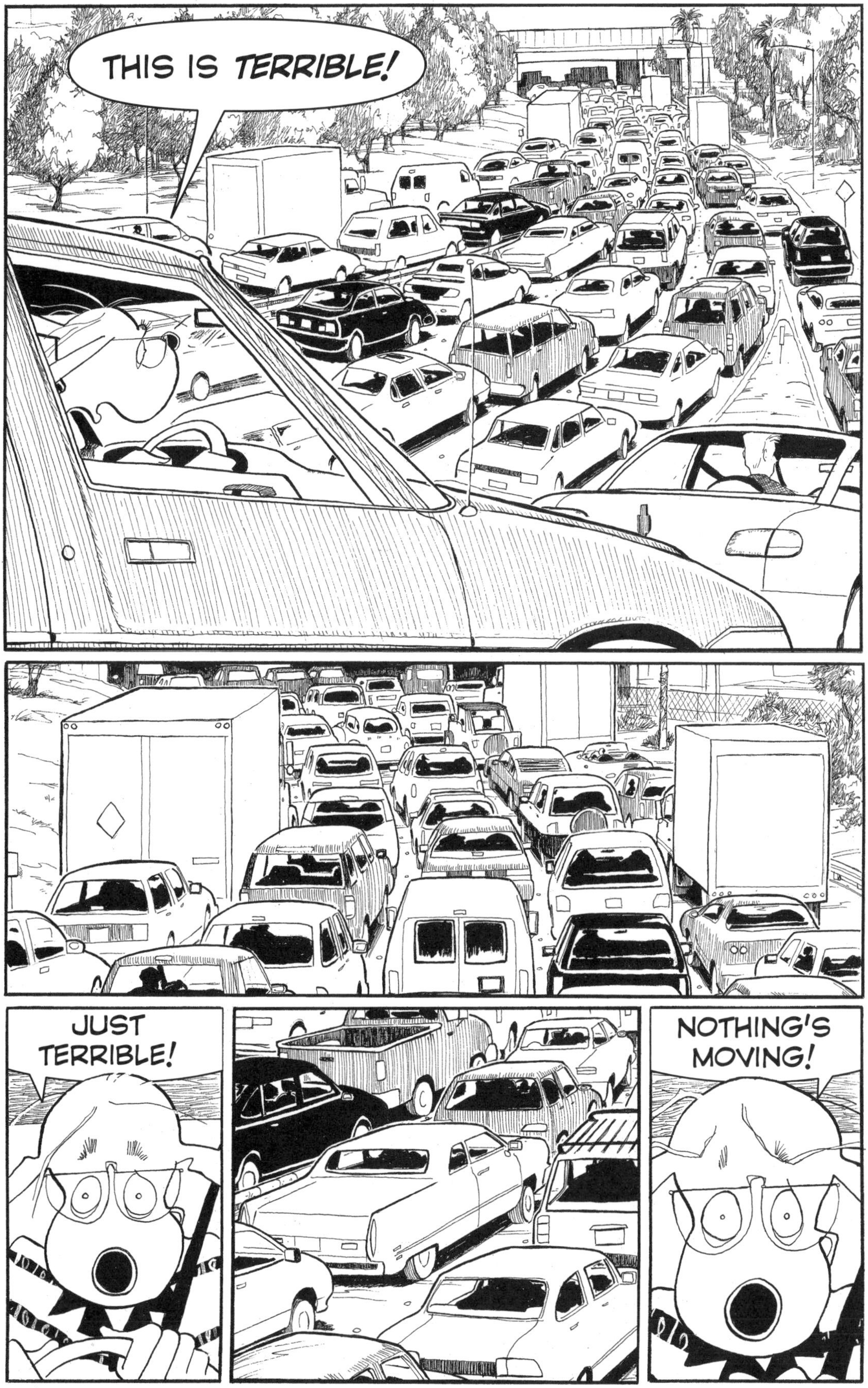
THIS IS *TERRIBLE!*
JUST TERRIBLE!
NOTHING'S MOVING!

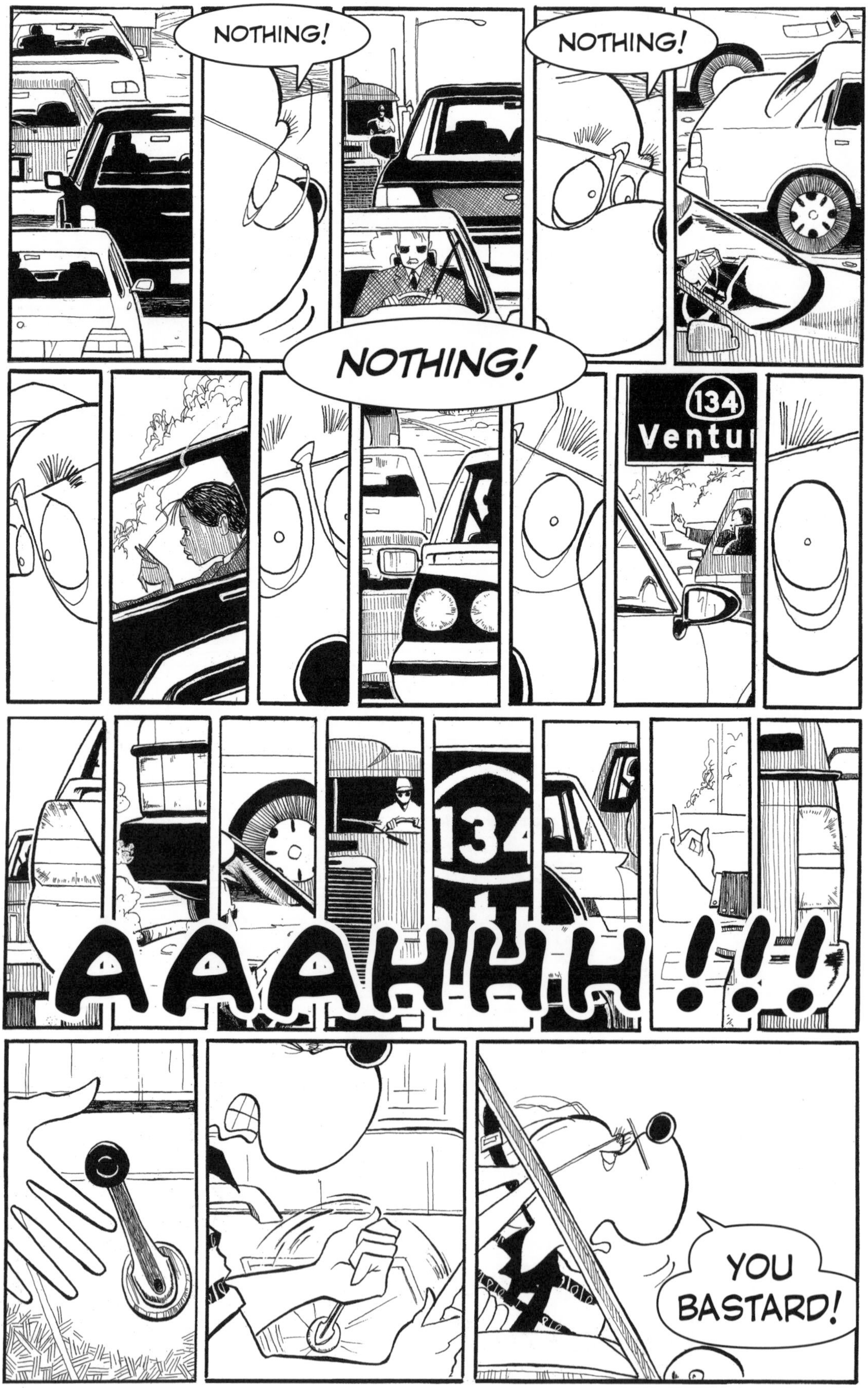
NOTHING!
NOTHING!
NOTHING!
134
Ventu
134
AAAHHH!!!
YOU BASTARD!

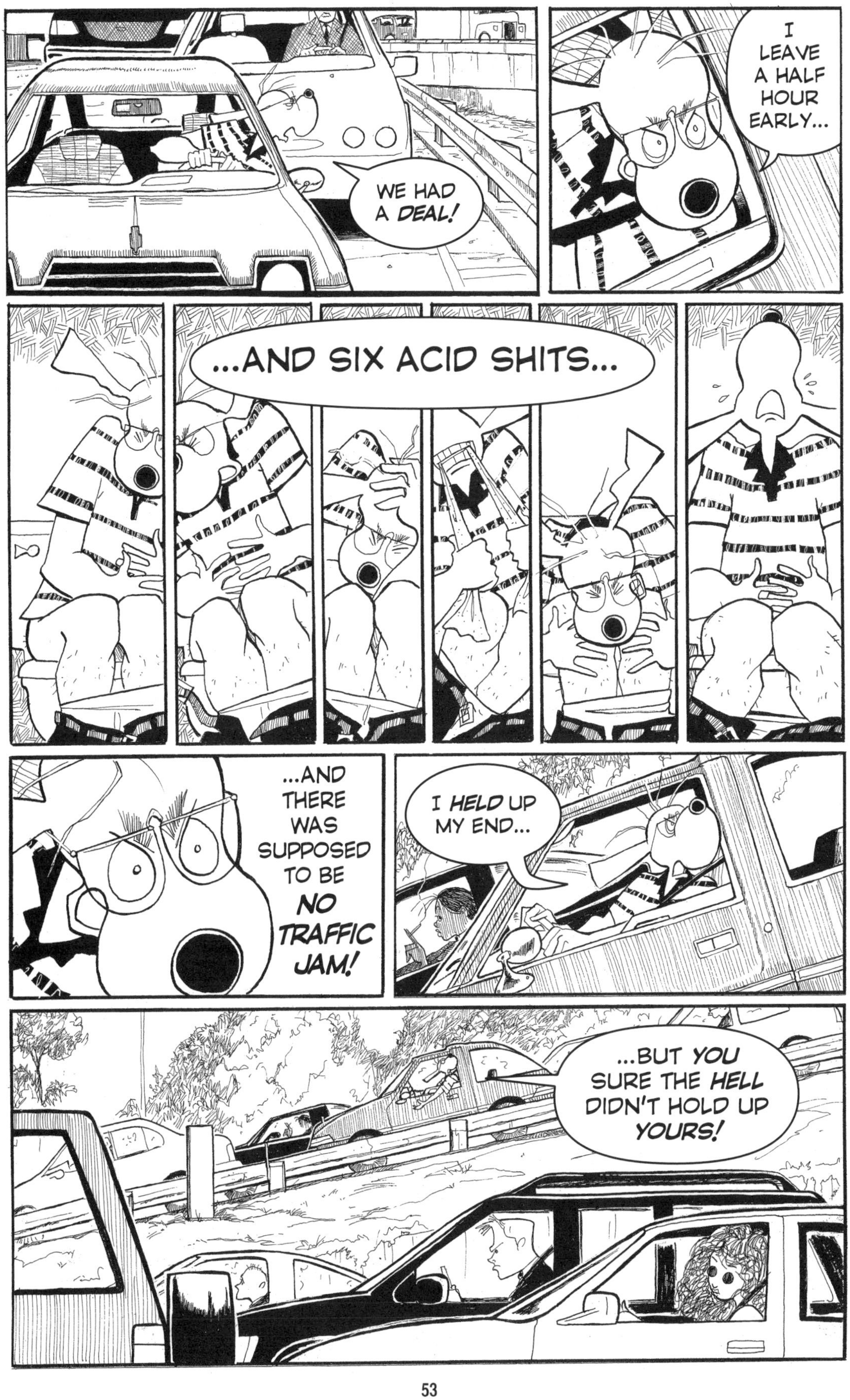
WE HAD A DEAL!
I LEAVE A HALF HOUR EARLY...
...AND SIX ACID SHITS...
...AND THERE WAS SUPPOSED TO BE NO TRAFFIC JAM!
I HELD UP MY END...
...BUT YOU SURE THE HELL DIDN'T HOLD UP YOURS!

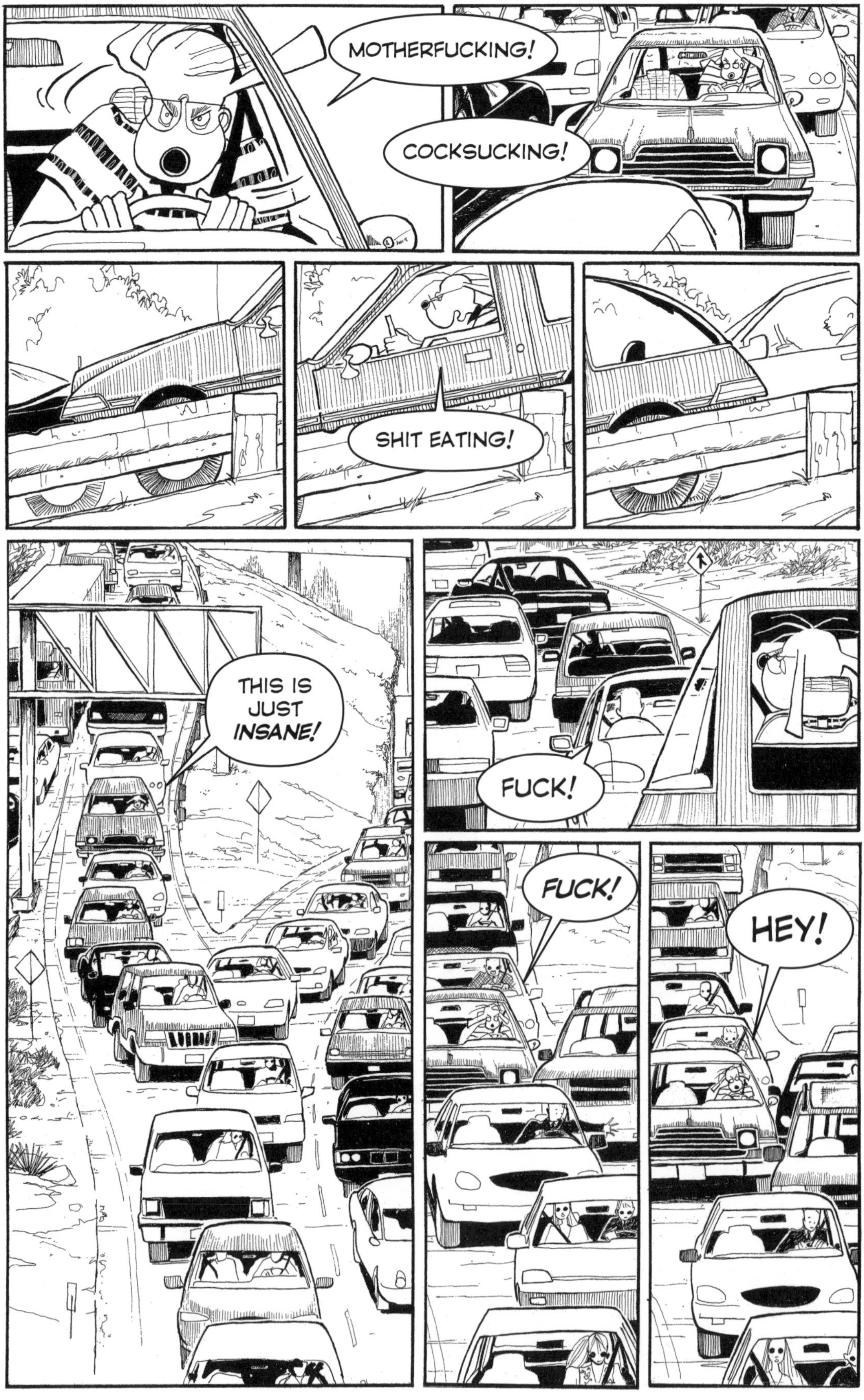
MOTHERFUCKING!
COCKSUCKING!
SHIT EATING!
THIS IS JUST *INSANE!*
FUCK!
FUCK!
HEY!

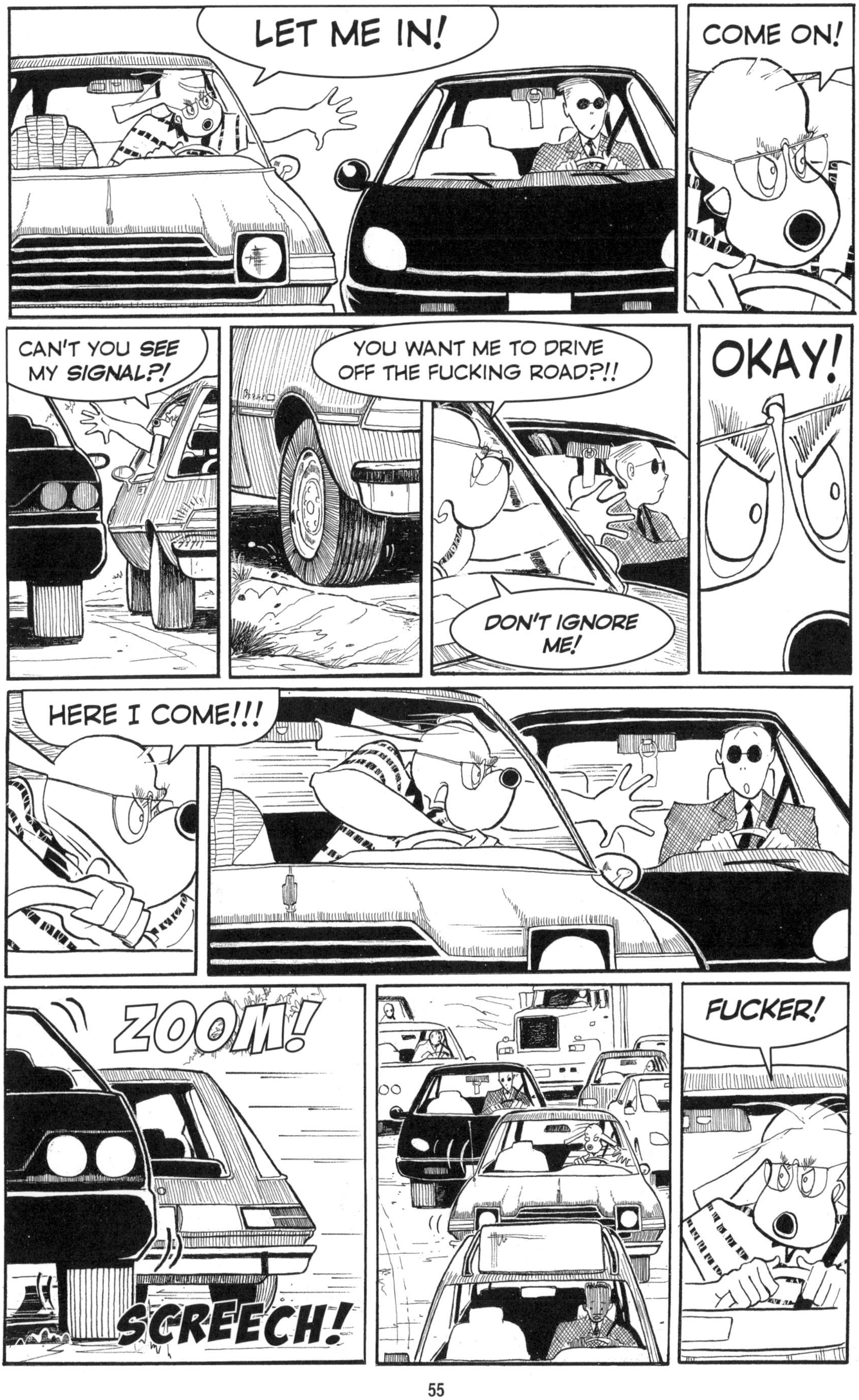
LET ME IN!
COME ON!
CAN'T YOU SEE MY SIGNAL?!
YOU WANT ME TO DRIVE OFF THE FUCKING ROAD?!!
DON'T IGNORE ME!
OKAY!
HERE I COME!!!
ZOOM!
SCREECH!
FUCKER!

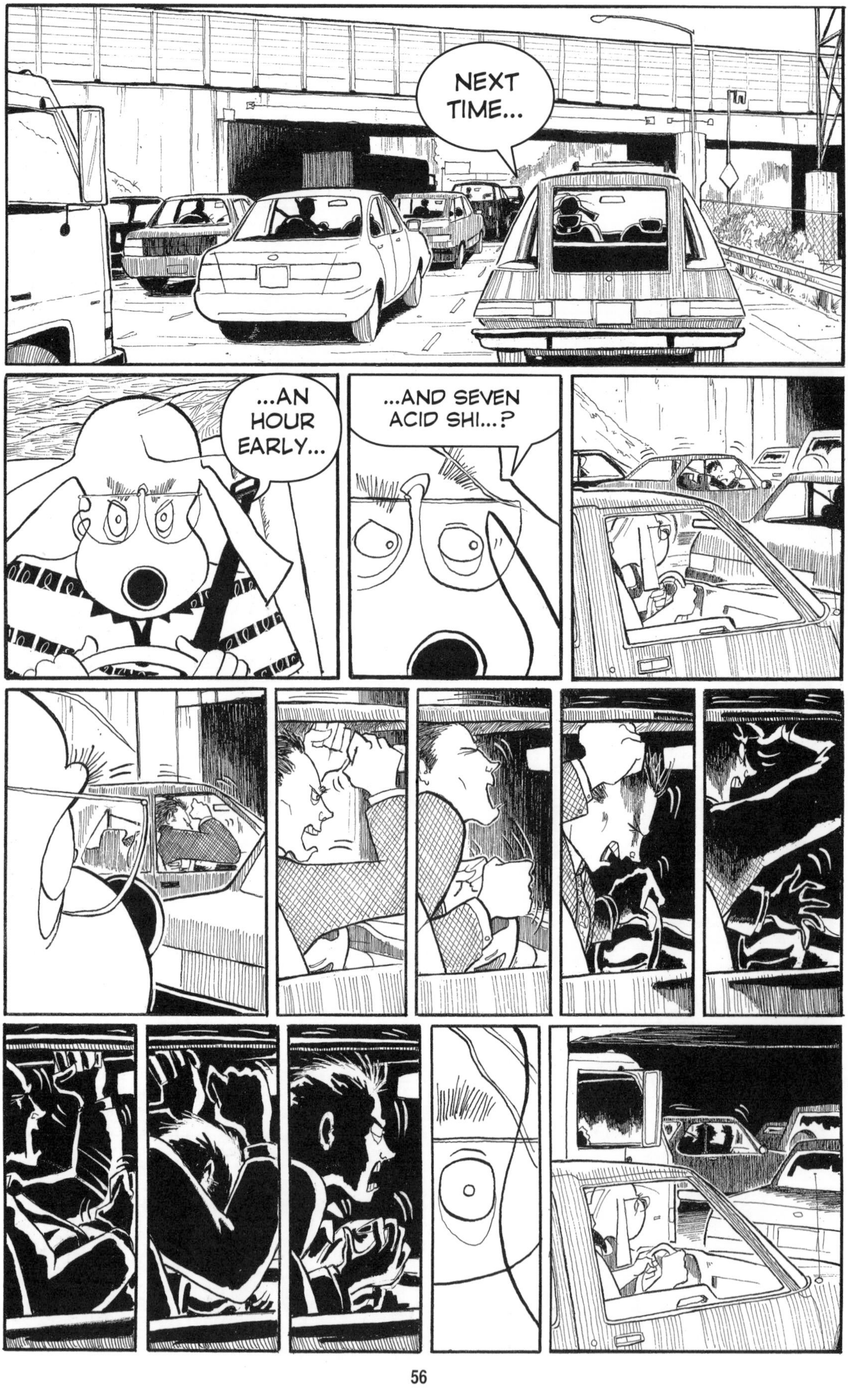
NEXT TIME...
...AN HOUR EARLY...
...AND SEVEN ACID SHI...?

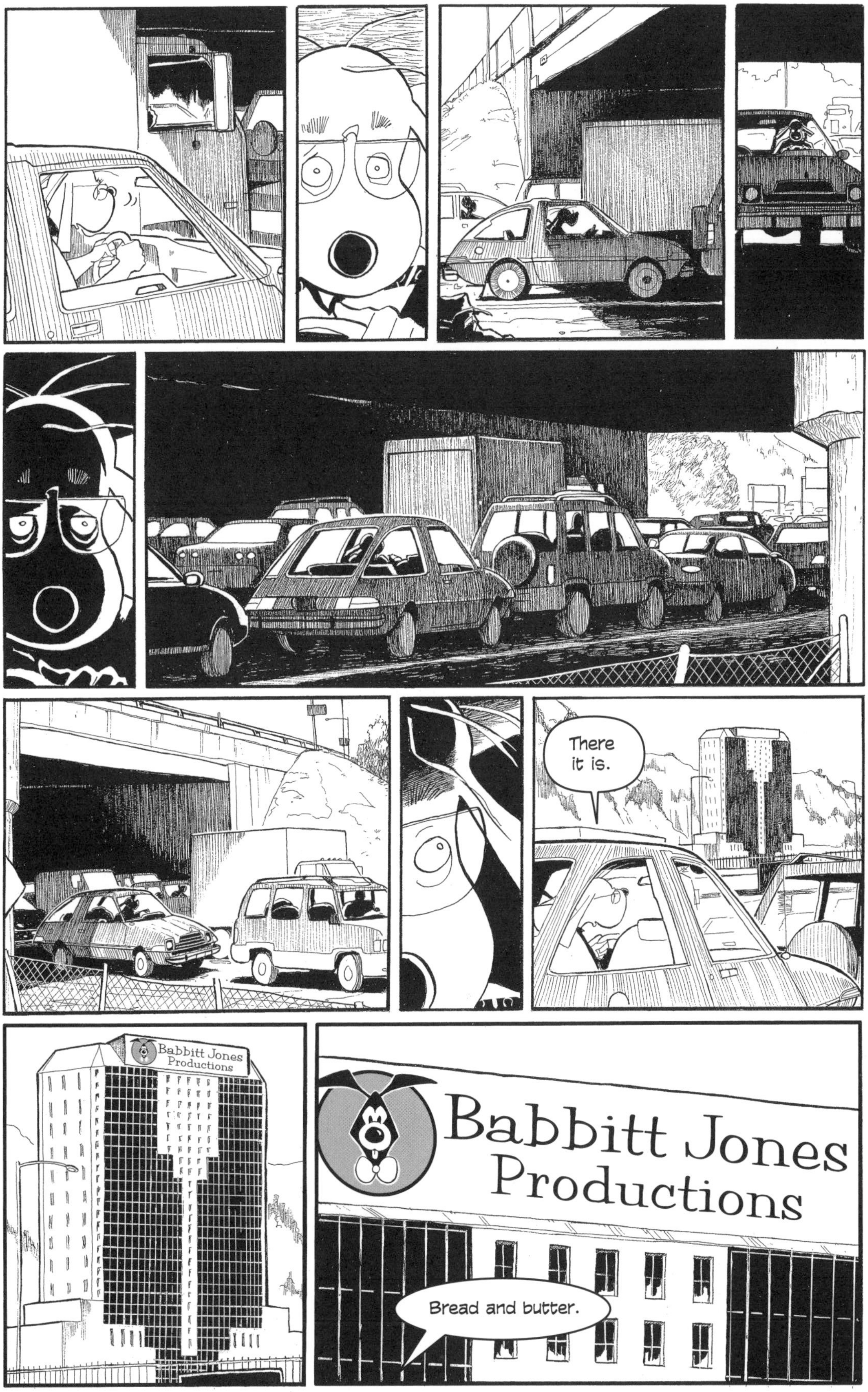
There it is.
Babbitt Jones Productions
Babbitt Jones Productions
Bread and butter.

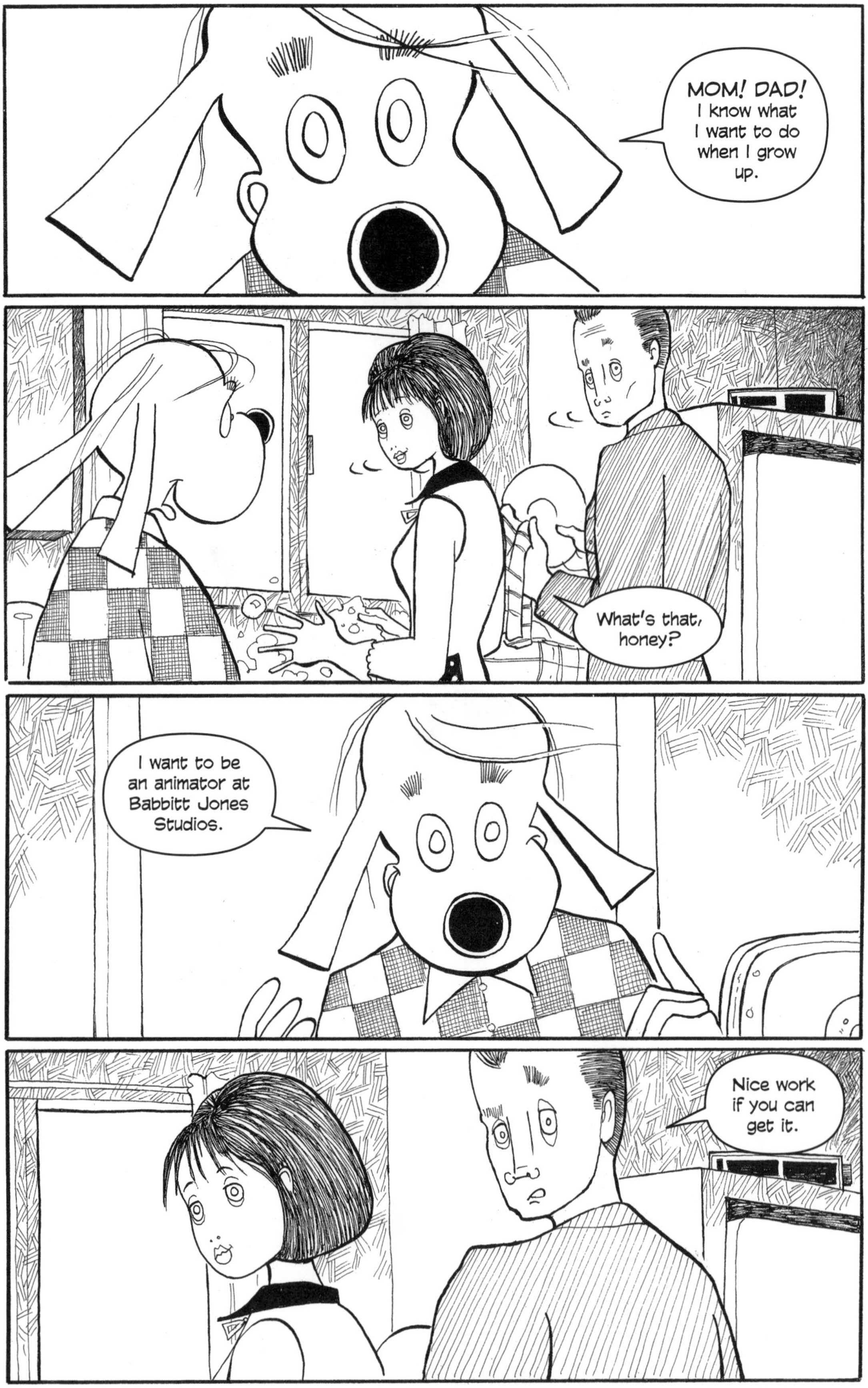
MOM! DAD! I know what I want to do when I grow up.
What's that, honey?
I want to be an animator at Babbitt Jones Studios.
Nice work if you can get it.

Babbitt Jones
Productions
AM
FM
Babbitt Jones
Drive
EXIT
EXIT
EXIT

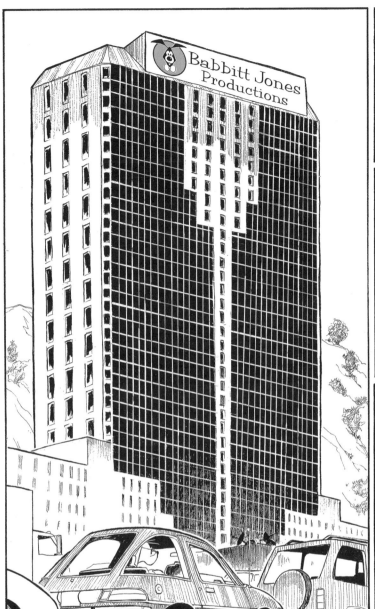

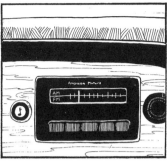

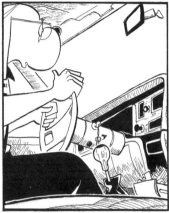

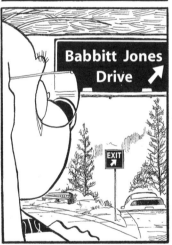

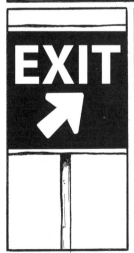

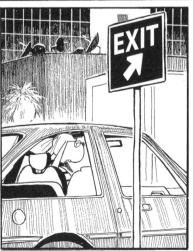

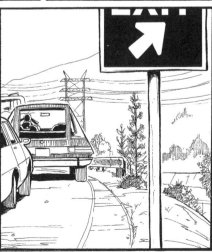

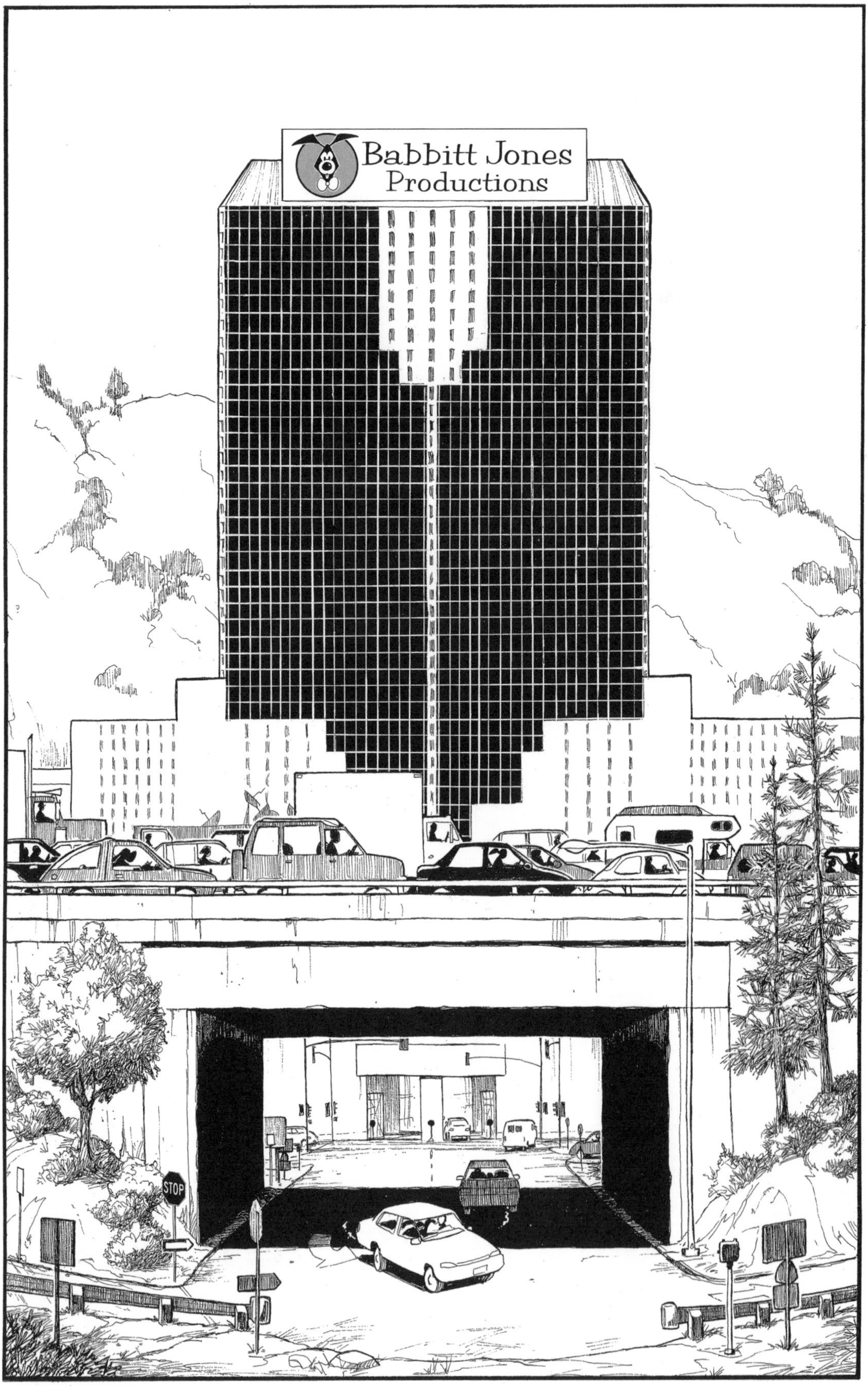
Babbitt Jones
Productions
STOP

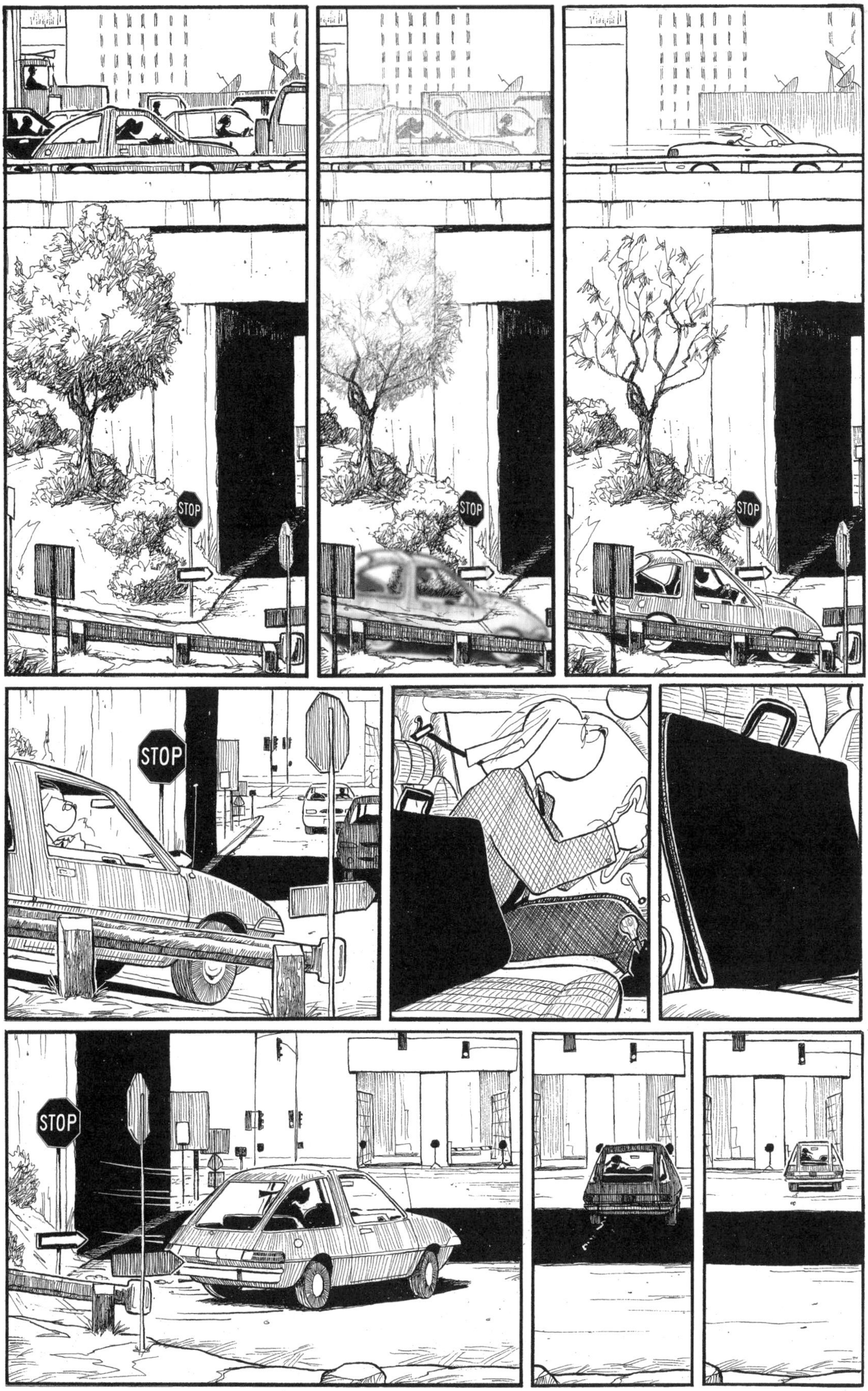
STOP
STOP
STOP
STOP
STOP

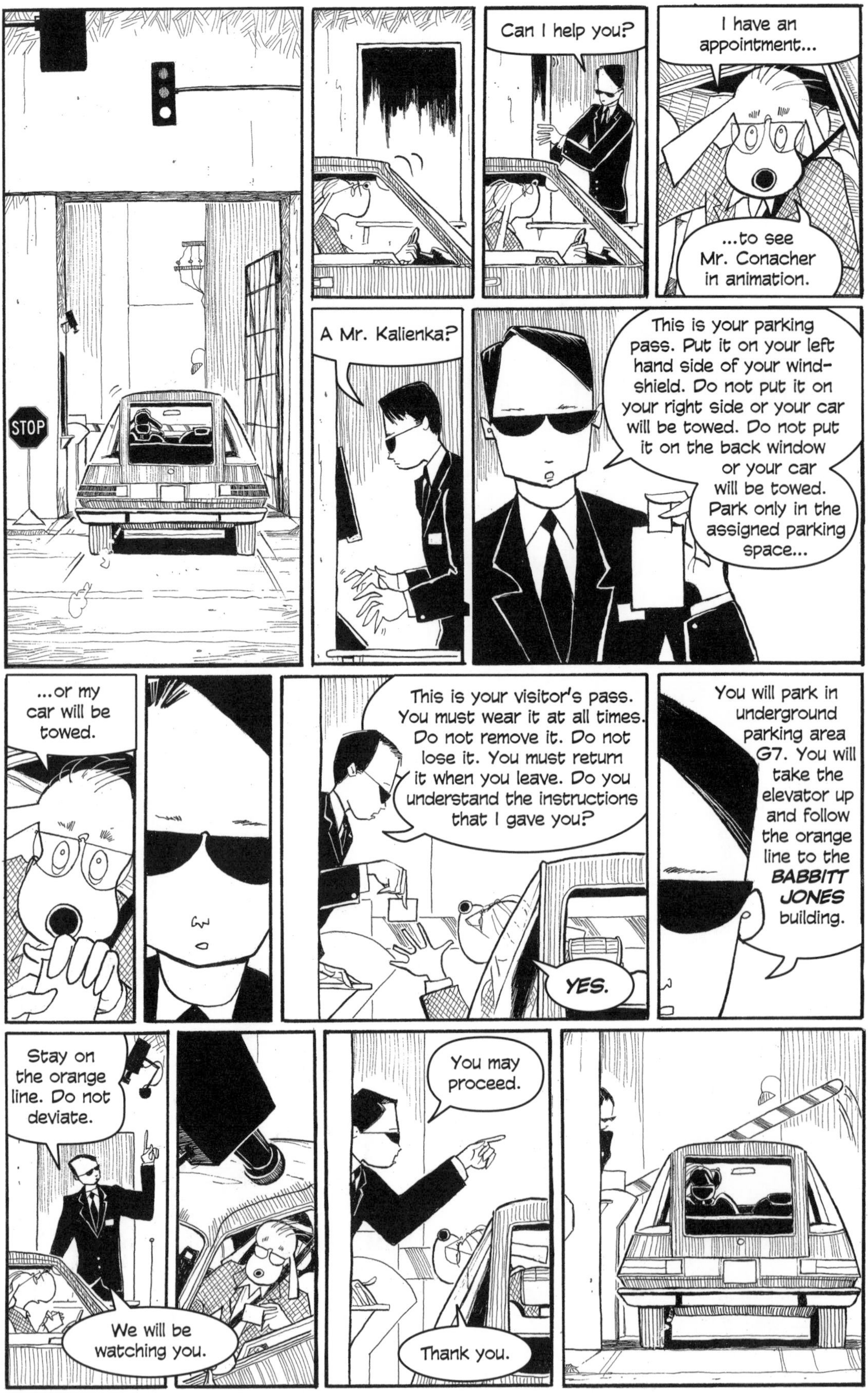

Can I help you?
I have an appointment...
...to see Mr. Conacher in animation.
A Mr. Kalienka?
This is your parking pass. Put it on your left hand side of your windshield. Do not put it on your right side or your car will be towed. Do not put it on the back window or your car will be towed. Park only in the assigned parking space...
...or my car will be towed.
This is your visitor's pass. You must wear it at all times. Do not remove it. Do not lose it. You must return it when you leave. Do you understand the instructions that I gave you?
YES.
You will park in underground parking area G7. You will take the elevator up and follow the orange line to the BABBITT JONES building.
Stay on the orange line. Do not deviate.
We will be watching you.
You may proceed.
Thank you.
STOP

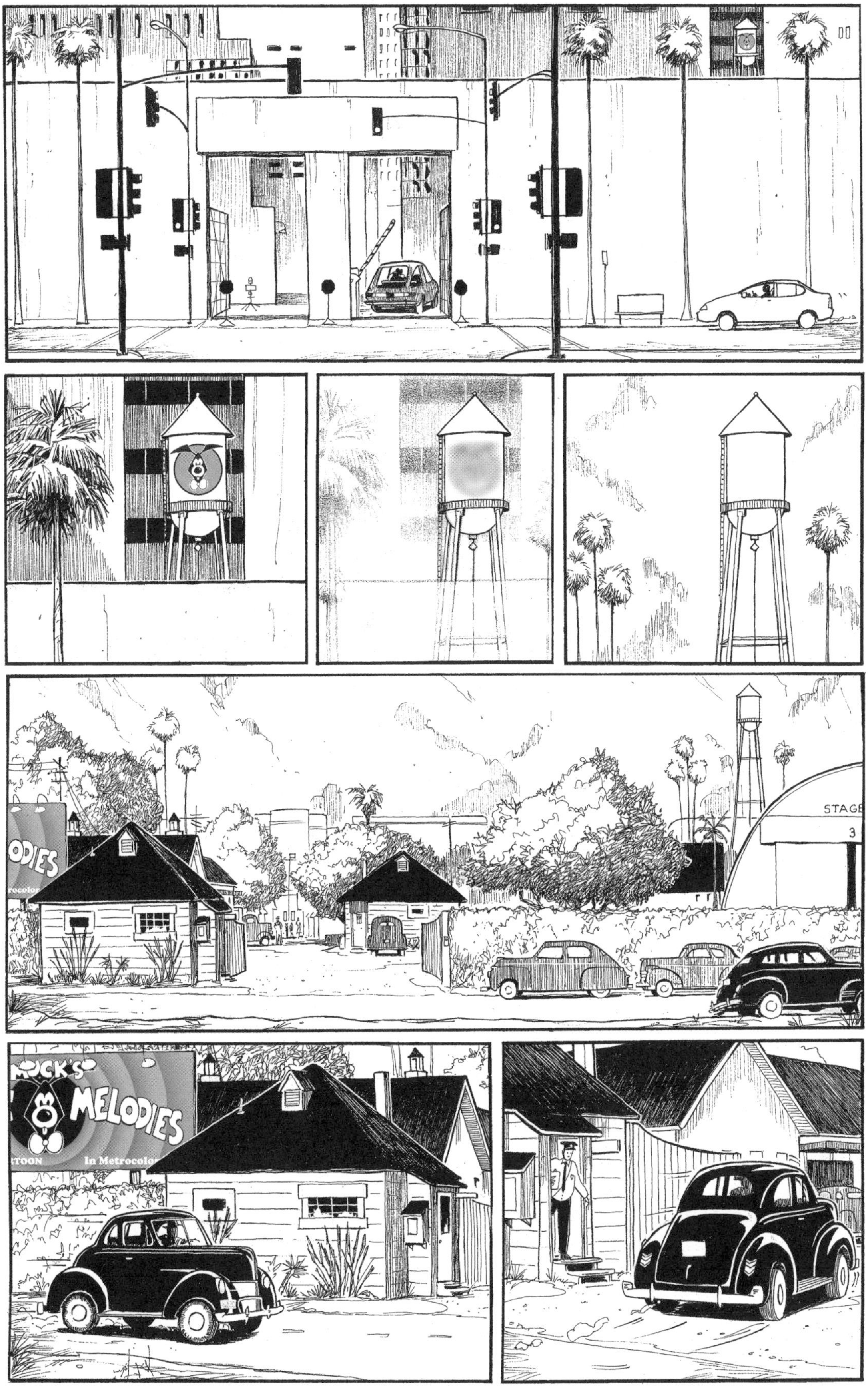
STAGE
3
ODIES
rocolor
CK'S
MELODIES
TOON
In Metrocolo

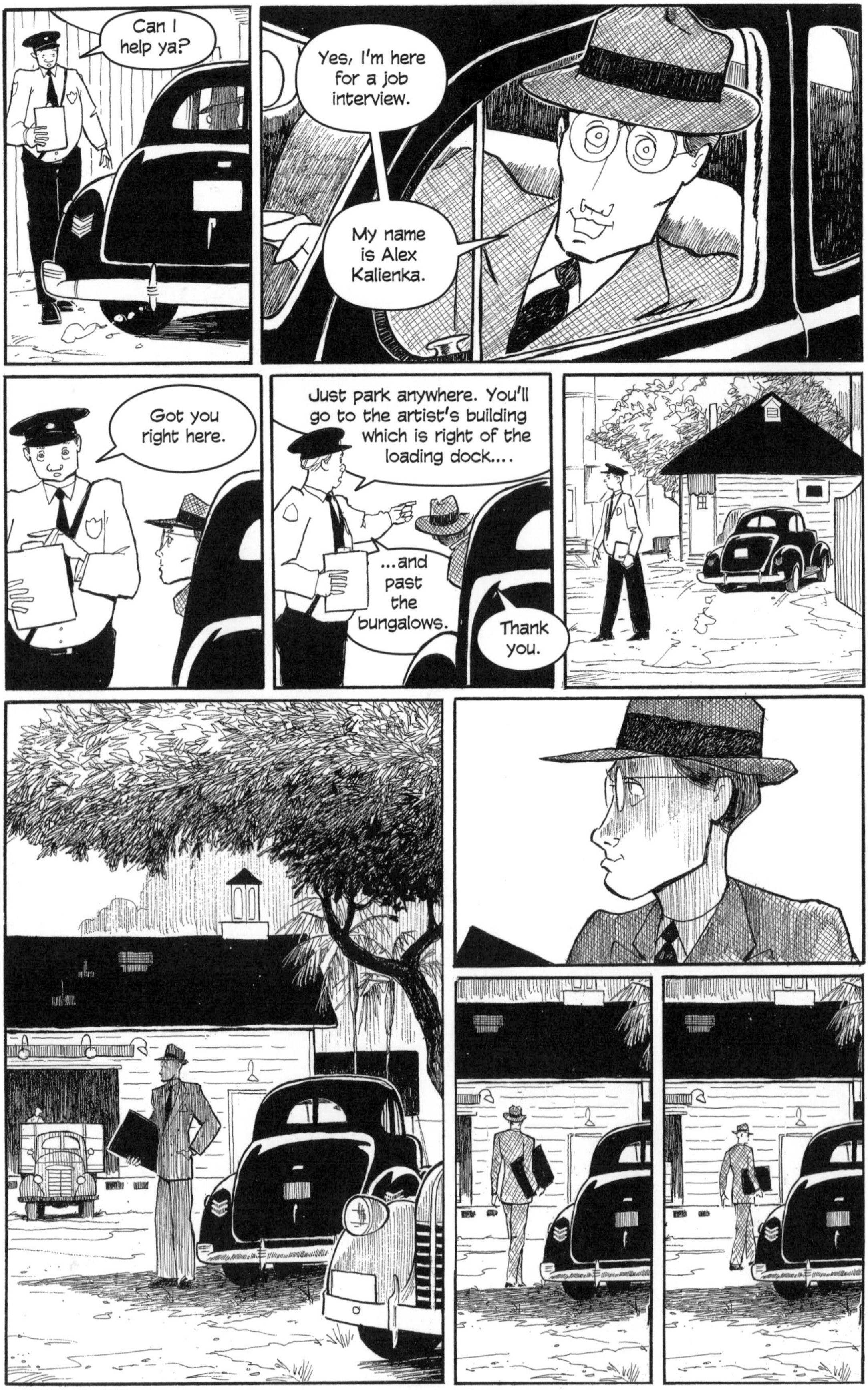
Can I help ya?
Yes, I'm here for a job interview.
My name is Alex Kalienka.
Got you right here.
Just park anywhere. You'll go to the artist's building which is right of the loading dock....
...and past the bungalows.
Thank you.

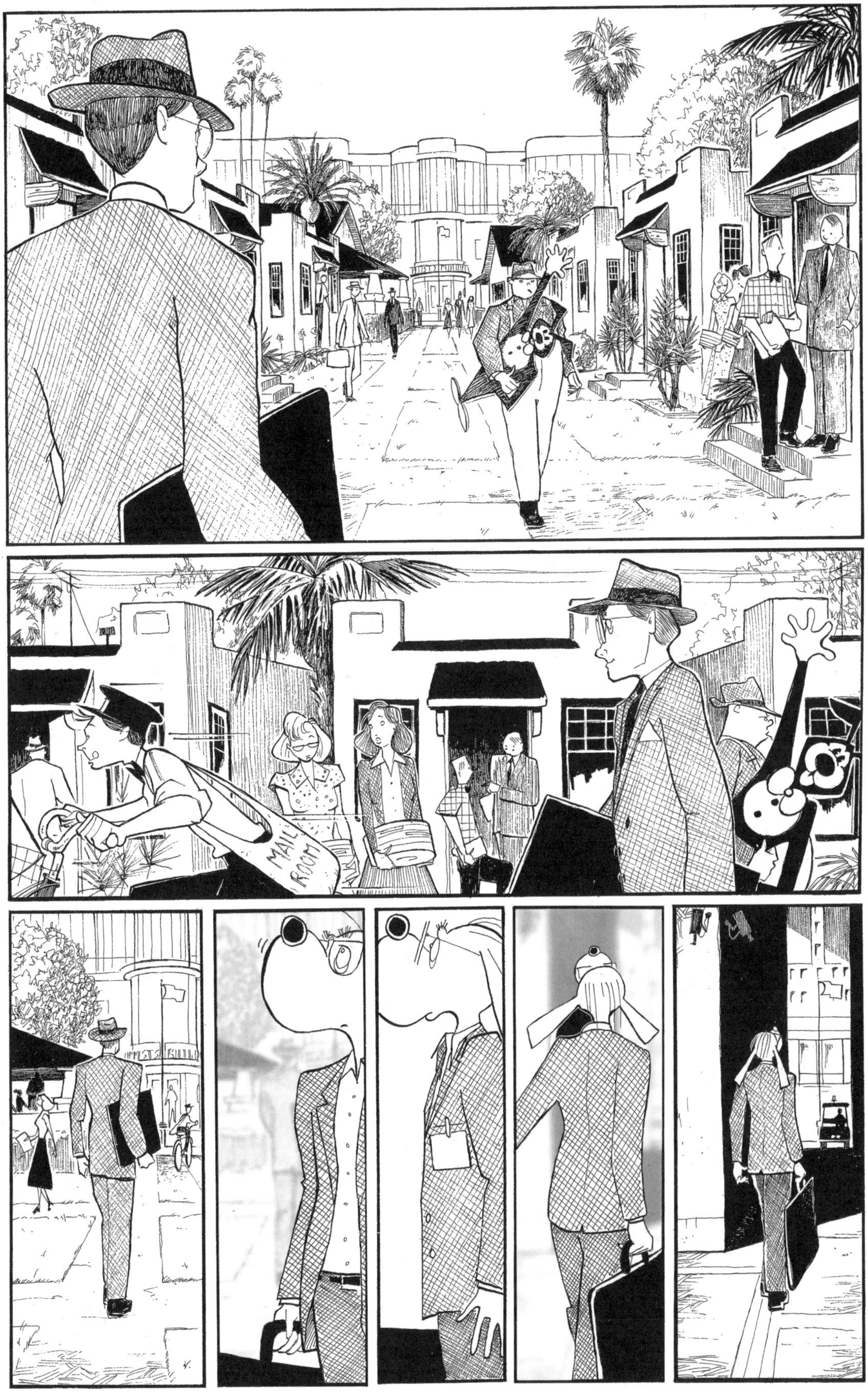
MAIL ROOM

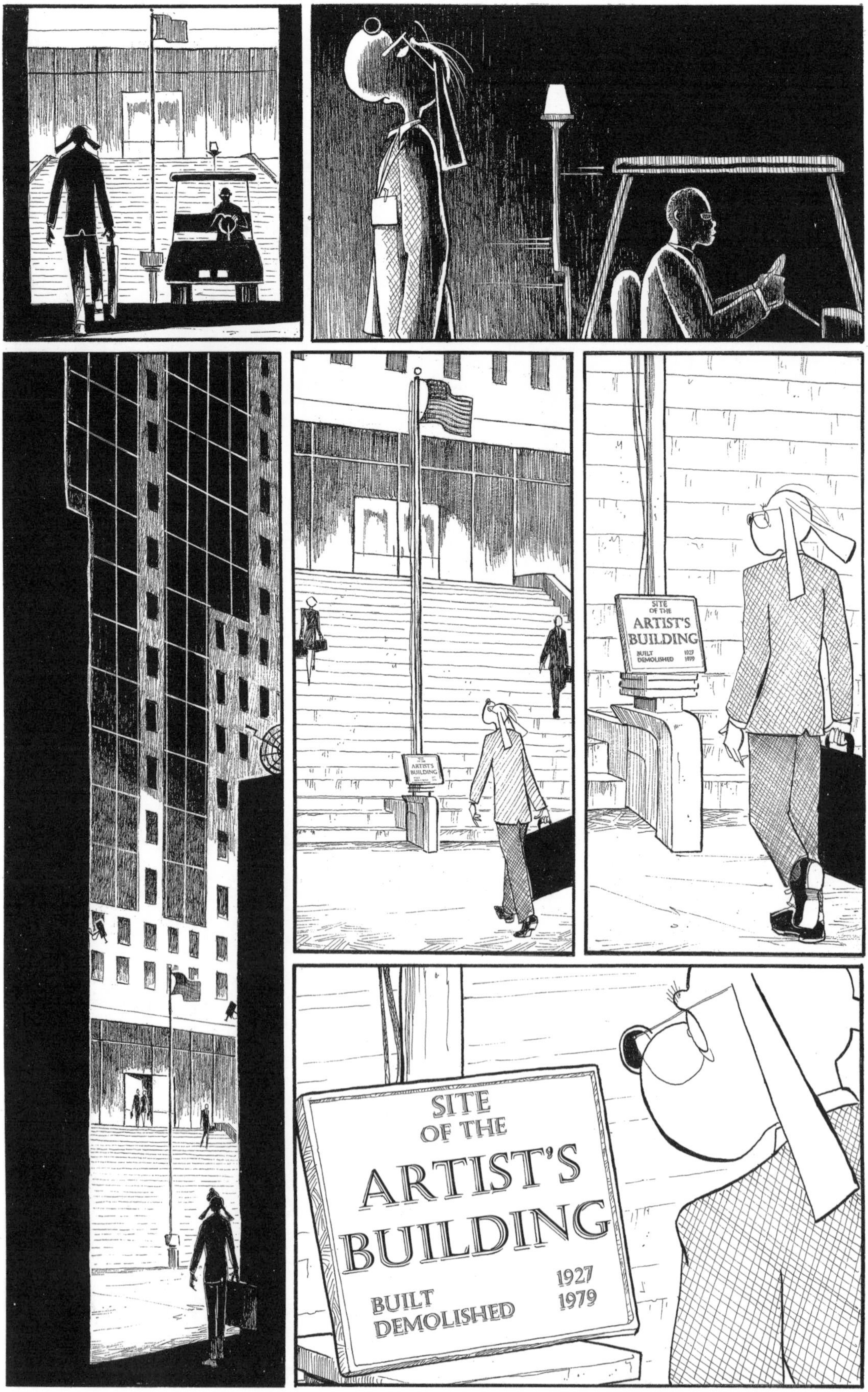
SITE OF THE ARTIST'S BUILDING
BUILT 1927
DEMOLISHED 1979
SITE OF THE
ARTIST'S
BUILDING
BUILT 1927
DEMOLISHED 1979

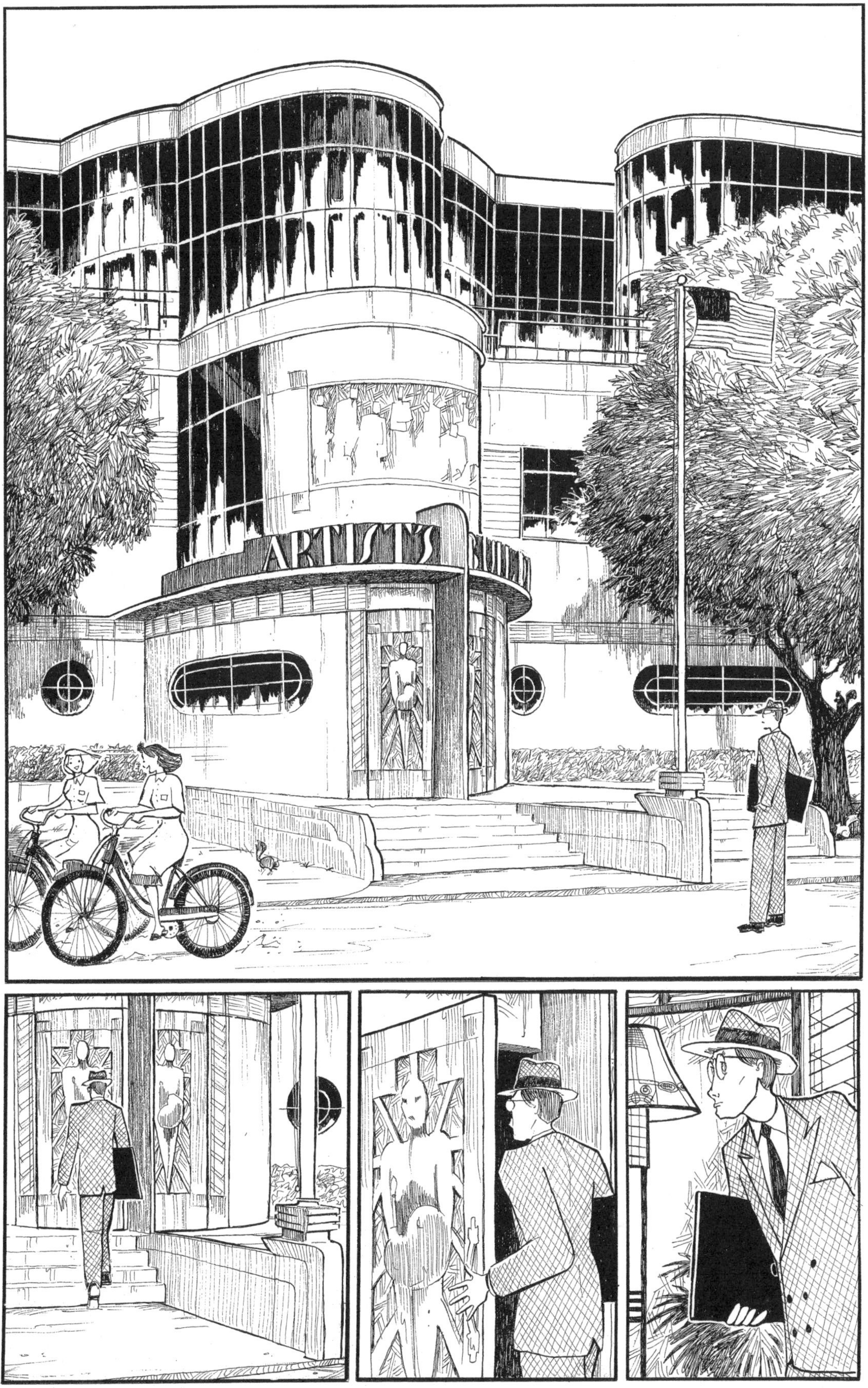
ARTIST'S

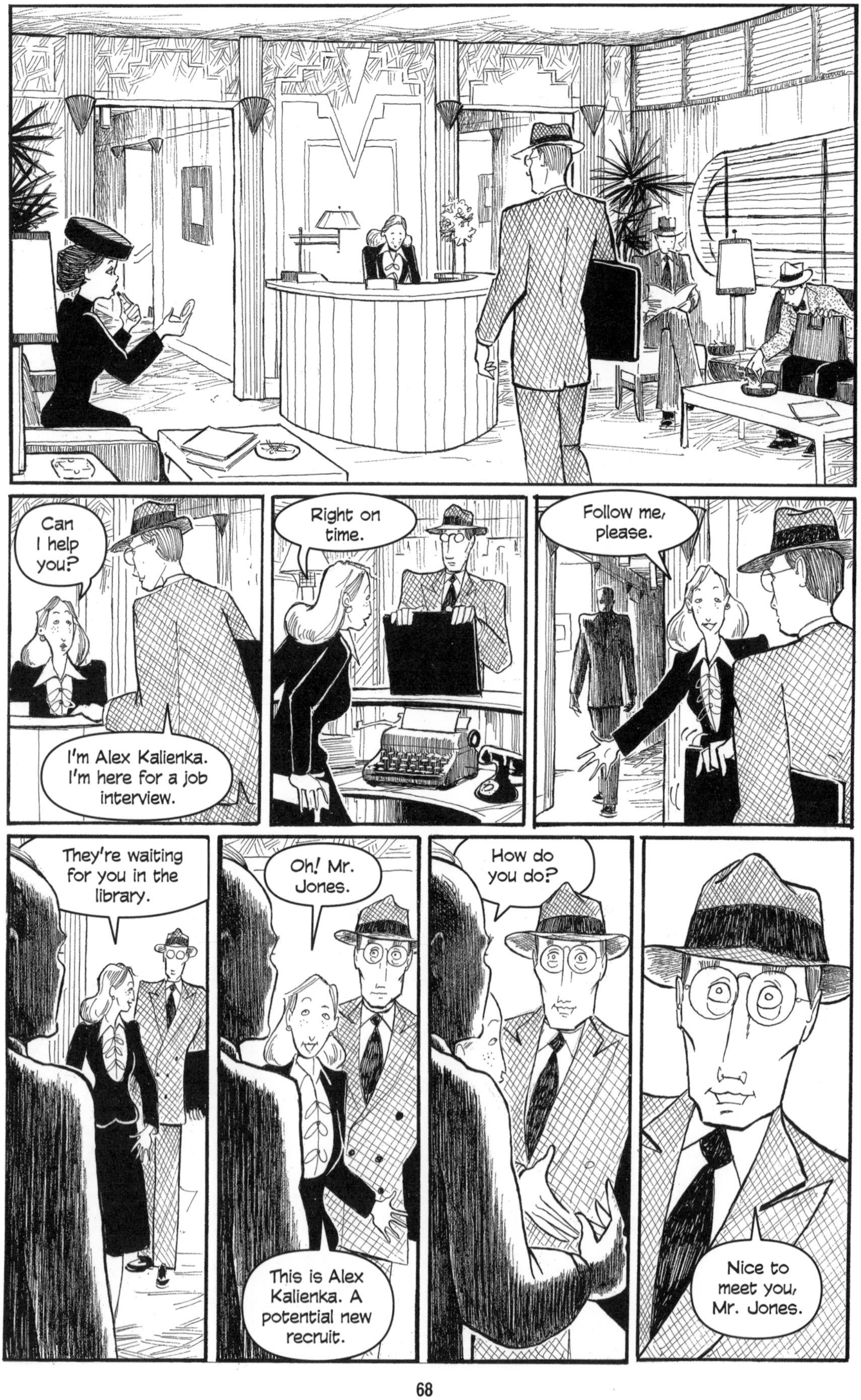
Can I help you?
I'm Alex Kalienka. I'm here for a job interview.
Right on time.
Follow me, please.
They're waiting for you in the library.
Oh! Mr. Jones.
This is Alex Kalienka. A potential new recruit.
How do you do?
Nice to meet you, Mr. Jones.

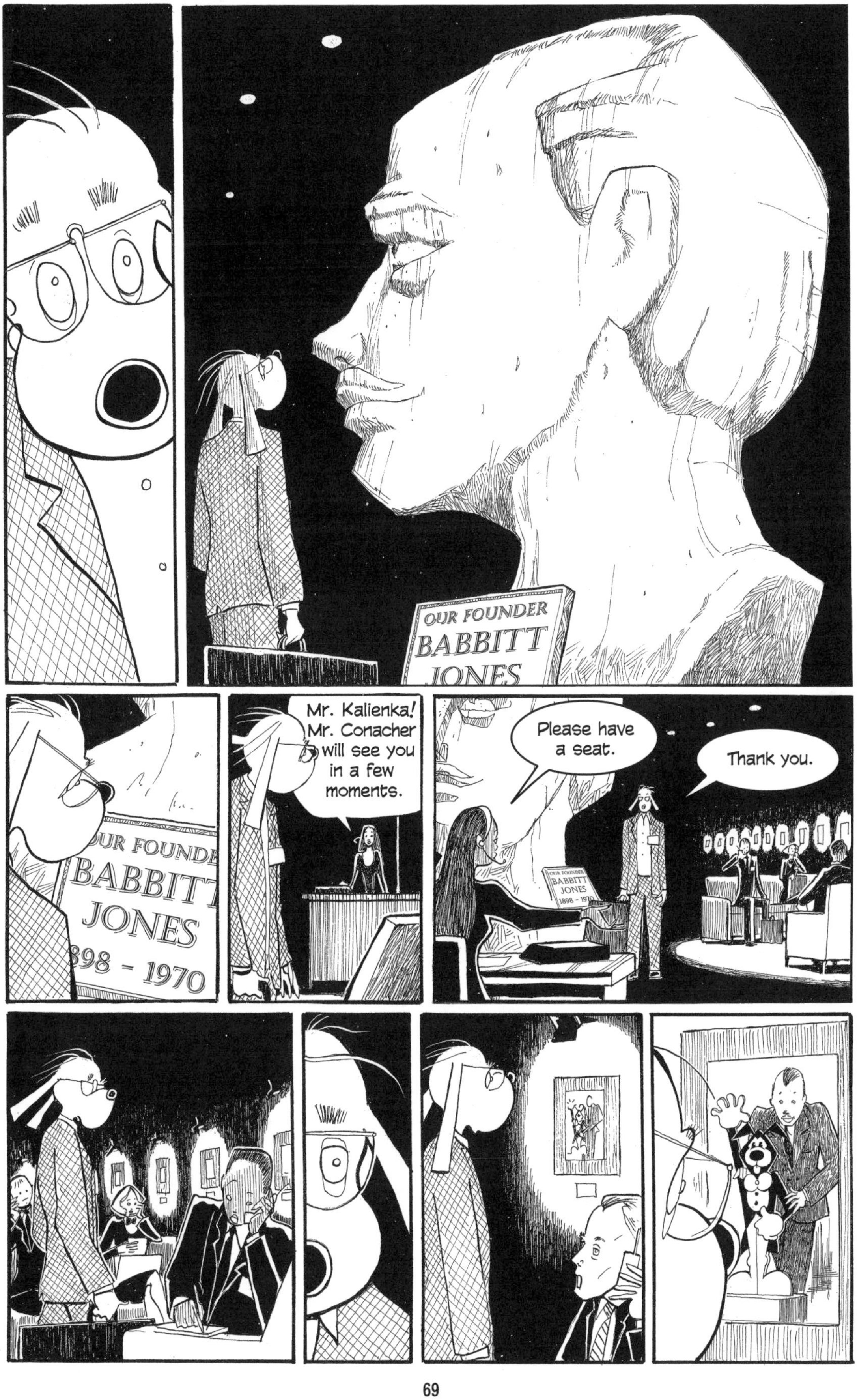
OUR FOUNDER
BABBITT
JONES
OUR FOUNDER
BABBITT
JONES
1898 - 1970
Mr. Kalienka! Mr. Conacher will see you in a few moments.
Please have a seat.
Thank you.

BABBITT
AND
MUCK

1919

INK
AND
PAINT
DEPT.

1946

THE
IRASCIBLES

1946

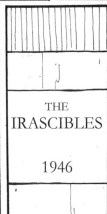

Who are the Irascibles?

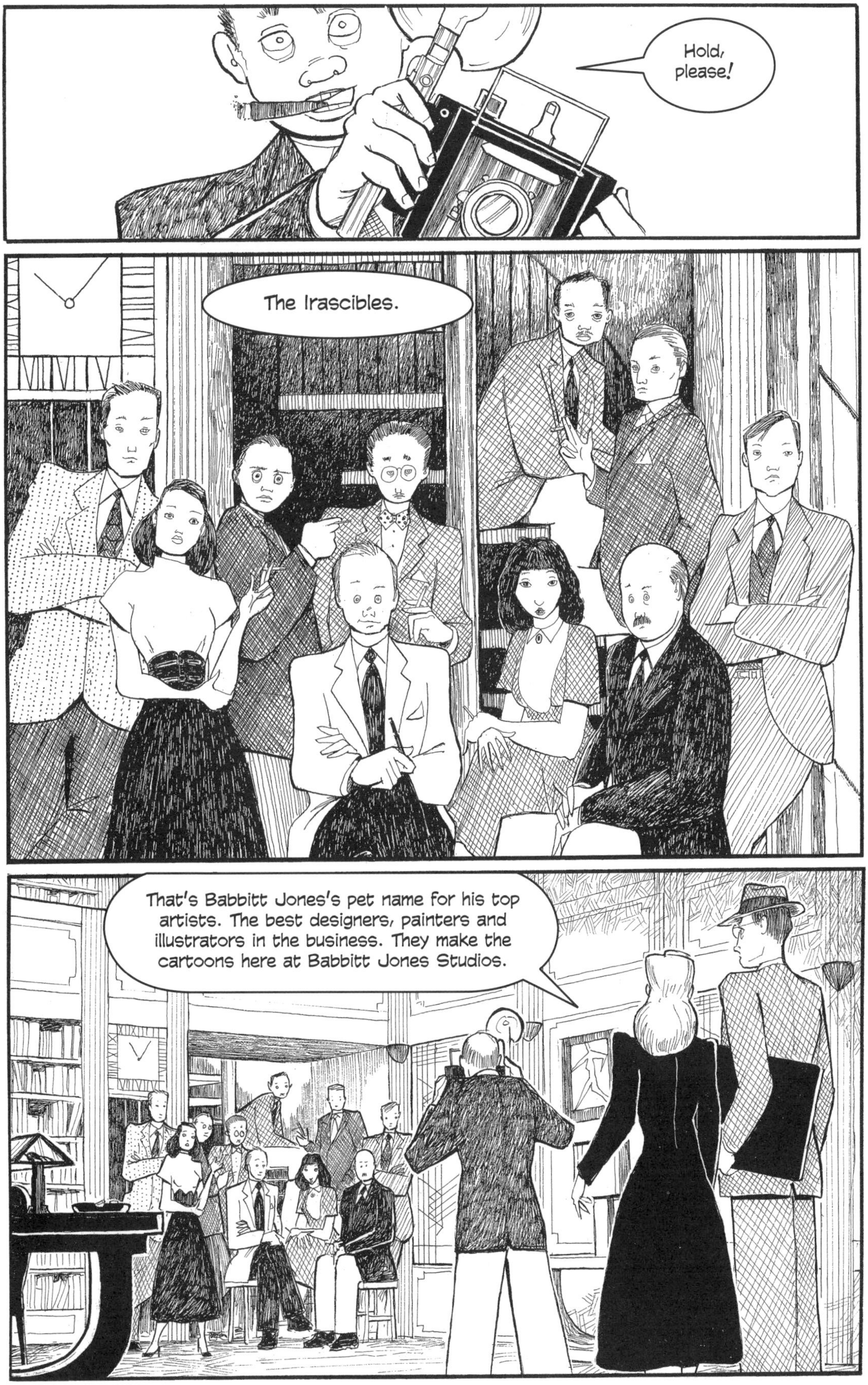
Hold, please!
The Irascibles.
That's Babbitt Jones's pet name for his top artists. The best designers, painters and illustrators in the business. They make the cartoons here at Babbitt Jones Studios.

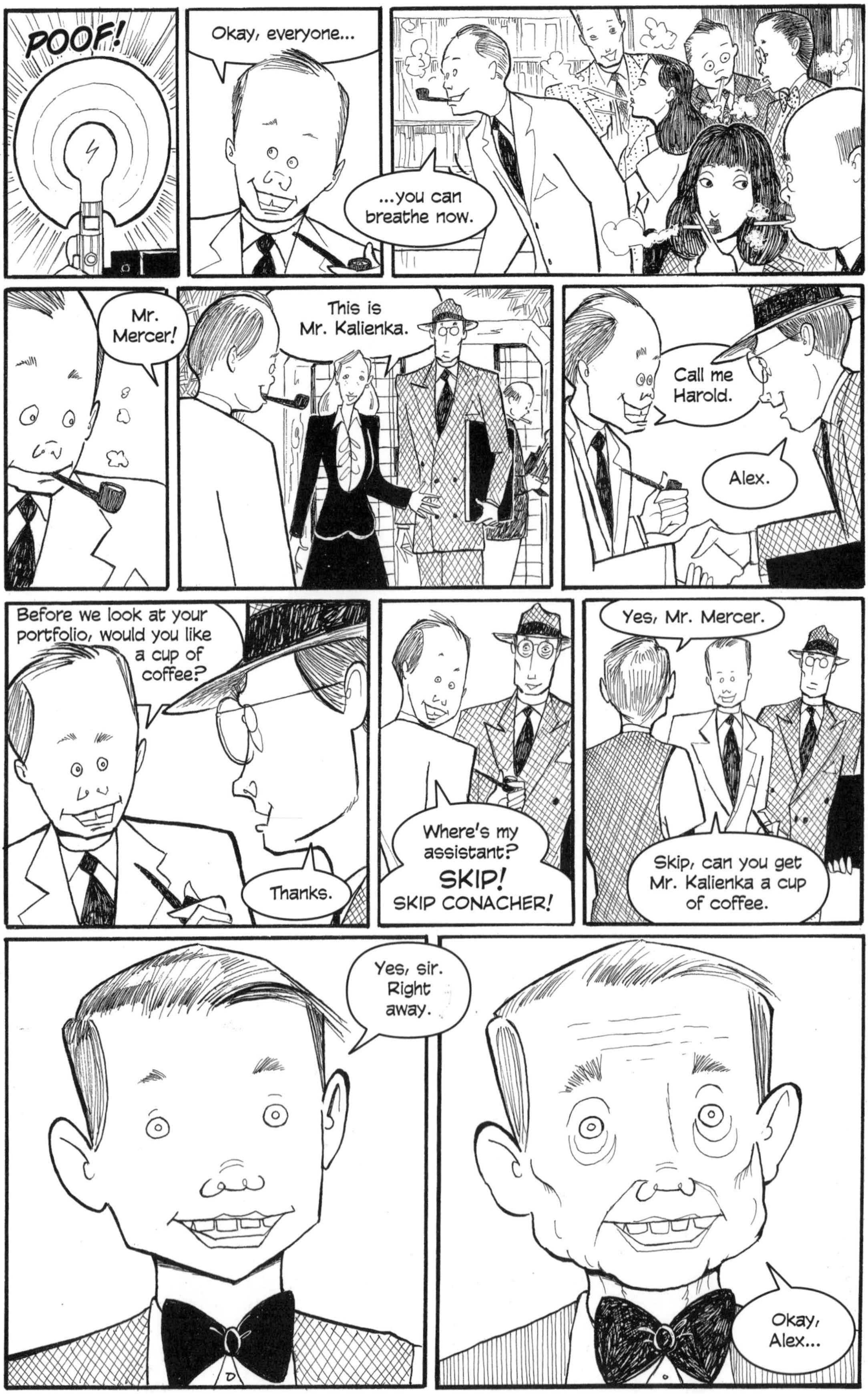
POOF!
Okay, everyone...
...you can breathe now.
Mr. Mercer!
This is Mr. Kalienka.
Call me Harold.
Alex.
Before we look at your portfolio, would you like a cup of coffee?
Thanks.
Where's my assistant? SKIP! SKIP CONACHER!
Yes, Mr. Mercer.
Skip, can you get Mr. Kalienka a cup of coffee.
Yes, sir. Right away.
Okay, Alex...

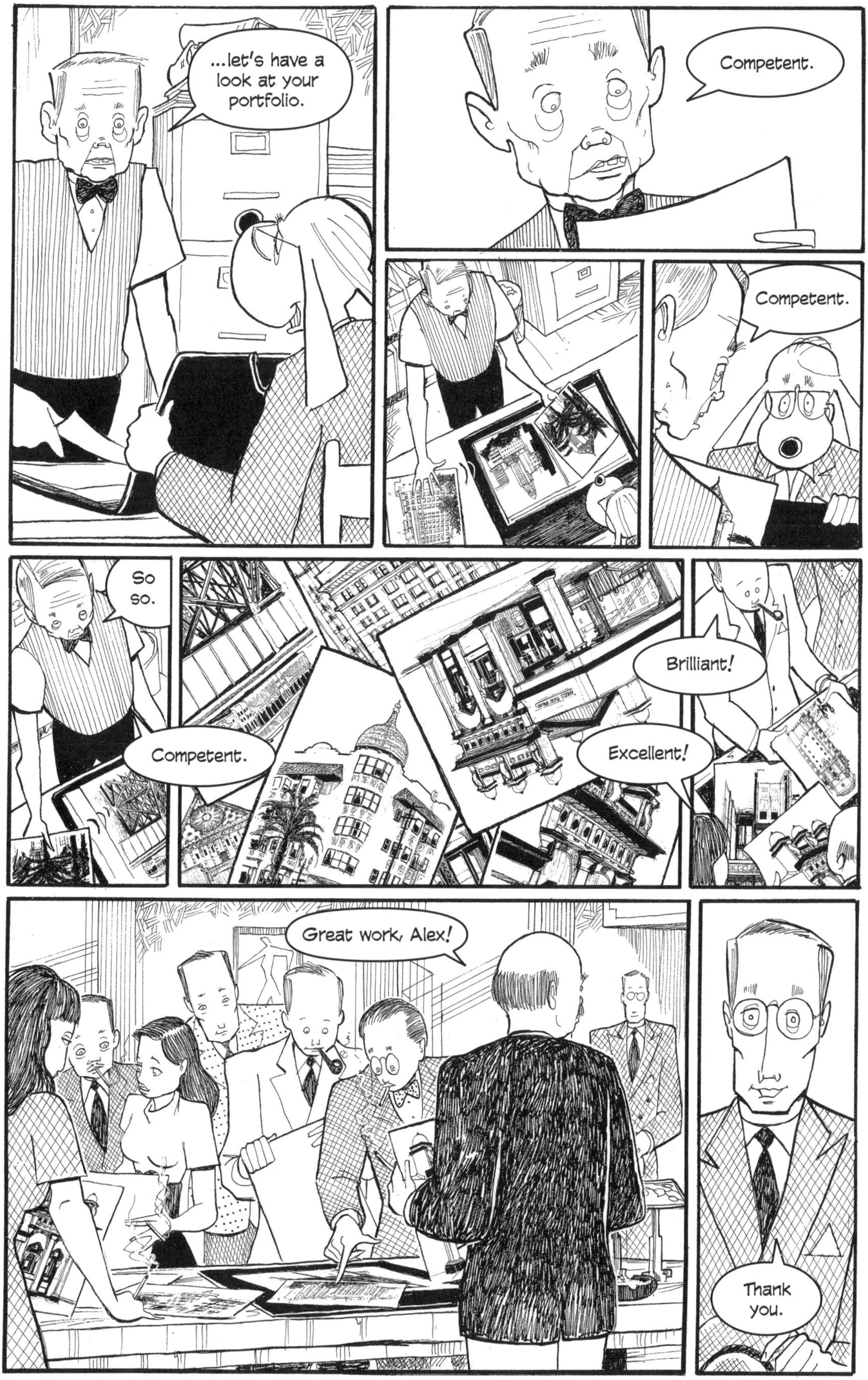
...let's have a look at your portfolio.
Competent.
Competent.
So so.
Competent.
Brilliant!
Excellent!
Great work, Alex!
Thank you.

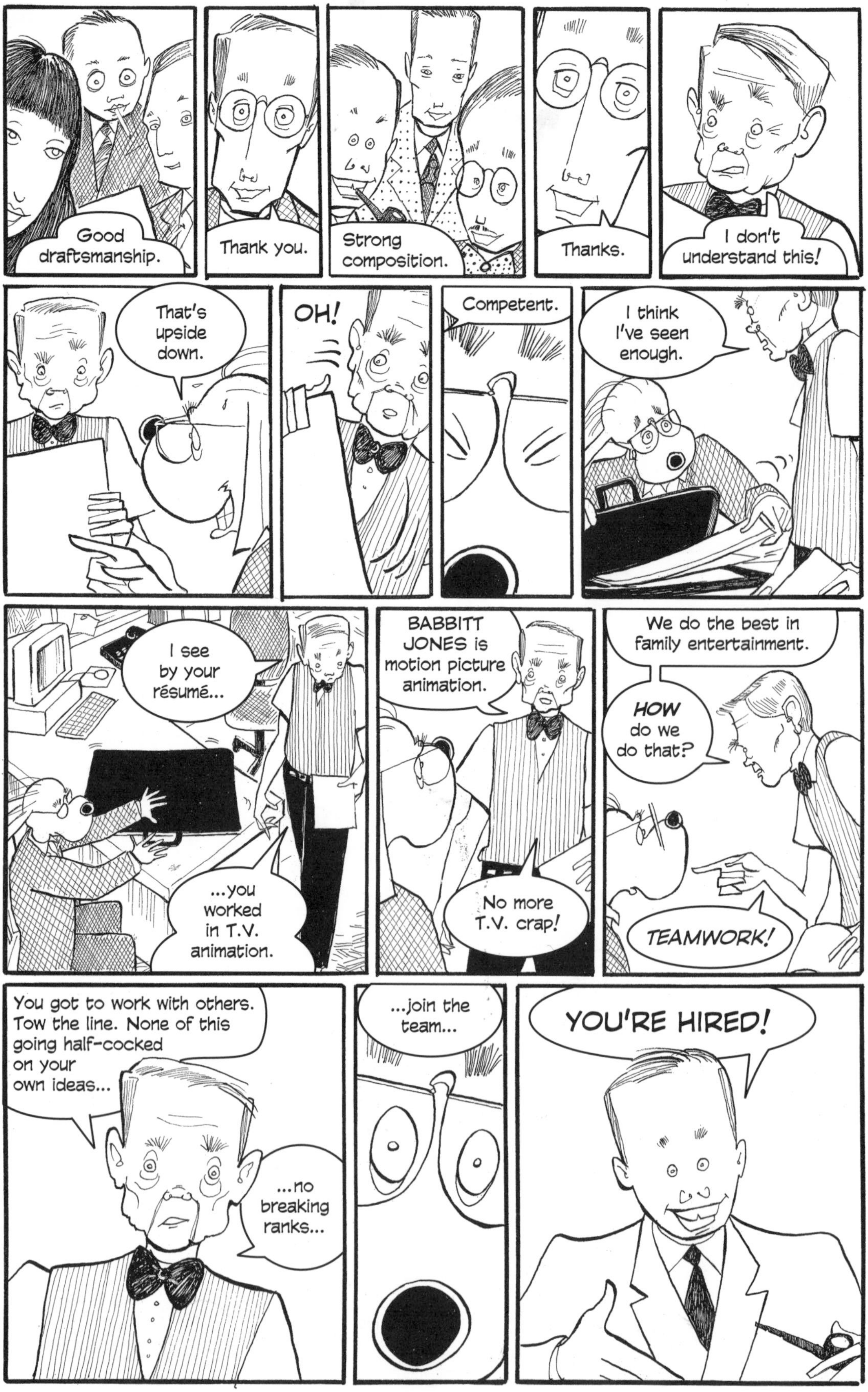
Good draftsmanship.
Thank you.
Strong composition.
Thanks.
I don't understand this!
That's upside down.
OH!
Competent.
I think I've seen enough.
I see by your résumé...
...you worked in T.V. animation.
BABBITT JONES is motion picture animation.
No more T.V. crap!
We do the best in family entertainment.
HOW do we do that?
TEAMWORK!
You got to work with others. Tow the line. None of this going half-cocked on your own ideas...
...no breaking ranks...
...join the team...
YOU'RE HIRED!

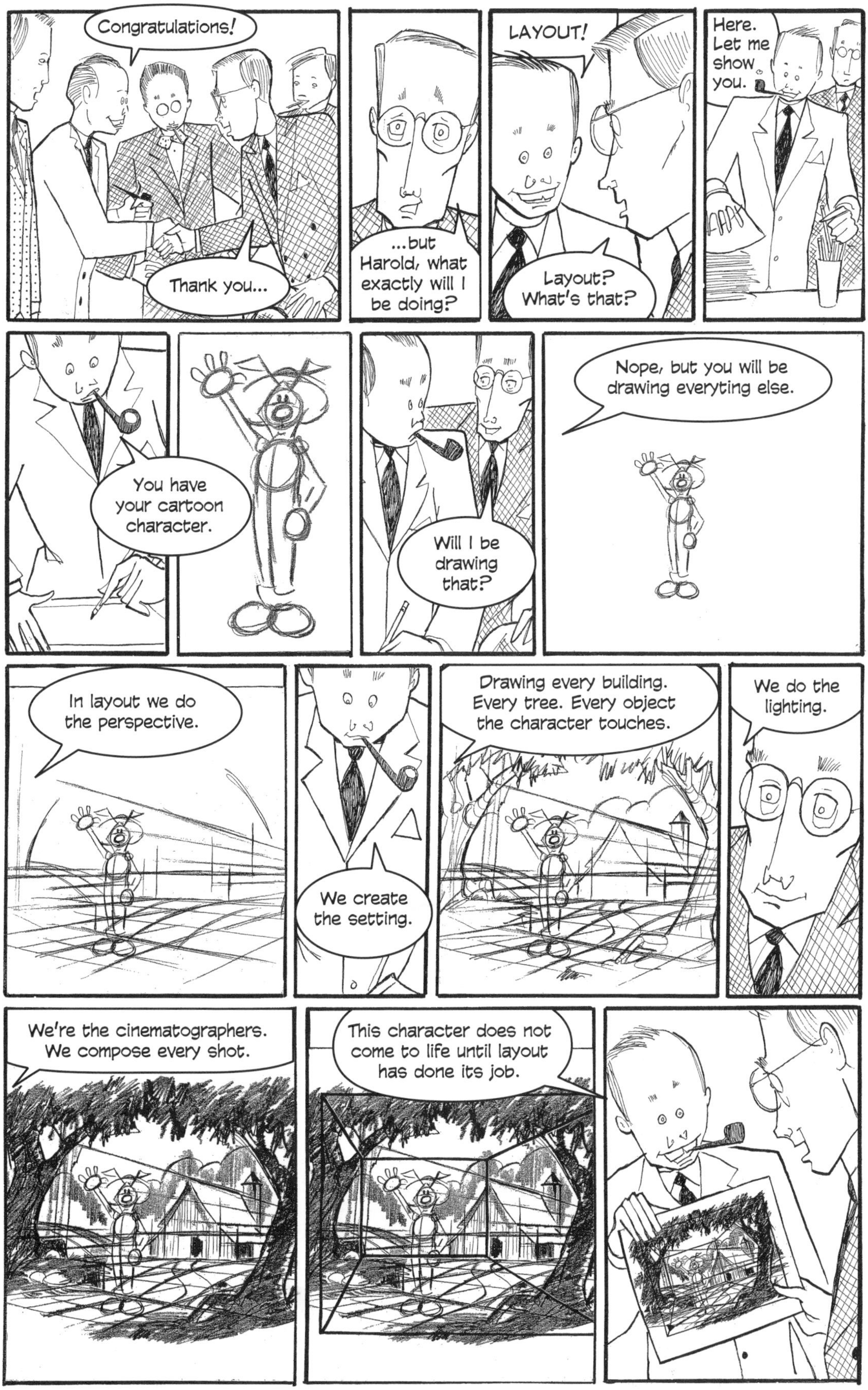
Congratulations!
Thank you...
...but Harold, what exactly will I be doing?
LAYOUT!
Layout? What's that?
Here. Let me show you.
You have your cartoon character.
Will I be drawing that?
Nope, but you will be drawing everyting else.
In layout we do the perspective.
We create the setting.
Drawing every building. Every tree. Every object the character touches.
We do the lighting.
We're the cinematographers. We compose every shot.
This character does not come to life until layout has done its job.

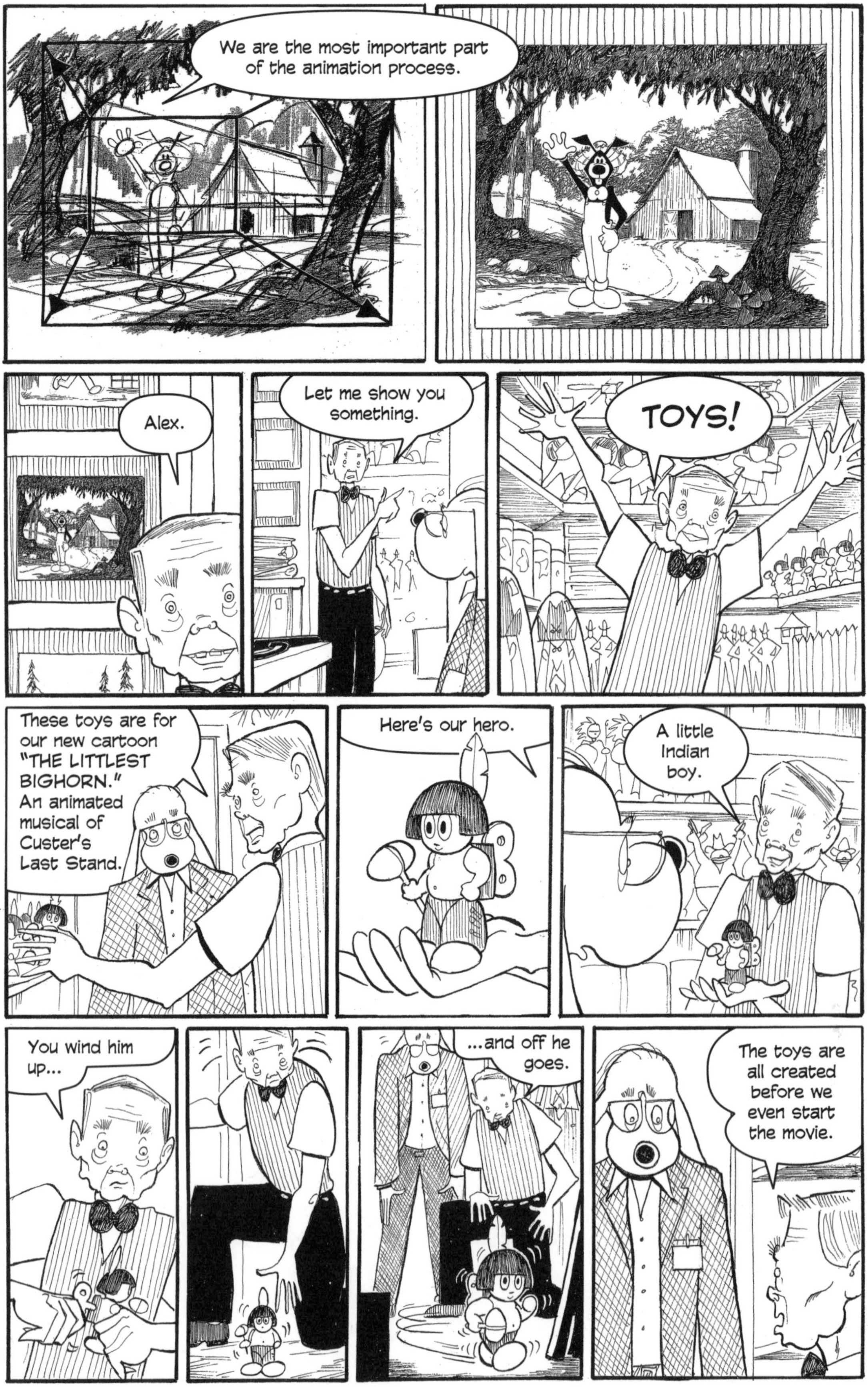

We are the most important part of the animation process.
Alex.
Let me show you something.
TOYS!
These toys are for our new cartoon "THE LITTLEST BIGHORN." An animated musical of Custer's Last Stand.
Here's our hero.
A little Indian boy.
You wind him up...
...and off he goes.
The toys are all created before we even start the movie.

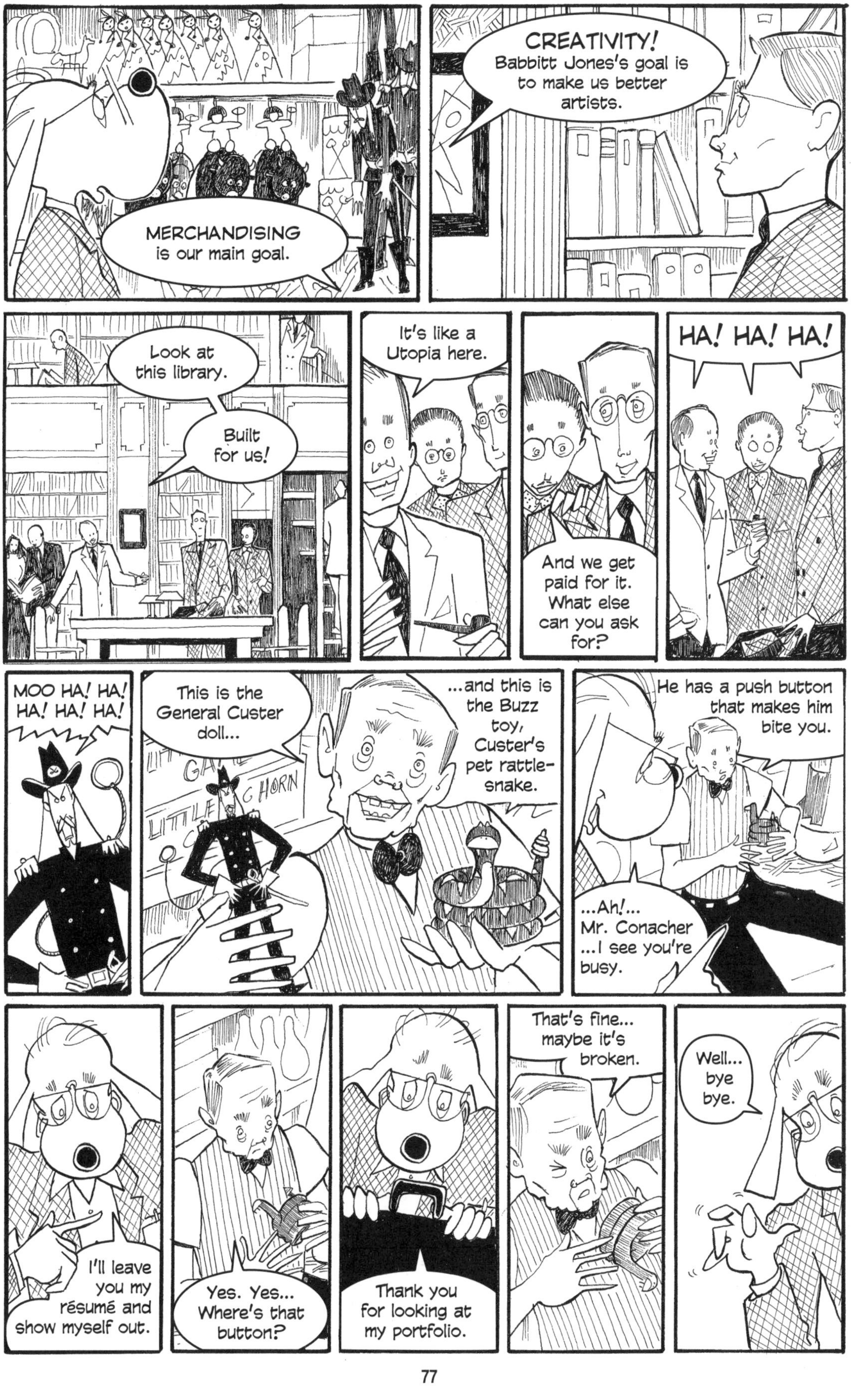
MERCHANDISING
is our main goal.
CREATIVITY!
Babbitt Jones's goal is to make us better artists.
Look at this library.
Built for us!
It's like a Utopia here.
And we get paid for it. What else can you ask for?
HA! HA! HA!
MOO HA! HA! HA! HA! HA!
This is the General Custer doll...
...and this is the Buzz toy, Custer's pet rattle-snake.
He has a push button that makes him bite you.
...Ah!... Mr. Conacher ...I see you're busy.
I'll leave you my résumé and show myself out.
Yes. Yes... Where's that button?
Thank you for looking at my portfolio.
That's fine... maybe it's broken.
Well... bye bye.

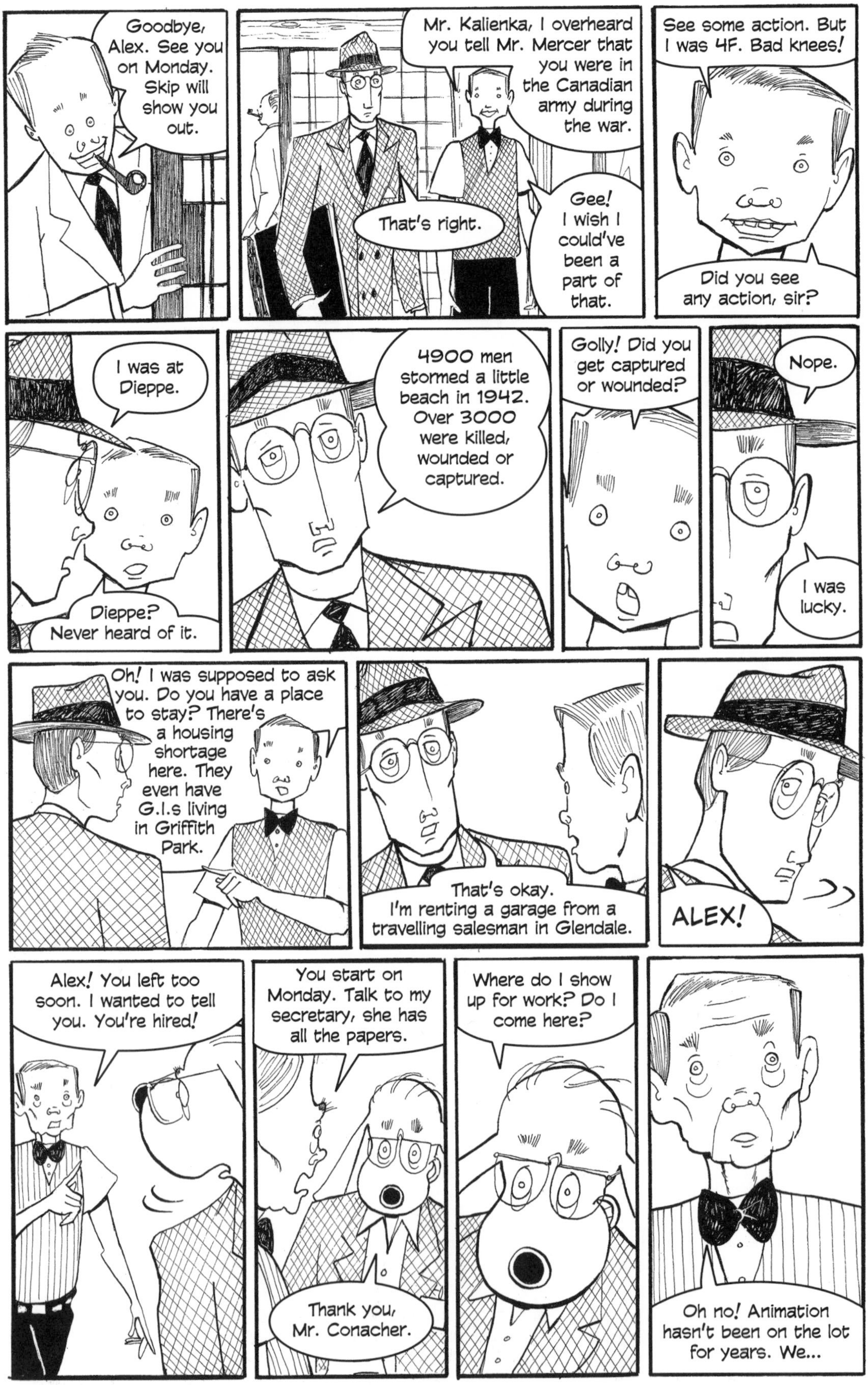
Goodbye, Alex. See you on Monday. Skip will show you out.
Mr. Kalienka, I overheard you tell Mr. Mercer that you were in the Canadian army during the war.
That's right.
Gee! I wish I could've been a part of that.
See some action. But I was 4F. Bad knees!
Did you see any action, sir?
I was at Dieppe.
Dieppe? Never heard of it.
4900 men stormed a little beach in 1942. Over 3000 were killed, wounded or captured.
Golly! Did you get captured or wounded?
Nope.
I was lucky.
Oh! I was supposed to ask you. Do you have a place to stay? There's a housing shortage here. They even have G.I.s living in Griffith Park.
That's okay. I'm renting a garage from a travelling salesman in Glendale.
ALEX!
Alex! You left too soon. I wanted to tell you. You're hired!
You start on Monday. Talk to my secretary, she has all the papers.
Thank you, Mr. Conacher.
Where do I show up for work? Do I come here?
Oh no! Animation hasn't been on the lot for years. We...

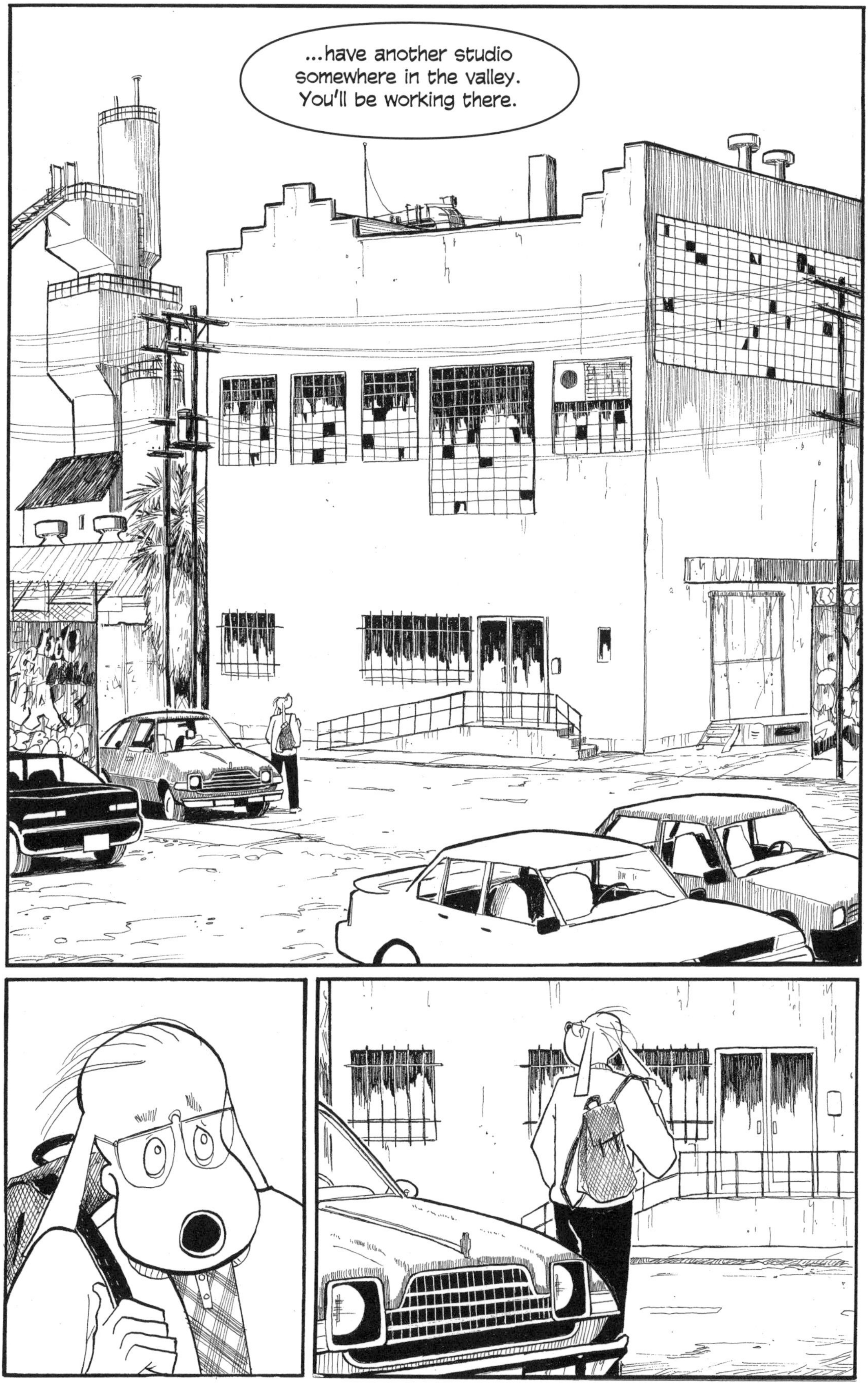
...have another studio somewhere in the valley. You'll be working there.

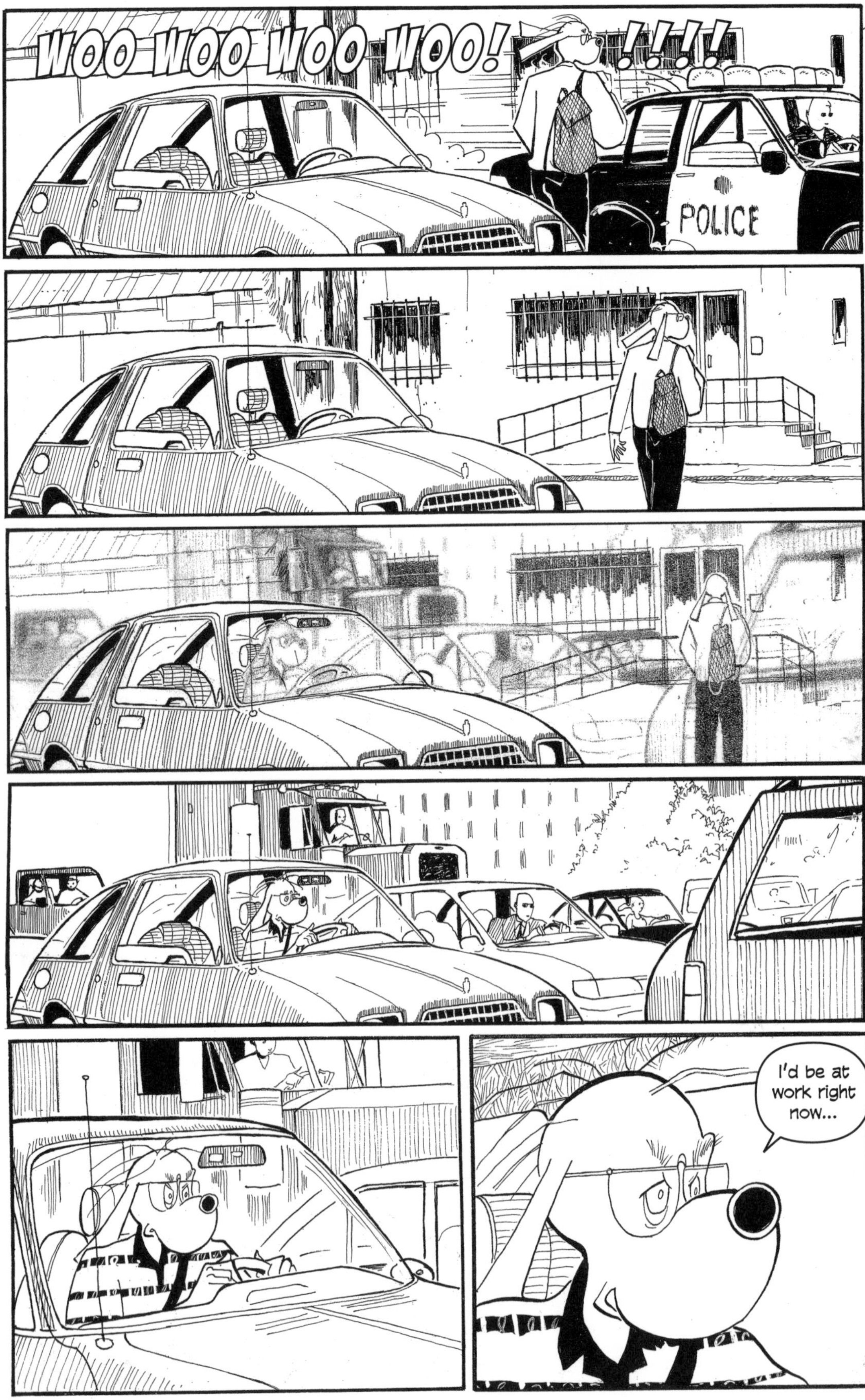
WOO WOO WOO WOO!
!!!!!
POLICE
I'd be at work right now...

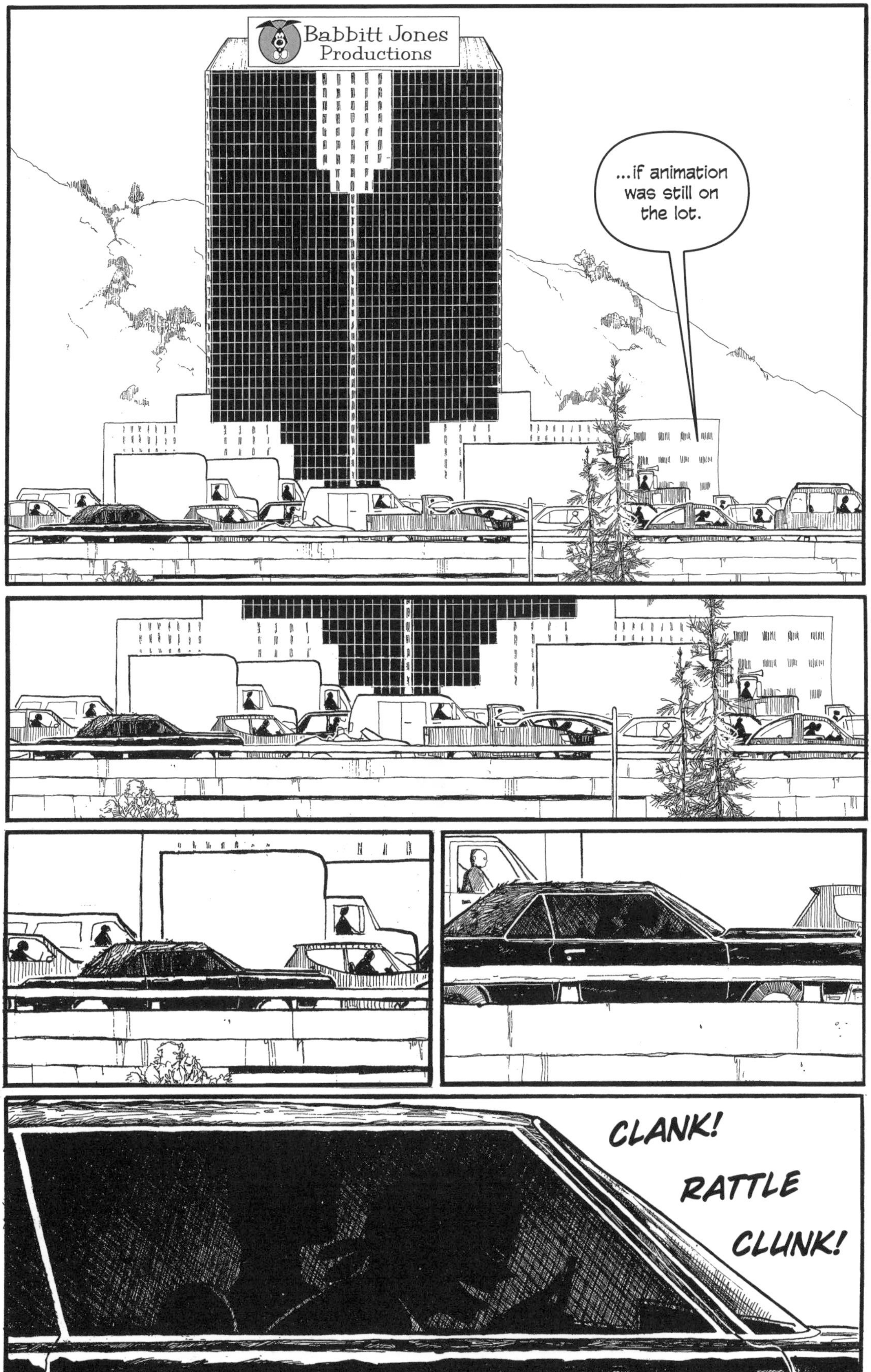
Babbitt Jones Productions
...if animation was still on the lot.
CLANK!
RATTLE
CLUNK!

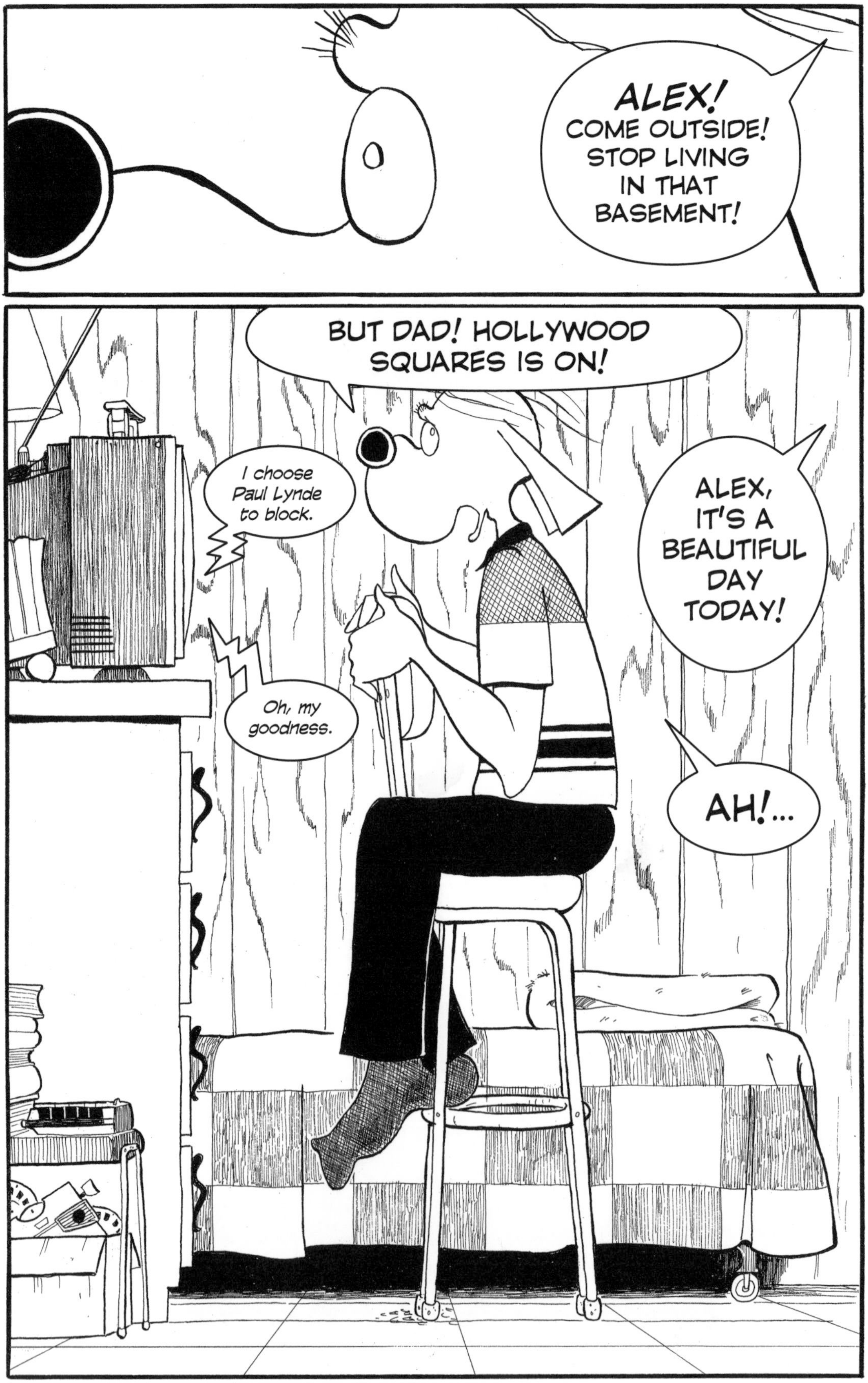
ALEX! COME OUTSIDE! STOP LIVING IN THAT BASEMENT!
BUT DAD! HOLLYWOOD SQUARES IS ON!
I choose Paul Lynde to block.
Oh, my goodness.
ALEX, IT'S A BEAUTIFUL DAY TODAY!
AH!...

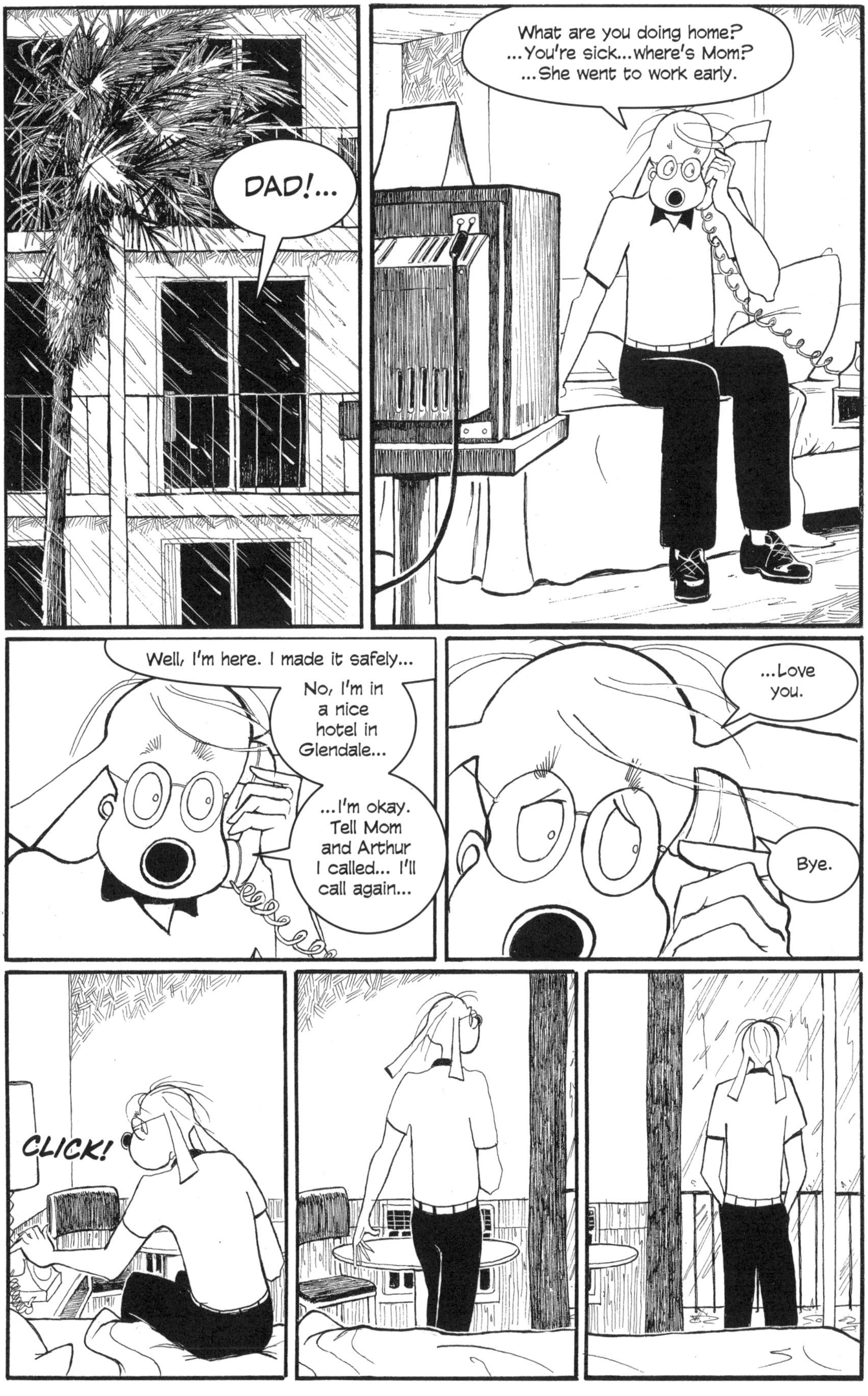
DAD!...
What are you doing home? ...You're sick...where's Mom? ...She went to work early.
Well, I'm here. I made it safely...
No, I'm in a nice hotel in Glendale...
...I'm okay. Tell Mom and Arthur I called... I'll call again...
...Love you.
Bye.
CLICK!

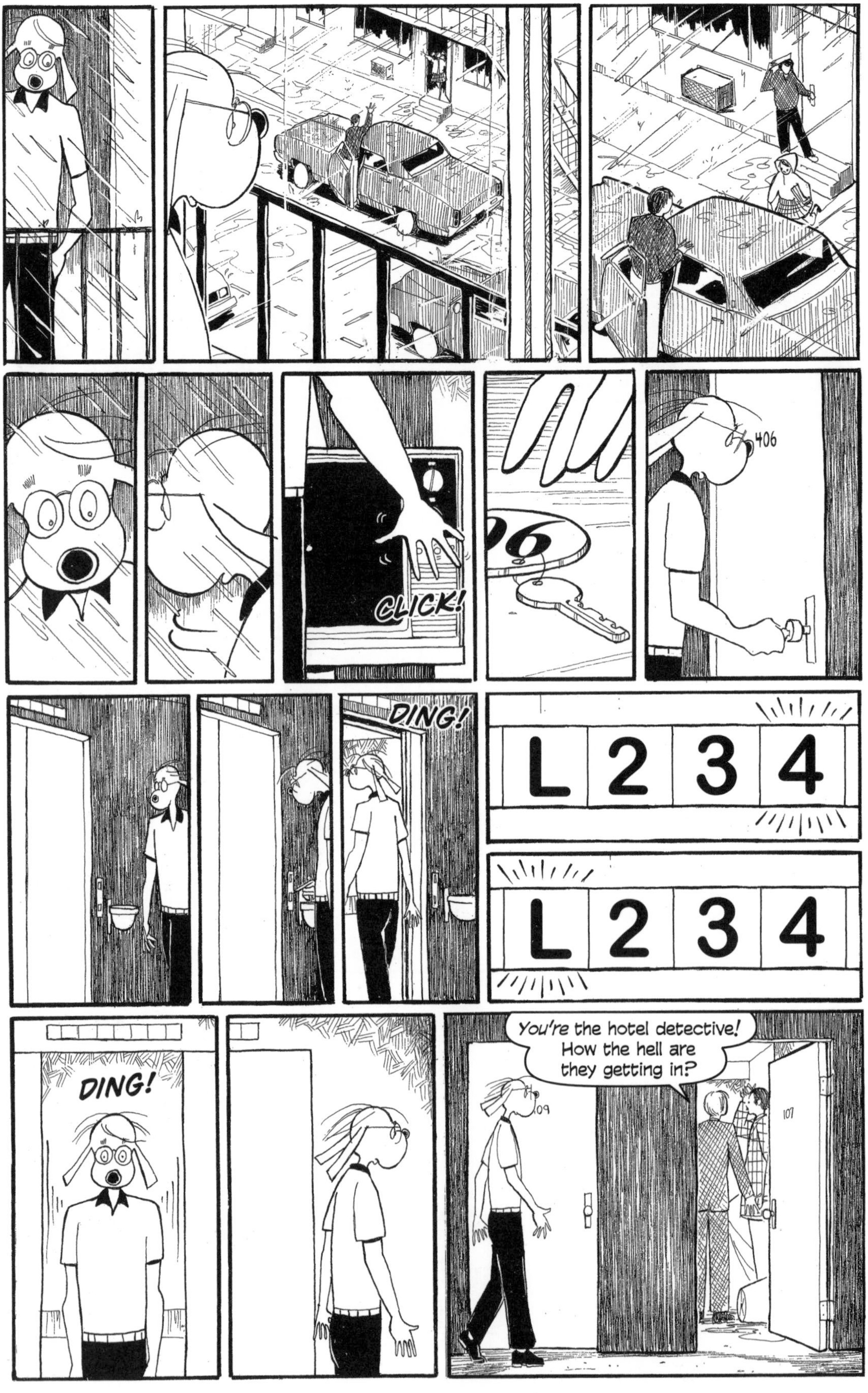
CLICK!
406
DING!
L 2 3 4
L 2 3 4
DING!
You're the hotel detective! How the hell are they getting in?
109
107

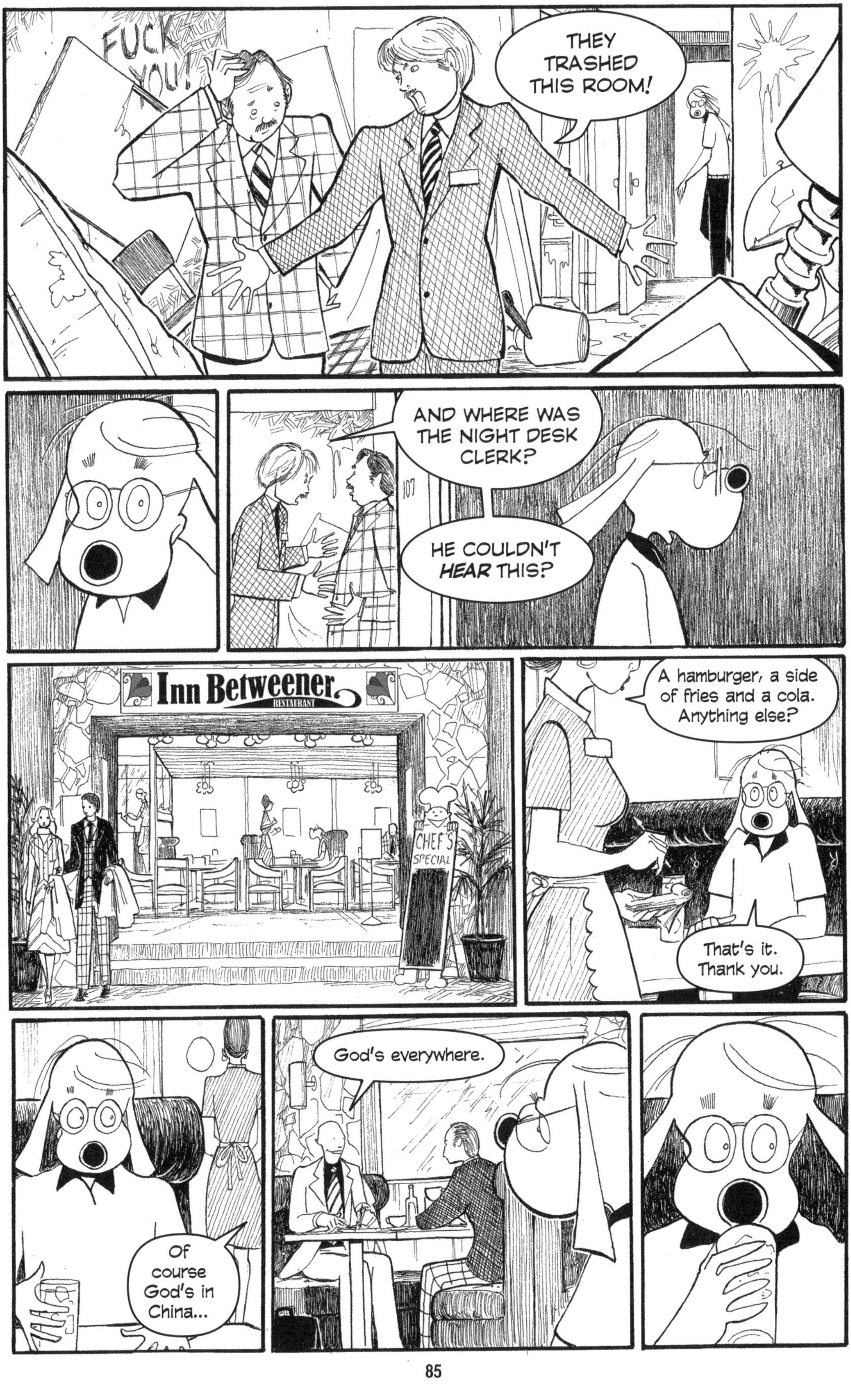
FUCK YOU!
THEY TRASHED THIS ROOM!
AND WHERE WAS THE NIGHT DESK CLERK?
107
HE COULDN'T **HEAR** THIS?
Inn Betweener
RESTAURANT
CHEF'S SPECIAL
A hamburger, a side of fries and a cola. Anything else?
That's it. Thank you.
Of course God's in China...
God's everywhere.

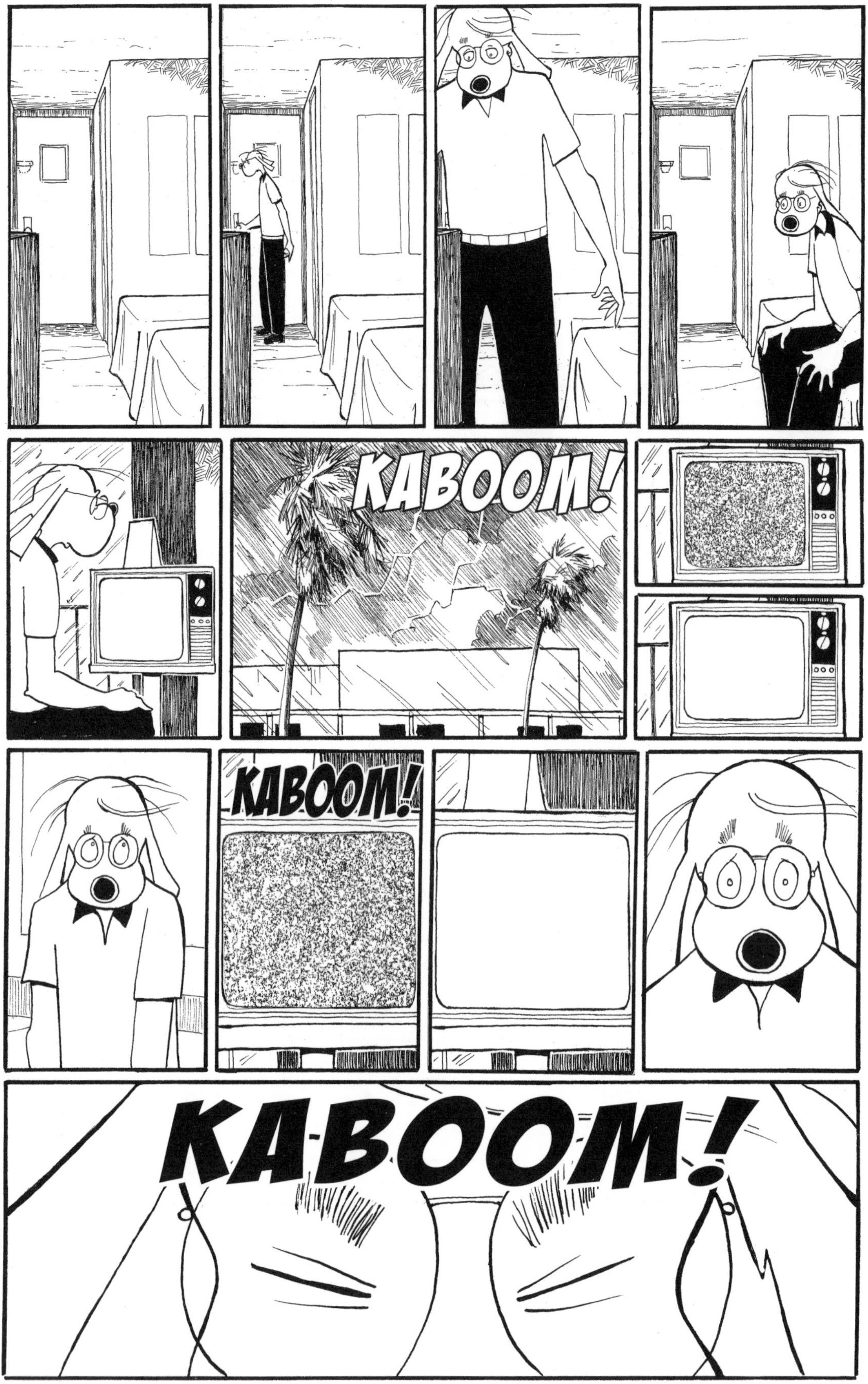
KABOOM!
KABOOM!
KABOOM!

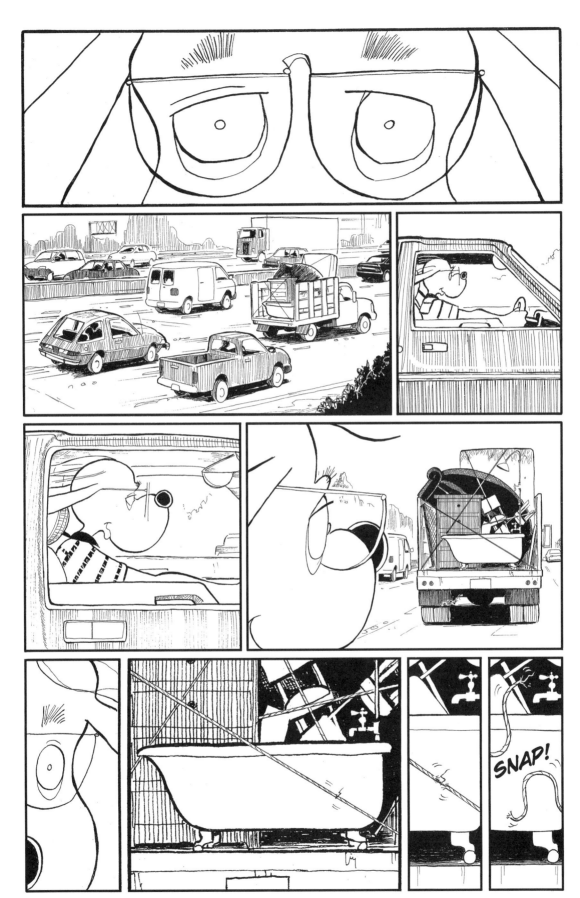

SNAP!

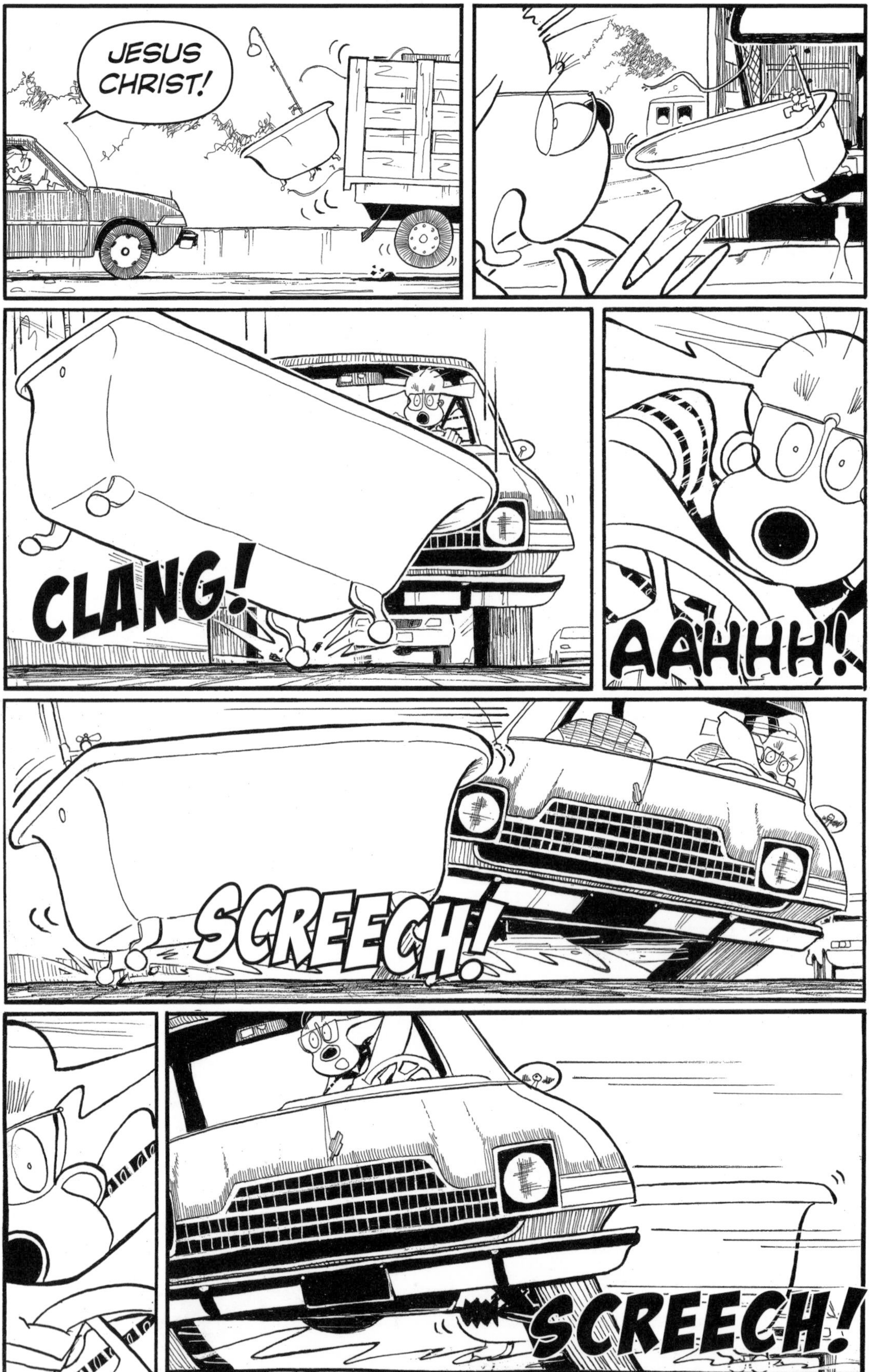
JESUS CHRIST!
CLANG!
AAHHH!
SCREECH!
SCREECH!

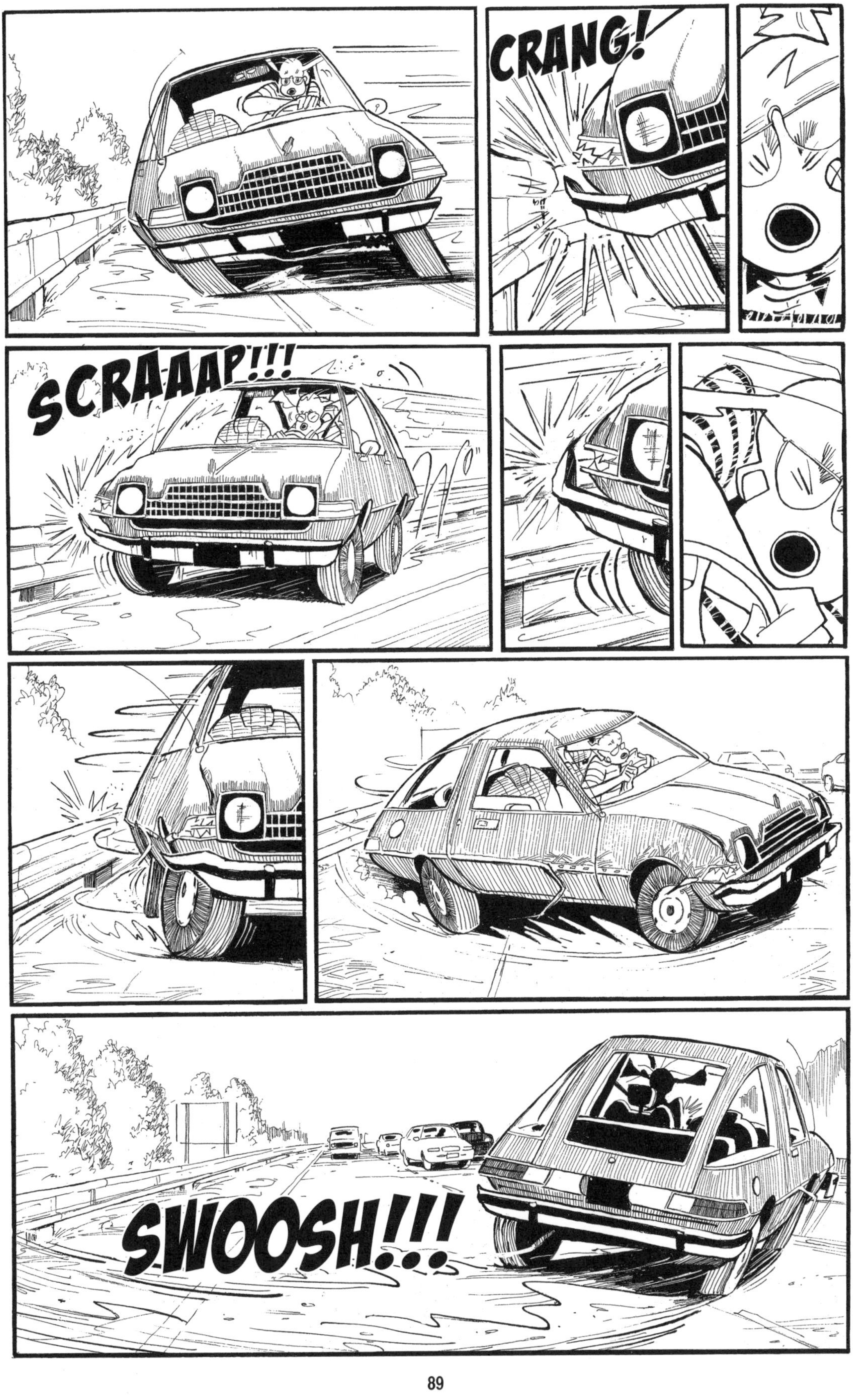
CRANG!
SCRAAAP!!!
SWOOSH!!!

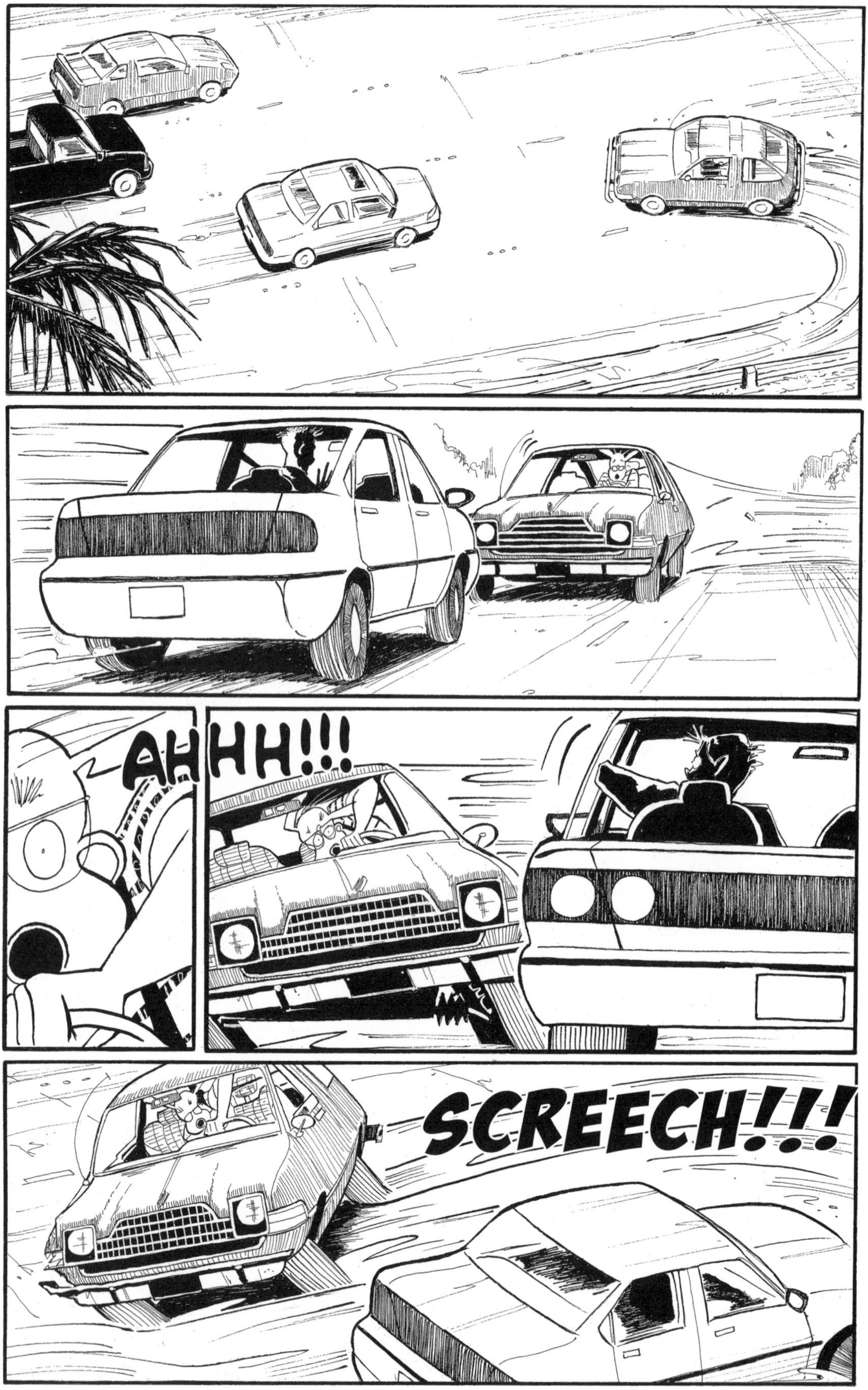
AHHH!!!
SCREECH!!!

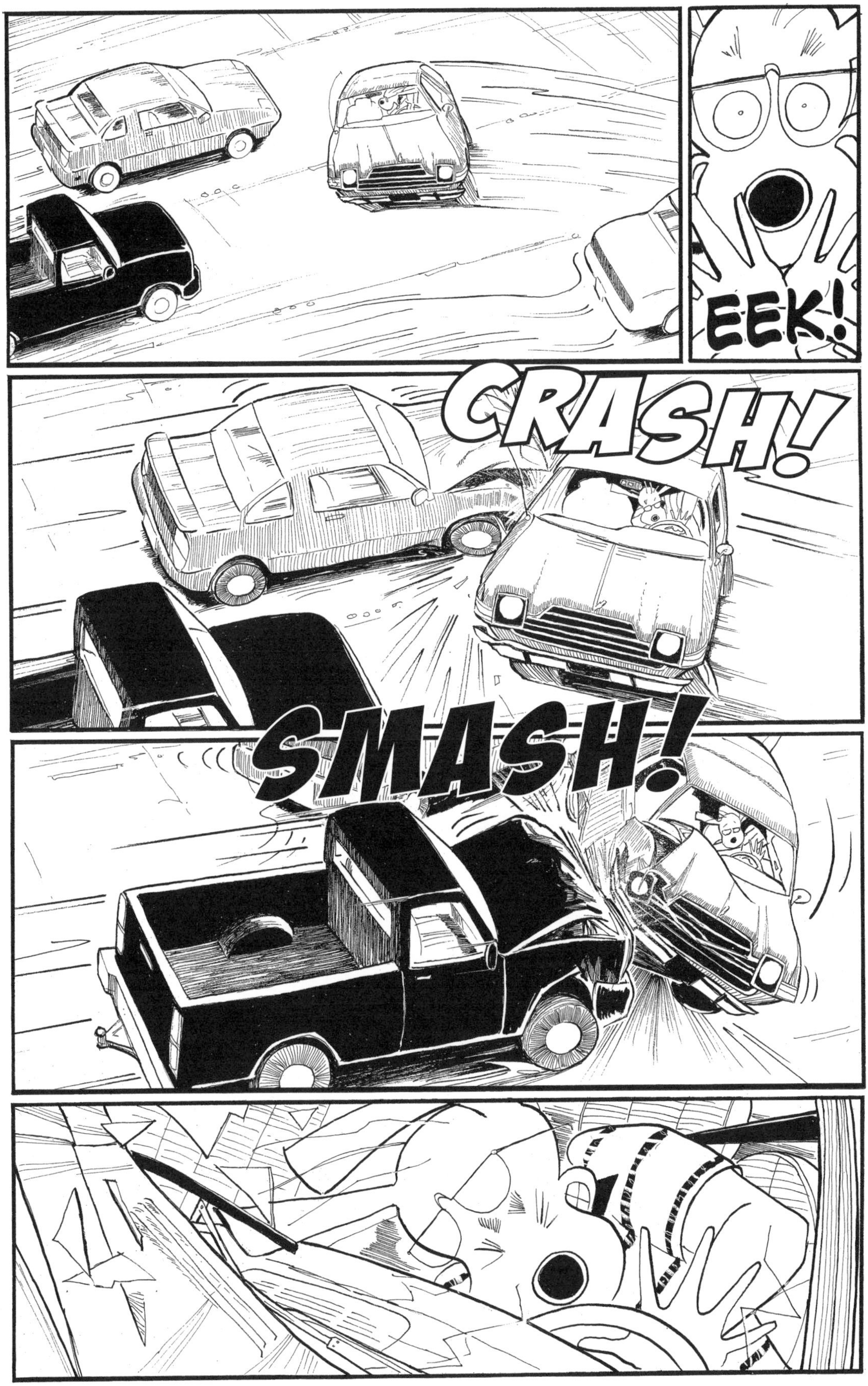
EEK!
CRASH!
SMASH!

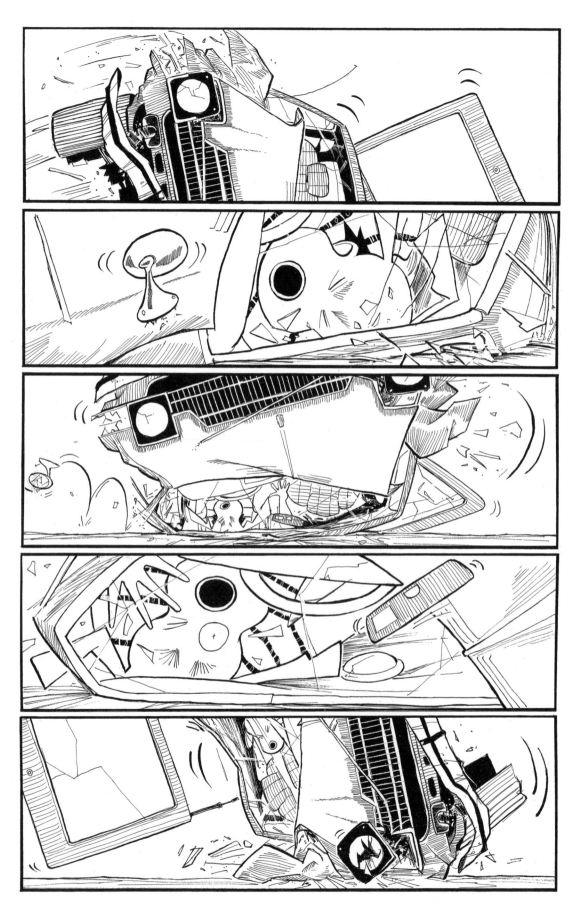

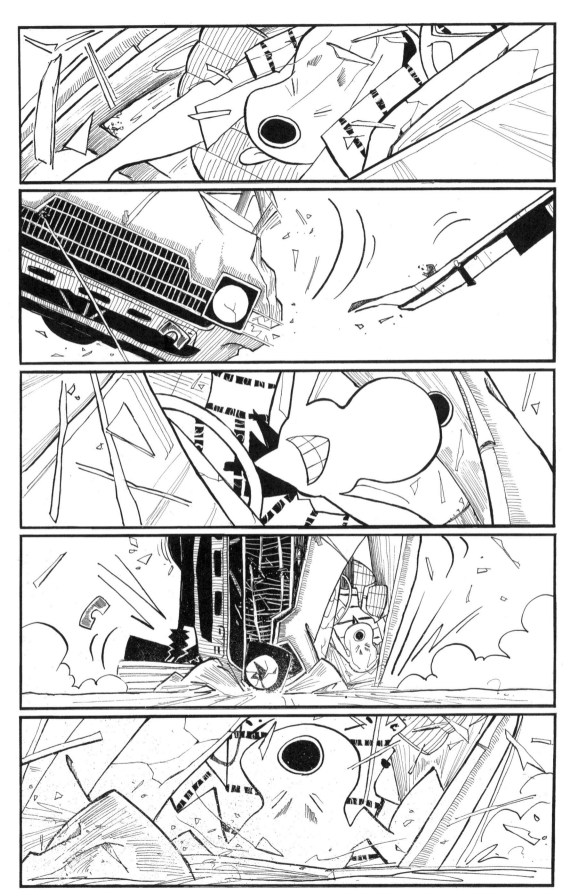

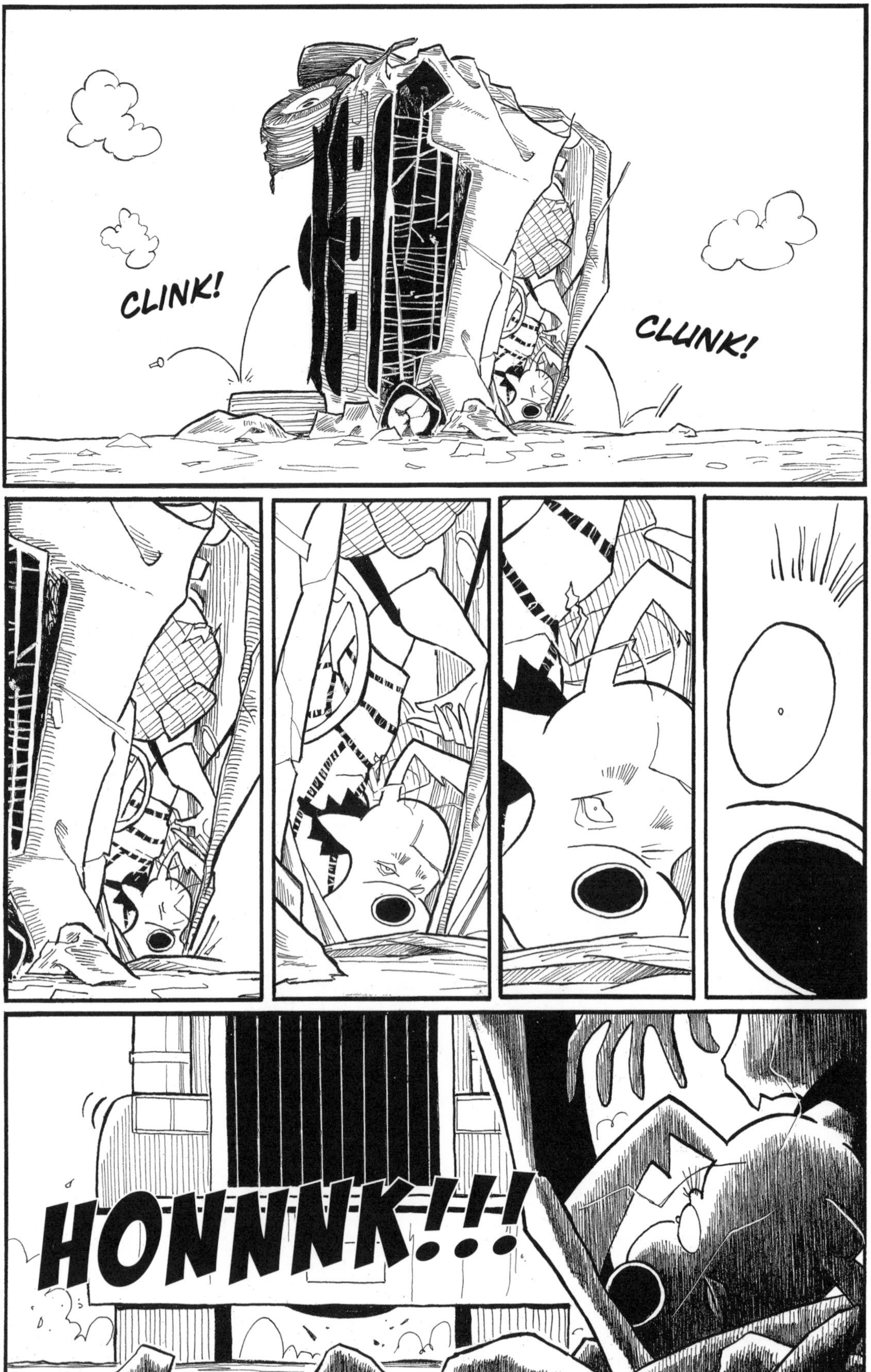
CLINK!
CLUNK!
HONNNK!!!

HONK!

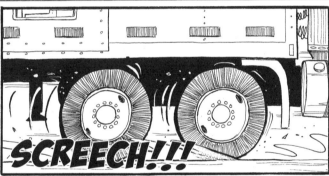

SCREECH!!!

CRASH!

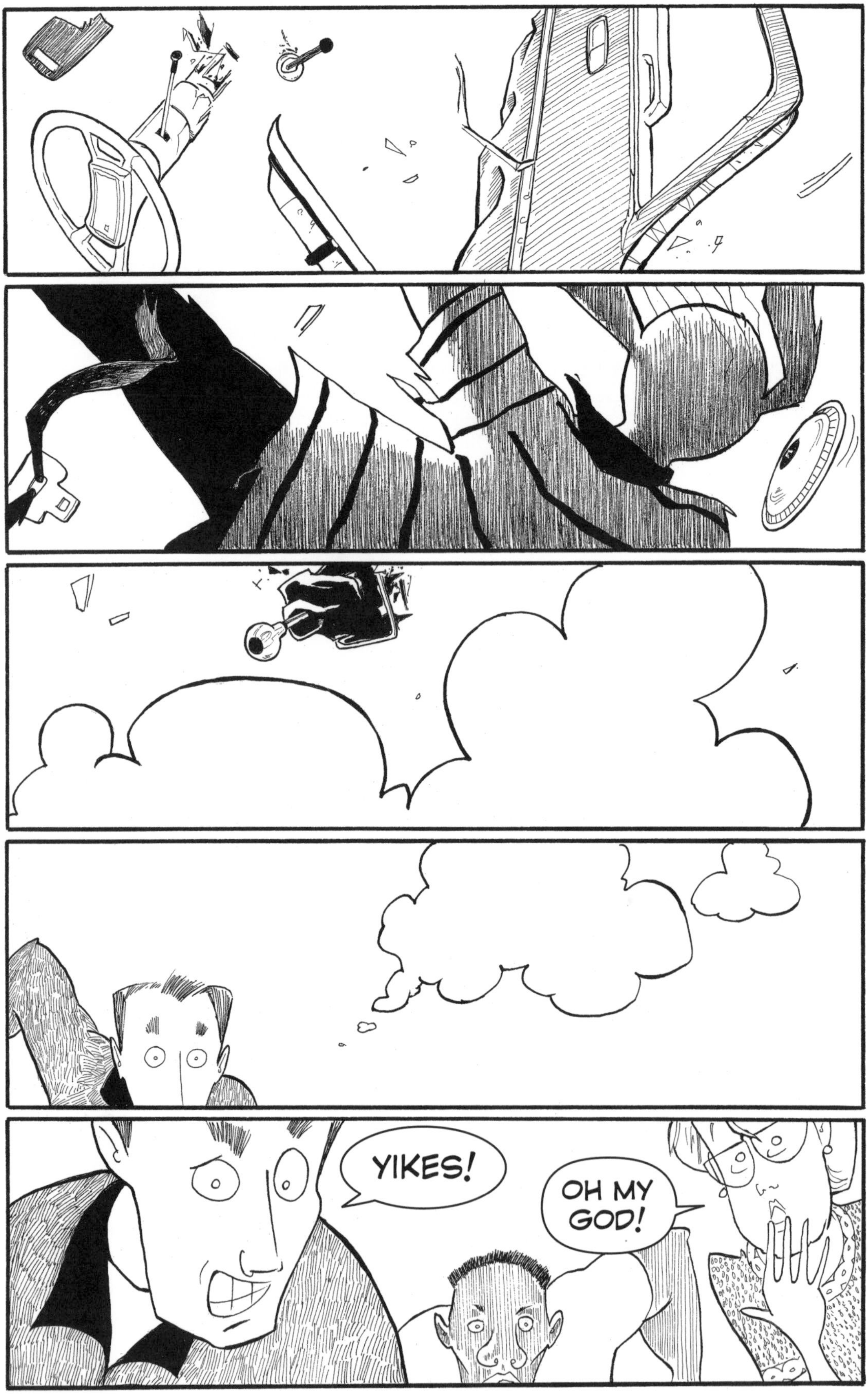
YIKES!
OH MY GOD!

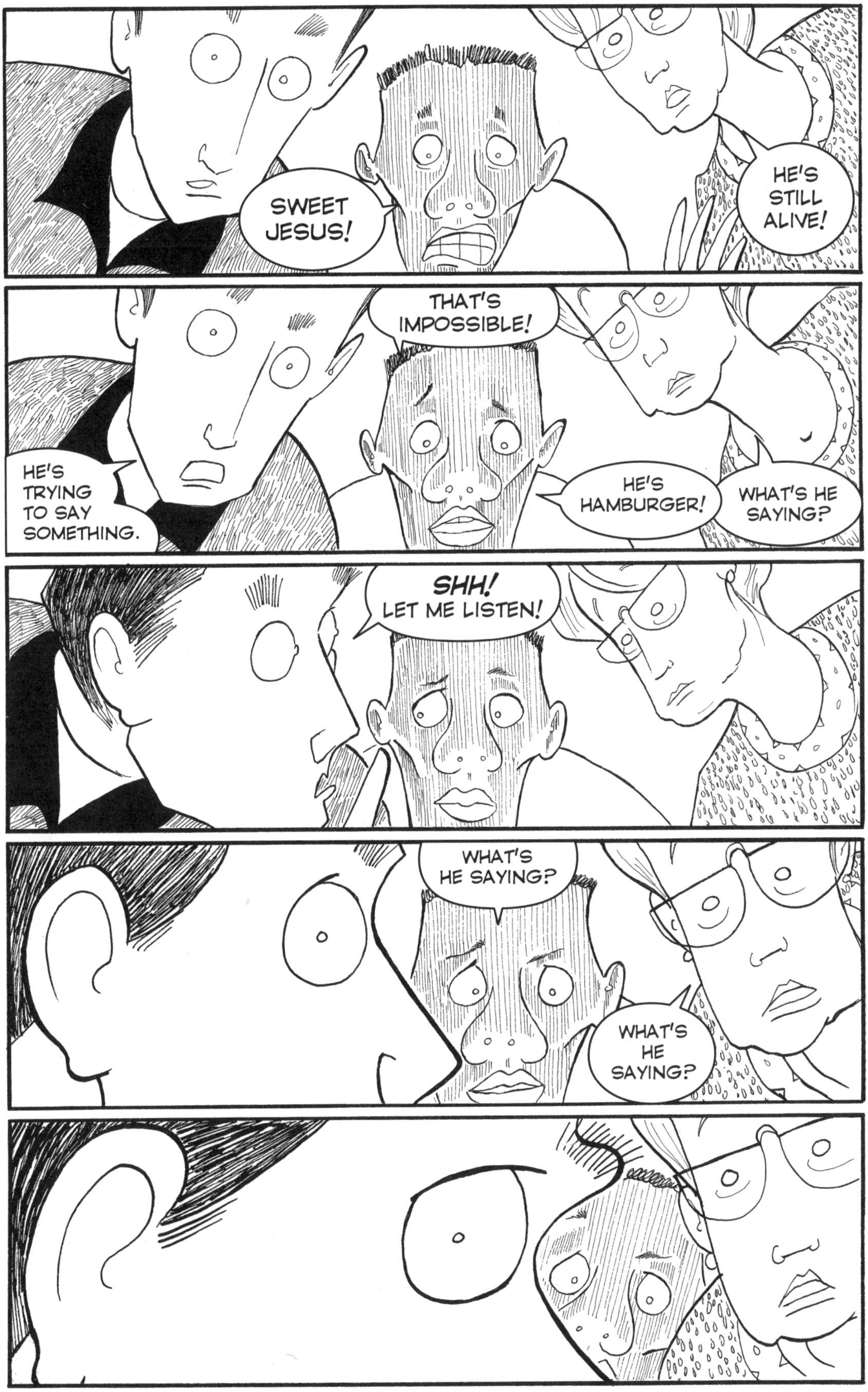
SWEET JESUS!
HE'S STILL ALIVE!
THAT'S IMPOSSIBLE!
HE'S TRYING TO SAY SOMETHING.
HE'S HAMBURGER!
WHAT'S HE SAYING?
SHH! LET ME LISTEN!
WHAT'S HE SAYING?
WHAT'S HE SAYING?

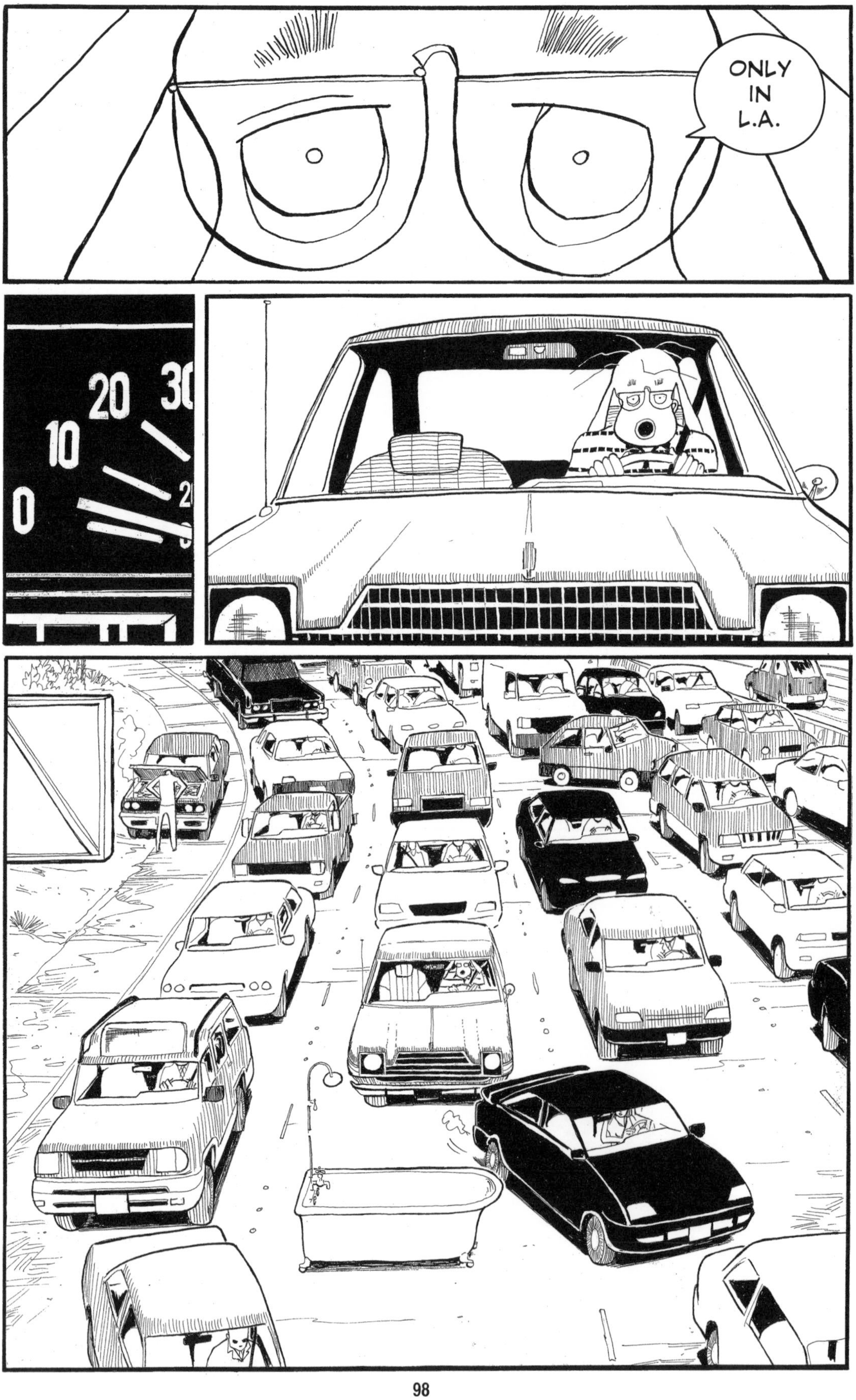
ONLY IN L.A.
0
10
20
30

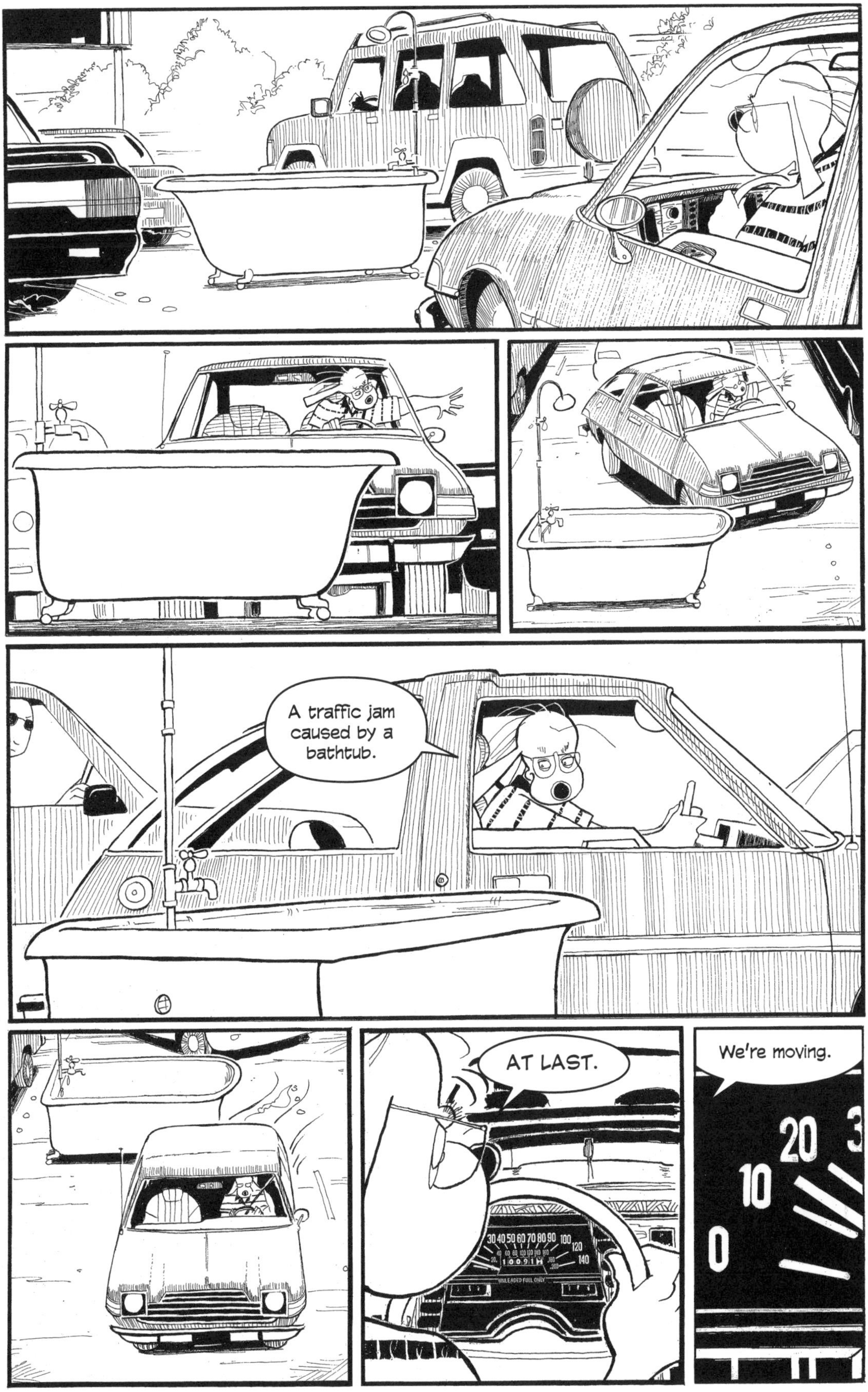
A traffic jam caused by a bathtub.
AT LAST.
We're moving.
UNLEADED FUEL ONLY

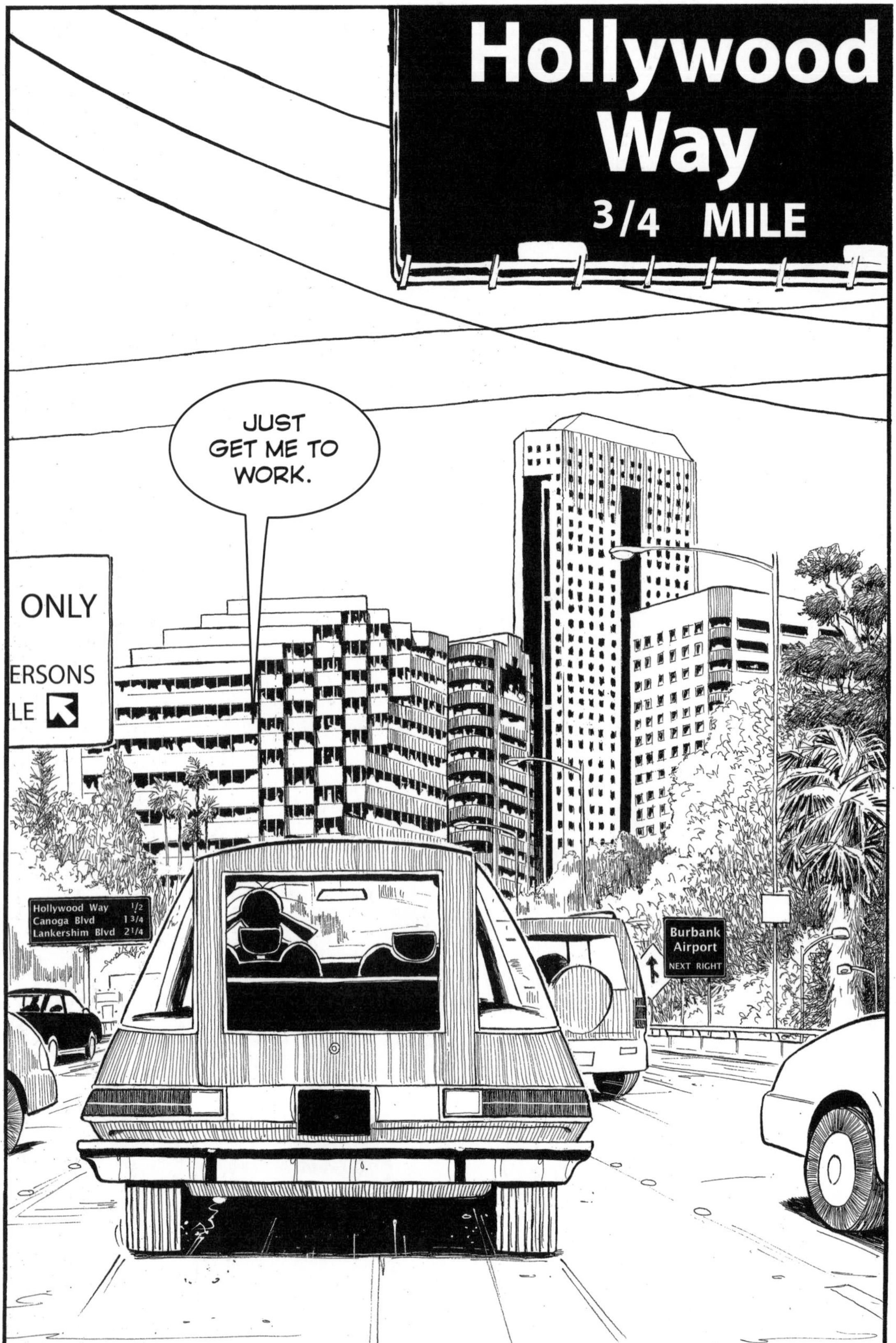
Hollywood
Way
3/4 MILE
JUST GET ME TO WORK.
ONLY
ERSONS
LE
Hollywood Way 1/2
Canoga Blvd 1 3/4
Lankershim Blvd 2 1/4
Burbank
Airport
NEXT RIGHT

CHAPTER 3

IF YOU WERE THE ONLY GIRL IN THE WORLD

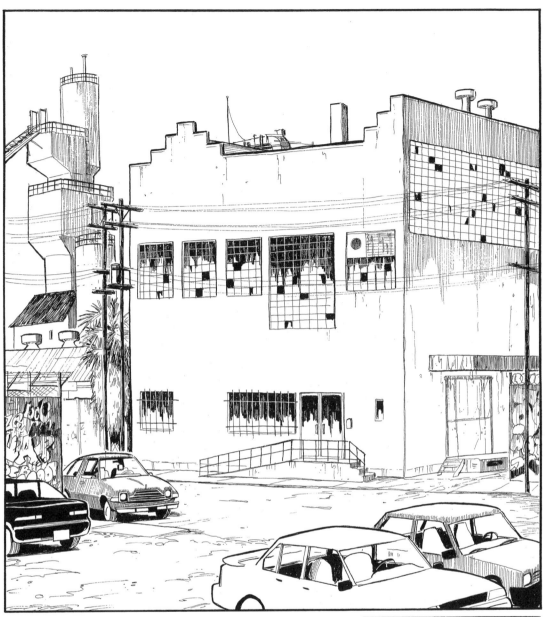

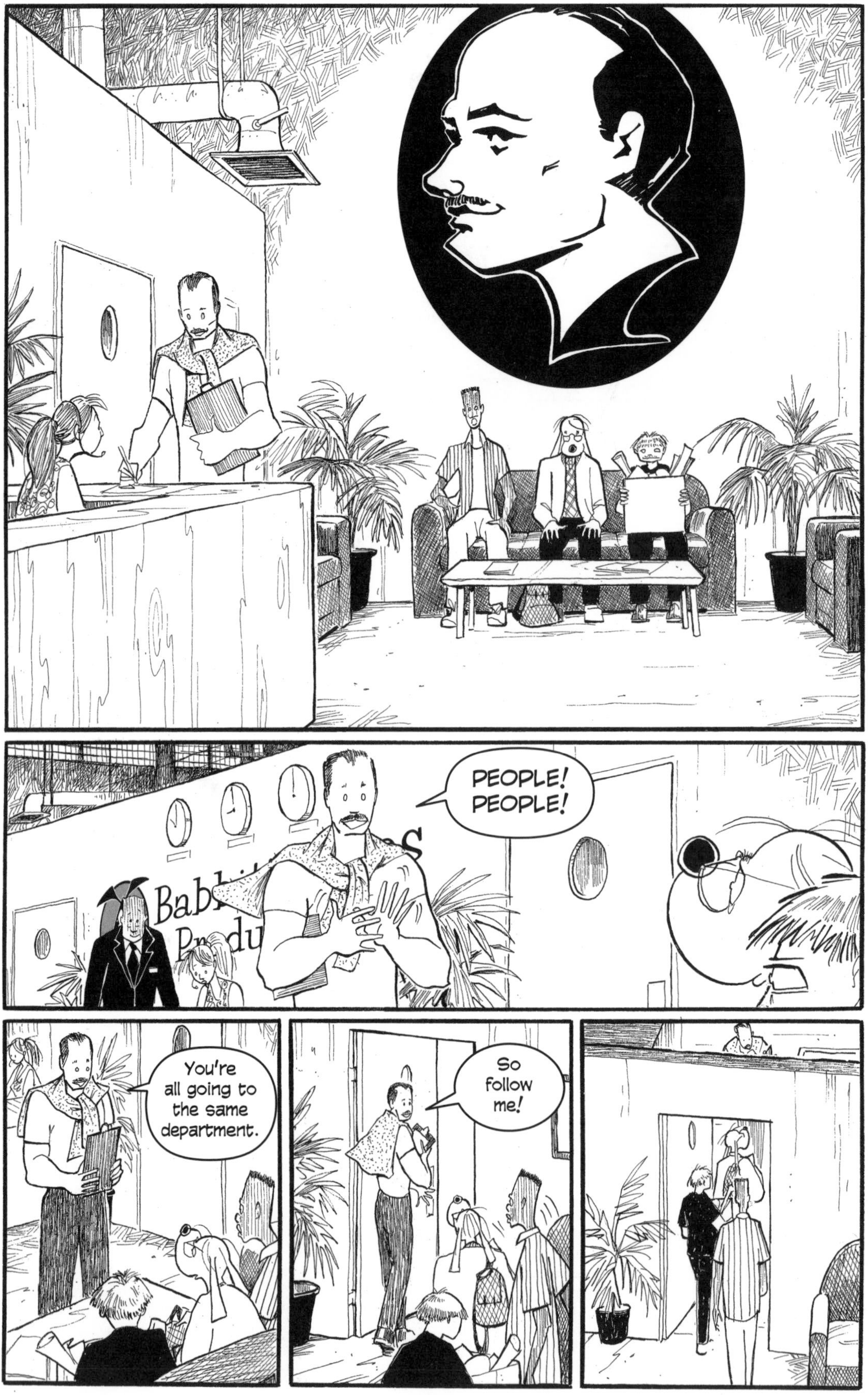
PEOPLE! PEOPLE!
You're all going to the same department.
So follow me!

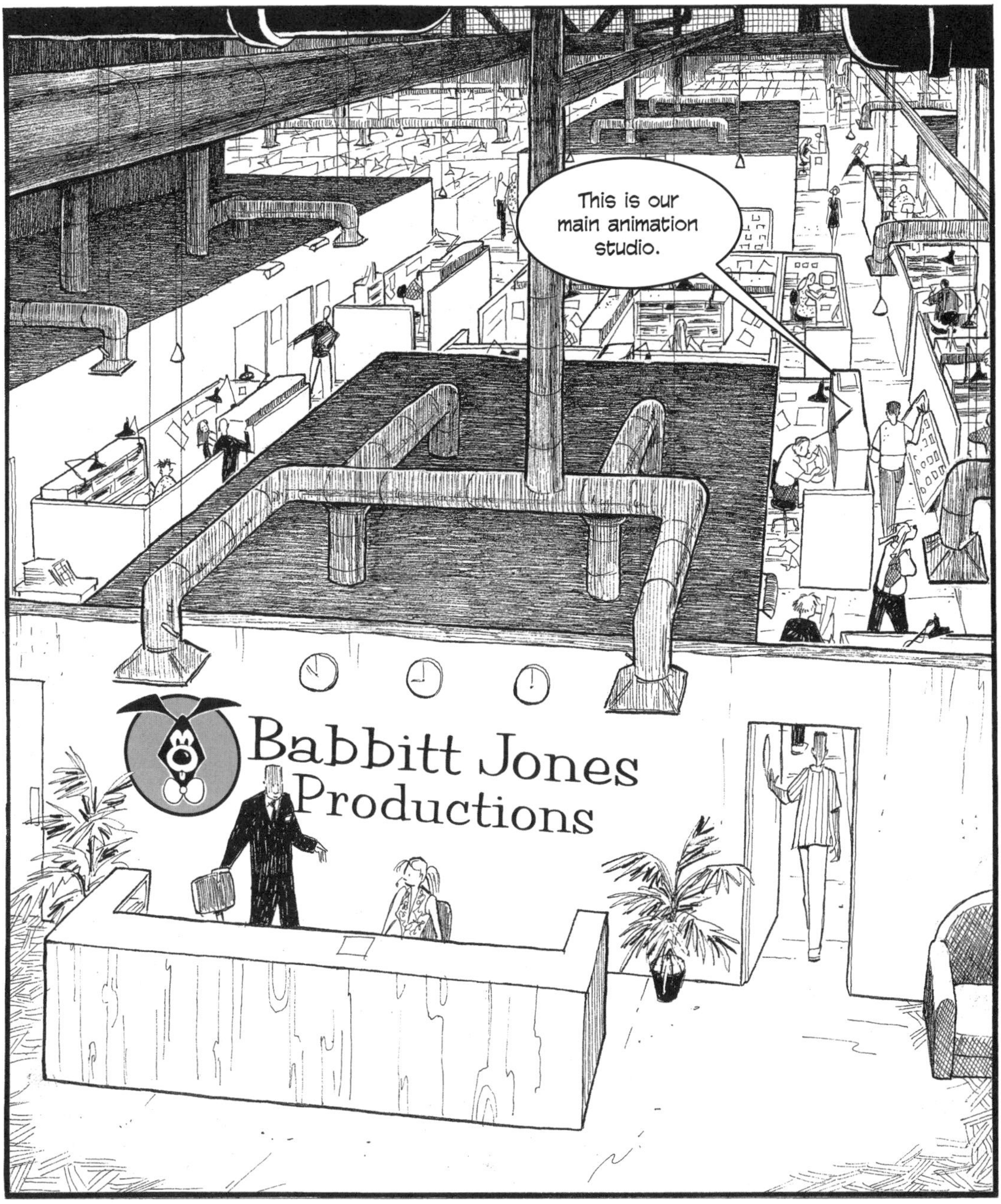
This is our main animation studio.
Babbitt Jones Productions

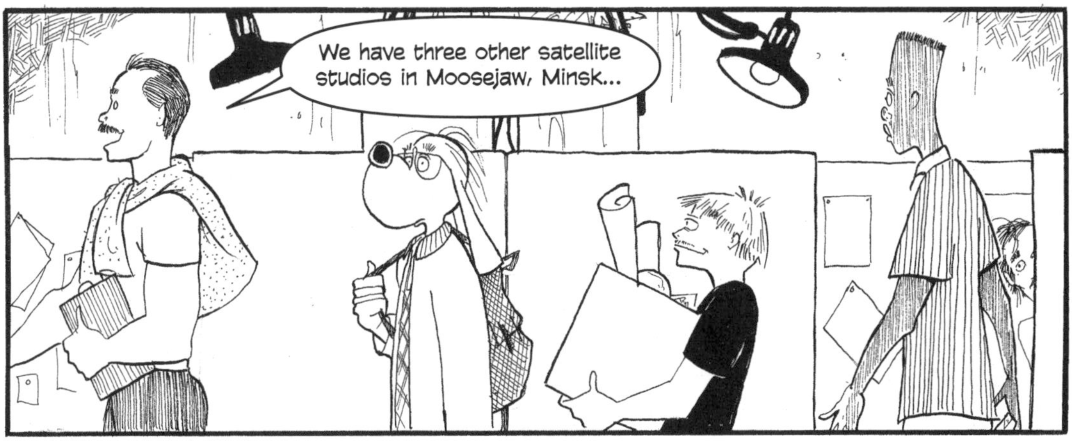
We have three other satellite studios in Moosejaw, Minsk...

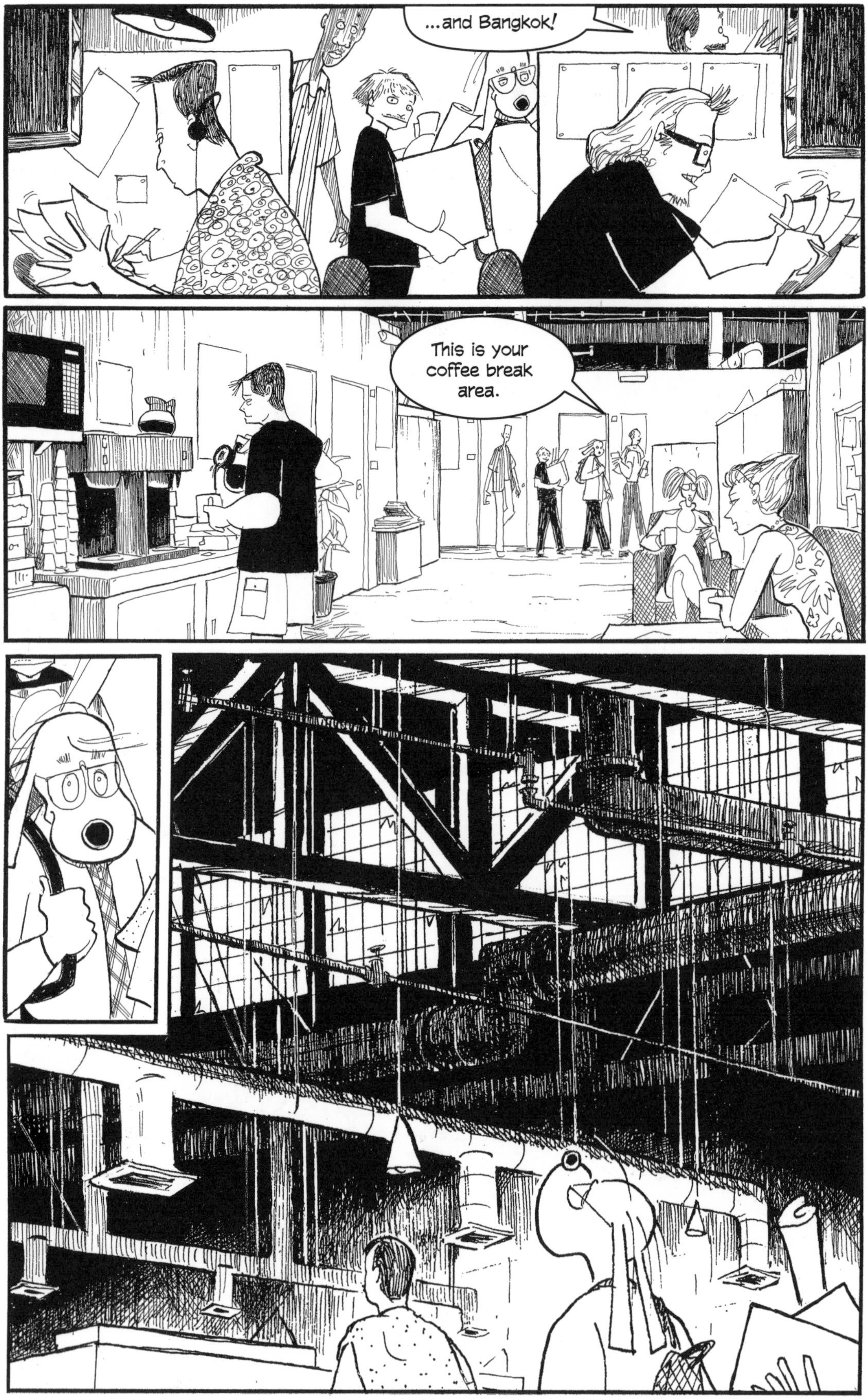
...and Bangkok!
This is your coffee break area.

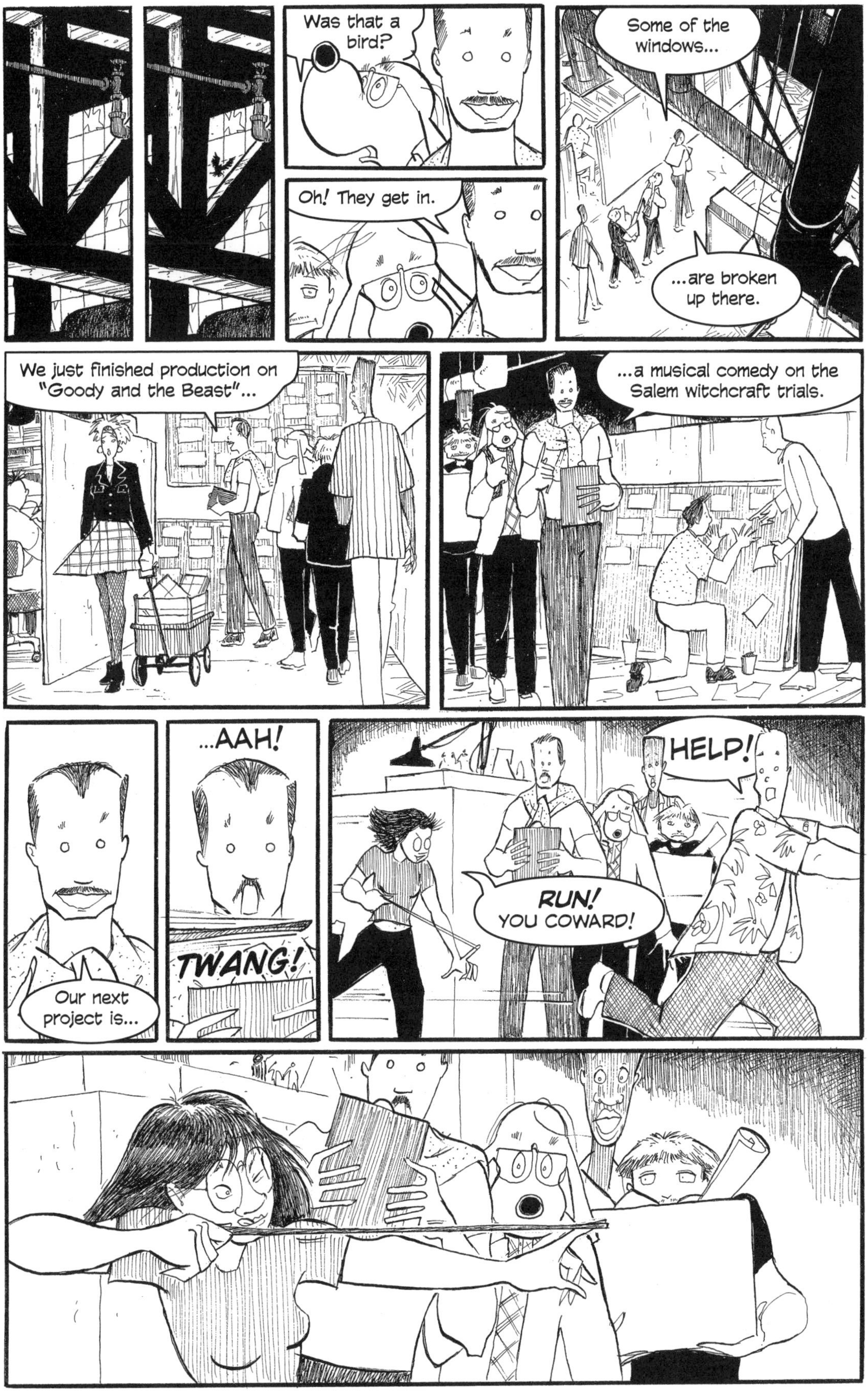
Was that a bird?
Oh! They get in.
Some of the windows...
...are broken up there.
We just finished production on "Goody and the Beast"...
...a musical comedy on the Salem witchcraft trials.
Our next project is...
...AAH!
TWANG!
HELP!
RUN! YOU COWARD!

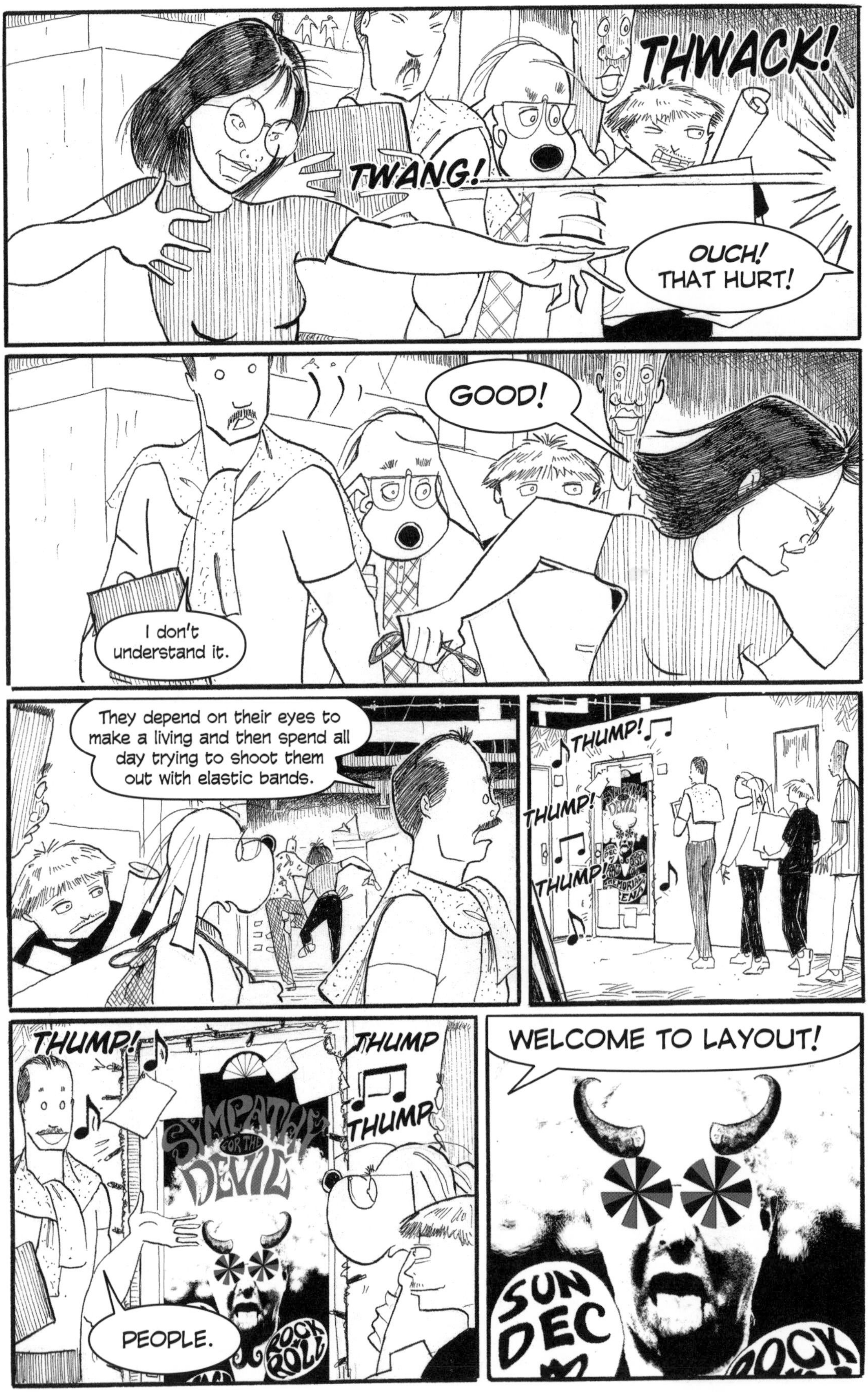
THWACK!
TWANG!
OUCH! THAT HURT!
GOOD!
I don't understand it.
They depend on their eyes to make a living and then spend all day trying to shoot them out with elastic bands.
THUMP!
THUMP!
THUMP!
THUMP!
THUMP
THUMP
SYMPATHY FOR THE DEVIL
PEOPLE.
ROCK ROLL
WELCOME TO LAYOUT!
SUN DEC

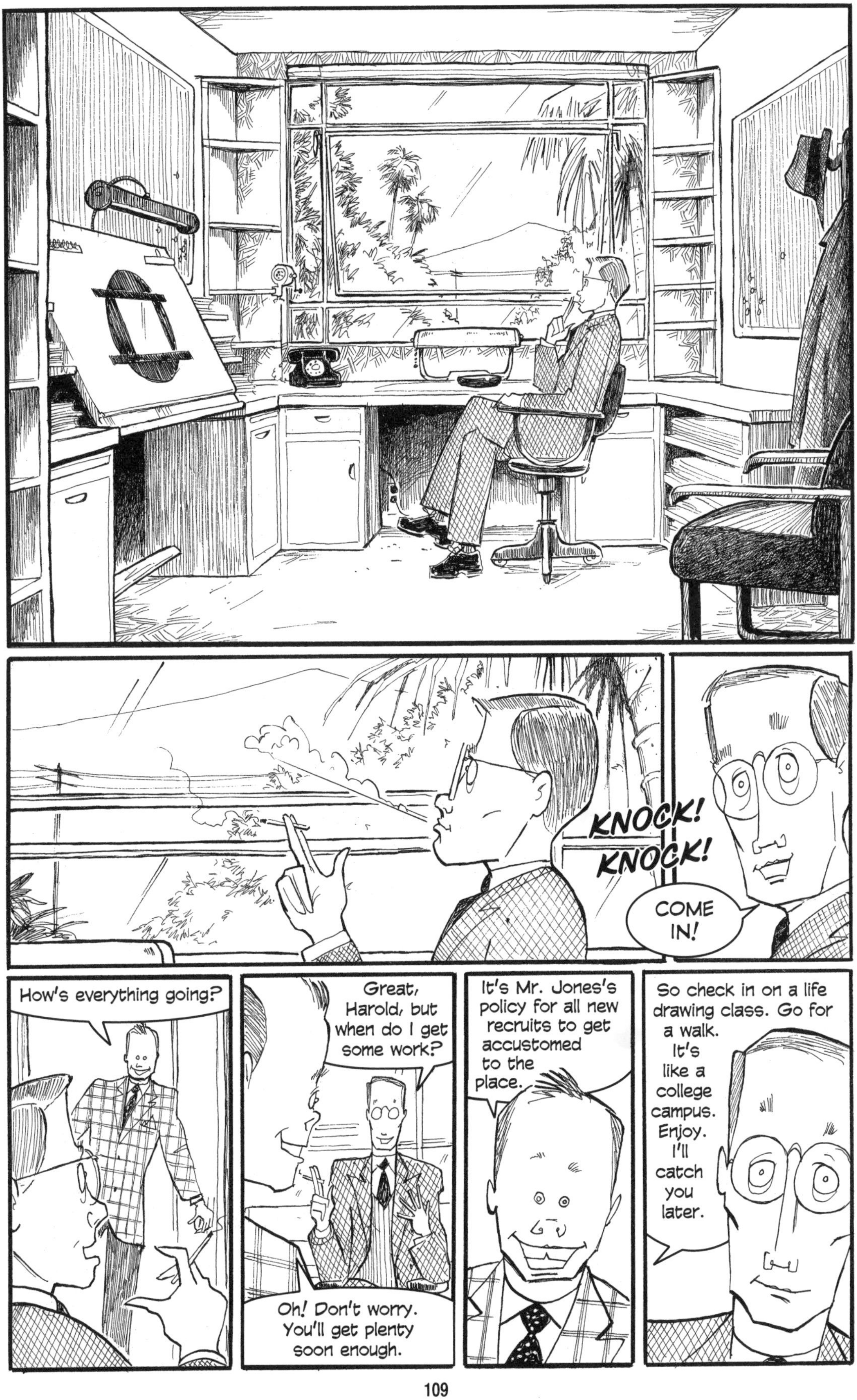
KNOCK! KNOCK!
COME IN!
How's everything going?
Great, Harold, but when do I get some work?
Oh! Don't worry. You'll get plenty soon enough.
It's Mr. Jones's policy for all new recruits to get accustomed to the place.
So check in on a life drawing class. Go for a walk. It's like a college campus. Enjoy. I'll catch you later.

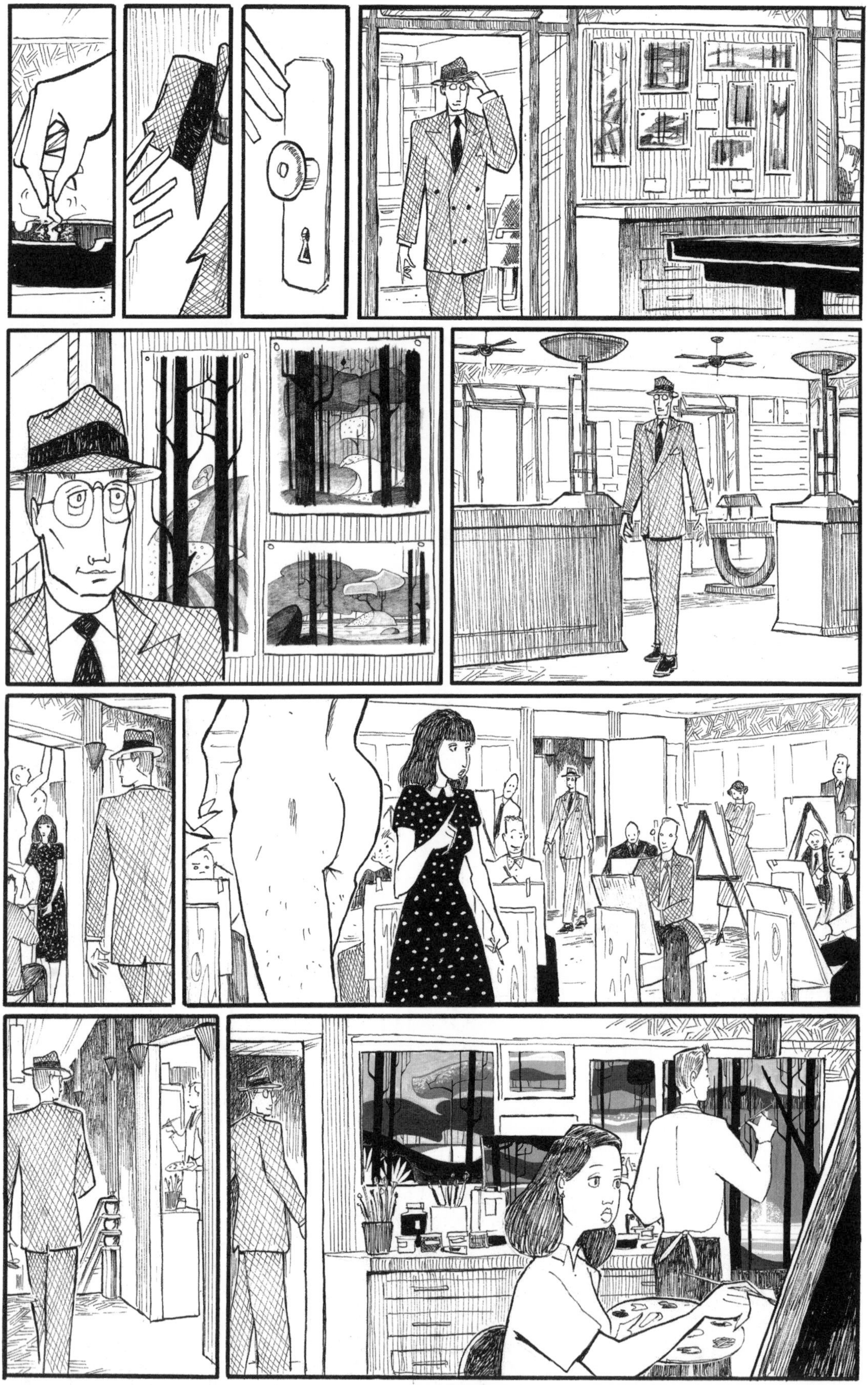

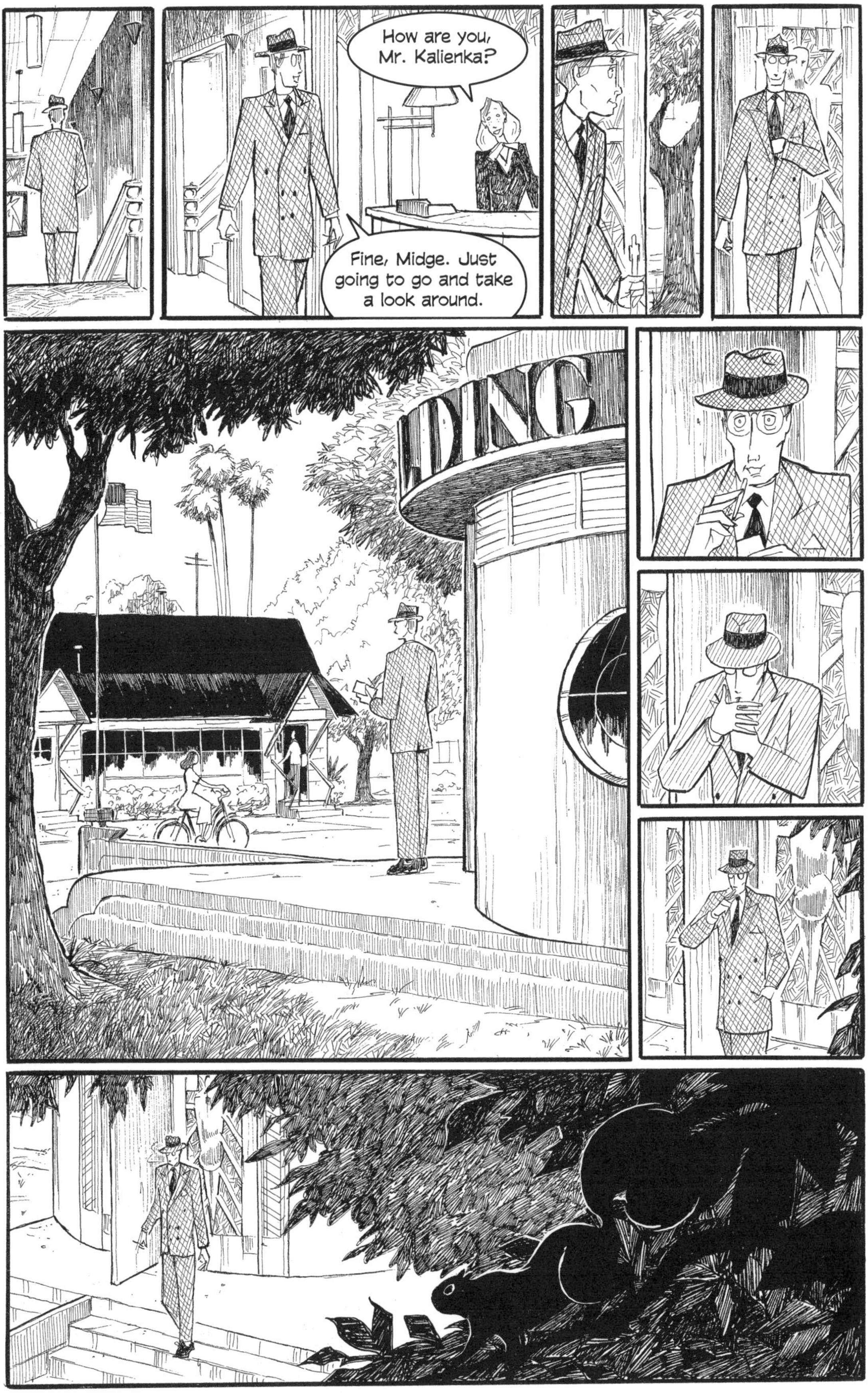
How are you, Mr. Kalienka?
Fine, Midge. Just going to go and take a look around.

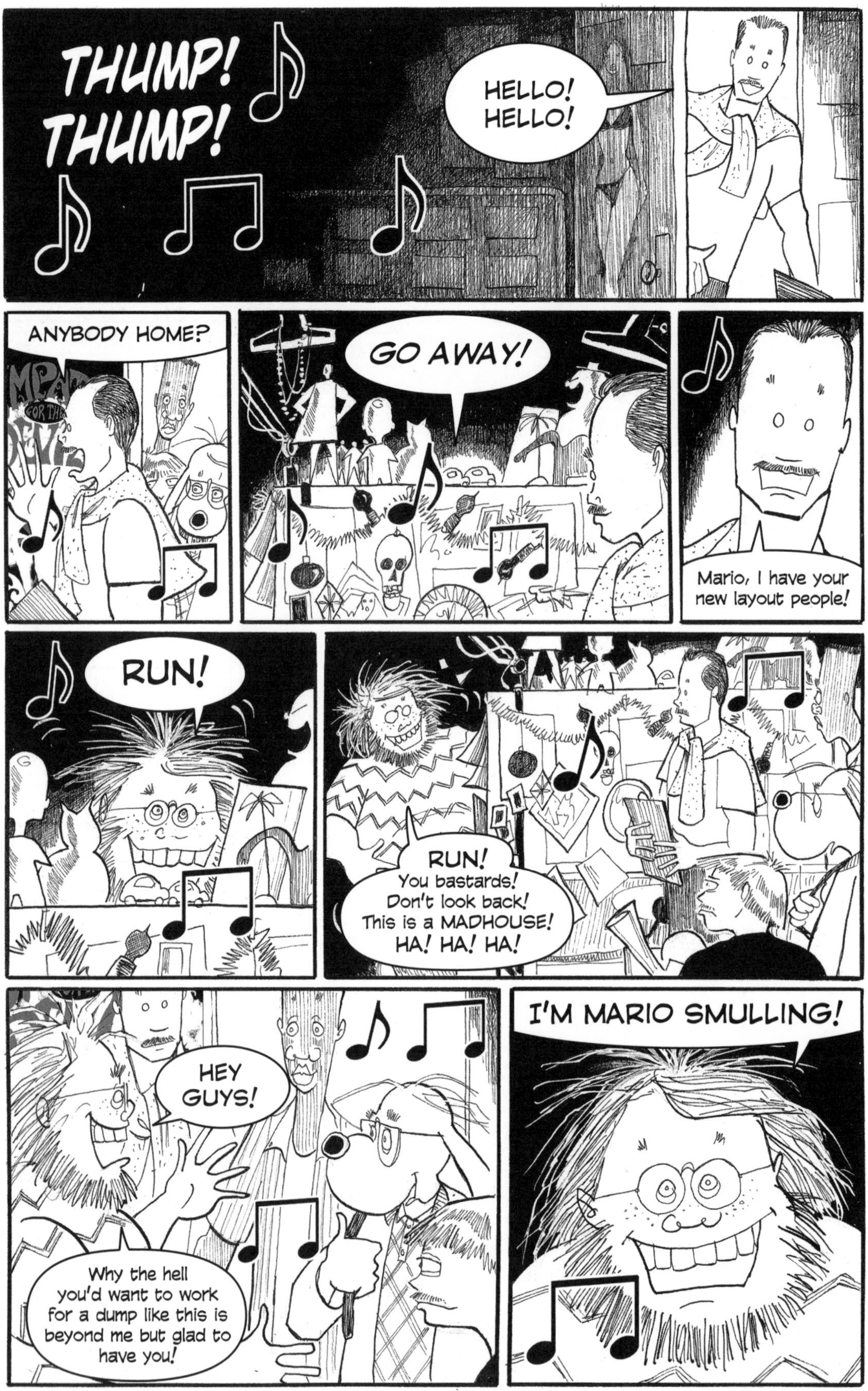
THUMP! THUMP!
HELLO! HELLO!
ANYBODY HOME?
GO AWAY!
Mario, I have your new layout people!
RUN!
RUN! You bastards! Don't look back! This is a MADHOUSE! HA! HA! HA!
HEY GUYS!
Why the hell you'd want to work for a dump like this is beyond me but glad to have you!
I'M MARIO SMULLING!

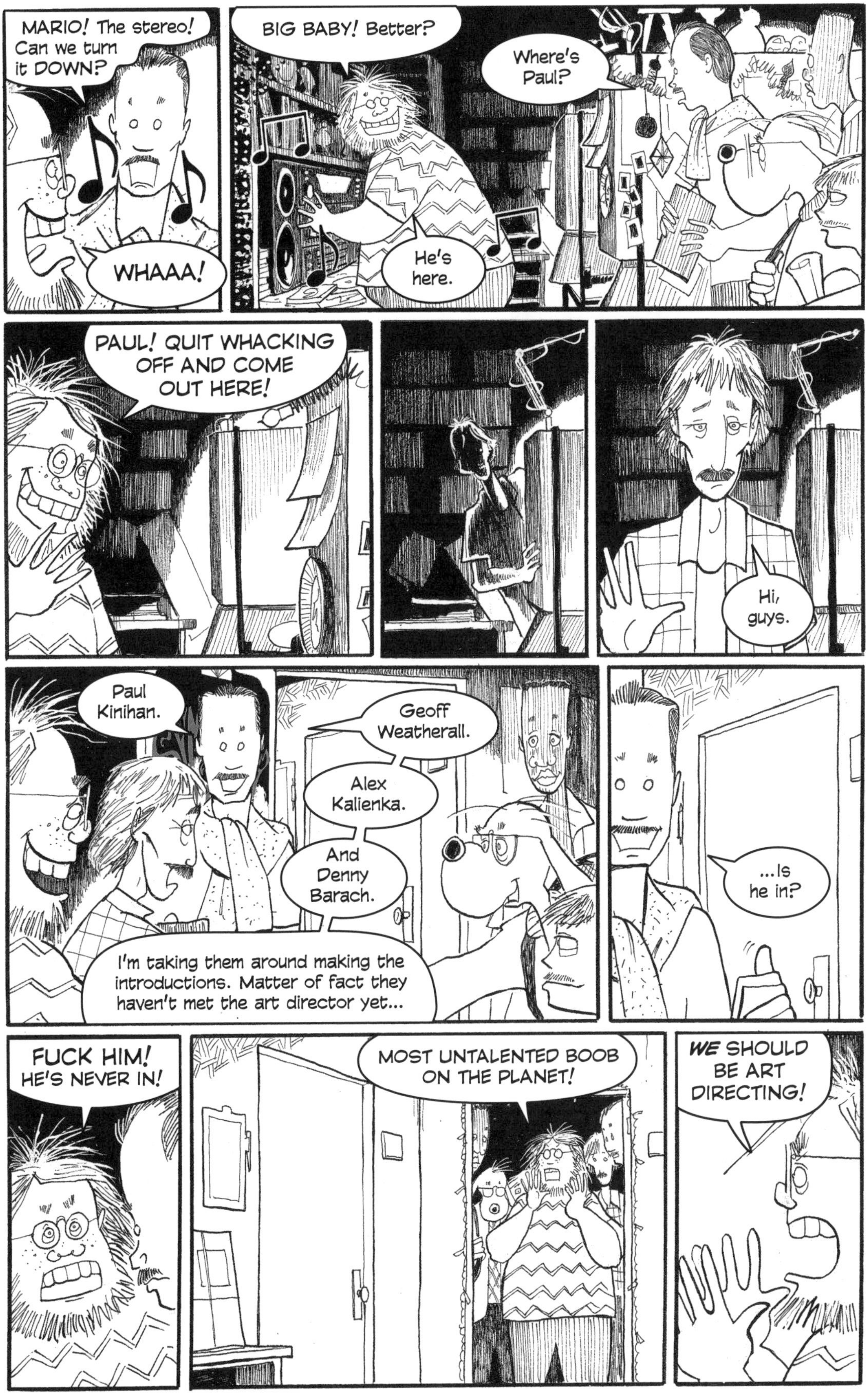
MARIO! The stereo! Can we turn it DOWN?
WHAAA!
BIG BABY! Better?
Where's Paul?
He's here.
PAUL! QUIT WHACKING OFF AND COME OUT HERE!
Hi, guys.
Paul Kinihan.
Geoff Weatherall.
Alex Kalienka.
And Denny Barach.
I'm taking them around making the introductions. Matter of fact they haven't met the art director yet...
...Is he in?
FUCK HIM! HE'S NEVER IN!
MOST UNTALENTED BOOB ON THE PLANET!
WE SHOULD BE ART DIRECTING!

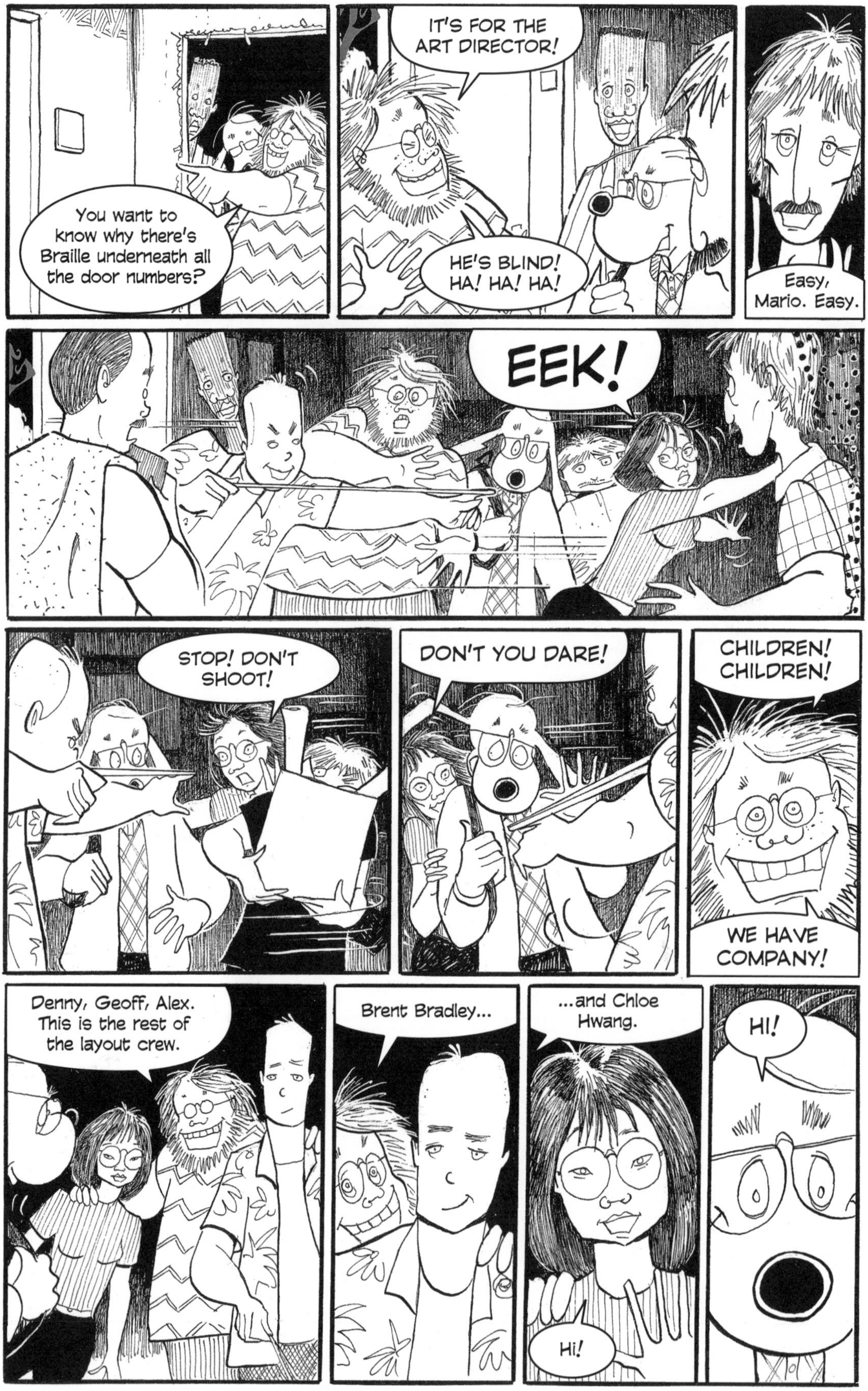
You want to know why there's Braille underneath all the door numbers?
IT'S FOR THE ART DIRECTOR!
HE'S BLIND! HA! HA! HA!
Easy, Mario. Easy.
EEK!
STOP! DON'T SHOOT!
DON'T YOU DARE!
CHILDREN! CHILDREN!
WE HAVE COMPANY!
Denny, Geoff, Alex. This is the rest of the layout crew.
Brent Bradley...
...and Chloe Hwang.
Hi!
HI!

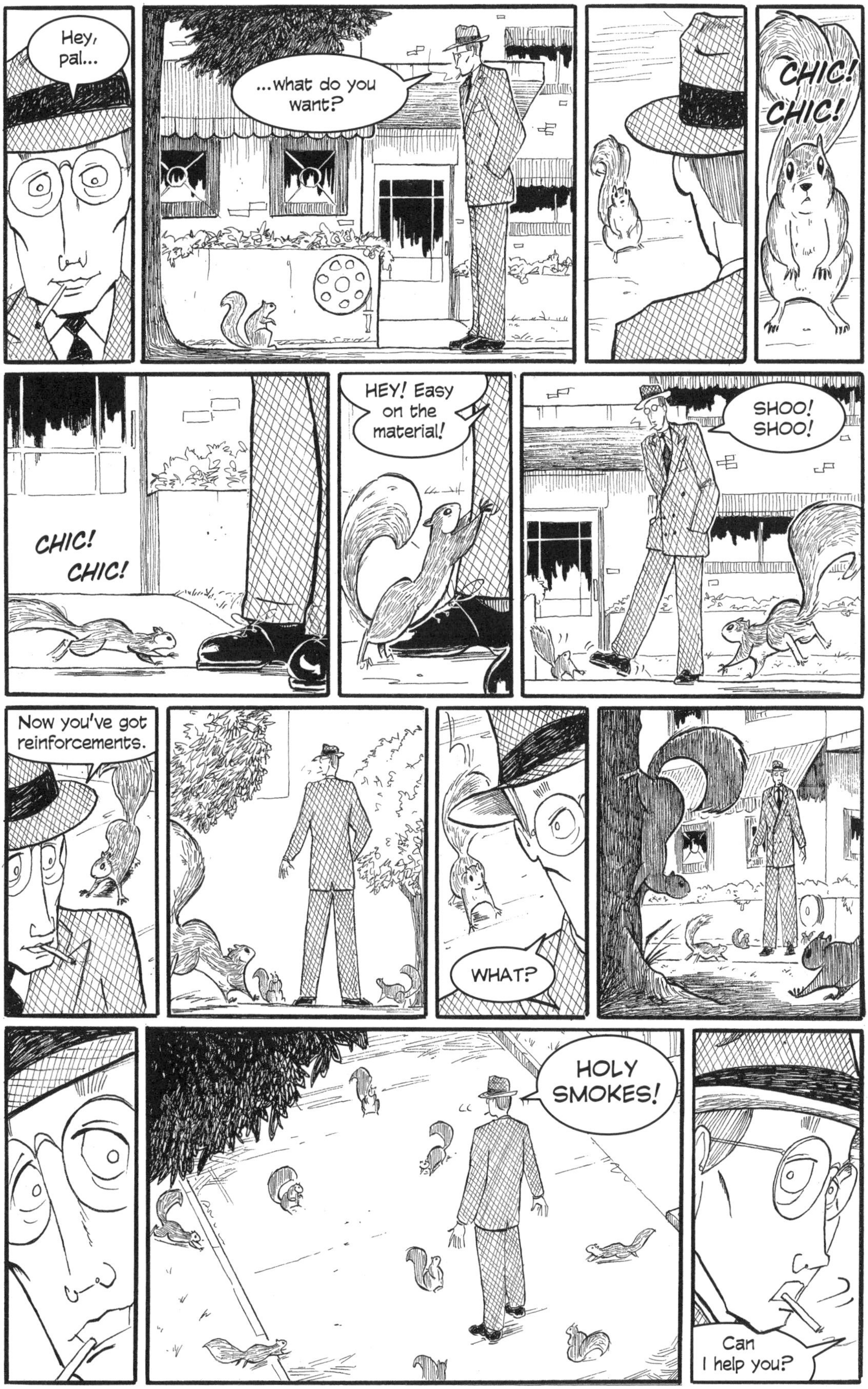

Hey, pal...
...what do you want?
CHIC! CHIC!
CHIC! CHIC!
HEY! Easy on the material!
SHOO! SHOO!
Now you've got reinforcements.
WHAT?
HOLY SMOKES!
Can I help you?

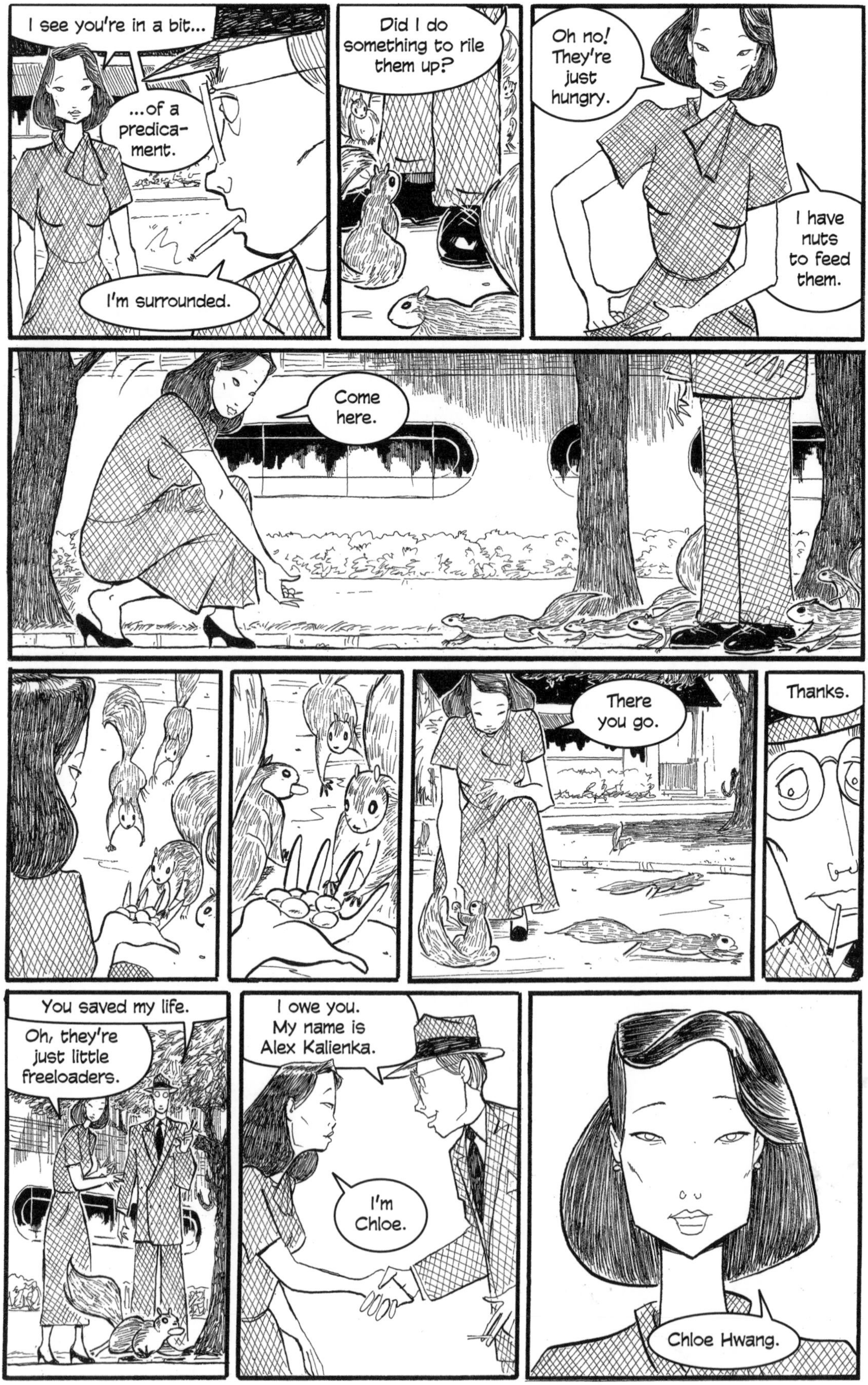

I see you're in a bit...
...of a predica-ment.
I'm surrounded.
Did I do something to rile them up?
Oh no! They're just hungry.
I have nuts to feed them.
Come here.
There you go.
Thanks.
You saved my life.
Oh, they're just little freeloaders.
I owe you. My name is Alex Kalienka.
I'm Chloe.
Chloe Hwang.

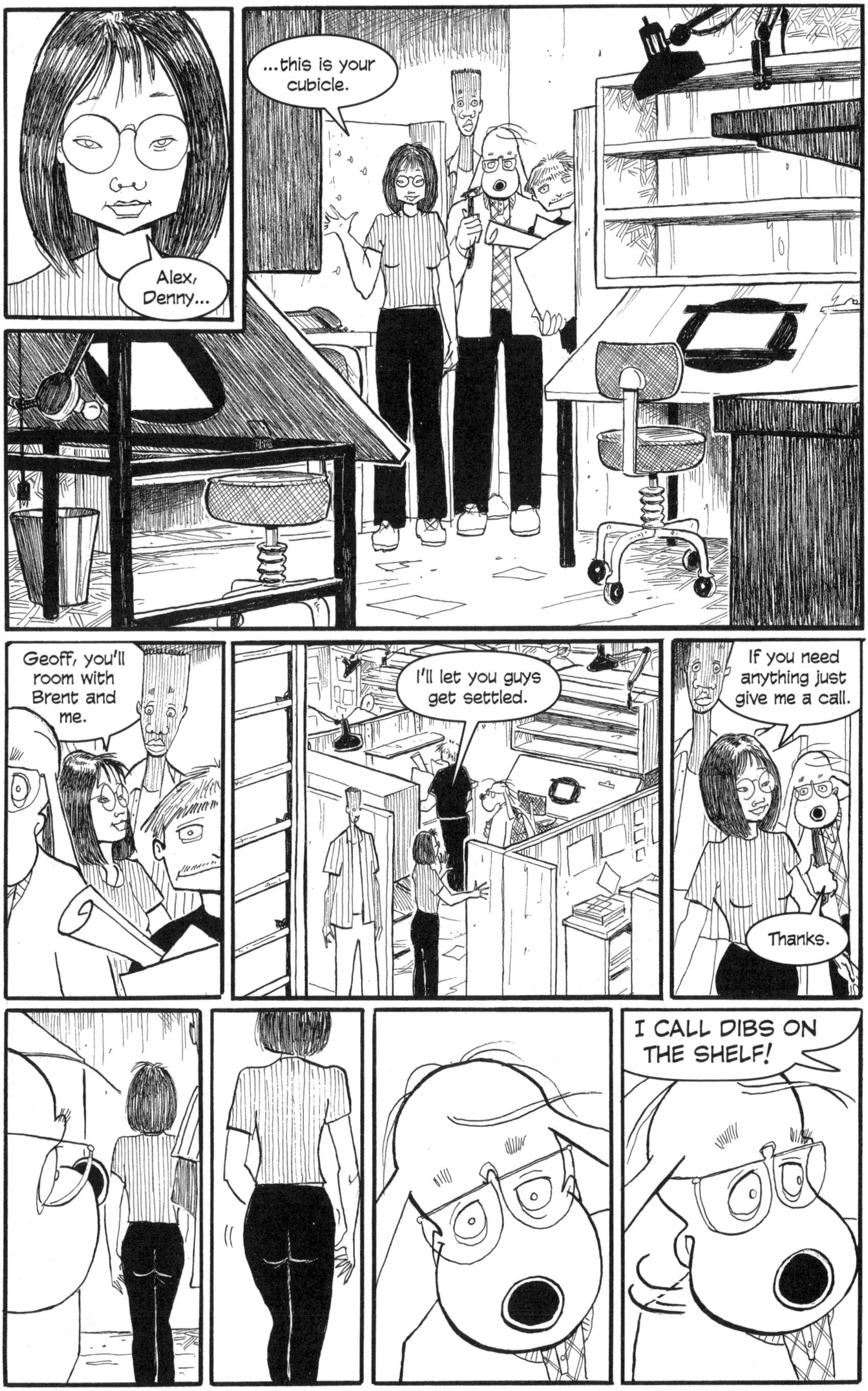
Alex, Denny...
...this is your cubicle.
Geoff, you'll room with Brent and me.
I'll let you guys get settled.
If you need anything just give me a call.
Thanks.
I CALL DIBS ON THE SHELF!

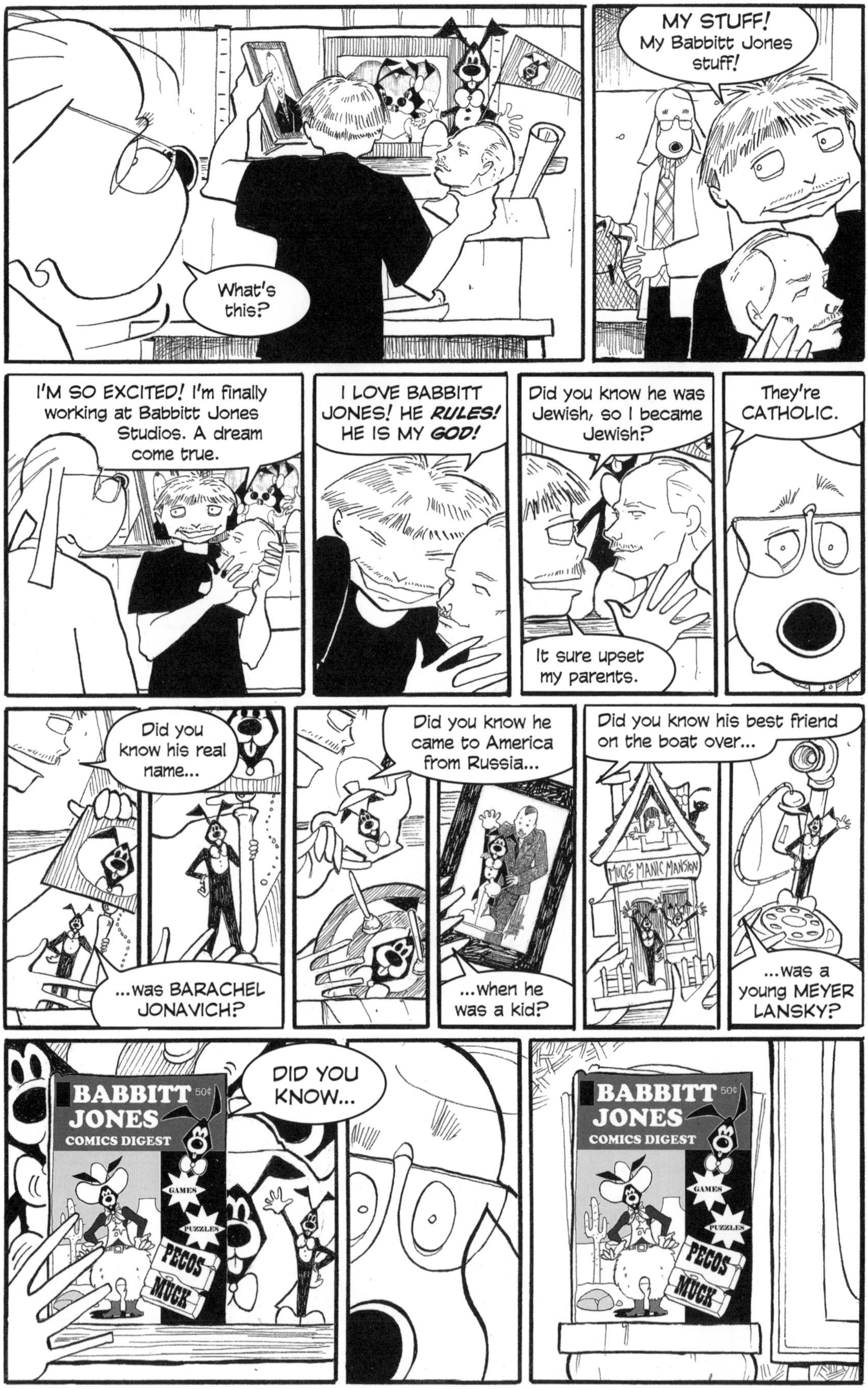
What's this?
MY STUFF! My Babbitt Jones stuff!
I'M SO EXCITED! I'm finally working at Babbitt Jones Studios. A dream come true.
I LOVE BABBITT JONES! HE RULES! HE IS MY GOD!
Did you know he was Jewish, so I became Jewish?
It sure upset my parents.
They're CATHOLIC.
Did you know his real name...
...was BARACHEL JONAVICH?
Did you know he came to America from Russia...
...when he was a kid?
Did you know his best friend on the boat over...
MUCK'S MANIC MANSION
...was a young MEYER LANSKY?
BABBITT JONES 50¢ COMICS DIGEST
GAMES
PUZZLES
PECOS MUCK
DID YOU KNOW...
BABBITT JONES 50¢ COMICS DIGEST
GAMES
PUZZLES
PECOS MUCK

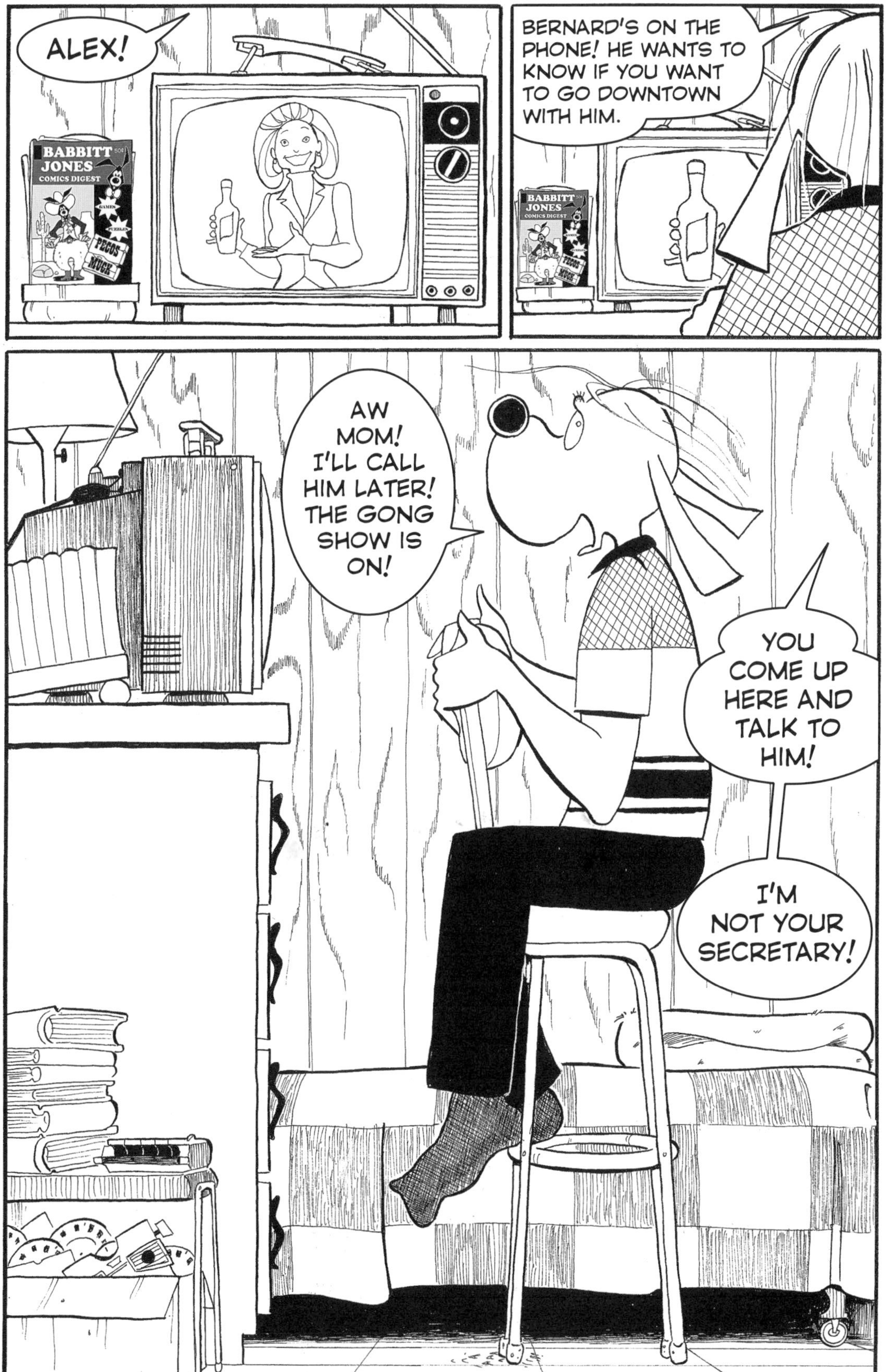
ALEX!
BABBITT JONES
COMICS DIGEST
GAMES
PUZZLES
PECOS
MUCK
BERNARD'S ON THE PHONE! HE WANTS TO KNOW IF YOU WANT TO GO DOWNTOWN WITH HIM.
AW MOM! I'LL CALL HIM LATER! THE GONG SHOW IS ON!
YOU COME UP HERE AND TALK TO HIM!
I'M NOT YOUR SECRETARY!

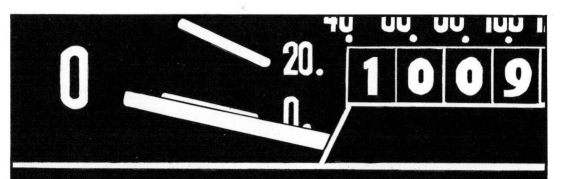

WHY?

WHY IS THE TRAFFIC *NOT MOVING?*

WHY IS THIS HAPPENING AGAIN?

WHY?

WHY?
WHY?
WHY?
WHY?
WHY?

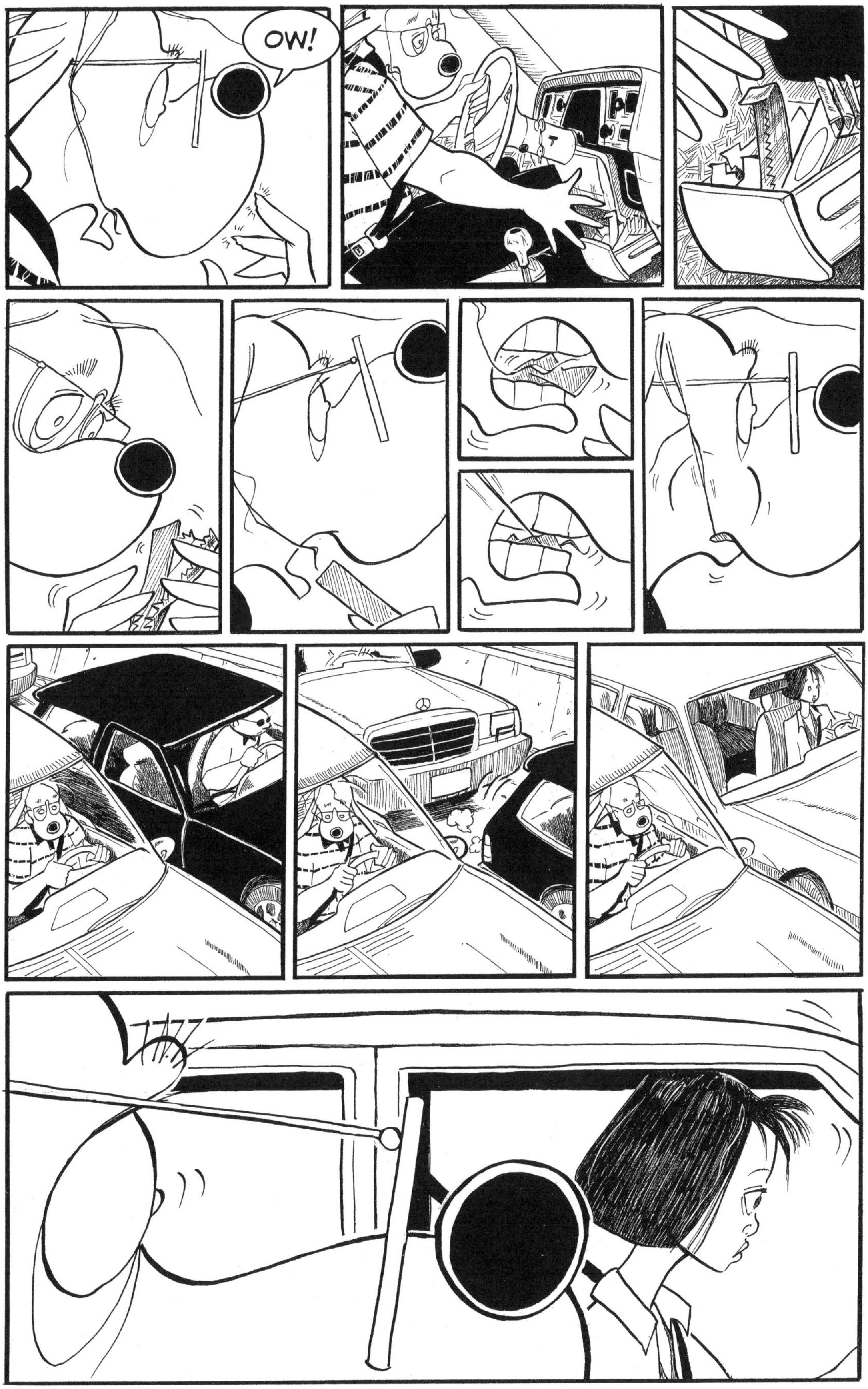
OW!

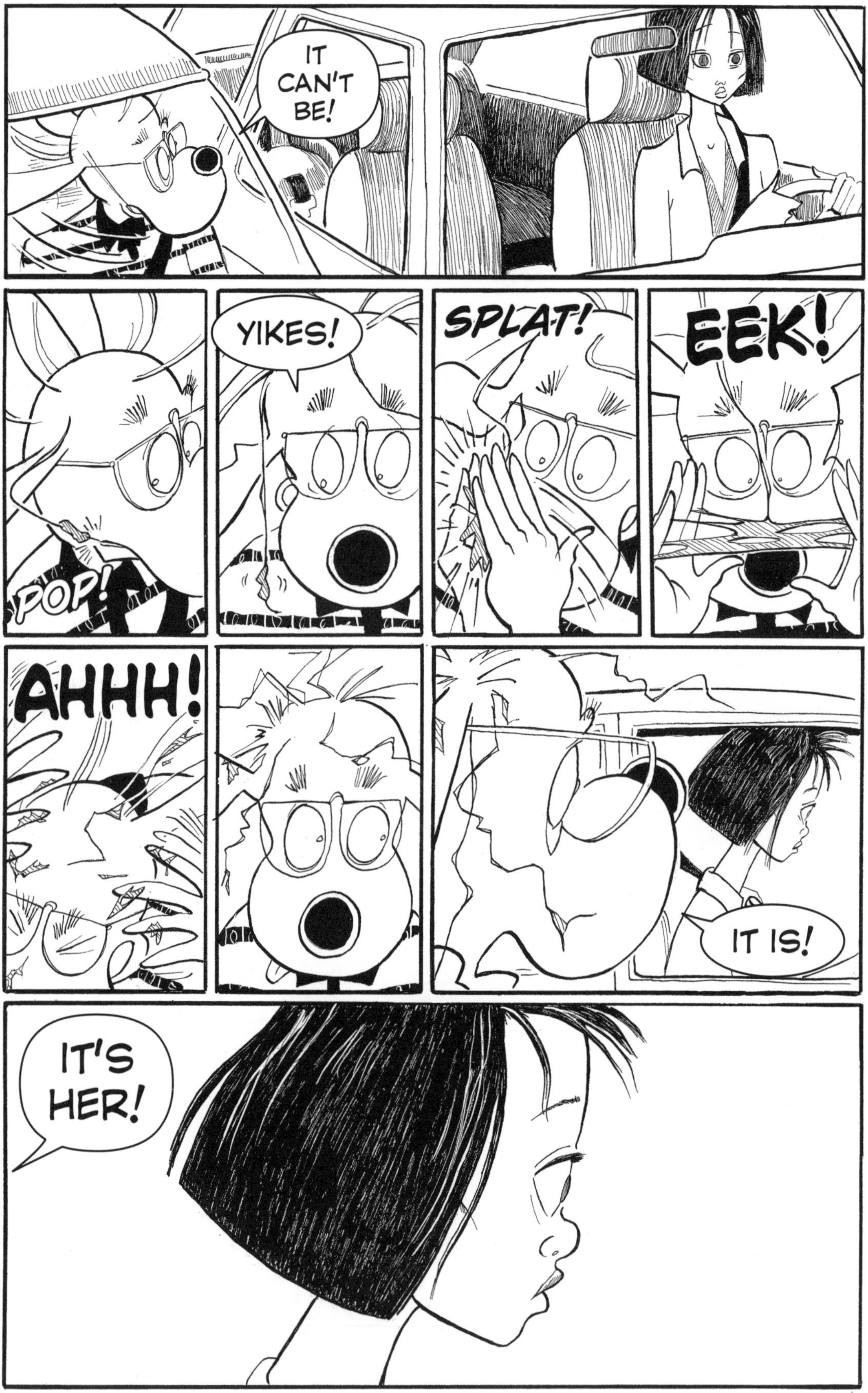
IT CAN'T BE!
POP!
YIKES!
SPLAT!
EEK!
AHHH!
IT IS!
IT'S HER!

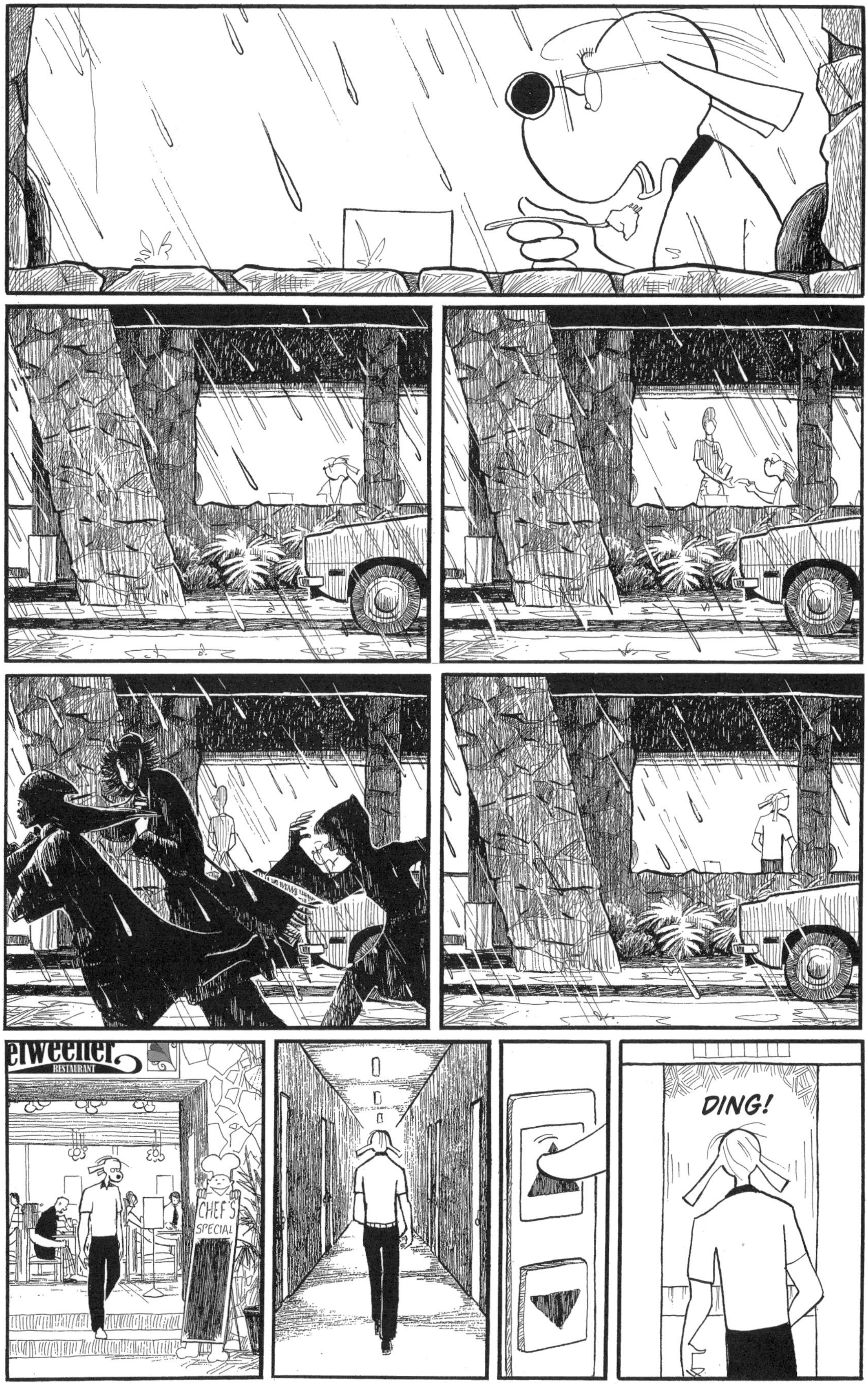
elweener
RESTAURANT
CHEF'S SPECIAL
DING!

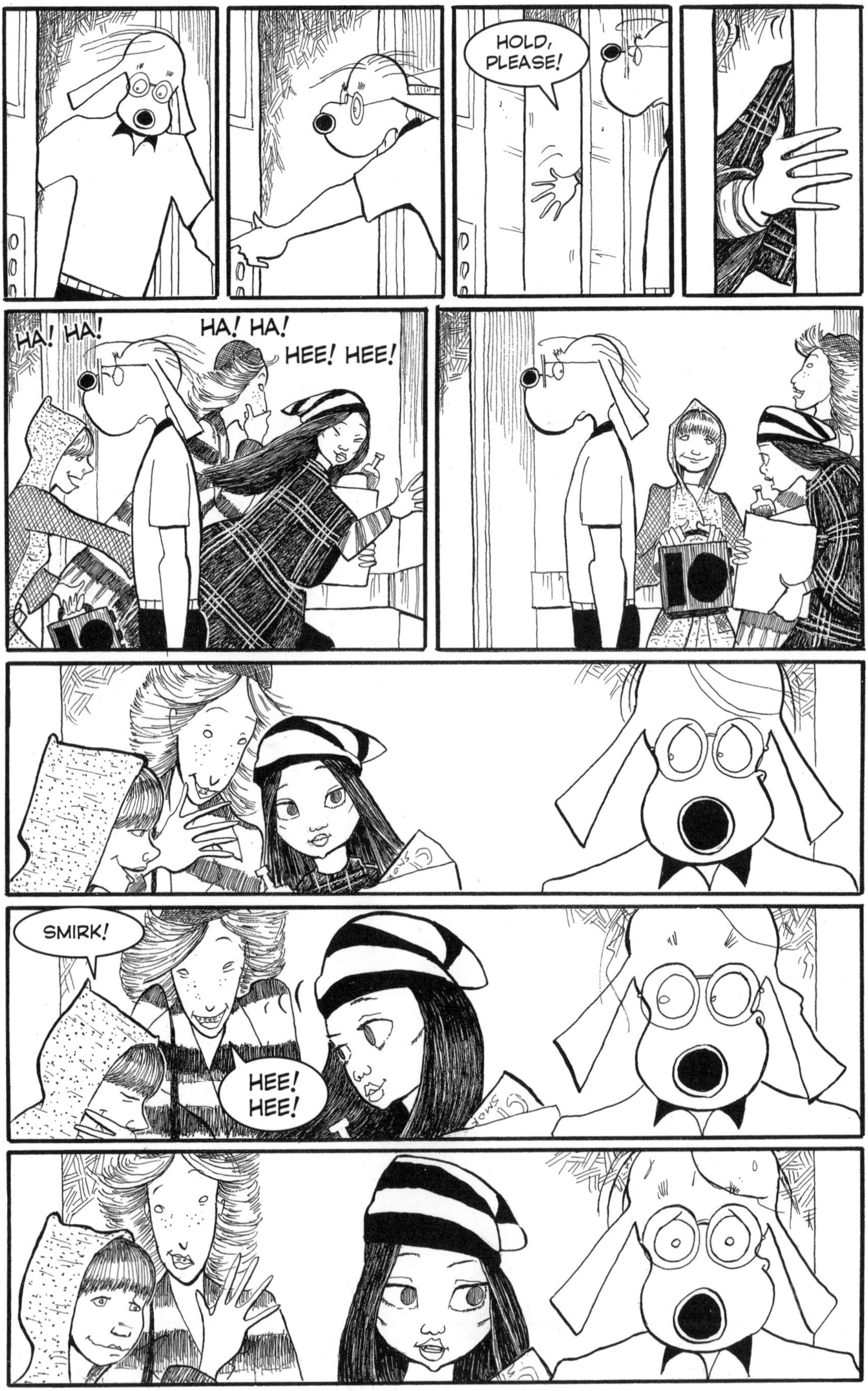
HOLD, PLEASE!
HA! HA!
HA! HA!
HEE! HEE!
SMIRK!
HEE! HEE!

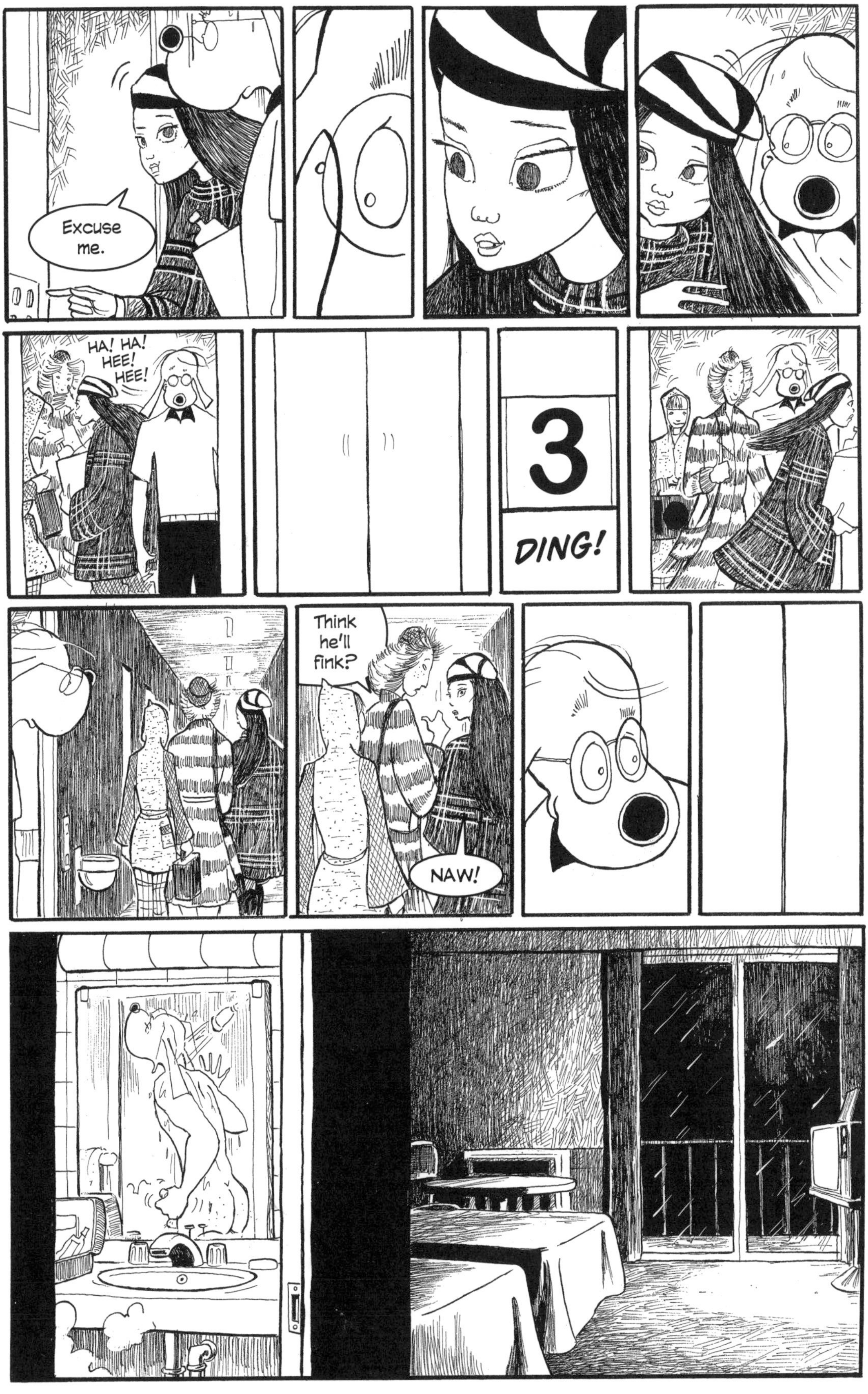
Excuse me.
HA! HA! HEE! HEE!
3
DING!
Think he'll fink?
NAW!

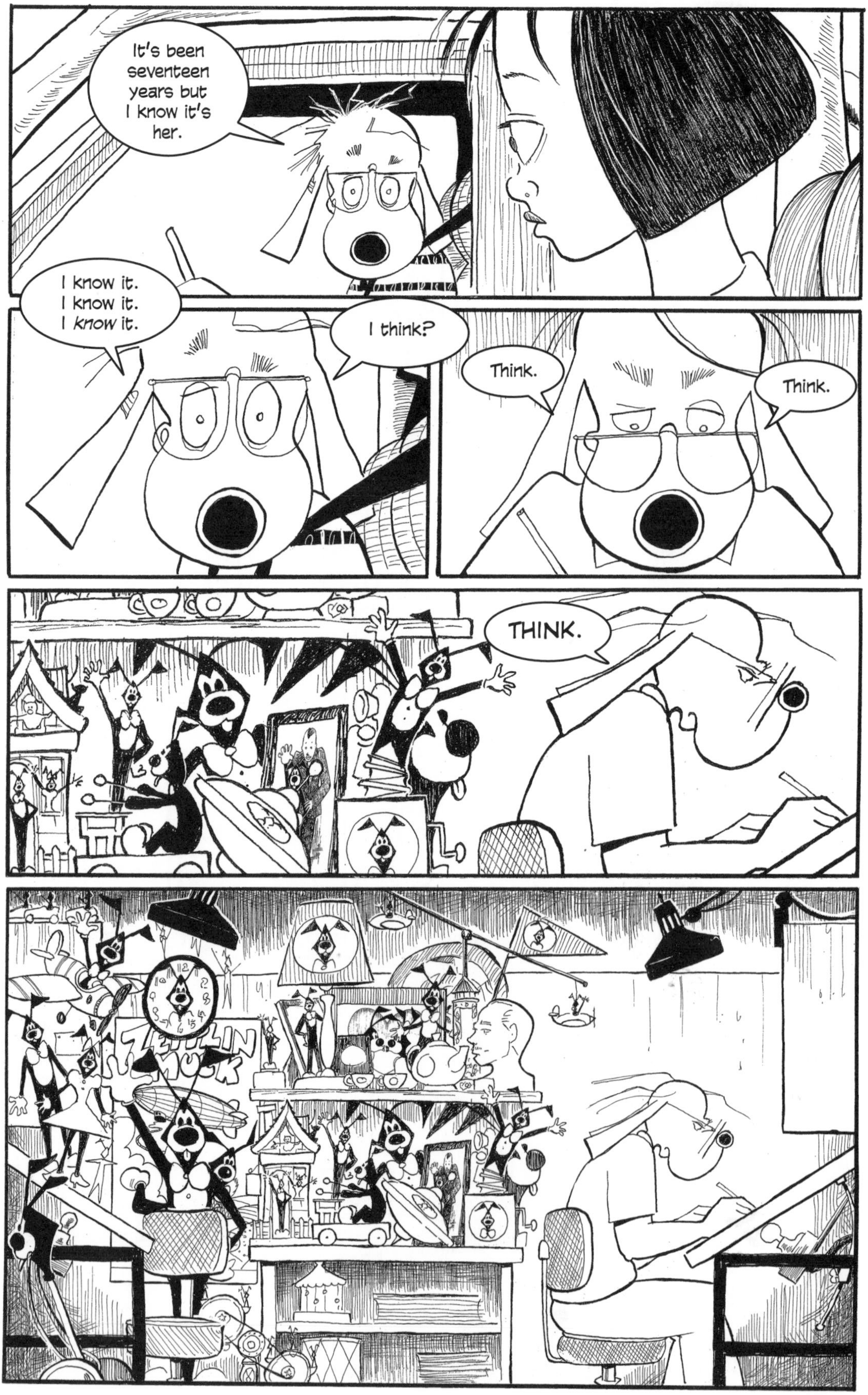
It's been seventeen years but I know it's her.
I know it.
I know it.
I *know* it.
I think?
Think.
Think.
THINK.

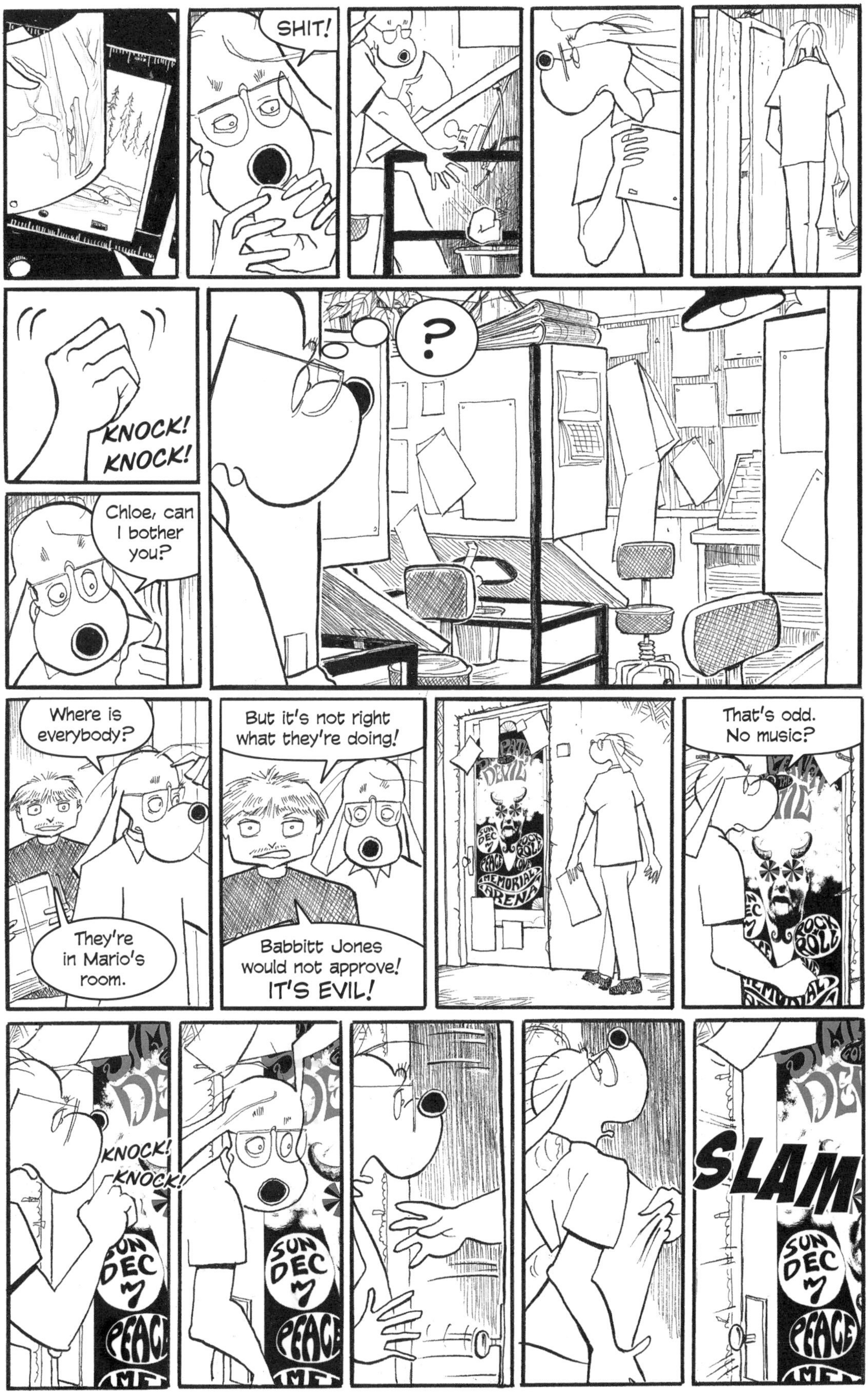
SHIT!
KNOCK! KNOCK!
?
Chloe, can I bother you?
Where is everybody?
They're in Mario's room.
But it's not right what they're doing!
Babbitt Jones would not approve! IT'S EVIL!
That's odd. No music?
KNOCK! KNOCK!
SLAM

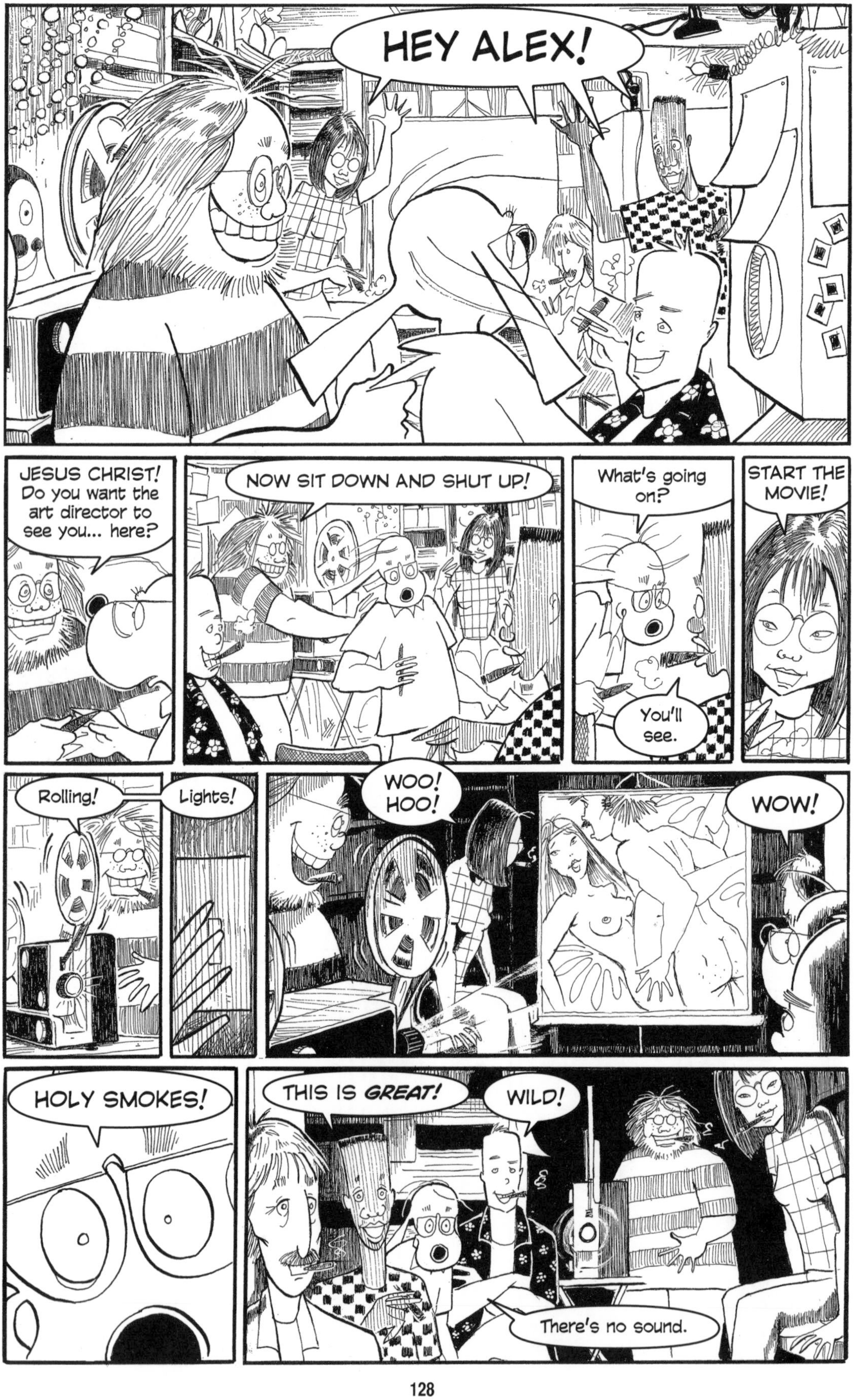

HEY ALEX!
JESUS CHRIST! Do you want the art director to see you... here?
NOW SIT DOWN AND SHUT UP!
What's going on?
You'll see.
START THE MOVIE!
Rolling!
Lights!
WOO! HOO!
WOW!
HOLY SMOKES!
THIS IS *GREAT!*
WILD!
There's no sound.

It doesn't work.

Where did you find this?

A garage sale. Some old widow was selling her husband's junk. This was hidden in a box of old records I bought.

It looks old.

I think the sixties.

Vintage porn. Look! Hippy girl is going down on afro guy.

Is she trying to talk while giving head?

What do you think she's saying?

MMUH! MMMUH! MMUH!

HA! HA! HA!

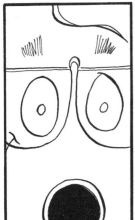

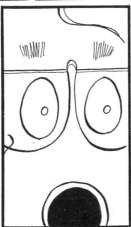

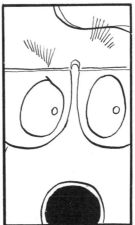

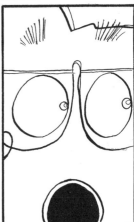

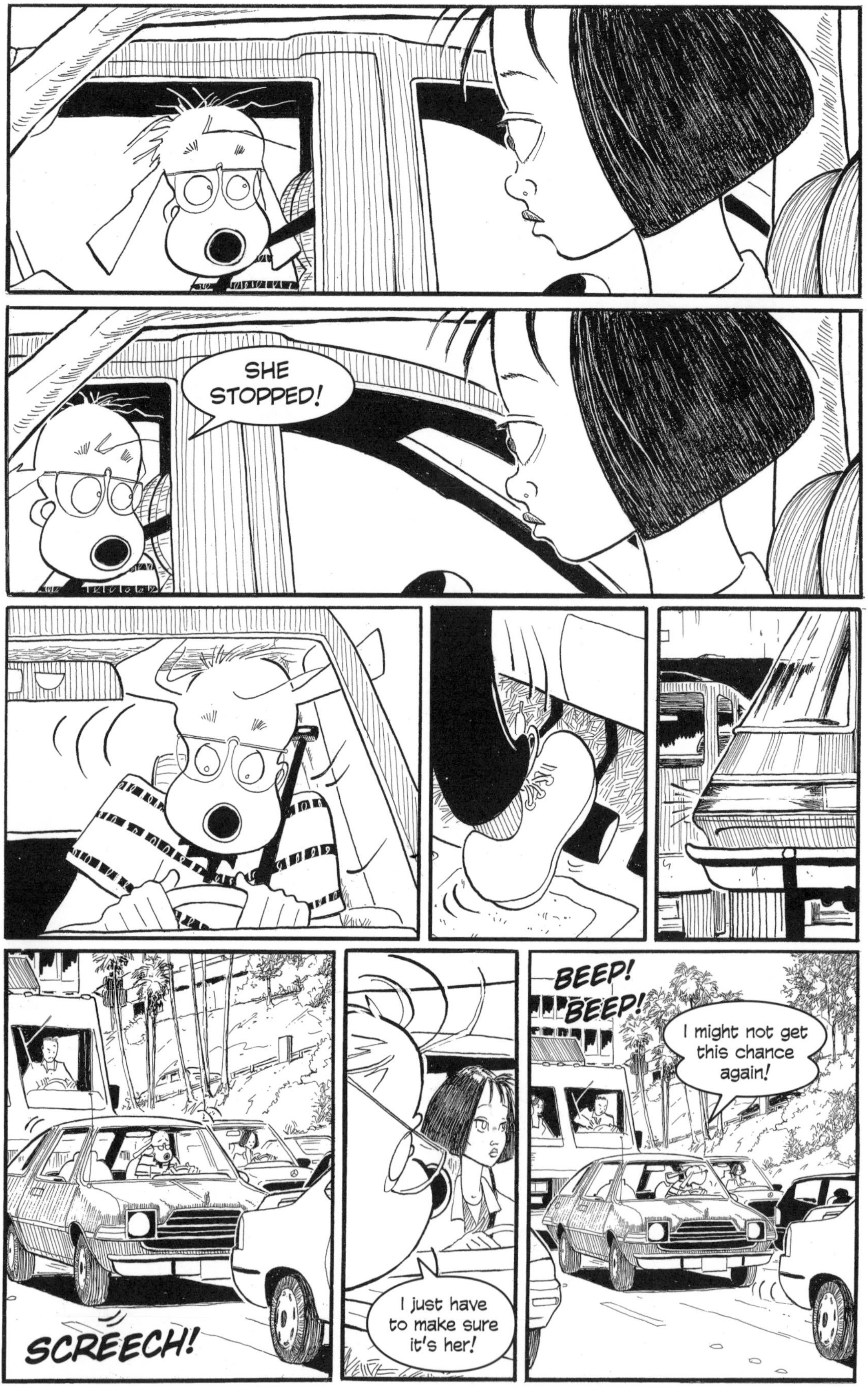
SHE STOPPED!
SCREECH!
I just have to make sure it's her!
BEEP! BEEP!
I might not get this chance again!

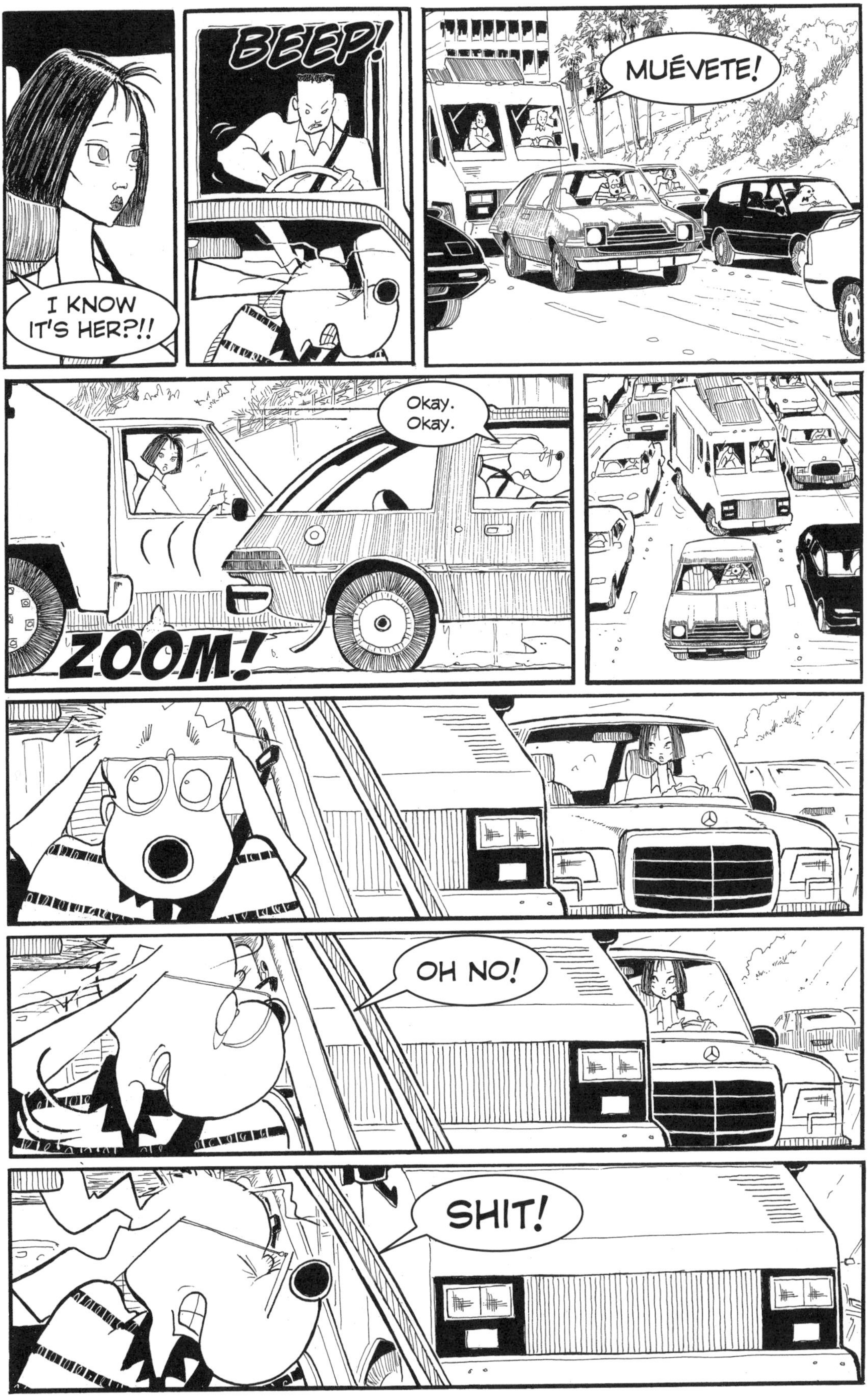
I KNOW IT'S HER?!!
BEEP!
MUÉVETE!
Okay. Okay.
ZOOM!
OH NO!
SHIT!

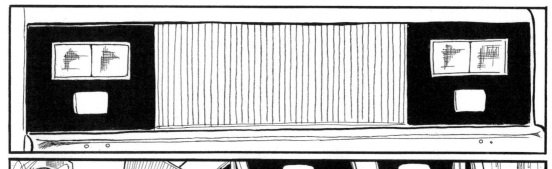

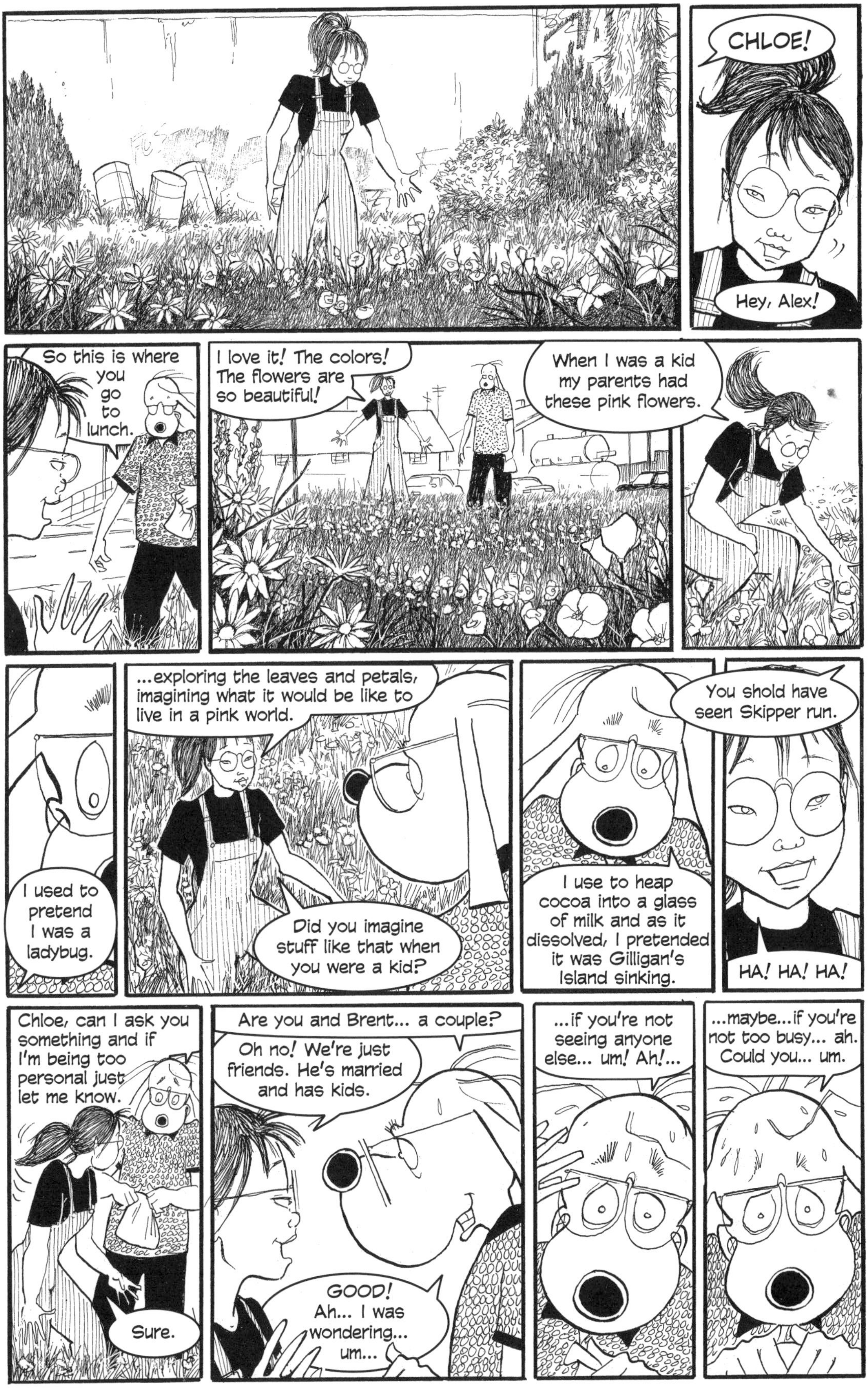
CHLOE!
Hey, Alex!
So this is where you go to lunch.
I love it! The colors! The flowers are so beautiful!
When I was a kid my parents had these pink flowers.
I used to pretend I was a ladybug.
...exploring the leaves and petals, imagining what it would be like to live in a pink world.
Did you imagine stuff like that when you were a kid?
I use to heap cocoa into a glass of milk and as it dissolved, I pretended it was Gilligan's Island sinking.
You shold have seen Skipper run.
HA! HA! HA!
Chloe, can I ask you something and if I'm being too personal just let me know.
Sure.
Are you and Brent... a couple?
Oh no! We're just friends. He's married and has kids.
GOOD! Ah... I was wondering... um...
...if you're not seeing anyone else... um! Ah!...
...maybe...if you're not too busy... ah. Could you... um.

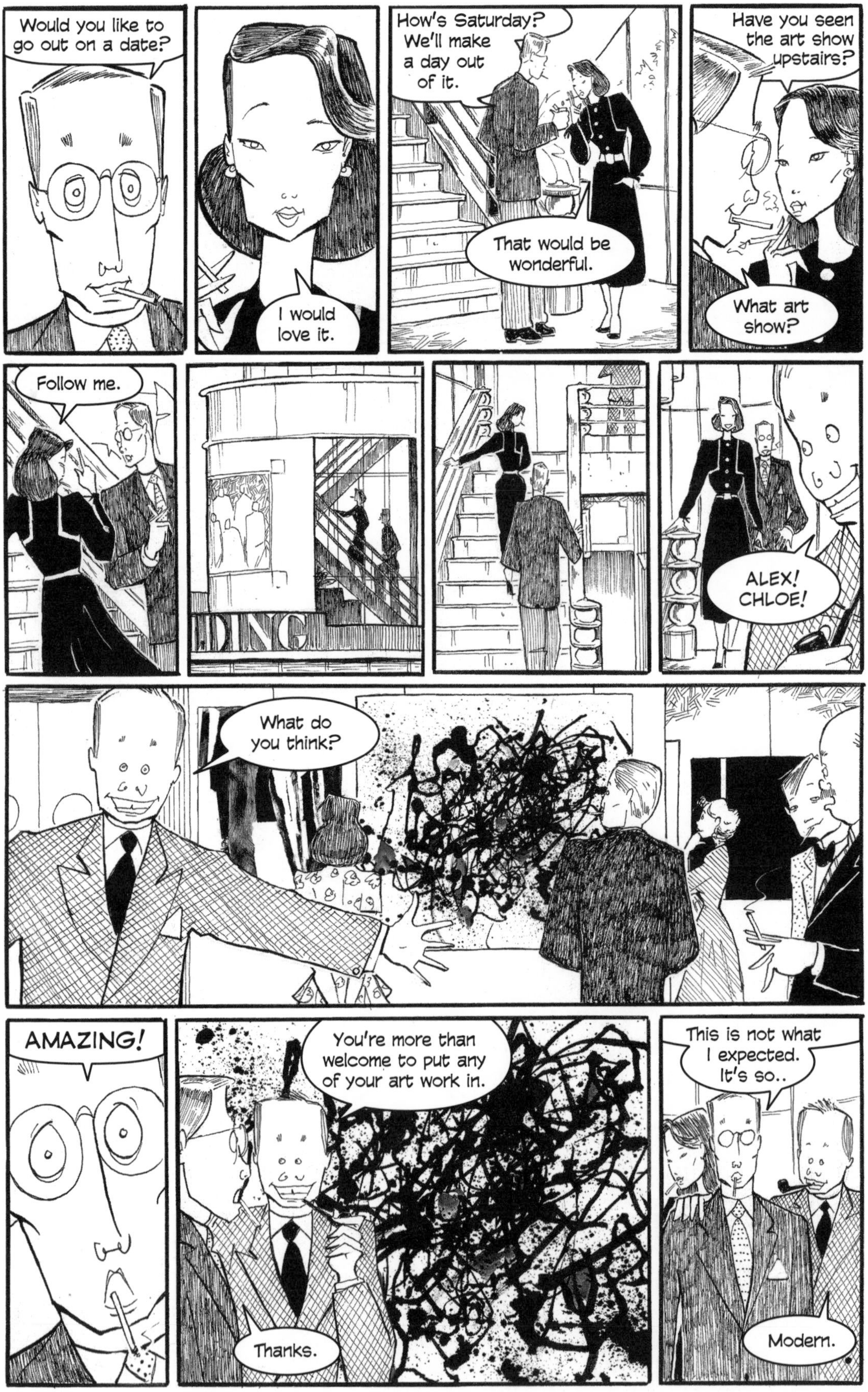

Would you like to go out on a date?
I would love it.
How's Saturday? We'll make a day out of it.
That would be wonderful.
Have you seen the art show upstairs?
What art show?
Follow me.
ALEX! CHLOE!
What do you think?
AMAZING!
You're more than welcome to put any of your art work in.
Thanks.
This is not what I expected. It's so..
Modern.

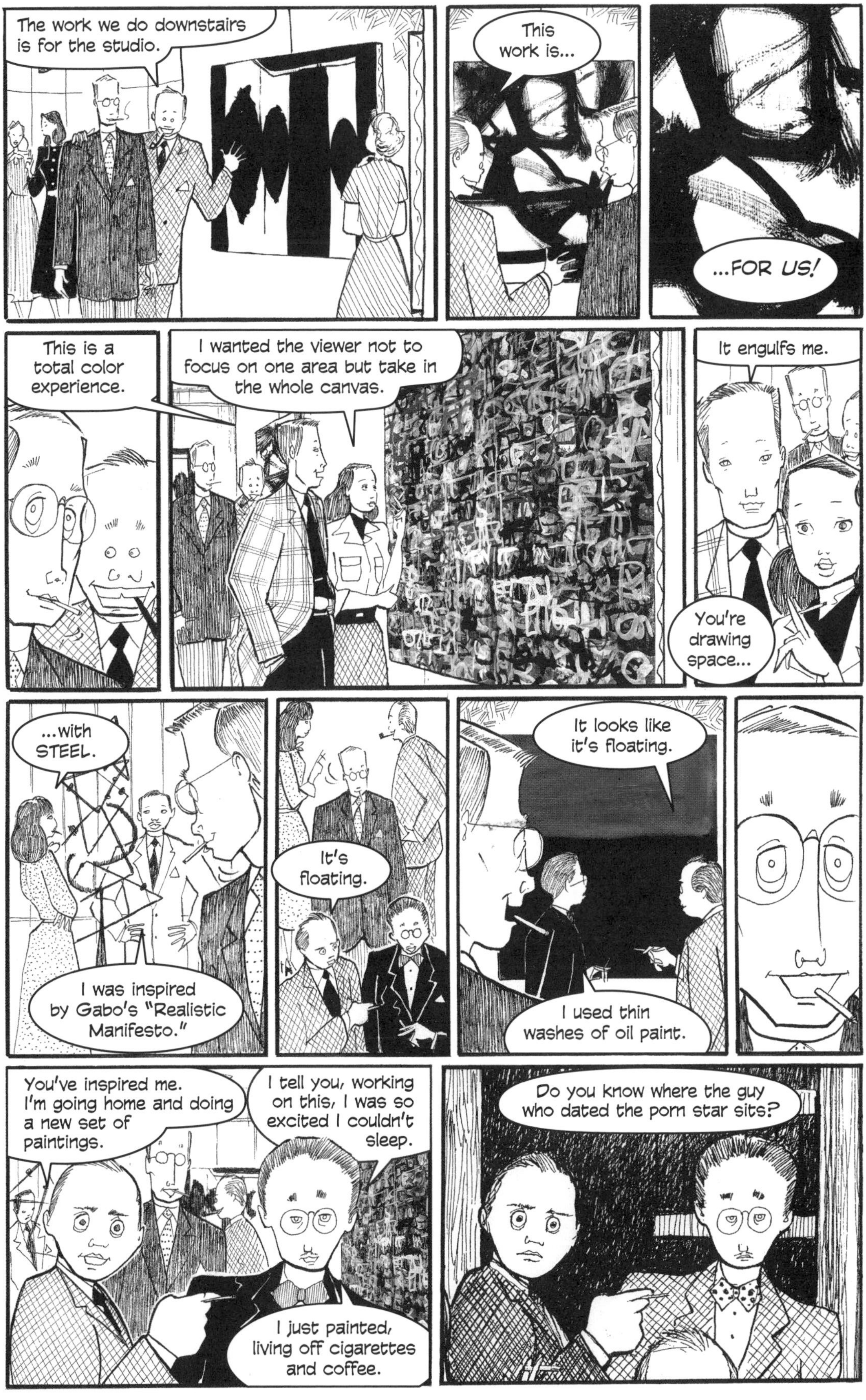

The work we do downstairs is for the studio.
This work is...
...FOR US!
This is a total color experience.
I wanted the viewer not to focus on one area but take in the whole canvas.
It engulfs me.
You're drawing space...
...with STEEL.
I was inspired by Gabo's "Realistic Manifesto."
It's floating.
It looks like it's floating.
I used thin washes of oil paint.
You've inspired me. I'm going home and doing a new set of paintings.
I tell you, working on this, I was so excited I couldn't sleep.
I just painted, living off cigarettes and coffee.
Do you know where the guy who dated the porn star sits?

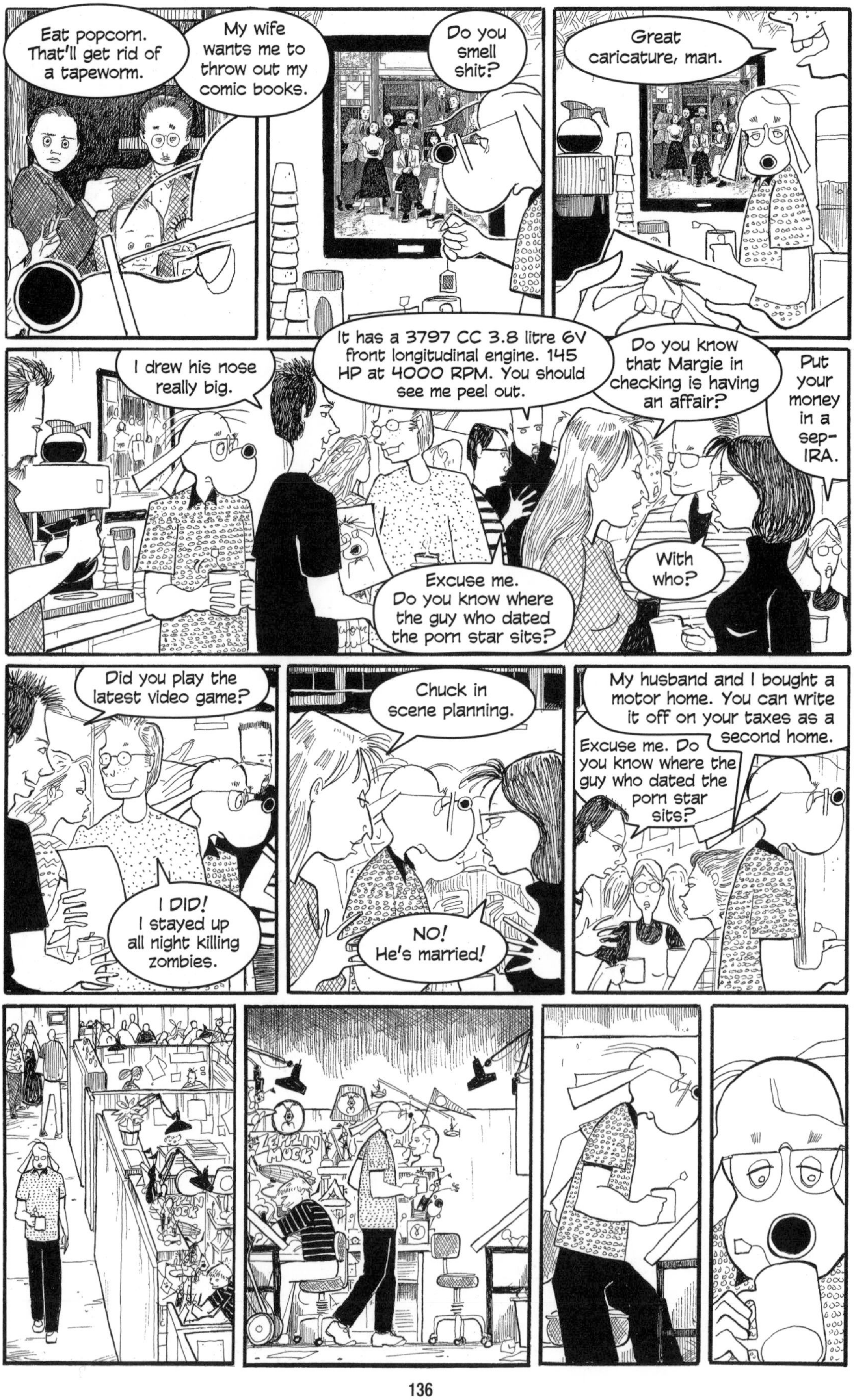
Eat popcorn. That'll get rid of a tapeworm.
My wife wants me to throw out my comic books.
Do you smell shit?
Great caricature, man.
I drew his nose really big.
It has a 3797 CC 3.8 litre 6V front longitudinal engine. 145 HP at 4000 RPM. You should see me peel out.
Do you know that Margie in checking is having an affair?
Put your money in a sep-IRA.
Excuse me. Do you know where the guy who dated the porn star sits?
With who?
Did you play the latest video game?
I DID! I stayed up all night killing zombies.
Chuck in scene planning.
NO! He's married!
My husband and I bought a motor home. You can write it off on your taxes as a second home.
Excuse me. Do you know where the guy who dated the porn star sits?
ZEPPLIN MUCK

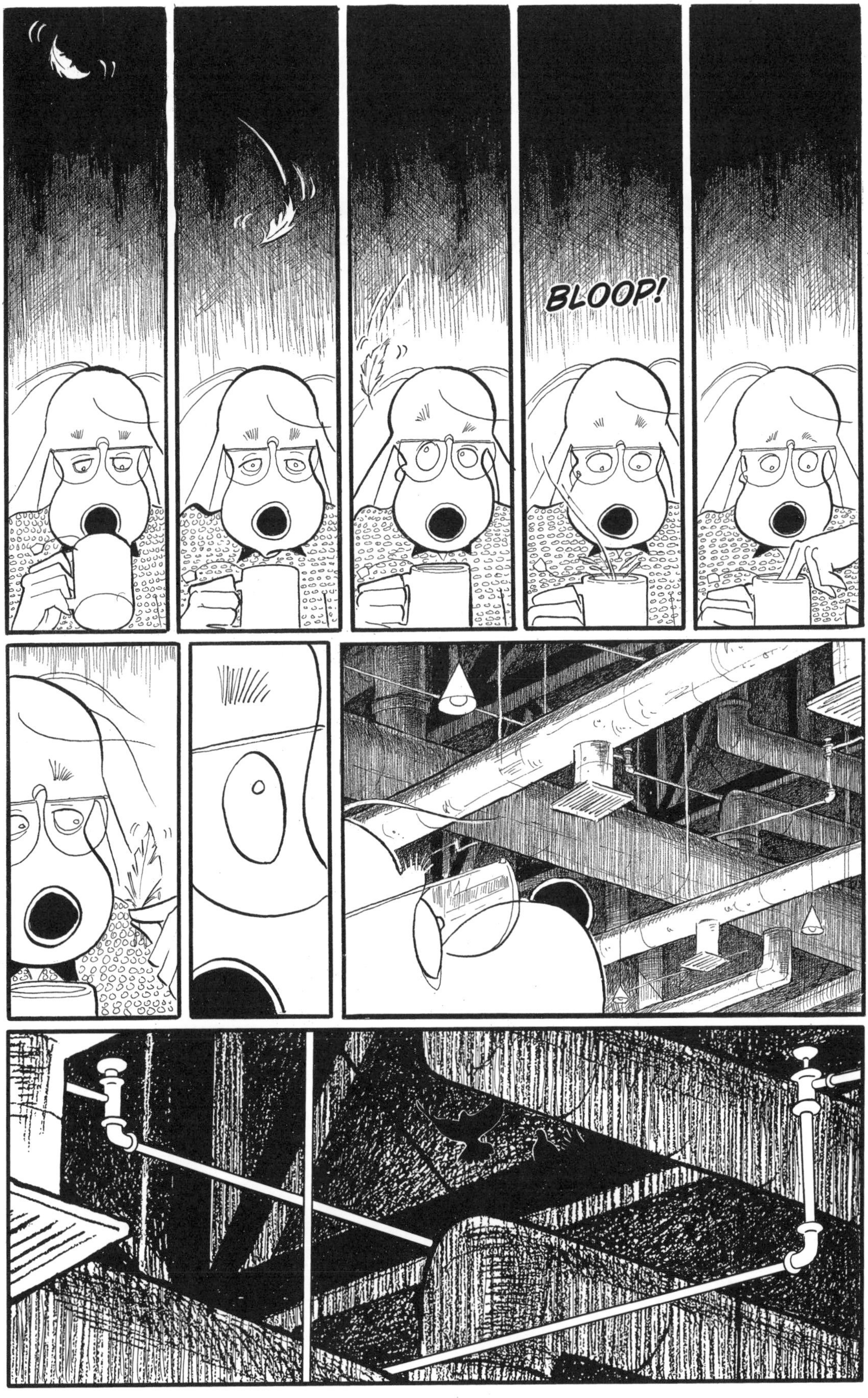
BLOOP!

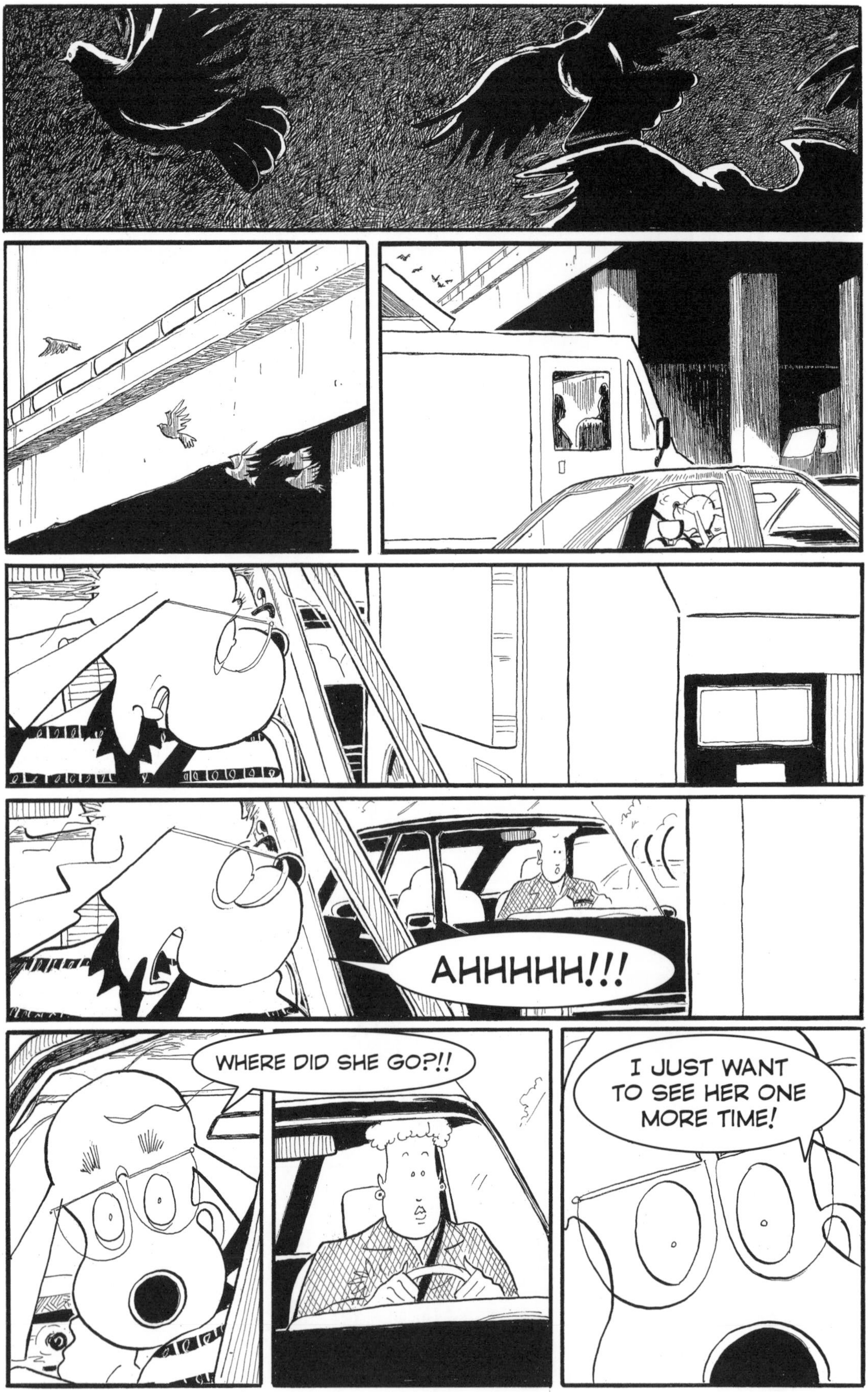
AHHHHH!!!
WHERE DID SHE GO?!!
I JUST WANT TO SEE HER ONE MORE TIME!

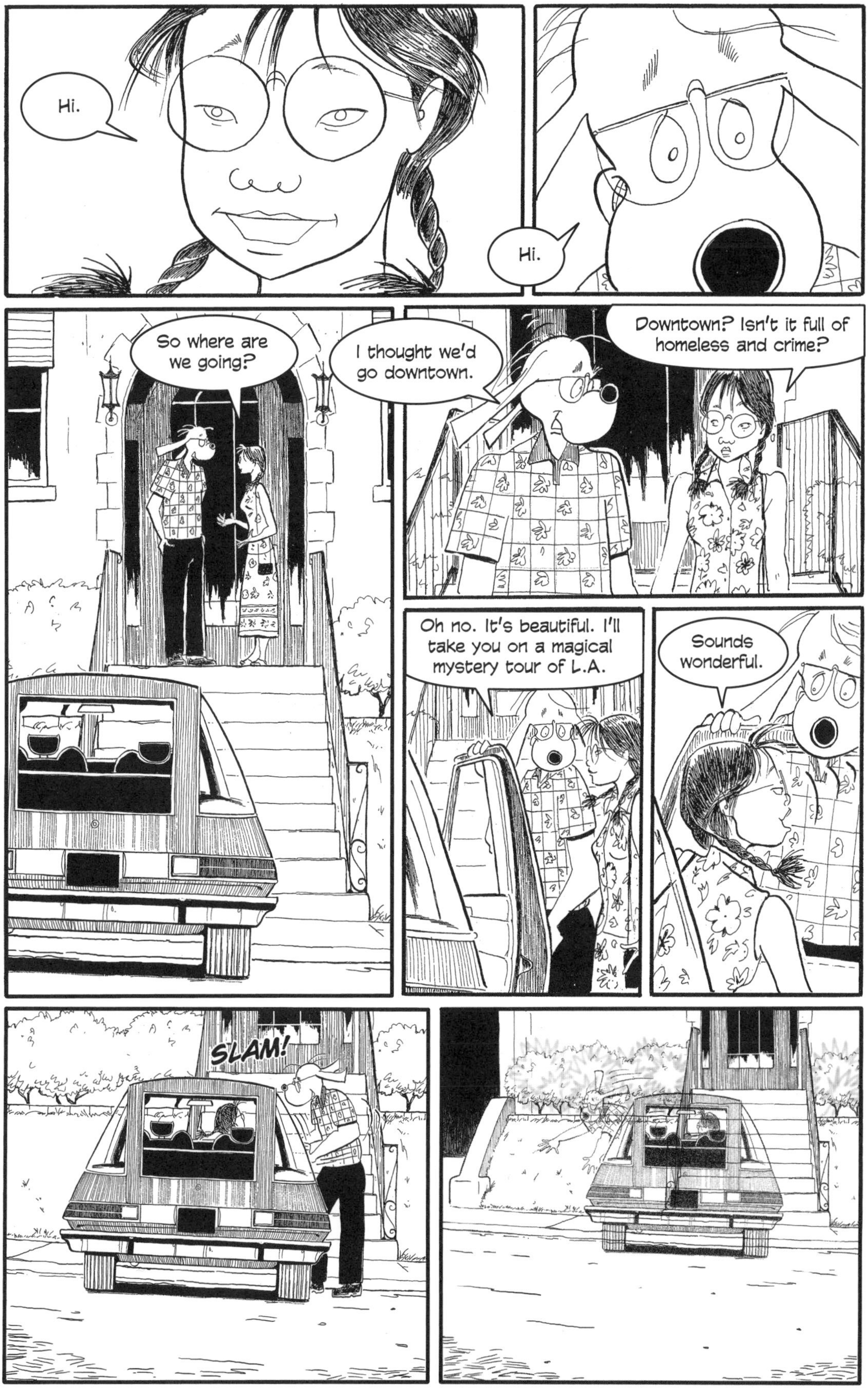
Hi.
Hi.
So where are we going?
I thought we'd go downtown.
Downtown? Isn't it full of homeless and crime?
Oh no. It's beautiful. I'll take you on a magical mystery tour of L.A.
Sounds wonderful.
SLAM!

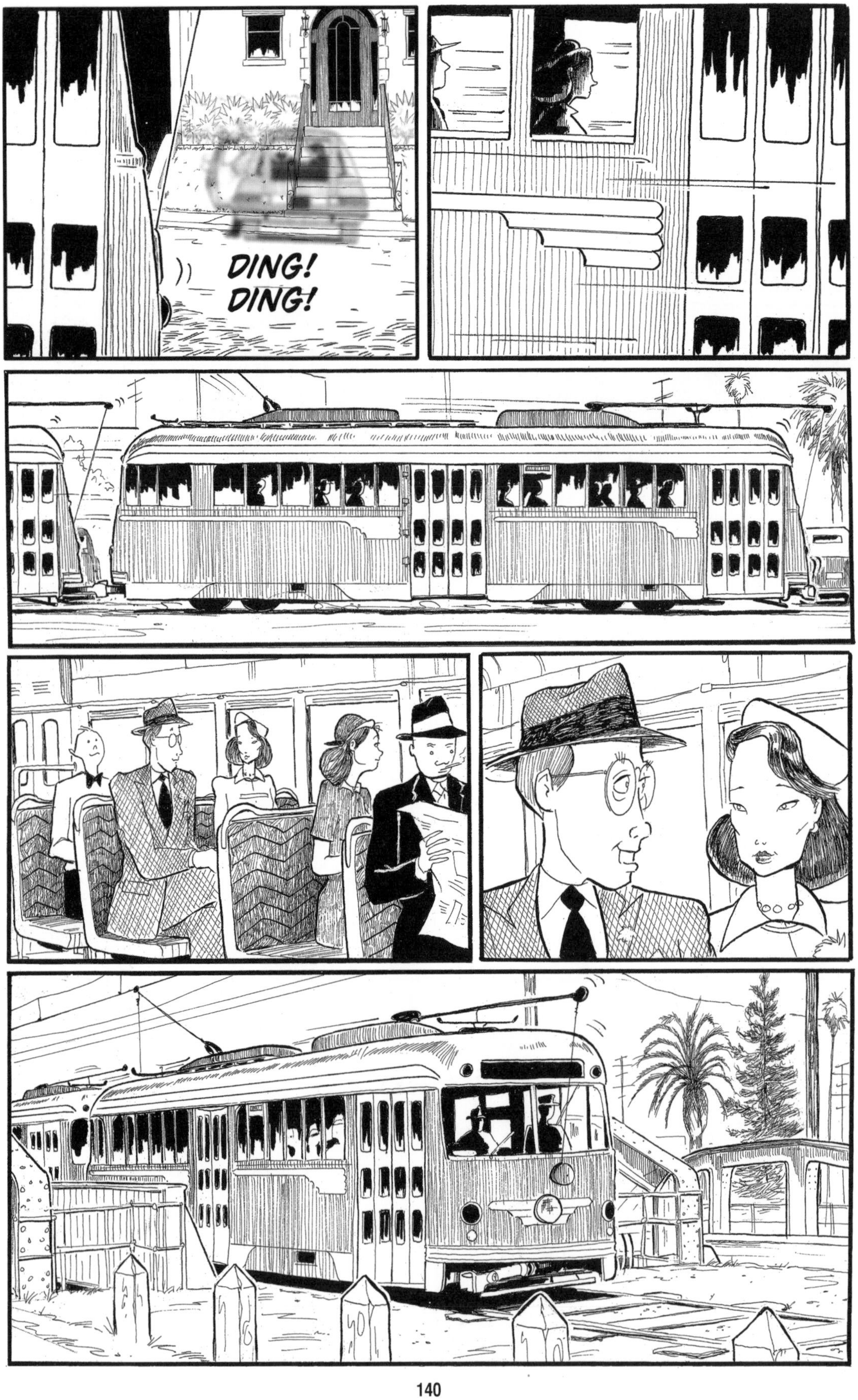
DING!
DING!

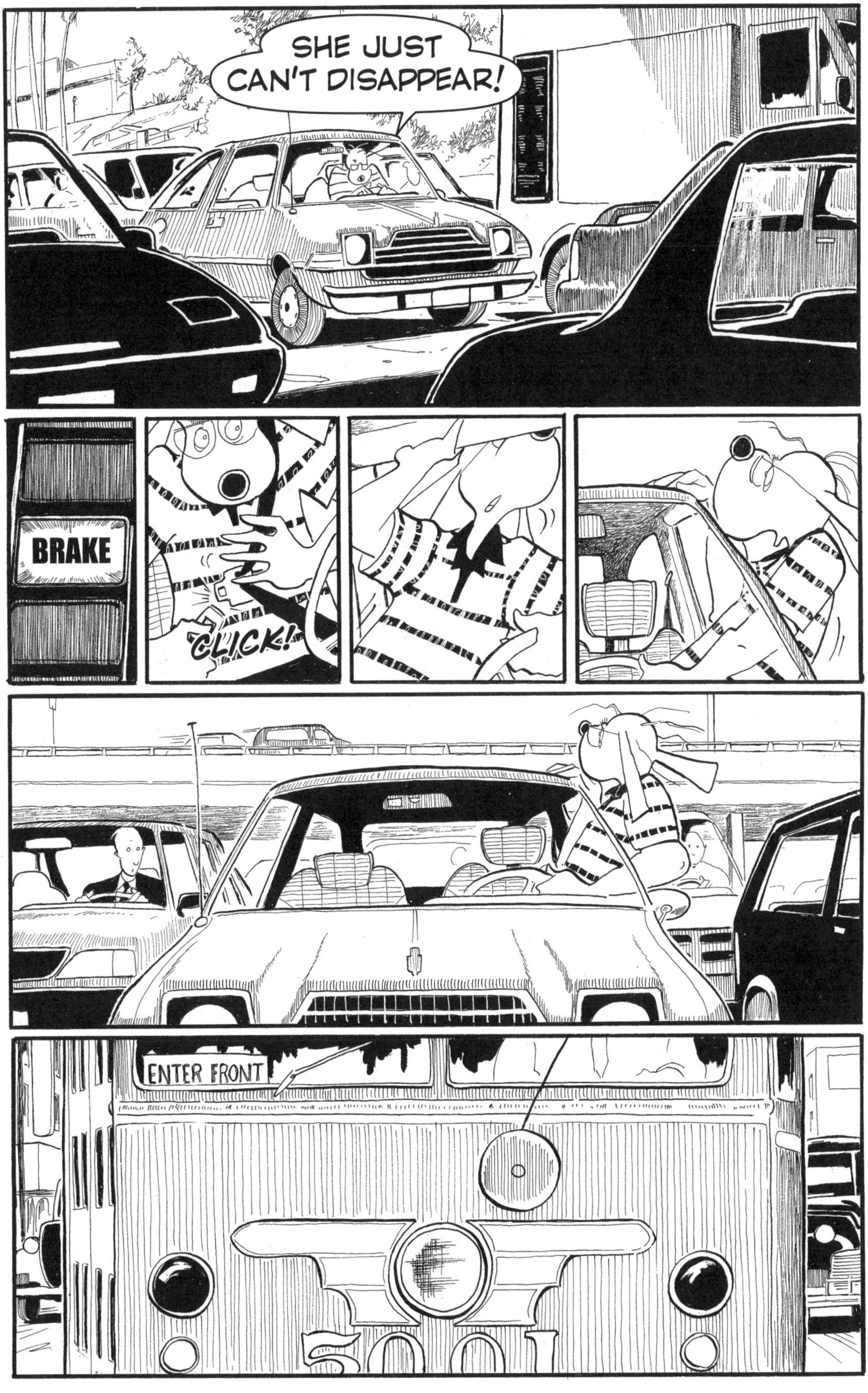
SHE JUST CAN'T DISAPPEAR!
BRAKE
CLICK!
ENTER FRONT

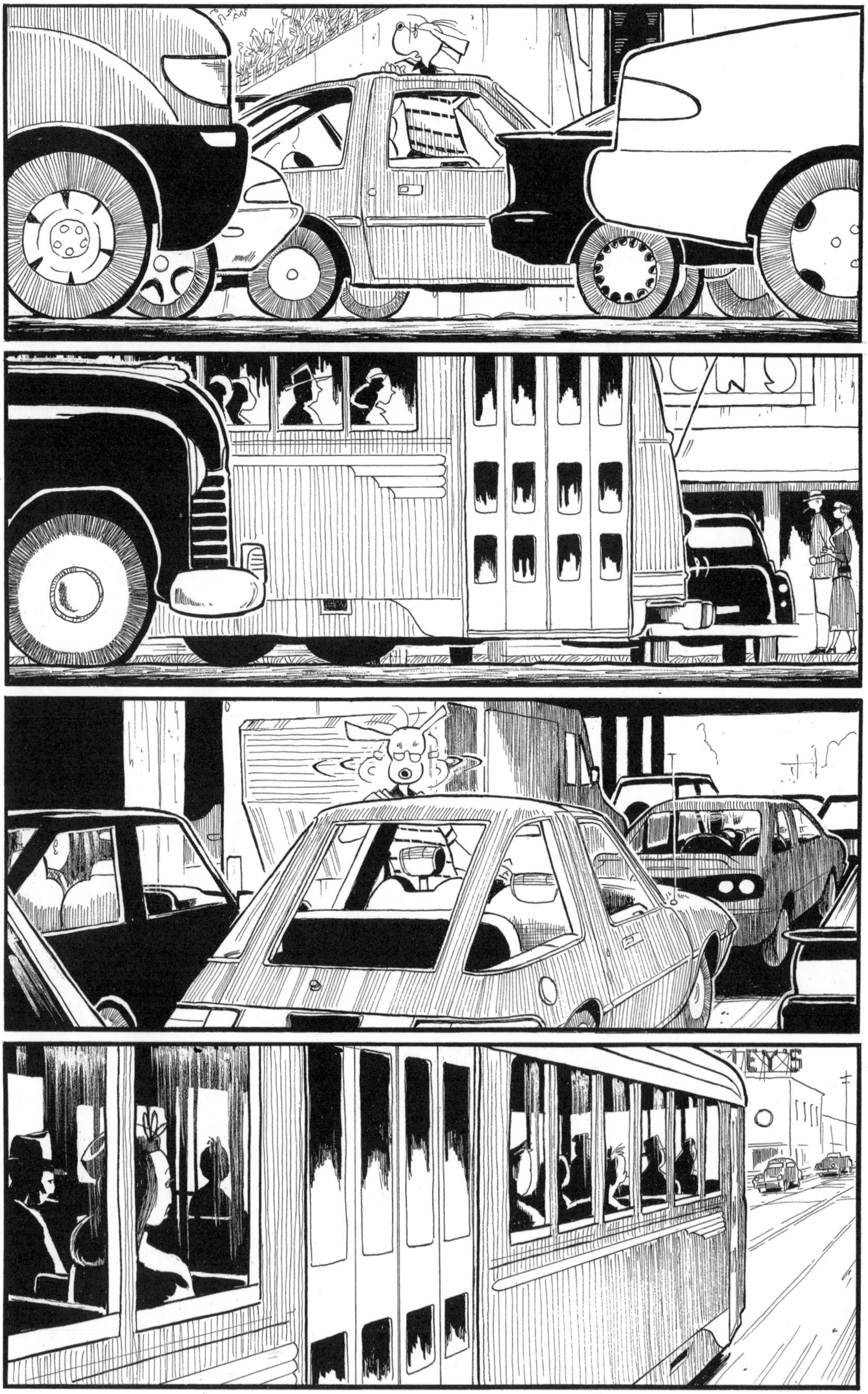

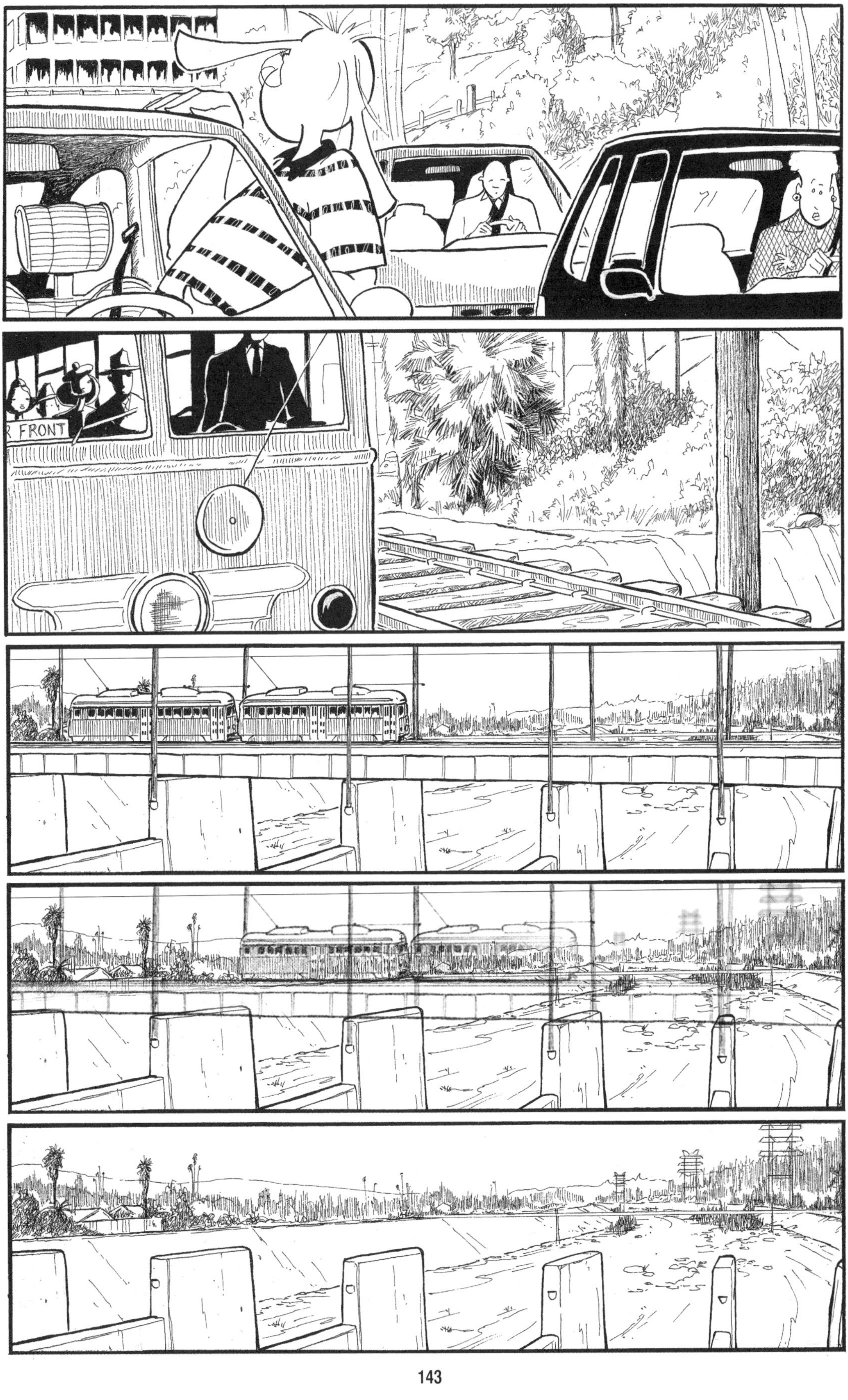
R FRONT

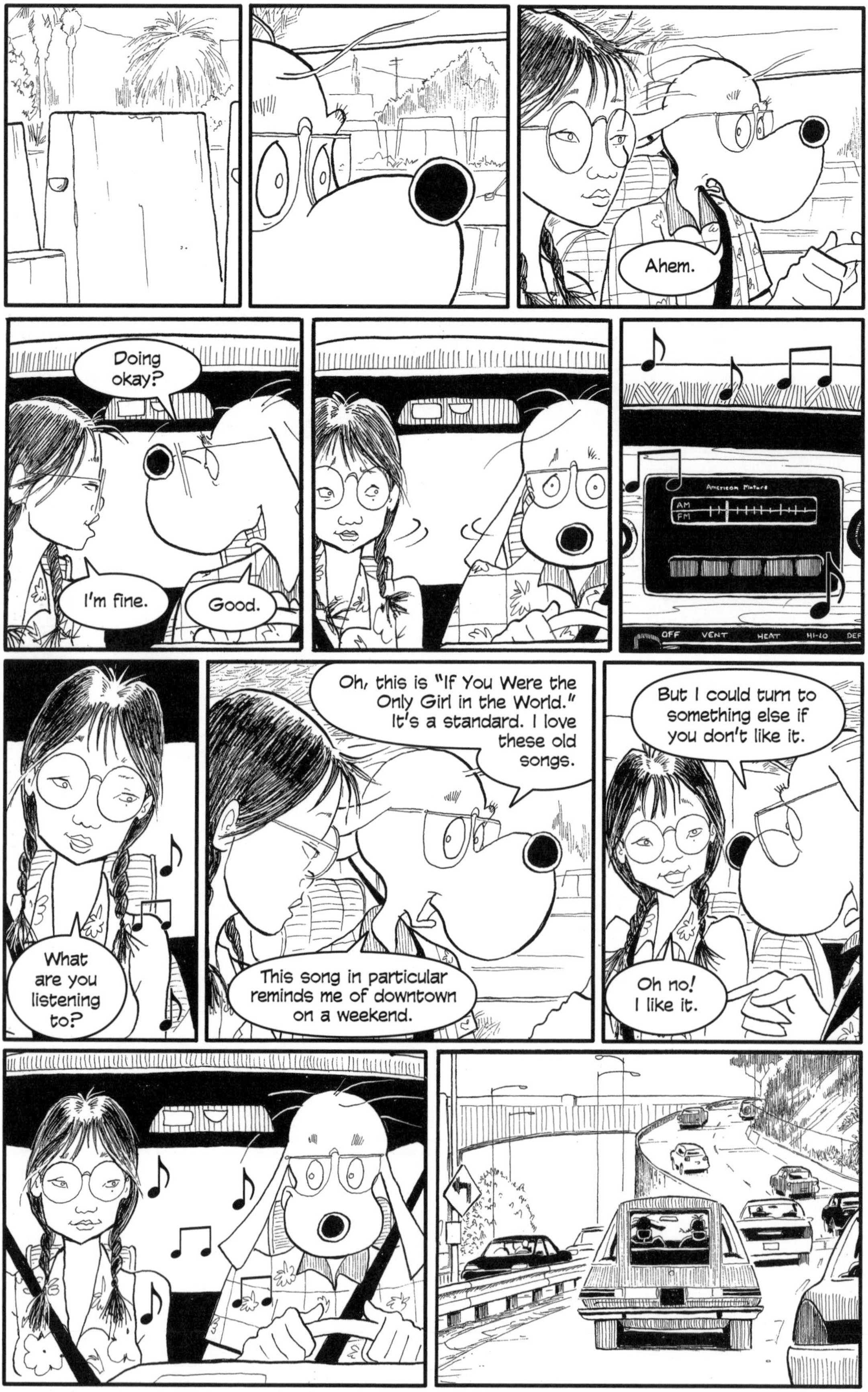

Ahem.
Doing okay?
I'm fine.
Good.
American Motors
AM
FM
OFF VENT HEAT HI-LO DEF
What are you listening to?
Oh, this is "If You Were the Only Girl in the World." It's a standard. I love these old songs.
This song in particular reminds me of downtown on a weekend.
But I could turn to something else if you don't like it.
Oh no! I like it.

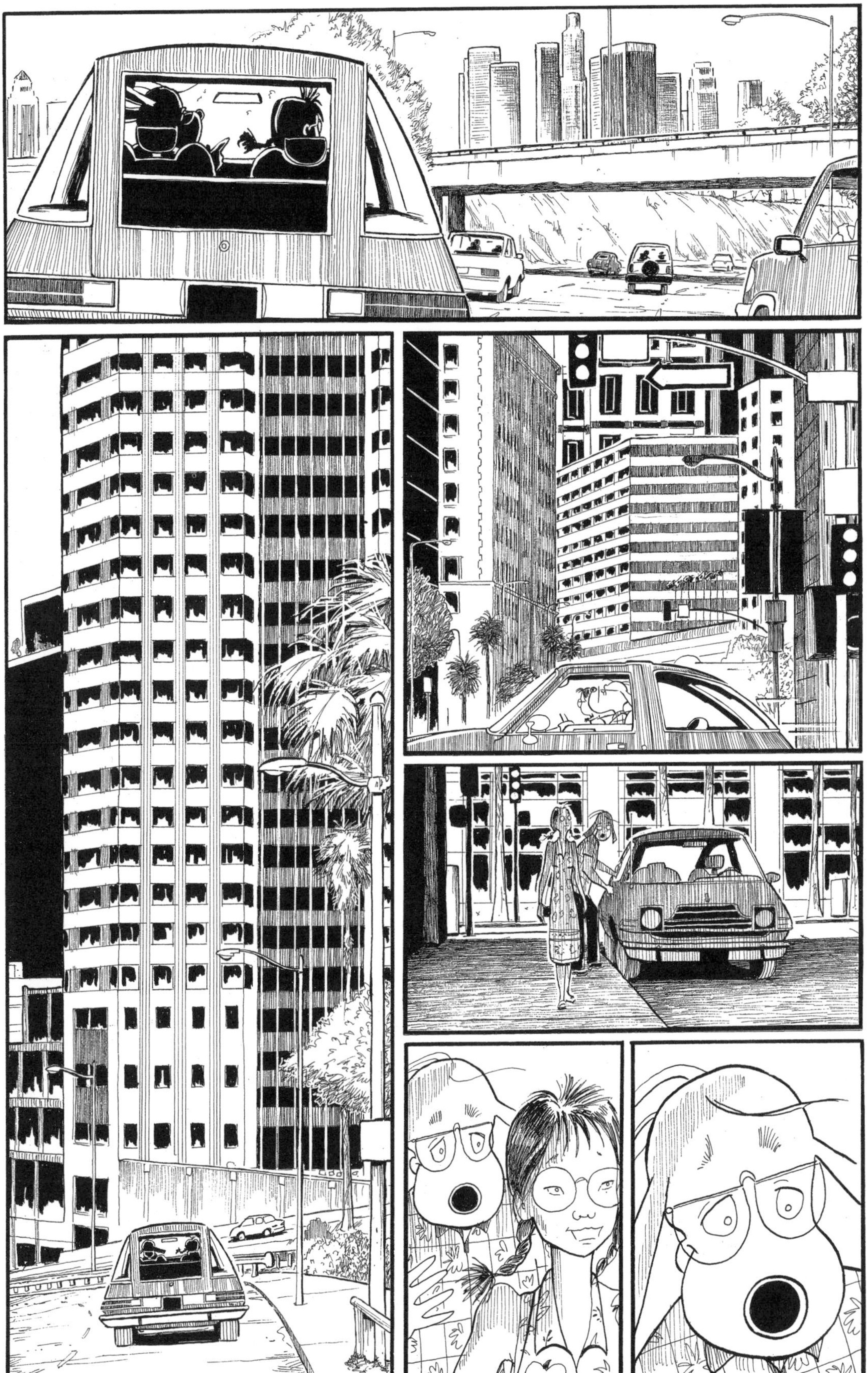

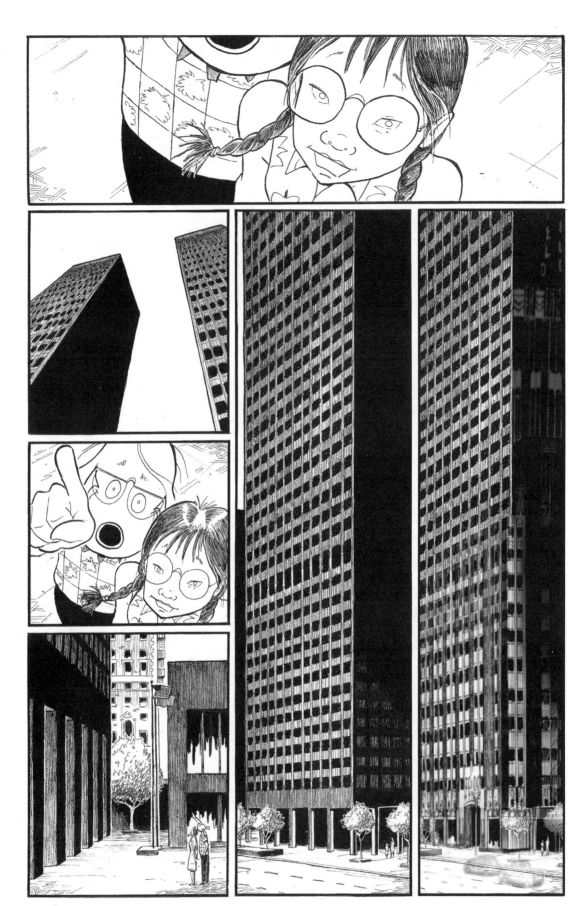

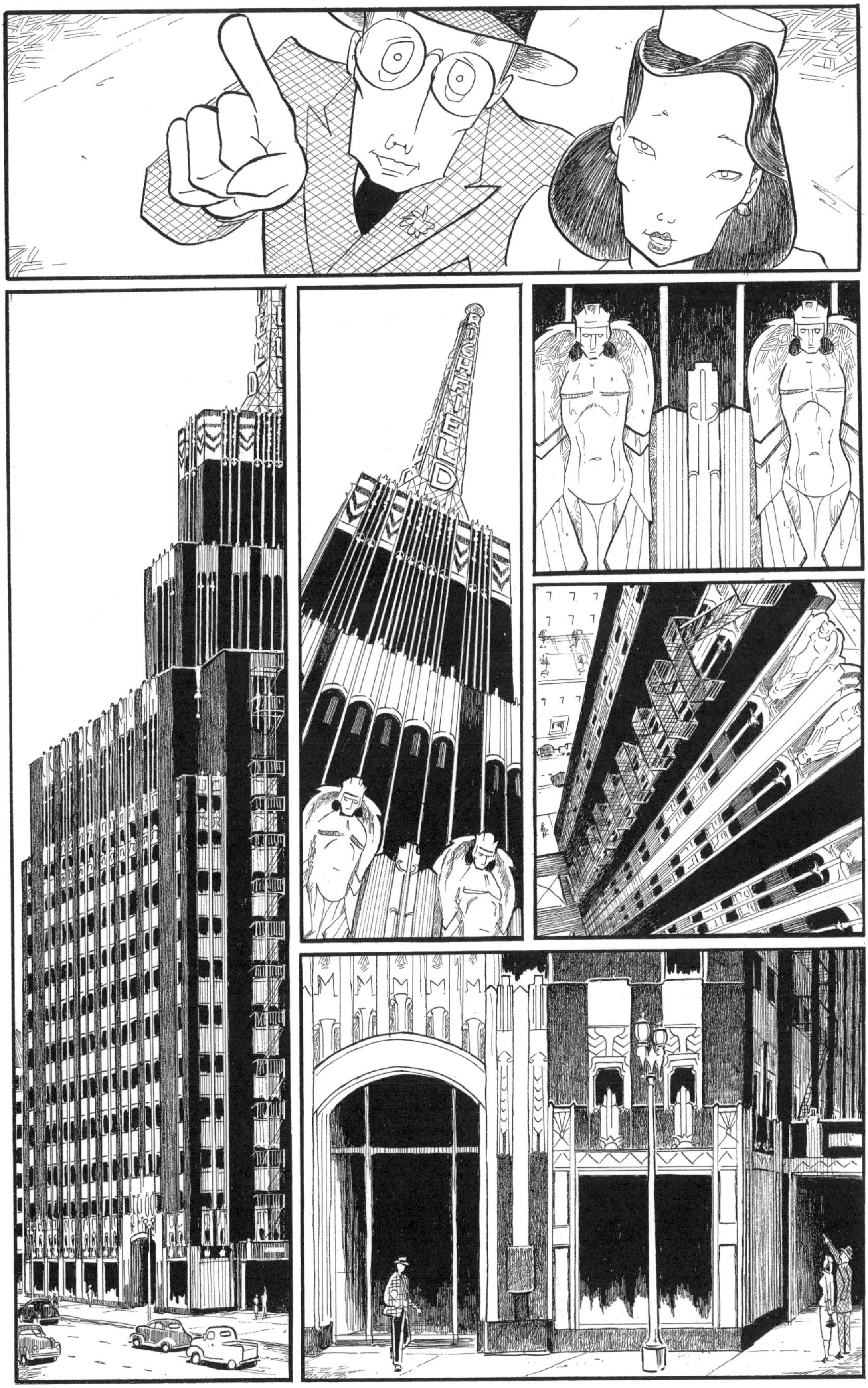
RICHFIELD

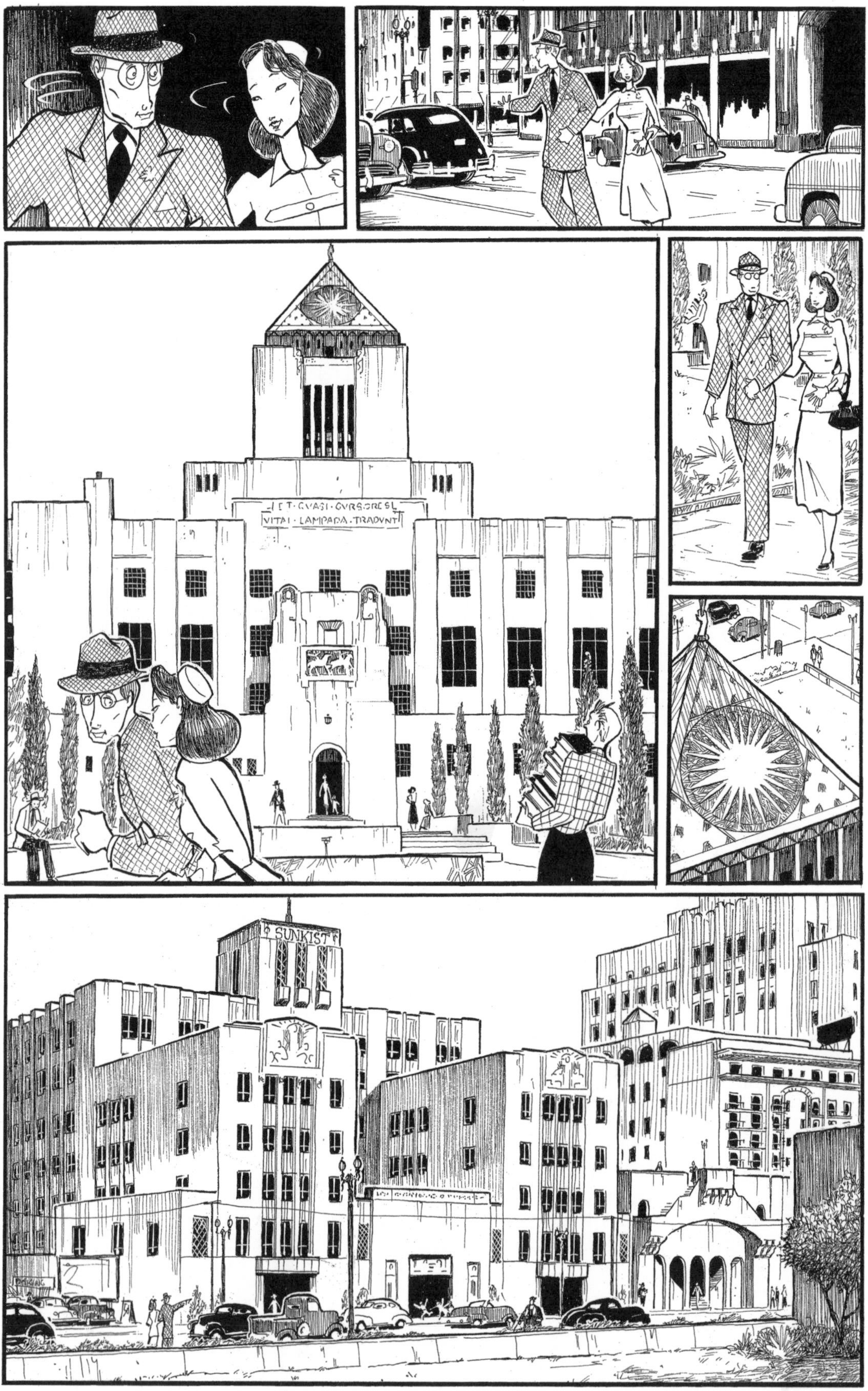
ET · QVASI · CVRSORES
VITAI · LAMPADA · TRADVNT
SUNKIST

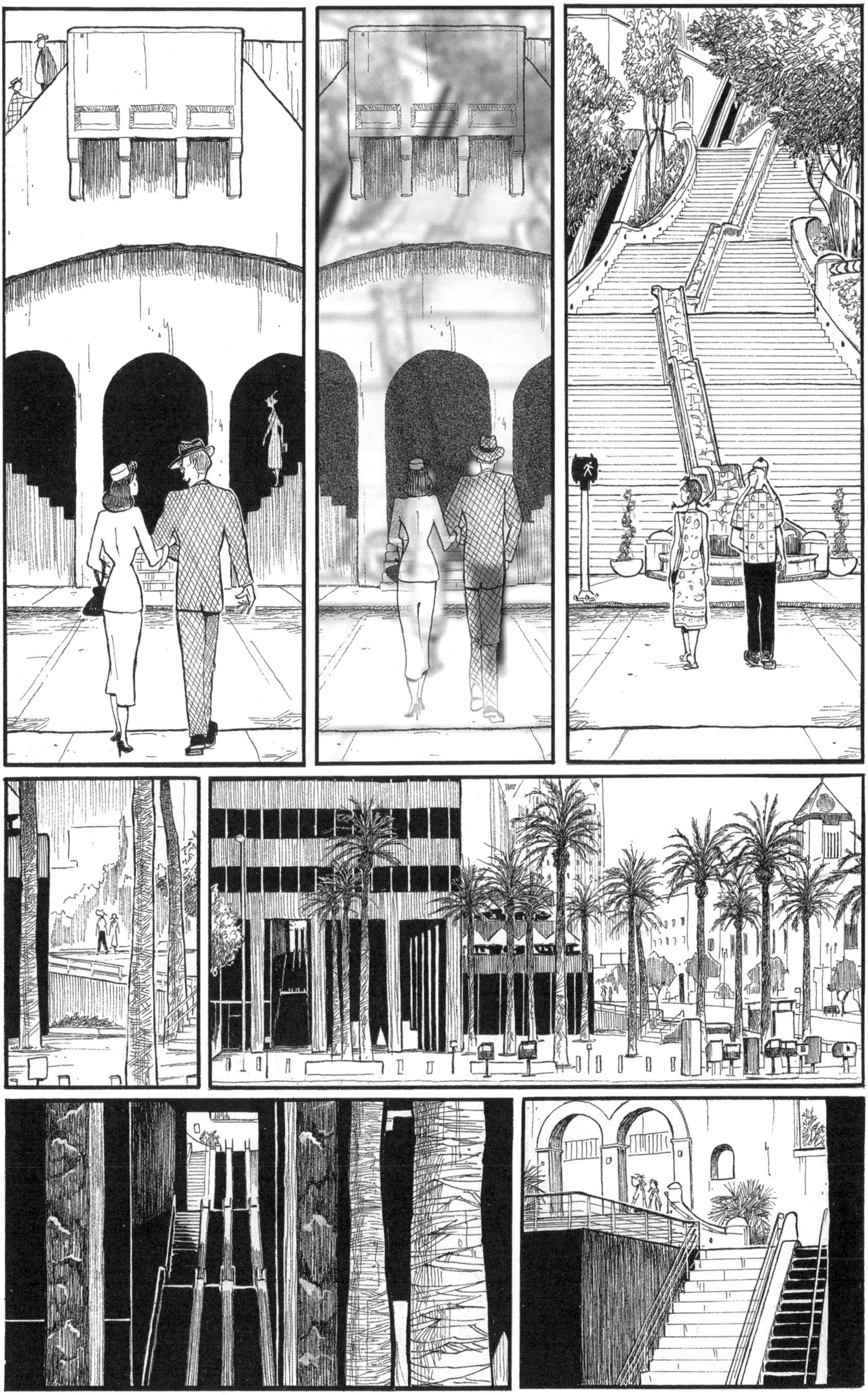

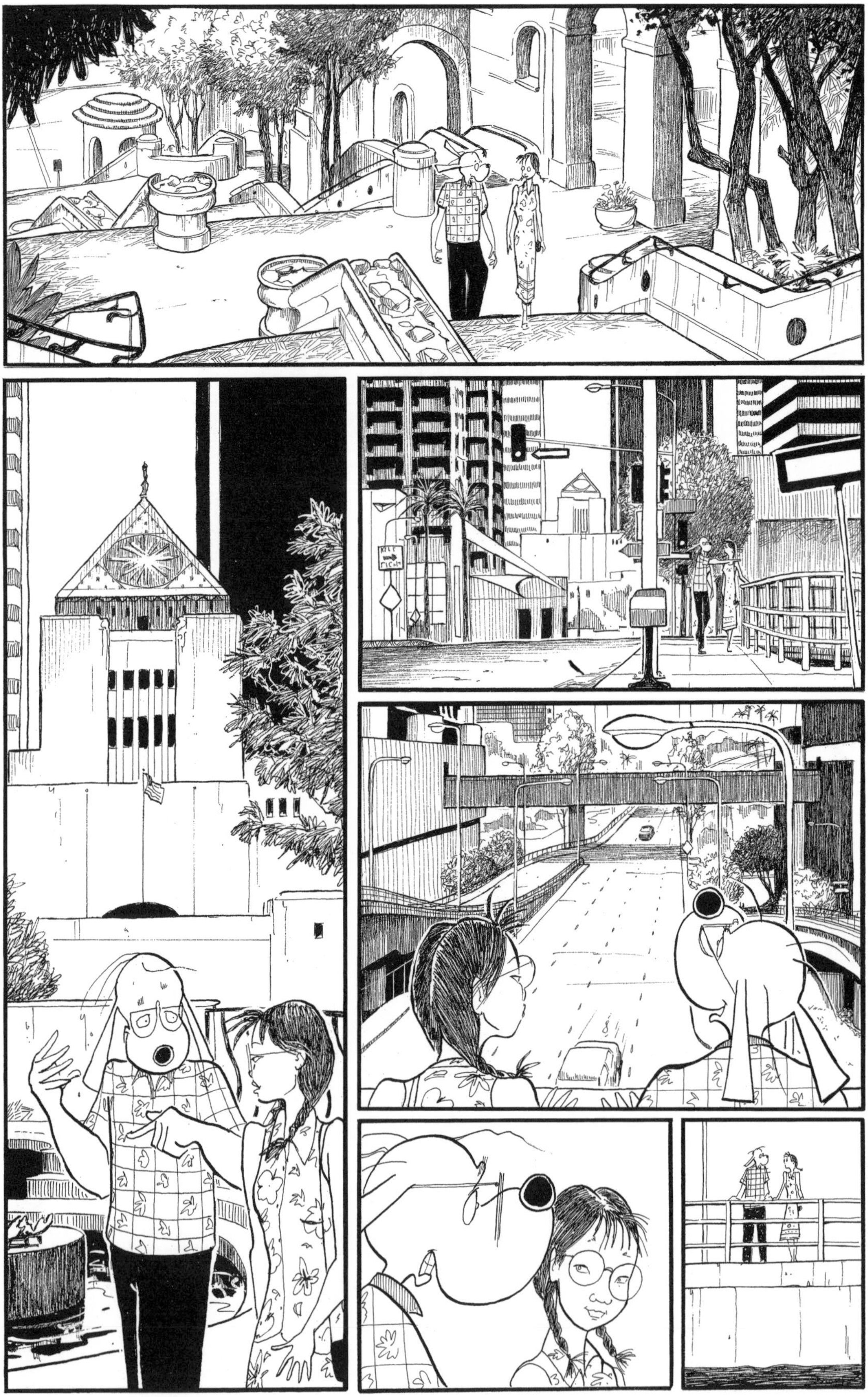

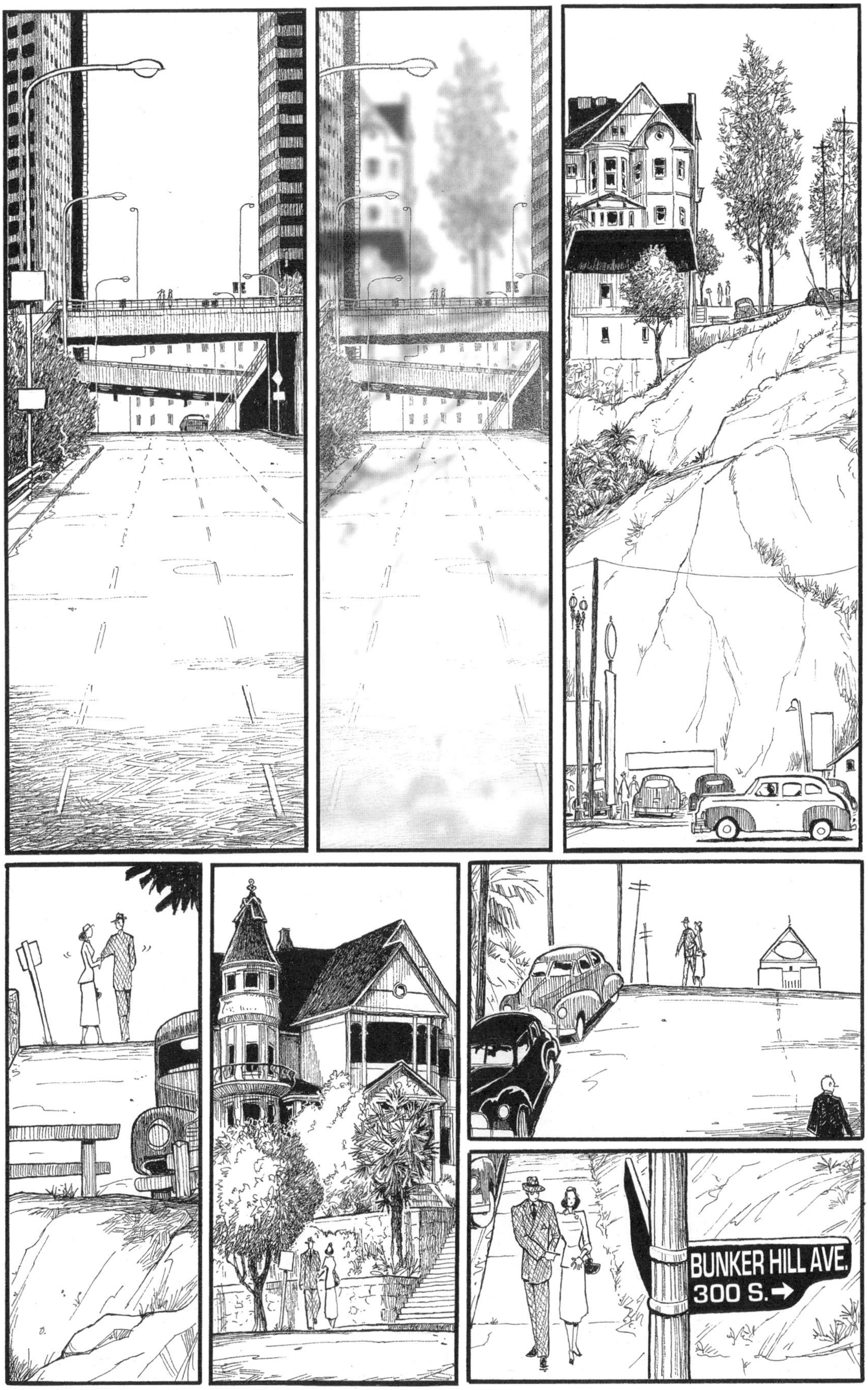
BUNKER HILL AVE.
300 S.

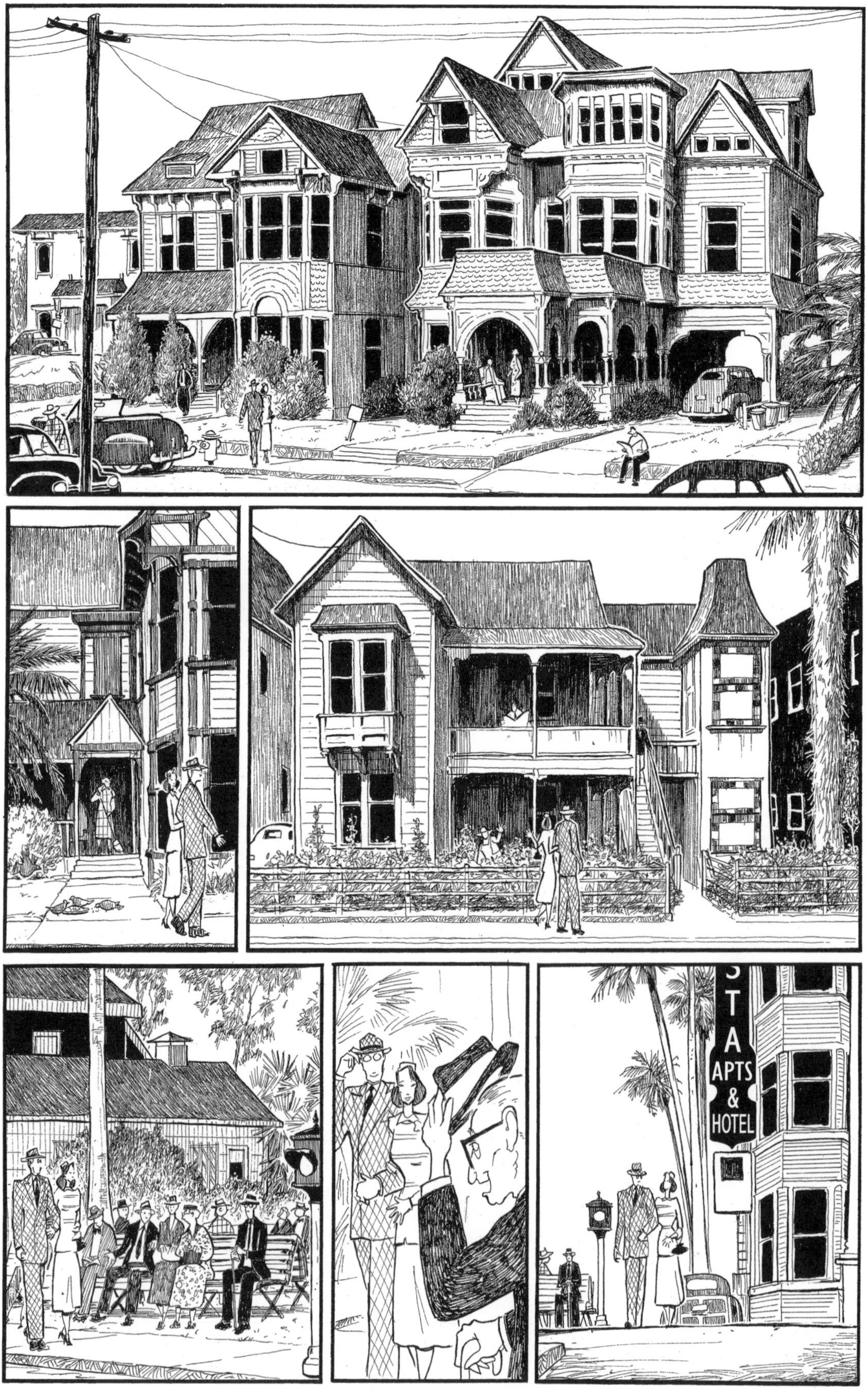
STA
APTS & HOTEL

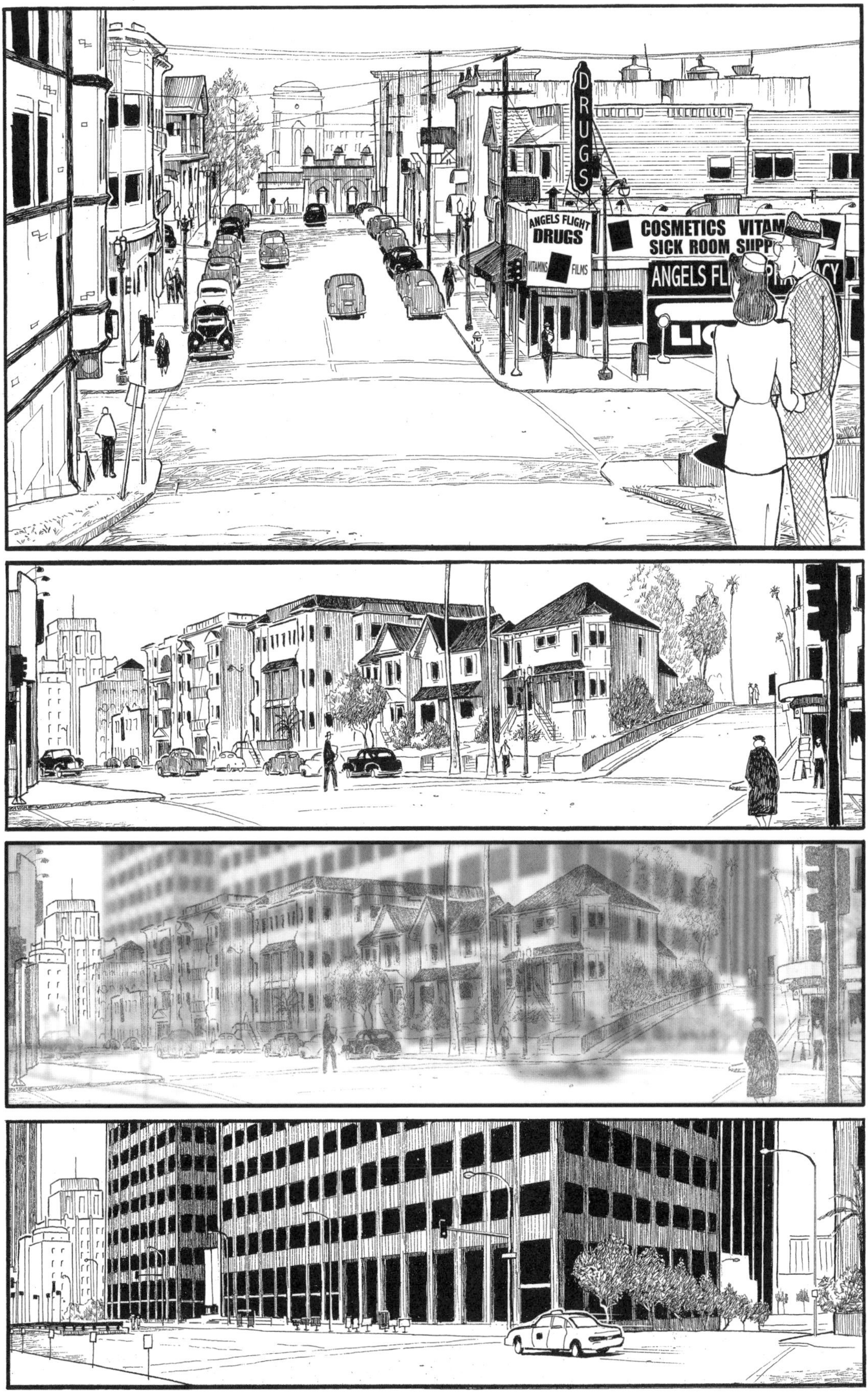
DRUGS
ANGELS FLIGHT DRUGS
VITAMINS
FILMS
COSMETICS VITAM
SICK ROOM SUPP

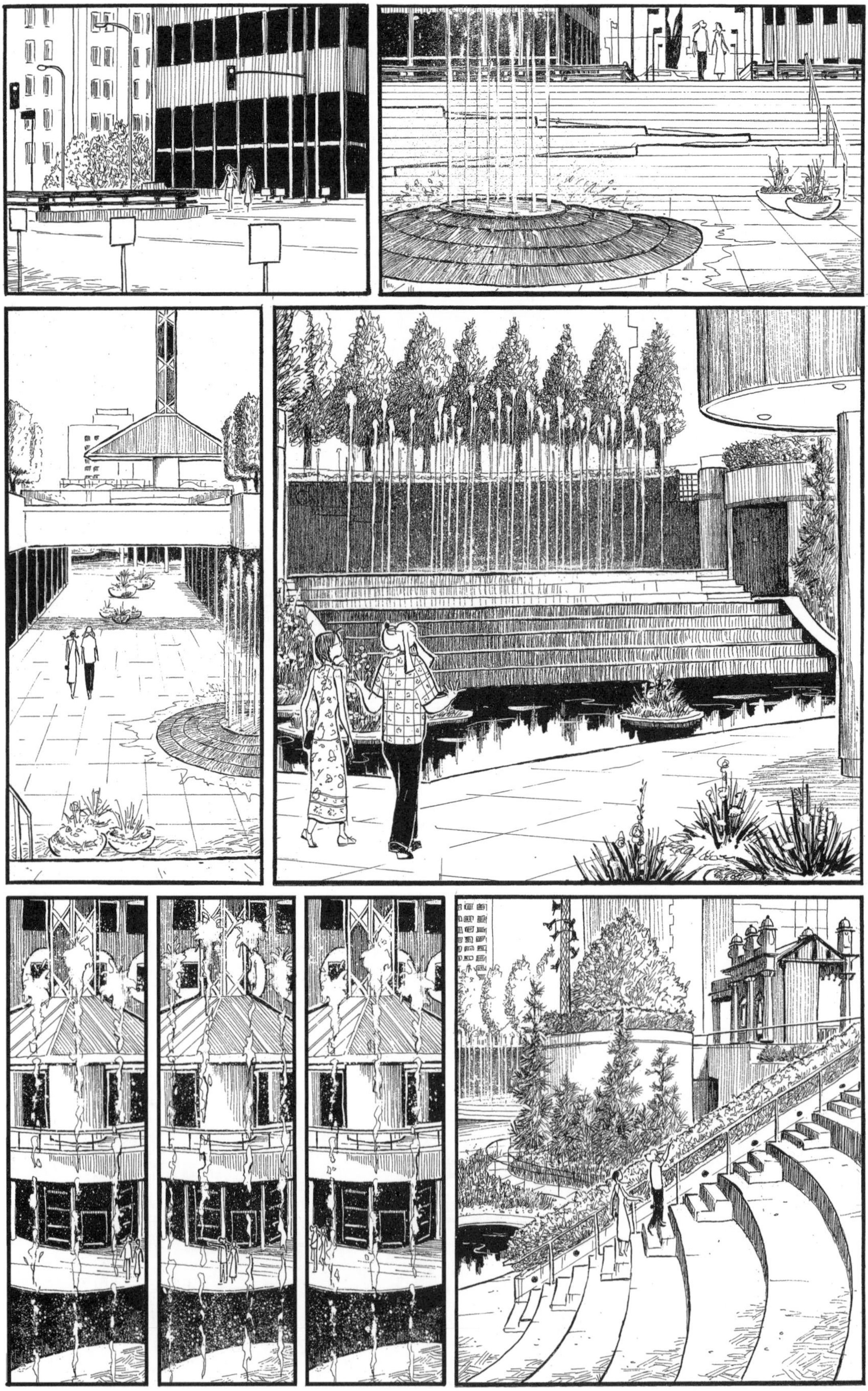

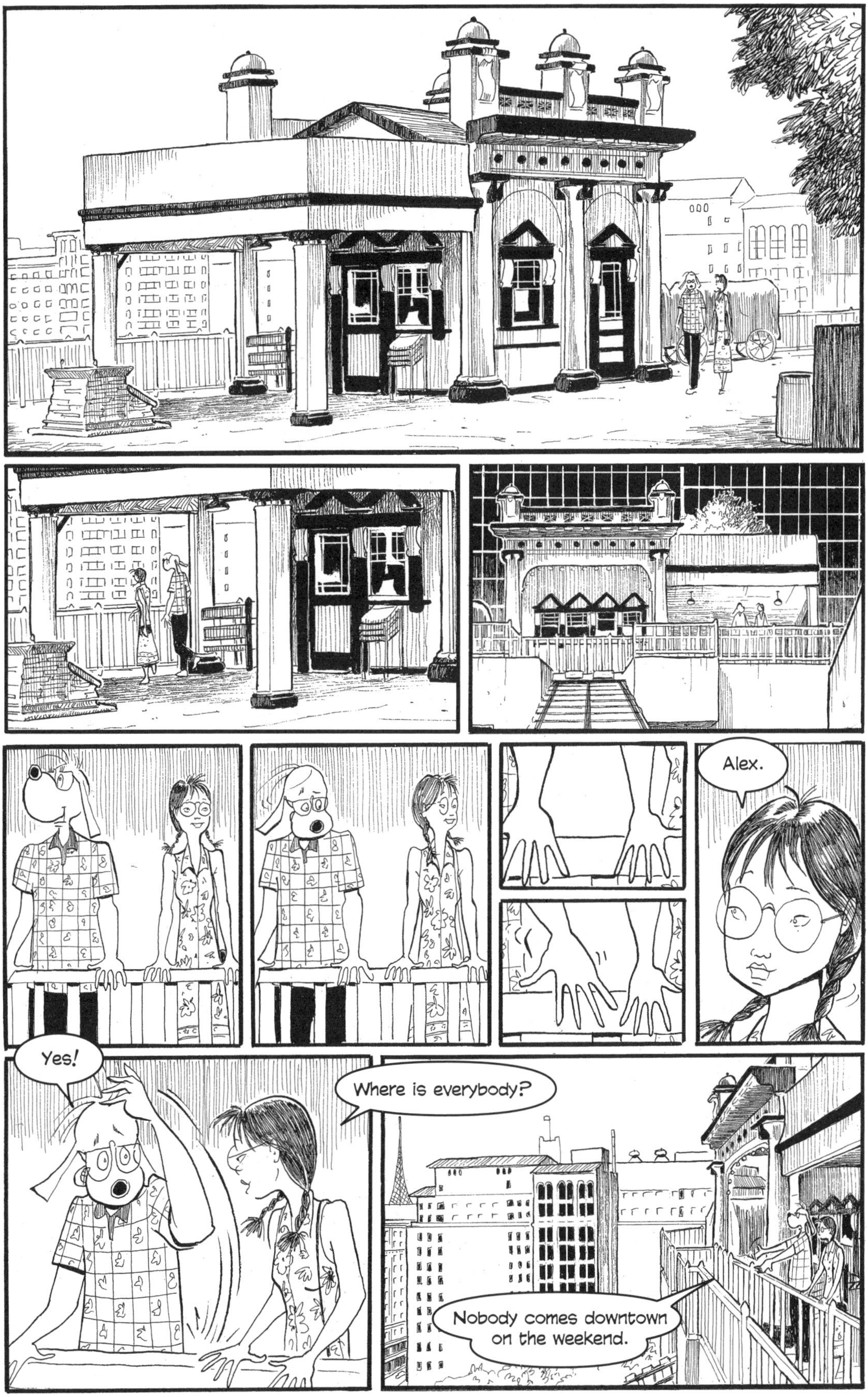
Alex.
Yes!
Where is everybody?
Nobody comes downtown on the weekend.

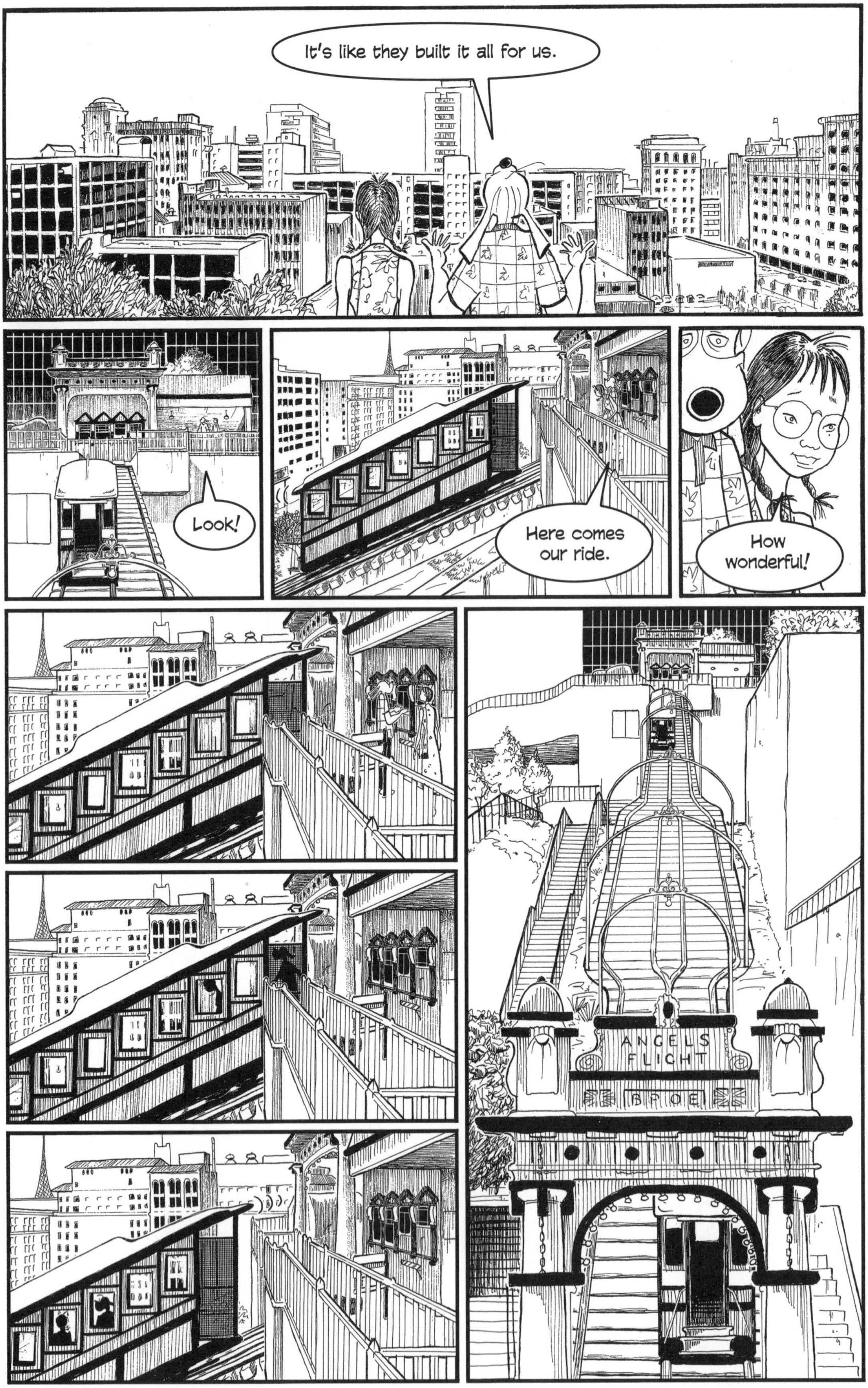
It's like they built it all for us.
Look!
Here comes our ride.
How wonderful!
ANGELS FLIGHT
B P O E

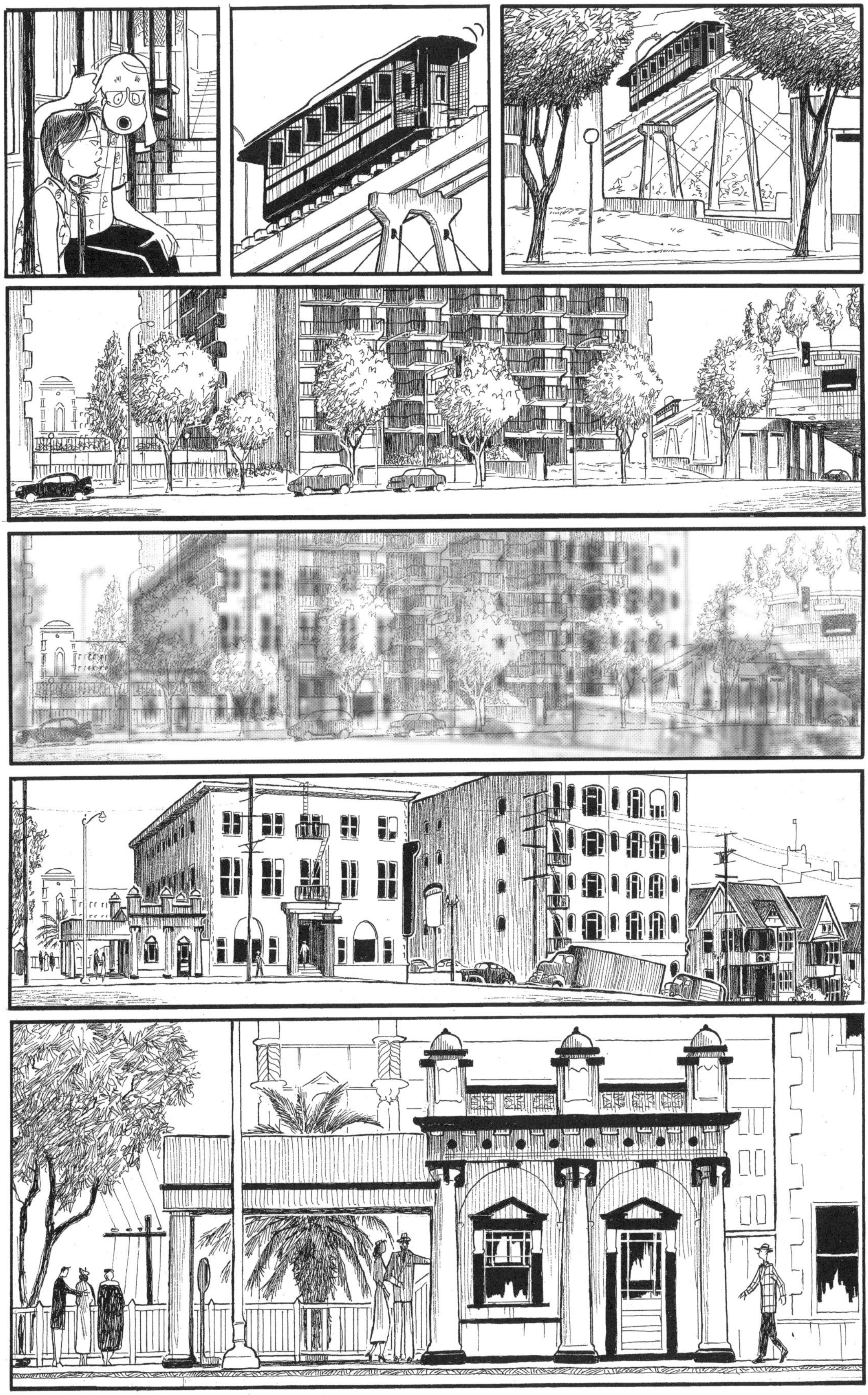

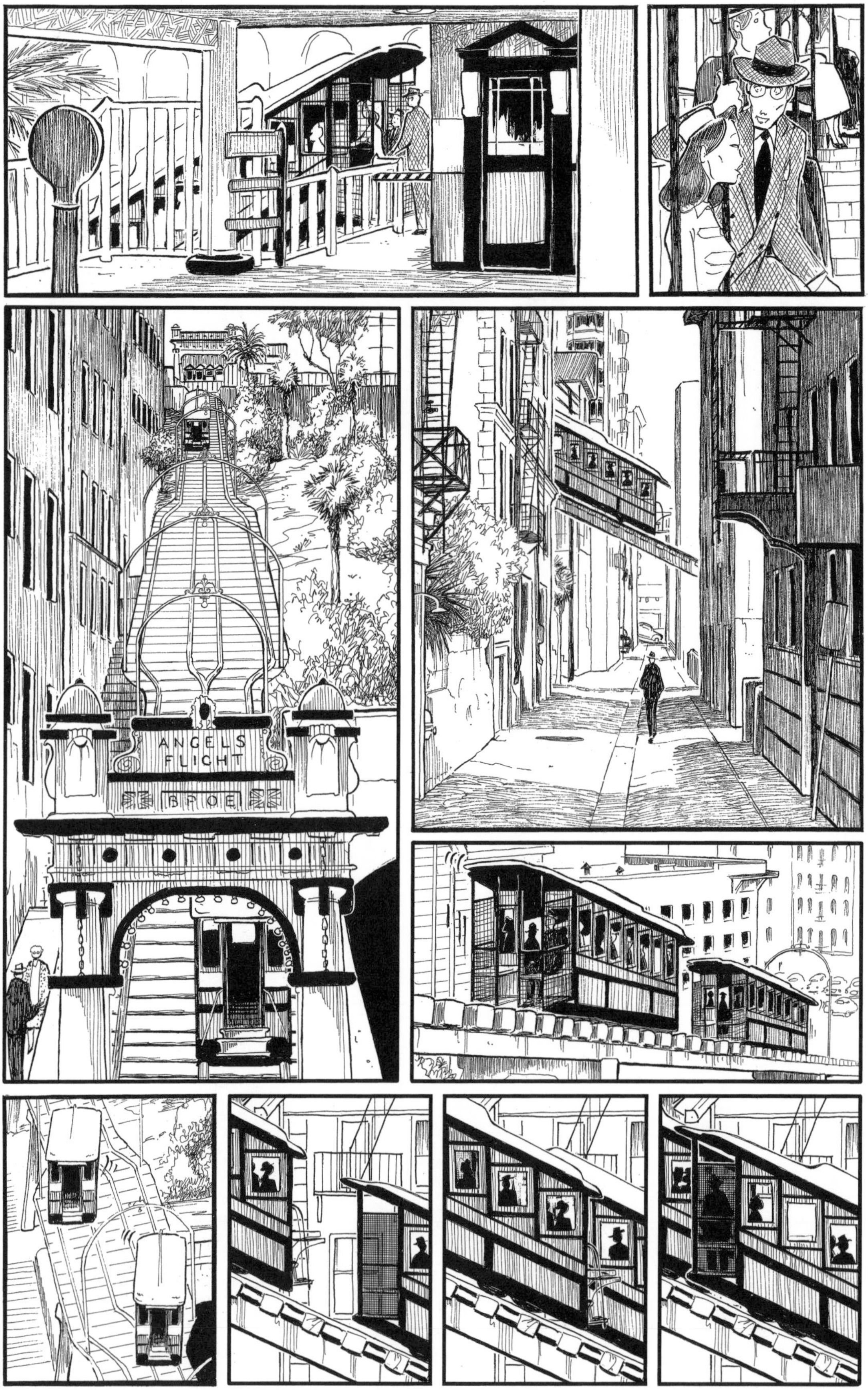
ANGELS FLIGHT
BPOE

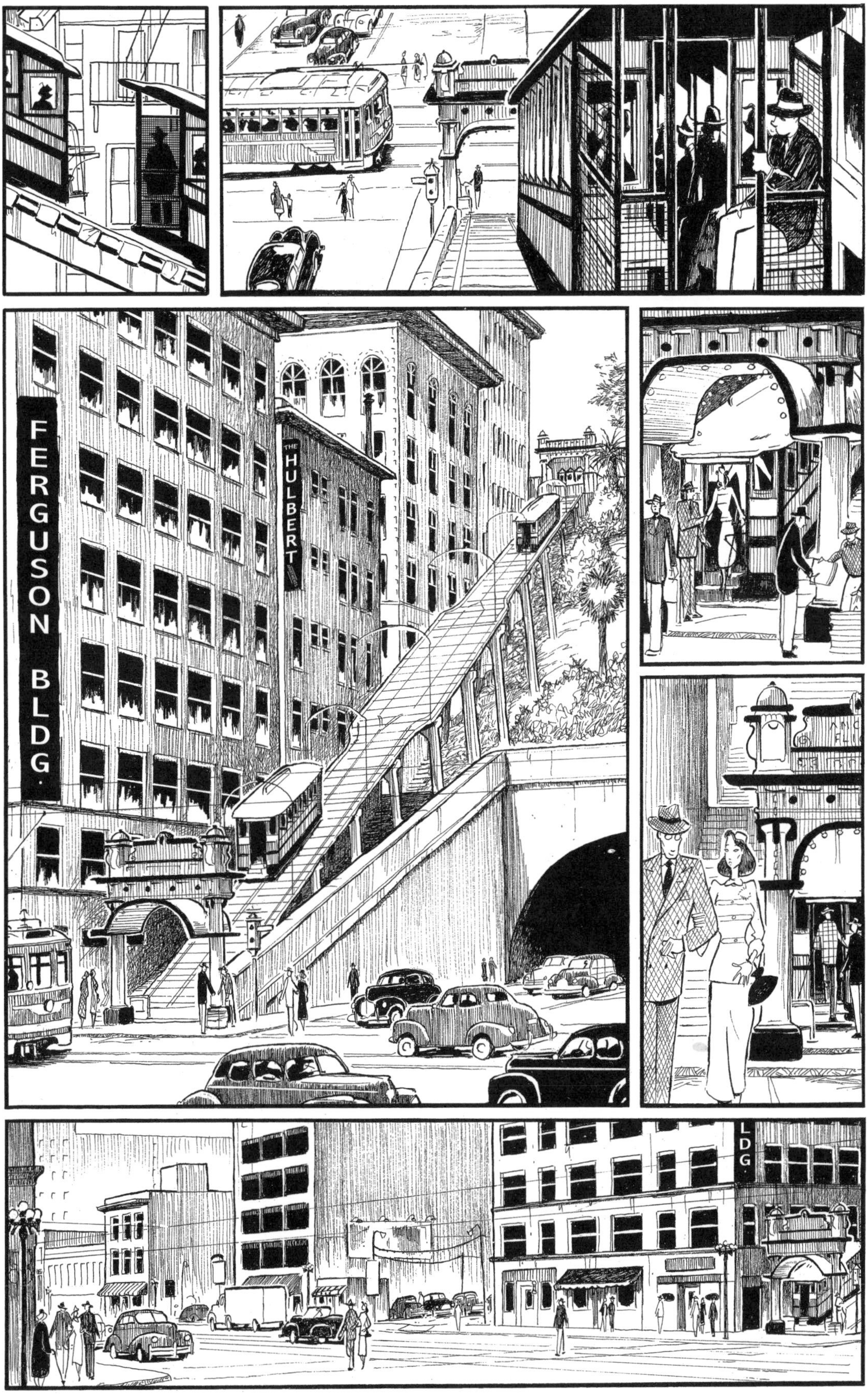
FERGUSON BLDG.
THE HULBERT
LDG.

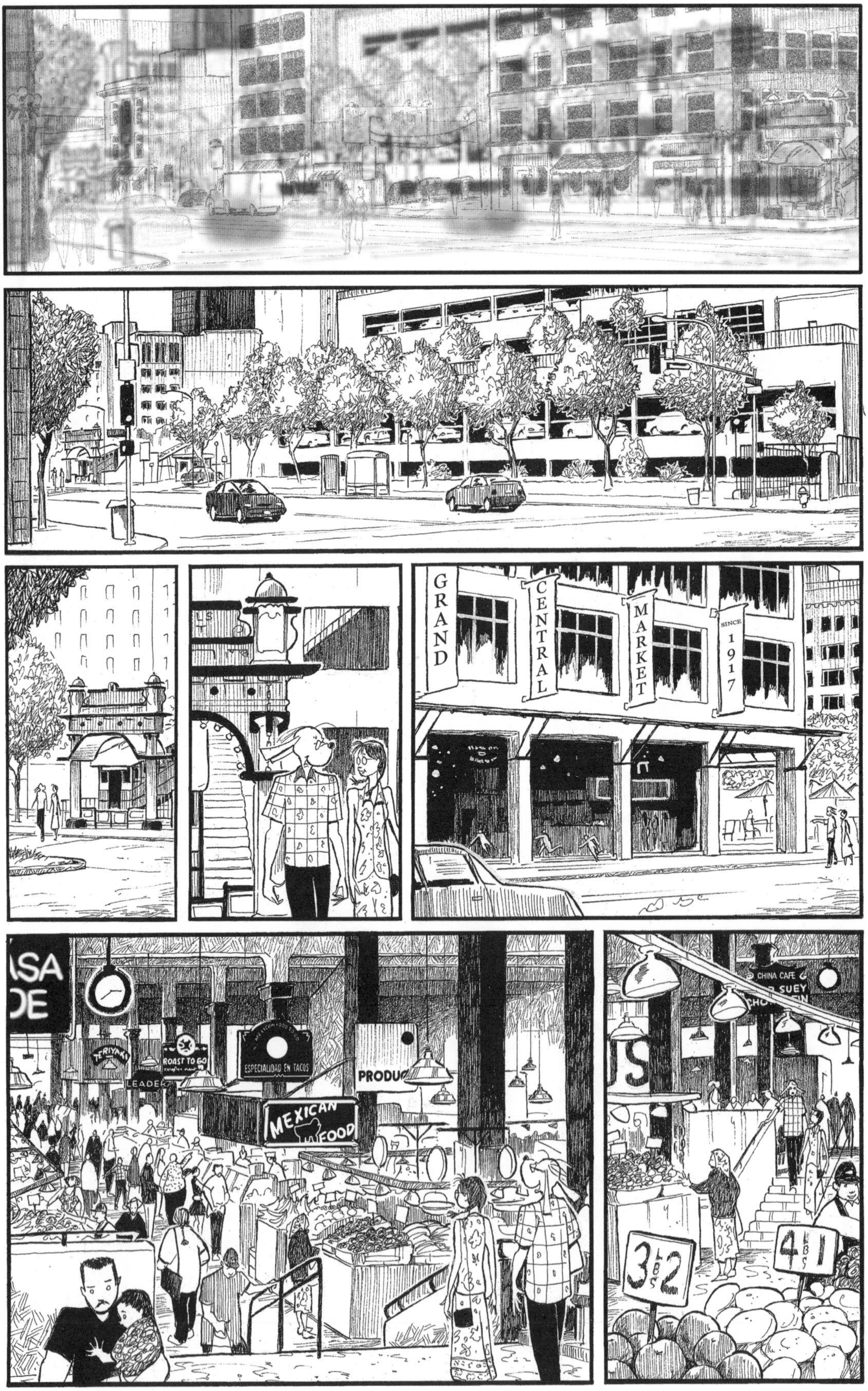
GRAND
CENTRAL
MARKET
SINCE 1917
ASA
DE
TERIYAKI
ROAST TO GO
LEADER
ESPECIALIDAD EN TACOS
PRODUC
MEXICAN FOOD
CHINA CAFE
3 lbs 2
4 lbs 1

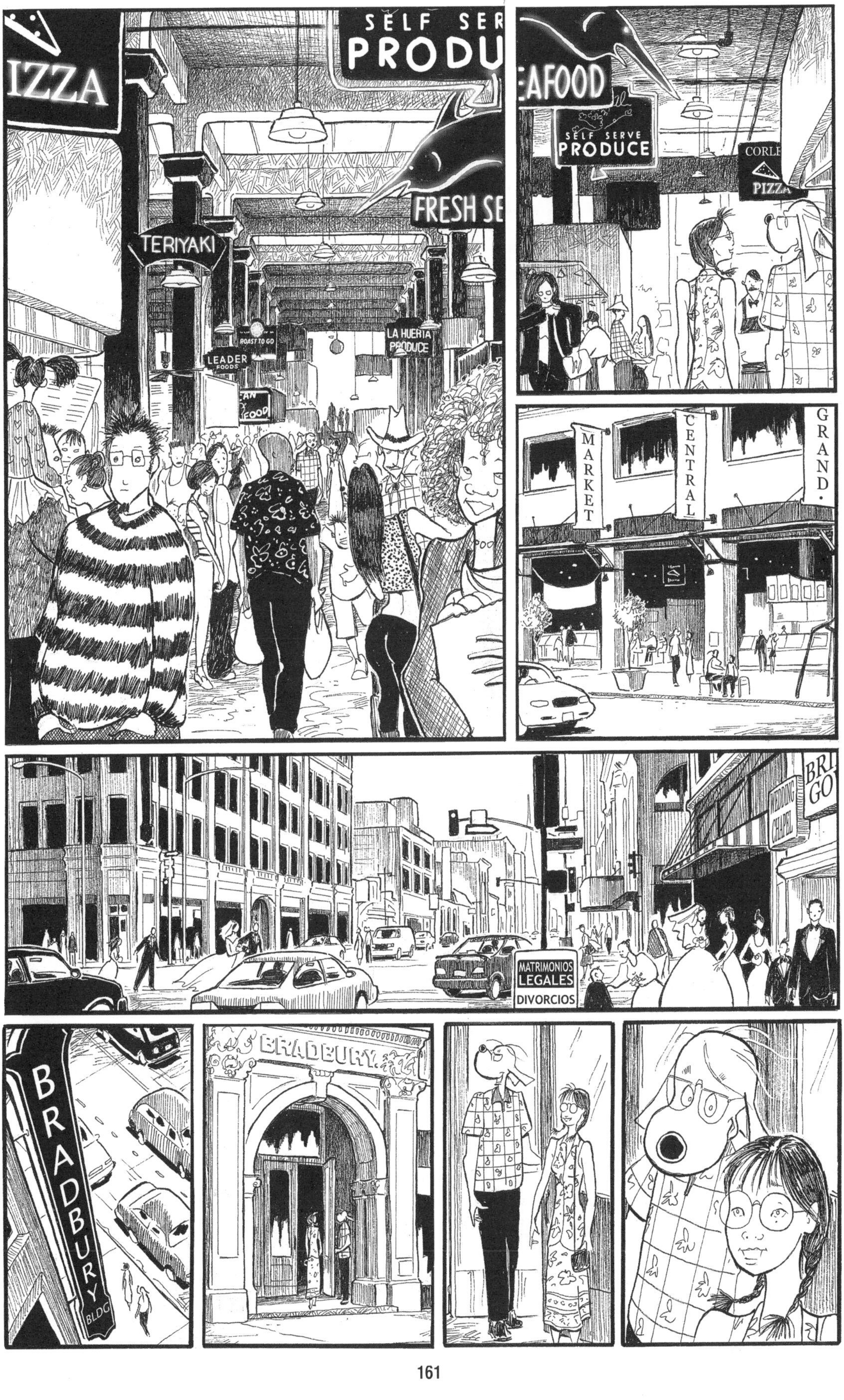
IZZA
SELF SER
PRODU
FRESH SE
TERIYAKI
ROAST TO GO
LA HUERTA PRODUCE
LEADER FOODS
EAFOOD
SELF SERVE PRODUCE
CORLE
PIZZA
MARKET
CENTRAL
GRAND
WEDDING CHAPEL
MATRIMONIOS LEGALES DIVORCIOS
BRADBURY BLDG
BRADBURY

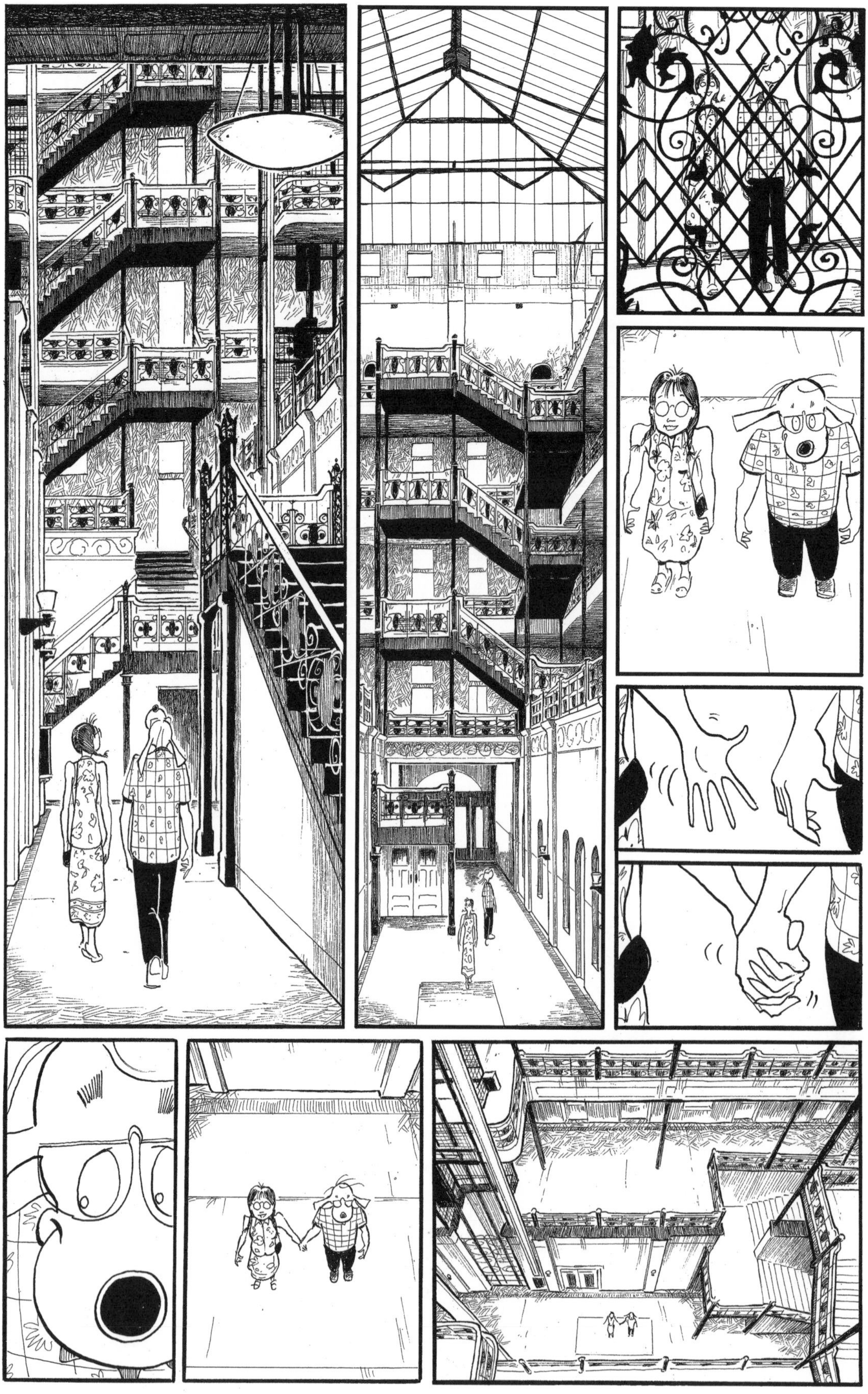

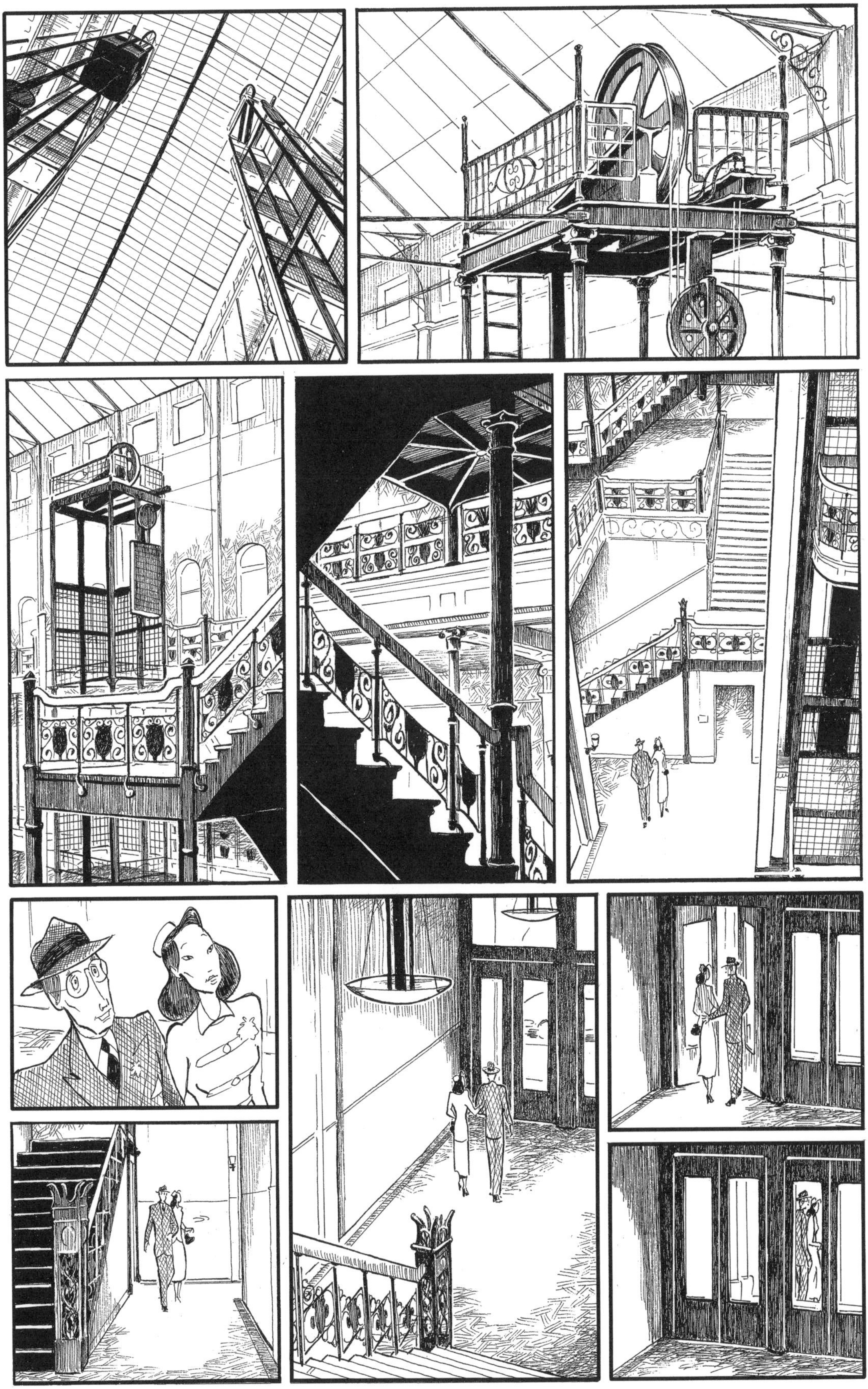

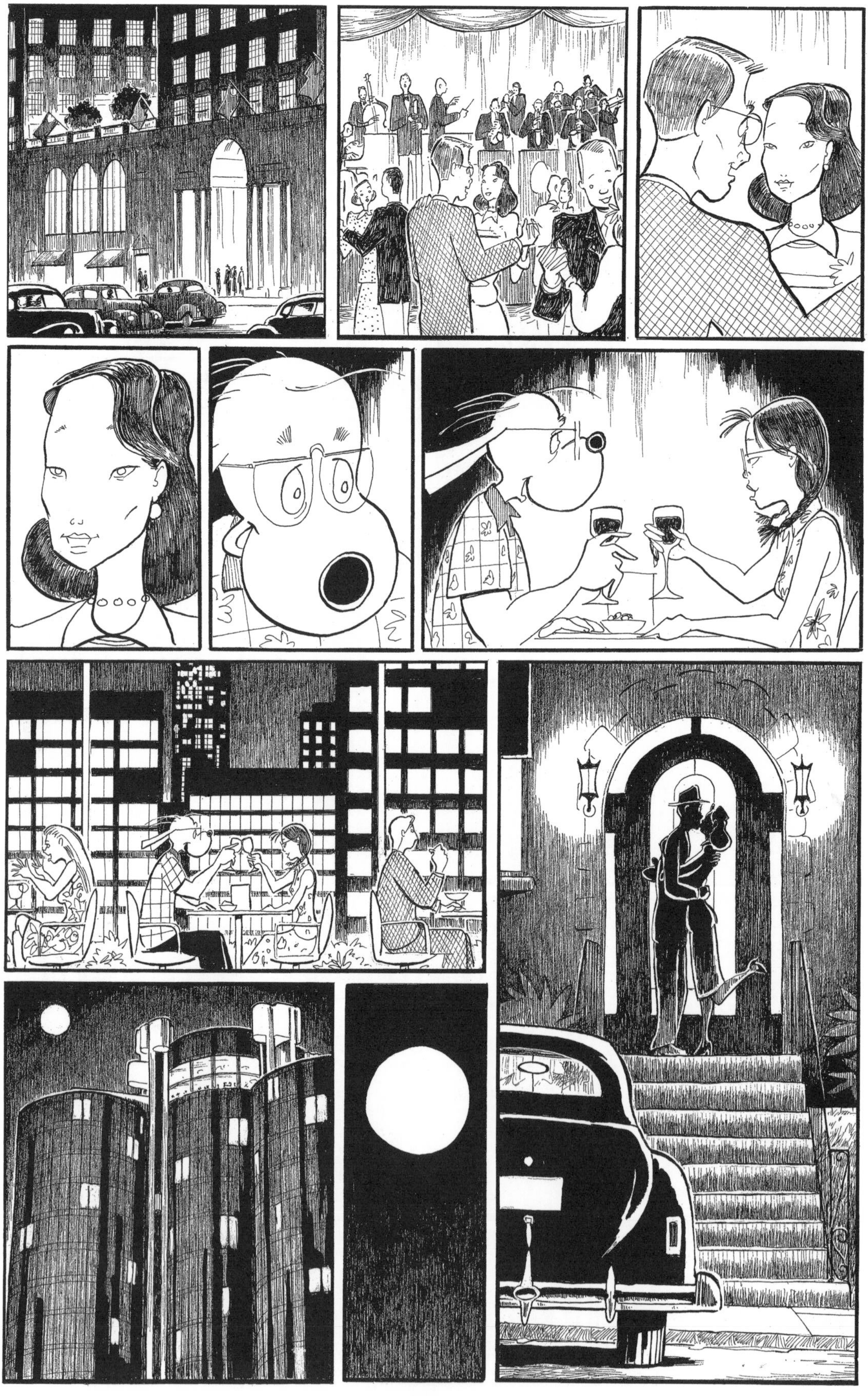

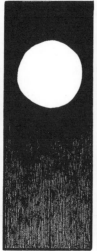

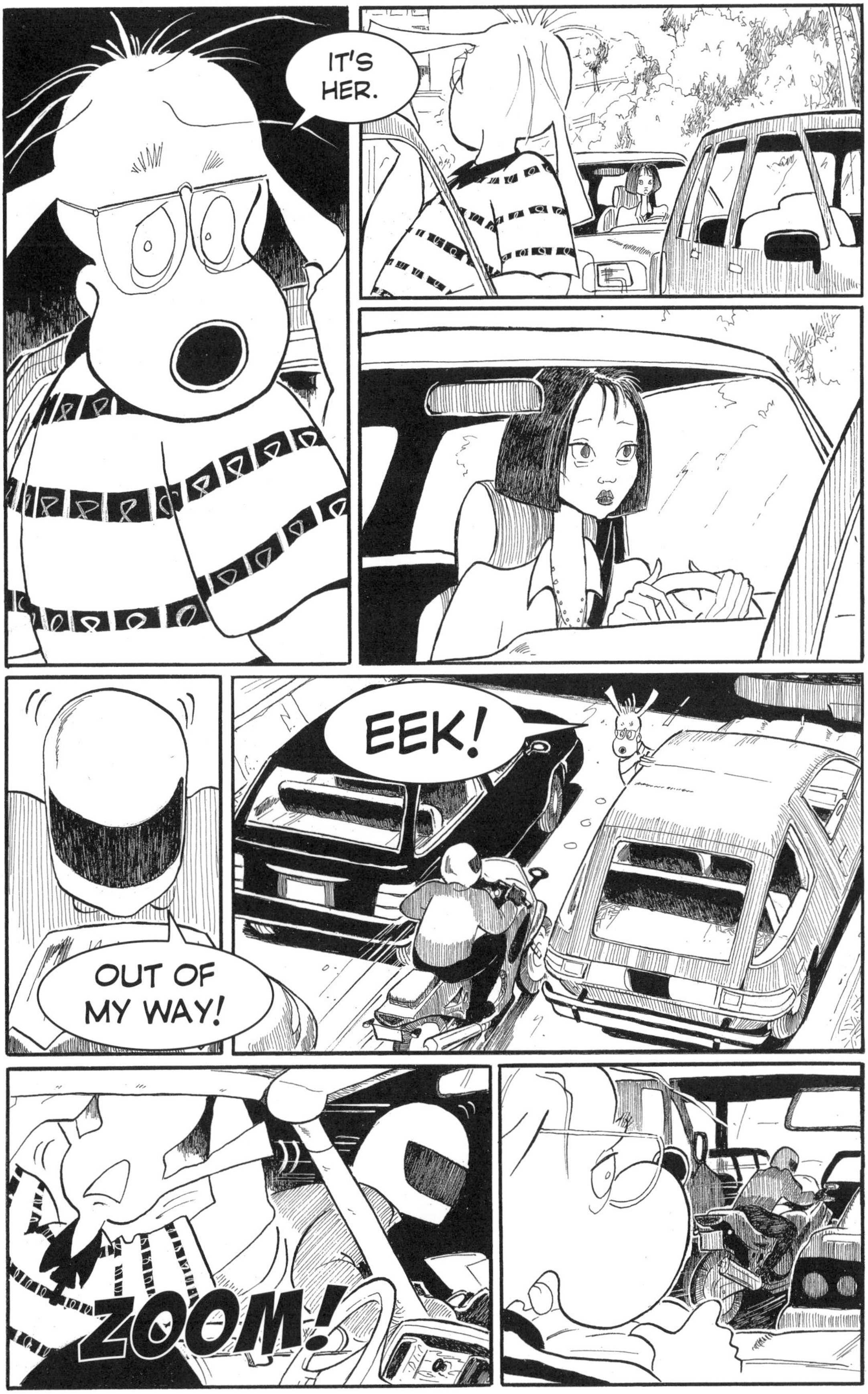
IT'S HER.
EEK!
OUT OF MY WAY!
ZOOM!

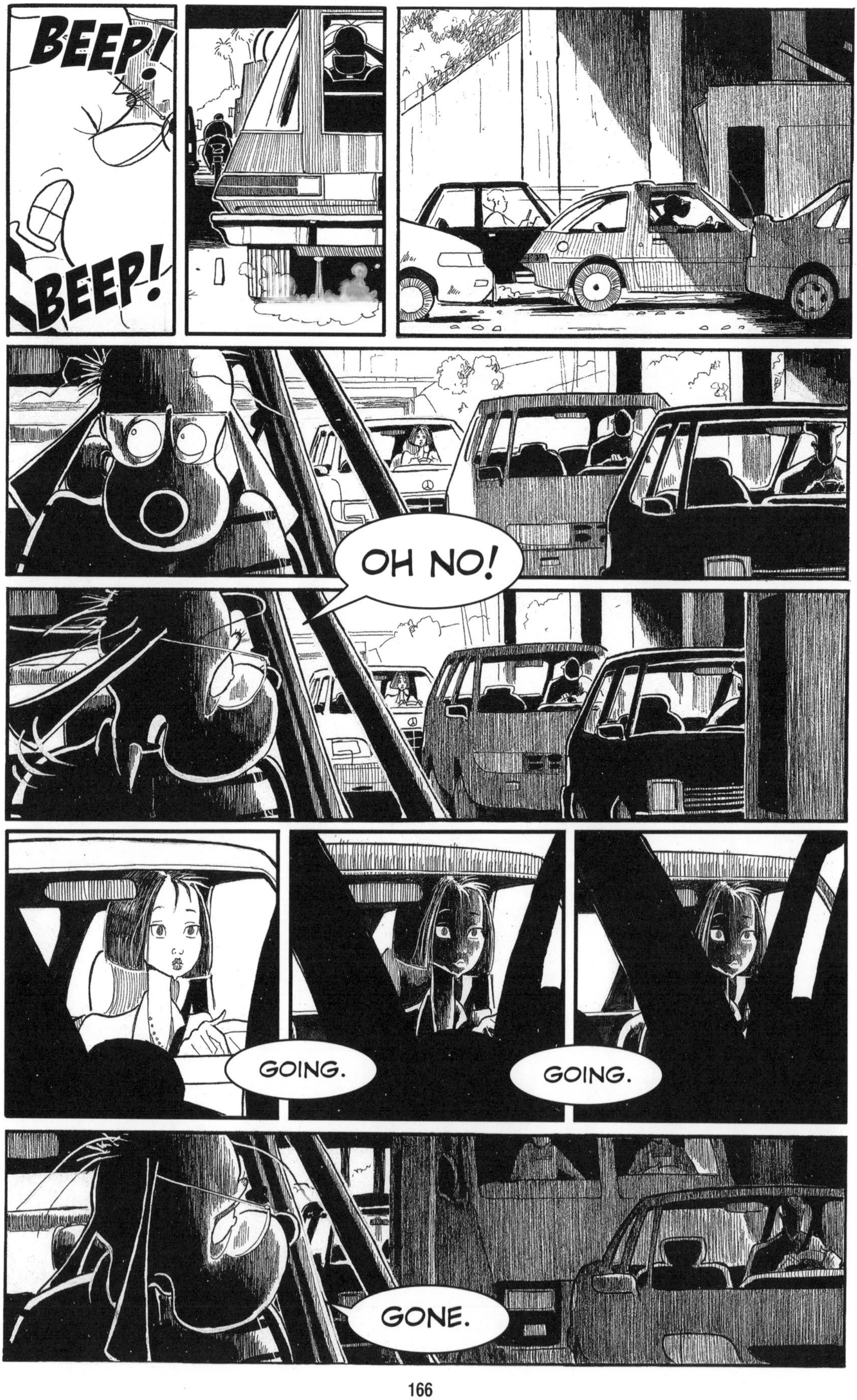
BEEP!
BEEP!
OH NO!
GOING.
GOING.
GONE.

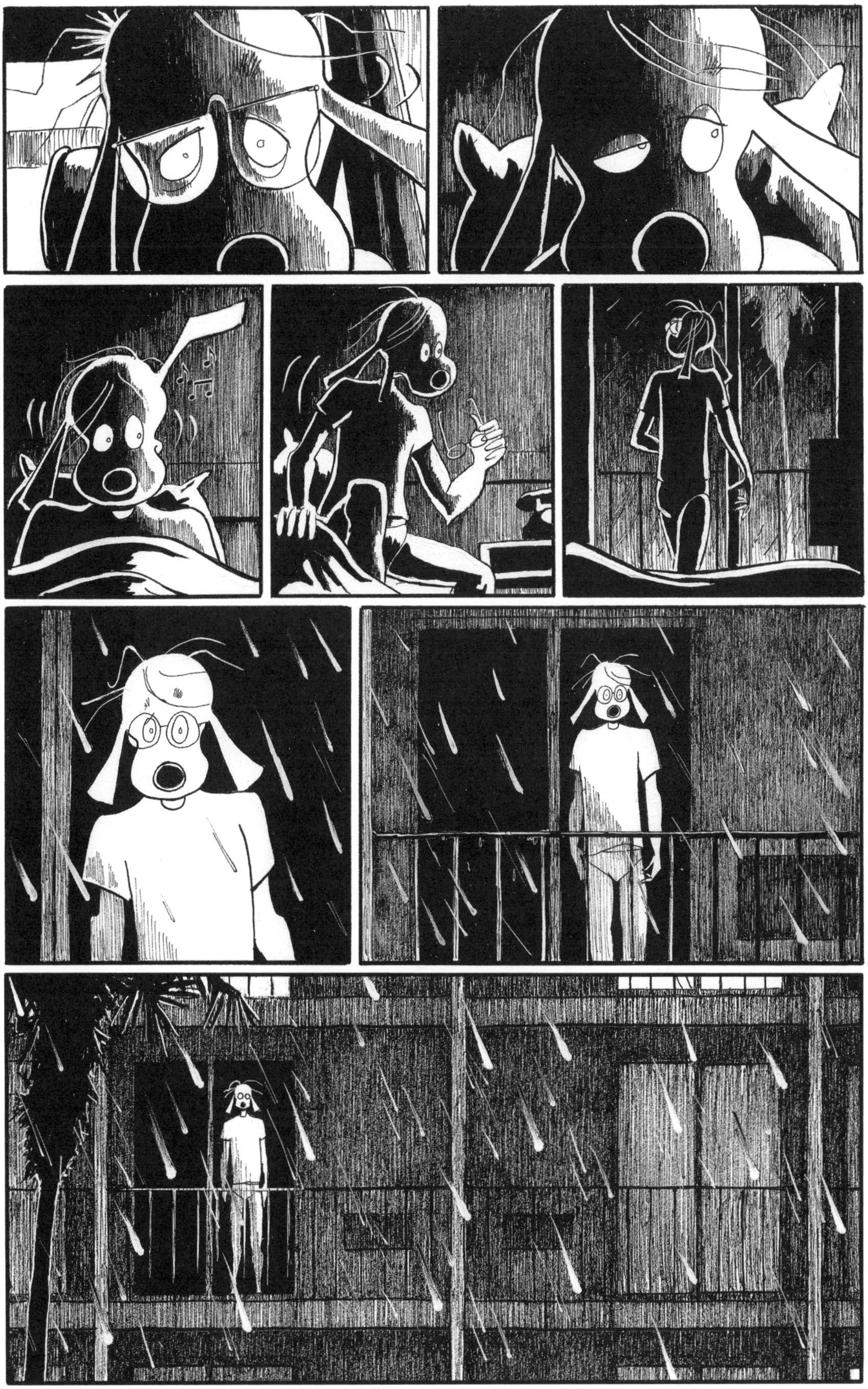

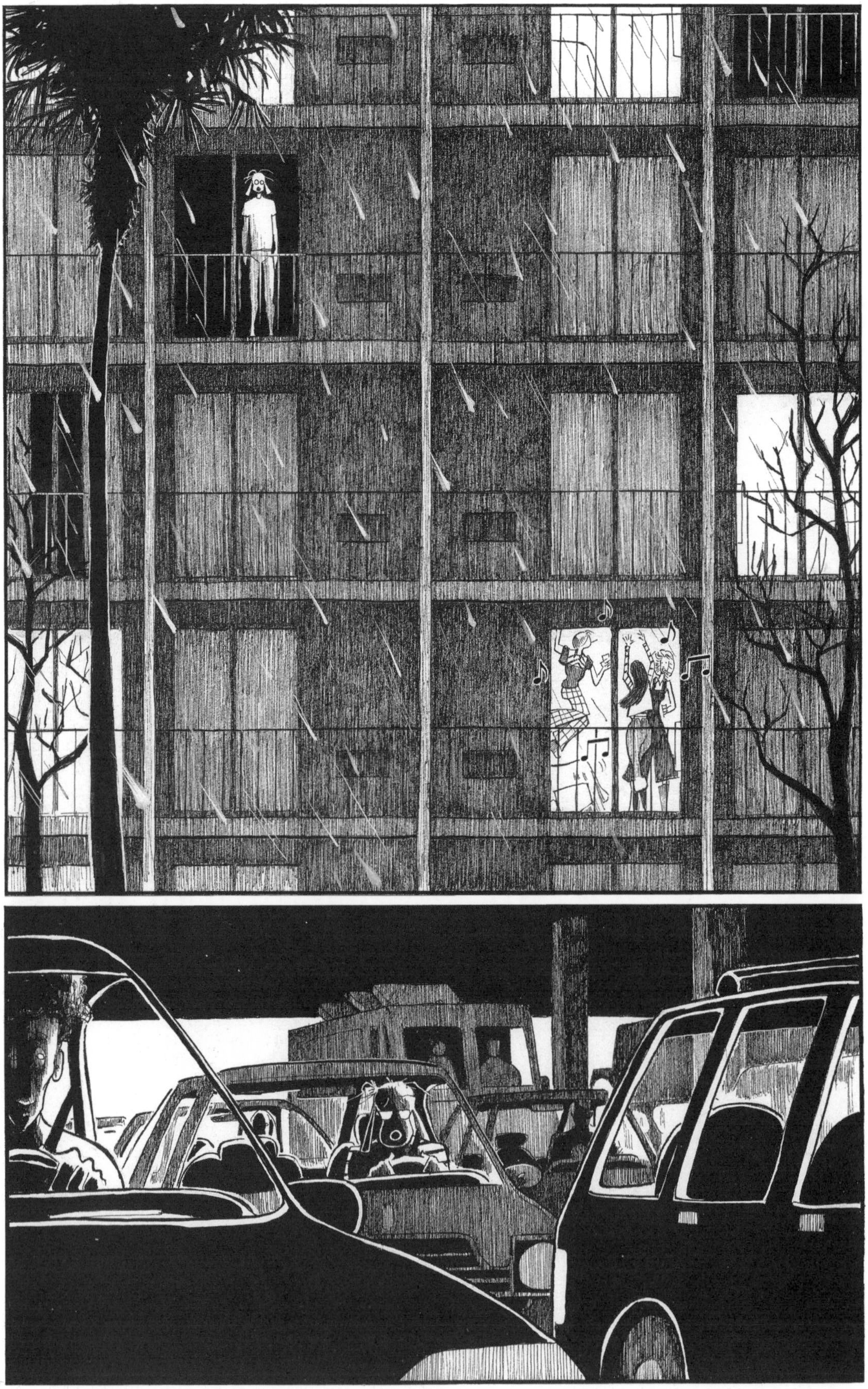

CHAPTER 4

AT LAST

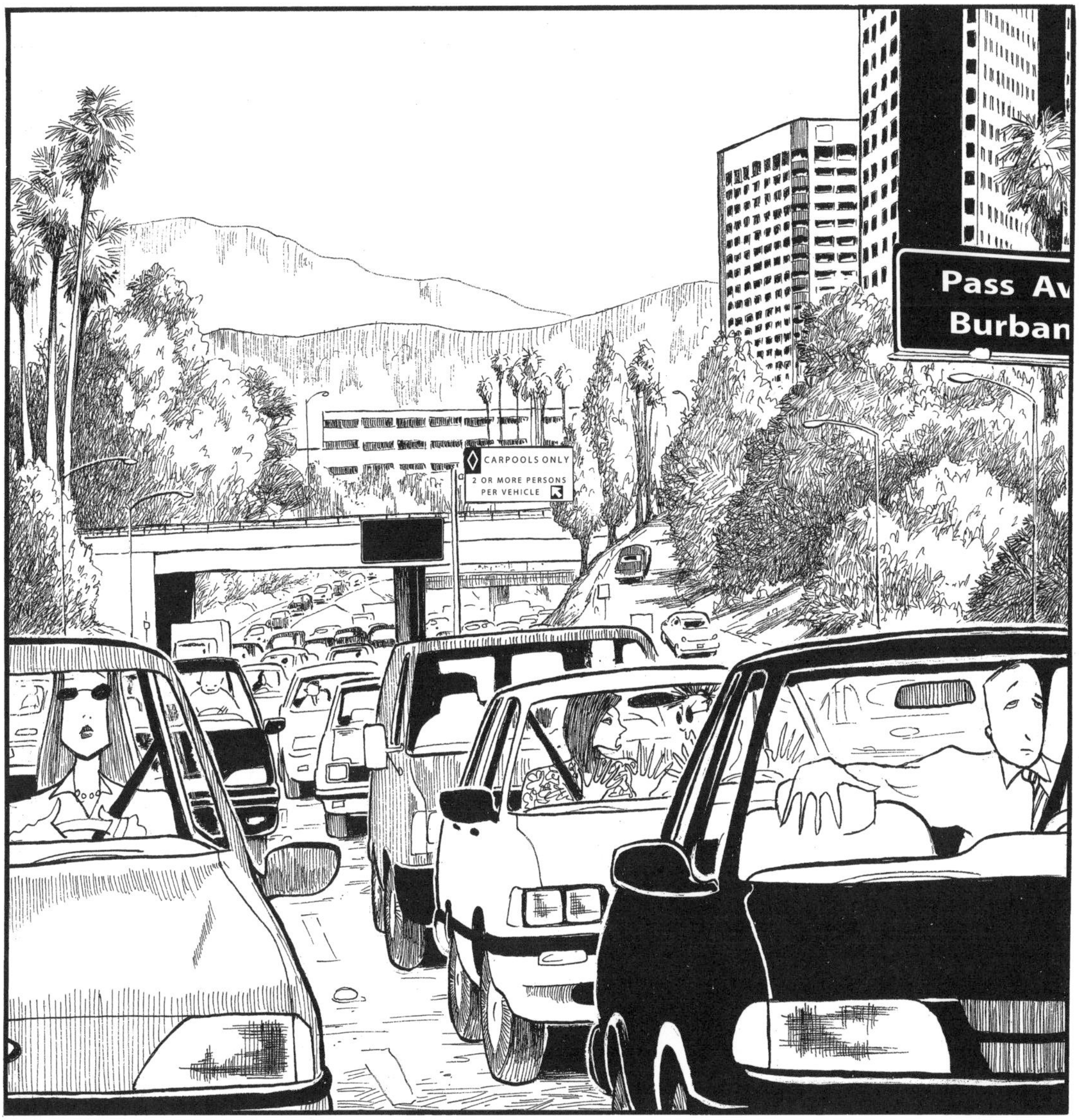
Pass Av
Burban
CARPOOLS ONLY
2 OR MORE PERSONS
PER VEHICLE

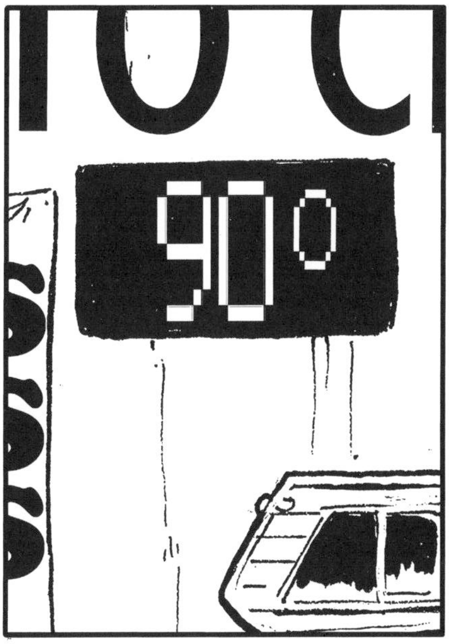
90°

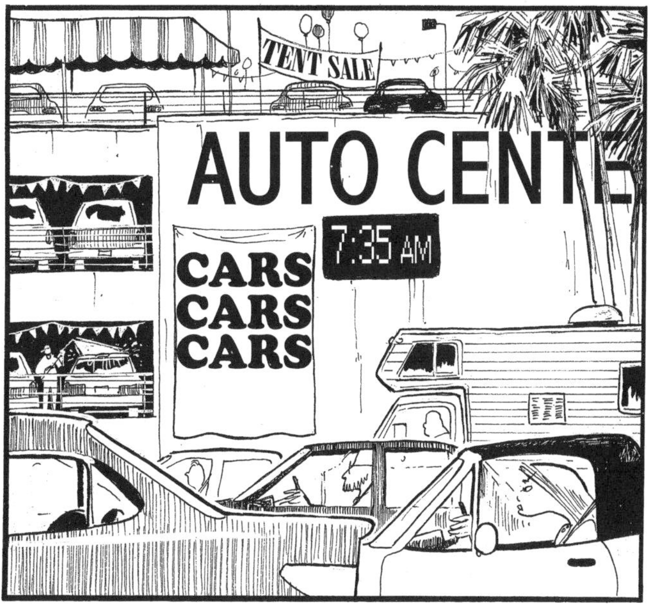
TENT SALE
AUTO CENTE
7:35 AM
CARS
CARS
CARS

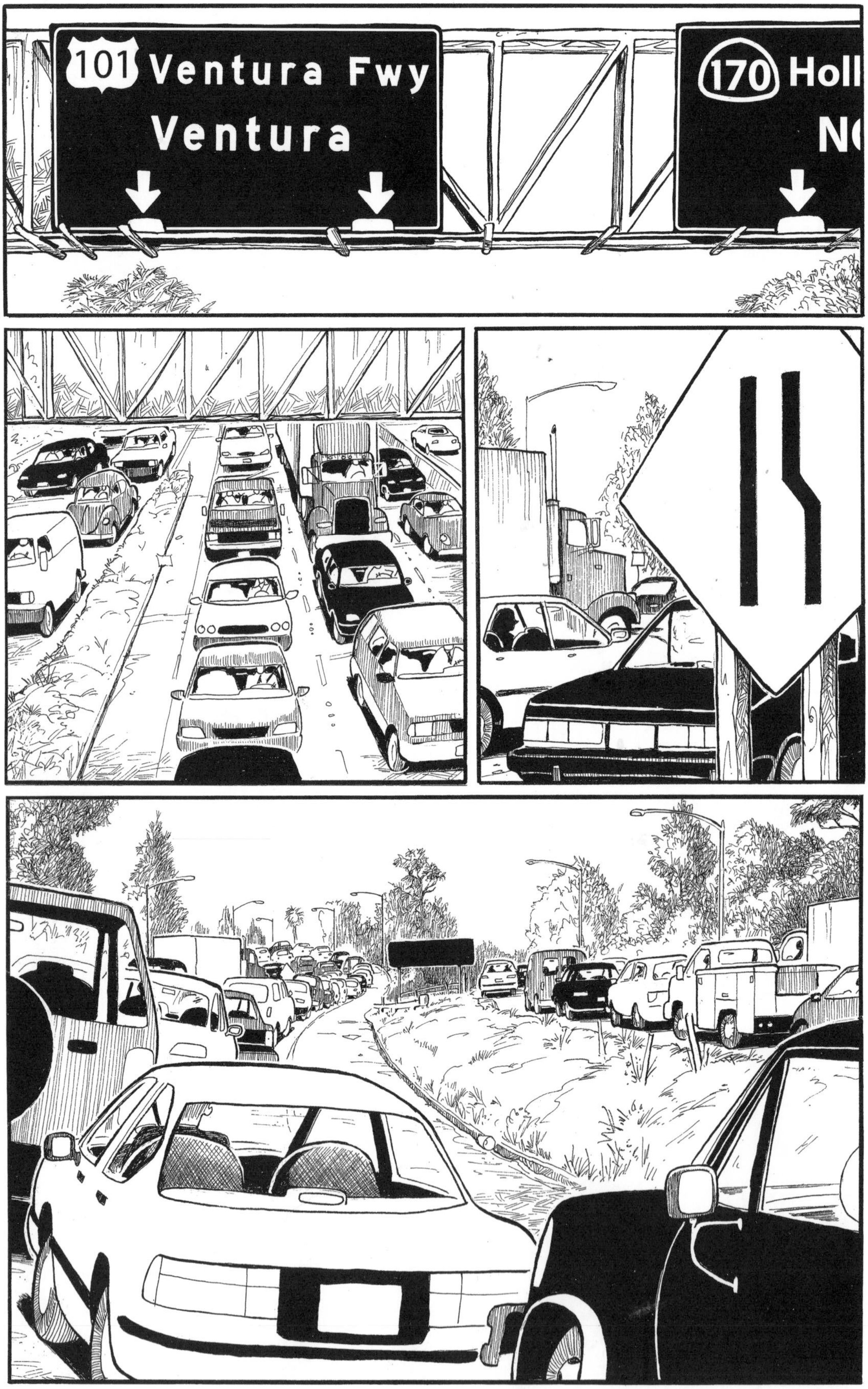
101 Ventura Fwy
Ventura
170 Holl

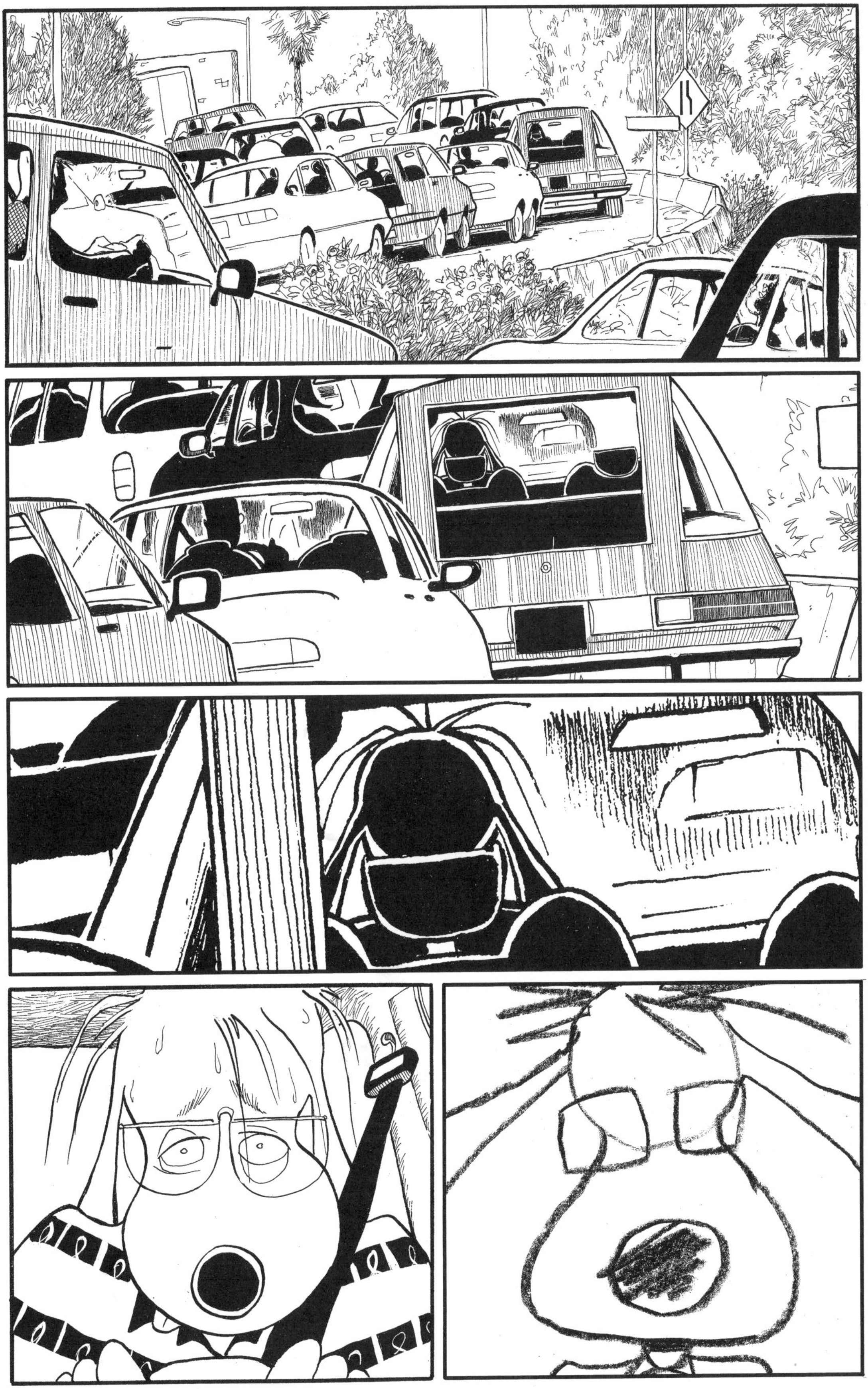

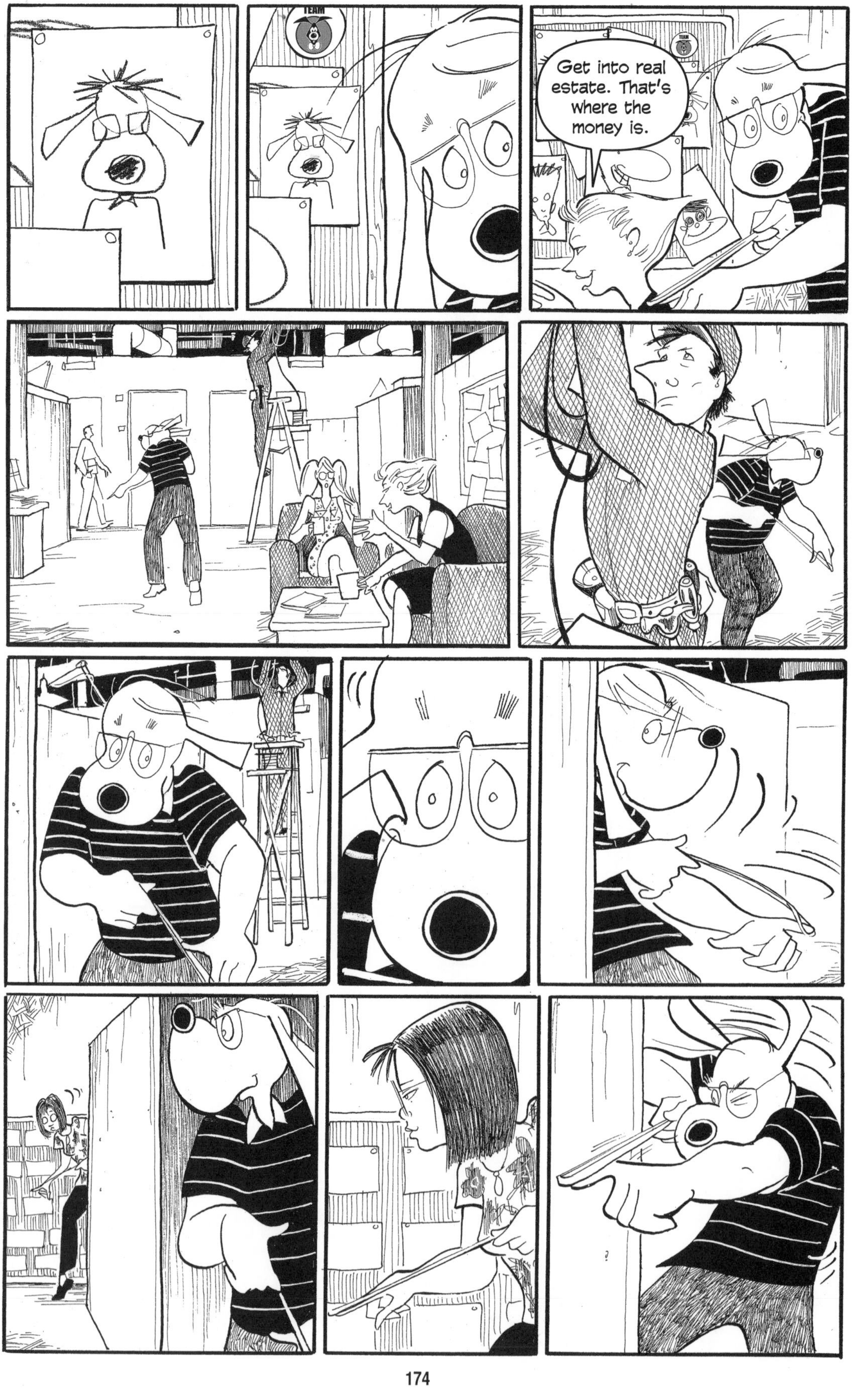
TEAM
Get into real estate. That's where the money is.

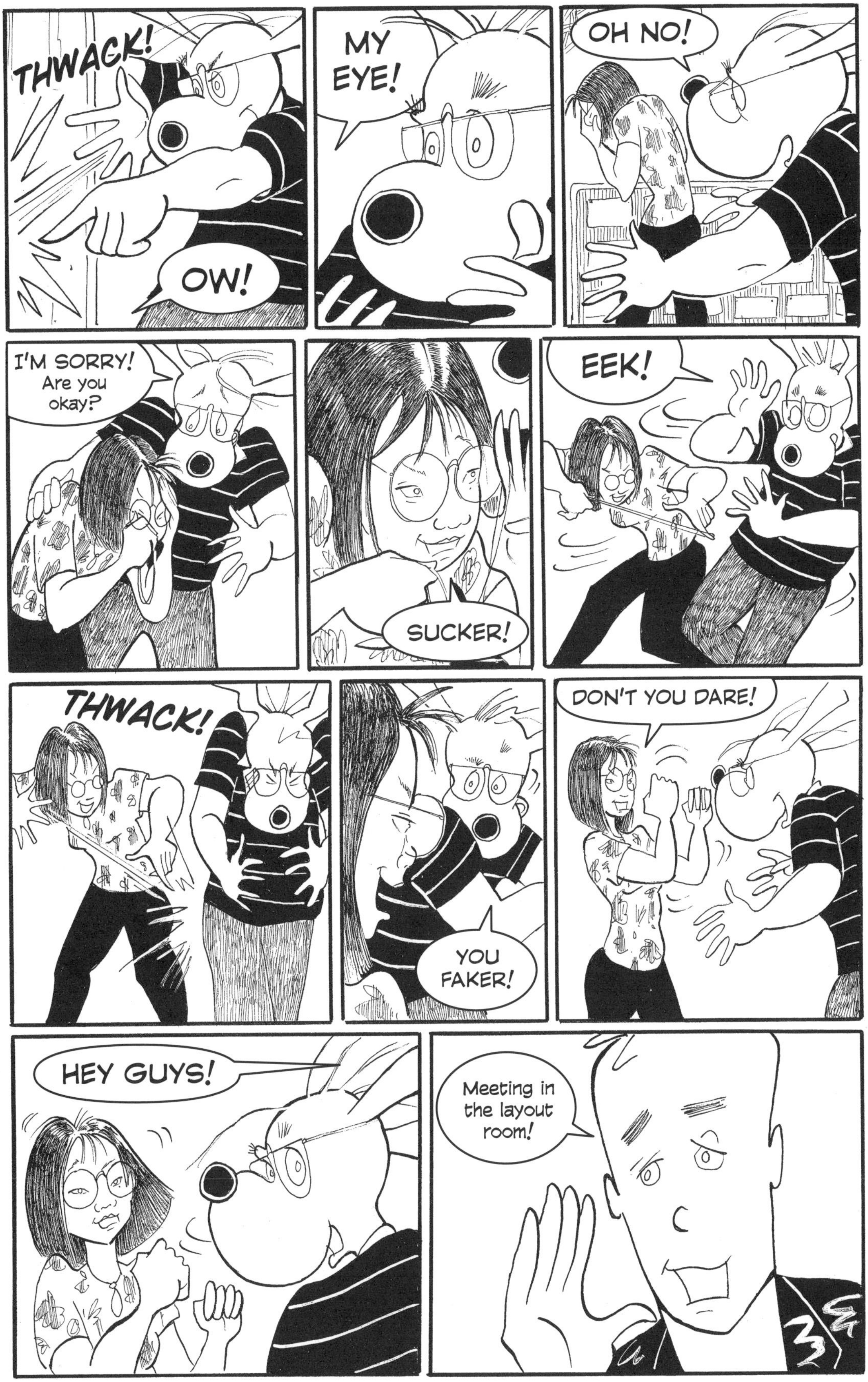
THWACK!
OW!
MY EYE!
OH NO!
I'M SORRY! Are you okay?
SUCKER!
EEK!
THWACK!
YOU FAKER!
DON'T YOU DARE!
HEY GUYS!
Meeting in the layout room!

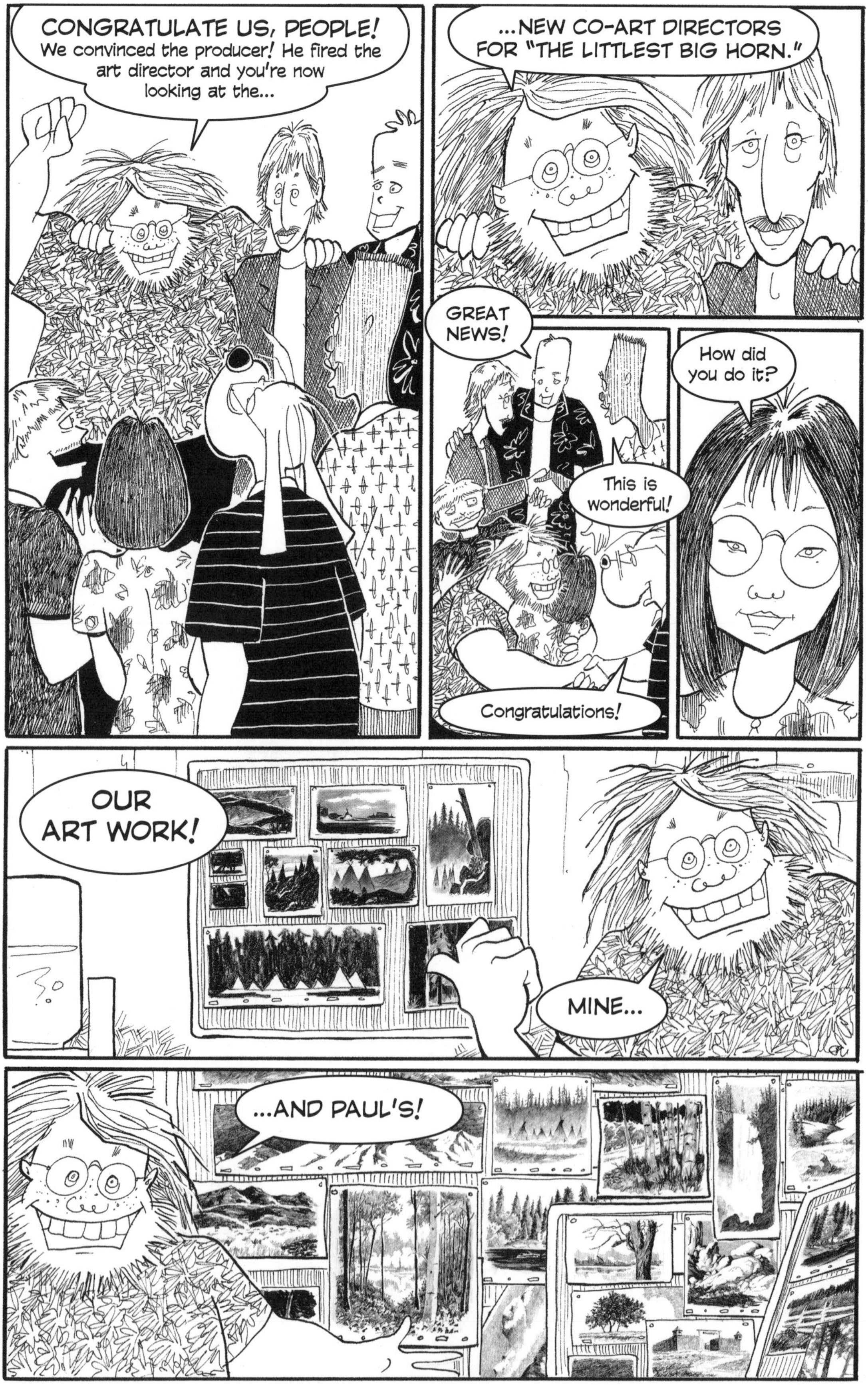
CONGRATULATE US, PEOPLE! We convinced the producer! He fired the art director and you're now looking at the...
...NEW CO-ART DIRECTORS FOR "THE LITTLEST BIG HORN."
GREAT NEWS!
This is wonderful!
Congratulations!
How did you do it?
OUR ART WORK!
MINE...
...AND PAUL'S!

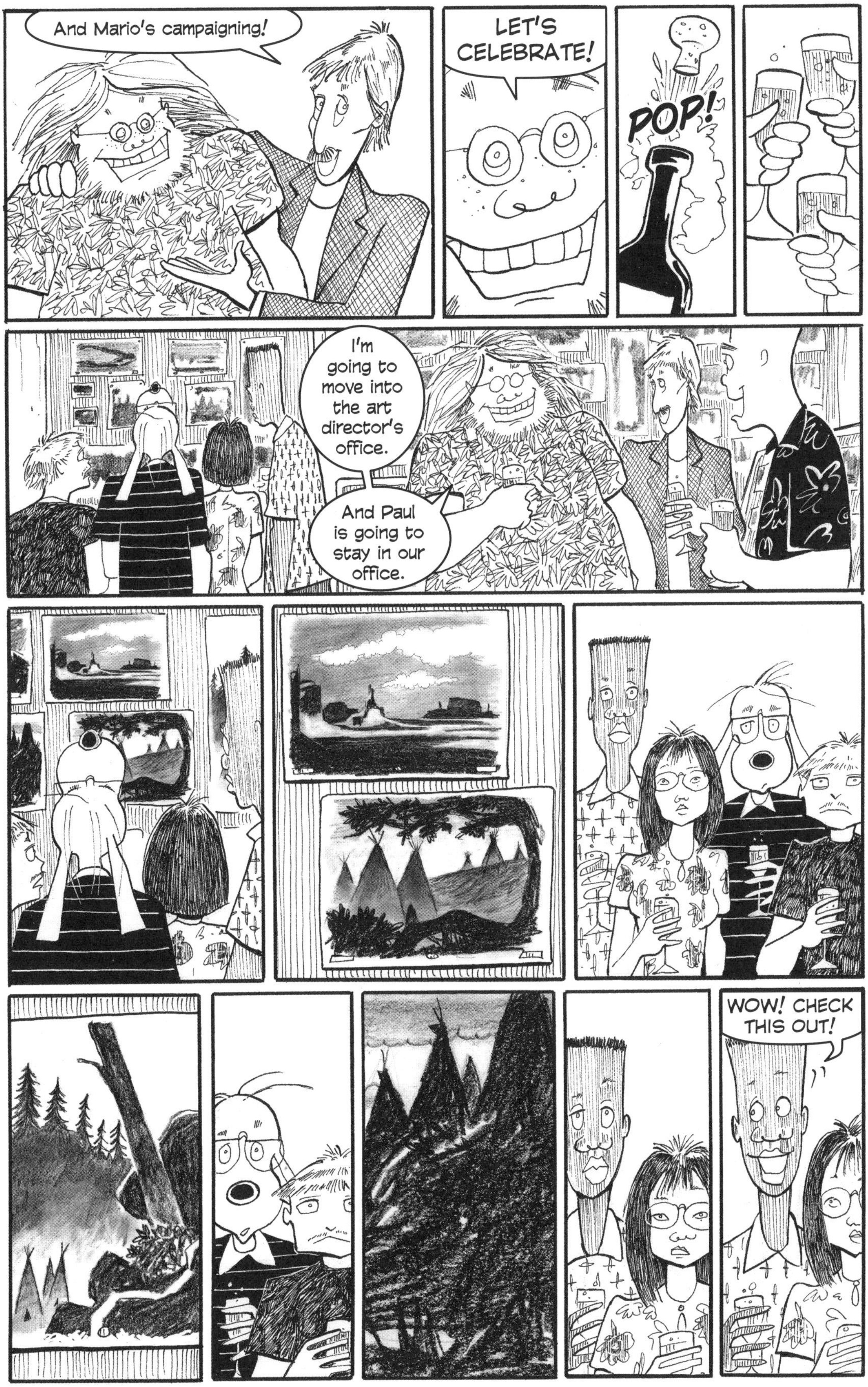
And Mario's campaigning!
LET'S CELEBRATE!
POP!
I'm going to move into the art director's office.
And Paul is going to stay in our office.
WOW! CHECK THIS OUT!

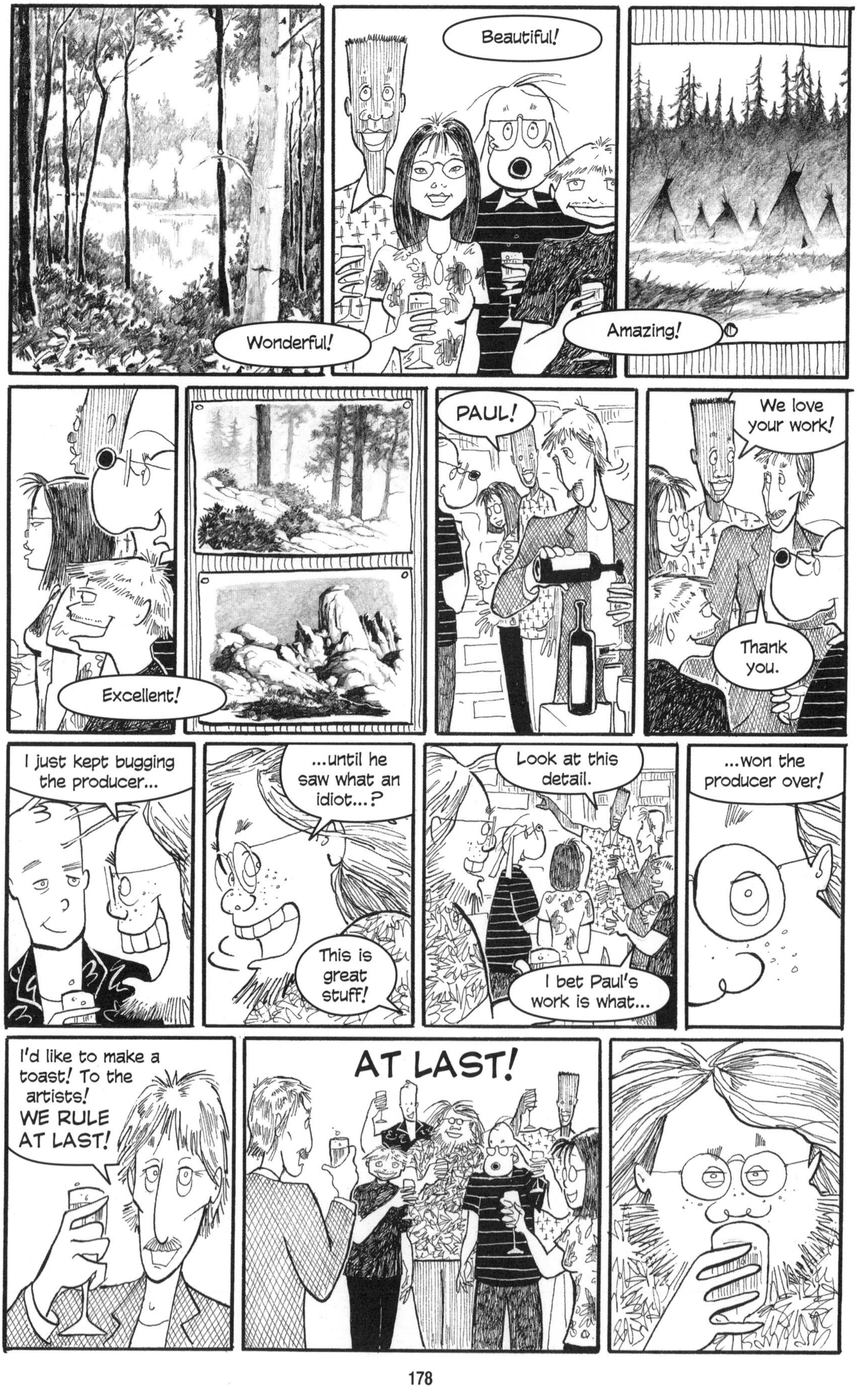
Beautiful!
Wonderful!
Amazing!
Excellent!
PAUL!
We love your work!
Thank you.
I just kept bugging the producer...
...until he saw what an idiot...?
This is great stuff!
Look at this detail.
I bet Paul's work is what...
...won the producer over!
I'd like to make a toast! To the artists! WE RULE AT LAST!
AT LAST!

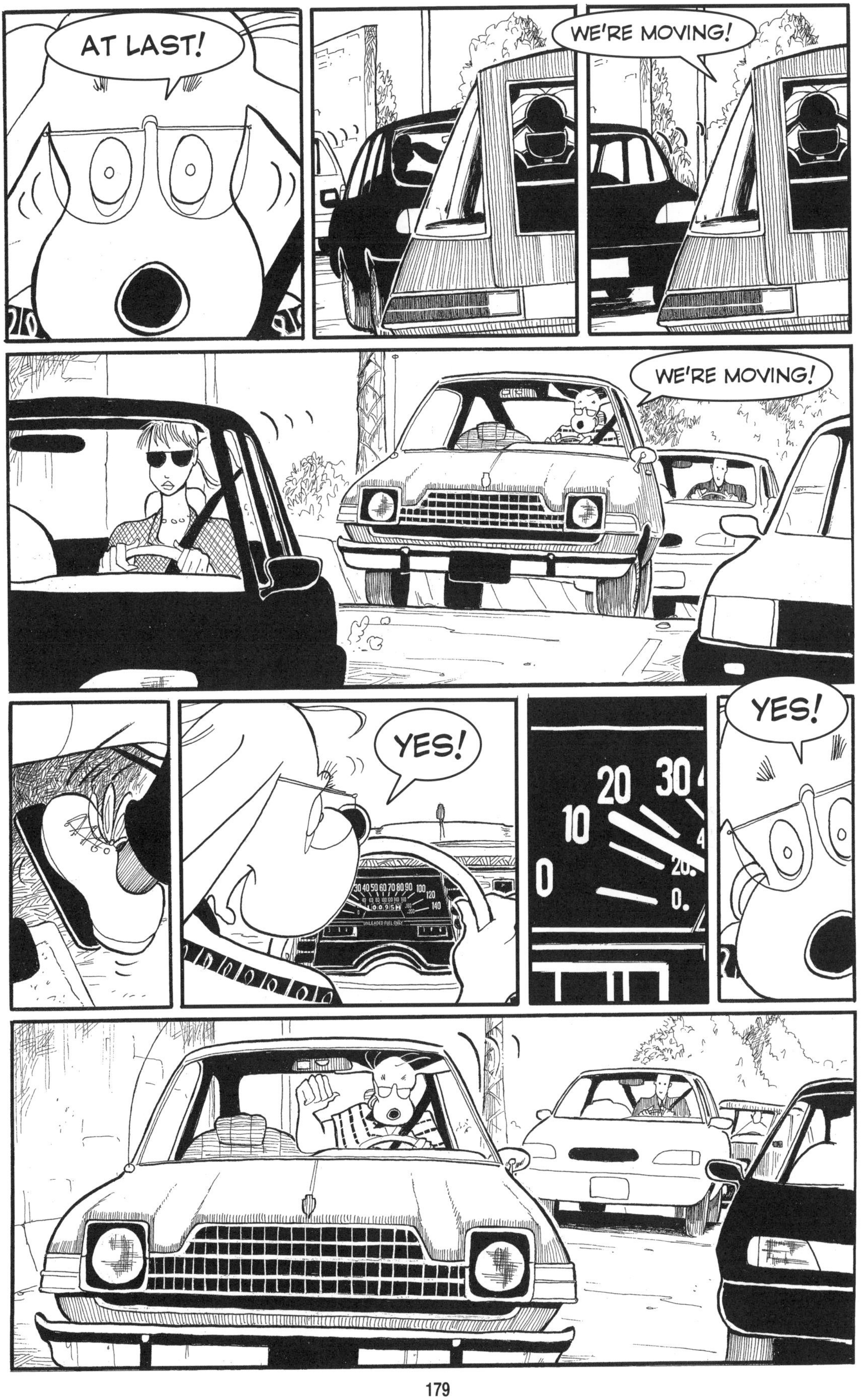
AT LAST!
WE'RE MOVING!
WE'RE MOVING!
YES!
20 30
10
0
YES!

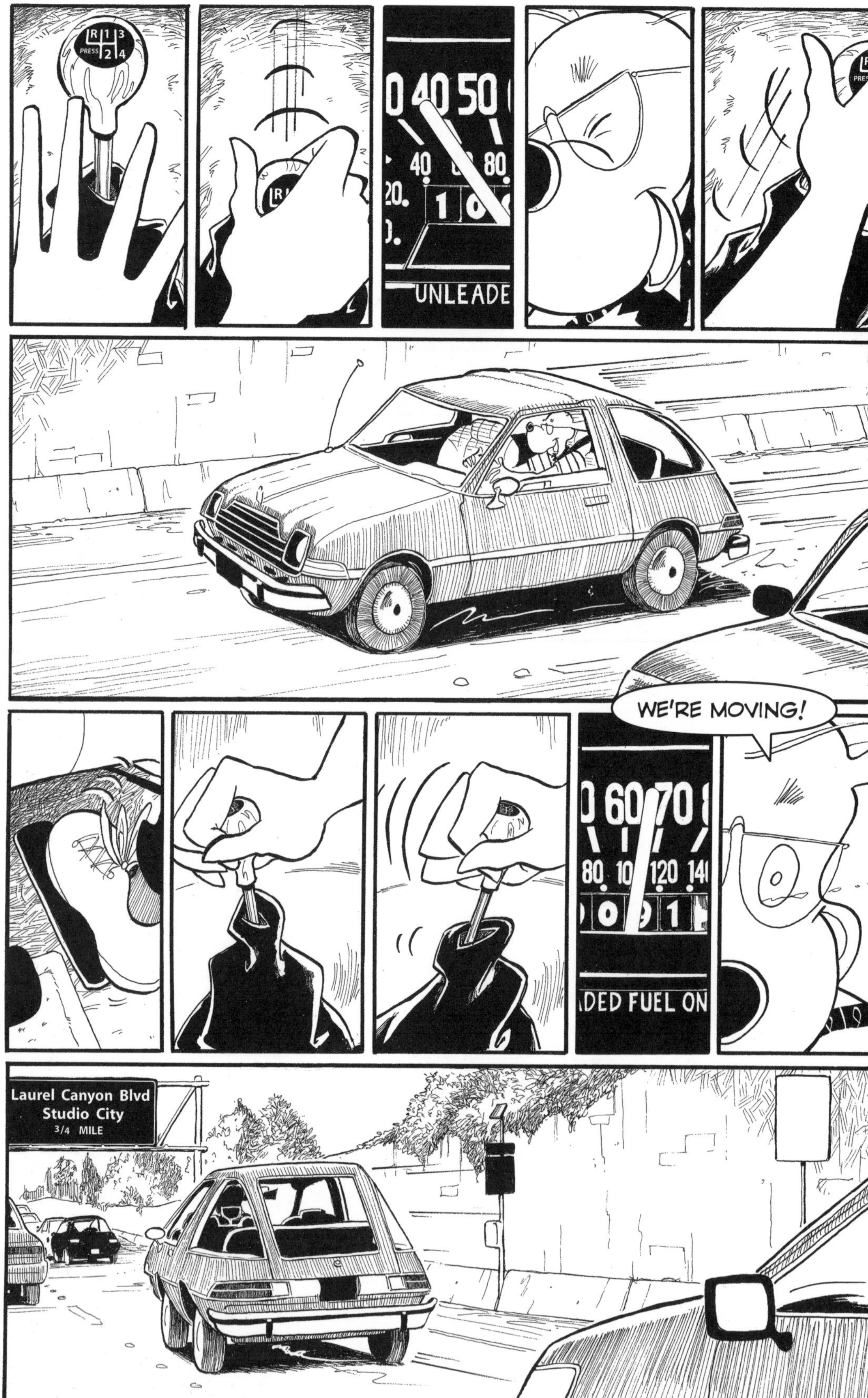
R 1 3
PRESS 2 4
0 40 50
40 80
UNLEADE
WE'RE MOVING!
0 60 70
80. 120 140
ADED FUEL ON
Laurel Canyon Blvd
Studio City
3/4 MILE

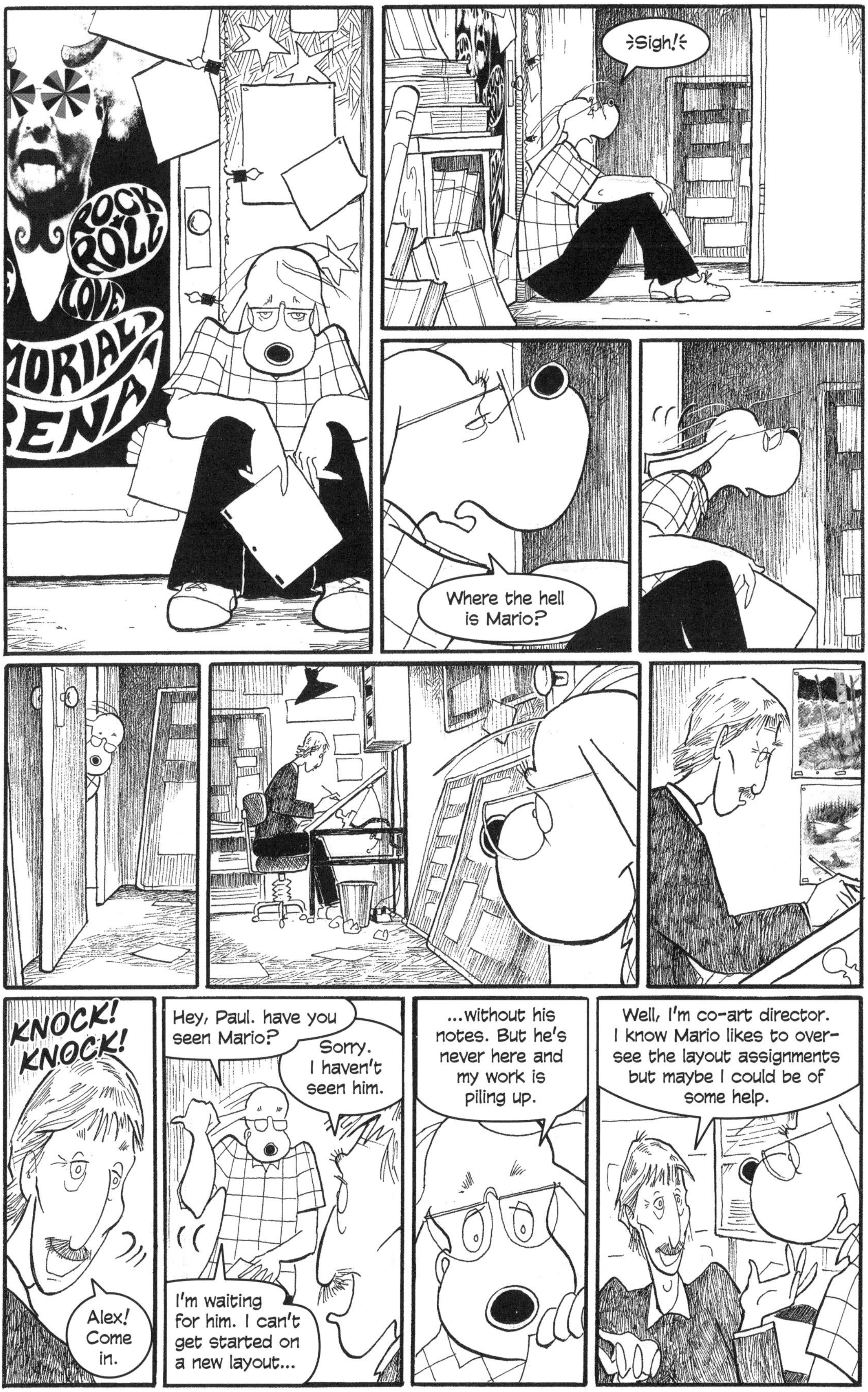
ROCK ROLL
LOVE
MORIAL
RENA
Sigh!
Where the hell is Mario?
KNOCK! KNOCK!
Alex! Come in.
Hey, Paul. have you seen Mario?
Sorry. I haven't seen him.
I'm waiting for him. I can't get started on a new layout...
...without his notes. But he's never here and my work is piling up.
Well, I'm co-art director. I know Mario likes to oversee the layout assignments but maybe I could be of some help.

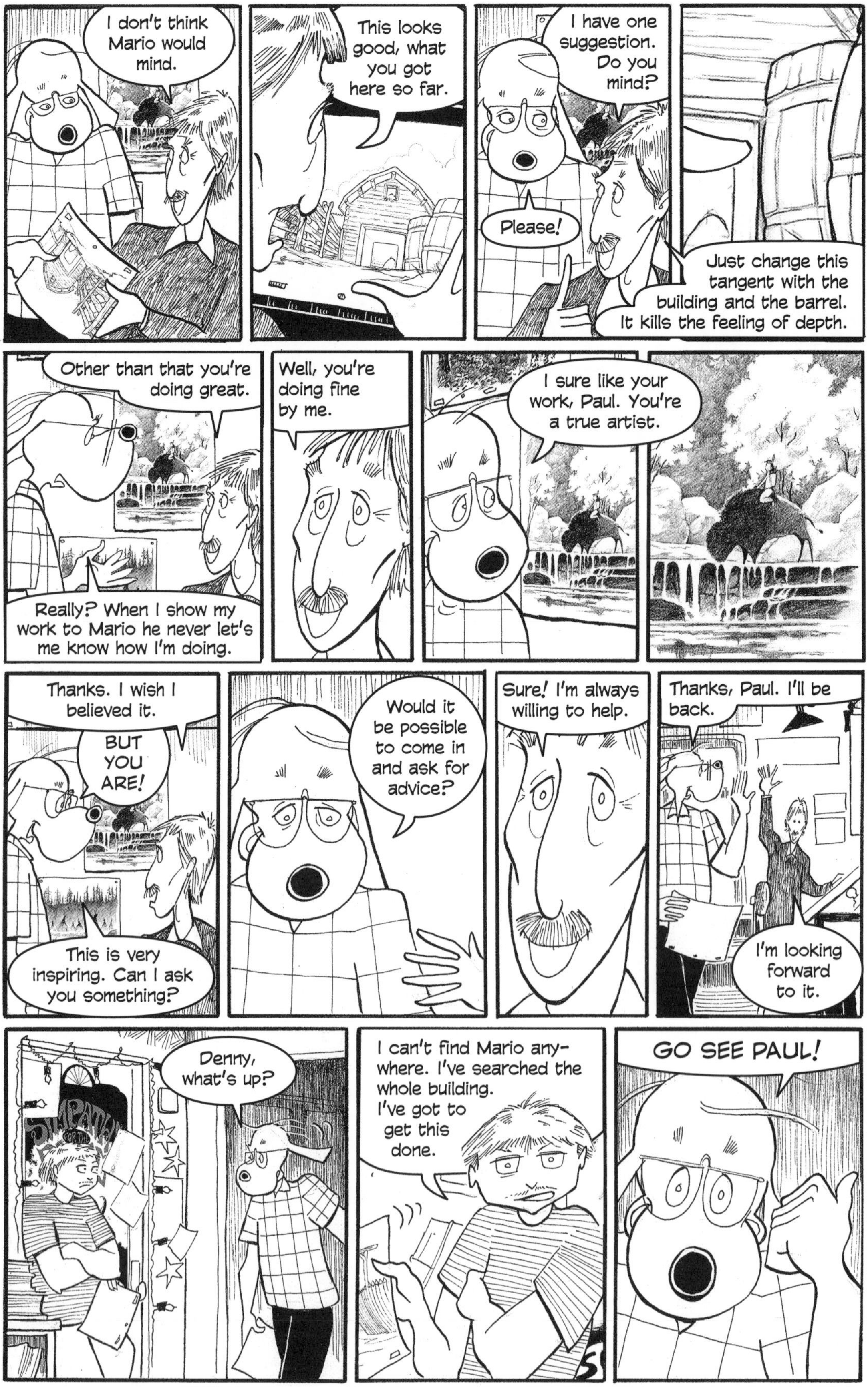
I don't think Mario would mind.
This looks good, what you got here so far.
I have one suggestion. Do you mind?
Please!
Just change this tangent with the building and the barrel. It kills the feeling of depth.
Other than that you're doing great.
Really? When I show my work to Mario he never let's me know how I'm doing.
Well, you're doing fine by me.
I sure like your work, Paul. You're a true artist.
Thanks. I wish I believed it.
BUT YOU ARE!
This is very inspiring. Can I ask you something?
Would it be possible to come in and ask for advice?
Sure! I'm always willing to help.
Thanks, Paul. I'll be back.
I'm looking forward to it.
Denny, what's up?
I can't find Mario any-where. I've searched the whole building. I've got to get this done.
GO SEE PAUL!

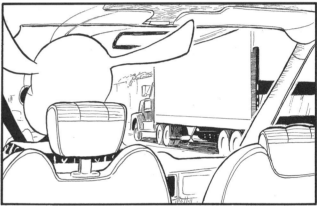

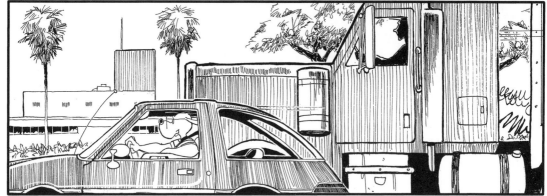

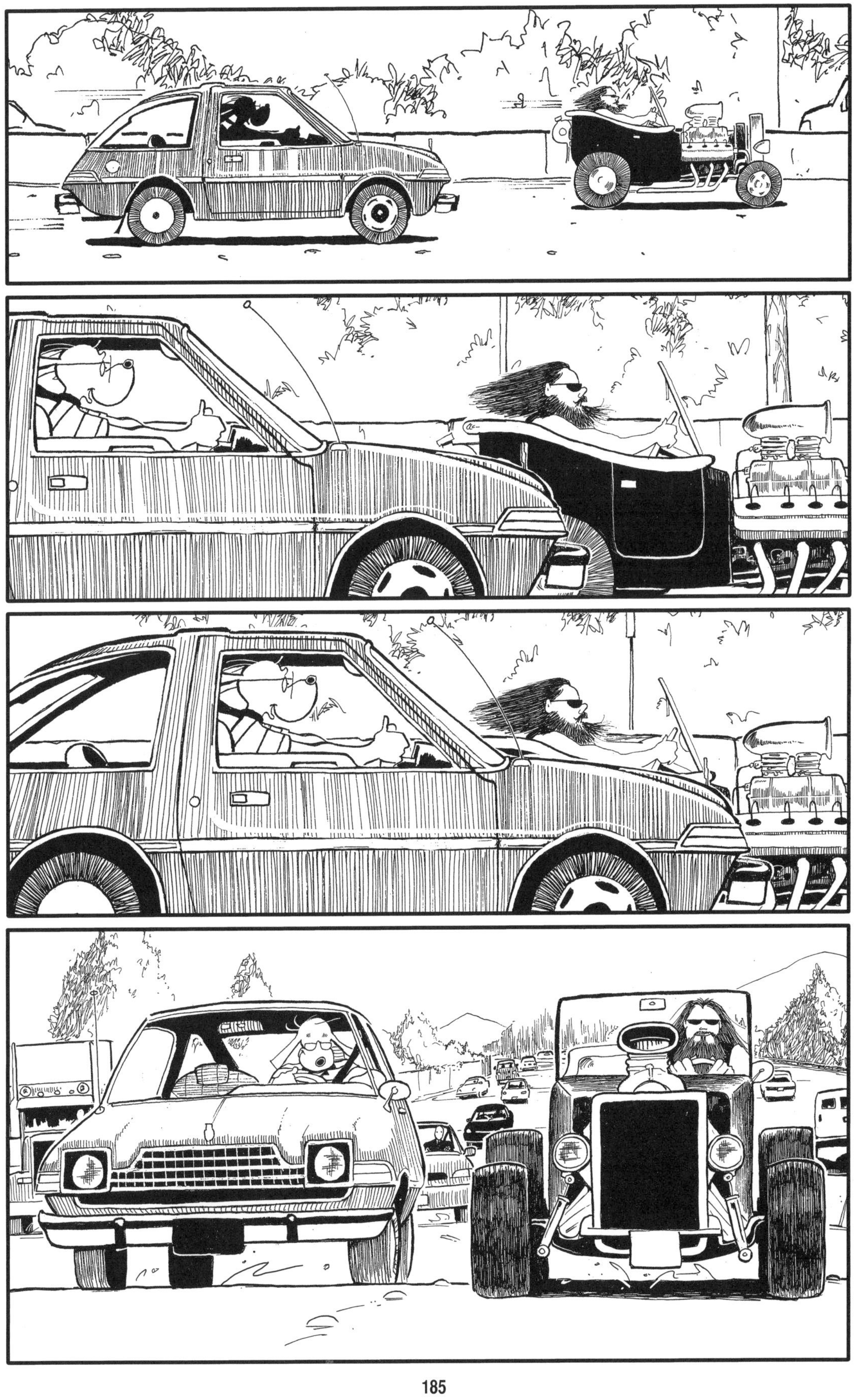

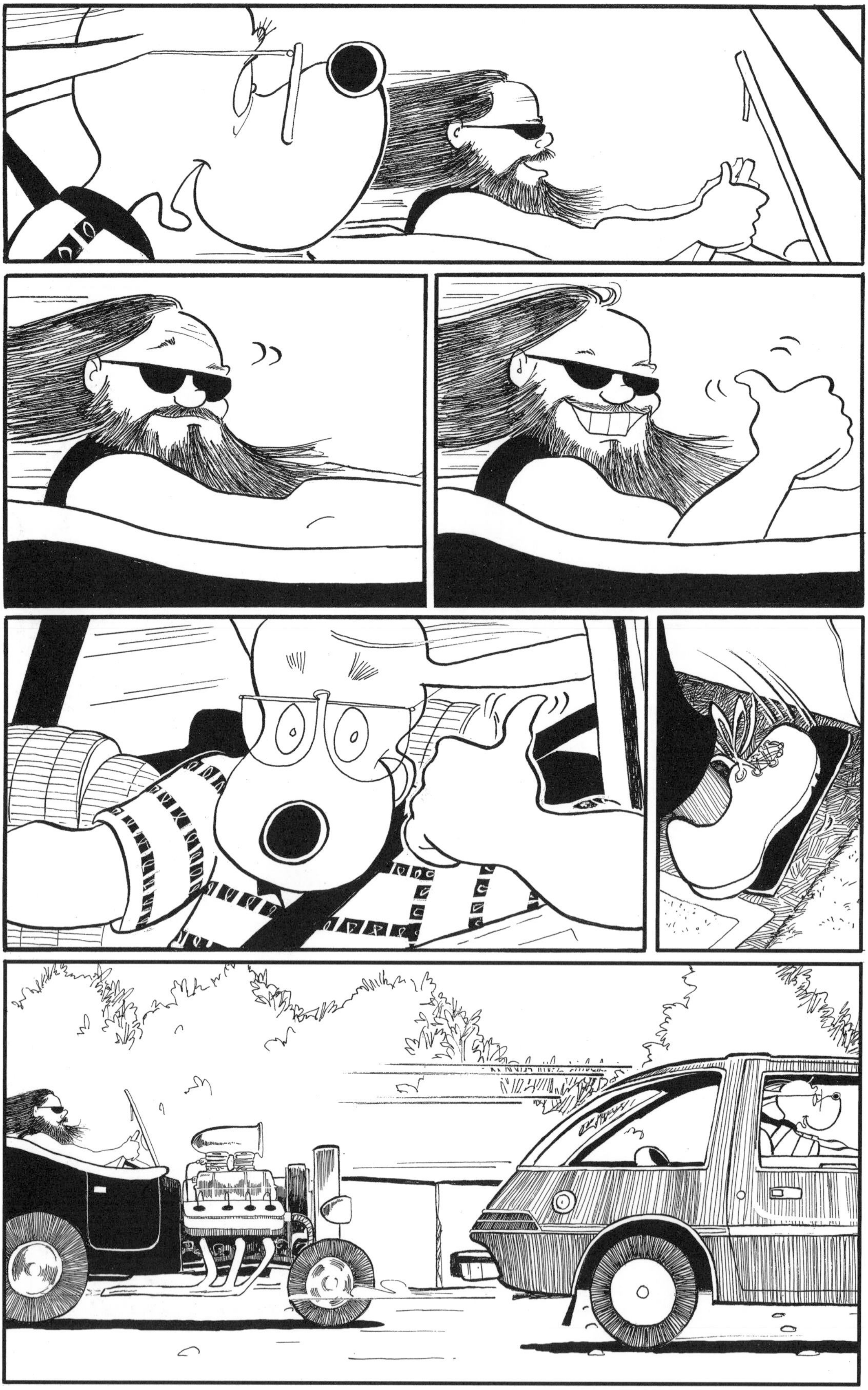

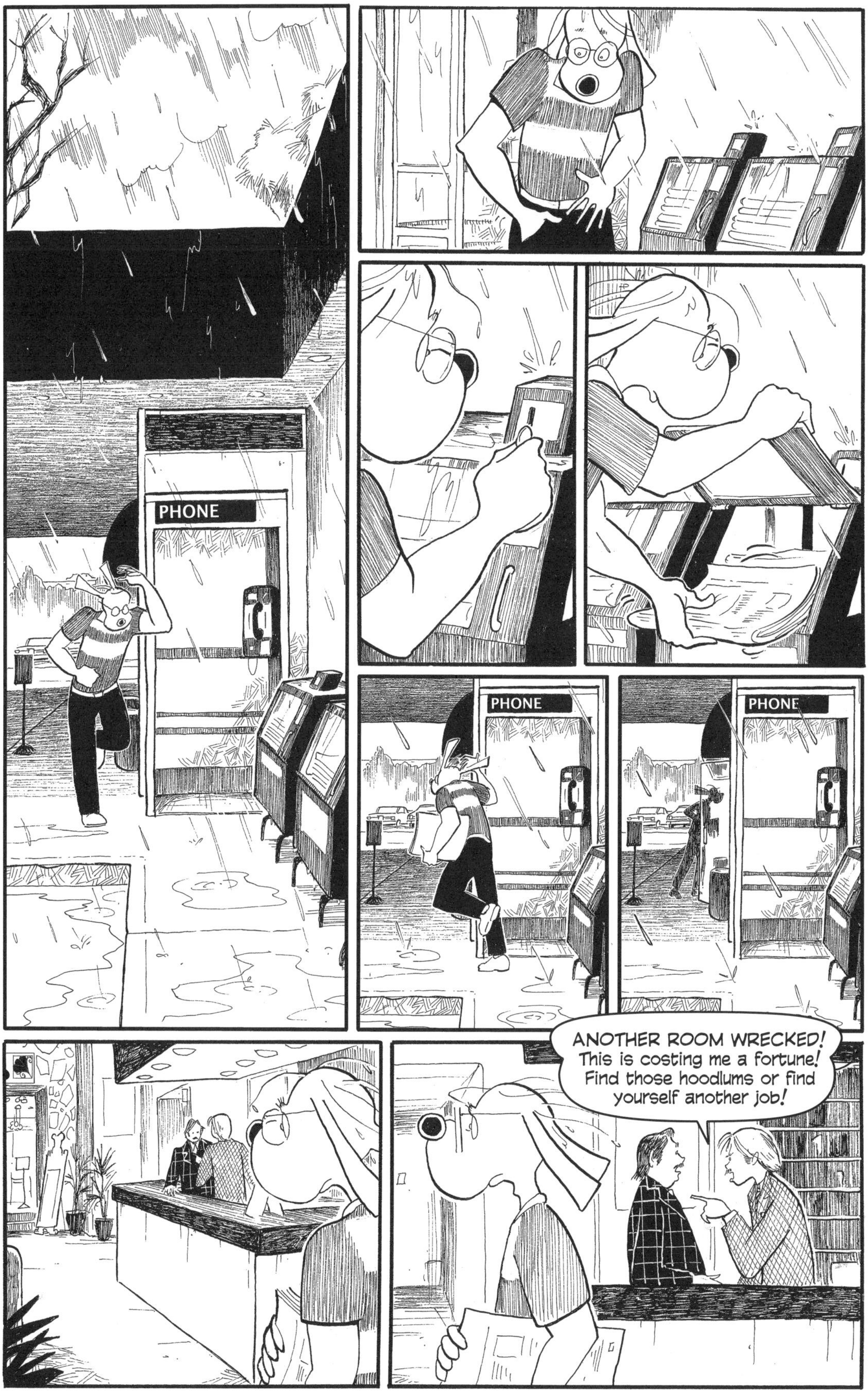
PHONE
PHONE
PHONE
ANOTHER ROOM WRECKED! This is costing me a fortune! Find those hoodlums or find yourself another job!

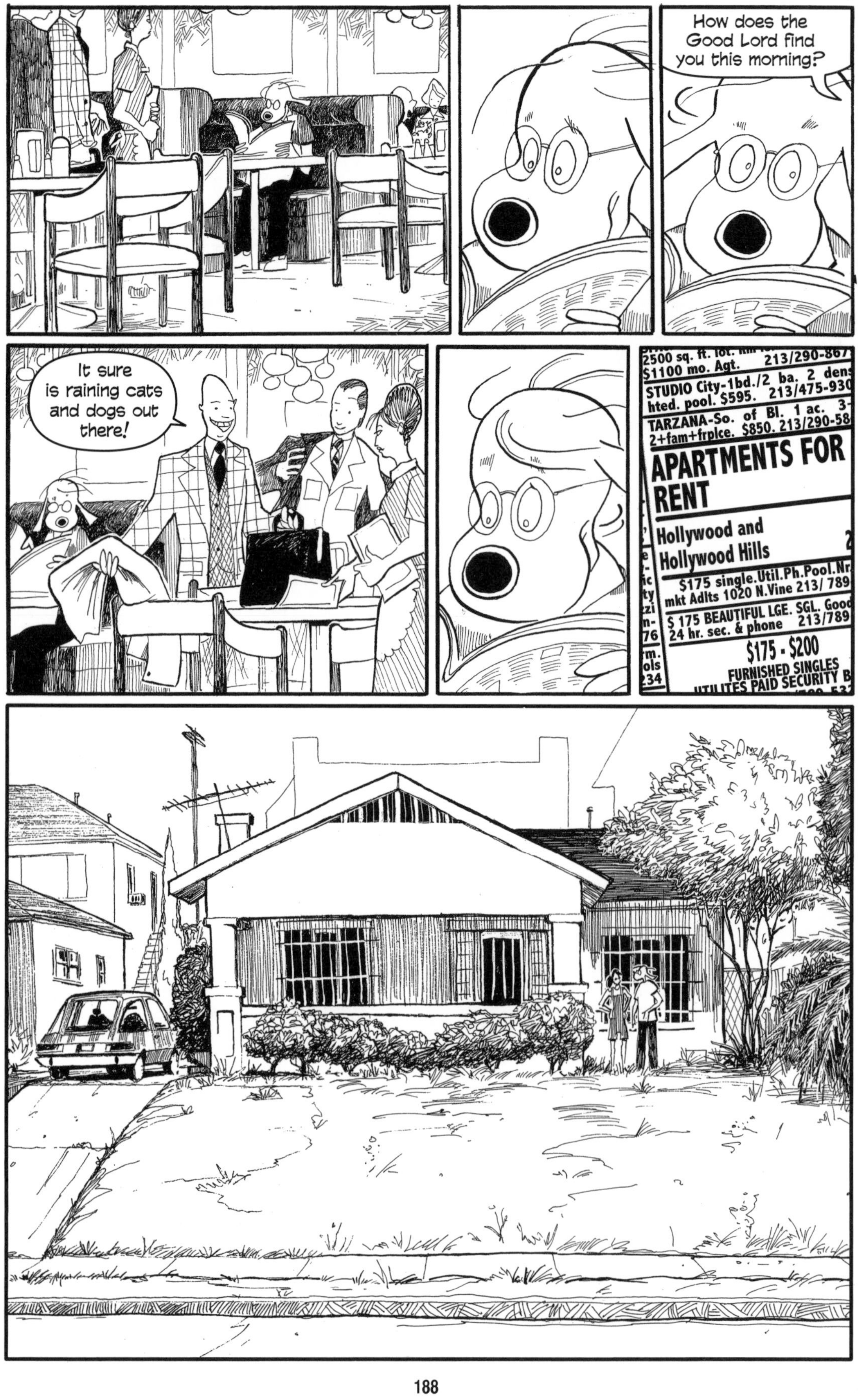
How does the Good Lord find you this morning?
It sure is raining cats and dogs out there!
2500 sq. ft. lot.
$1100 mo. Agt.
STUDIO City-1bd./2 ba. 2 dens
hted. pool. $595.
TARZANA-So. of Bl. 1 ac.
2+fam+frplce. $850.
APARTMENTS FOR RENT
Hollywood and Hollywood Hills
$175 single.Util.Ph.Pool.Nr.
mkt Adlts 1020 N.Vine
$ 175 BEAUTIFUL LGE. SGL. Good
24 hr. sec. & phone
$175 - $200
FURNISHED SINGLES

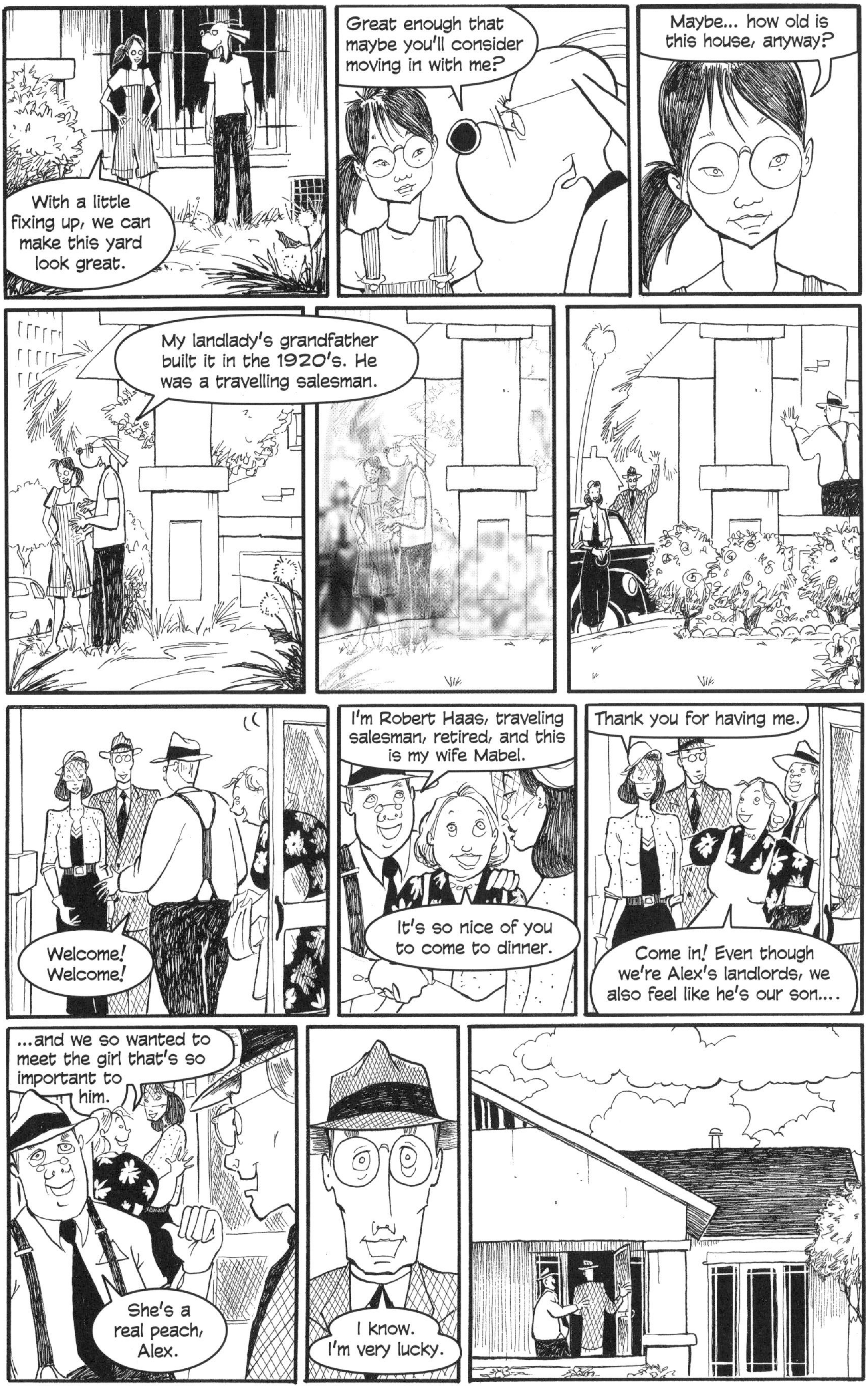
With a little fixing up, we can make this yard look great.
Great enough that maybe you'll consider moving in with me?
Maybe... how old is this house, anyway?
My landlady's grandfather built it in the 1920's. He was a travelling salesman.
Welcome! Welcome!
I'm Robert Haas, traveling salesman, retired, and this is my wife Mabel.
It's so nice of you to come to dinner.
Thank you for having me.
Come in! Even though we're Alex's landlords, we also feel like he's our son....
...and we so wanted to meet the girl that's so important to him.
She's a real peach, Alex.
I know. I'm very lucky.

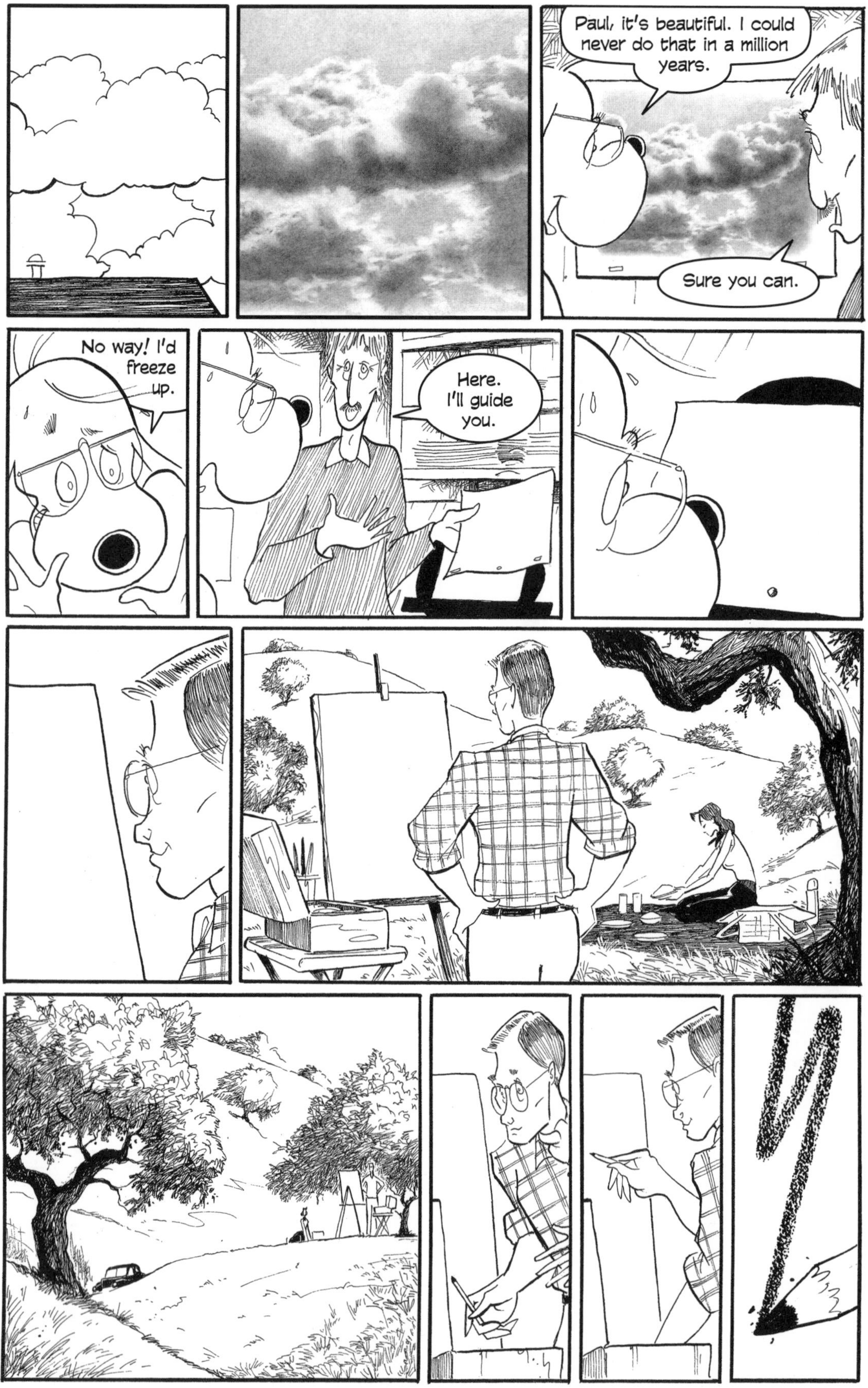
Paul, it's beautiful. I could never do that in a million years.
Sure you can.
No way! I'd freeze up.
Here. I'll guide you.

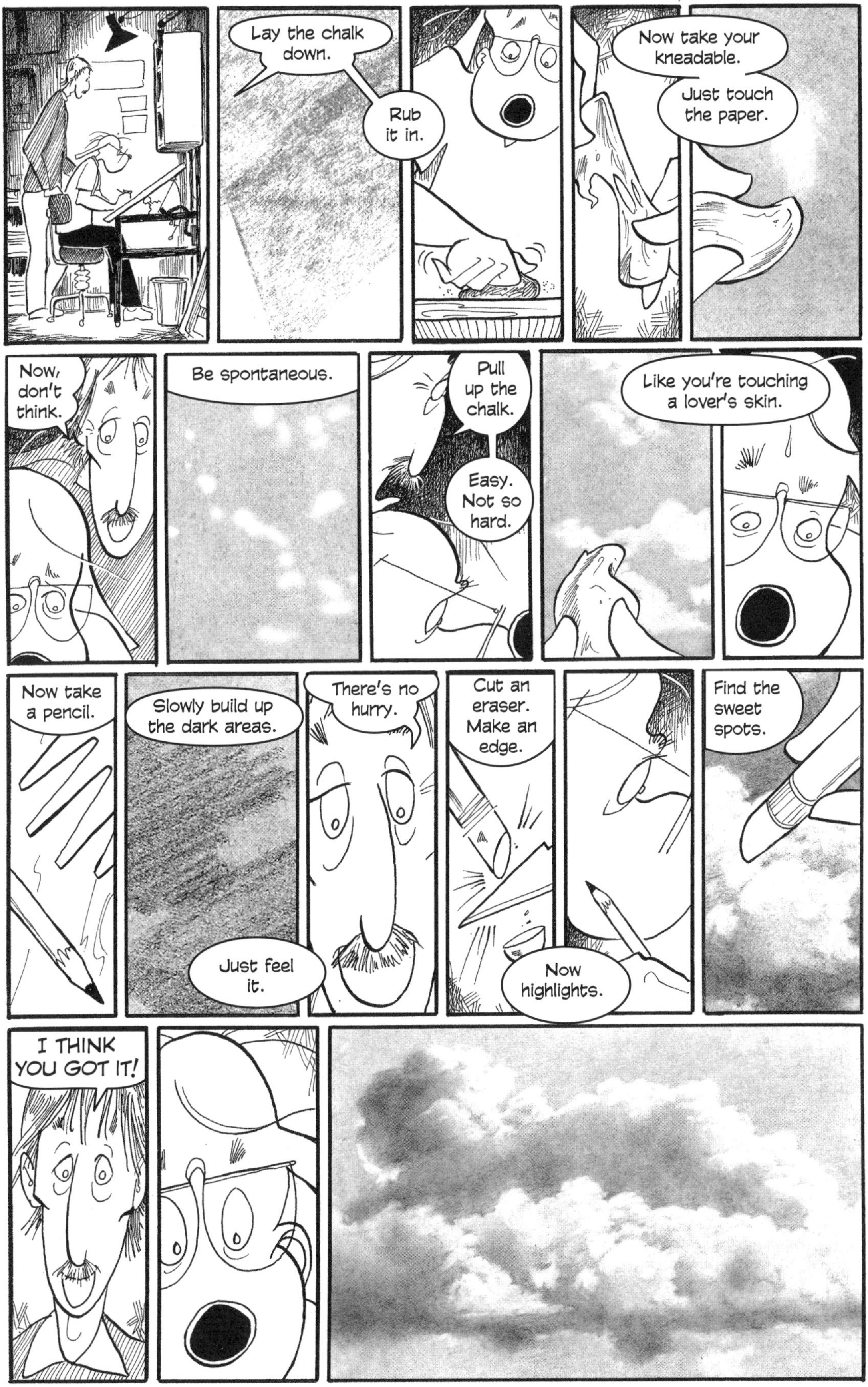
Lay the chalk down.
Rub it in.
Now take your kneadable.
Just touch the paper.
Now, don't think.
Be spontaneous.
Pull up the chalk.
Easy. Not so hard.
Like you're touching a lover's skin.
Now take a pencil.
Slowly build up the dark areas.
Just feel it.
There's no hurry.
Cut an eraser. Make an edge.
Now highlights.
Find the sweet spots.
I THINK YOU GOT IT!

CLAP! CLAP! CLAP!

CLAP!

COOL!

Can you show me how to do that?

Sure. Have a seat.

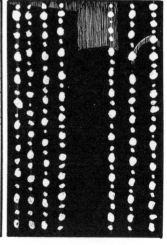

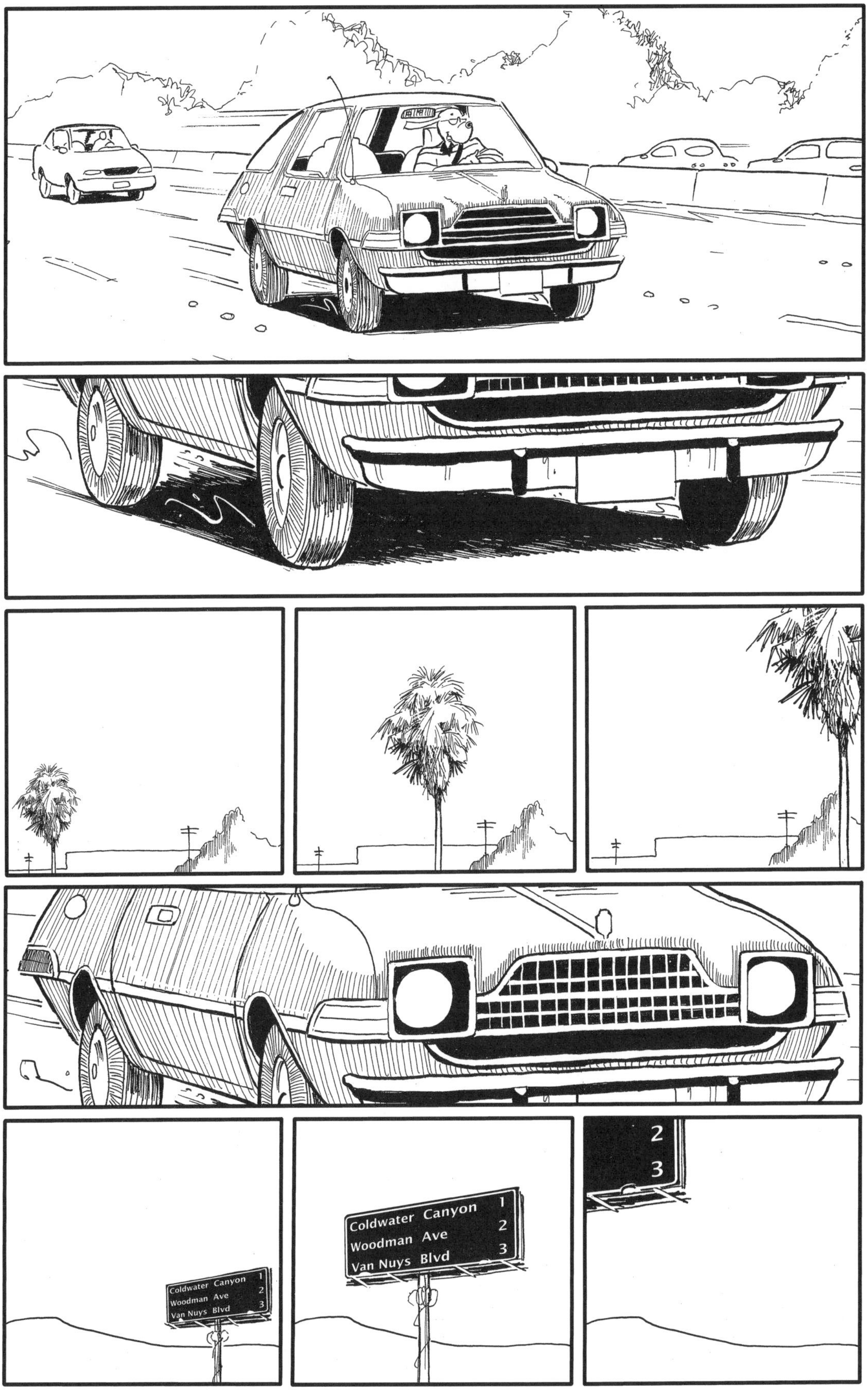
Coldwater Canyon 1
Woodman Ave 2
Van Nuys Blvd 3
Coldwater Canyon 1
Woodman Ave 2
Van Nuys Blvd 3
2
3

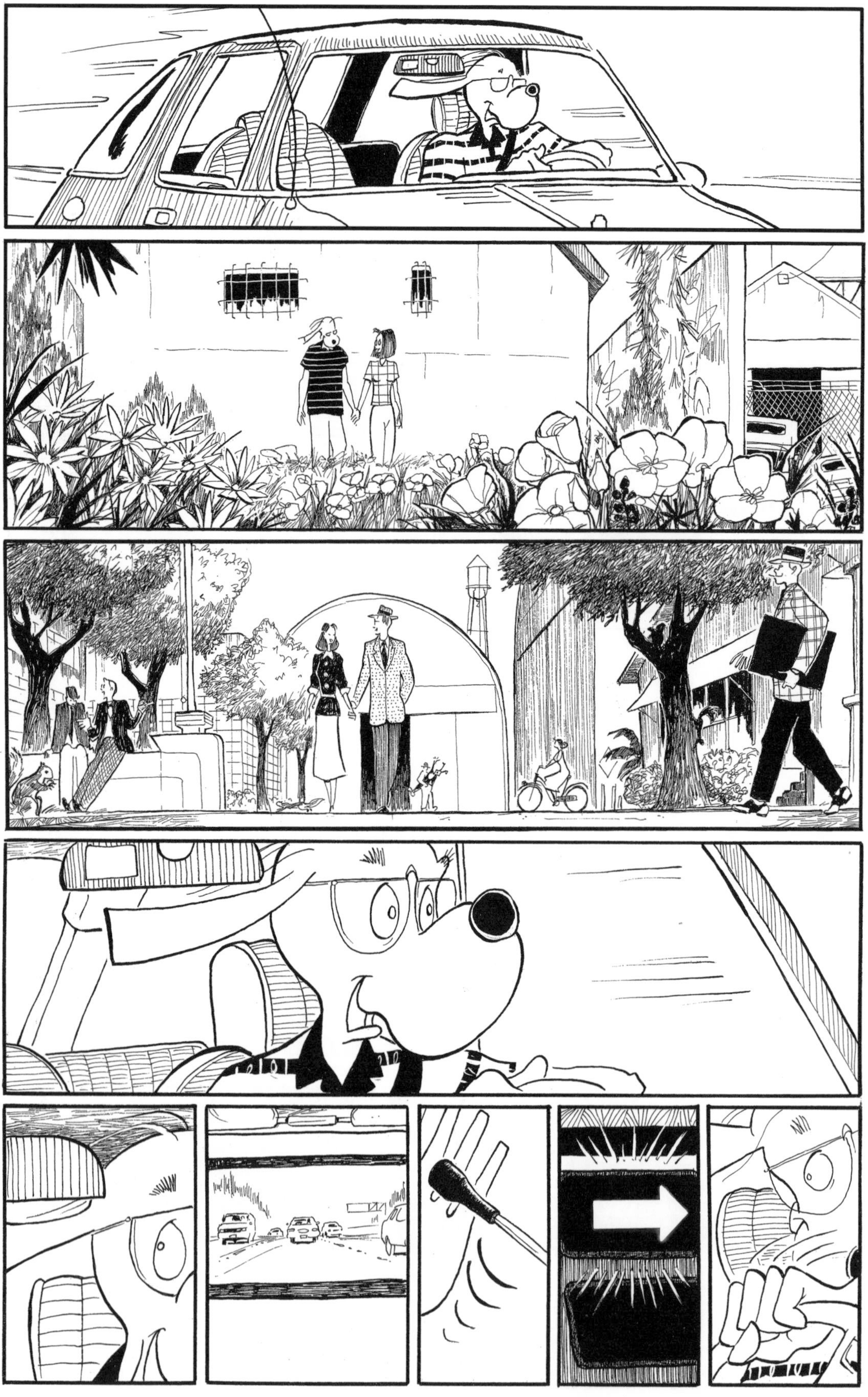

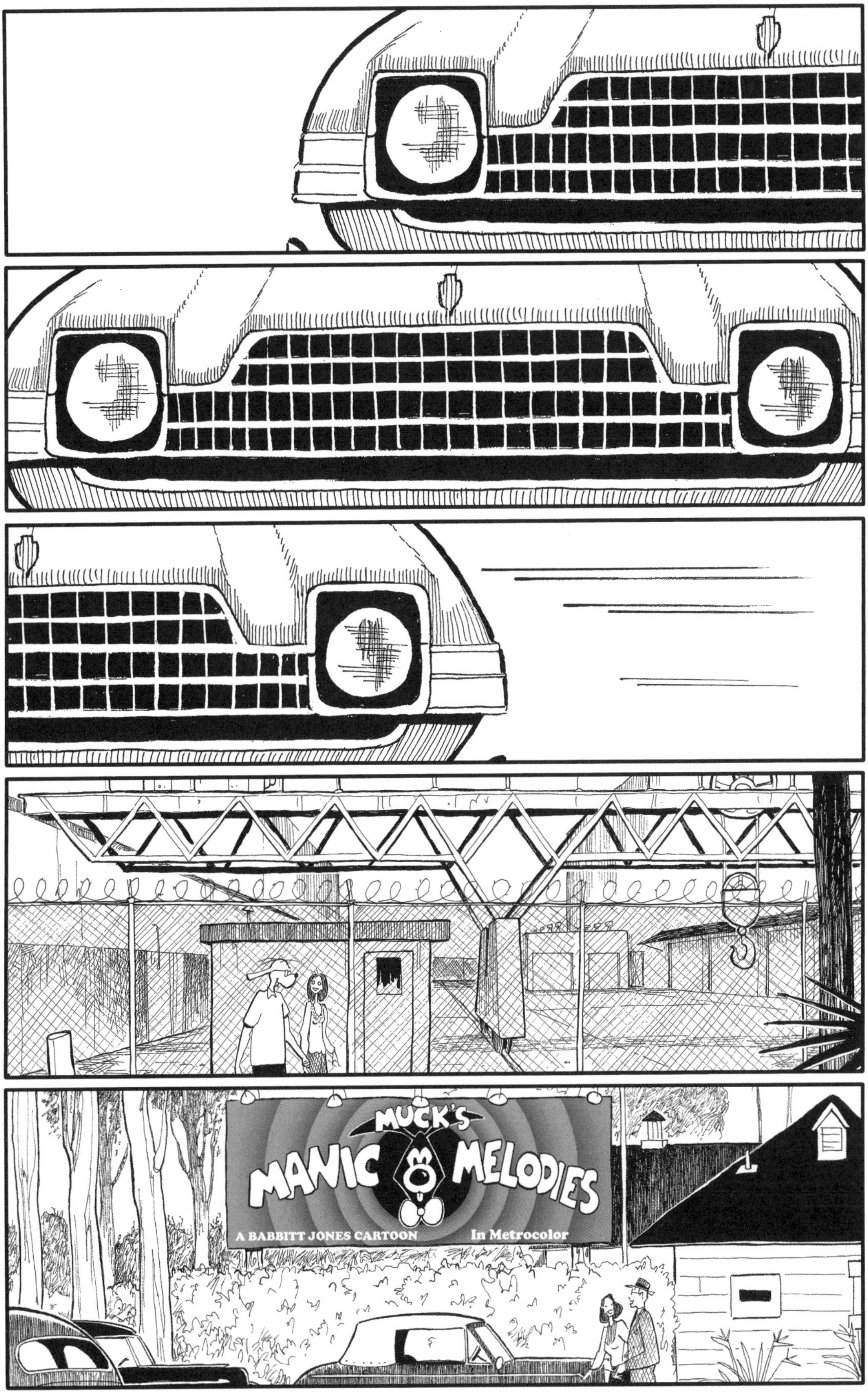
MUCK'S
MANIC MELODIES
A BABBITT JONES CARTOON
In Metrocolor

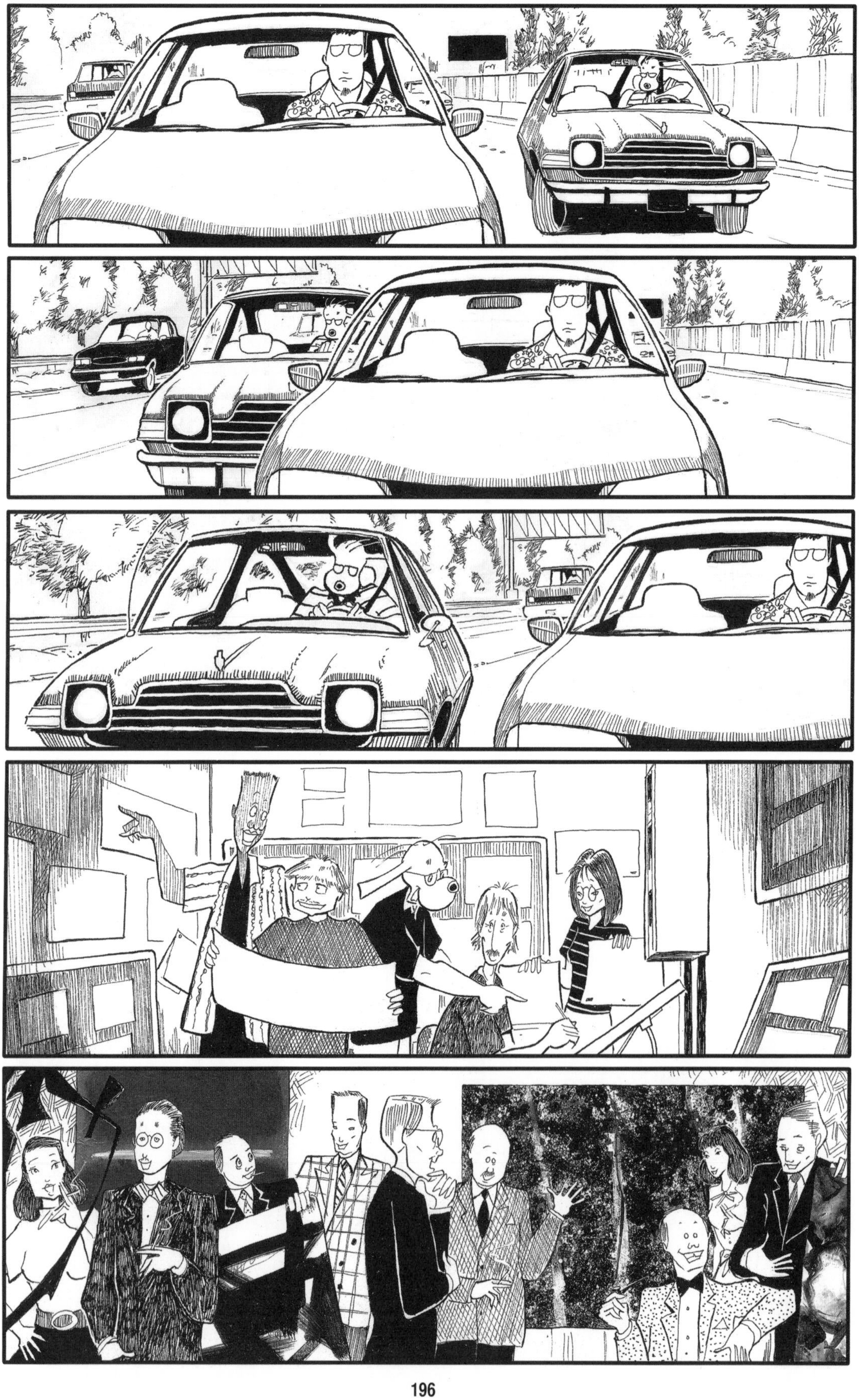

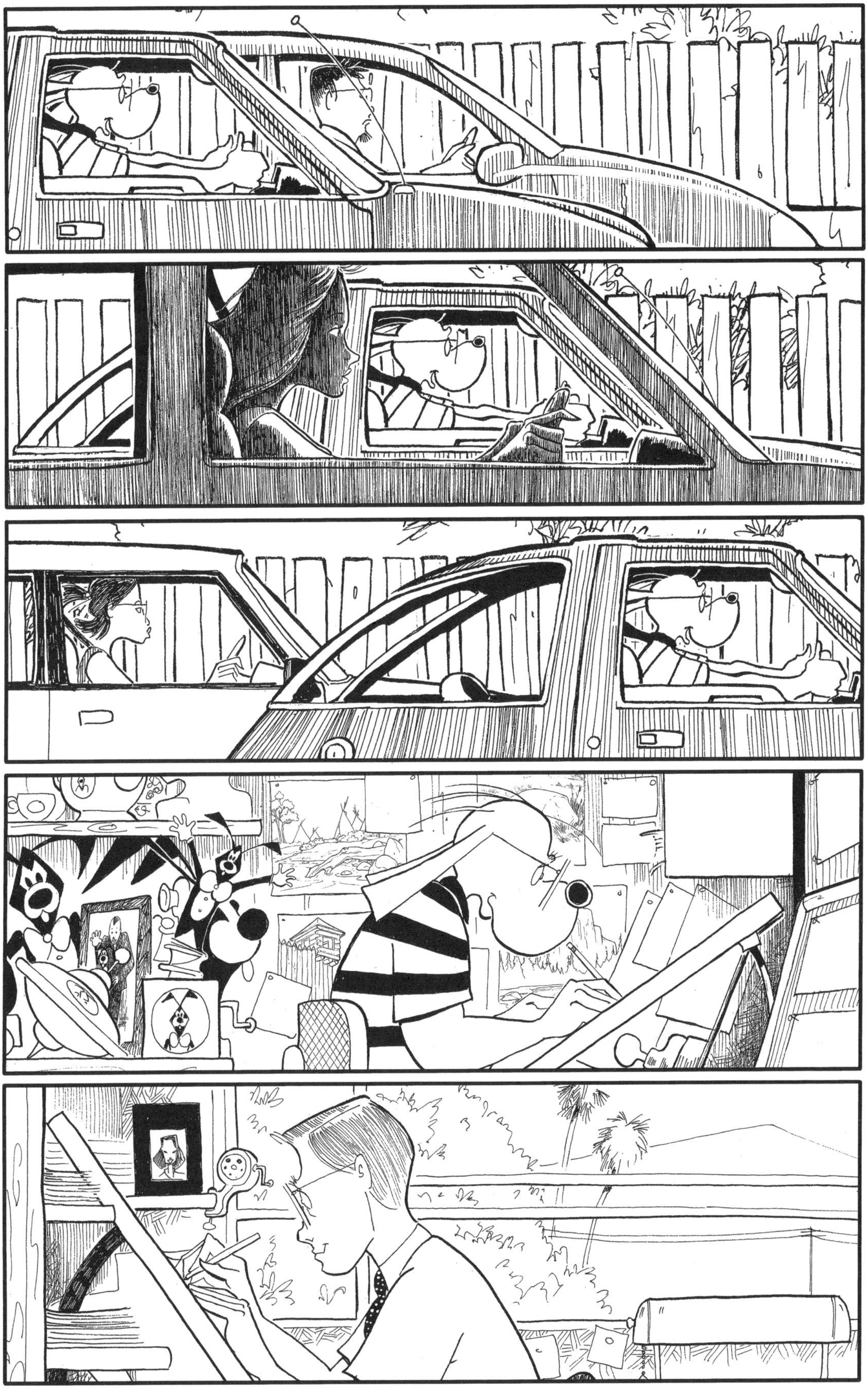

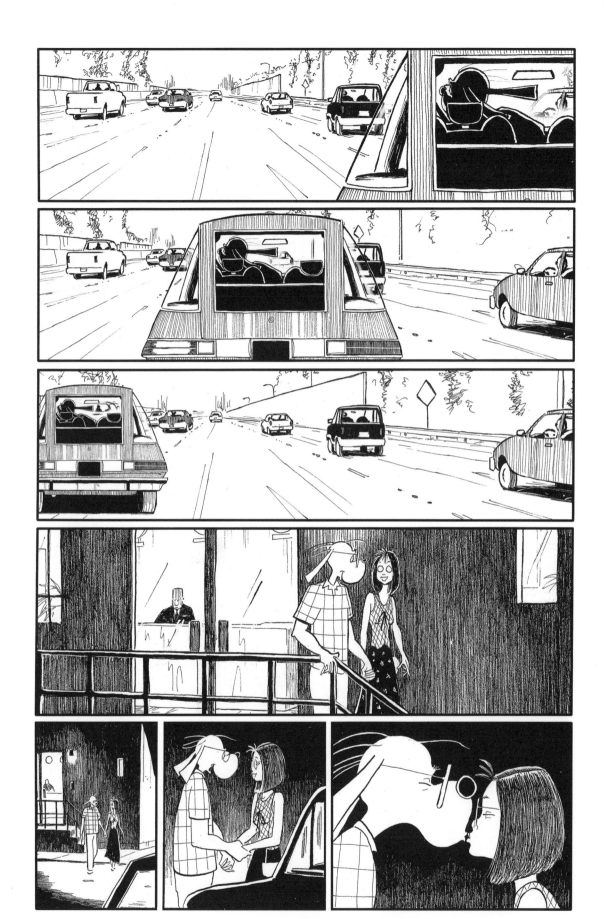

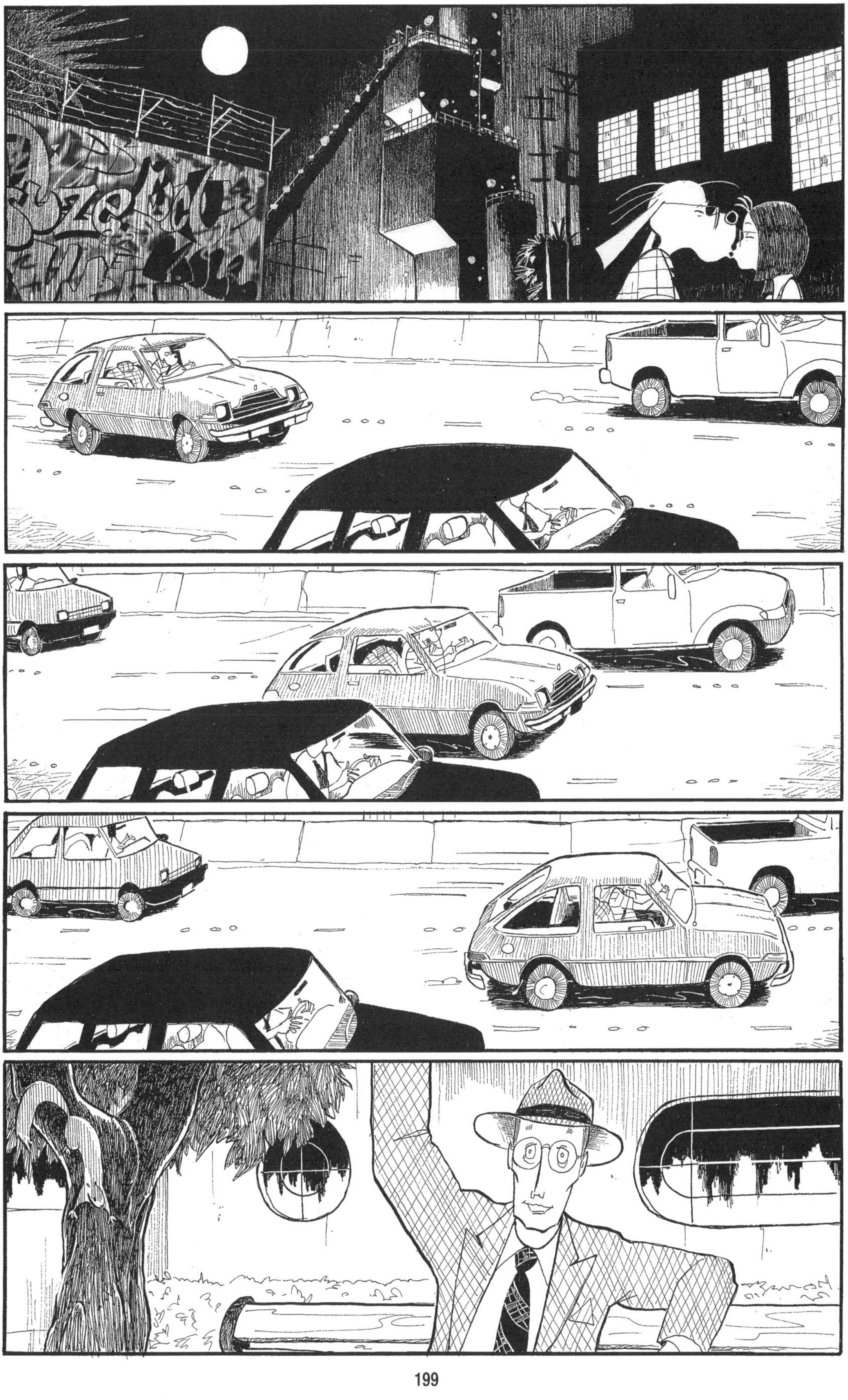

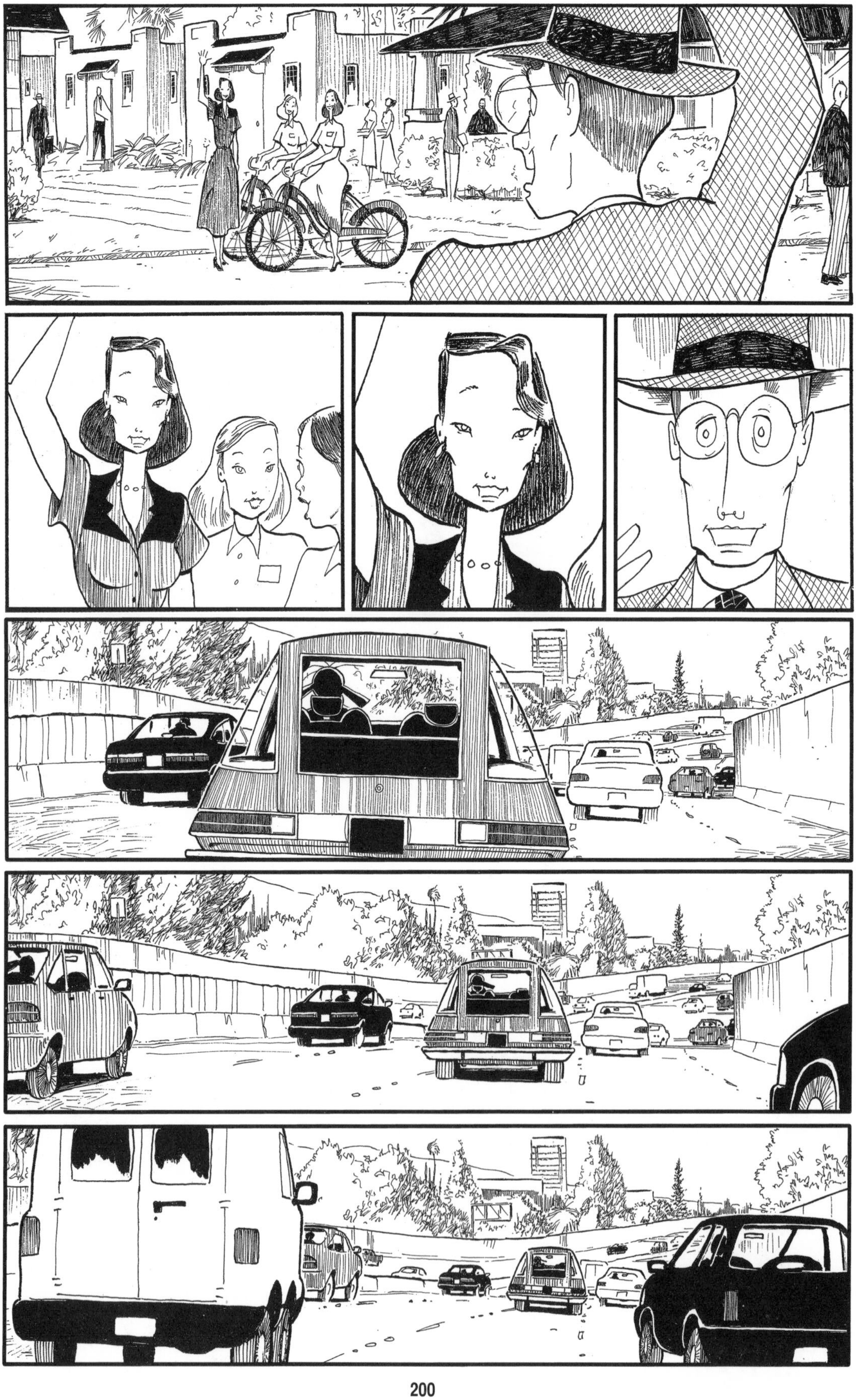

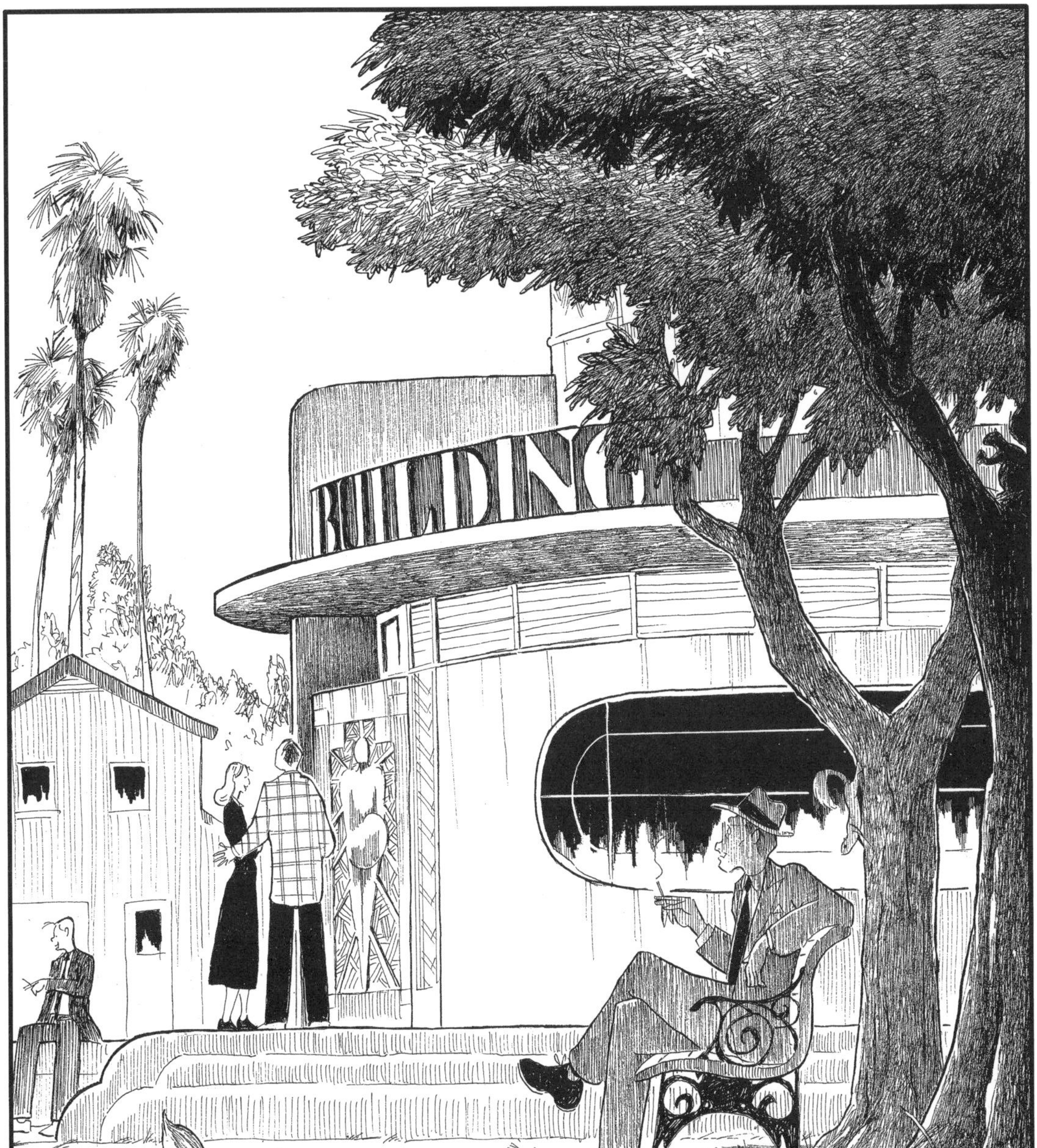
BUILDING

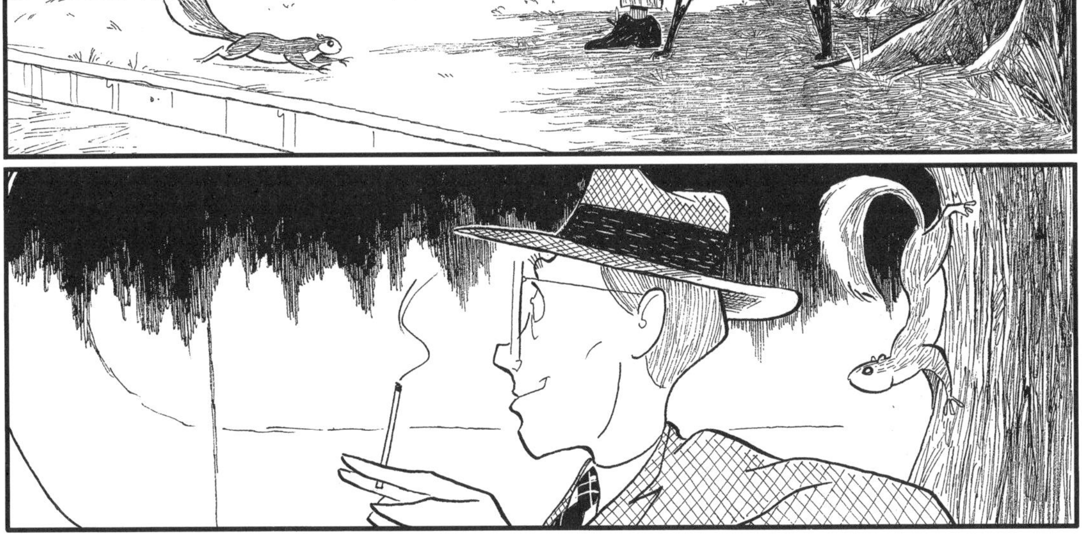

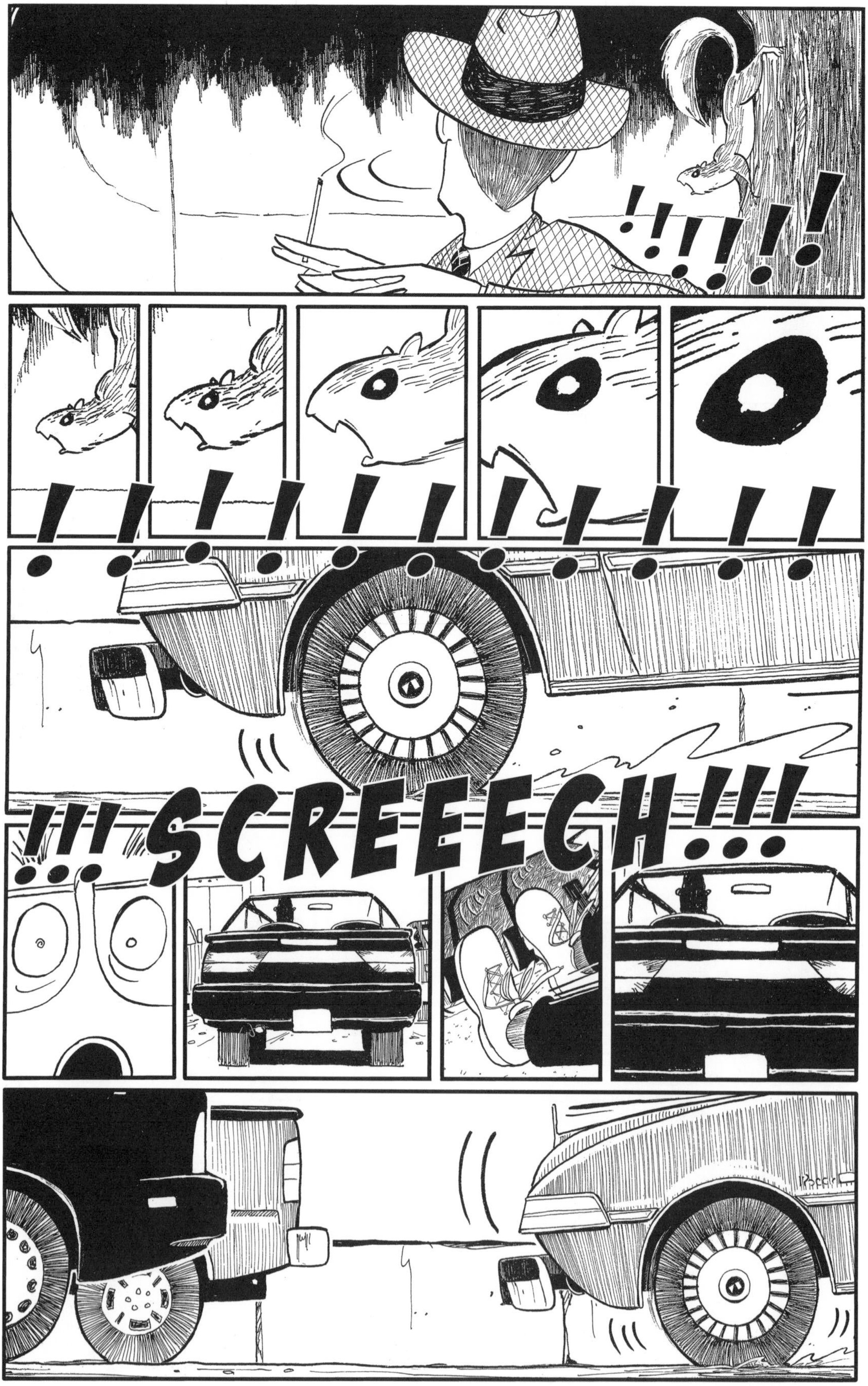
!!!!!!
!!!!!!!!!!!!!!!!!!
!!! SCREEECH!!!

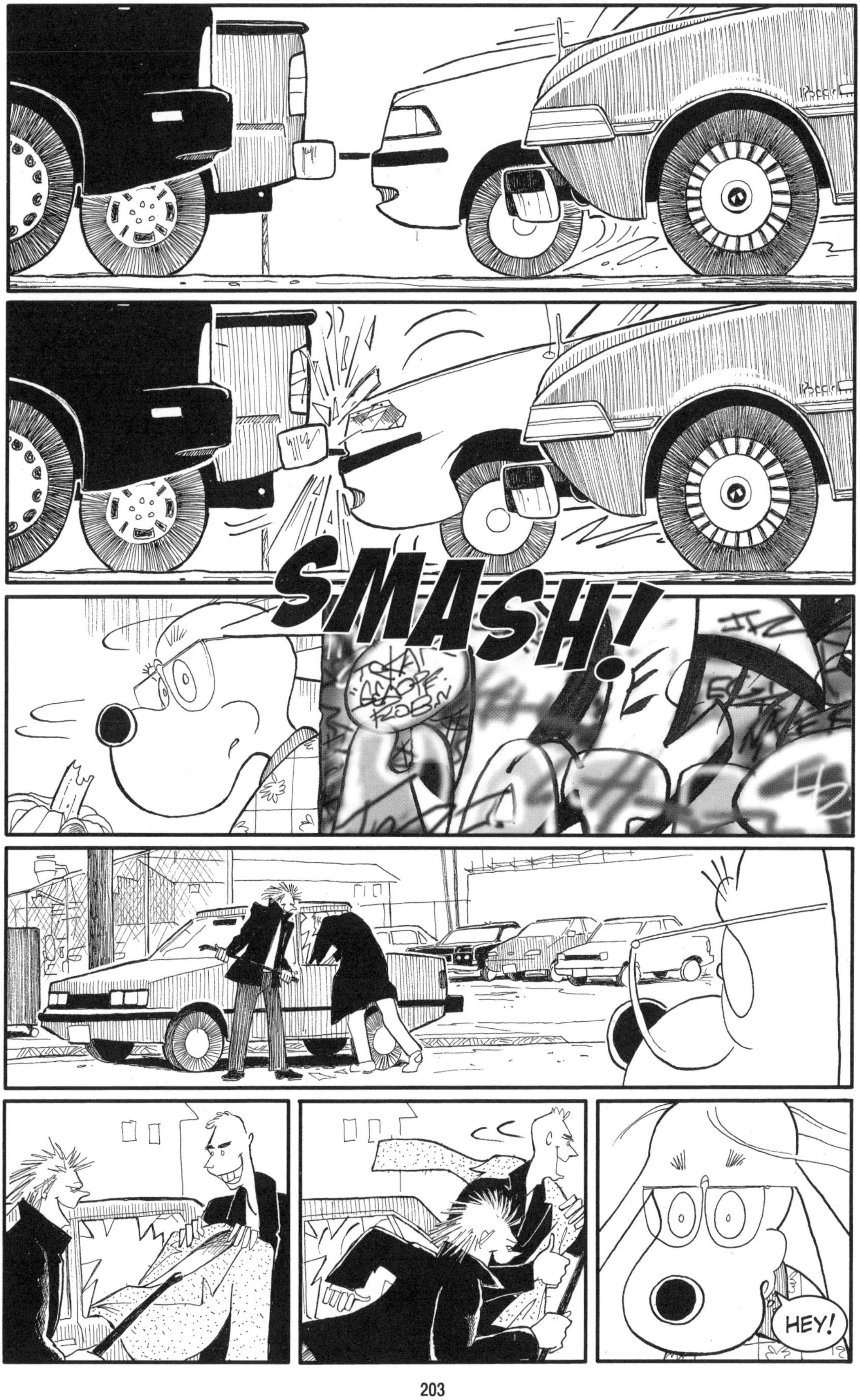
SMASH!
HEY!

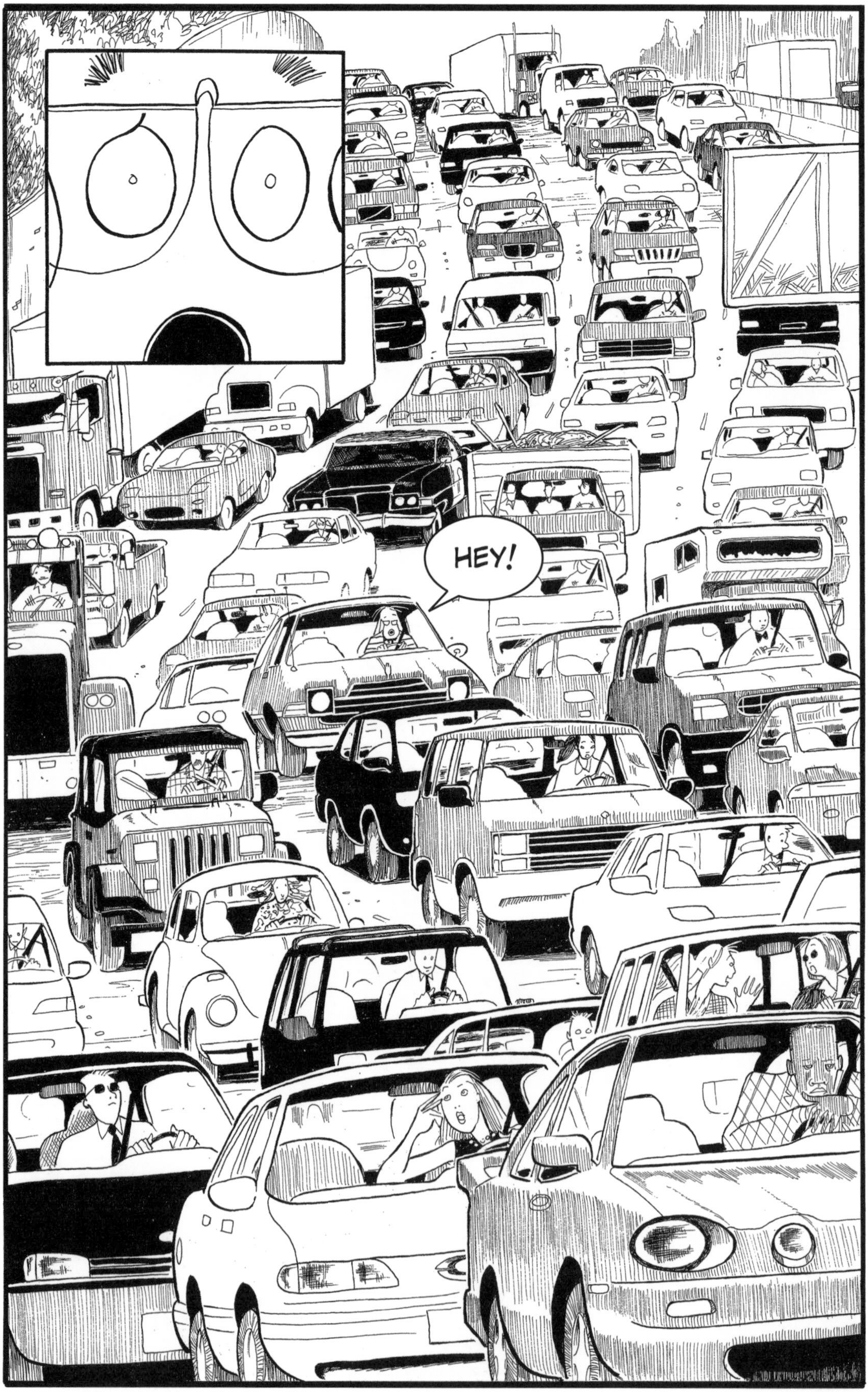
HEY!

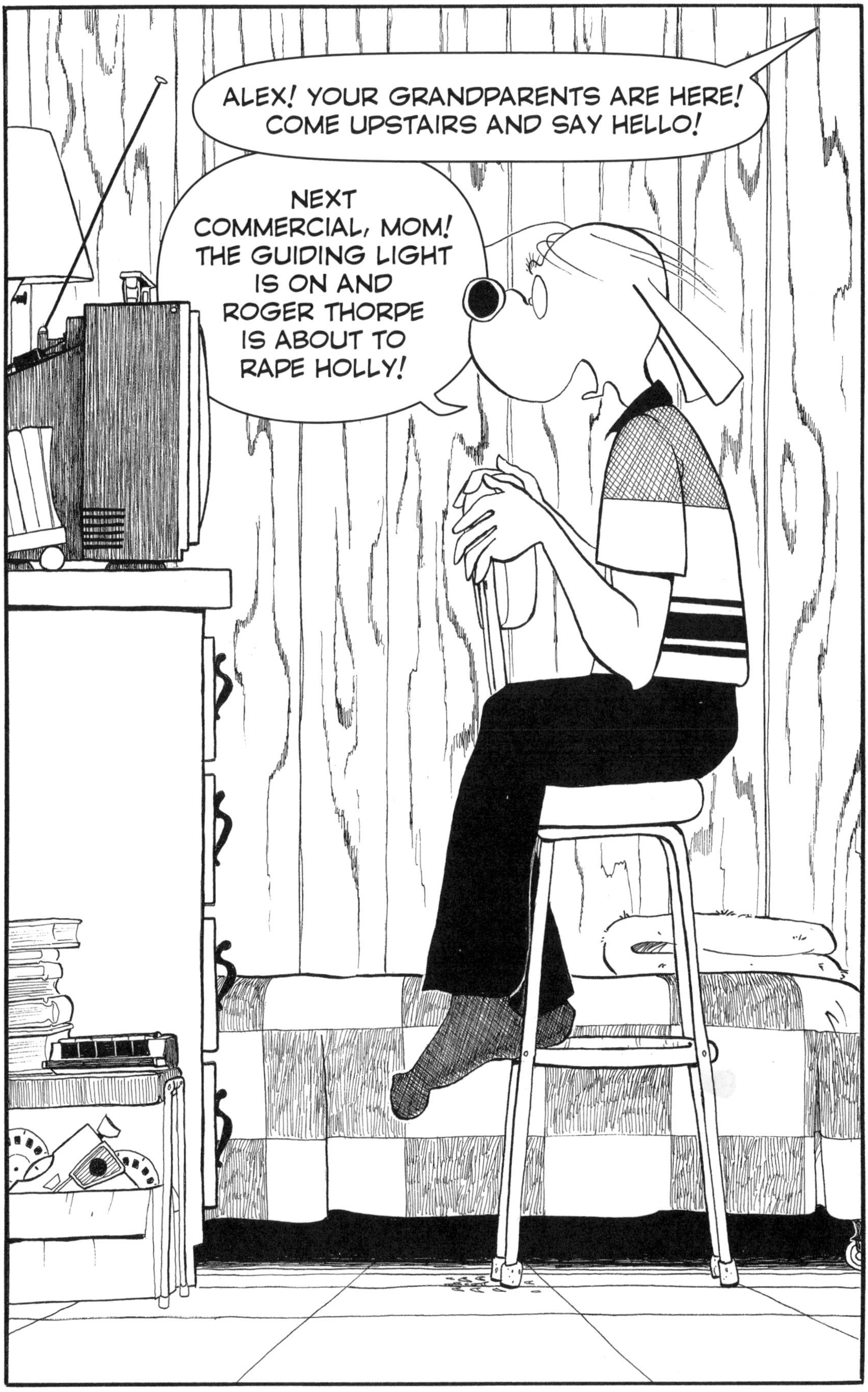
ALEX! YOUR GRANDPARENTS ARE HERE! COME UPSTAIRS AND SAY HELLO!
NEXT COMMERCIAL, MOM! THE GUIDING LIGHT IS ON AND ROGER THORPE IS ABOUT TO RAPE HOLLY!

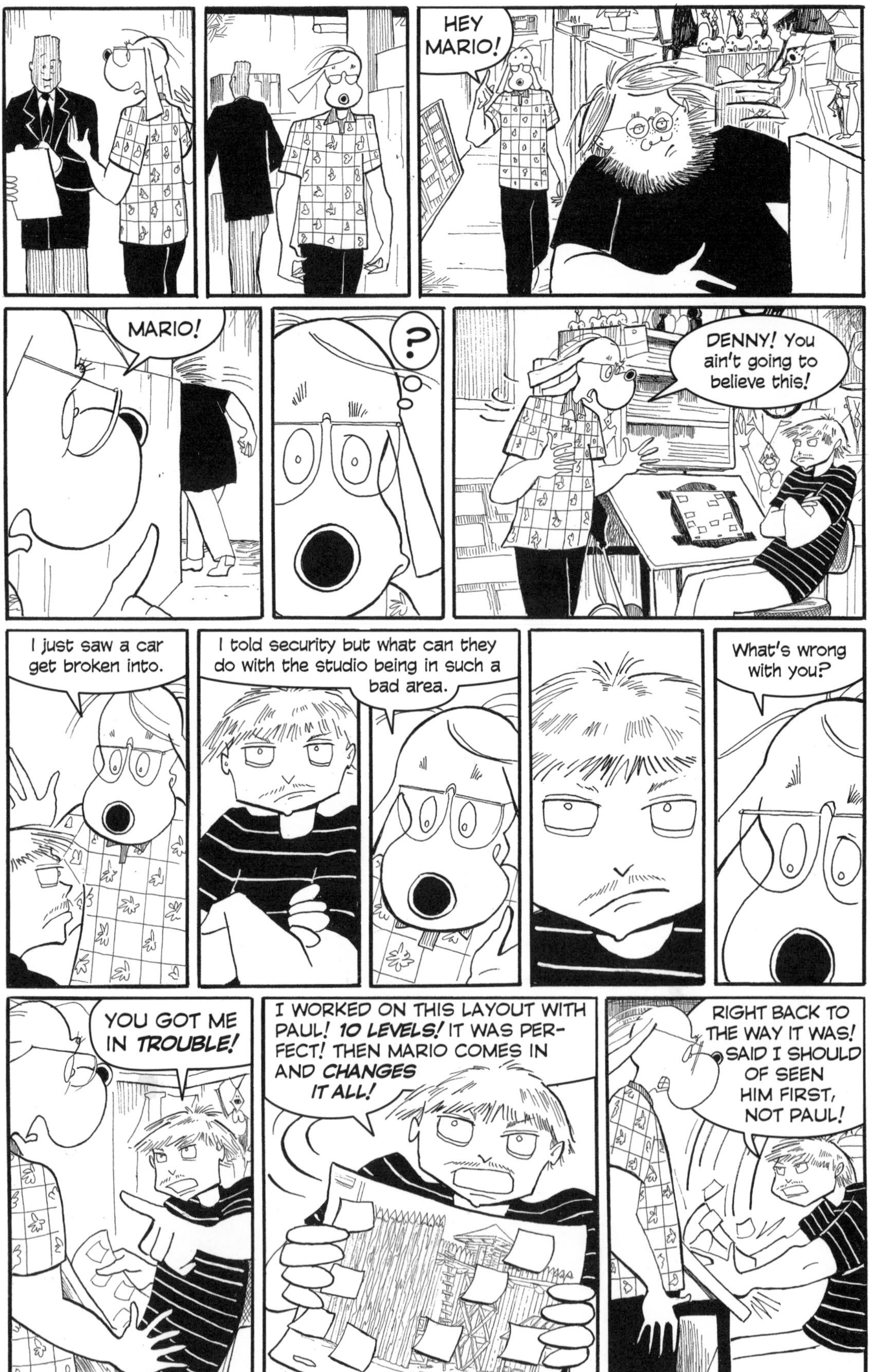
HEY MARIO!
MARIO!
?
DENNY! You ain't going to believe this!
I just saw a car get broken into.
I told security but what can they do with the studio being in such a bad area.
What's wrong with you?
YOU GOT ME IN TROUBLE!
I WORKED ON THIS LAYOUT WITH PAUL! 10 LEVELS! IT WAS PERFECT! THEN MARIO COMES IN AND CHANGES IT ALL!
RIGHT BACK TO THE WAY IT WAS! SAID I SHOULD OF SEEN HIM FIRST, NOT PAUL!

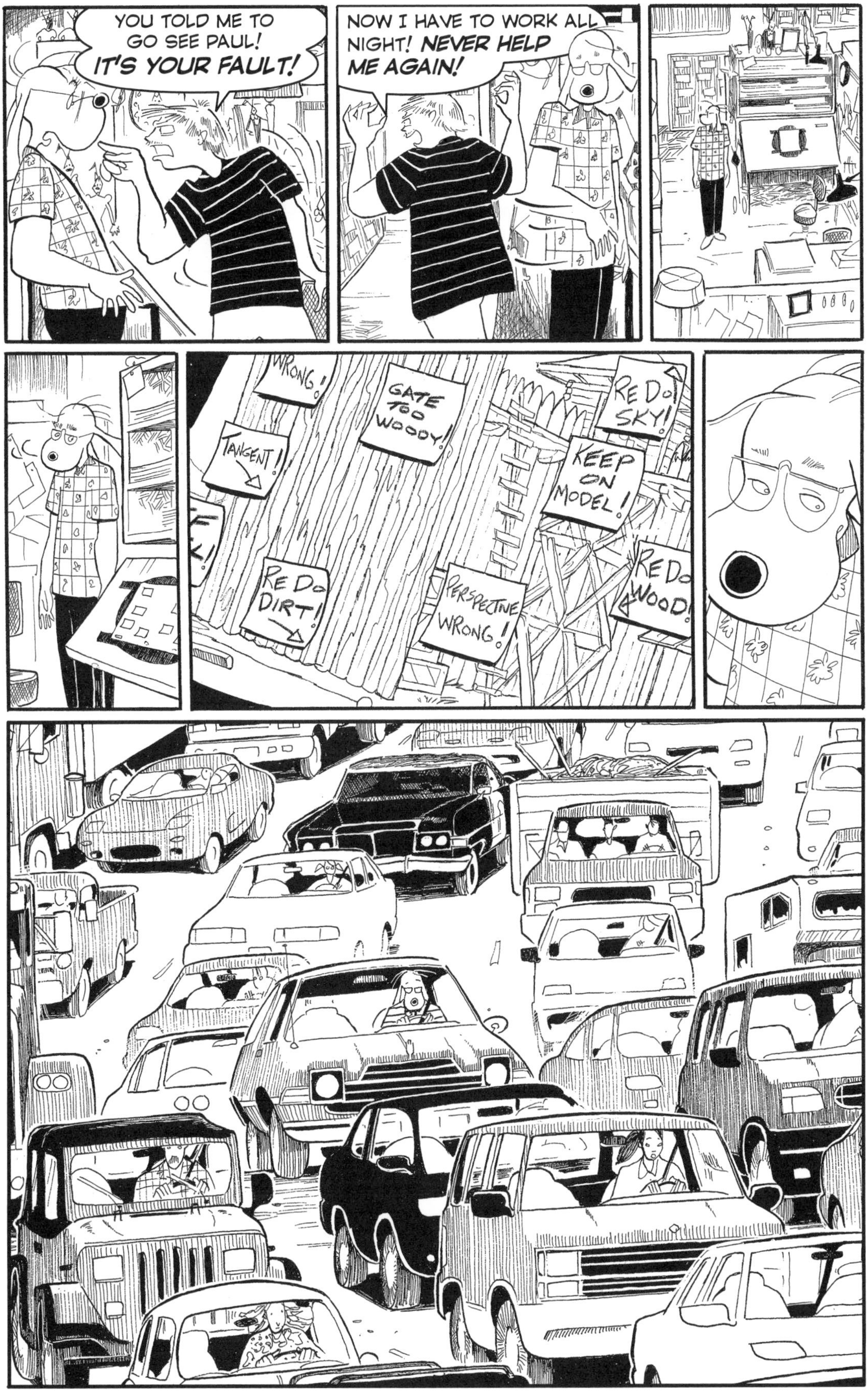
YOU TOLD ME TO GO SEE PAUL! IT'S YOUR FAULT!
NOW I HAVE TO WORK ALL NIGHT! NEVER HELP ME AGAIN!
WRONG!
GATE TOO WOODY!
RE DO SKY!
TANGENT!
KEEP ON MODEL!
RE DO DIRT!
PERSPECTIVE WRONG!
RE DO WOOD!

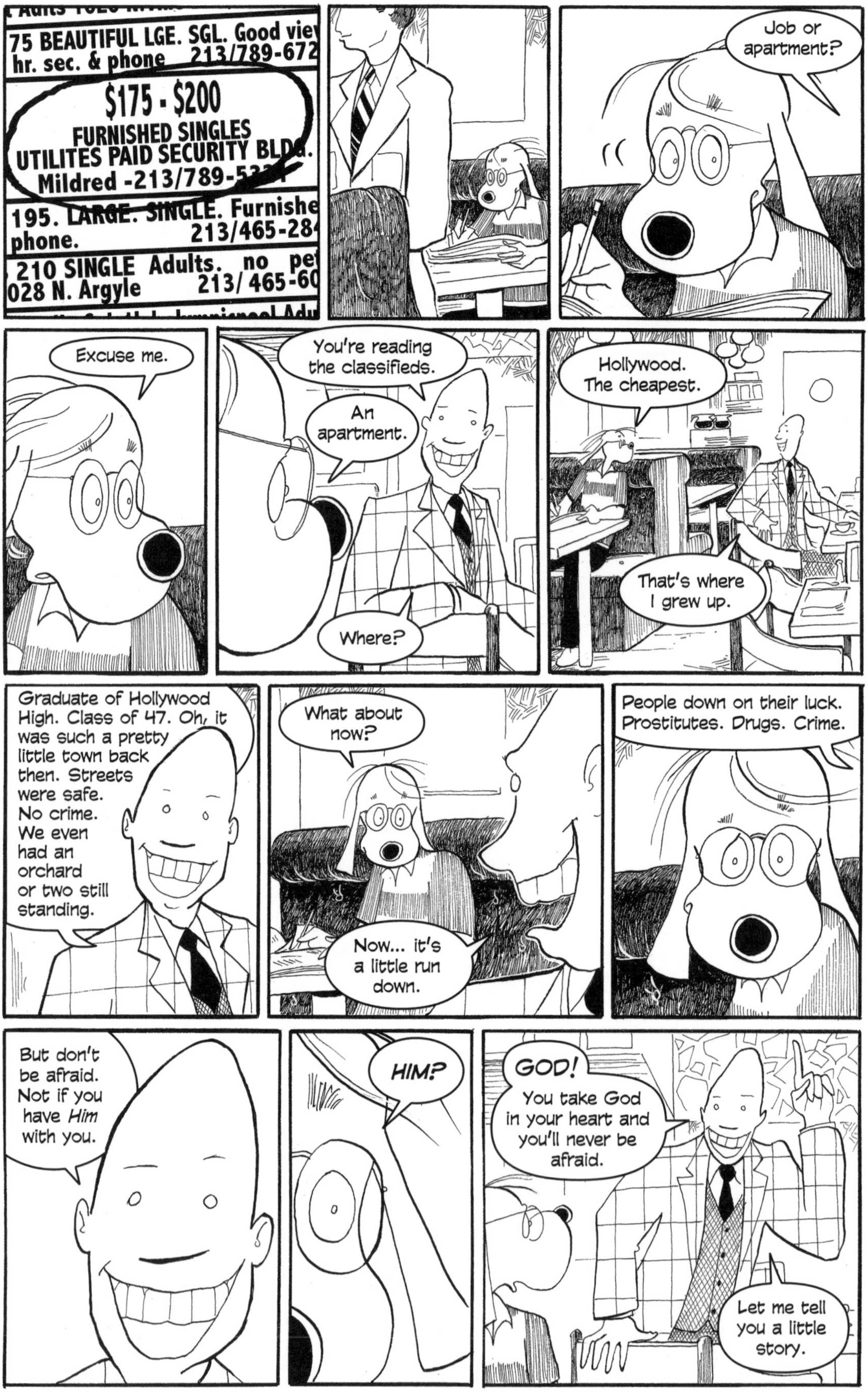
75 BEAUTIFUL LGE. SGL. Good view
hr. sec. & phone 213/789-672
$175 - $200
FURNISHED SINGLES
UTILITES PAID SECURITY BLDG.
Mildred -213/789-5
195. LARGE. SINGLE. Furnishe
phone. 213/465-284
210 SINGLE Adults. no pe
028 N. Argyle 213/ 465-60
Job or apartment?
Excuse me.
You're reading the classifieds.
An apartment.
Where?
Hollywood. The cheapest.
That's where I grew up.
Graduate of Hollywood High. Class of 47. Oh, it was such a pretty little town back then. Streets were safe. No crime. We even had an orchard or two still standing.
What about now?
Now... it's a little run down.
People down on their luck. Prostitutes. Drugs. Crime.
But don't be afraid. Not if you have *Him* with you.
HIM?
GOD!
You take God in your heart and you'll never be afraid.
Let me tell you a little story.

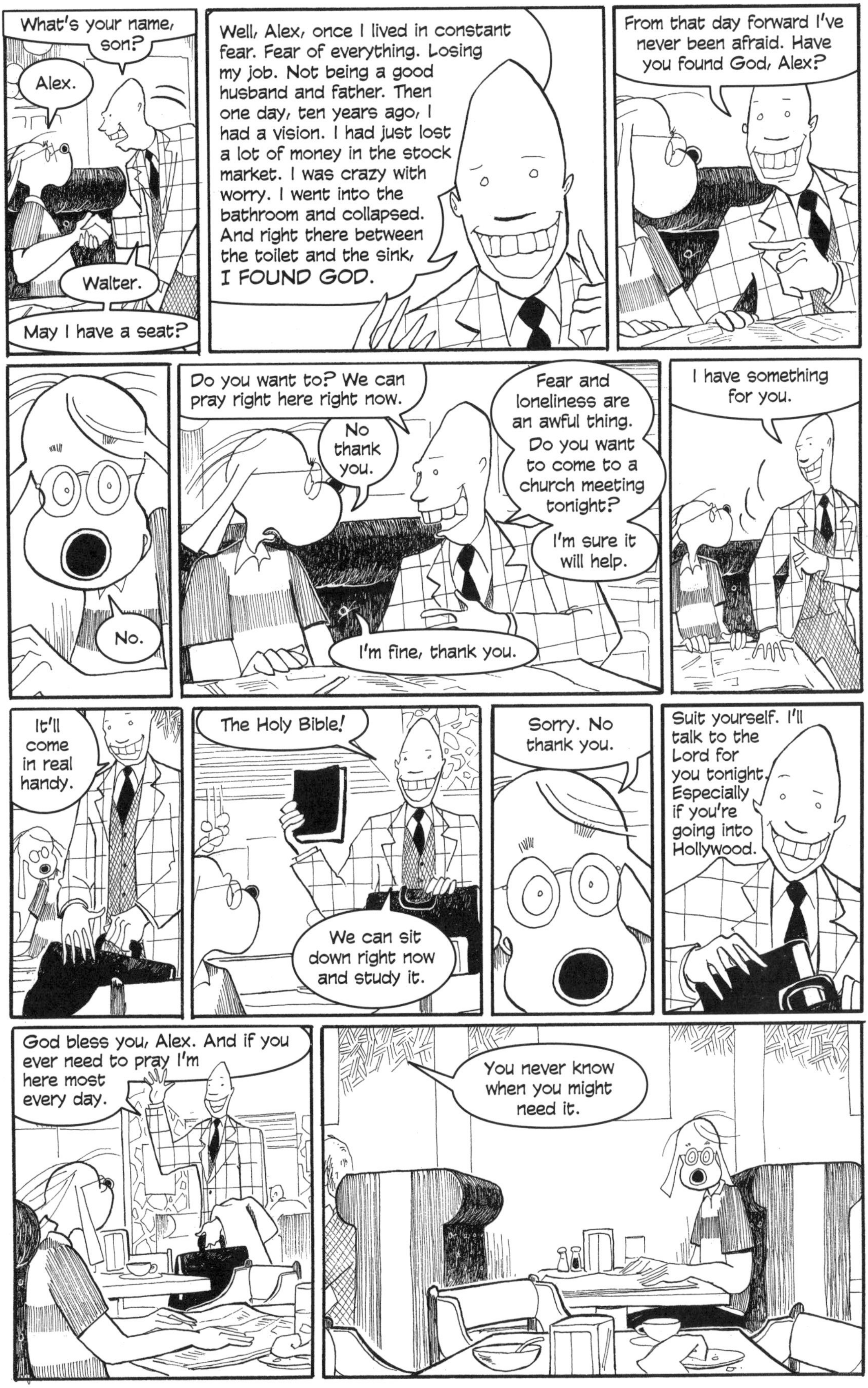

What's your name, son?
Alex.
Walter.
May I have a seat?
Well, Alex, once I lived in constant fear. Fear of everything. Losing my job. Not being a good husband and father. Then one day, ten years ago, I had a vision. I had just lost a lot of money in the stock market. I was crazy with worry. I went into the bathroom and collapsed. And right there between the toilet and the sink, I FOUND GOD.
From that day forward I've never been afraid. Have you found God, Alex?
No.
Do you want to? We can pray right here right now.
No thank you.
Fear and loneliness are an awful thing.
Do you want to come to a church meeting tonight?
I'm sure it will help.
I'm fine, thank you.
I have something for you.
It'll come in real handy.
The Holy Bible!
We can sit down right now and study it.
Sorry. No thank you.
Suit yourself. I'll talk to the Lord for you tonight. Especially if you're going into Hollywood.
God bless you, Alex. And if you ever need to pray I'm here most every day.
You never know when you might need it.

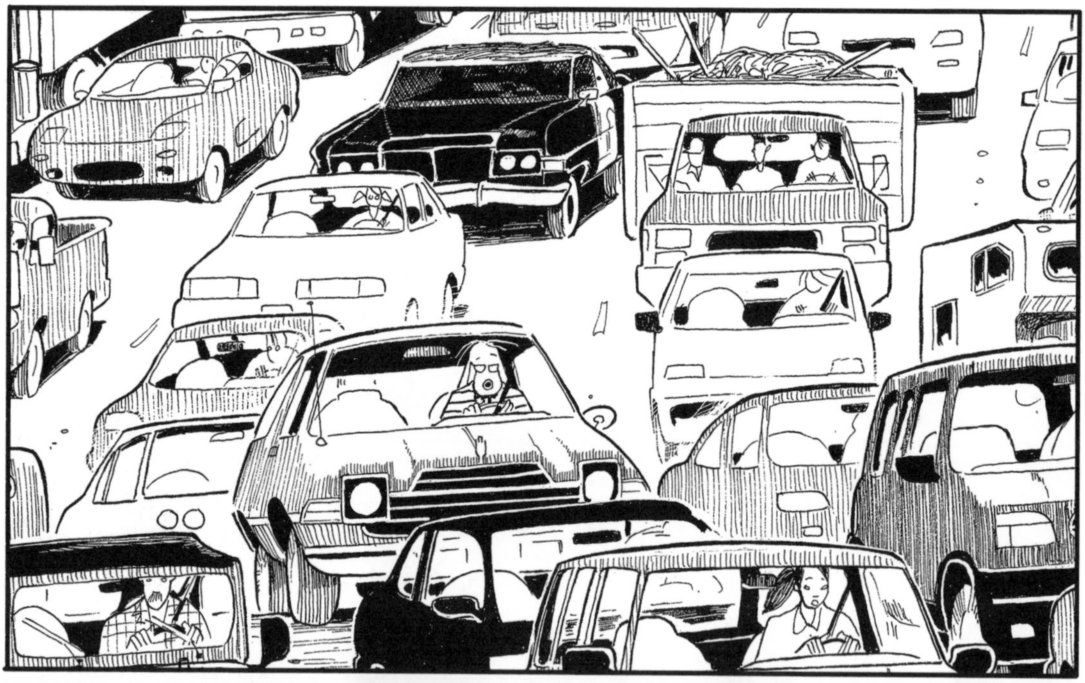

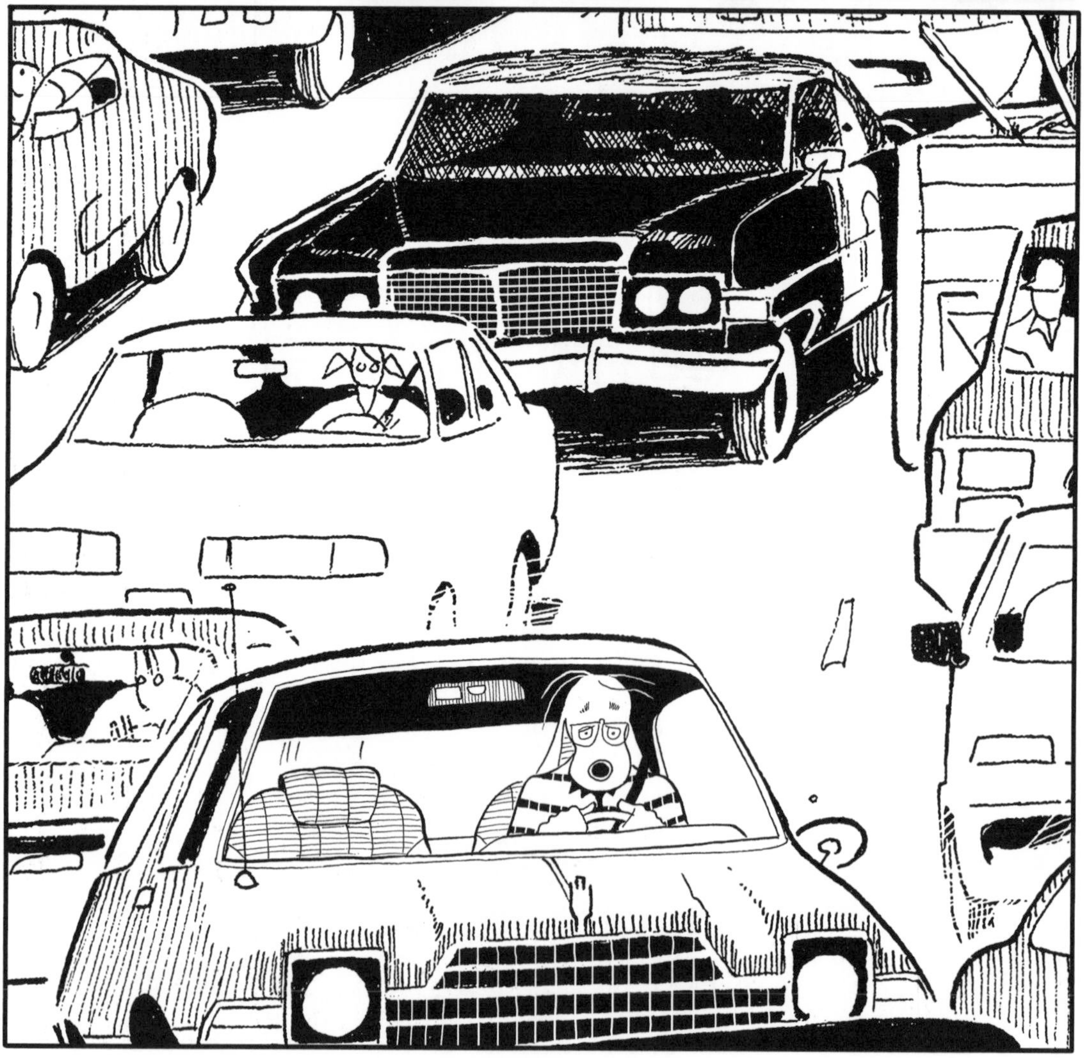

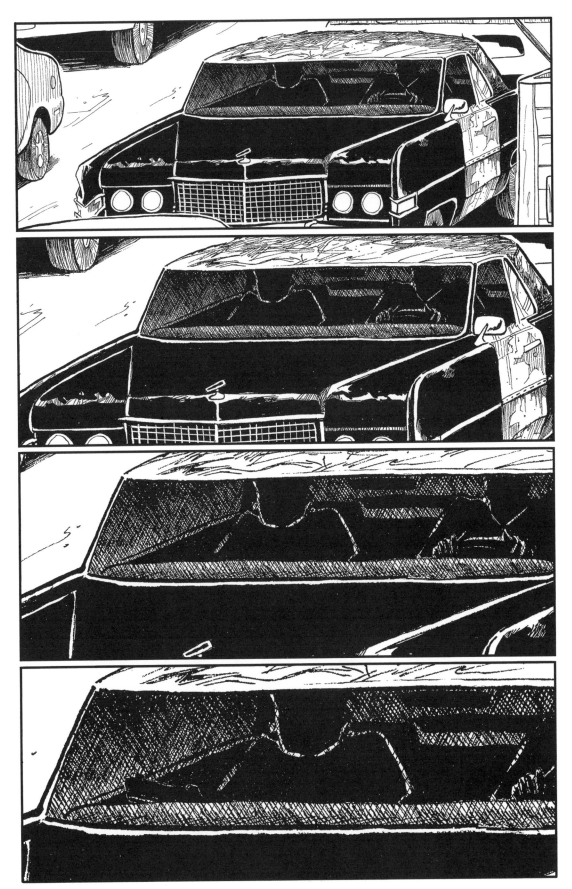

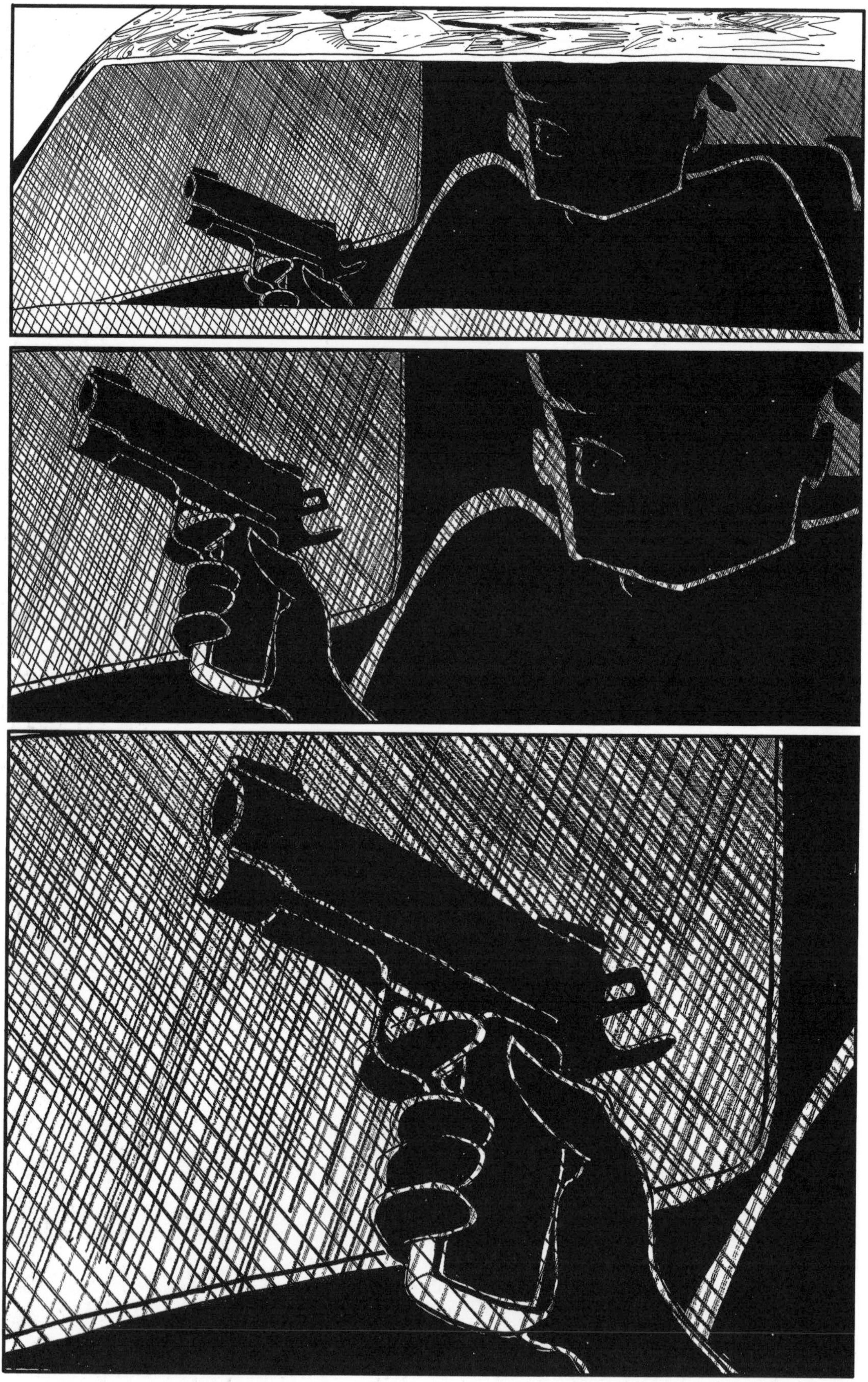

CHAPTER 5

SAN FERNANDO VALLEY

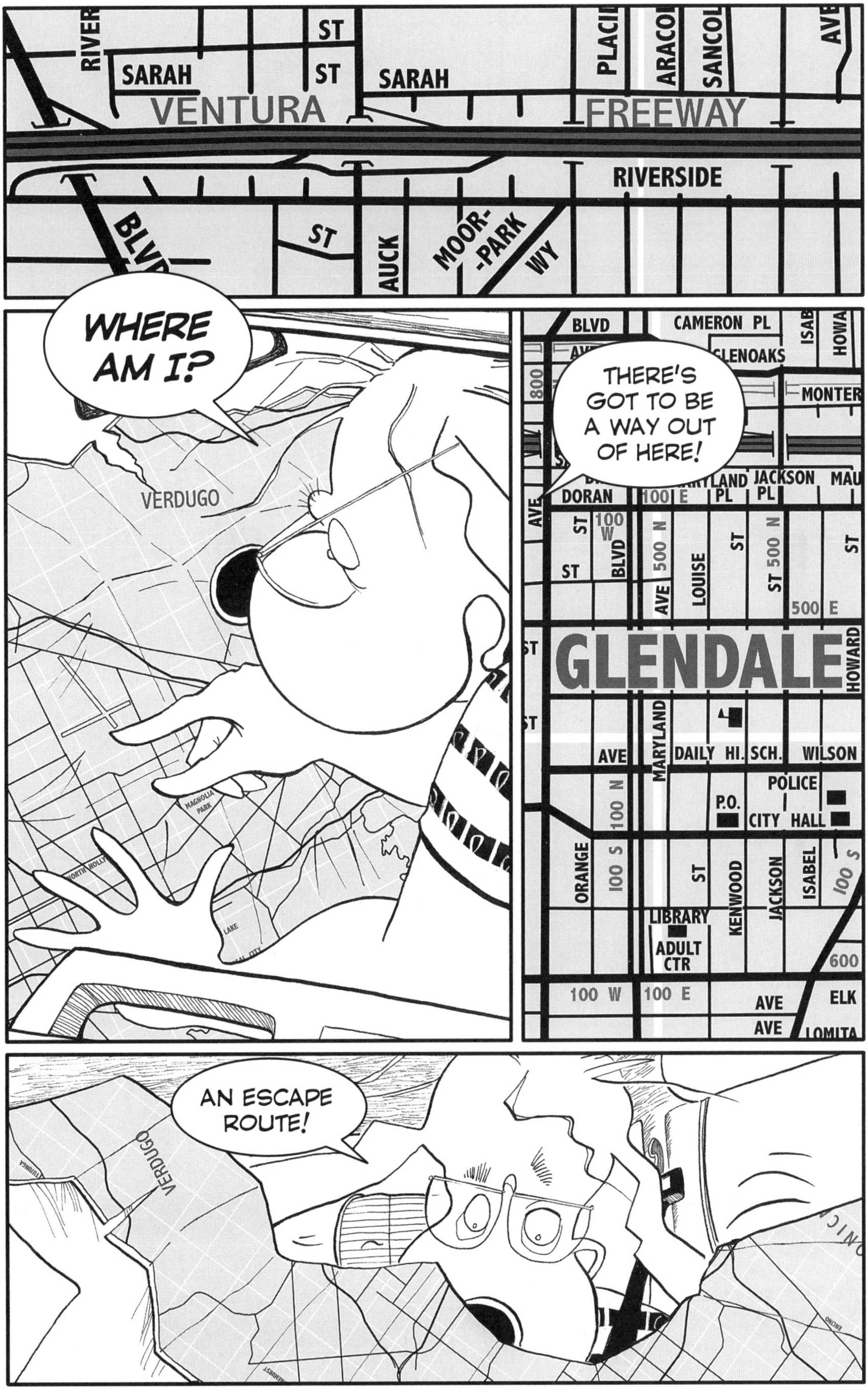
RIVER
SARAH
ST
ST
SARAH
PLACI
ARACO
SANCO
AVE
VENTURA
FREEWAY
RIVERSIDE
BLVD
ST
AUCK
MOOR-
-PARK
WY
WHERE AM I?
VERDUGO
MAGNOLIA PARK
NORTH HOLLY
LAKE
BLVD
CAMERON PL
GLENOAKS
MONTER
THERE'S GOT TO BE A WAY OUT OF HERE!
800
AVE
DORAN
MARYLAND PL
JACKSON PL
100 E
100 W
ST
BLVD
500 N
LOUISE
500 E
GLENDALE
HOWARD
MARYLAND
AVE
DAILY HI. SCH.
WILSON
POLICE
P.O.
CITY HALL
100 N
ORANGE
100 S
KENWOOD
JACKSON
ISABEL
LIBRARY
ADULT CTR
600
100 W
100 E
AVE
ELK
LOMITA
AN ESCAPE ROUTE!
VERDUGO

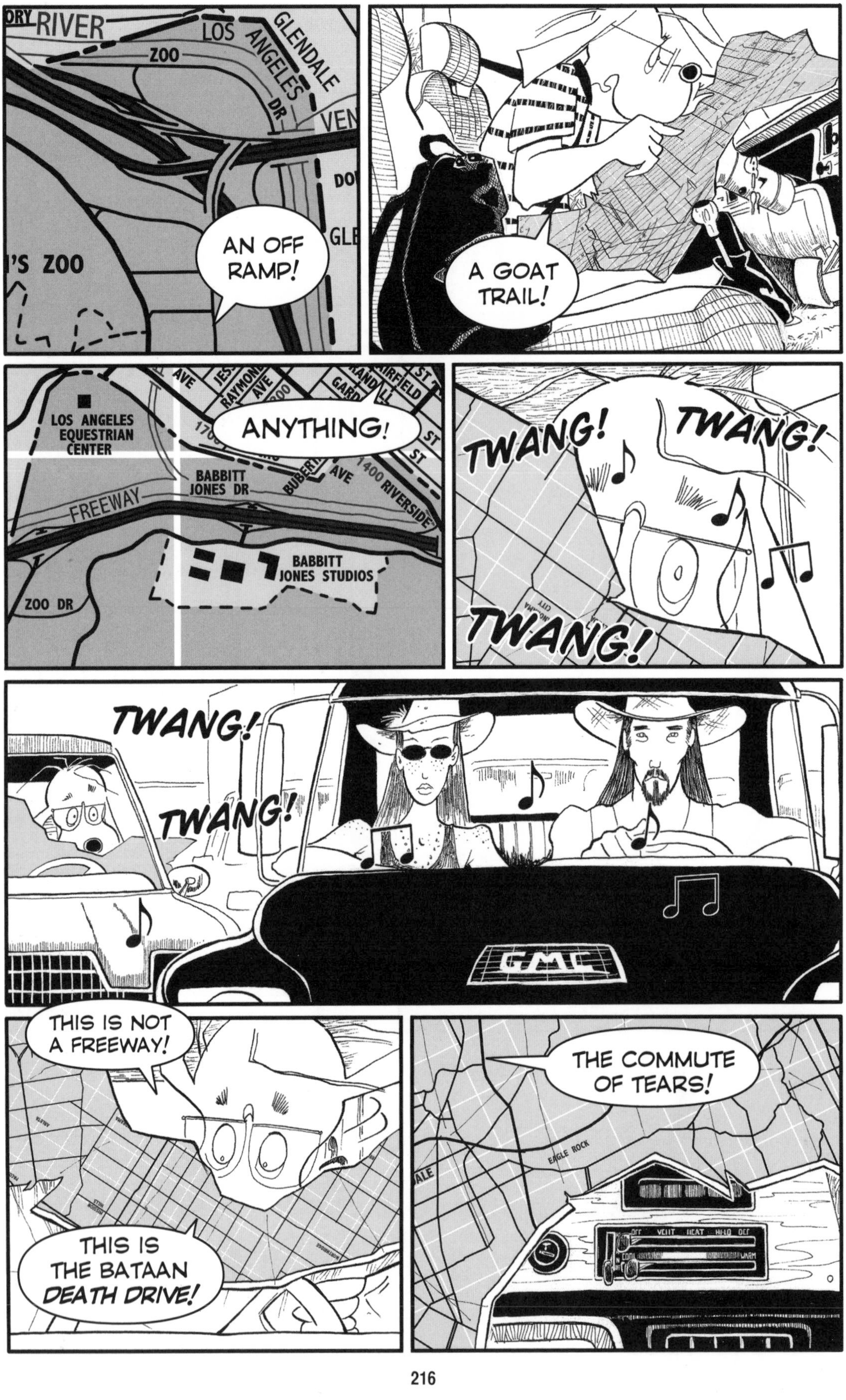
RIVER
LOS ANGELES DR
GLENDALE
ZOO
AN OFF RAMP!
A GOAT TRAIL!
LOS ANGELES EQUESTRIAN CENTER
ANYTHING!
BABBITT JONES DR
FREEWAY
RIVERSIDE
BABBITT JONES STUDIOS
ZOO DR
TWANG!
TWANG!
TWANG!
TWANG!
TWANG!
GMC
THIS IS NOT A FREEWAY!
THIS IS THE BATAAN *DEATH DRIVE!*
THE COMMUTE OF TEARS!
EAGLE ROCK

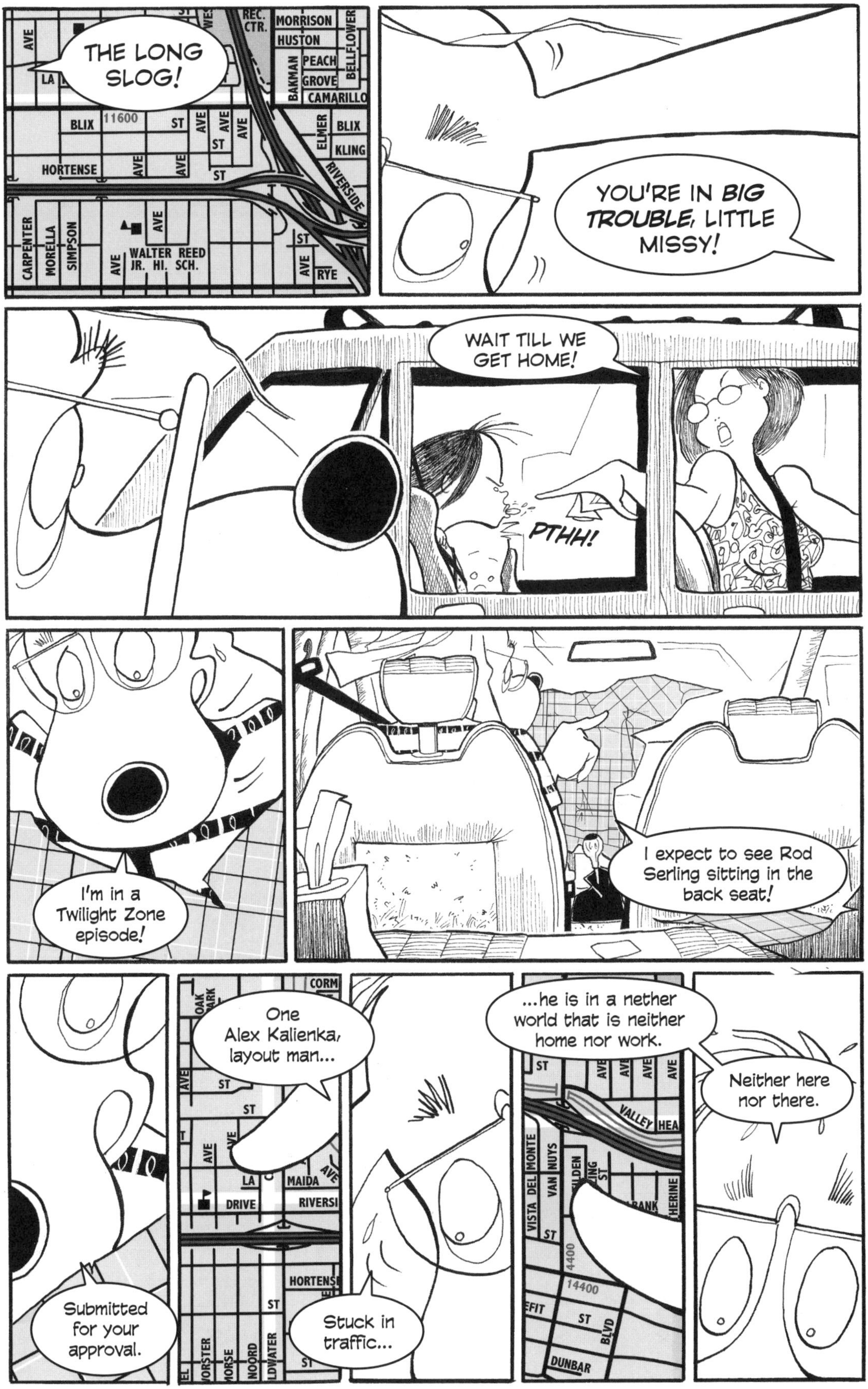
THE LONG SLOG!
REC. CTR.
MORRISON
HUSTON
PEACH
GROVE
CAMARILLO
BAKMAN
BELLFLOWER
BLIX
11600
HORTENSE
ELMER
KLING
RIVERSIDE
CARPENTER
MORELLA
SIMPSON
WALTER REED JR. HI. SCH.
RYE
YOU'RE IN *BIG TROUBLE*, LITTLE MISSY!
WAIT TILL WE GET HOME!
PTHH!
I'm in a Twilight Zone episode!
I expect to see Rod Serling sitting in the back seat!
Submitted for your approval.
One Alex Kalienka, layout man...
MAIDA
DRIVE
HORTENSE
NOORD
Stuck in traffic...
...he is in a nether world that is neither home nor work.
VALLEY
VISTA DEL MONTE
VAN NUYS
14400
DUNBAR
Neither here nor there.

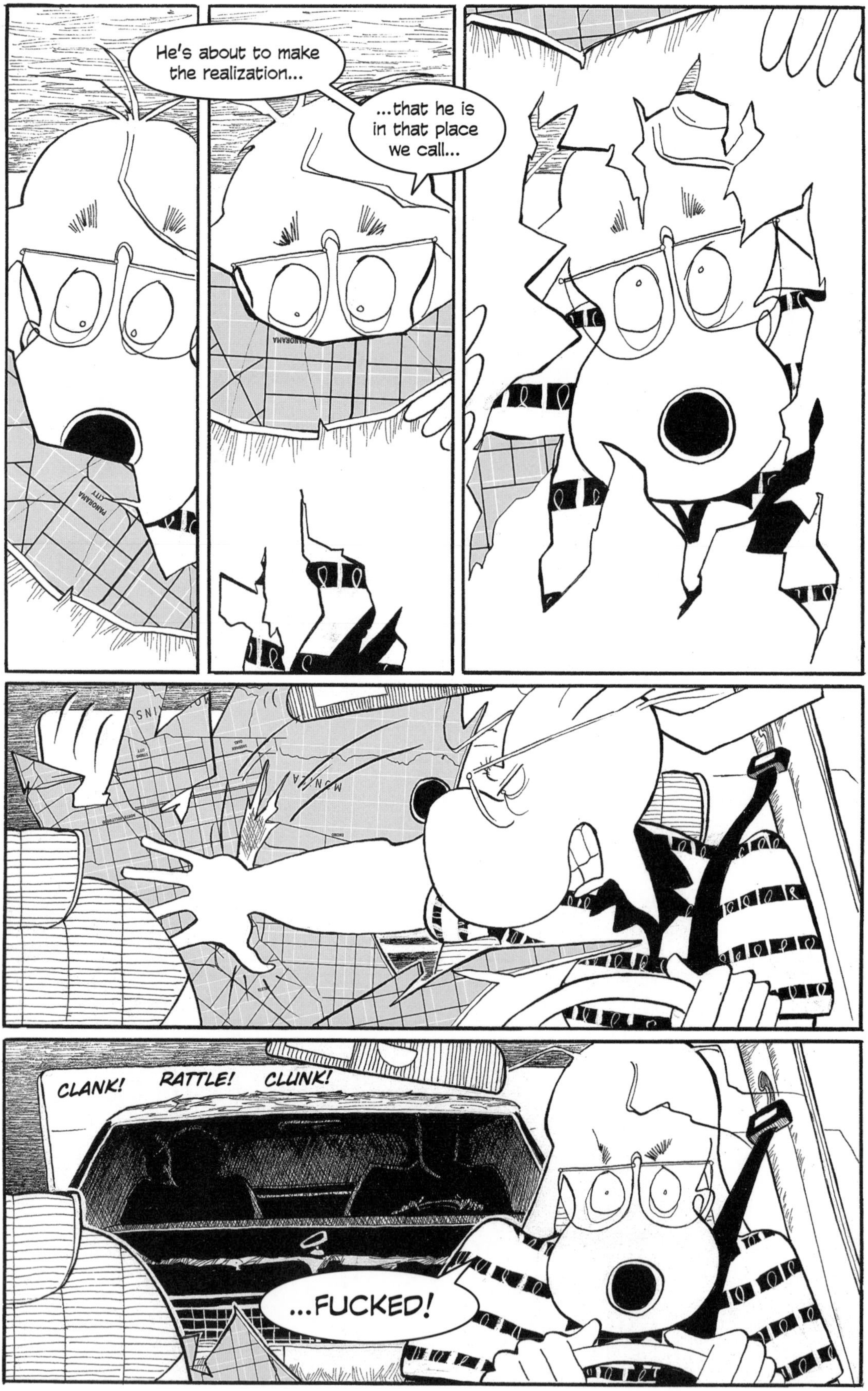
He's about to make the realization...
...that he is in that place we call...
CLANK!
RATTLE!
CLUNK!
...FUCKED!

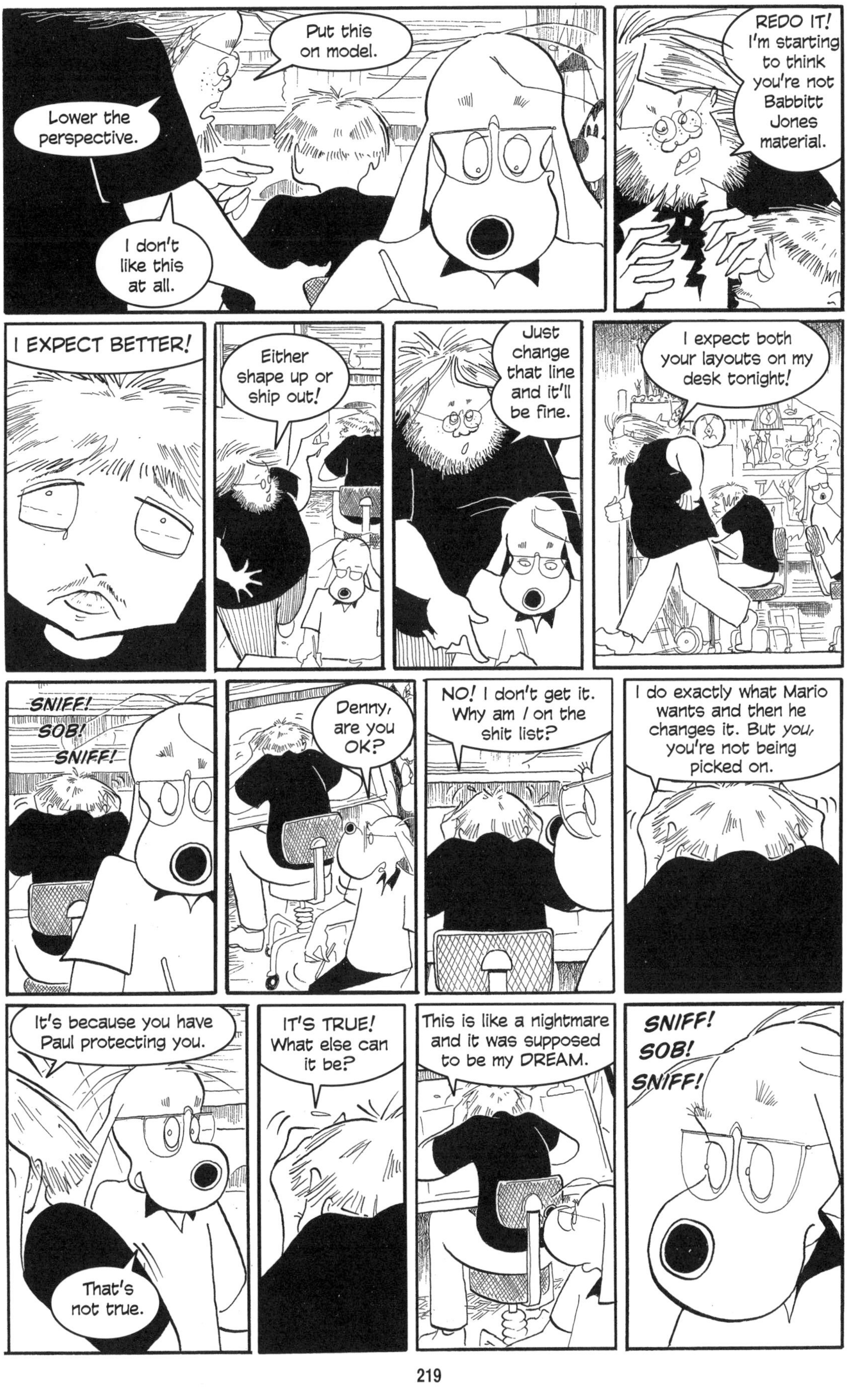
Put this on model.
Lower the perspective.
I don't like this at all.
REDO IT! I'm starting to think you're not Babbitt Jones material.
I EXPECT BETTER!
Either shape up or ship out!
Just change that line and it'll be fine.
I expect both your layouts on my desk tonight!
SNIFF! SOB! SNIFF!
Denny, are you OK?
NO! I don't get it. Why am I on the shit list?
I do exactly what Mario wants and then he changes it. But you, you're not being picked on.
It's because you have Paul protecting you.
That's not true.
IT'S TRUE! What else can it be?
This is like a nightmare and it was supposed to be my DREAM.
SNIFF! SOB! SNIFF!

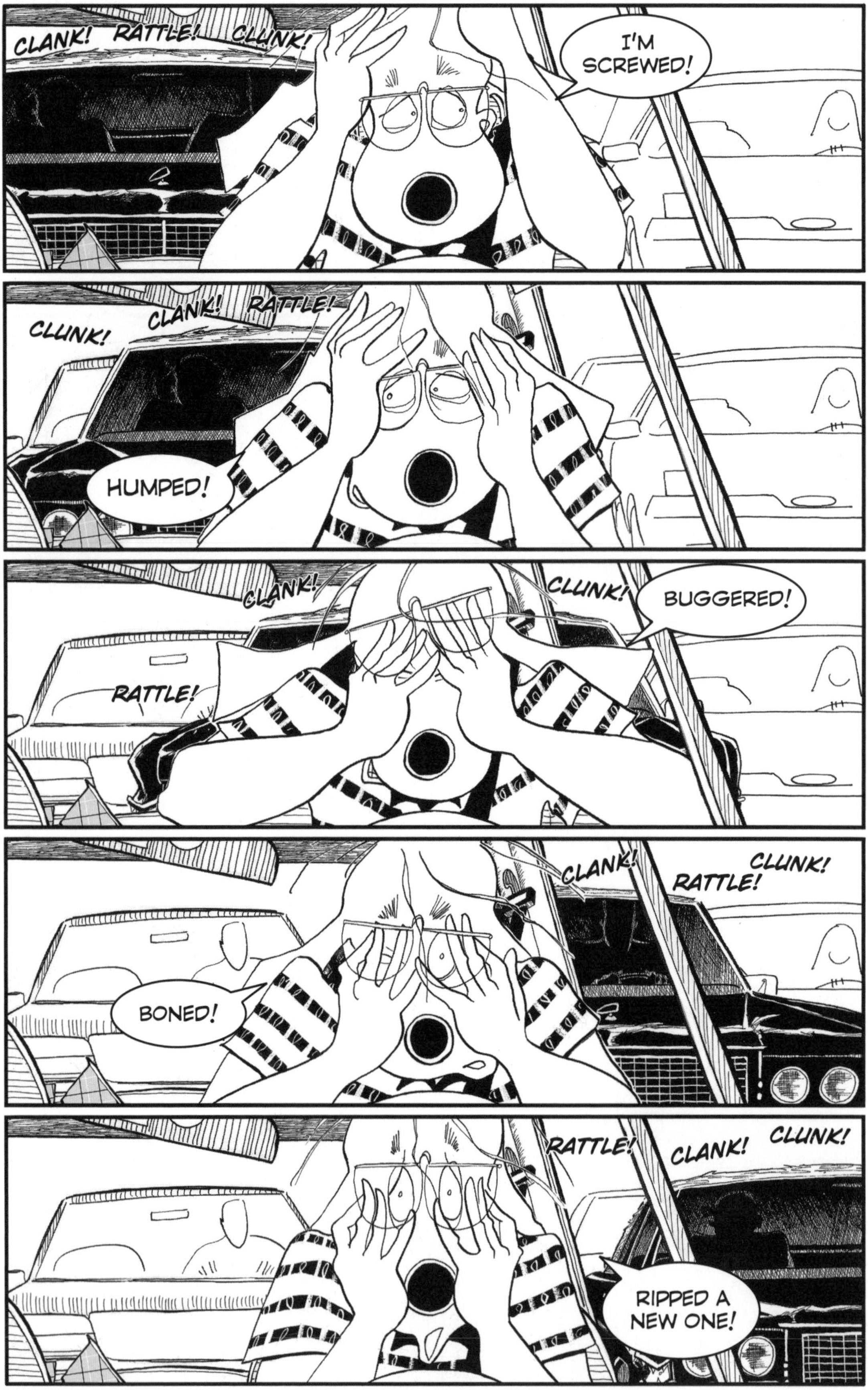
CLANK! RATTLE! CLUNK!
I'M SCREWED!
CLUNK! CLANK! RATTLE!
HUMPED!
CLANK! CLUNK!
BUGGERED!
RATTLE!
CLANK! CLUNK! RATTLE!
BONED!
RATTLE! CLANK! CLUNK!
RIPPED A NEW ONE!

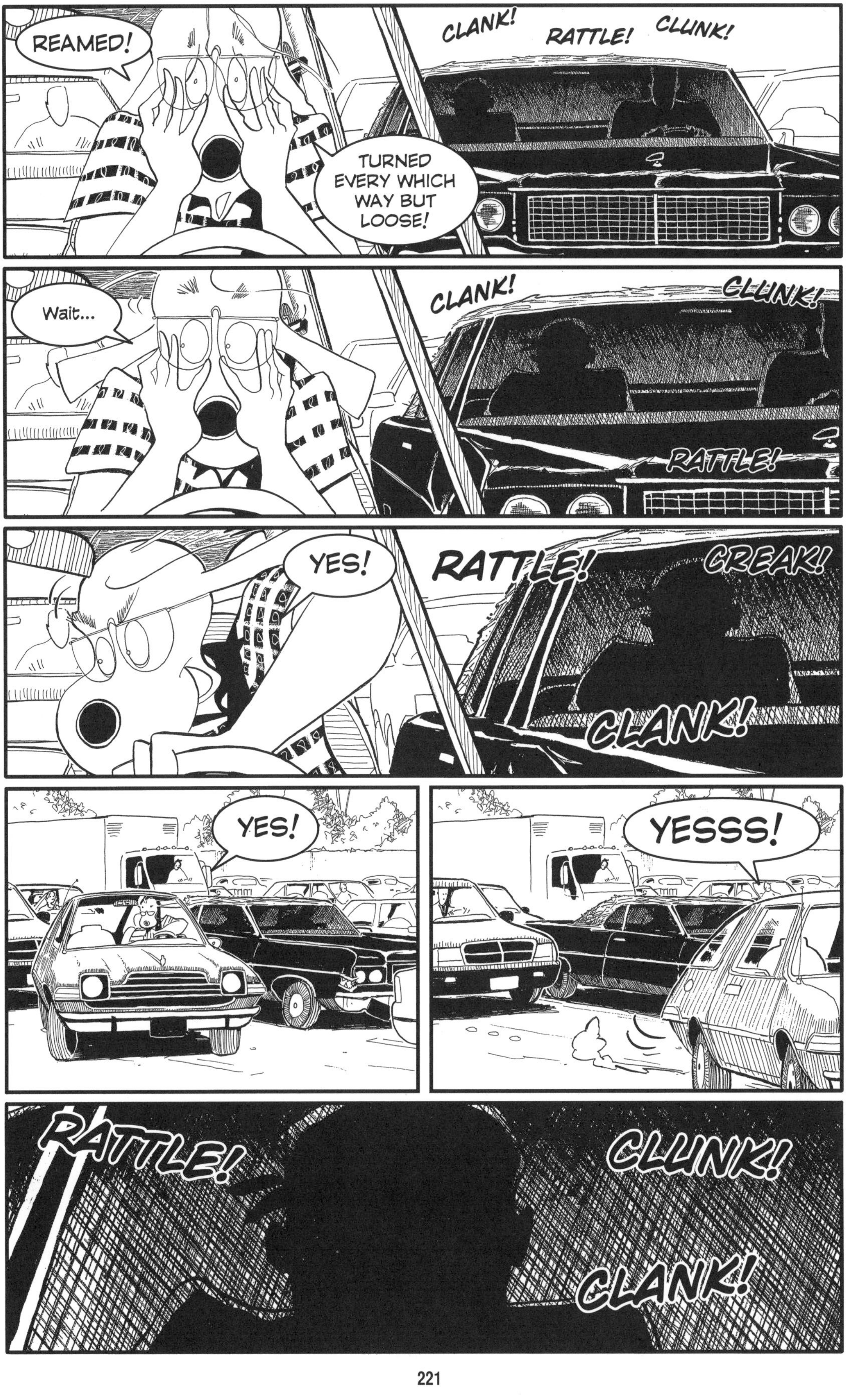
REAMED!
TURNED EVERY WHICH WAY BUT LOOSE!
CLANK!
RATTLE!
CLUNK!
Wait...
CLANK!
CLUNK!
RATTLE!
YES!
RATTLE!
CREAK!
CLANK!
YES!
YESSS!
RATTLE!
CLUNK!
CLANK!

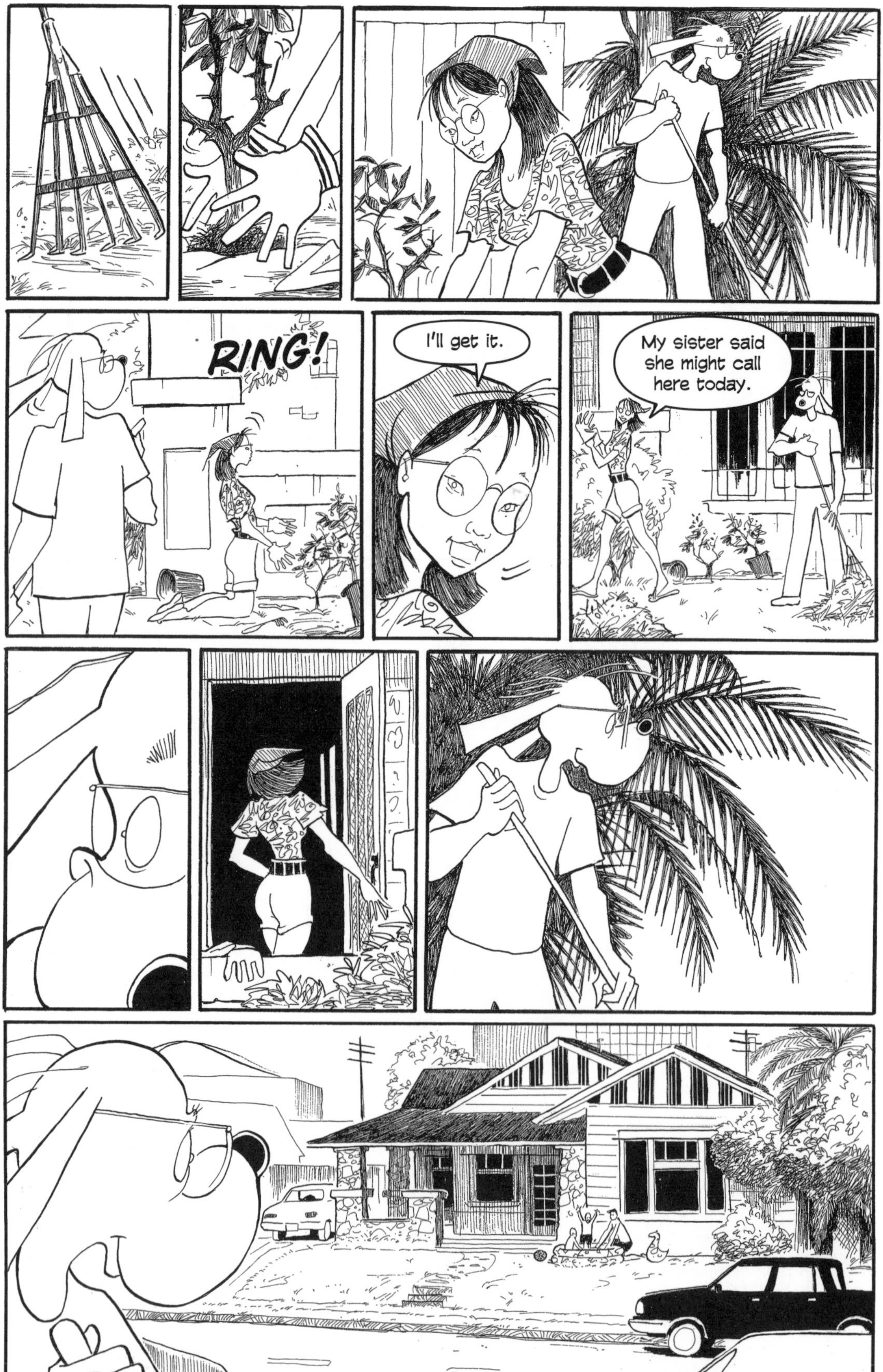
RING!
I'll get it.
My sister said she might call here today.

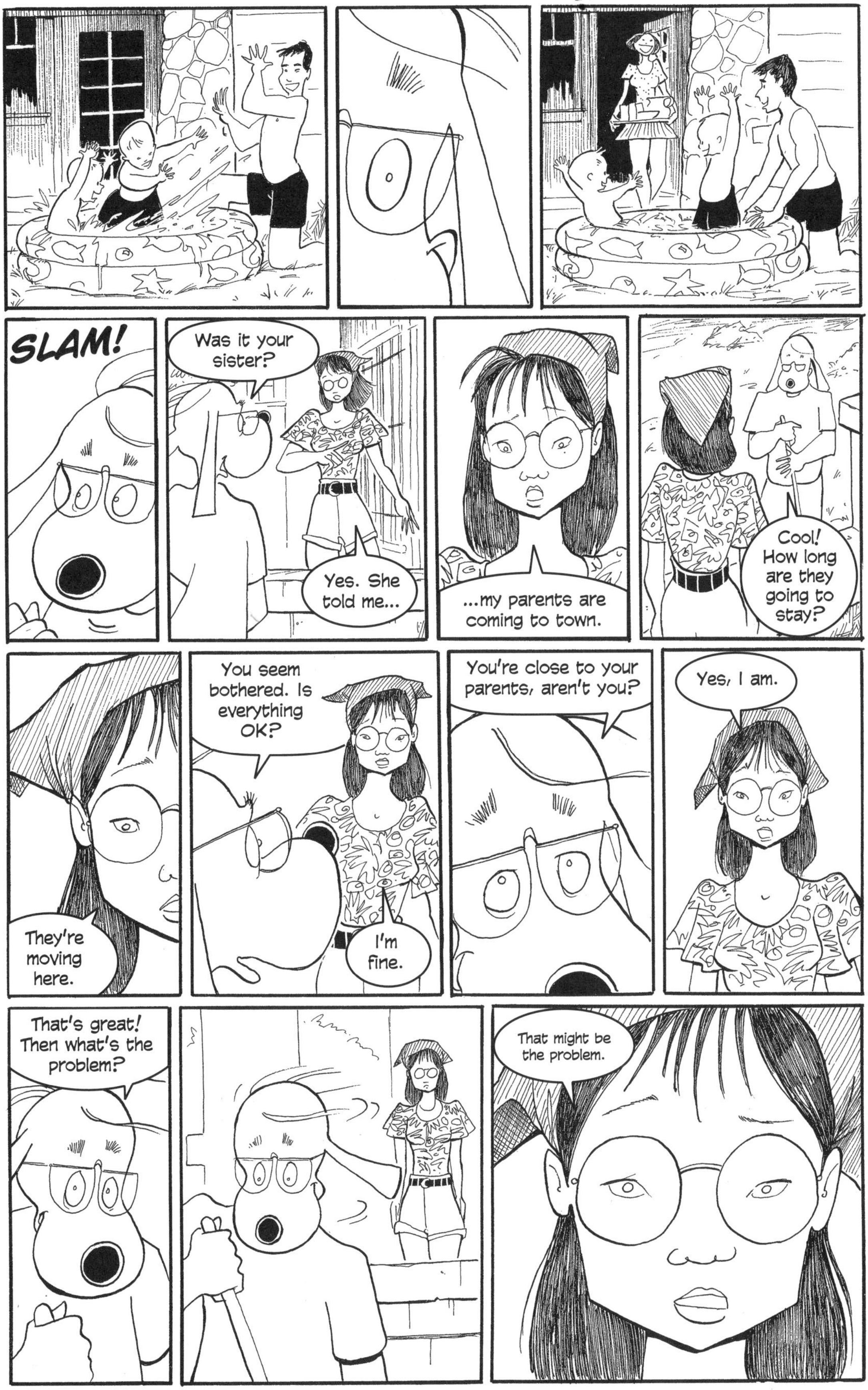
SLAM!
Was it your sister?
Yes. She told me...
...my parents are coming to town.
Cool! How long are they going to stay?
They're moving here.
You seem bothered. Is everything OK?
I'm fine.
You're close to your parents, aren't you?
Yes, I am.
That's great! Then what's the problem?
That might be the problem.

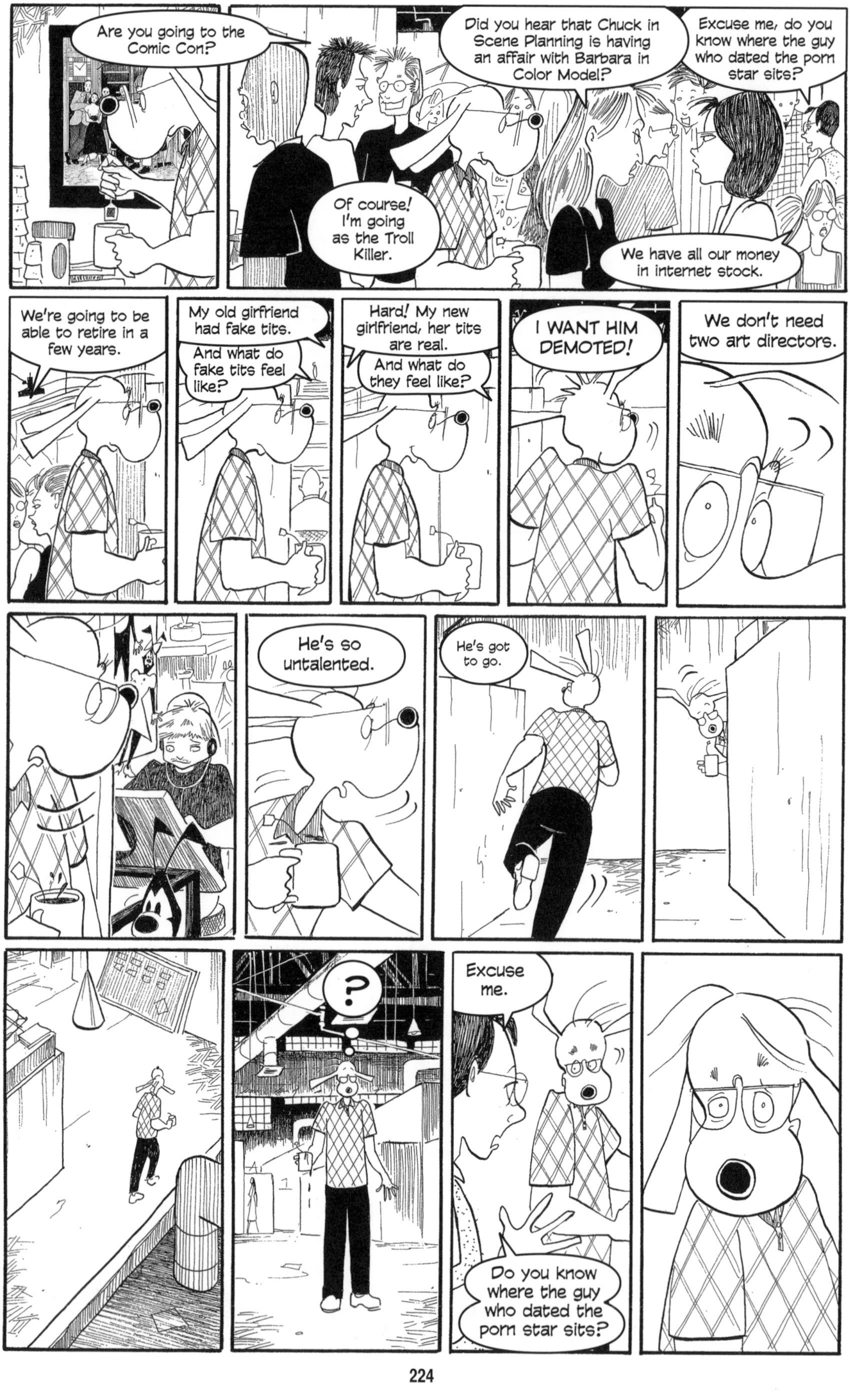
Are you going to the Comic Con?
Did you hear that Chuck in Scene Planning is having an affair with Barbara in Color Model?
Excuse me, do you know where the guy who dated the porn star sits?
Of course! I'm going as the Troll Killer.
We have all our money in internet stock.
We're going to be able to retire in a few years.
My old girfriend had fake tits.
And what do fake tits feel like?
Hard! My new girlfriend, her tits are real.
And what do they feel like?
I WANT HIM DEMOTED!
We don't need two art directors.
He's so untalented.
He's got to go.
?
Excuse me.
Do you know where the guy who dated the porn star sits?

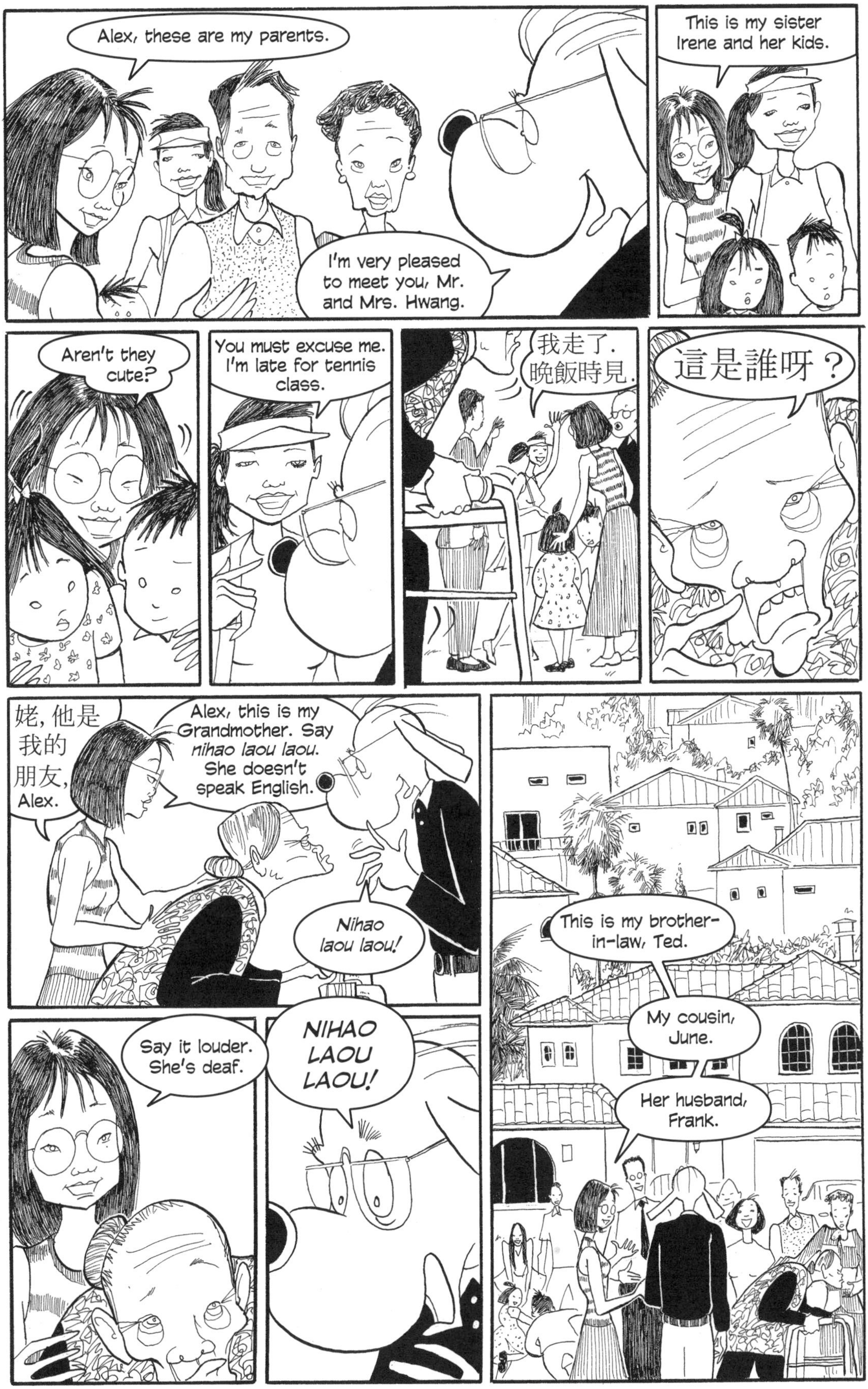

Alex, these are my parents.
I'm very pleased to meet you, Mr. and Mrs. Hwang.
This is my sister Irene and her kids.
Aren't they cute?
You must excuse me. I'm late for tennis class.
我走了.
晚飯時見.
這是誰呀？
姥, 他是我的朋友, Alex.
Alex, this is my Grandmother. Say *nihao laou laou.* She doesn't speak English.
Nihao laou laou!
This is my brother-in-law, Ted.
My cousin, June.
Her husband, Frank.
Say it louder. She's deaf.
NIHAO LAOU LAOU!

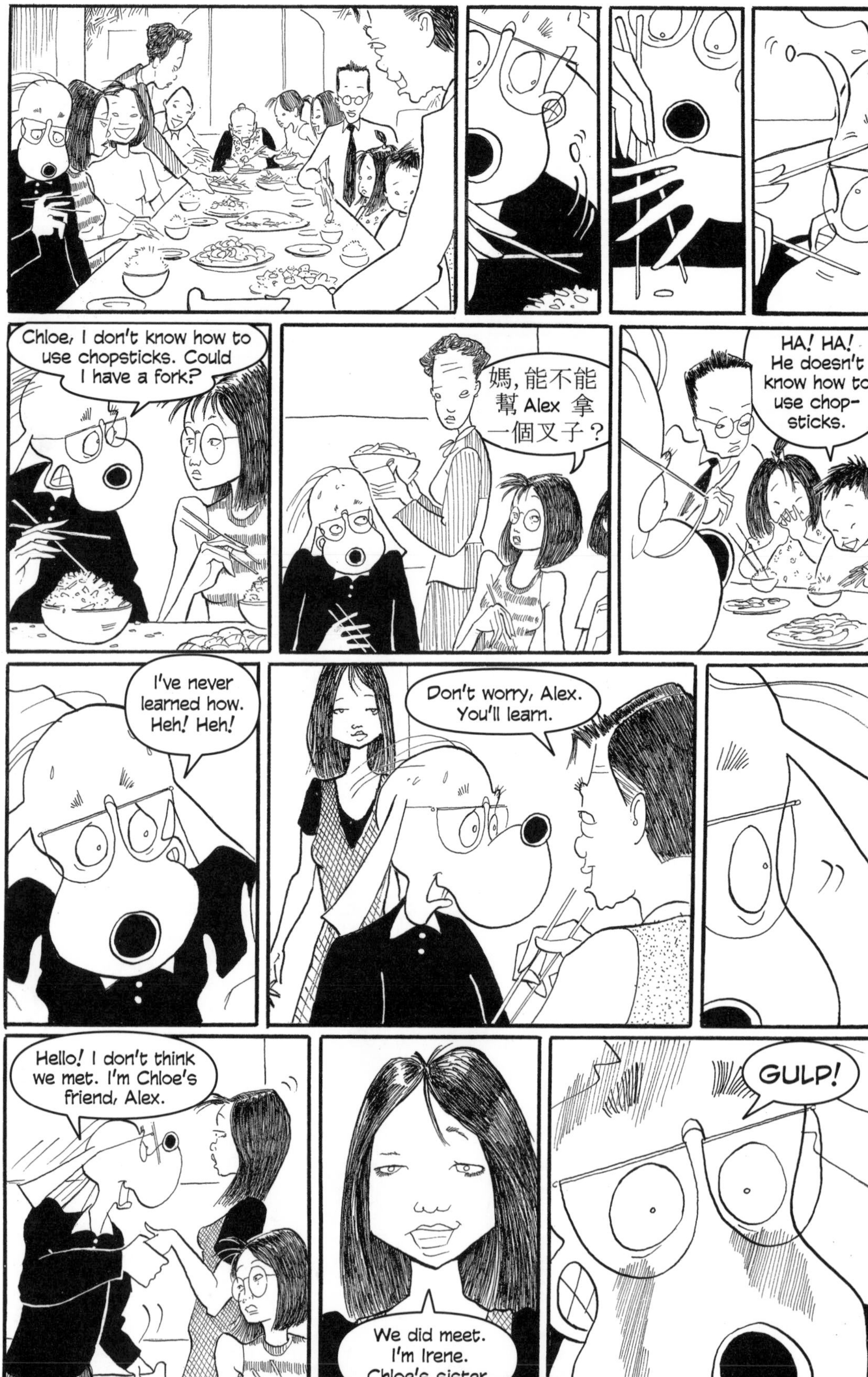
Chloe, I don't know how to use chopsticks. Could I have a fork?
媽,能不能幫 Alex 拿一個叉子?
HA! HA! He doesn't know how to use chop-sticks.
I've never learned how. Heh! Heh!
Don't worry, Alex. You'll learn.
Hello! I don't think we met. I'm Chloe's friend, Alex.
We did meet. I'm Irene. Chloe's sister.
GULP!

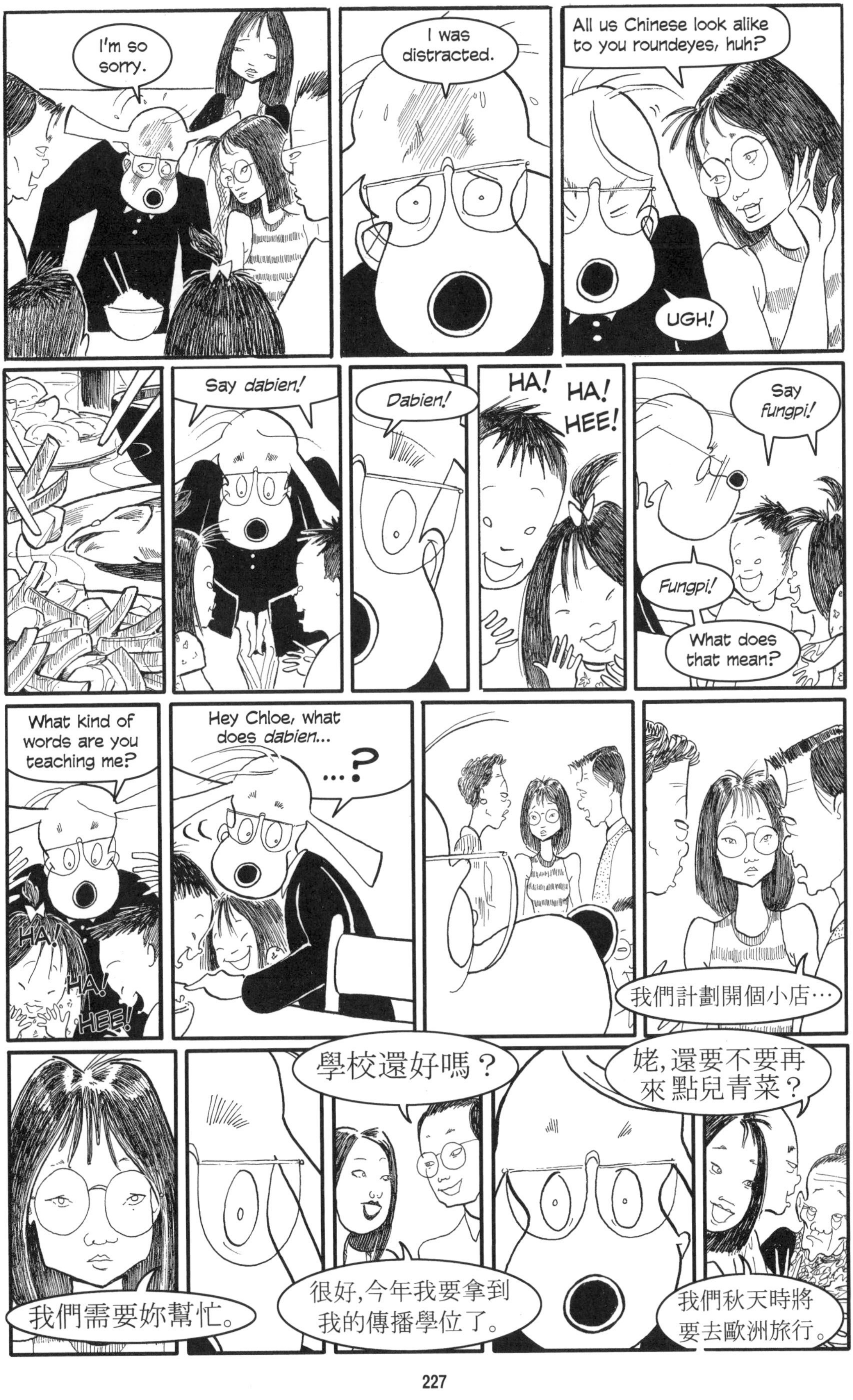
I'm so sorry.
I was distracted.
All us Chinese look alike to you roundeyes, huh?
UGH!
Say dabien!
Dabien!
HA! HA! HEE!
Say fungpi!
Fungpi!
What does that mean?
What kind of words are you teaching me?
HA! HA! HEE!
Hey Chloe, what does dabien...
...?
我們計劃開個小店…
我們需要妳幫忙。
學校還好嗎？
很好,今年我要拿到我的傳播學位了。
姥,還要不要再來點兒青菜？
我們秋天時將要去歐洲旅行。

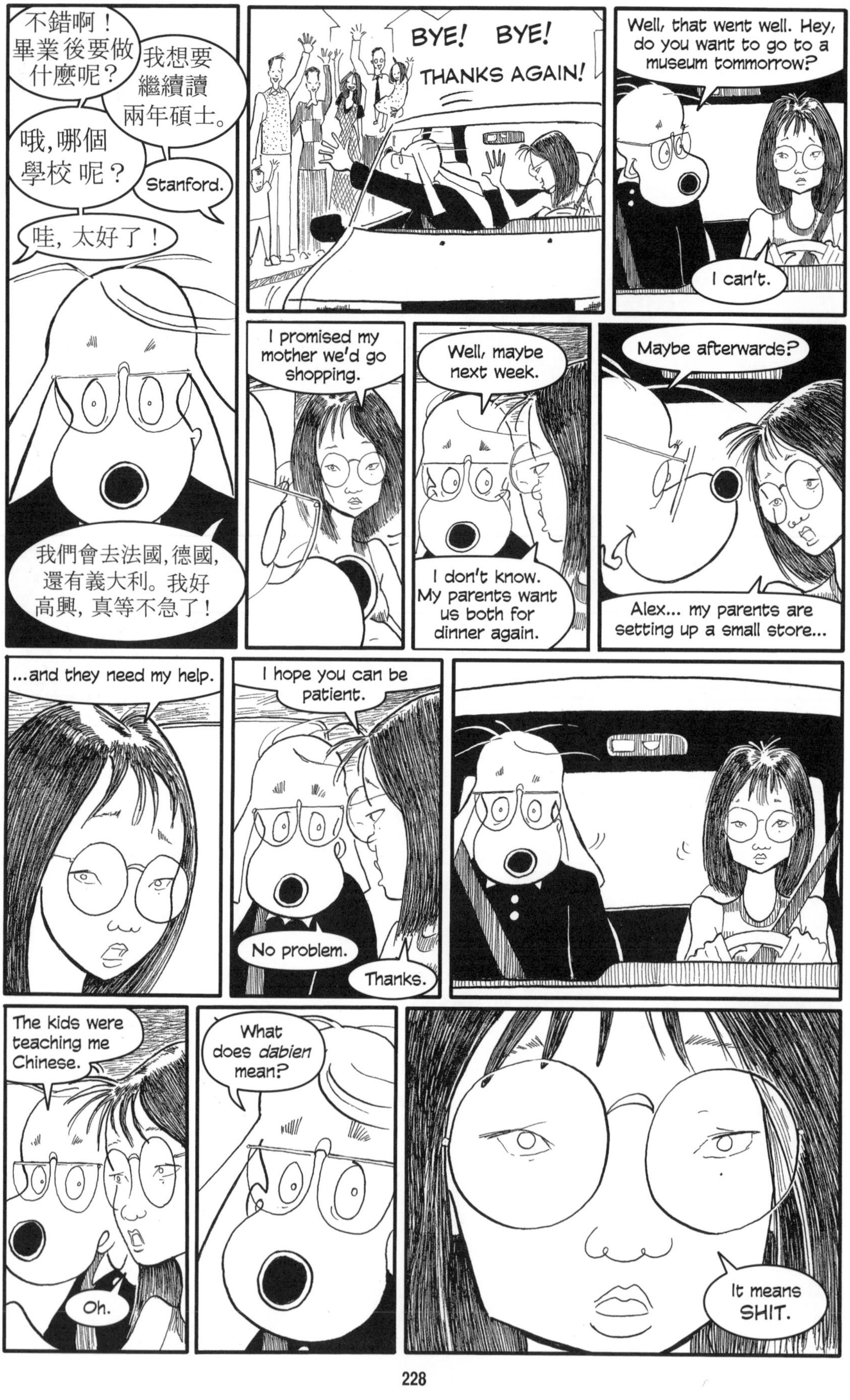
不錯啊！畢業後要做什麼呢？
我想要繼續讀兩年碩士。
哦,哪個學校呢？
Stanford.
哇, 太好了！
我們會去法國,德國,還有義大利。我好高興, 真等不急了！
BYE! BYE!
THANKS AGAIN!
Well, that went well. Hey, do you want to go to a museum tommorrow?
I can't.
I promised my mother we'd go shopping.
Well, maybe next week.
I don't know. My parents want us both for dinner again.
Maybe afterwards?
Alex... my parents are setting up a small store...
...and they need my help.
I hope you can be patient.
No problem.
Thanks.
The kids were teaching me Chinese.
Oh.
What does *dabien* mean?
It means SHIT.

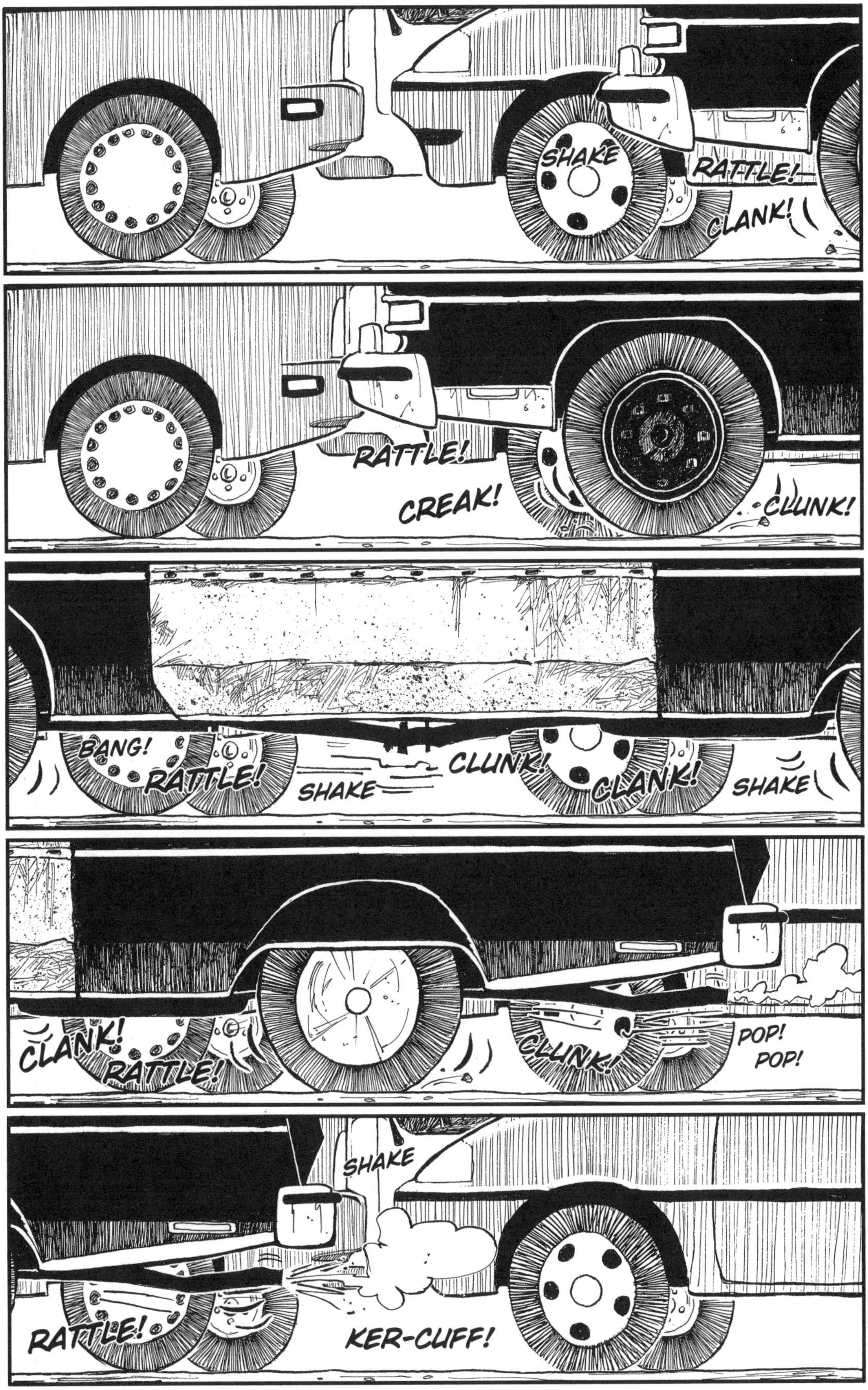
SHAKE
RATTLE!
CLANK!
RATTLE!
CREAK!
CLUNK!
BANG!
RATTLE!
SHAKE
CLUNK!
CLANK!
SHAKE
CLANK!
RATTLE!
CLUNK!
POP!
POP!
SHAKE
RATTLE!
KER-CUFF!

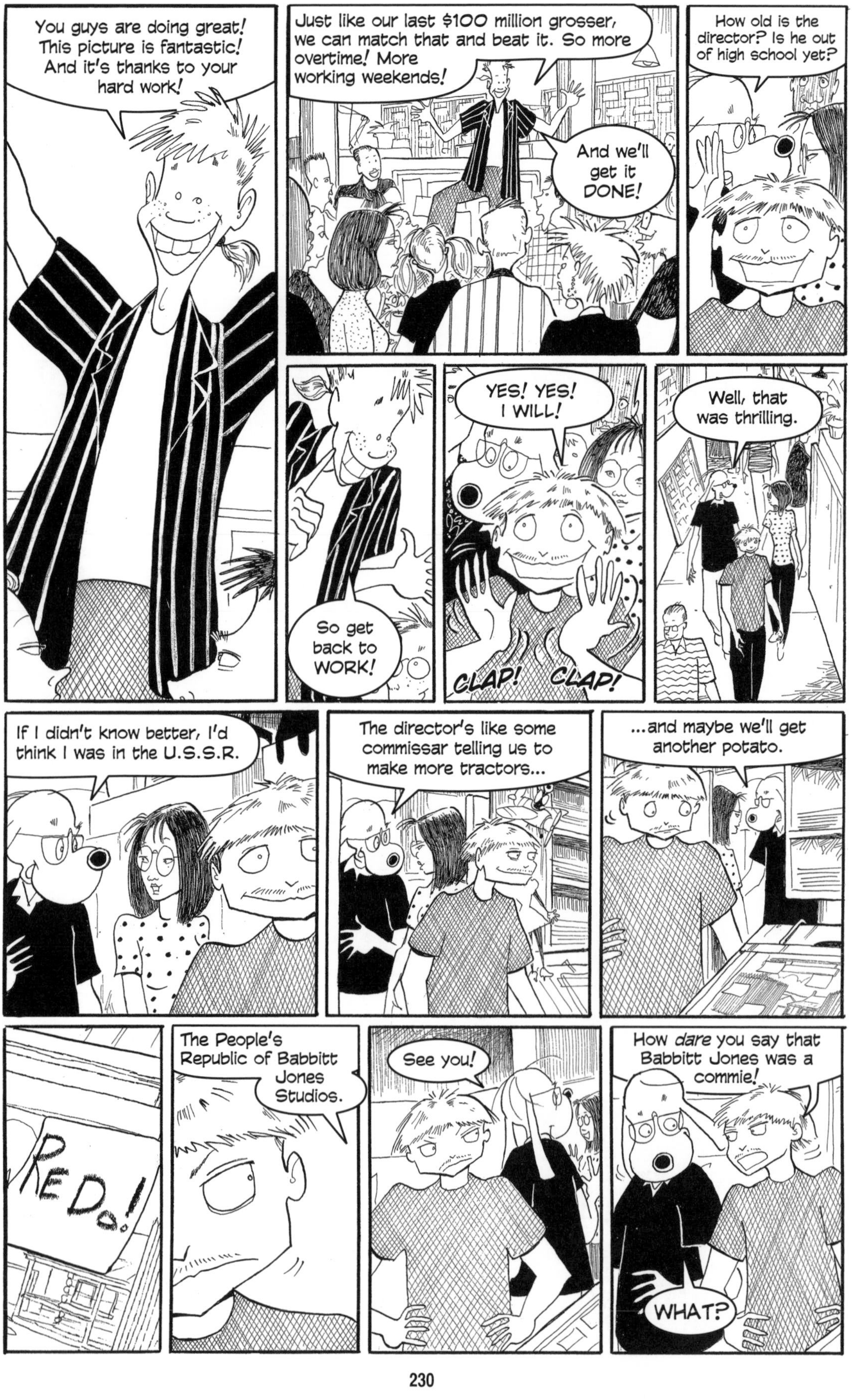
You guys are doing great! This picture is fantastic! And it's thanks to your hard work!
Just like our last $100 million grosser, we can match that and beat it. So more overtime! More working weekends!
And we'll get it DONE!
How old is the director? Is he out of high school yet?
So get back to WORK!
YES! YES! I WILL!
CLAP! CLAP!
Well, that was thrilling.
If I didn't know better, I'd think I was in the U.S.S.R.
The director's like some commissar telling us to make more tractors...
...and maybe we'll get another potato.
REDO!
The People's Republic of Babbitt Jones Studios.
See you!
How dare you say that Babbitt Jones was a commie!
WHAT?

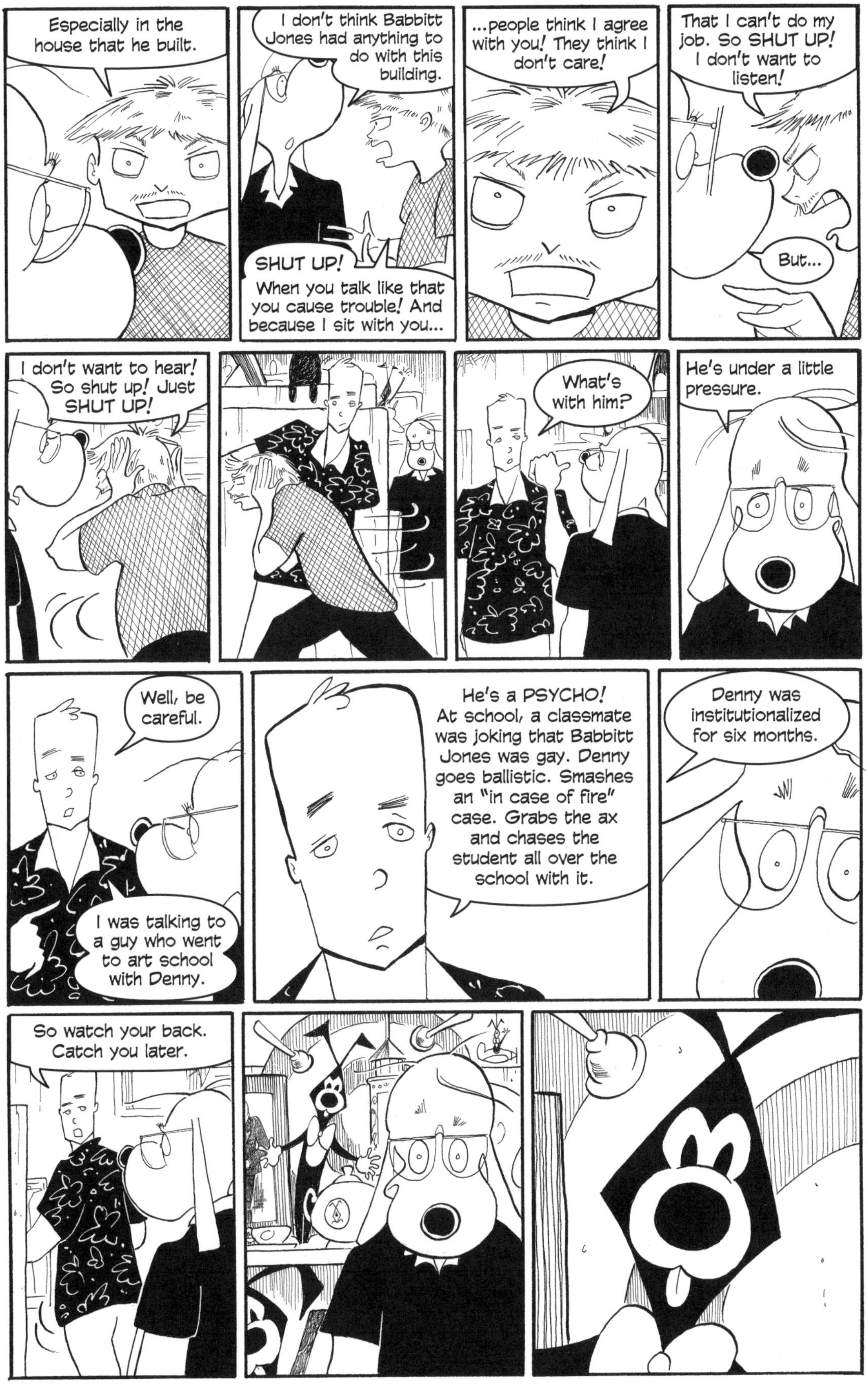
Especially in the house that he built.
I don't think Babbitt Jones had anything to do with this building.
SHUT UP! When you talk like that you cause trouble! And because I sit with you...
...people think I agree with you! They think I don't care!
That I can't do my job. So SHUT UP! I don't want to listen!
But...
I don't want to hear! So shut up! Just SHUT UP!
What's with him?
He's under a little pressure.
Well, be careful.
I was talking to a guy who went to art school with Denny.
He's a PSYCHO! At school, a classmate was joking that Babbitt Jones was gay. Denny goes ballistic. Smashes an "in case of fire" case. Grabs the ax and chases the student all over the school with it.
Denny was institutionalized for six months.
So watch your back. Catch you later.

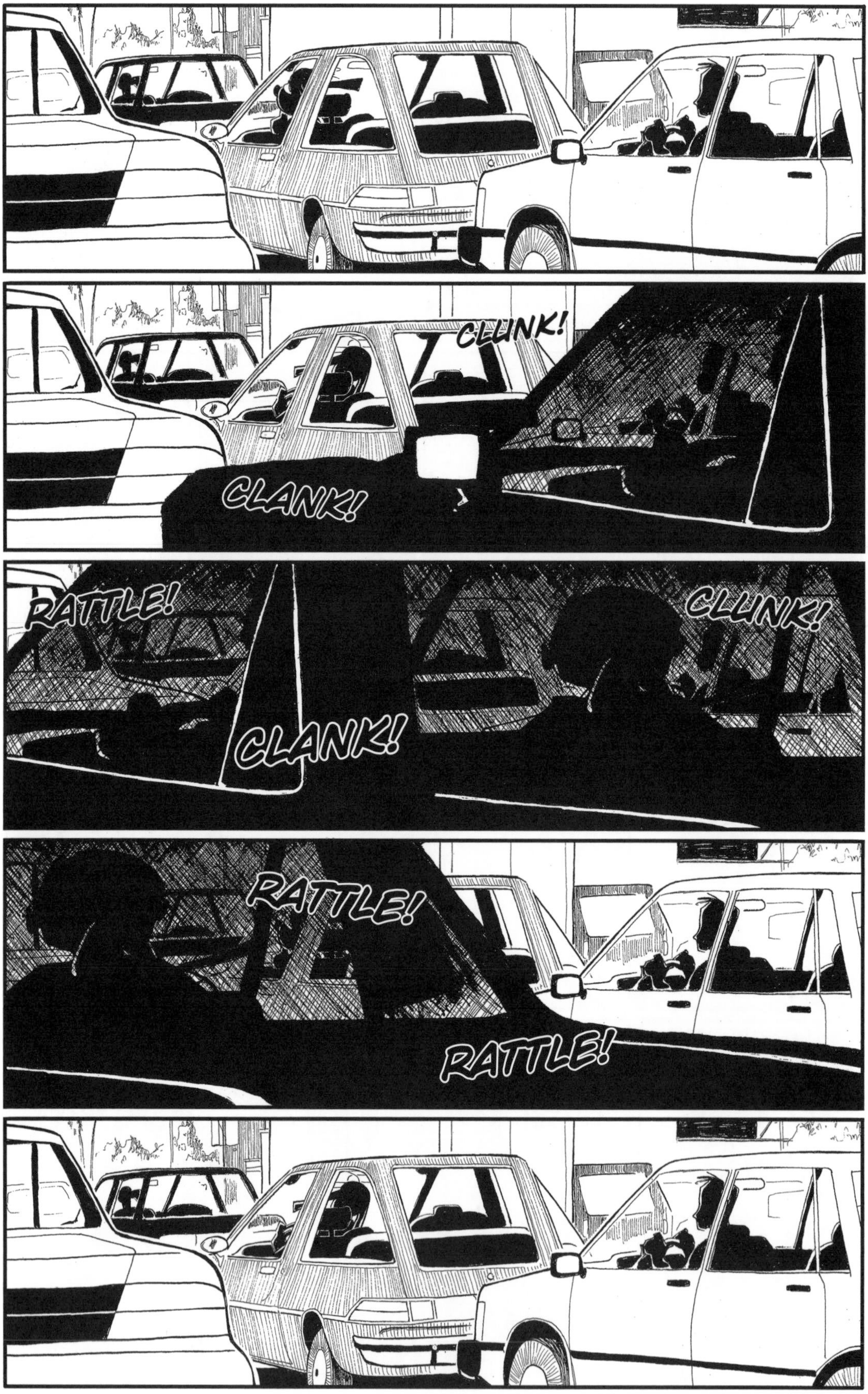
CLUNK!
CLANK!
RATTLE!
CLUNK!
CLANK!
RATTLE!
RATTLE!

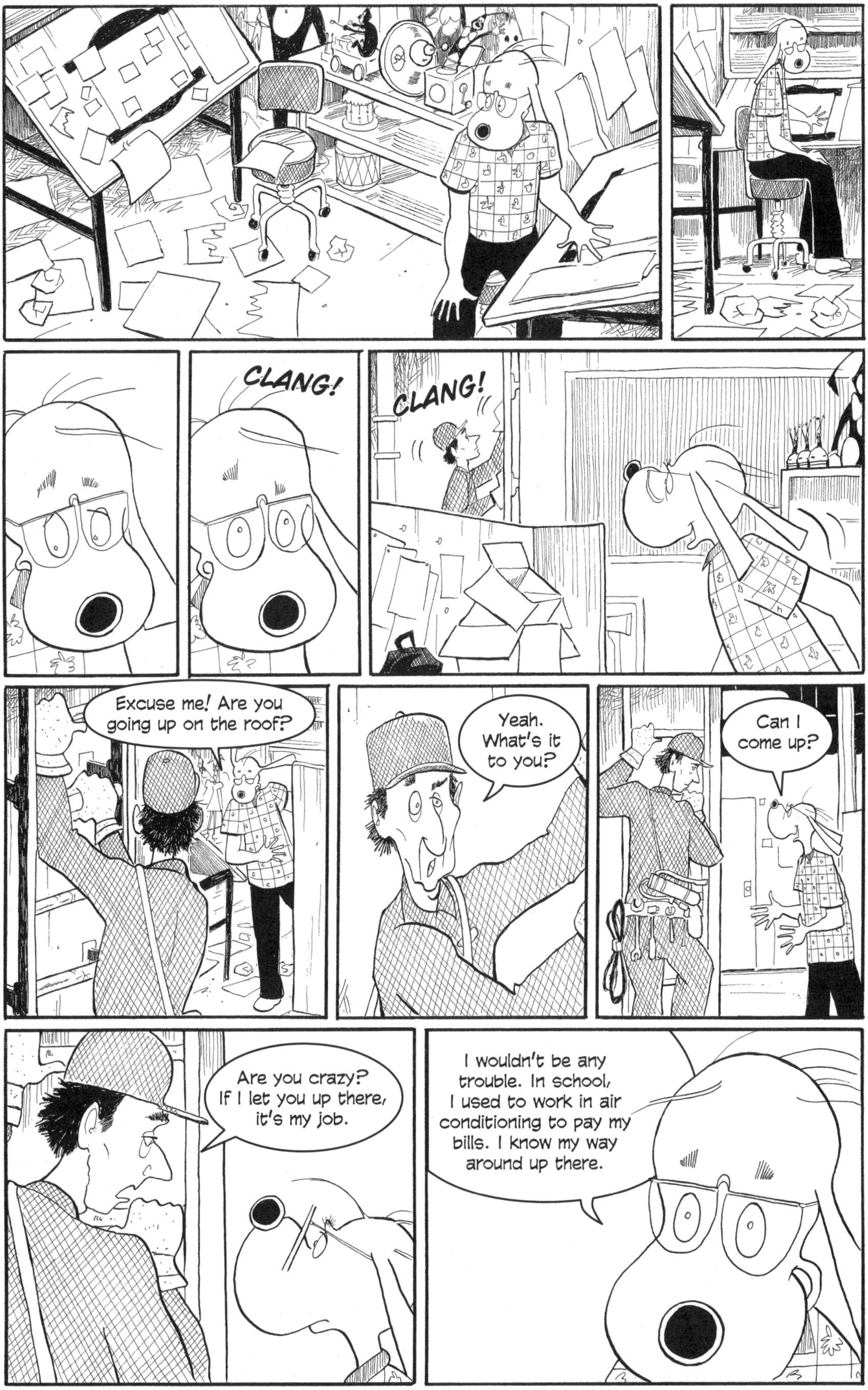
CLANG!
CLANG!
Excuse me! Are you going up on the roof?
Yeah. What's it to you?
Can I come up?
Are you crazy? If I let you up there, it's my job.
I wouldn't be any trouble. In school, I used to work in air conditioning to pay my bills. I know my way around up there.

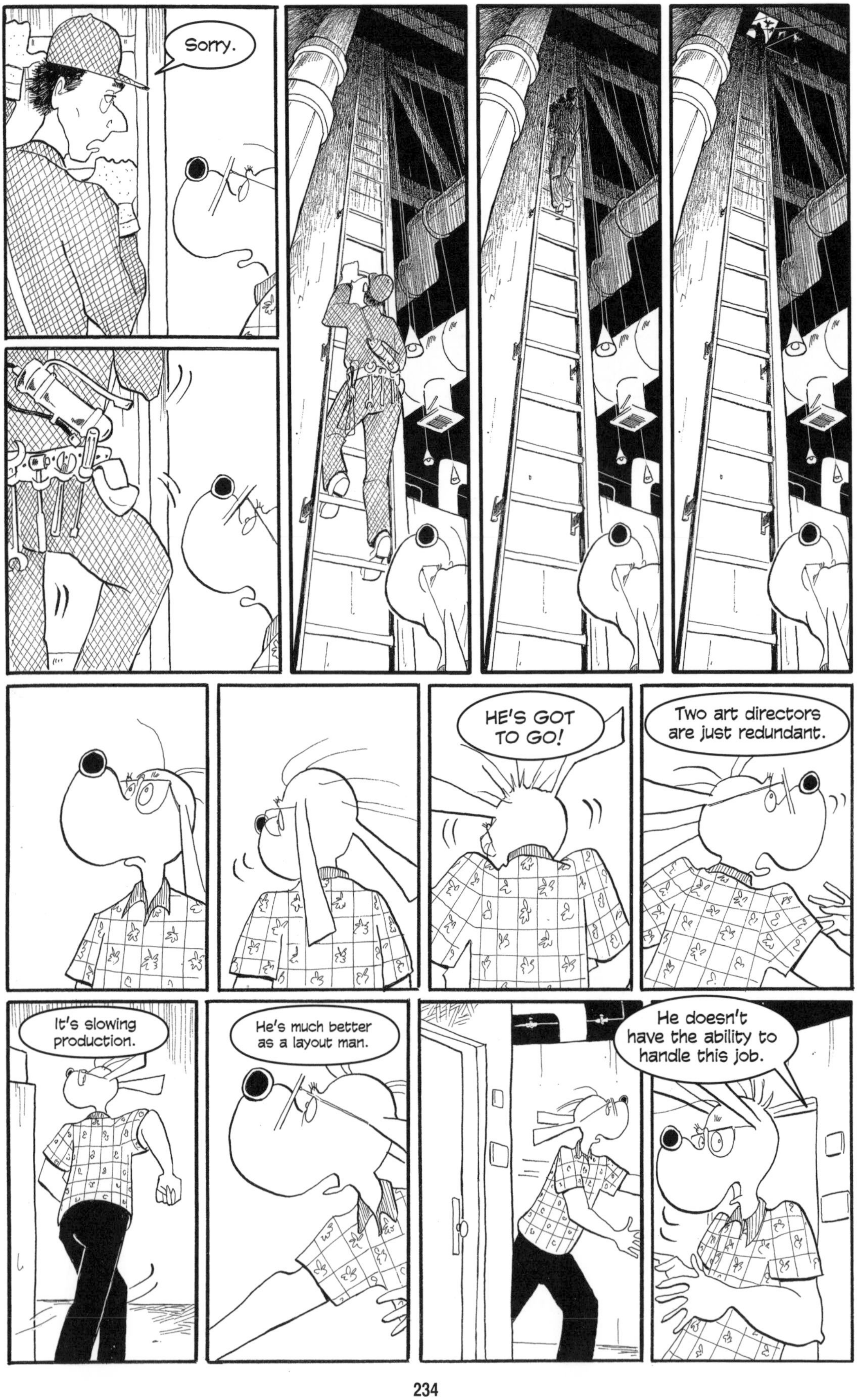
Sorry.
HE'S GOT TO GO!
Two art directors are just redundant.
It's slowing production.
He's much better as a layout man.
He doesn't have the ability to handle this job.

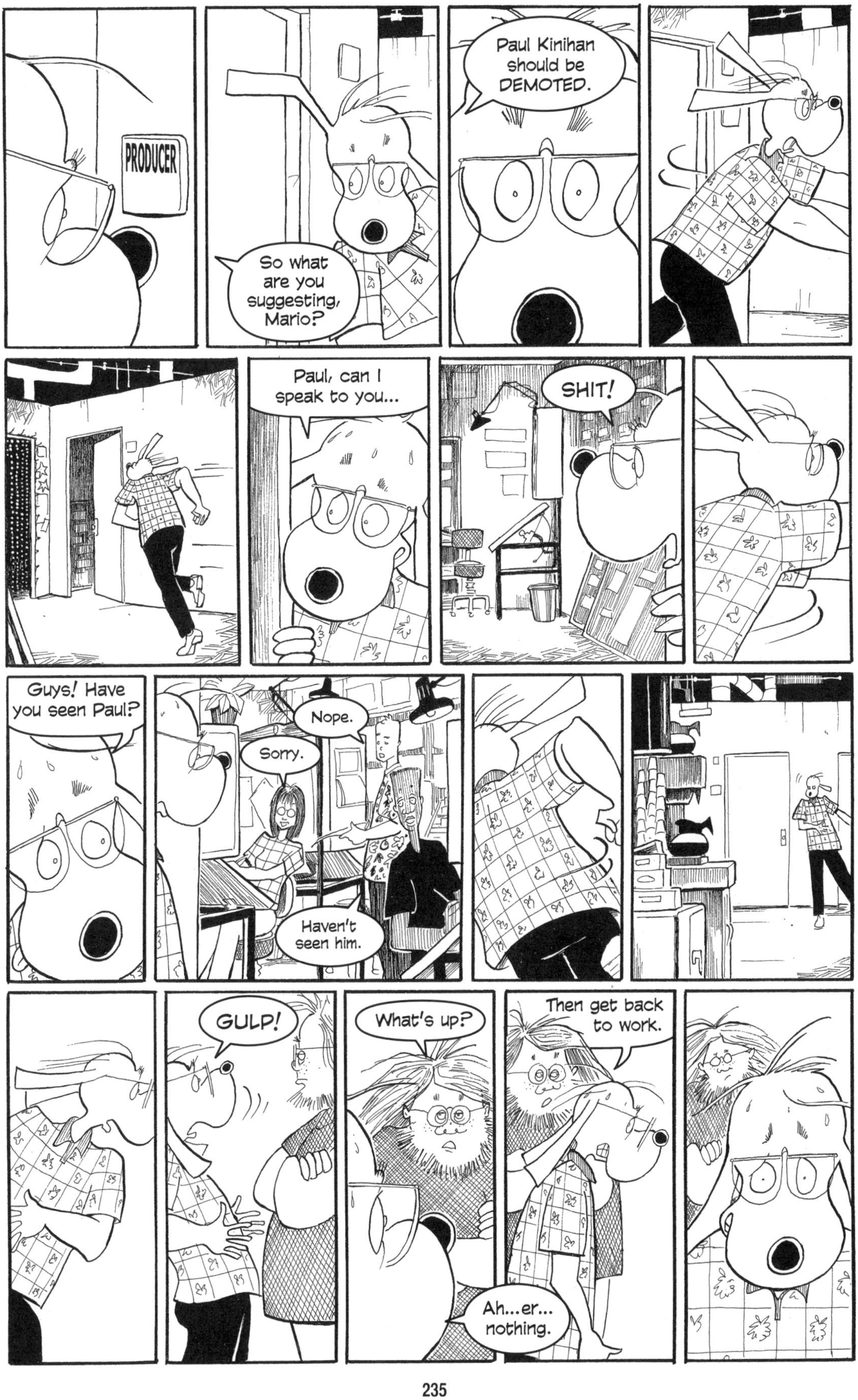
PRODUCER
So what are you suggesting, Mario?
Paul Kinihan should be DEMOTED.
Paul, can I speak to you...
SHIT!
Guys! Have you seen Paul?
Nope.
Sorry.
Haven't seen him.
GULP!
What's up?
Ah...er... nothing.
Then get back to work.

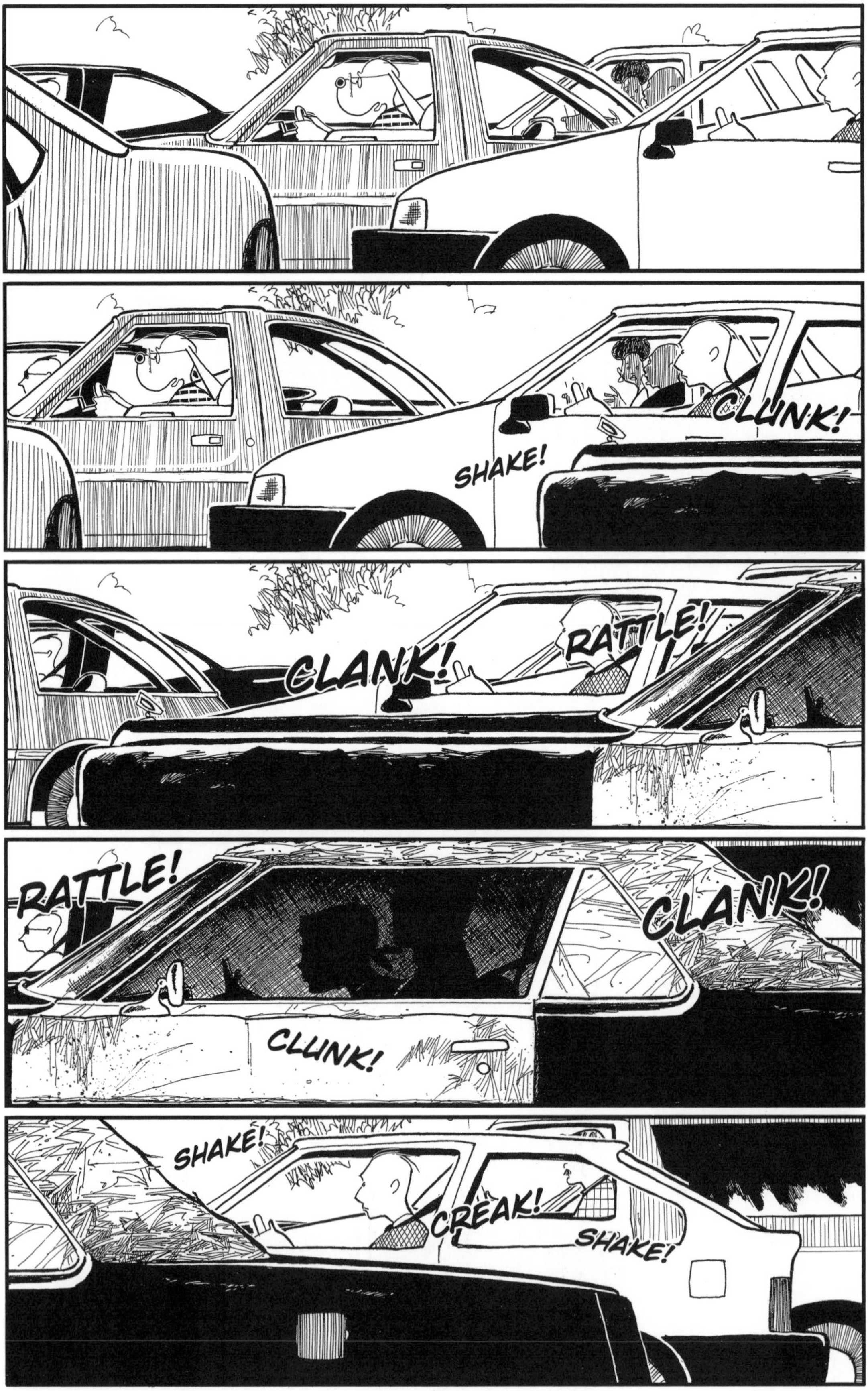
SHAKE!
CLUNK!
CLANK!
RATTLE!
RATTLE!
CLANK!
CLUNK!
SHAKE!
CREAK!
SHAKE!

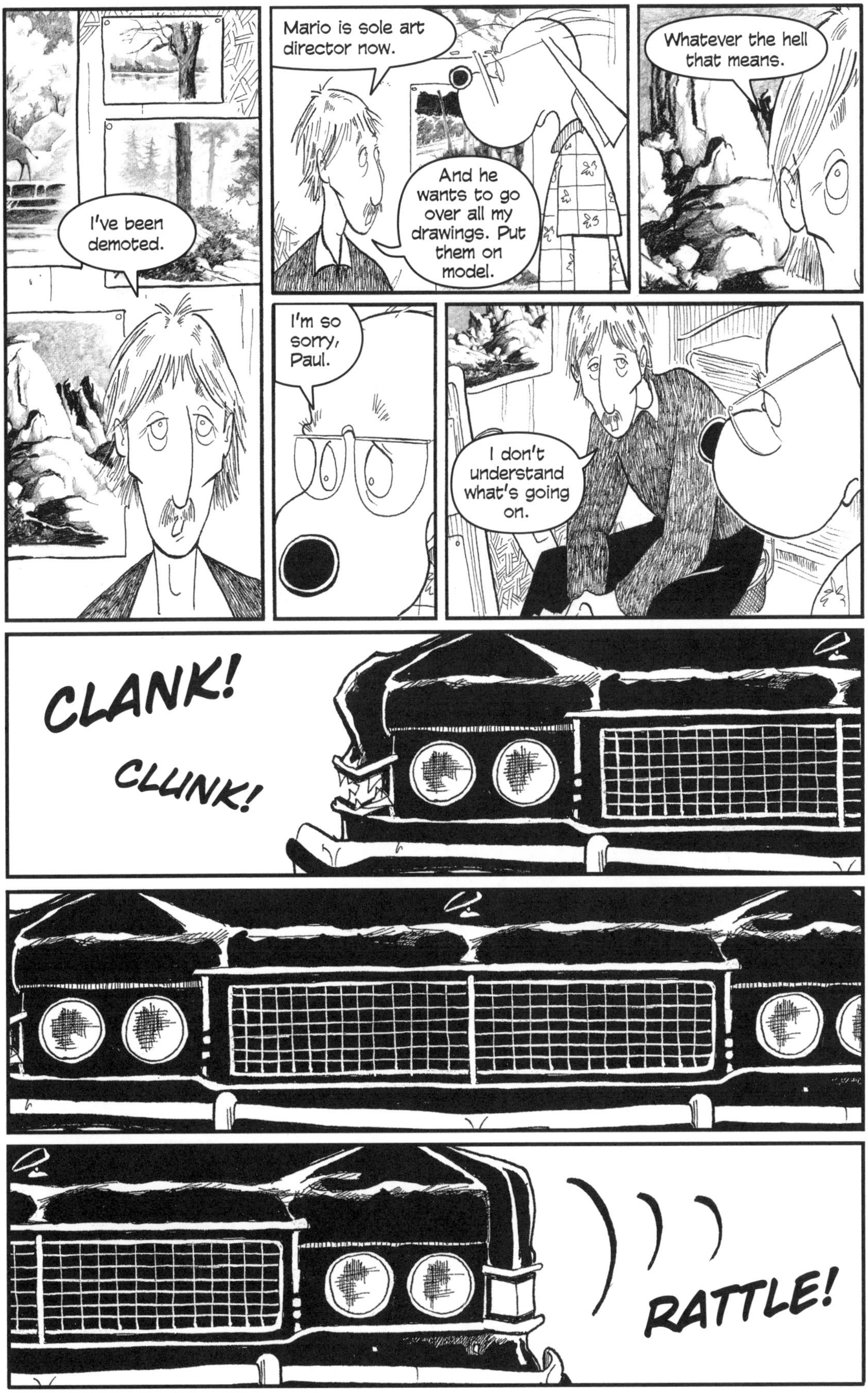
I've been demoted.
Mario is sole art director now.
And he wants to go over all my drawings. Put them on model.
Whatever the hell that means.
I'm so sorry, Paul.
I don't understand what's going on.
CLANK!
CLUNK!
RATTLE!

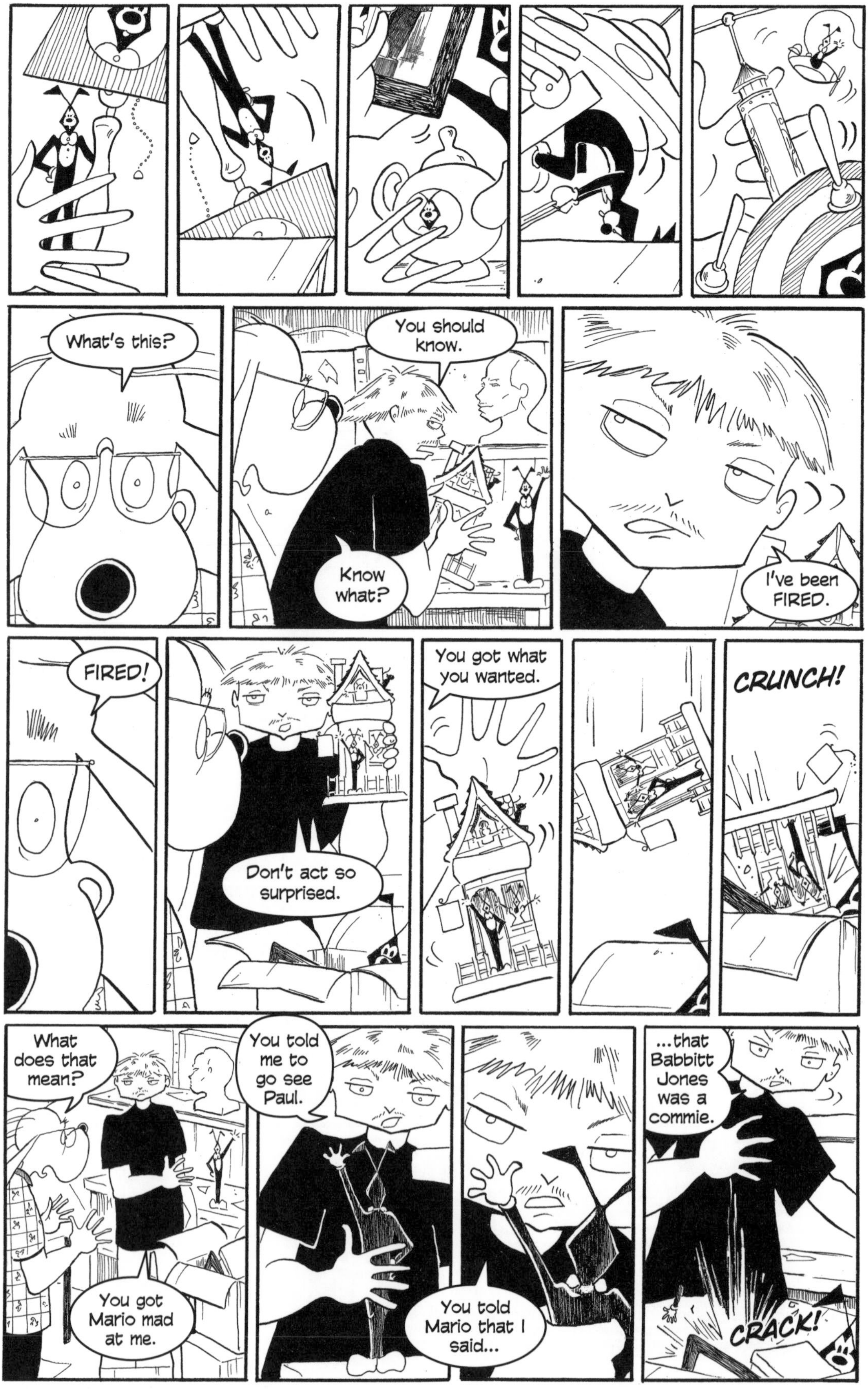
What's this?
You should know.
Know what?
I've been FIRED.
FIRED!
Don't act so surprised.
You got what you wanted.
CRUNCH!
What does that mean?
You got Mario mad at me.
You told me to go see Paul.
You told Mario that I said...
...that Babbitt Jones was a commie.
CRACK!

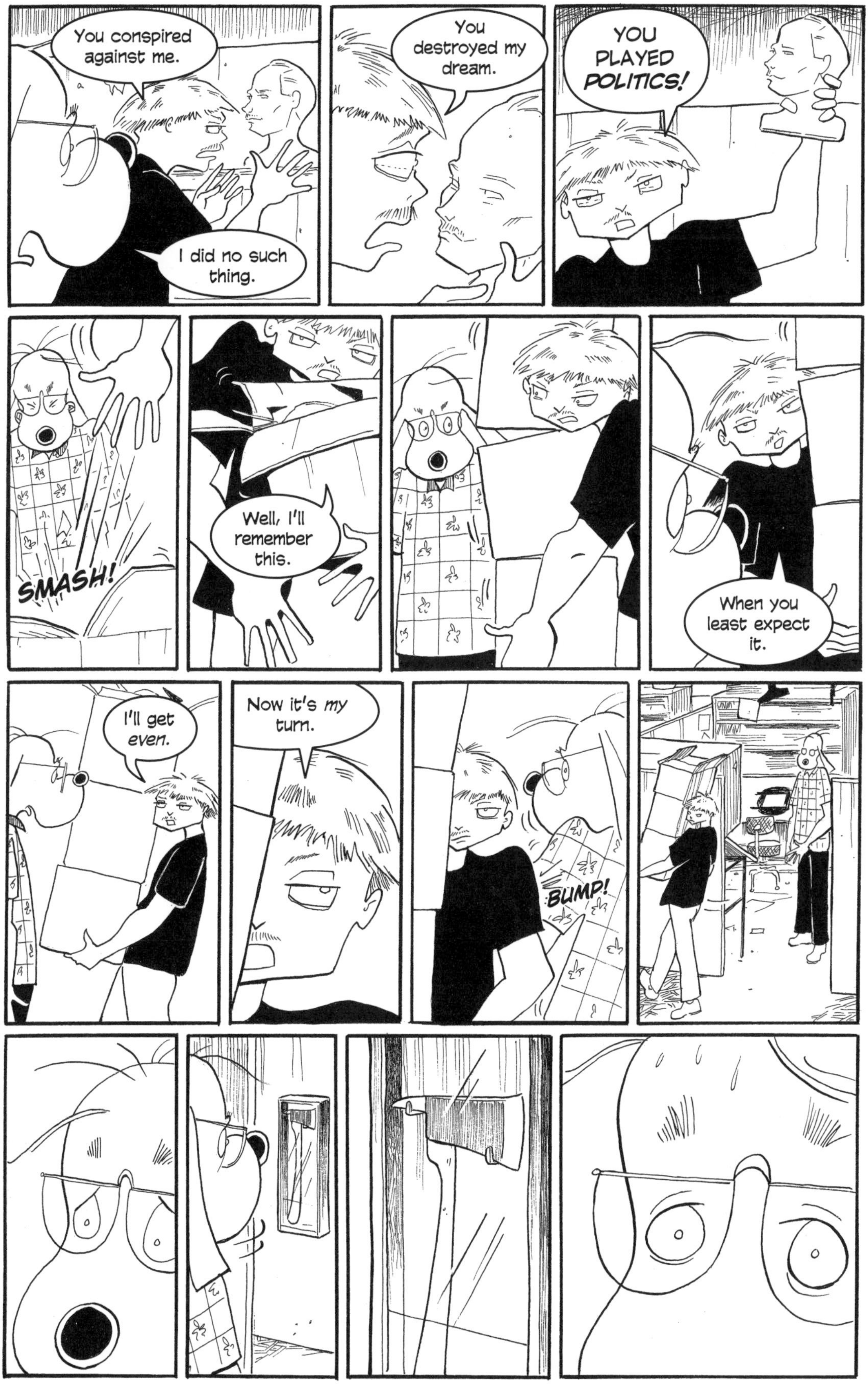
You conspired against me.
I did no such thing.
You destroyed my dream.
YOU PLAYED POLITICS!
SMASH!
Well, I'll remember this.
When you least expect it.
I'll get even.
Now it's my turn.
BUMP!

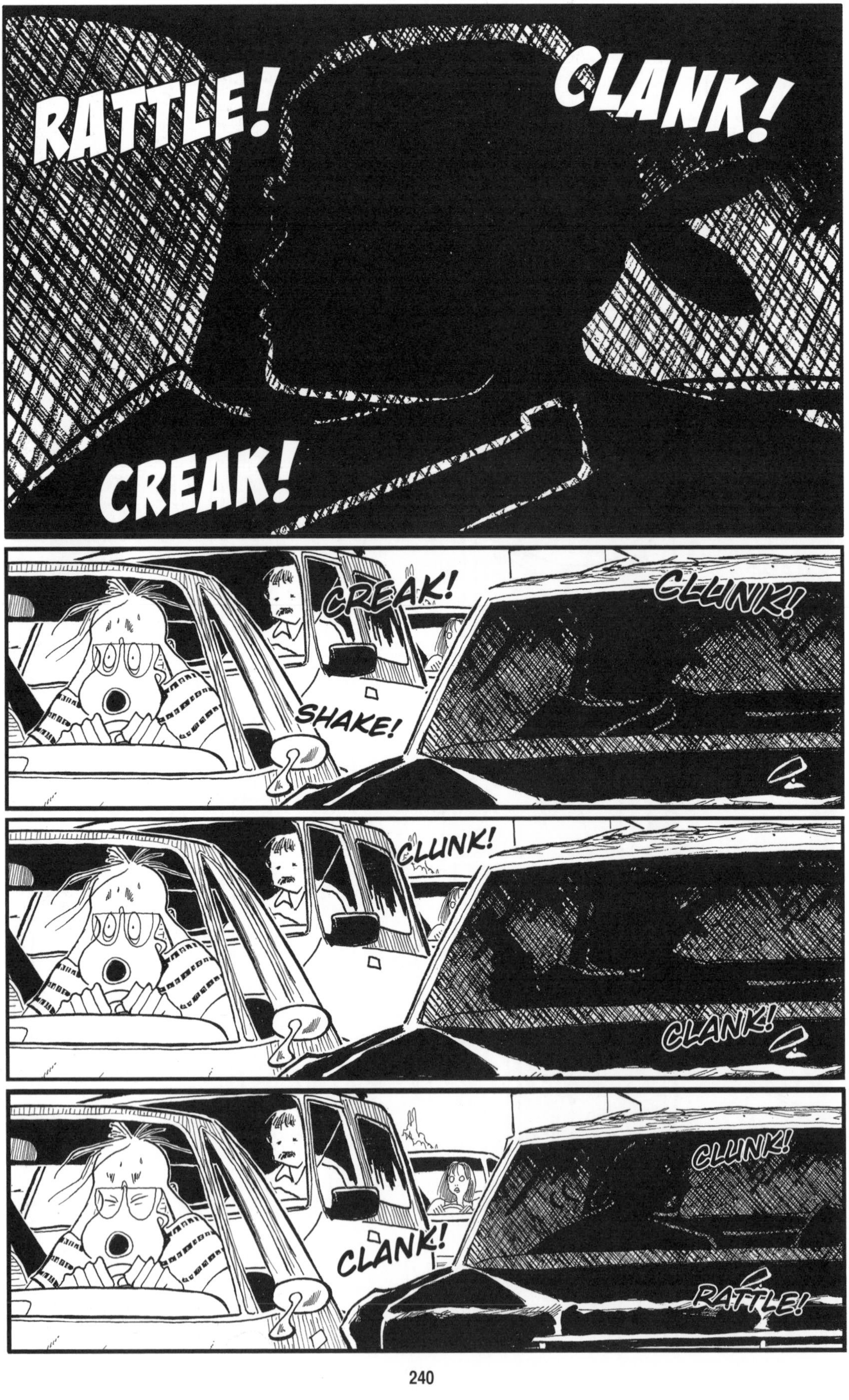
RATTLE!
CLANK!
CREAK!
CREAK!
CLUNK!
SHAKE!
CLUNK!
CLANK!
CLUNK!
CLANK!
RATTLE!

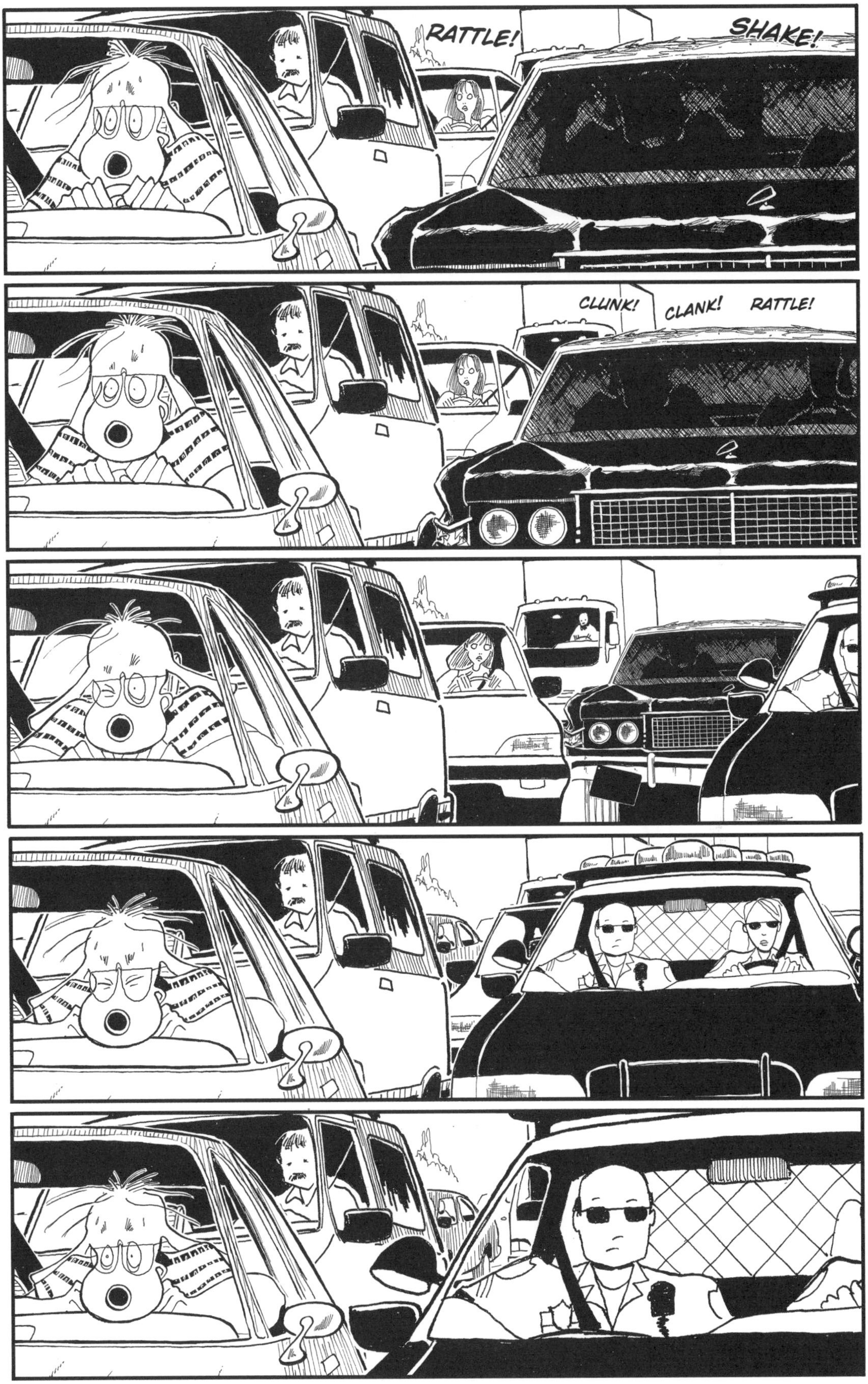
RATTLE!
SHAKE!
CLUNK!
CLANK!
RATTLE!

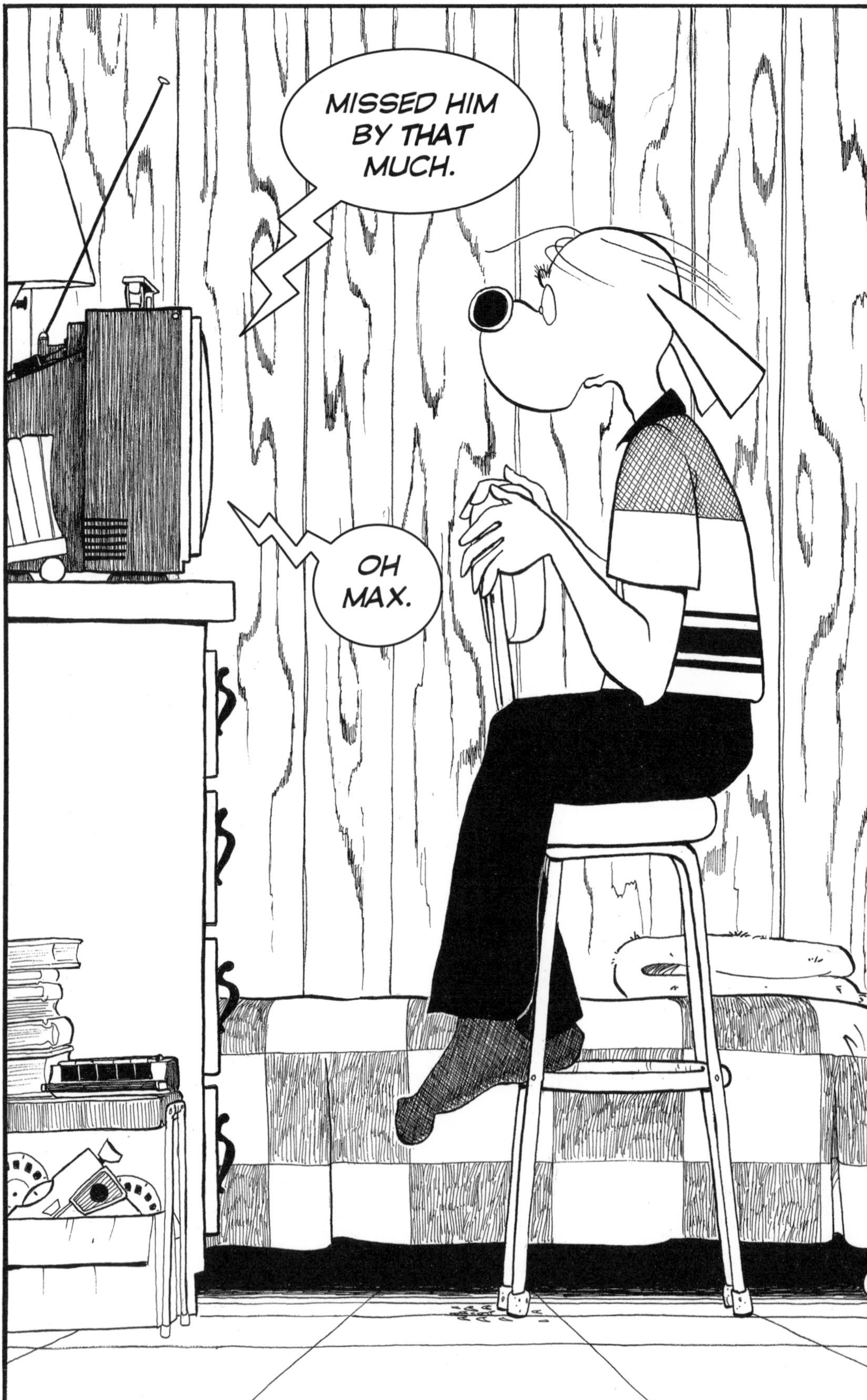
MISSED HIM
BY THAT
MUCH.
OH
MAX.

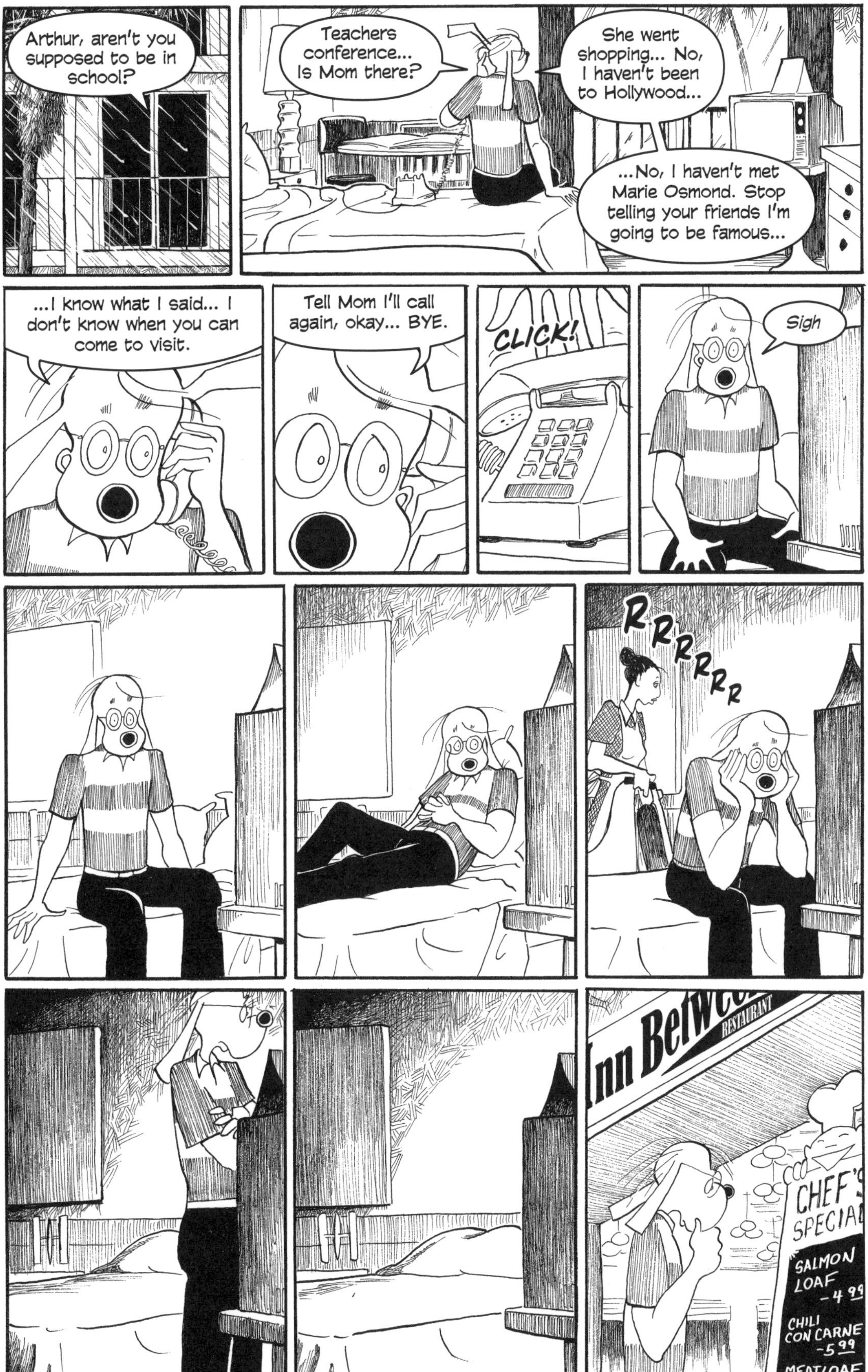
Arthur, aren't you supposed to be in school?
Teachers conference... Is Mom there?
She went shopping... No, I haven't been to Hollywood...
...No, I haven't met Marie Osmond. Stop telling your friends I'm going to be famous...
...I know what I said... I don't know when you can come to visit.
Tell Mom I'll call again, okay... BYE.
CLICK!
Sigh
RRRRRRR
Inn Betwe
RESTAURANT
CHEF'S
SPECIAL
SALMON LOAF -4.99
CHILI CON CARNE -5.99
MEATLOAF

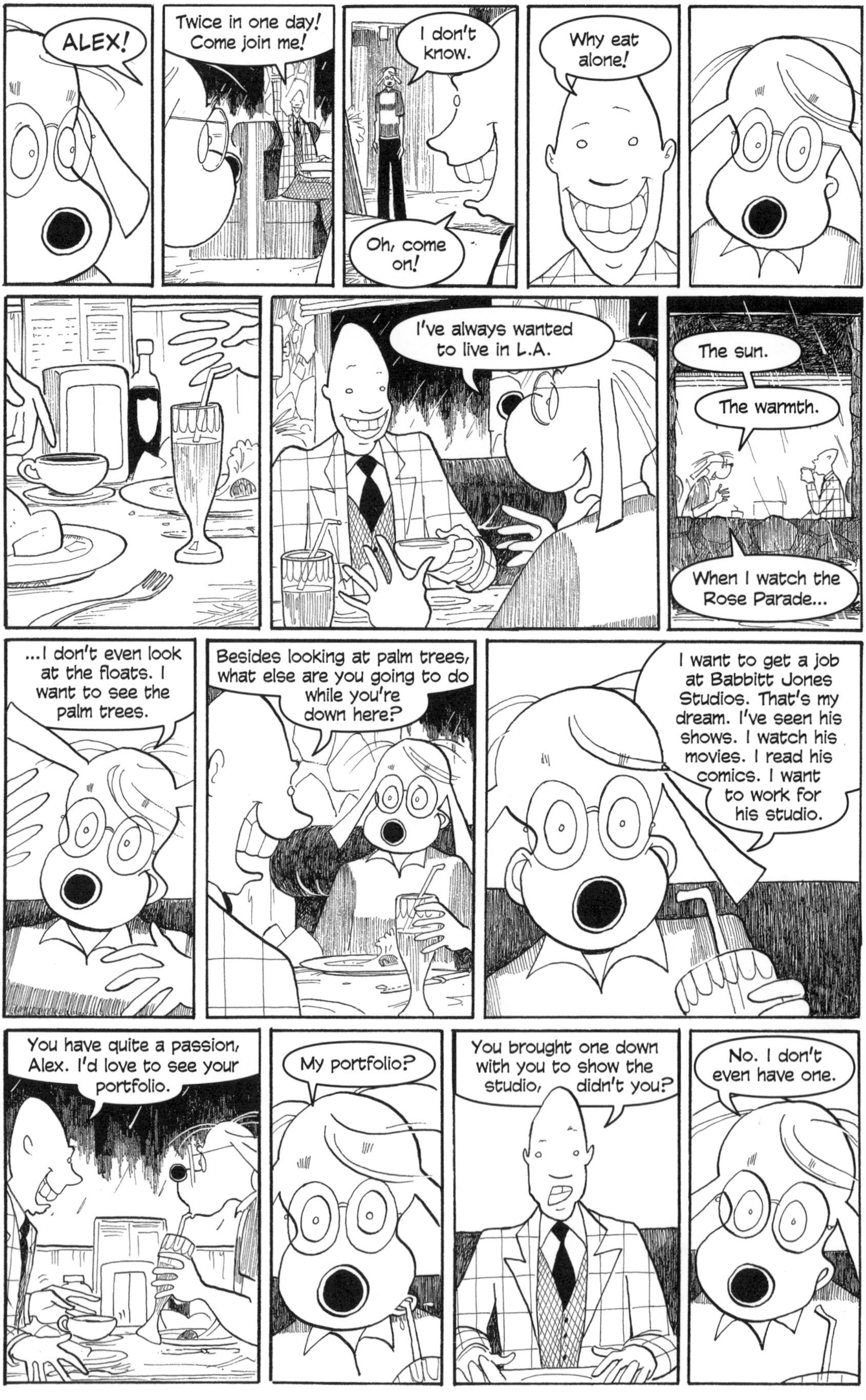
ALEX!
Twice in one day! Come join me!
I don't know.
Oh, come on!
Why eat alone!
I've always wanted to live in L.A.
The sun.
The warmth.
When I watch the Rose Parade...
...I don't even look at the floats. I want to see the palm trees.
Besides looking at palm trees, what else are you going to do while you're down here?
I want to get a job at Babbitt Jones Studios. That's my dream. I've seen his shows. I watch his movies. I read his comics. I want to work for his studio.
You have quite a passion, Alex. I'd love to see your portfolio.
My portfolio?
You brought one down with you to show the studio, didn't you?
No. I don't even have one.

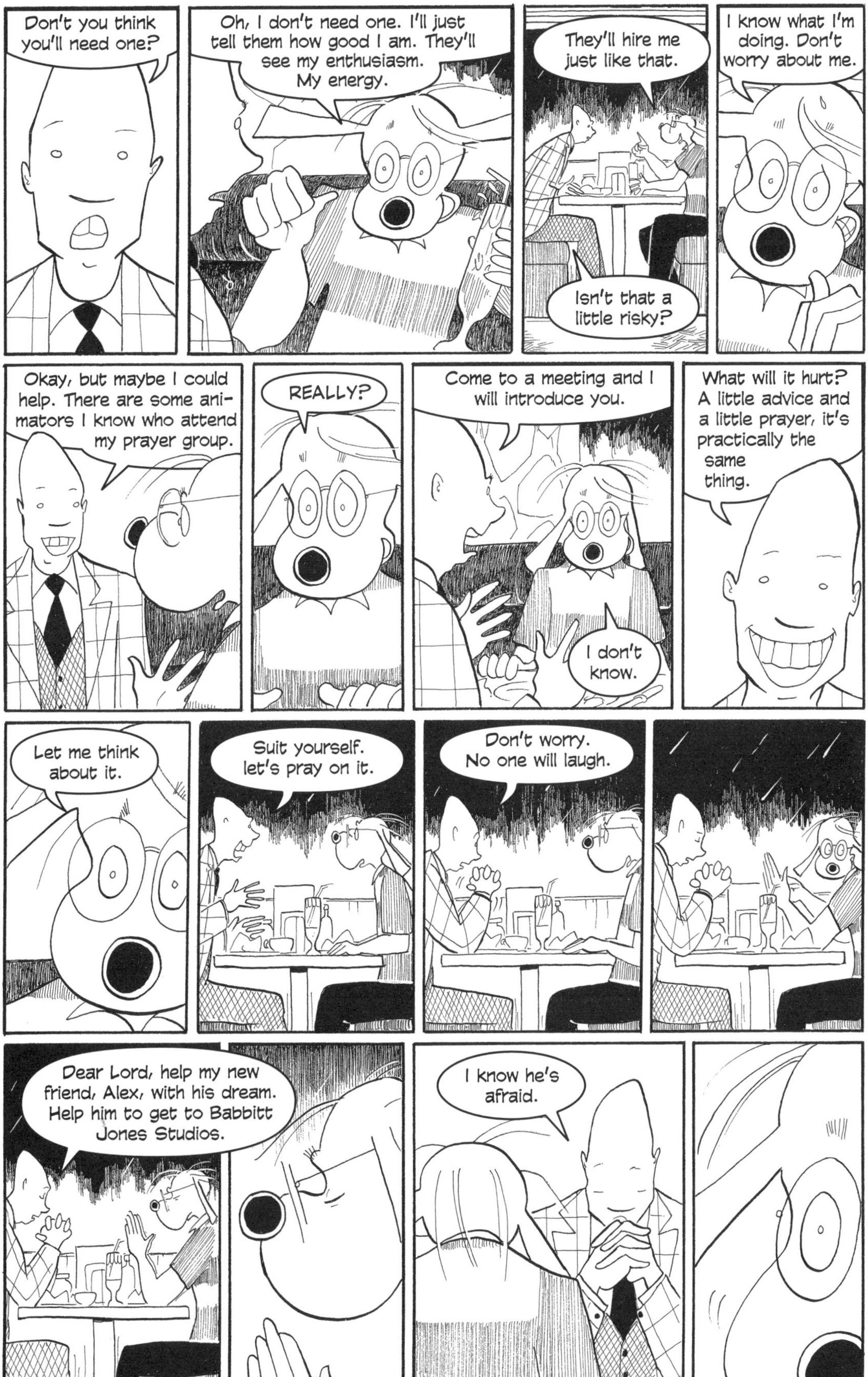

Don't you think you'll need one?
Oh, I don't need one. I'll just tell them how good I am. They'll see my enthusiasm. My energy.
They'll hire me just like that.
Isn't that a little risky?
I know what I'm doing. Don't worry about me.
Okay, but maybe I could help. There are some animators I know who attend my prayer group.
REALLY?
Come to a meeting and I will introduce you.
I don't know.
What will it hurt? A little advice and a little prayer, it's practically the same thing.
Let me think about it.
Suit yourself. let's pray on it.
Don't worry. No one will laugh.
Dear Lord, help my new friend, Alex, with his dream. Help him to get to Babbitt Jones Studios.
I know he's afraid.

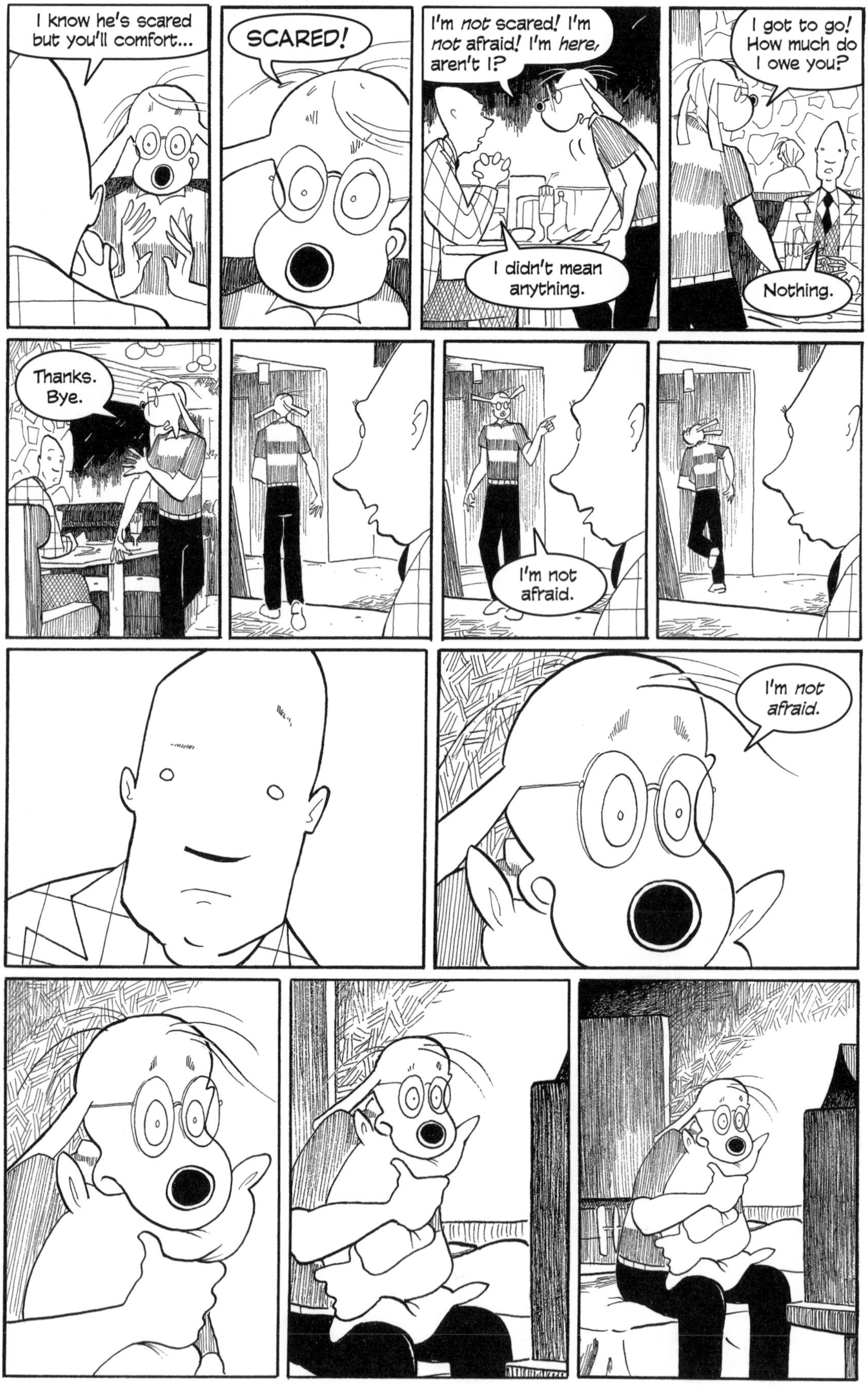
I know he's scared but you'll comfort...
SCARED!
I'm *not* scared! I'm *not* afraid! I'm *here*, aren't I?
I didn't mean anything.
I got to go! How much do I owe you?
Nothing.
Thanks. Bye.
I'm not afraid.
I'm *not afraid*.

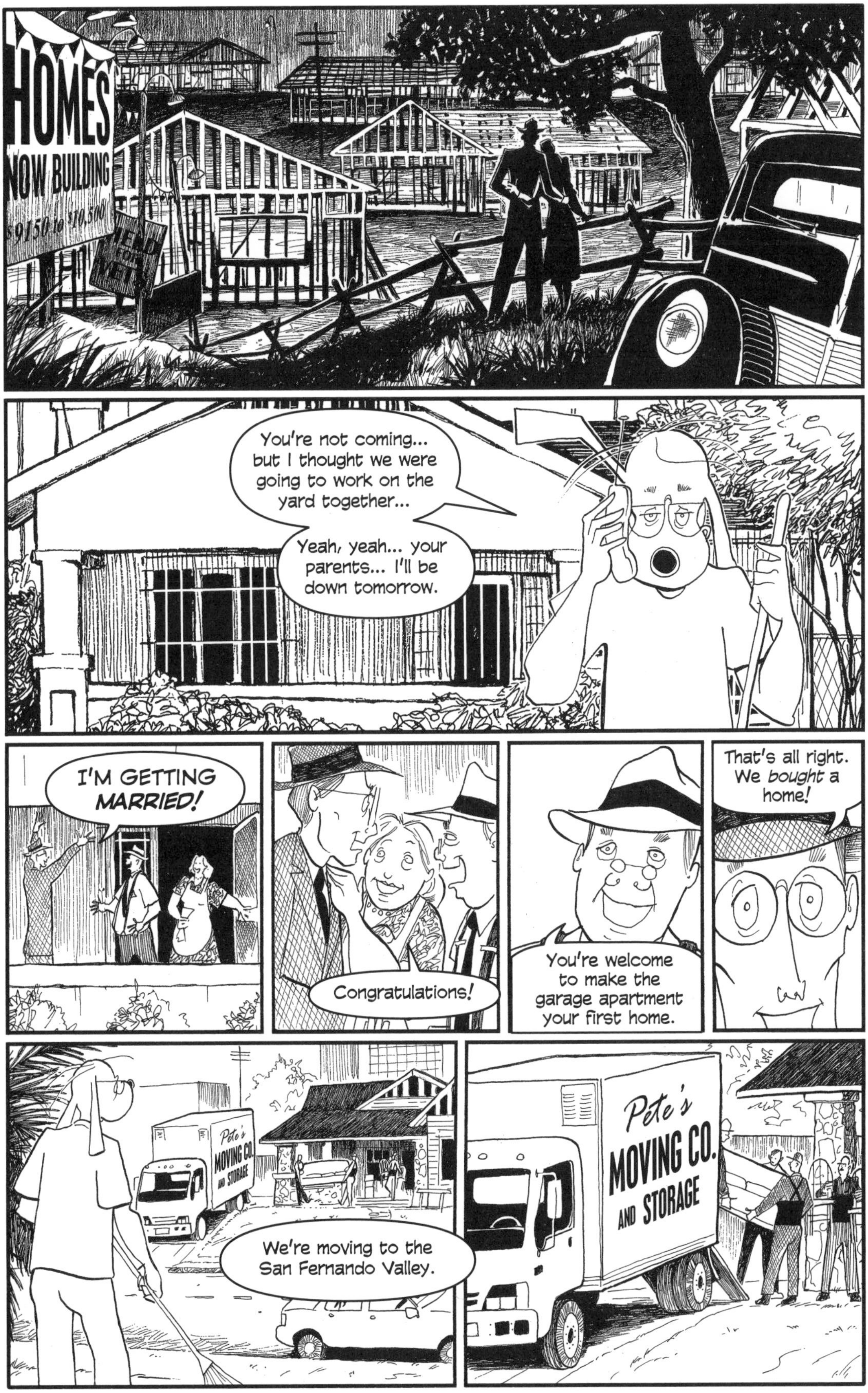
HOMES
NOW BUILDING
You're not coming... but I thought we were going to work on the yard together...
Yeah, yeah... your parents... I'll be down tomorrow.
I'M GETTING MARRIED!
Congratulations!
You're welcome to make the garage apartment your first home.
That's all right. We bought a home!
We're moving to the San Fernando Valley.
Pete's
MOVING CO.
AND STORAGE

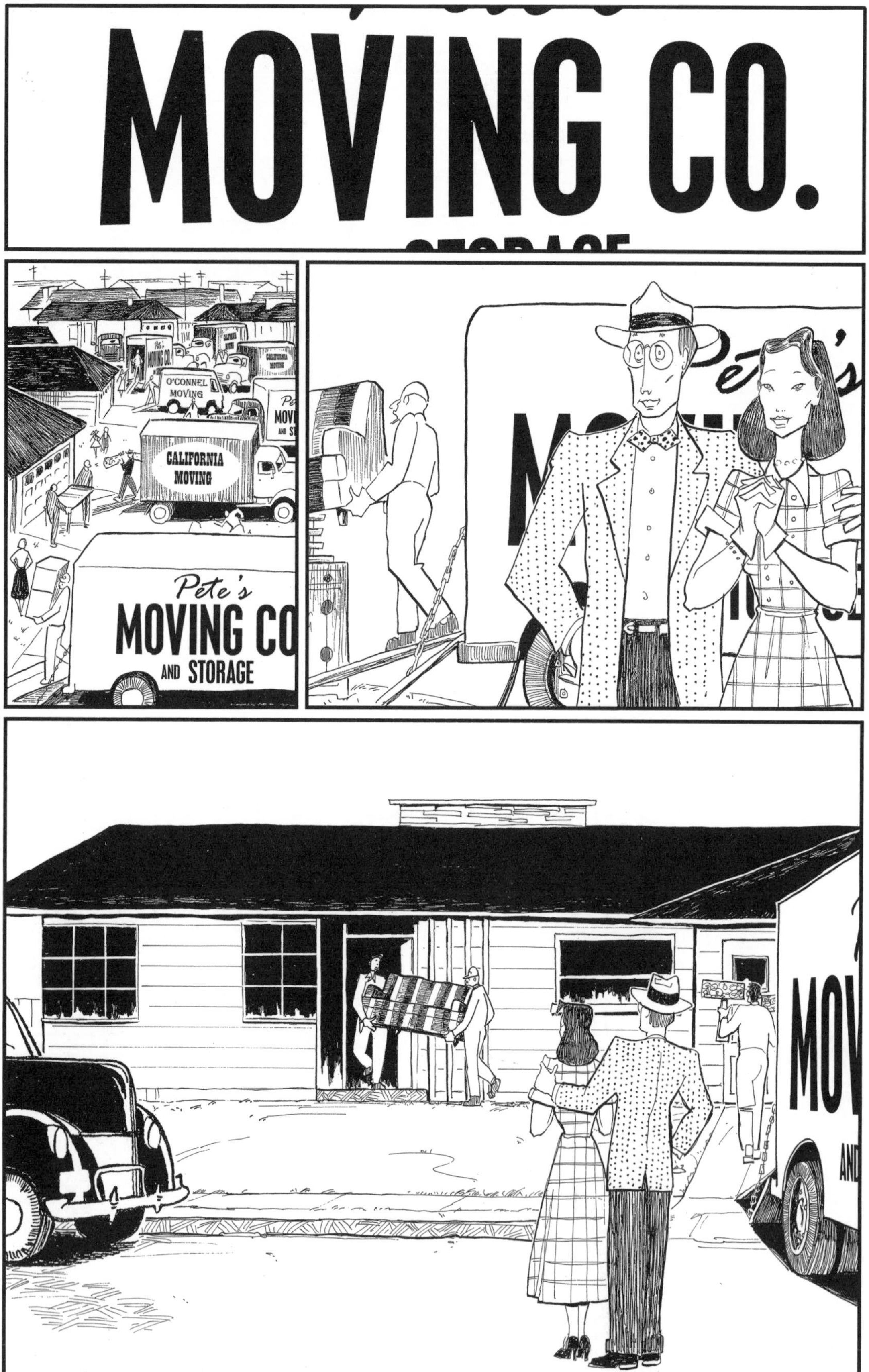
MOVING CO.
O'CONNEL MOVING
CALIFORNIA MOVING
Pete's
MOVING CO
AND STORAGE

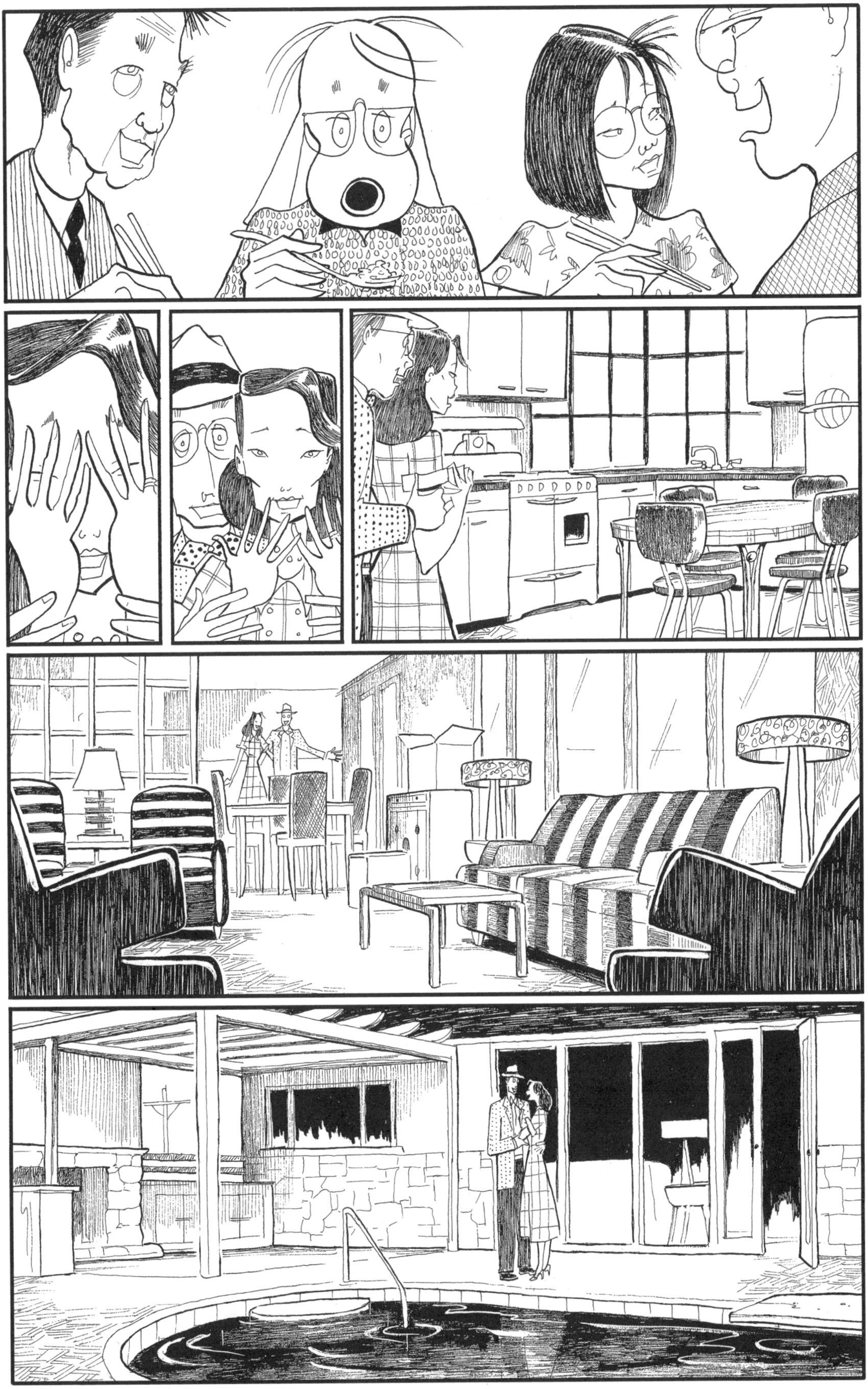

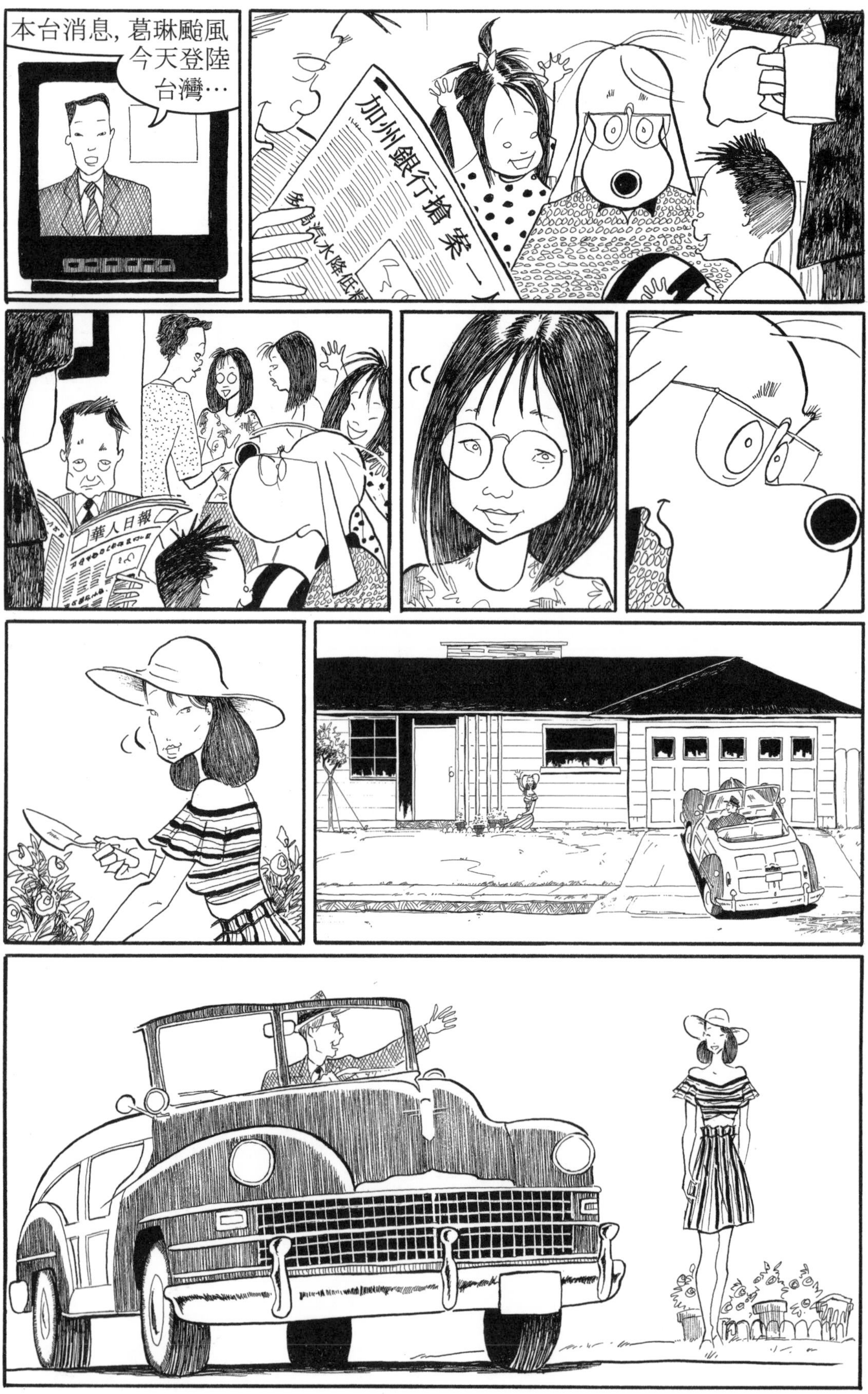
本台消息，葛琳颱風今天登陸台灣…
加州銀行搶案一
汽水降低
華人日報

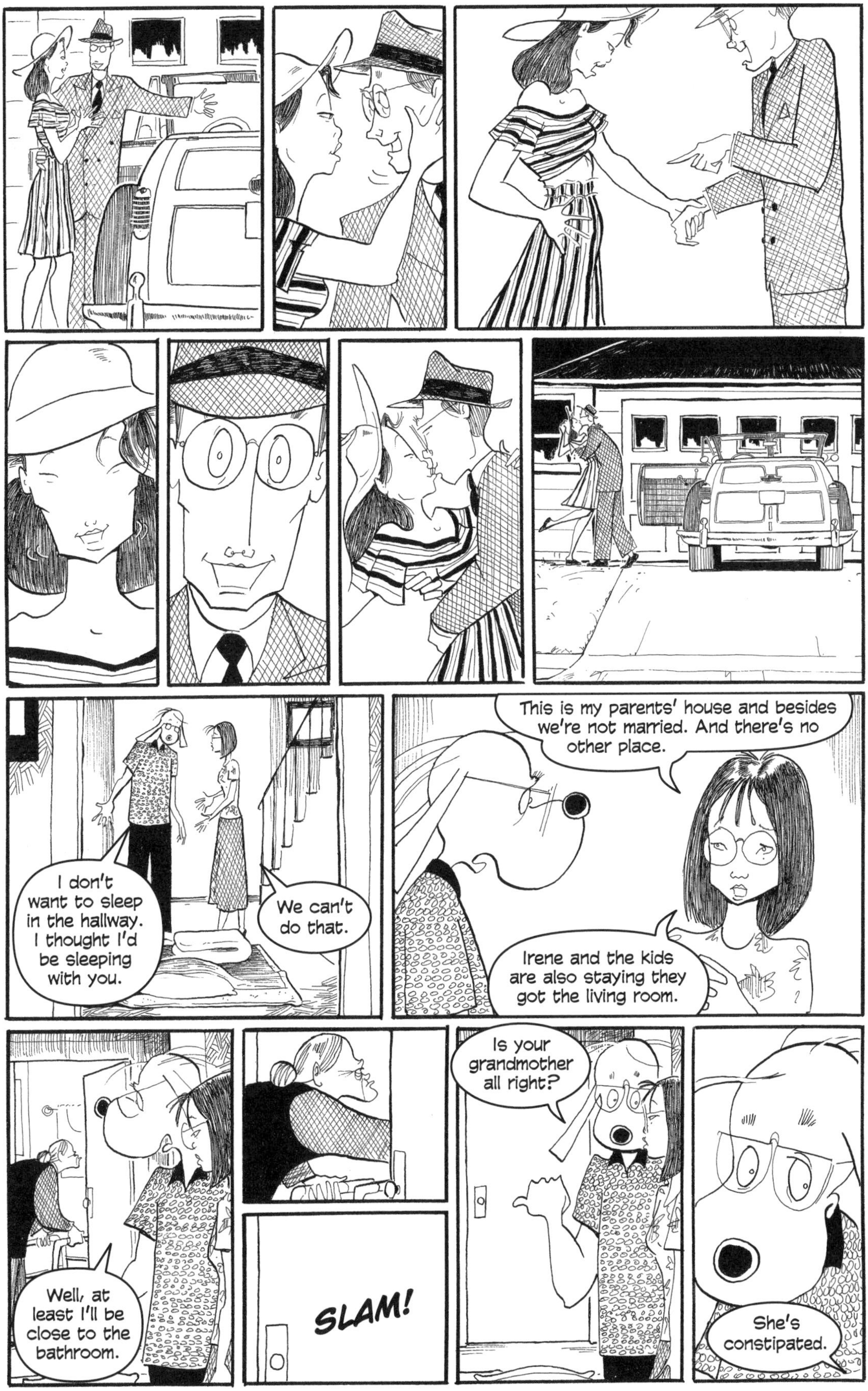
I don't want to sleep in the hallway. I thought I'd be sleeping with you.
We can't do that.
This is my parents' house and besides we're not married. And there's no other place.
Irene and the kids are also staying they got the living room.
Well, at least I'll be close to the bathroom.
SLAM!
Is your grandmother all right?
She's constipated.

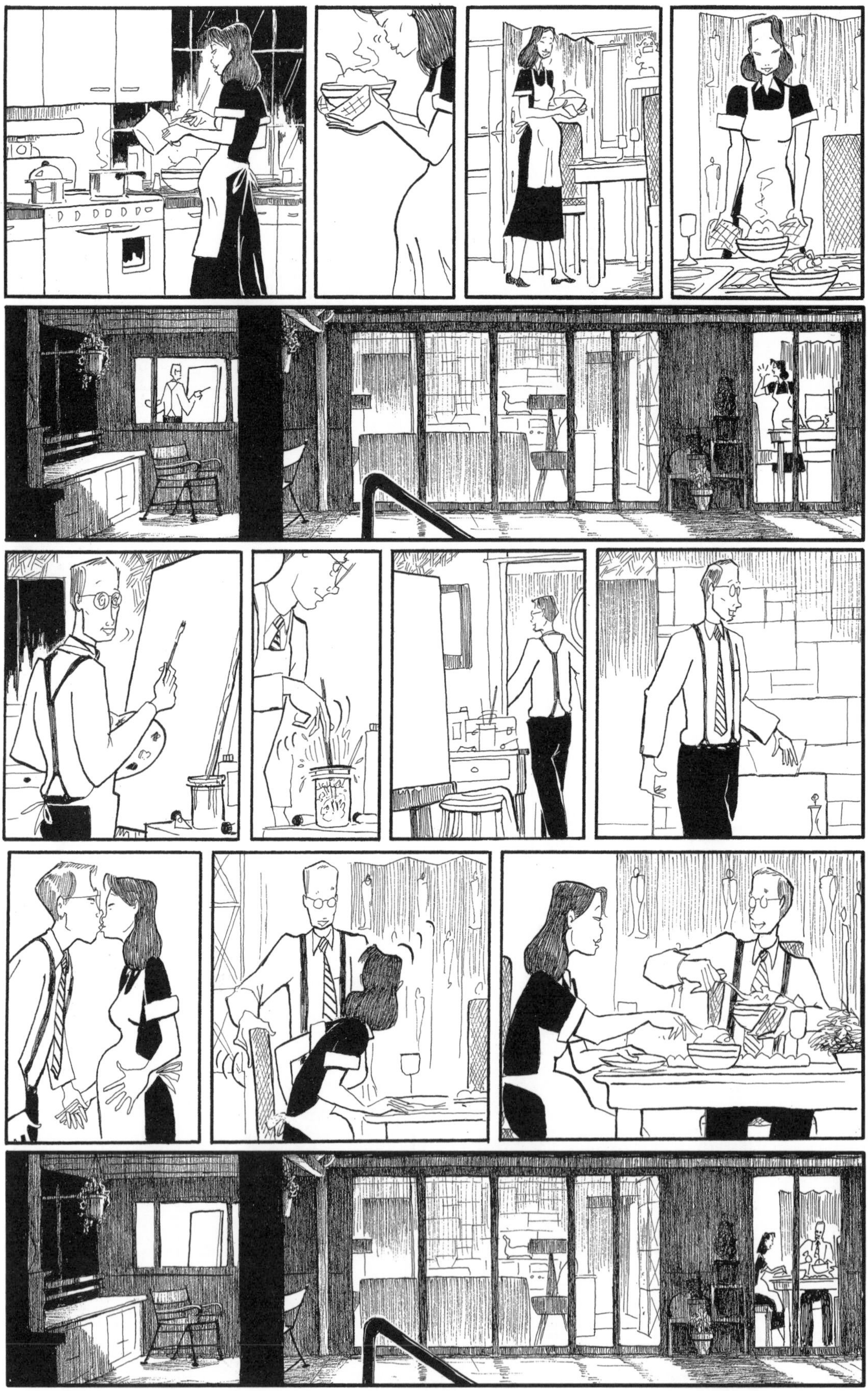

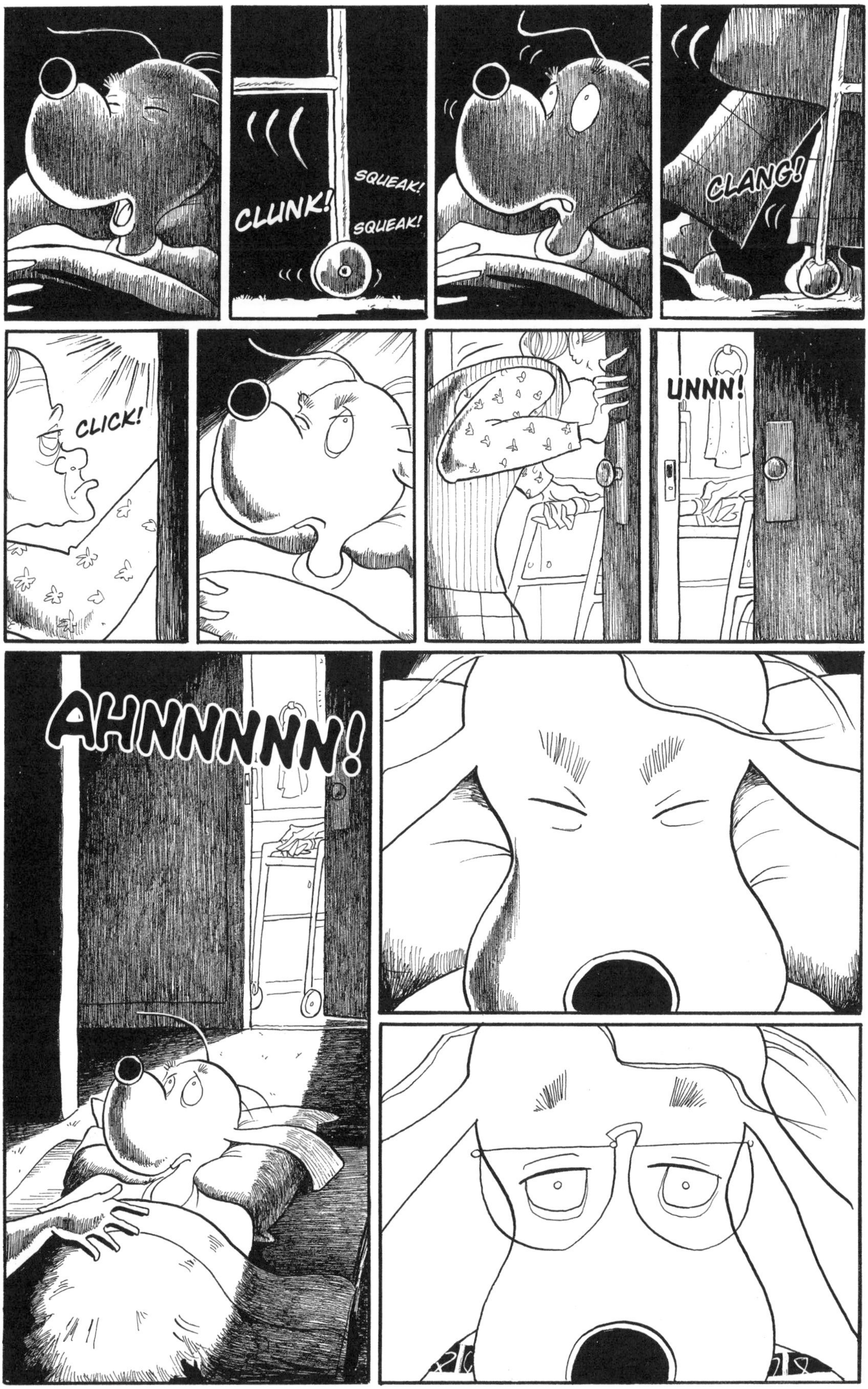
SQUEAK!
CLUNK!
SQUEAK!
CLANG!
CLICK!
UNNN!
AHNNNNNN!

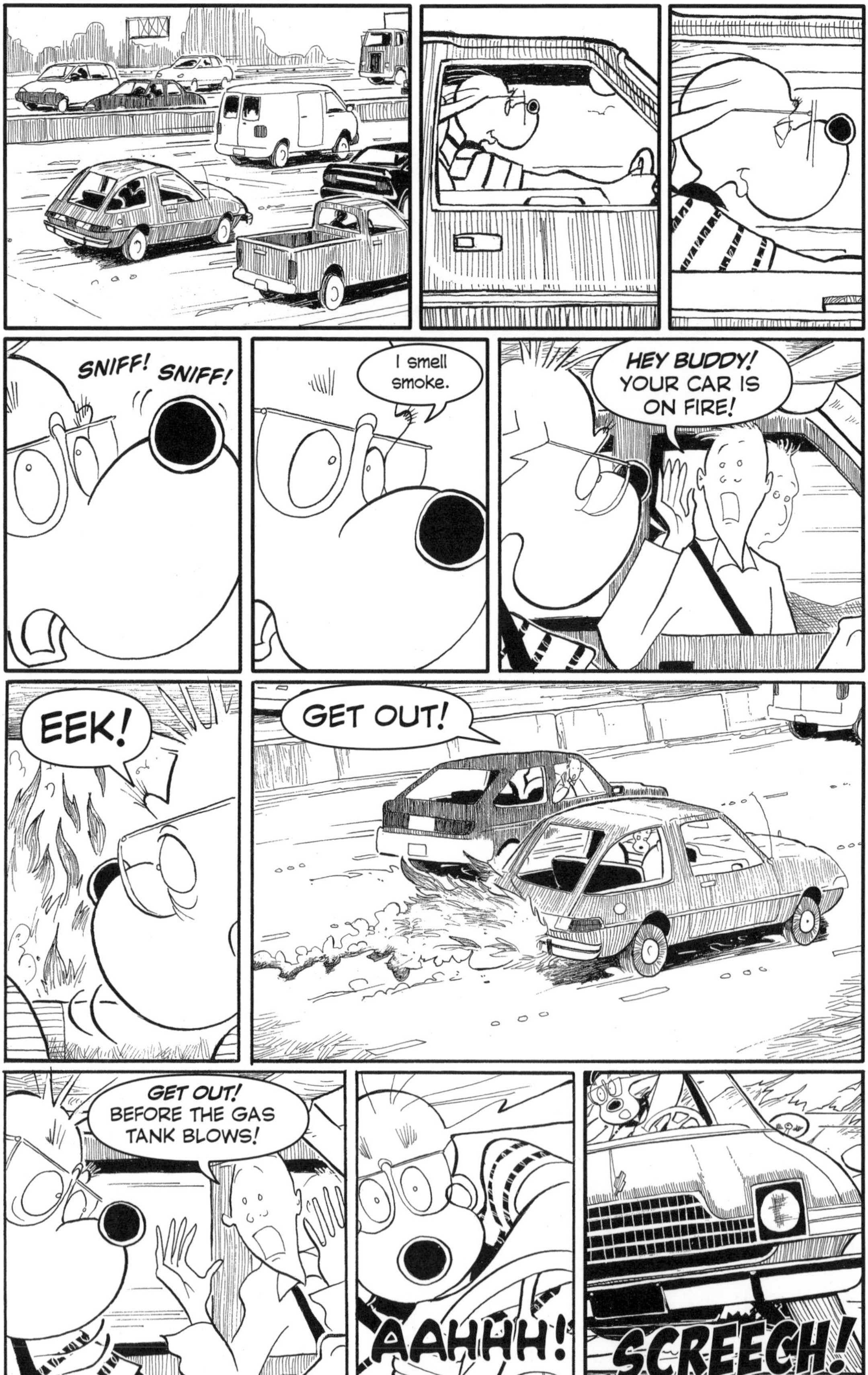
SNIFF! SNIFF!
I smell smoke.
HEY BUDDY! YOUR CAR IS ON FIRE!
EEK!
GET OUT!
GET OUT! BEFORE THE GAS TANK BLOWS!
AAHHH!
SCREECH!

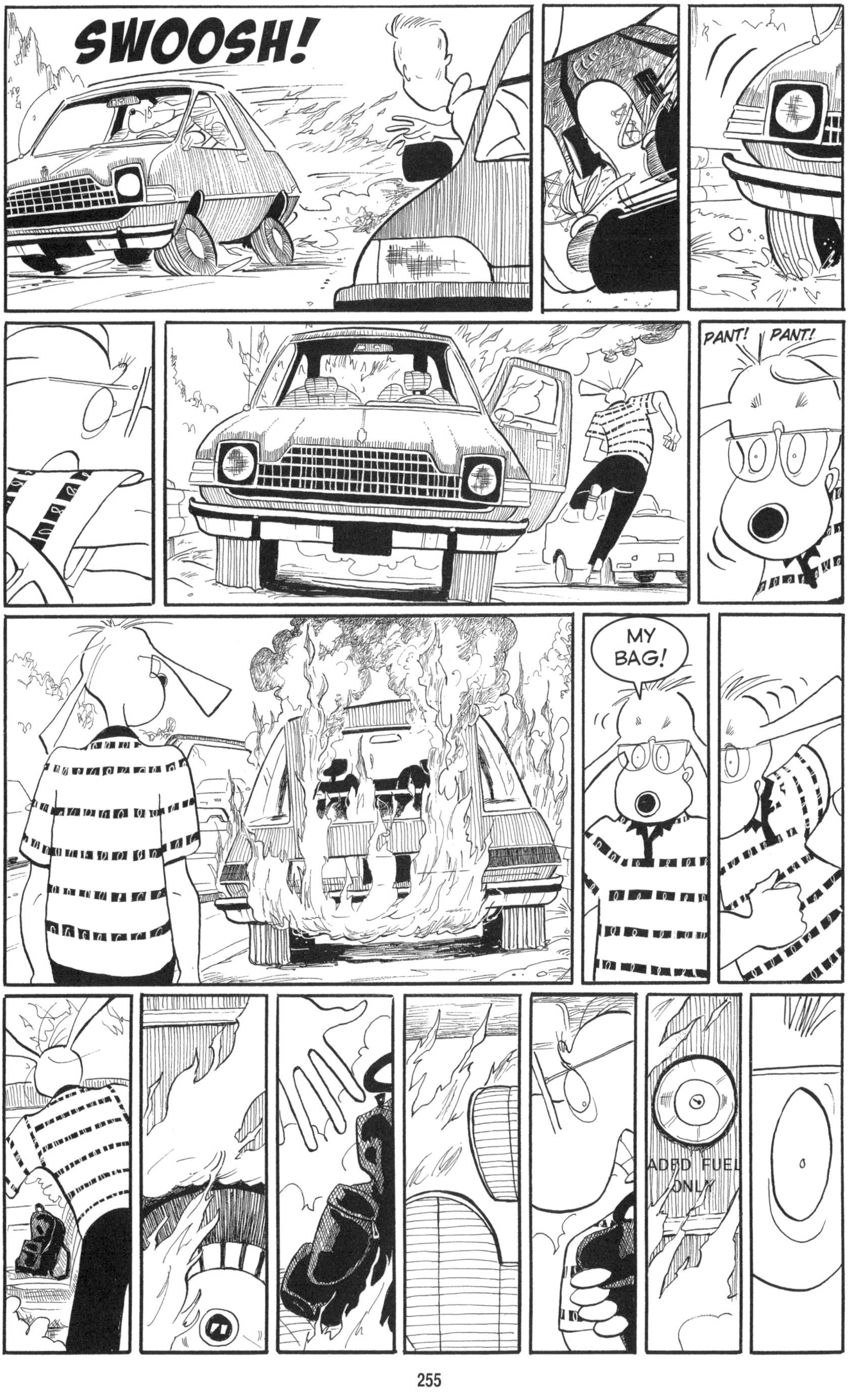
SWOOSH!
PANT! PANT!
MY BAG!
ADED FUEL ONLY

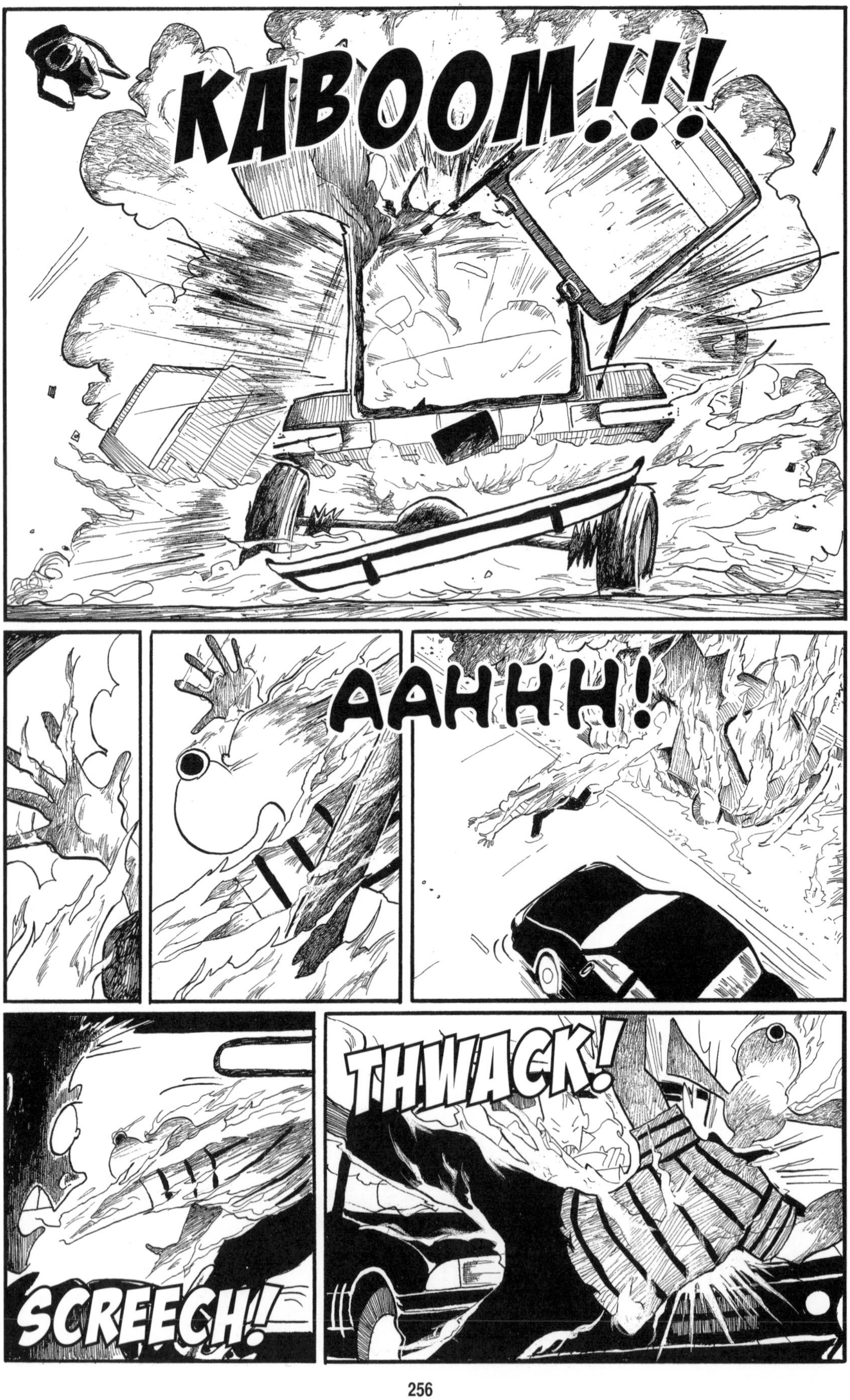
KABOOM!!!
AAHHH!
SCREECH!
THWACK!

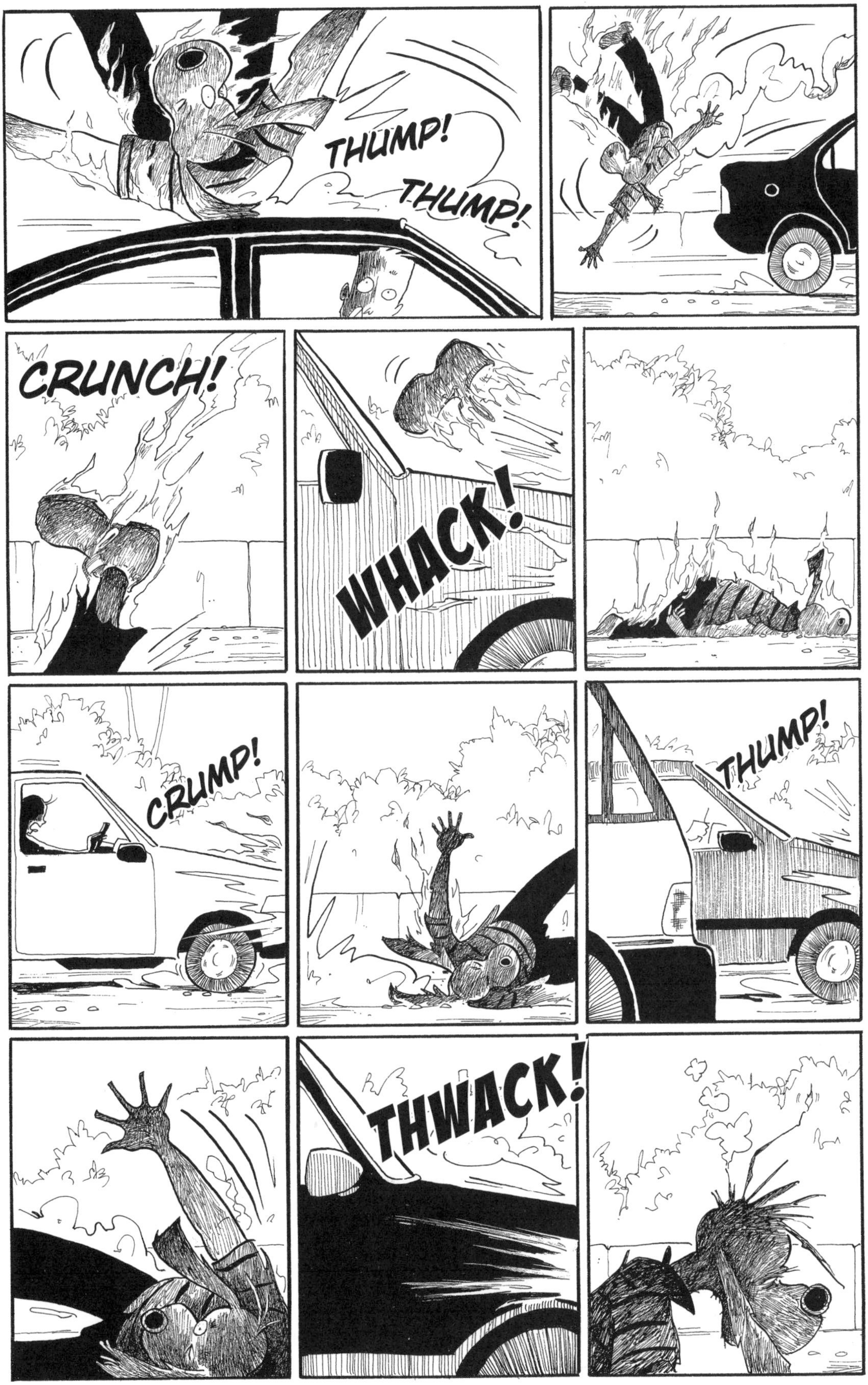
THUMP!
THUMP!
CRUNCH!
WHACK!
CRUMP!
THUMP!
THWACK!

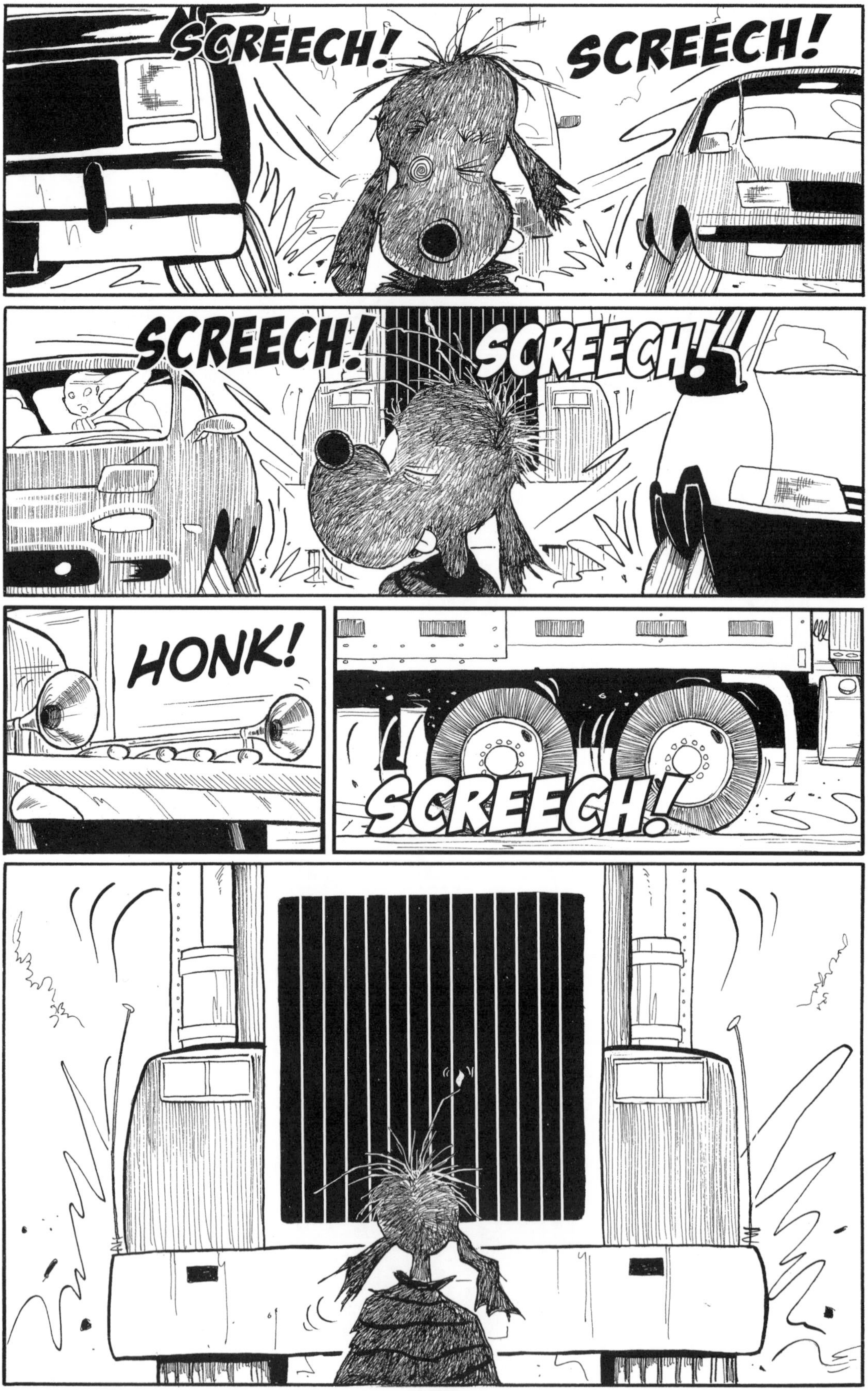
SCREECH!
SCREECH!
SCREECH!
SCREECH!
HONK!
SCREECH!

THRUMP!

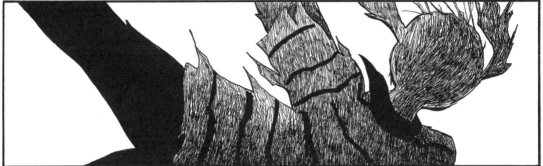

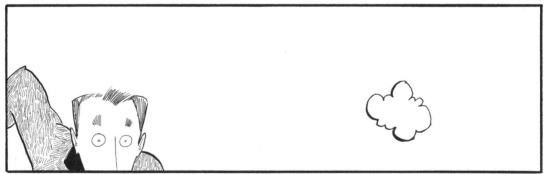

YIKES!

OH MY GOD!

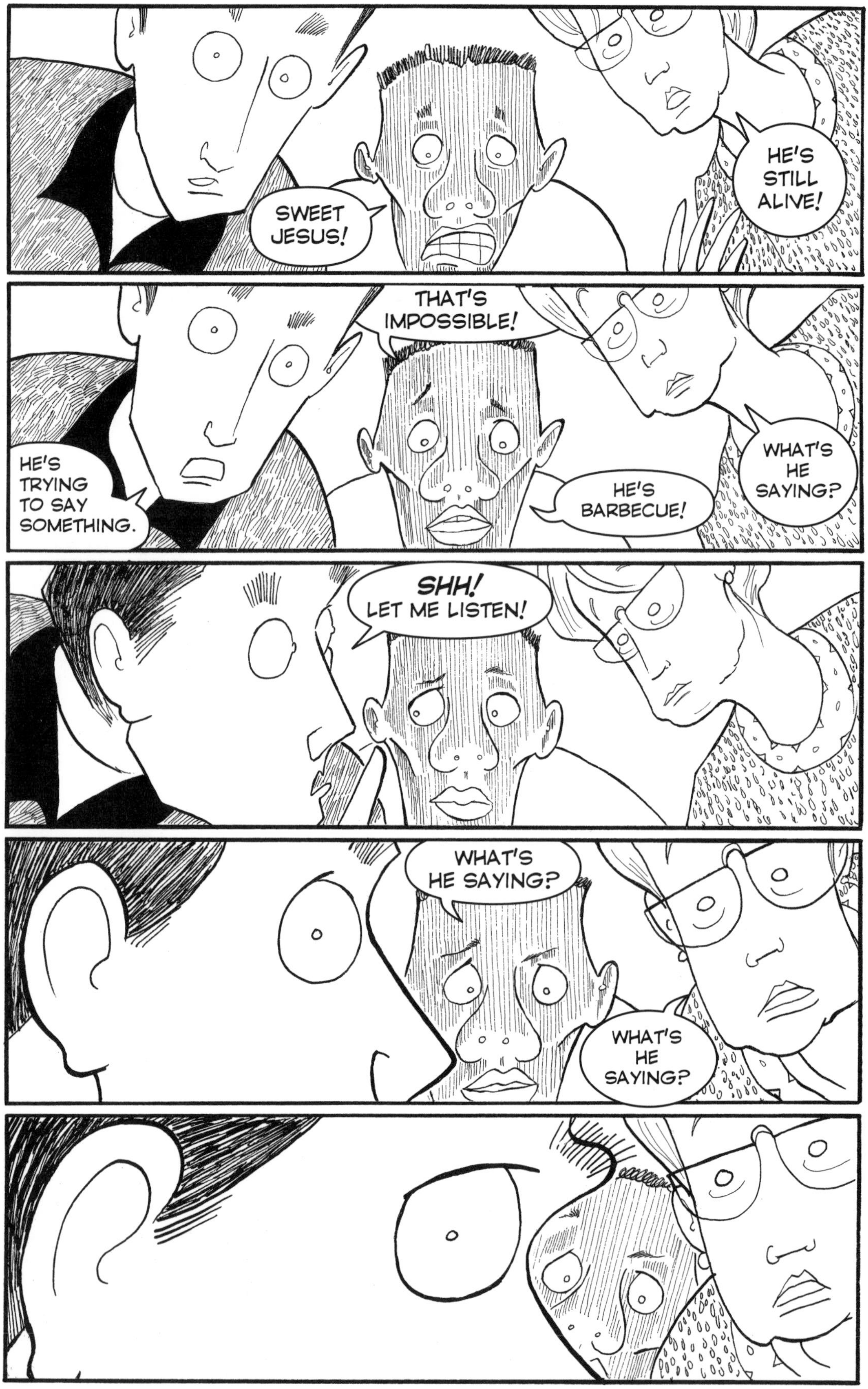
SWEET JESUS!
HE'S STILL ALIVE!
THAT'S IMPOSSIBLE!
HE'S TRYING TO SAY SOMETHING.
HE'S BARBECUE!
WHAT'S HE SAYING?
SHH! LET ME LISTEN!
WHAT'S HE SAYING?
WHAT'S HE SAYING?

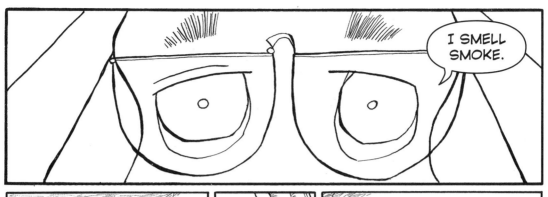

I SMELL SMOKE.

SNIFF! SNIFF!

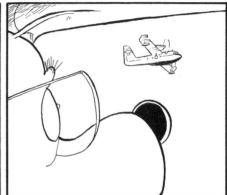

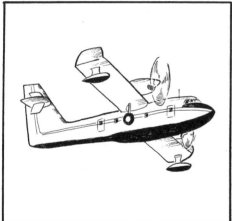

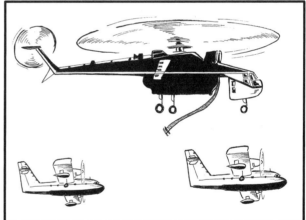

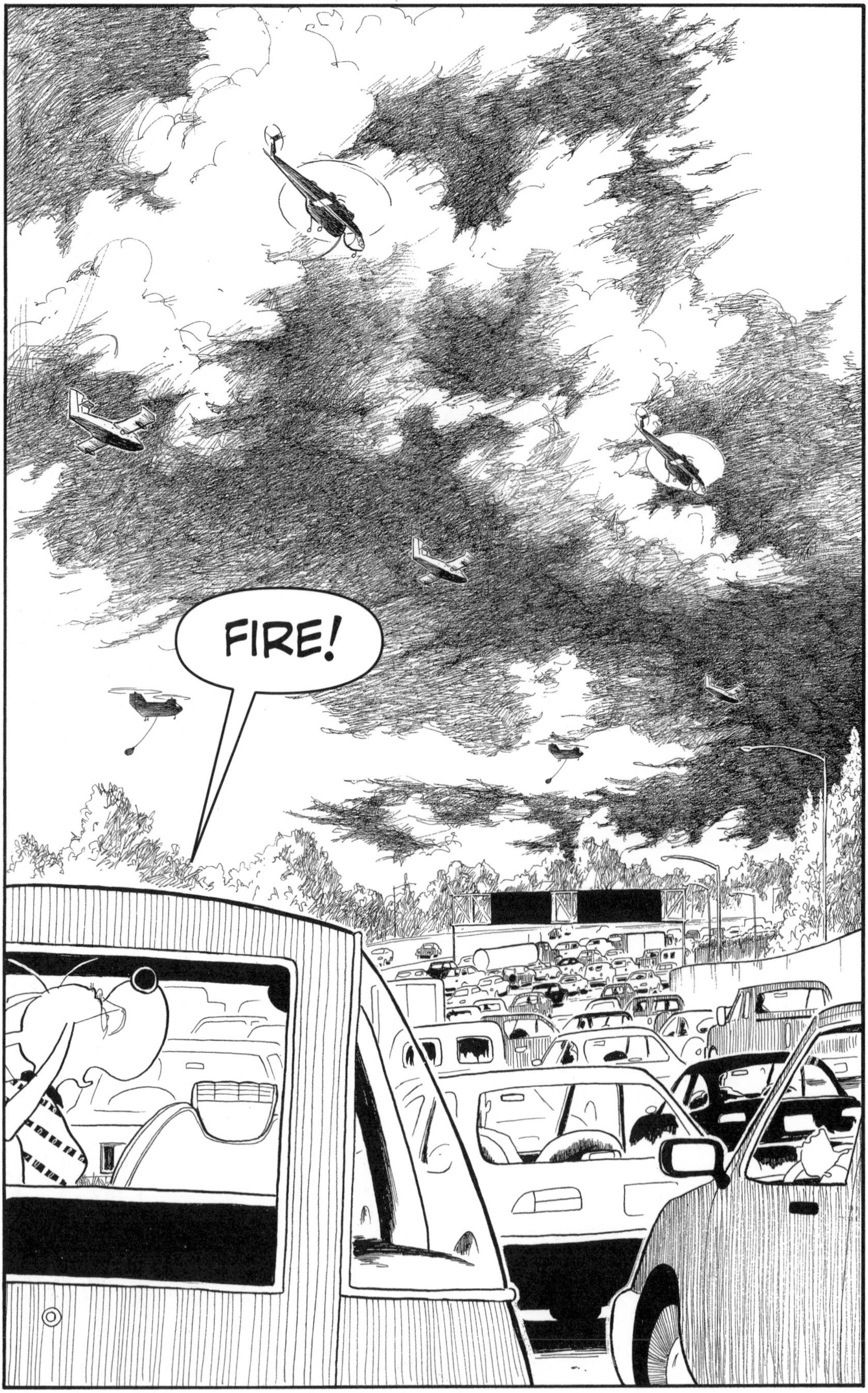
FIRE!

CHAPTER 6

I THOUGHT ABOUT YOU

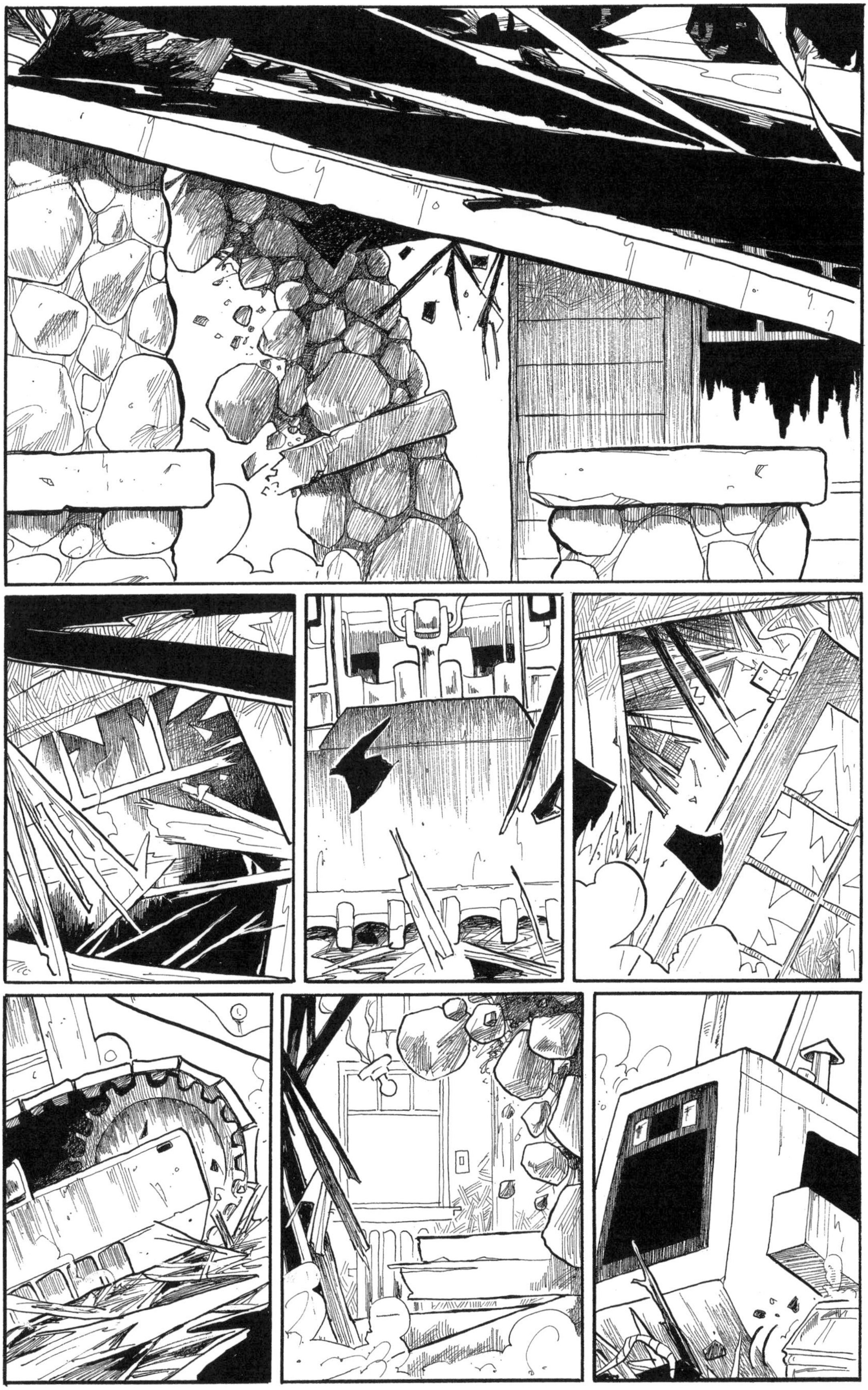

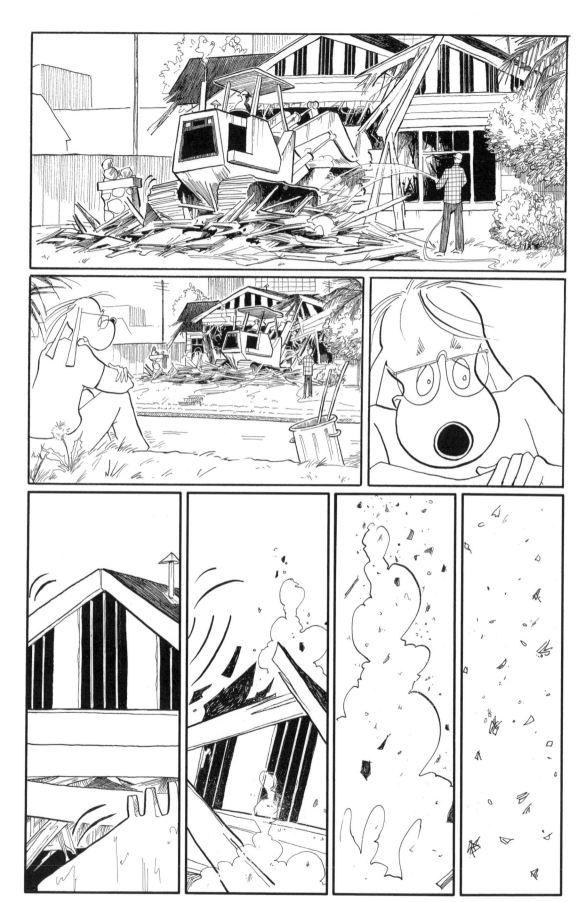

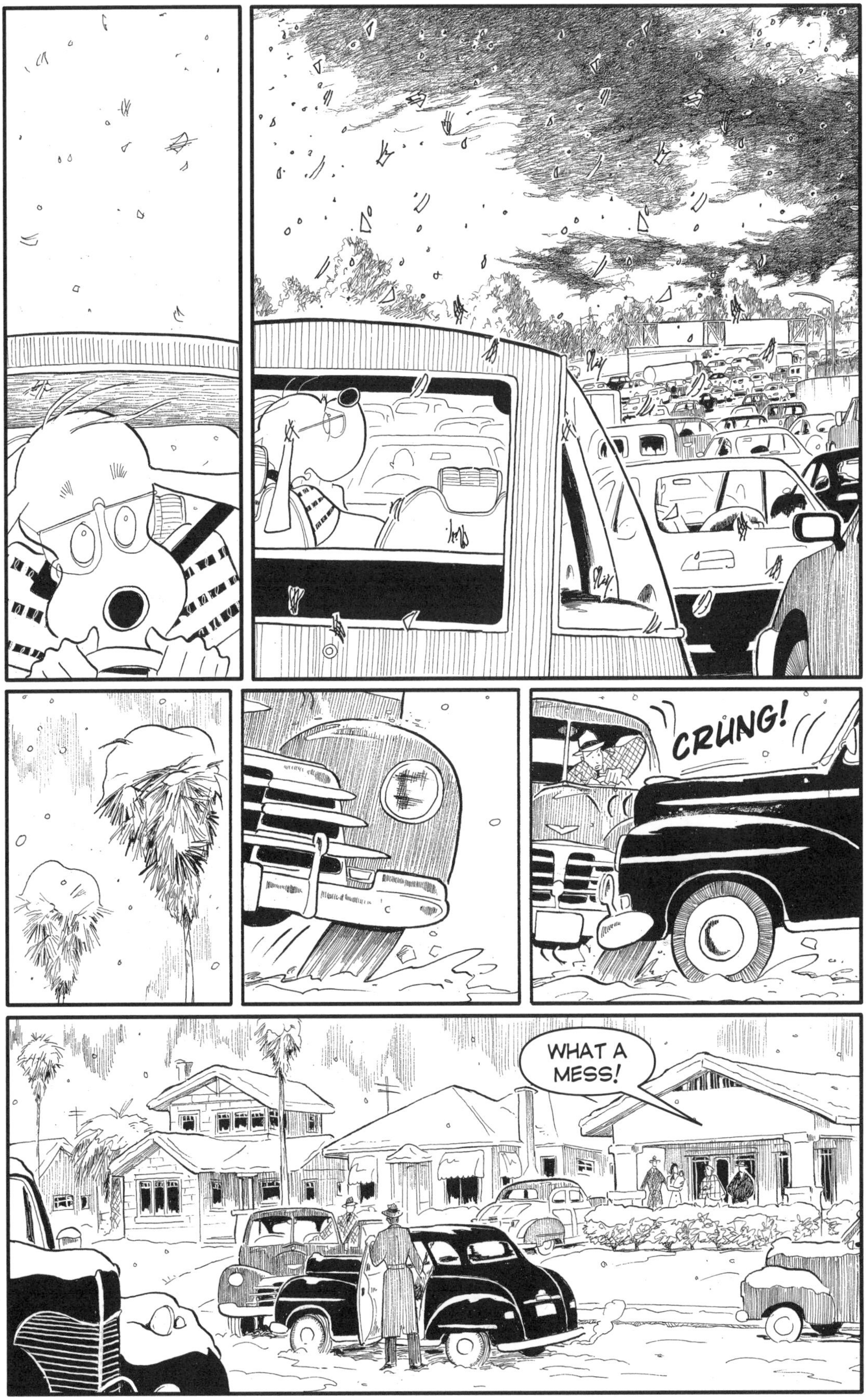
CRUNG!
WHAT A MESS!

How did you drive through this?
I'm Canadian.
Driving in snow is easy.
Ash... from the fires.

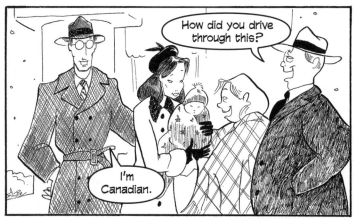

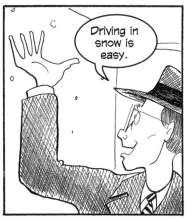

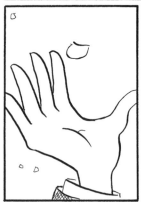

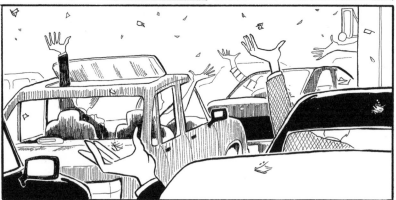

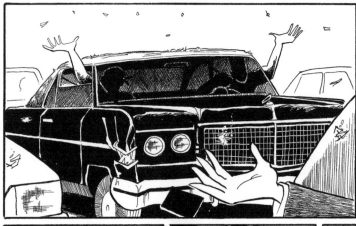

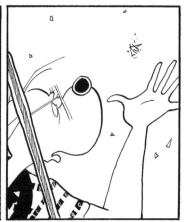

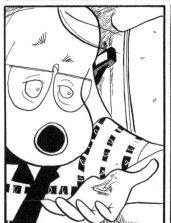

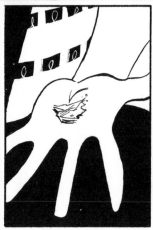

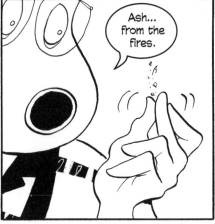

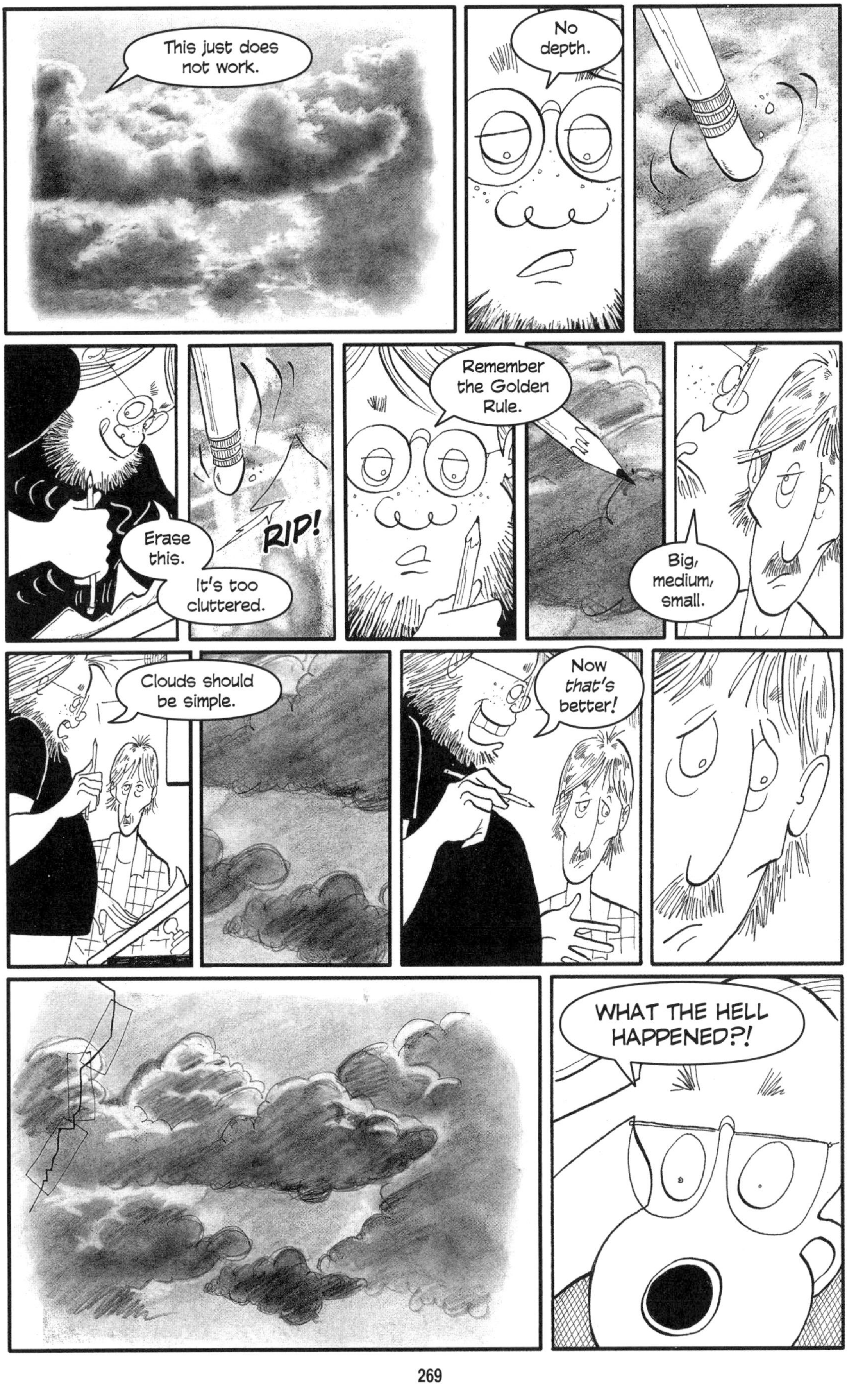
This just does not work.
No depth.
Erase this.
It's too cluttered.
RIP!
Remember the Golden Rule.
Big, medium, small.
Clouds should be simple.
Now *that's* better!
WHAT THE HELL HAPPENED?!

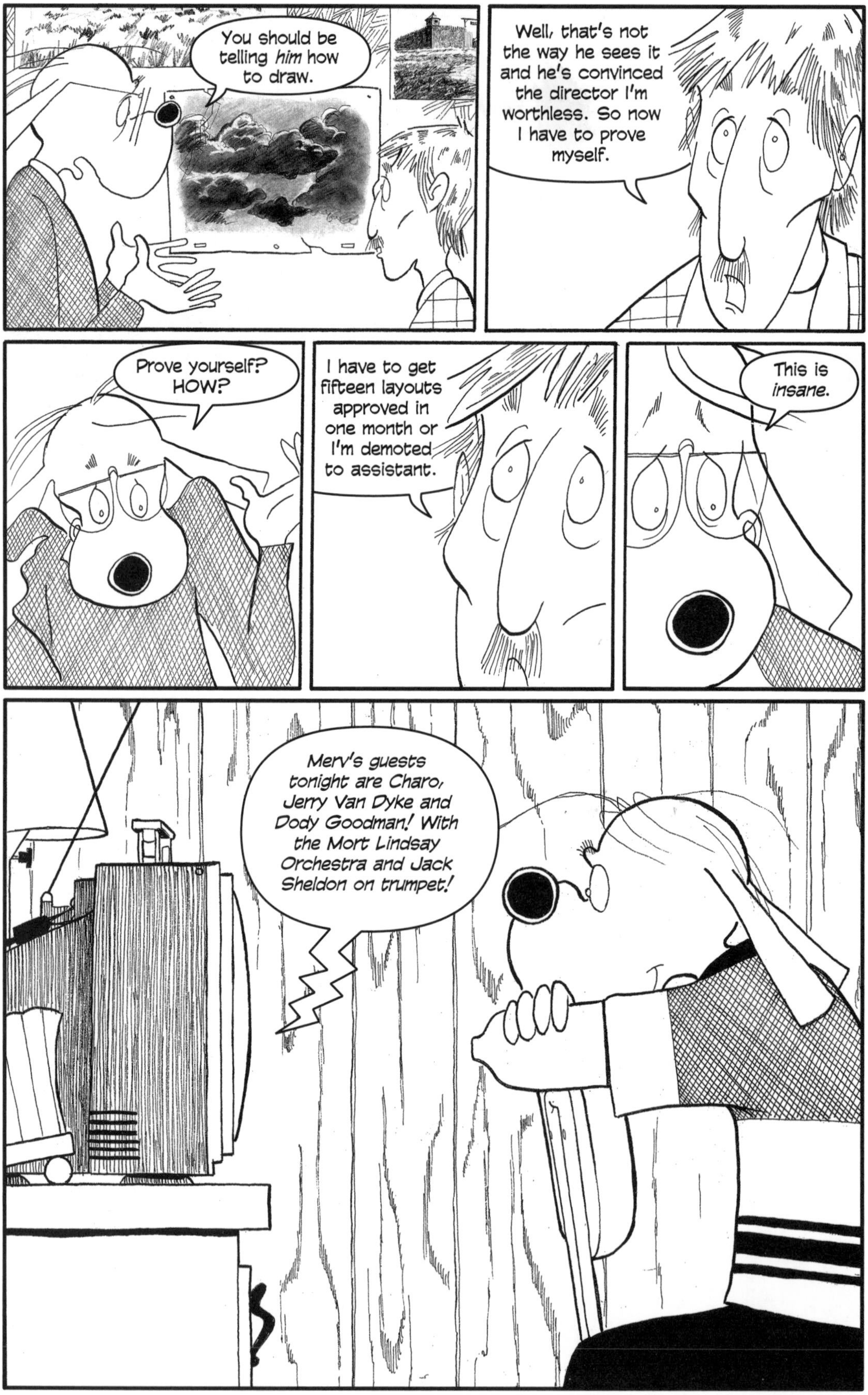
You should be telling *him* how to draw.
Well, that's not the way he sees it and he's convinced the director I'm worthless. So now I have to prove myself.
Prove yourself? HOW?
I have to get fifteen layouts approved in one month or I'm demoted to assistant.
This is *insane*.
Merv's guests tonight are Charo, Jerry Van Dyke and Dody Goodman! With the Mort Lindsay Orchestra and Jack Sheldon on trumpet!

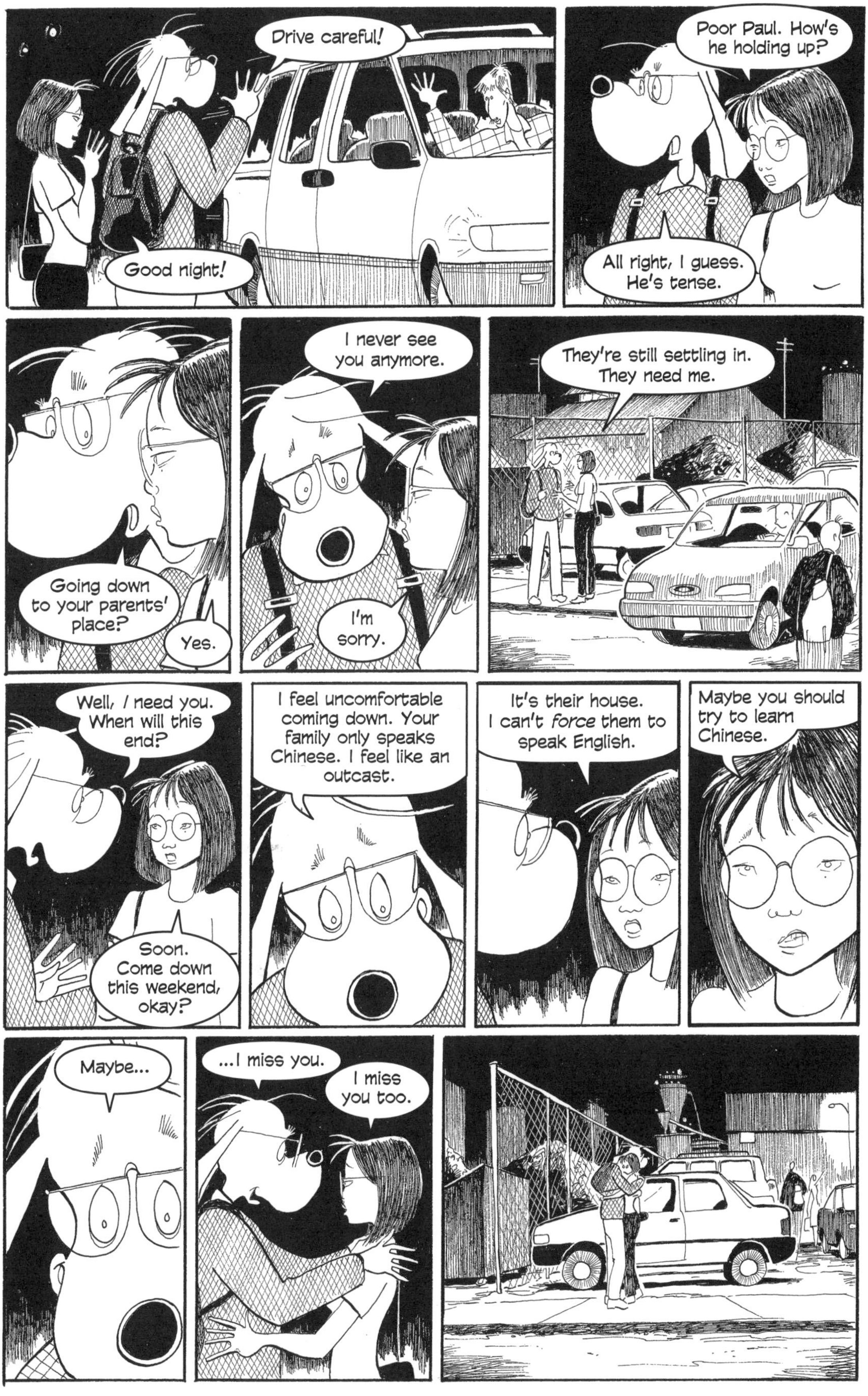
Drive careful!
Good night!
Poor Paul. How's he holding up?
All right, I guess. He's tense.
Going down to your parents' place?
Yes.
I never see you anymore.
I'm sorry.
They're still settling in. They need me.
Well, I need you. When will this end?
Soon. Come down this weekend, okay?
I feel uncomfortable coming down. Your family only speaks Chinese. I feel like an outcast.
It's their house. I can't *force* them to speak English.
Maybe you should try to learn Chinese.
Maybe...
...I miss you.
I miss you too.

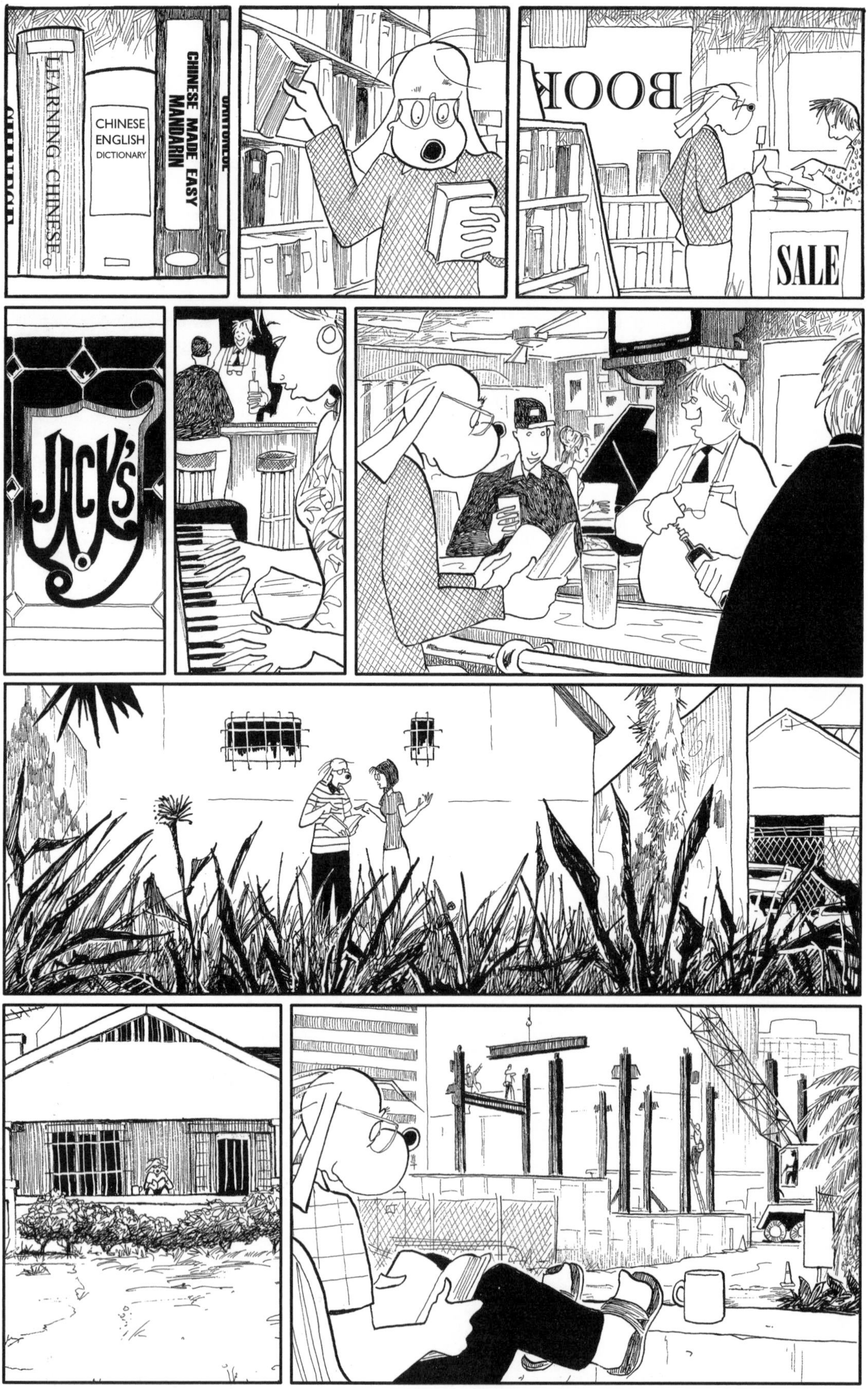
LEARNING CHINESE
CHINESE ENGLISH DICTIONARY
CHINESE MADE EASY MANDARIN
BOOK
SALE
JACK'S

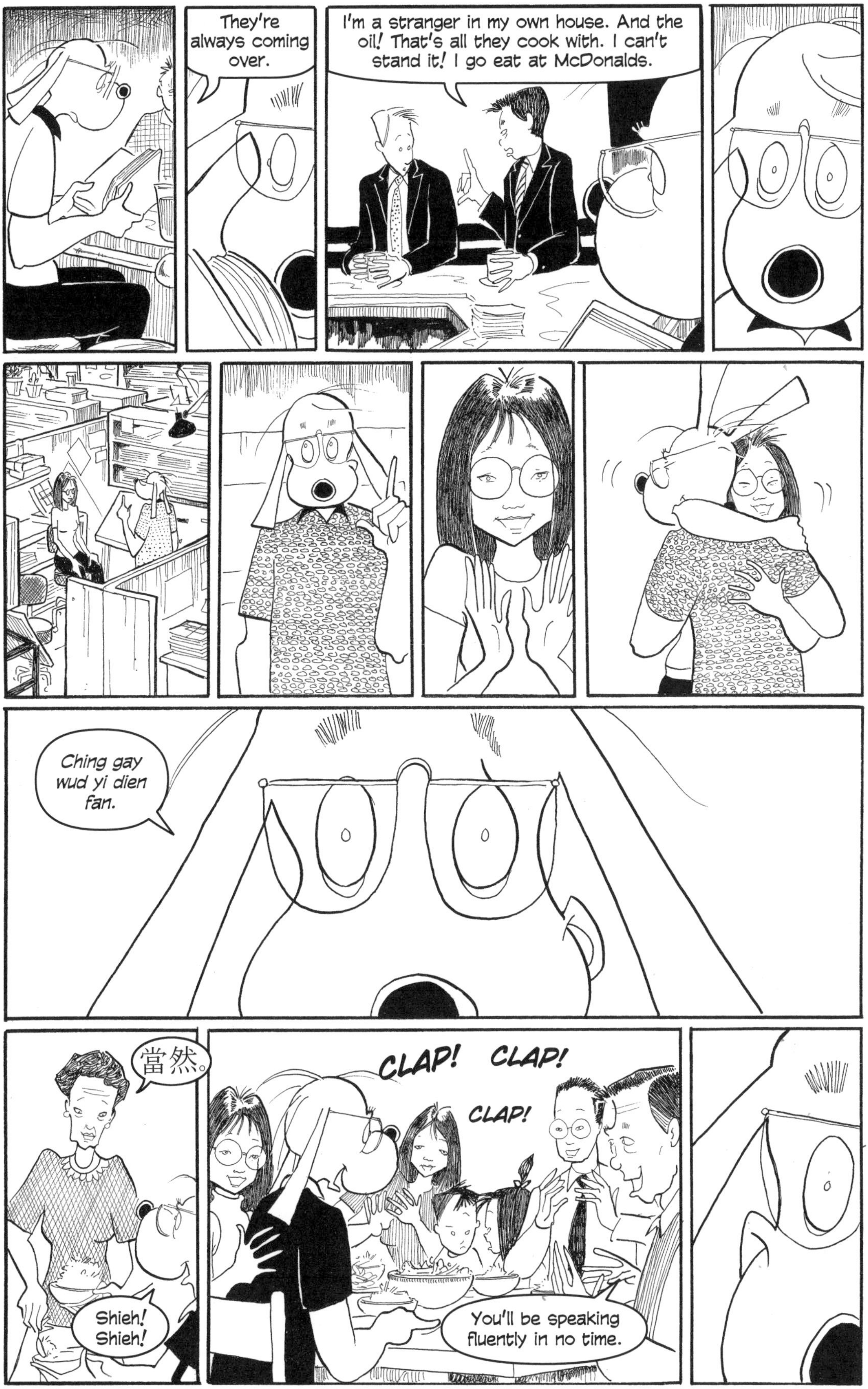
They're always coming over.
I'm a stranger in my own house. And the oil! That's all they cook with. I can't stand it! I go eat at McDonalds.
Ching gay wud yi dien fan.
當然。
Shieh! Shieh!
CLAP! CLAP!
CLAP!
You'll be speaking fluently in no time.

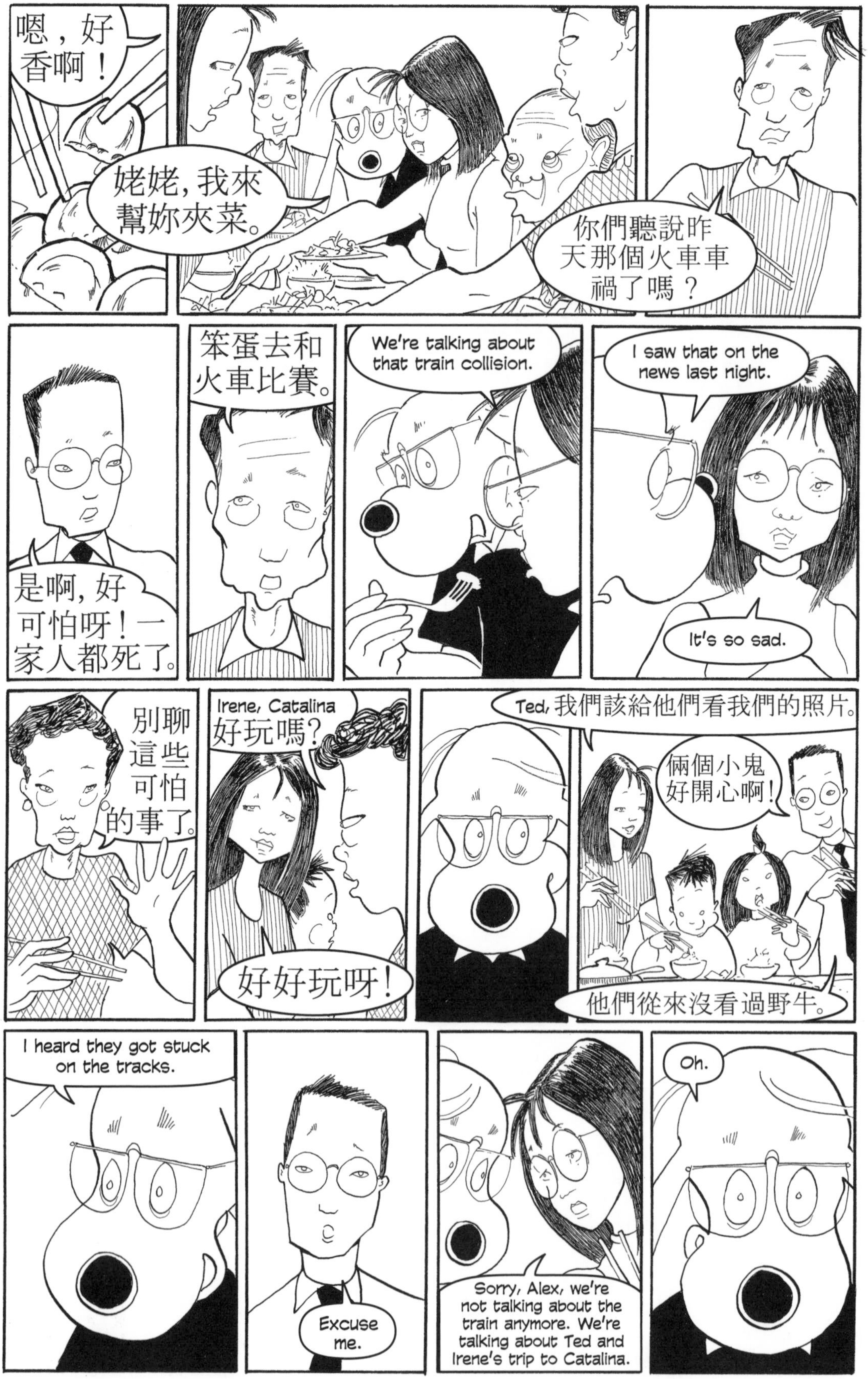

嗯，好香啊！
姥姥, 我來幫妳夾菜。
你們聽說昨天那個火車車禍了嗎？
是啊, 好可怕呀！一家人都死了。
笨蛋去和火車比賽。
We're talking about that train collision.
I saw that on the news last night.
It's so sad.
別聊這些可怕的事了。
Irene, Catalina 好玩嗎?
好好玩呀！
Ted, 我們該給他們看我們的照片。
倆個小鬼好開心啊!
他們從來沒看過野牛。
I heard they got stuck on the tracks.
Excuse me.
Sorry, Alex, we're not talking about the train anymore. We're talking about Ted and Irene's trip to Catalina.
Oh.

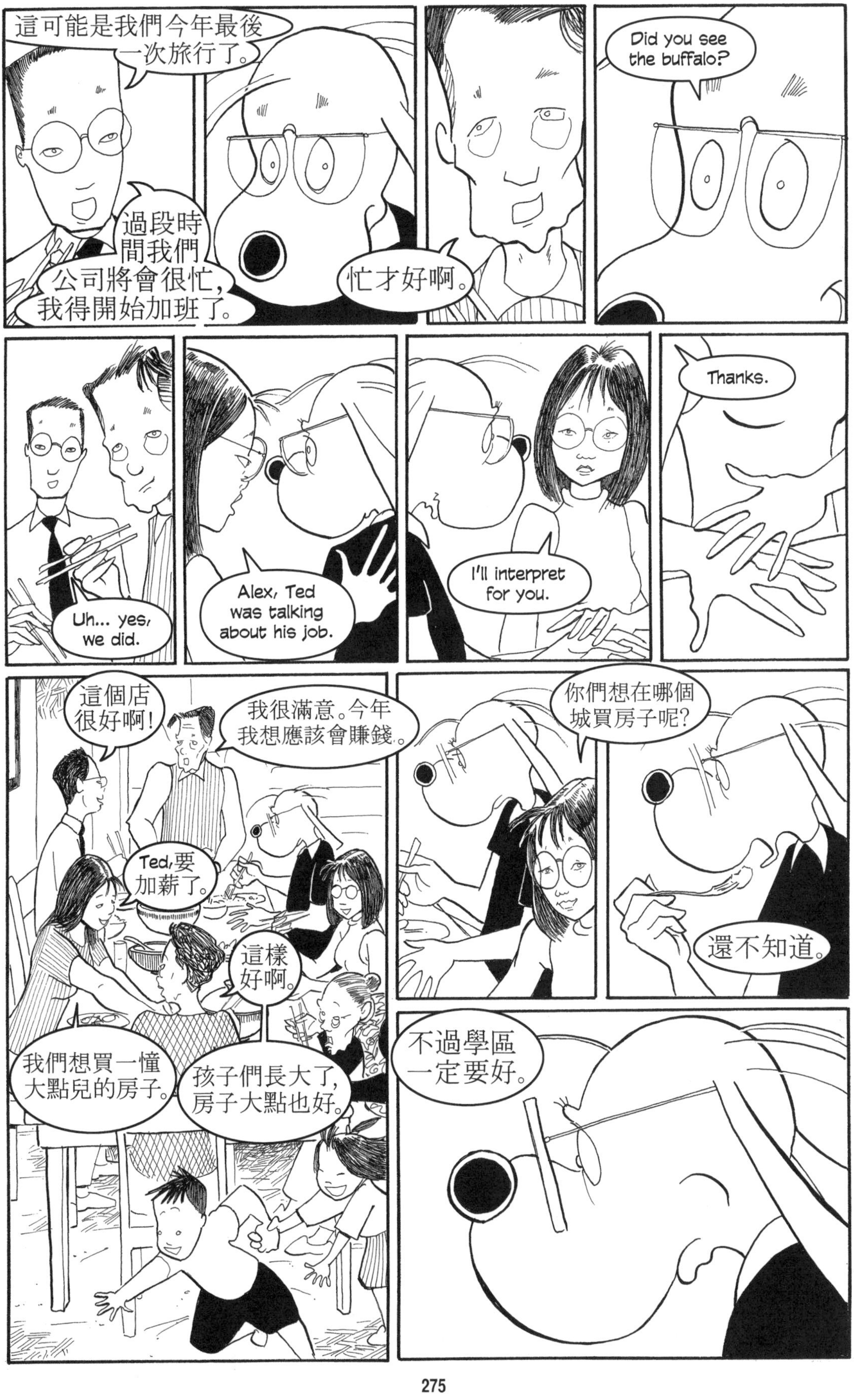
這可能是我們今年最後一次旅行了。
過段時間我們公司將會很忙，我得開始加班了。
忙才好啊。
Did you see the buffalo?
Uh... yes, we did.
Alex, Ted was talking about his job.
I'll interpret for you.
Thanks.
這個店很好啊!
我很滿意。今年我想應該會賺錢。
Ted,要加薪了。
這樣好啊。
我們想買一幢大點兒的房子。
孩子們長大了，房子大點也好。
你們想在哪個城買房子呢?
還不知道。
不過學區一定要好。

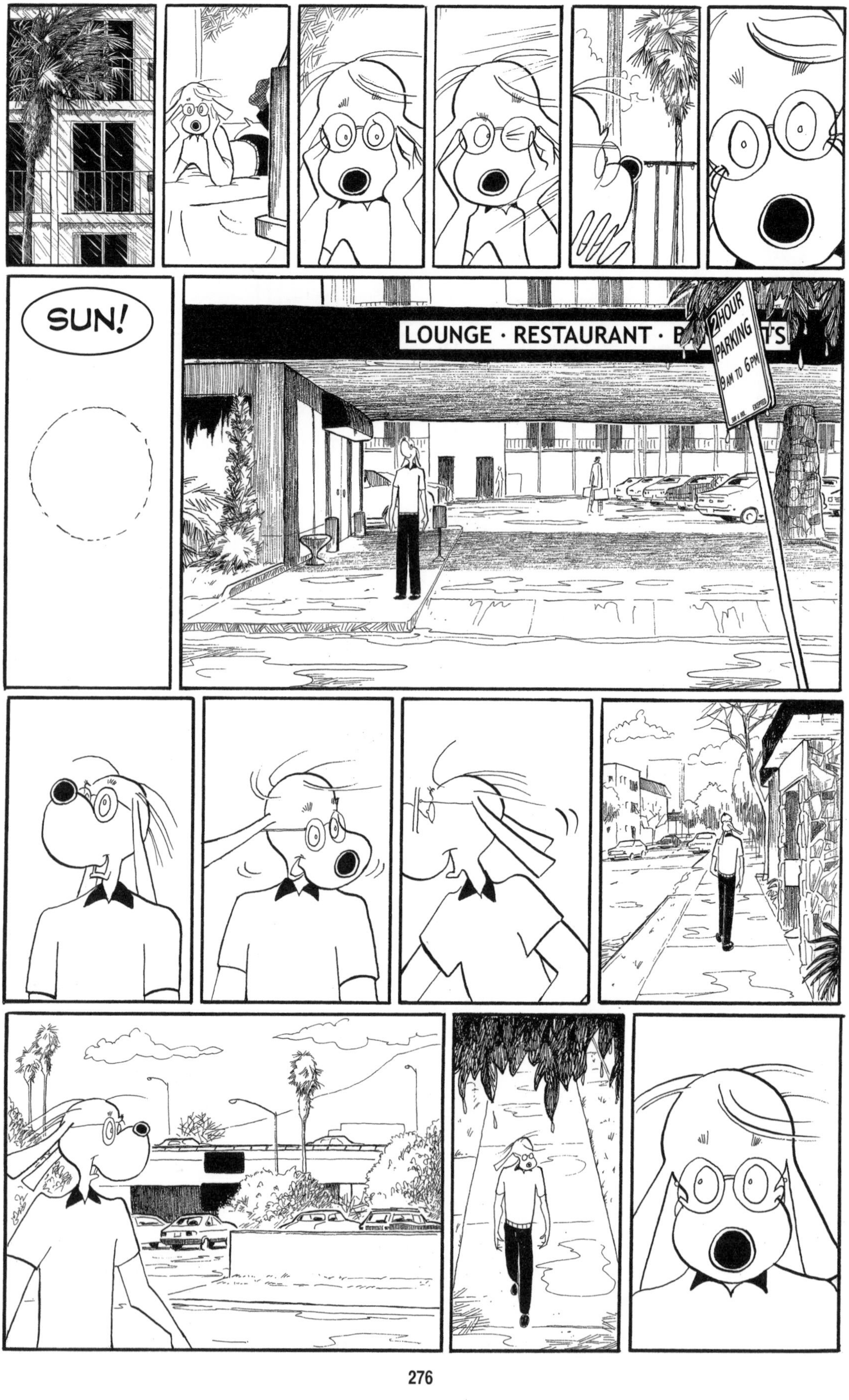
SUN!
LOUNGE · RESTAURANT ·
2 HOUR PARKING 9AM TO 6PM

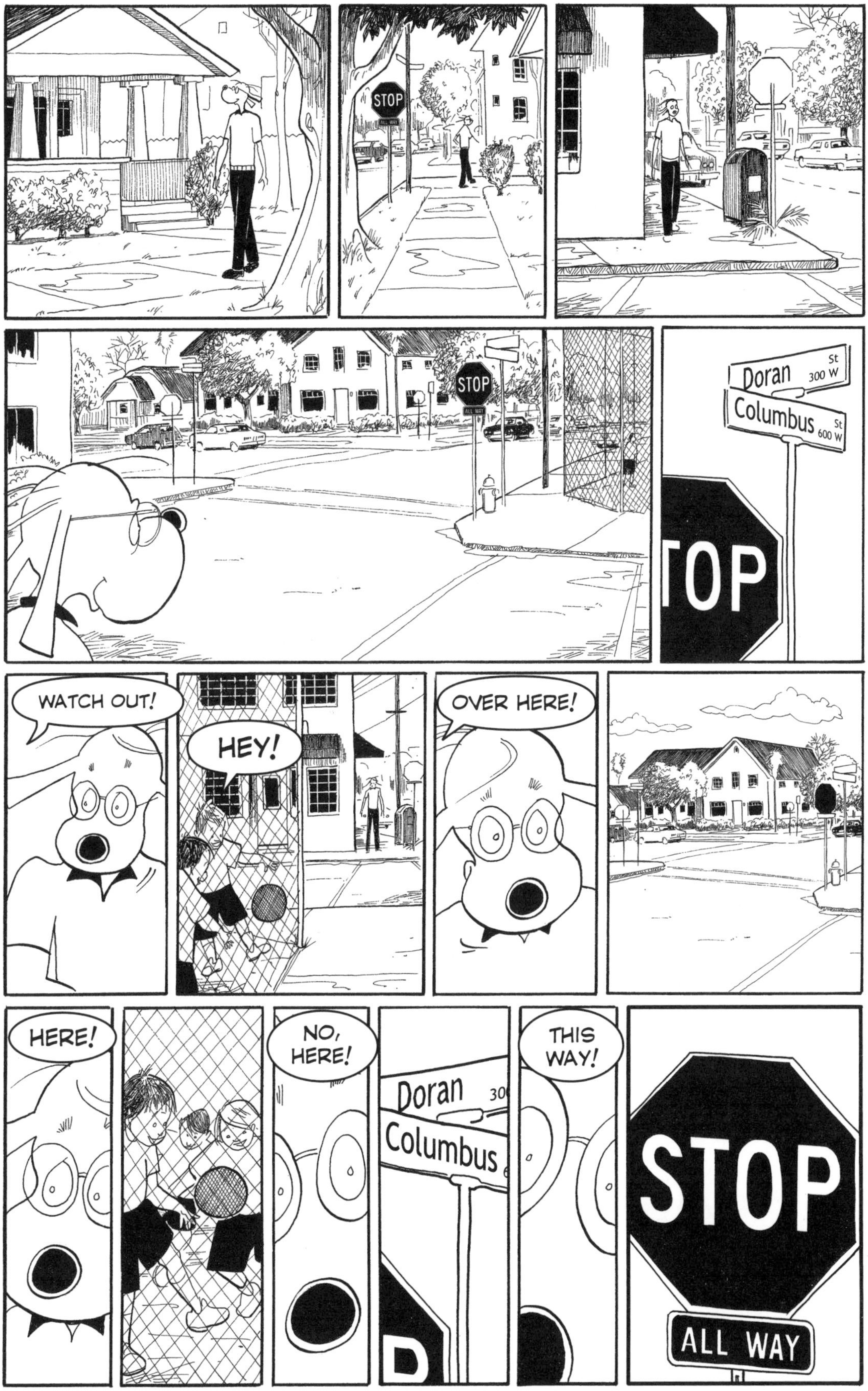
STOP
ALL WAY
Doran St 300 W
Columbus St 600 W
STOP
TOP
WATCH OUT!
HEY!
OVER HERE!
HERE!
NO, HERE!
Doran 30
Columbus
THIS WAY!
STOP
ALL WAY

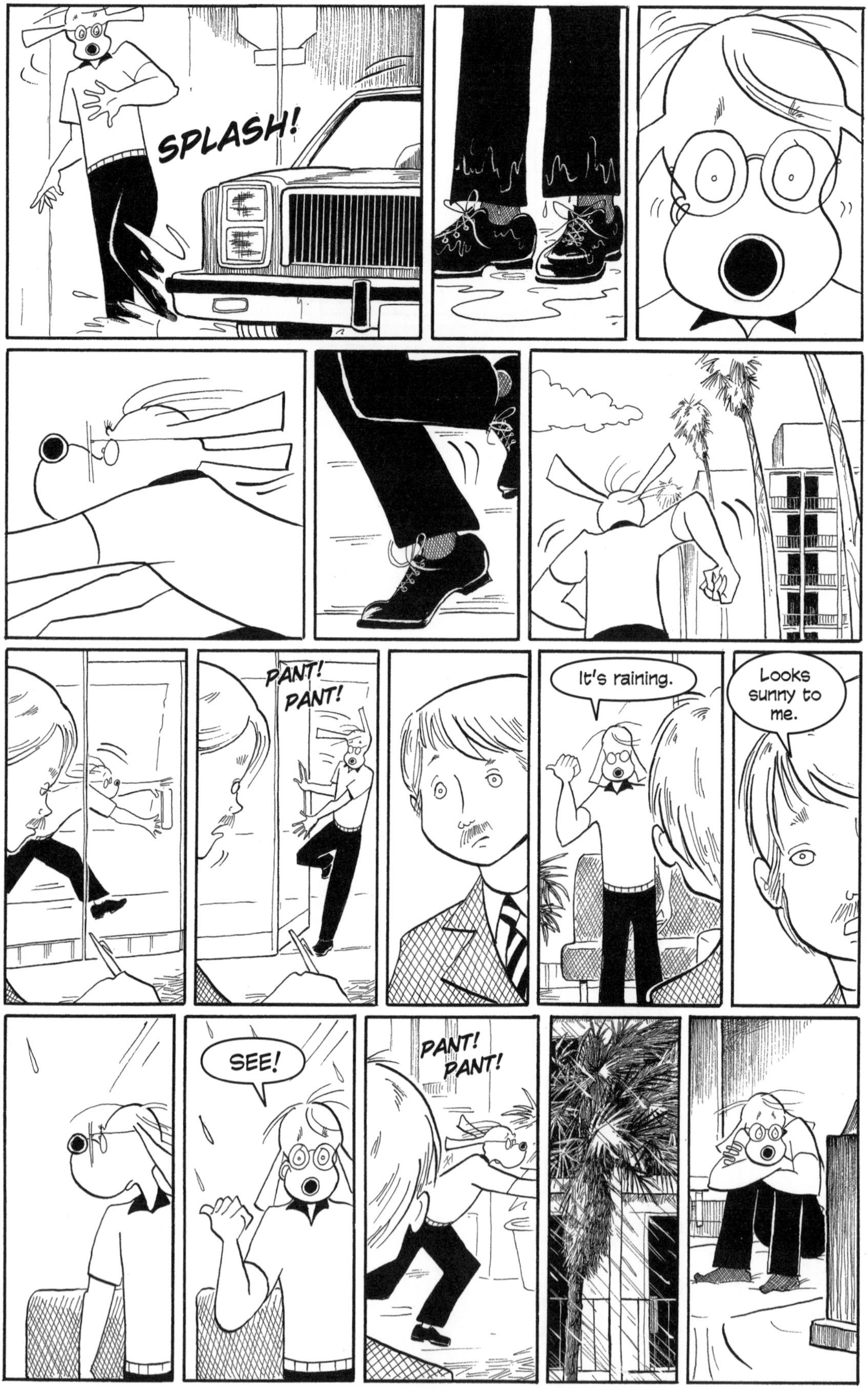
SPLASH!
PANT! PANT!
It's raining.
Looks sunny to me.
SEE!
PANT! PANT!

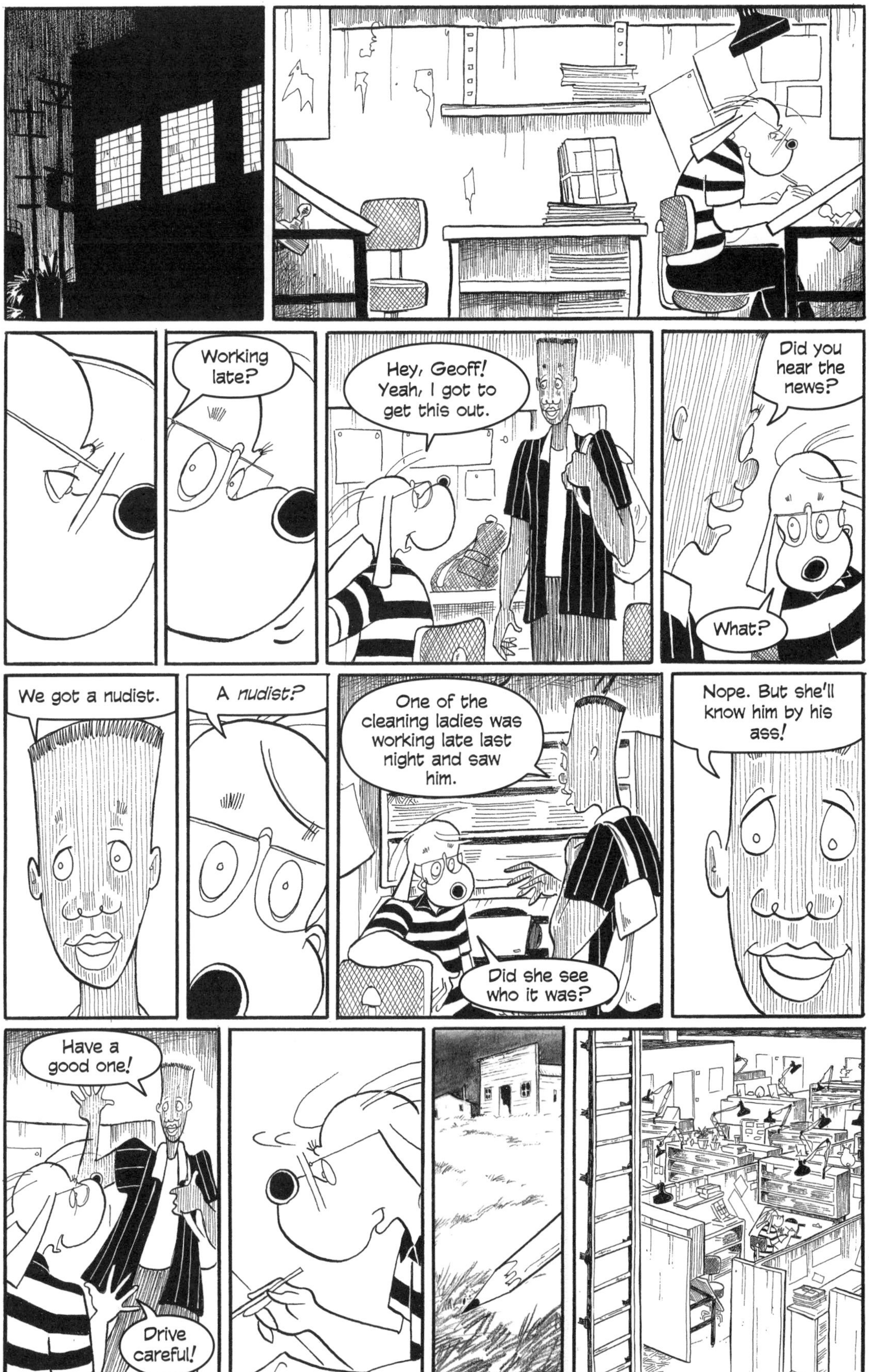

Working late?
Hey, Geoff! Yeah, I got to get this out.
Did you hear the news?
What?
We got a nudist.
A *nudist?*
One of the cleaning ladies was working late last night and saw him.
Did she see who it was?
Nope. But she'll know him by his ass!
Have a good one!
Drive careful!

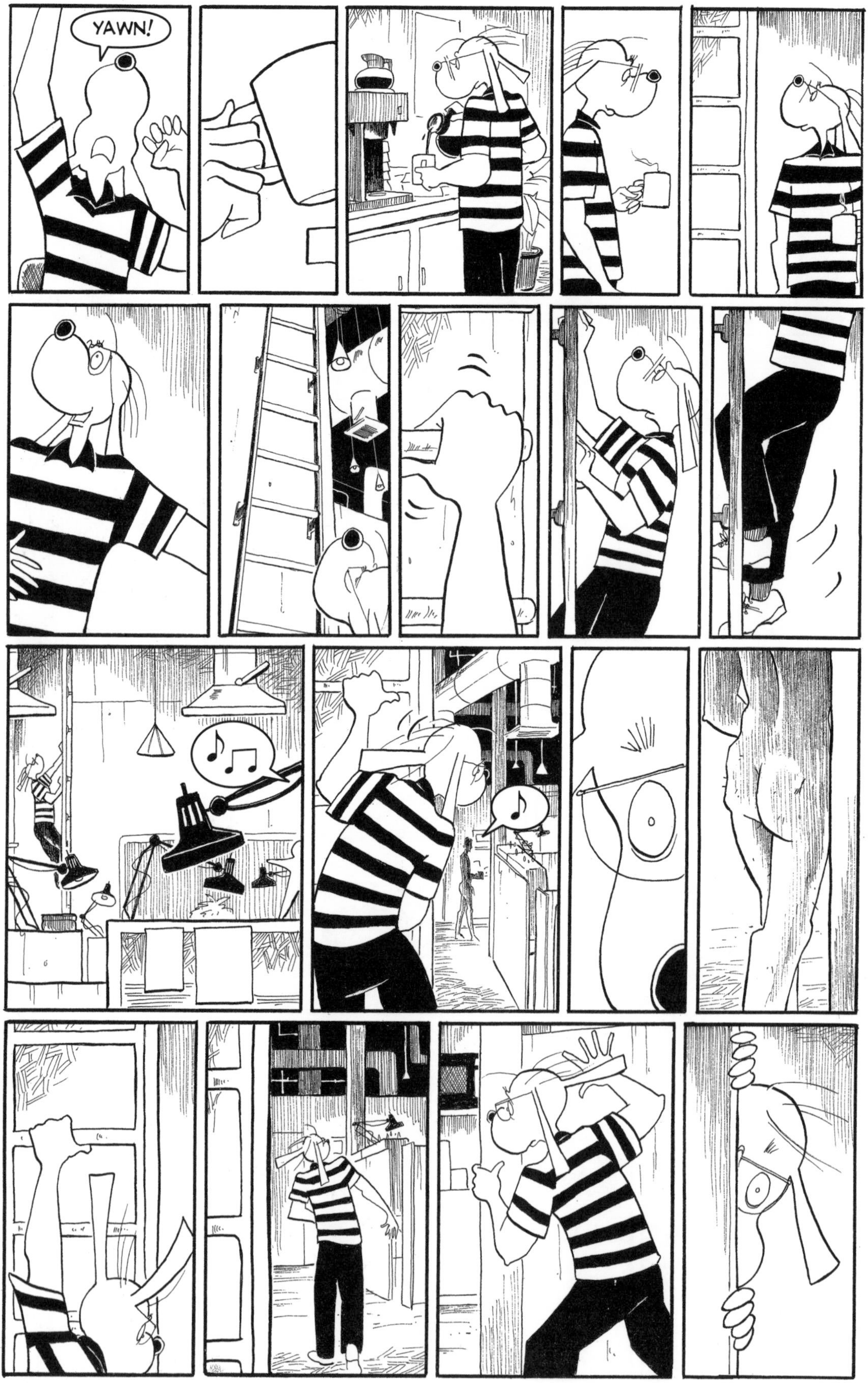
YAWN!

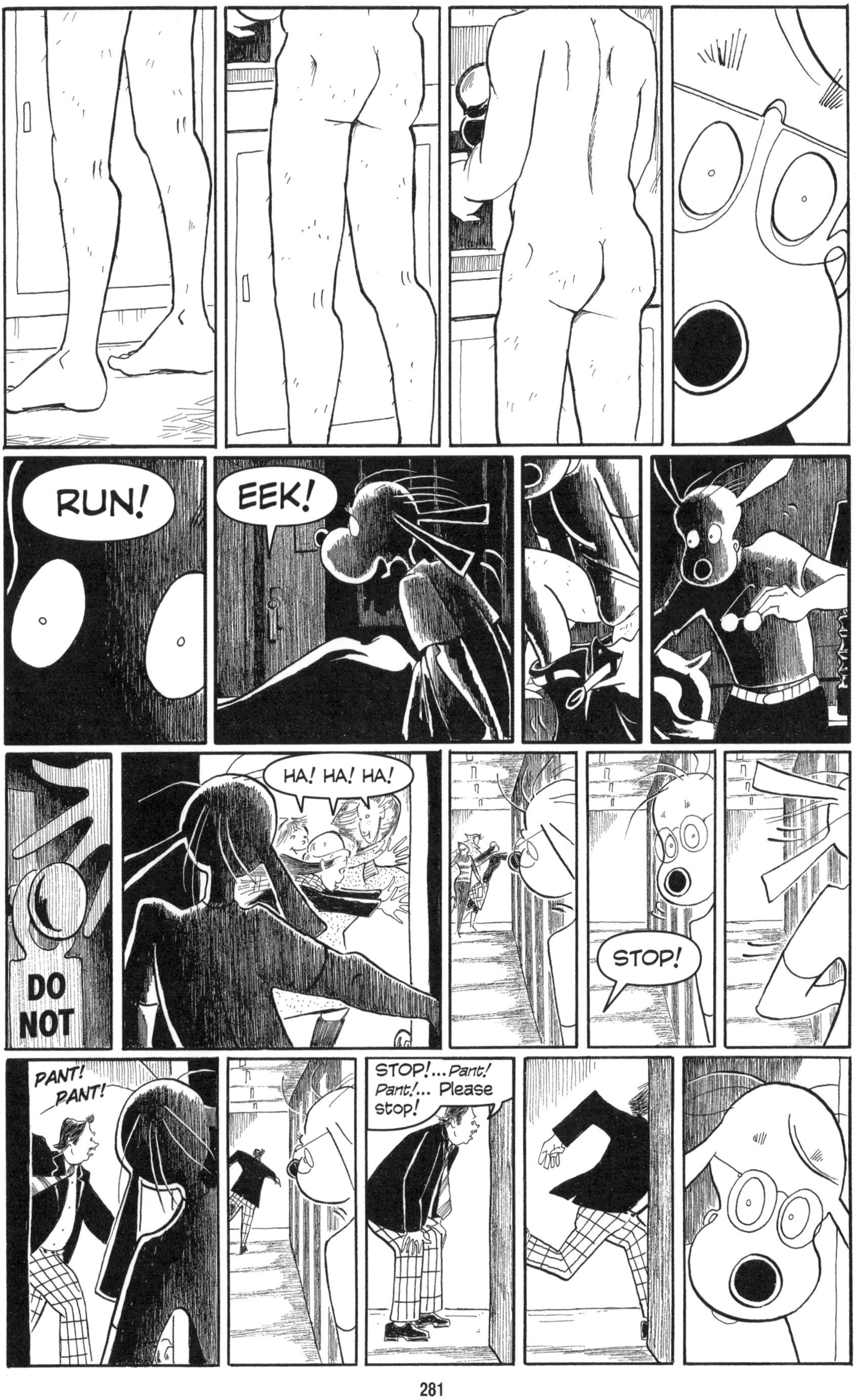
RUN!
EEK!
DO
NOT
HA! HA! HA!
STOP!
PANT!
PANT!
STOP!...Pant!
Pant!... Please
stop!

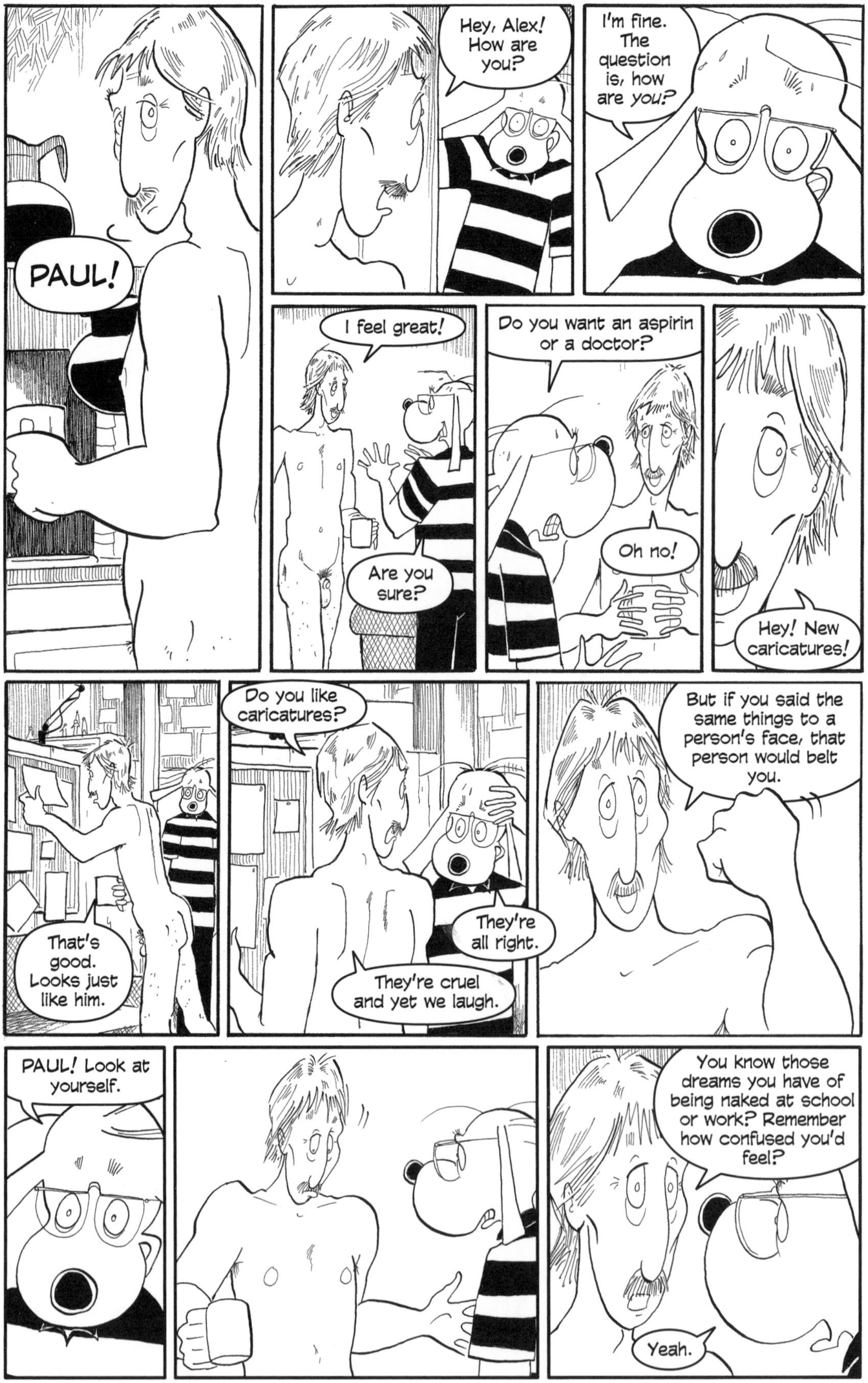
PAUL!
Hey, Alex! How are you?
I'm fine. The question is, how are you?
I feel great!
Are you sure?
Do you want an aspirin or a doctor?
Oh no!
Hey! New caricatures!
That's good. Looks just like him.
Do you like caricatures?
They're all right.
They're cruel and yet we laugh.
But if you said the same things to a person's face, that person would belt you.
PAUL! Look at yourself.
You know those dreams you have of being naked at school or work? Remember how confused you'd feel?
Yeah.

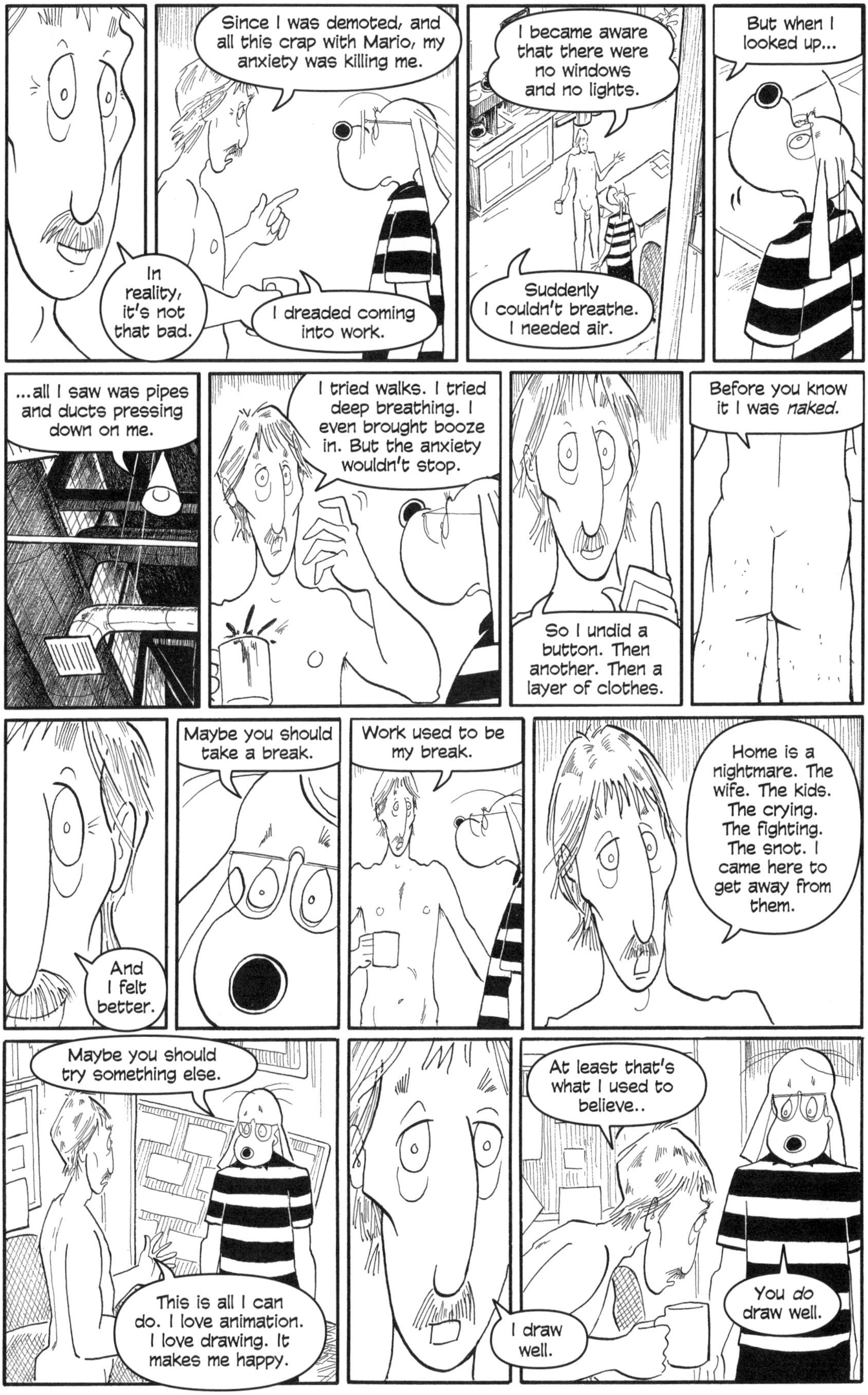

Since I was demoted, and all this crap with Mario, my anxiety was killing me.
In reality, it's not that bad.
I dreaded coming into work.
I became aware that there were no windows and no lights.
Suddenly I couldn't breathe. I needed air.
But when I looked up...
...all I saw was pipes and ducts pressing down on me.
I tried walks. I tried deep breathing. I even brought booze in. But the anxiety wouldn't stop.
So I undid a button. Then another. Then a layer of clothes.
Before you know it I was *naked.*
And I felt better.
Maybe you should take a break.
Work used to be my break.
Home is a nightmare. The wife. The kids. The crying. The fighting. The snot. I came here to get away from them.
Maybe you should try something else.
This is all I can do. I love animation. I love drawing. It makes me happy.
I draw well.
At least that's what I used to believe..
You *do* draw well.

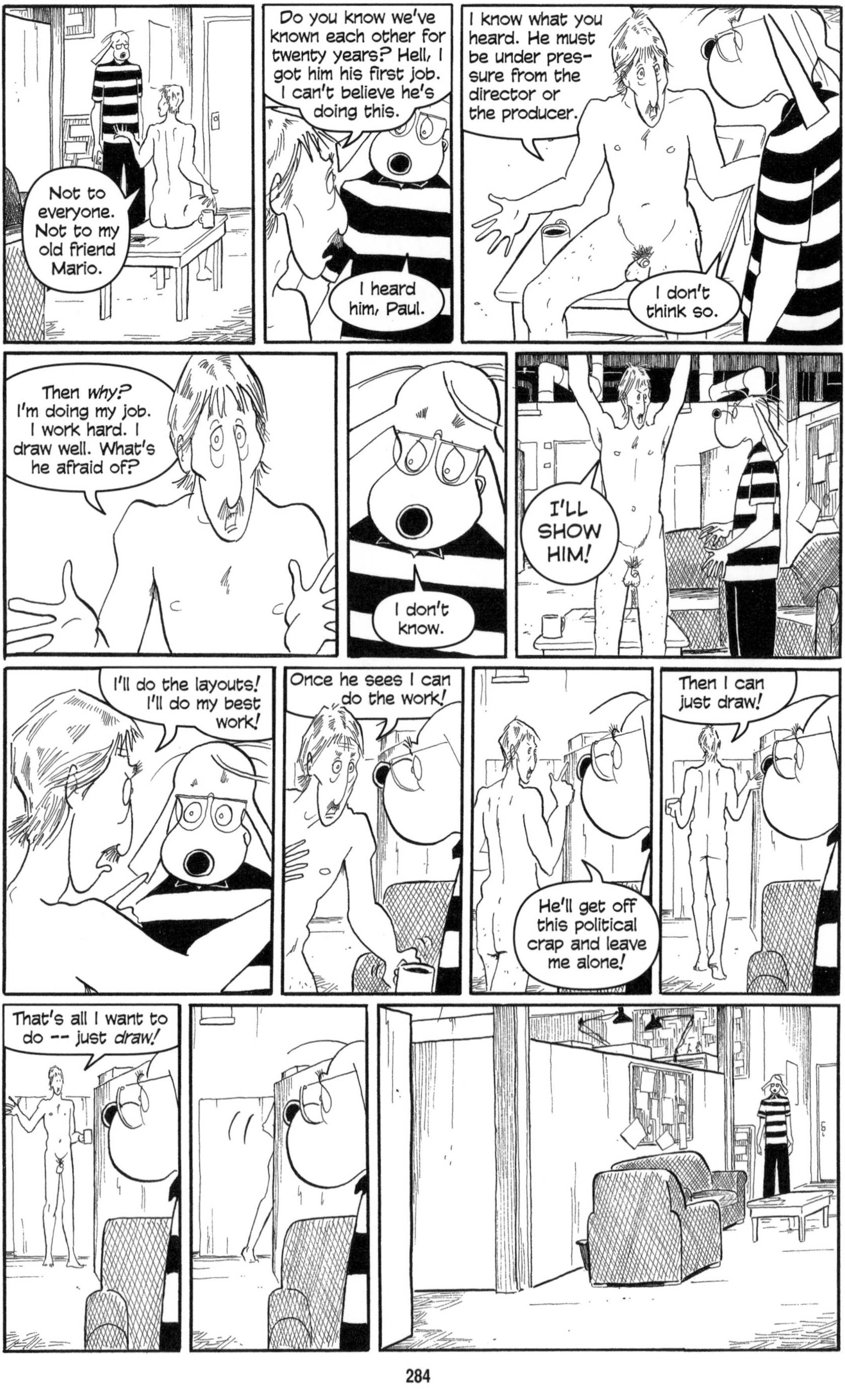
Not to everyone. Not to my old friend Mario.
Do you know we've known each other for twenty years? Hell, I got him his first job. I can't believe he's doing this.
I heard him, Paul.
I know what you heard. He must be under pressure from the director or the producer.
I don't think so.
Then *why?* I'm doing my job. I work hard. I draw well. What's he afraid of?
I don't know.
I'LL SHOW HIM!
I'll do the layouts! I'll do my best work!
Once he sees I can do the work!
He'll get off this political crap and leave me alone!
Then I can just draw!
That's all I want to do -- just *draw!*

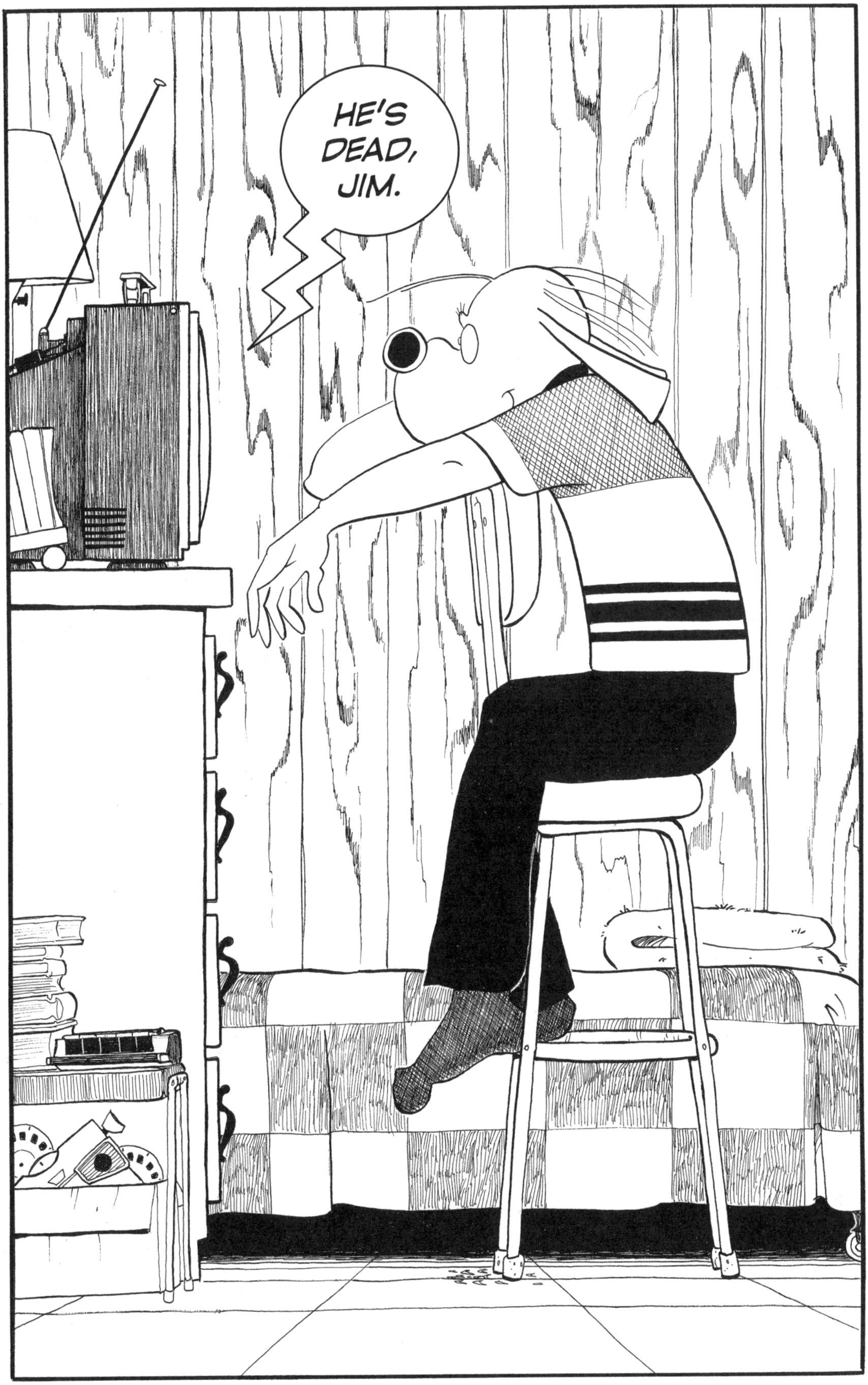
HE'S DEAD, JIM.

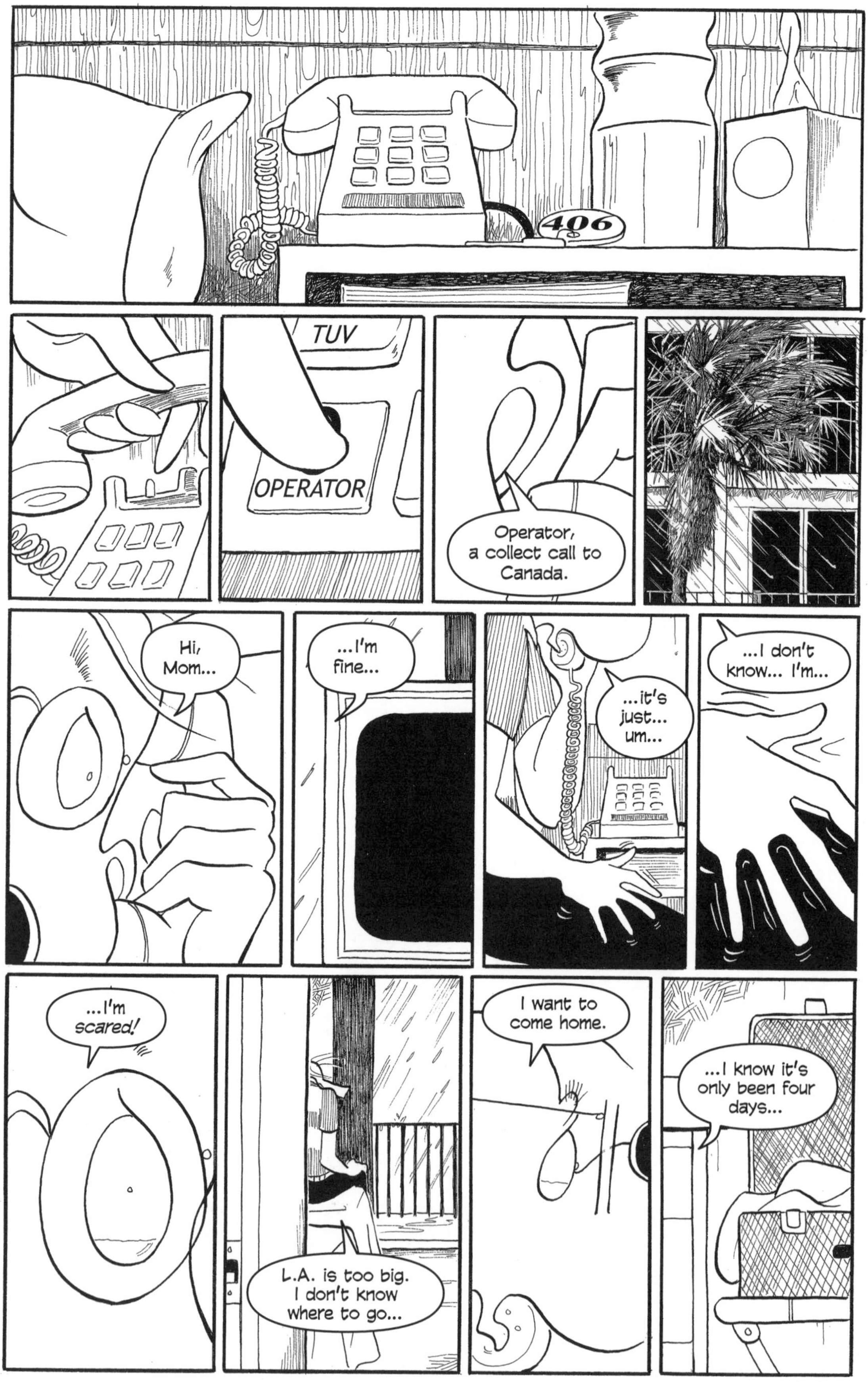
406
TUV
OPERATOR
Operator, a collect call to Canada.
Hi, Mom...
...I'm fine...
...it's just... um...
...I don't know... I'm...
...I'm scared!
L.A. is too big. I don't know where to go...
I want to come home.
...I know it's only been four days...

...I know it was my idea to come here...

...I'm homesick...

...I miss you and Dad and Arthur...

...I'm so lonely... *sniff*...

...uh huh... uh huh... but I don't want to...

...just one month...

...see what happens... okay, I'll try to stick it out...

DO NOT DISTURB!

...I'm sorry... don't tell Dad...

...I love you... bye, Mom.

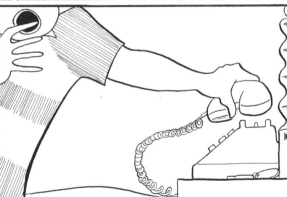

287

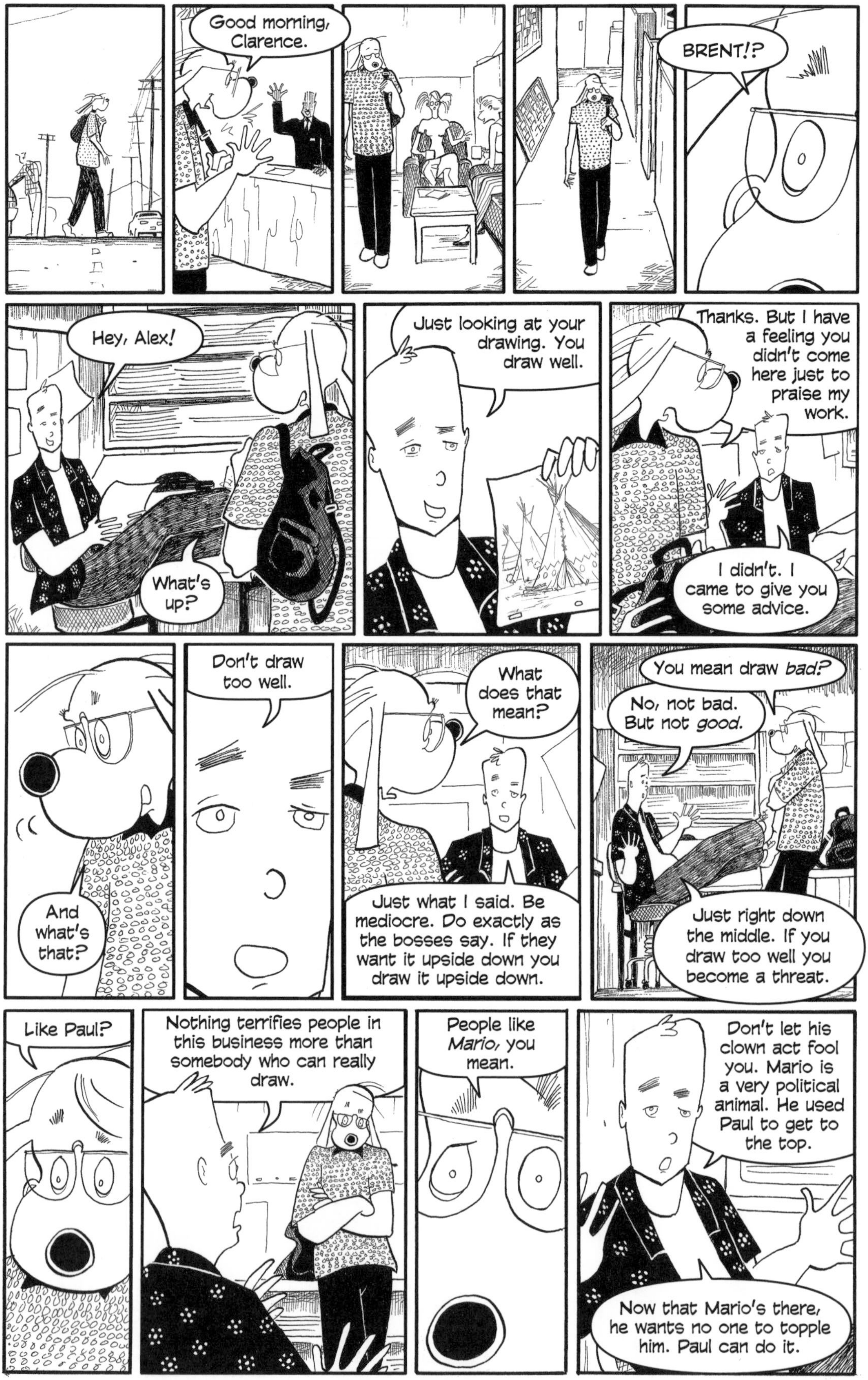
Good morning, Clarence.
BRENT!?
Hey, Alex!
What's up?
Just looking at your drawing. You draw well.
Thanks. But I have a feeling you didn't come here just to praise my work.
I didn't. I came to give you some advice.
And what's that?
Don't draw too well.
What does that mean?
Just what I said. Be mediocre. Do exactly as the bosses say. If they want it upside down you draw it upside down.
You mean draw *bad?*
No, not bad. But not *good.*
Just right down the middle. If you draw too well you become a threat.
Like Paul?
Nothing terrifies people in this business more than somebody who can really draw.
People like *Mario,* you mean.
Don't let his clown act fool you. Mario is a very political animal. He used Paul to get to the top.
Now that Mario's there, he wants no one to topple him. Paul can do it.

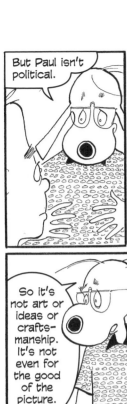

But Paul isn't political.

It doesn't matter. Mario can't have anyone saying there's someone who can draw better than him.

But what about the director or the producer? Can't they see how great Paul's work is?

People see with their ears. Mario says Paul's bad. He's bad.

So it's not art or ideas or craftsmanship. It's not even for the good of the picture.

It's office politics.

It's nothing personal.

So what do I tell Paul? Not to draw well?

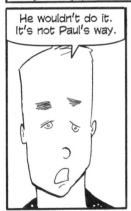

He wouldn't do it. It's not Paul's way.

This is just some helpful advice.

See ya.

It's not fair.

Animation is a lot like sausages. You shouldn't see how it's made.

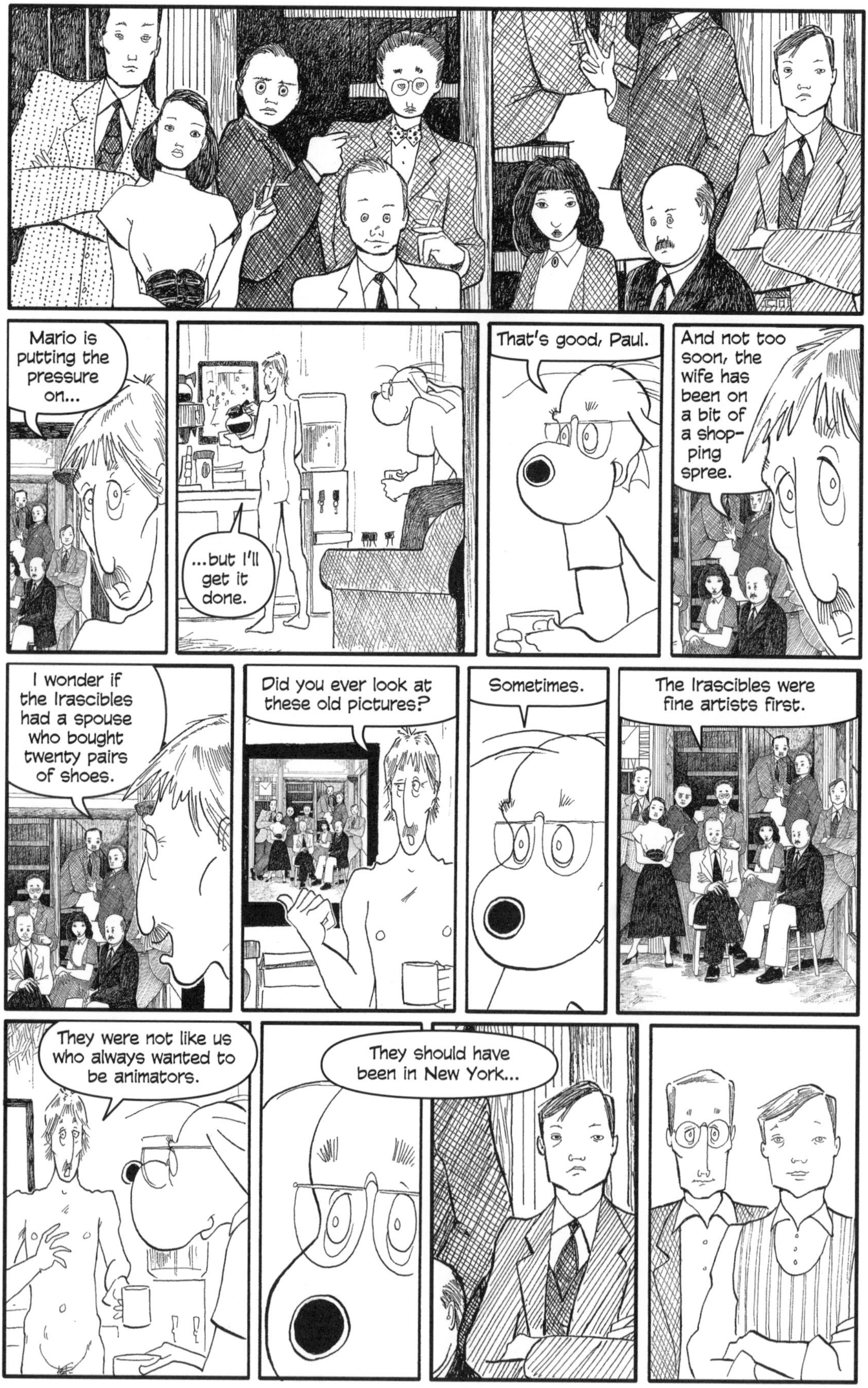
Mario is putting the pressure on...
...but I'll get it done.
That's good, Paul.
And not too soon, the wife has been on a bit of a shop-ping spree.
I wonder if the Irascibles had a spouse who bought twenty pairs of shoes.
Did you ever look at these old pictures?
Sometimes.
The Irascibles were fine artists first.
They were not like us who always wanted to be animators.
They should have been in New York...

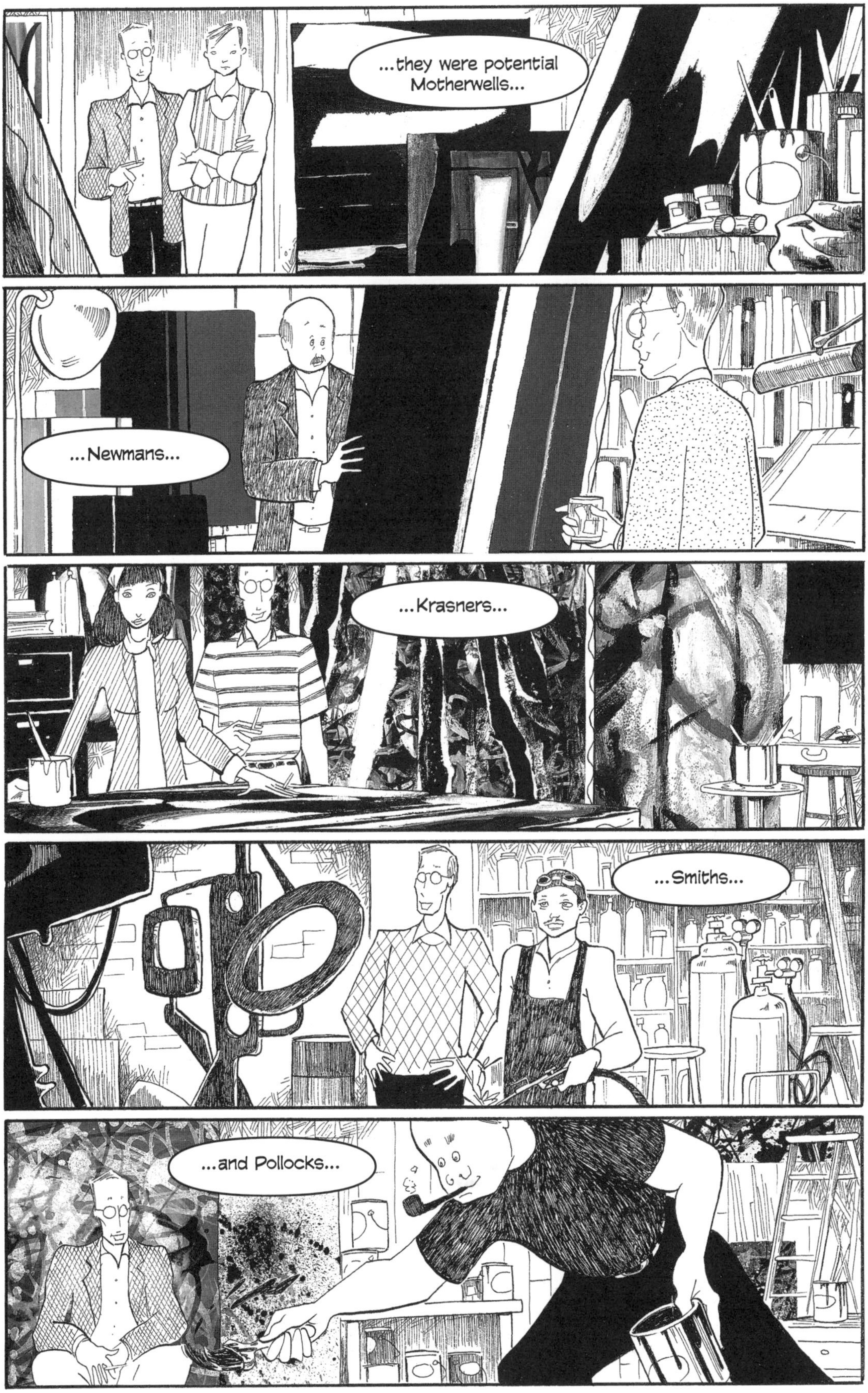
...they were potential Motherwells...
...Newmans...
...Krasners...
...Smiths...
...and Pollocks...

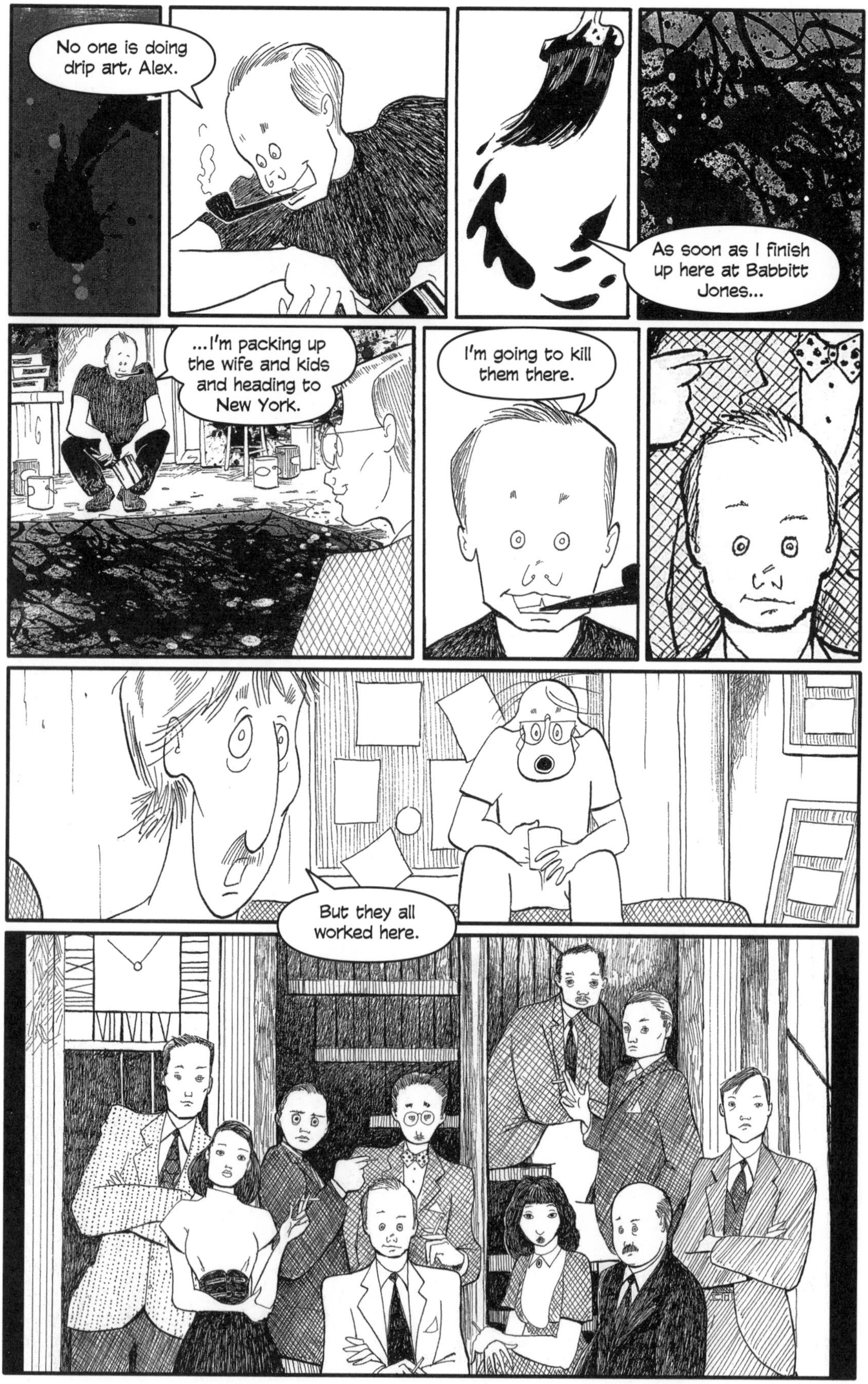
No one is doing drip art, Alex.
As soon as I finish up here at Babbitt Jones...
...I'm packing up the wife and kids and heading to New York.
I'm going to kill them there.
But they all worked here.

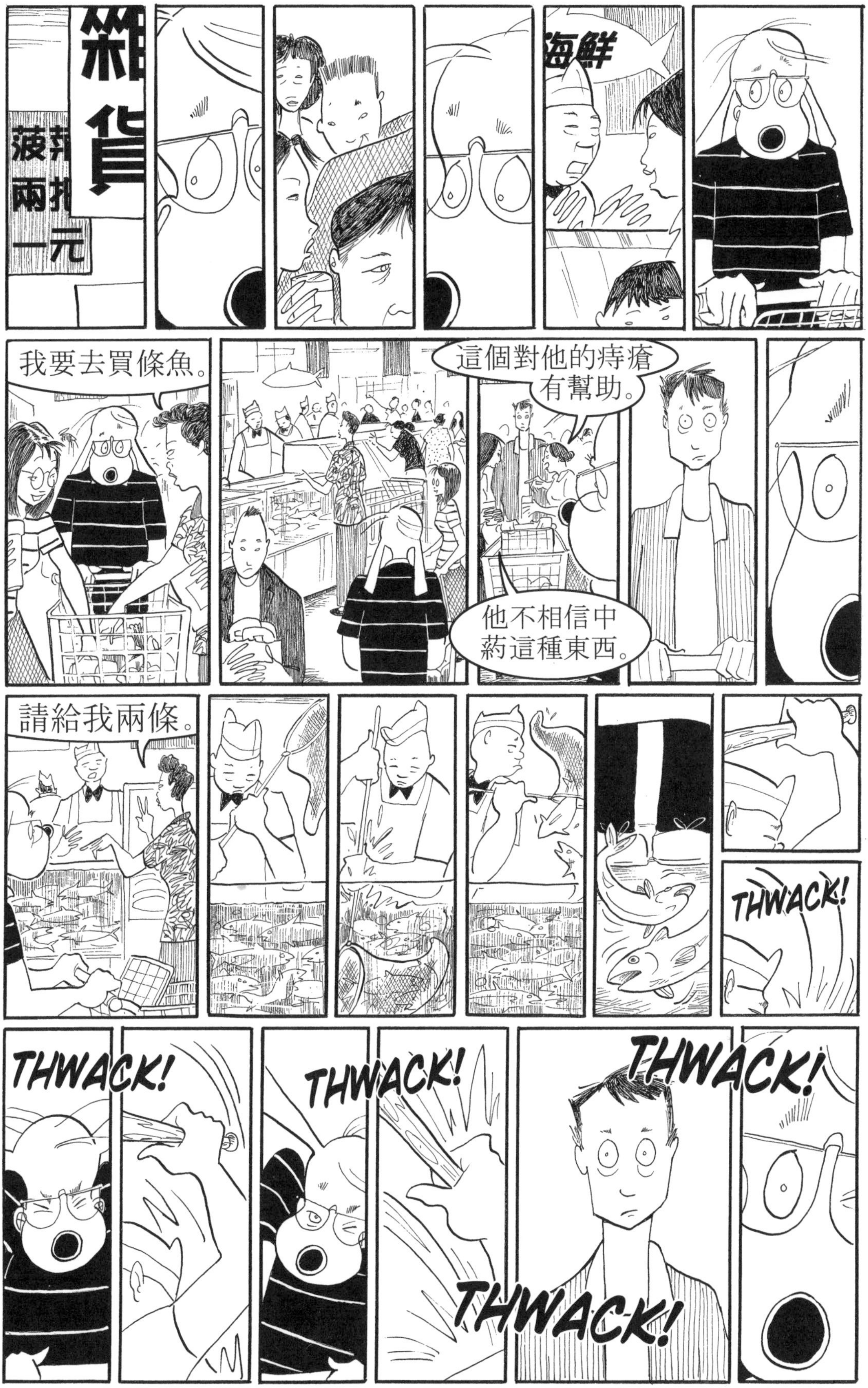
一元
海鮮
我要去買條魚。
這個對他的痔瘡有幫助。
他不相信中藥這種東西。
請給我兩條。
THWACK!
THWACK!
THWACK!
THWACK!
THWACK!

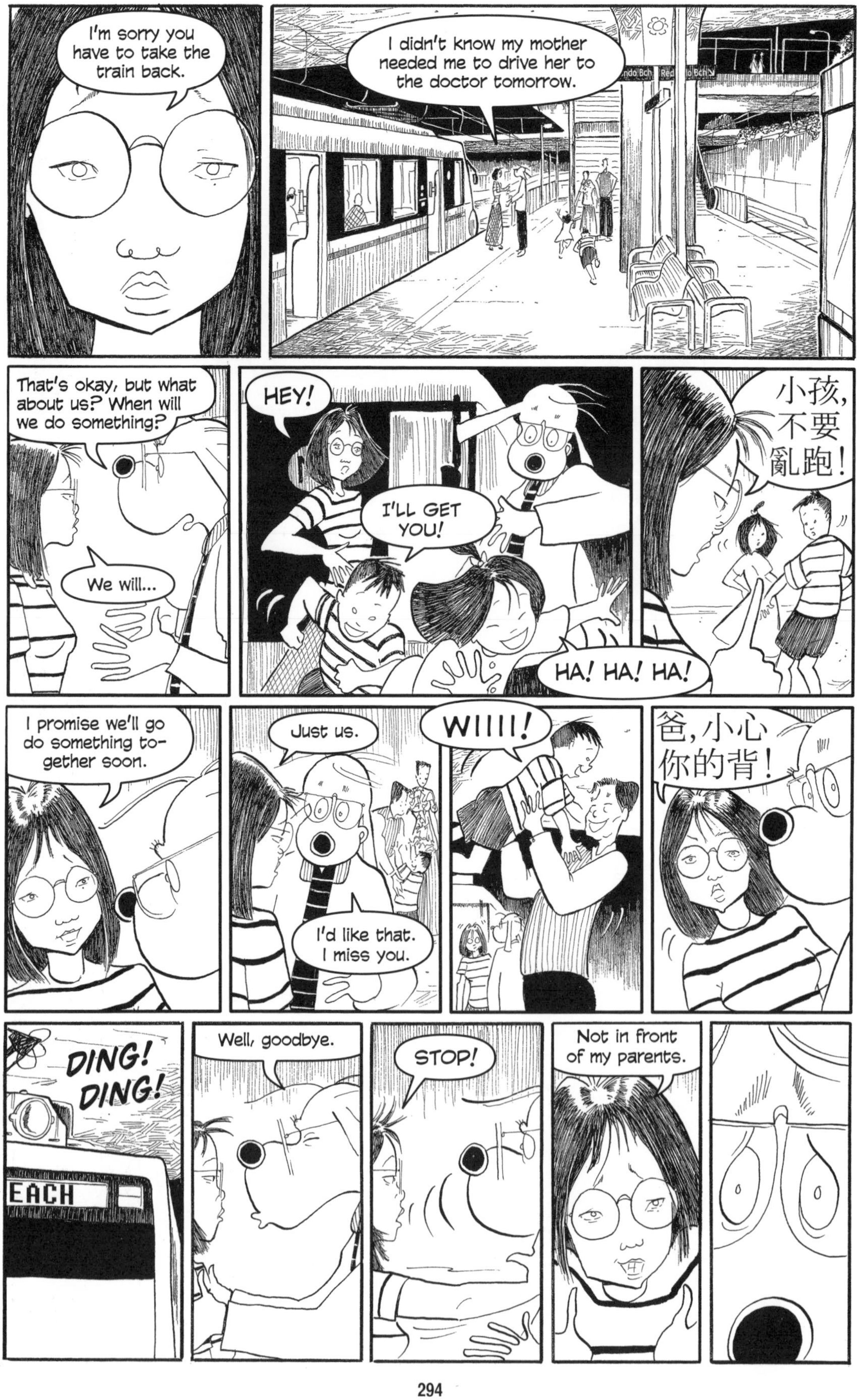

I'm sorry you have to take the train back.
I didn't know my mother needed me to drive her to the doctor tomorrow.
That's okay, but what about us? When will we do something?
We will...
HEY!
I'LL GET YOU!
HA! HA! HA!
小孩,不要亂跑!
I promise we'll go do something together soon.
Just us.
I'd like that. I miss you.
WIIII!
爸,小心你的背!
DING! DING!
EACH
Well, goodbye.
STOP!
Not in front of my parents.

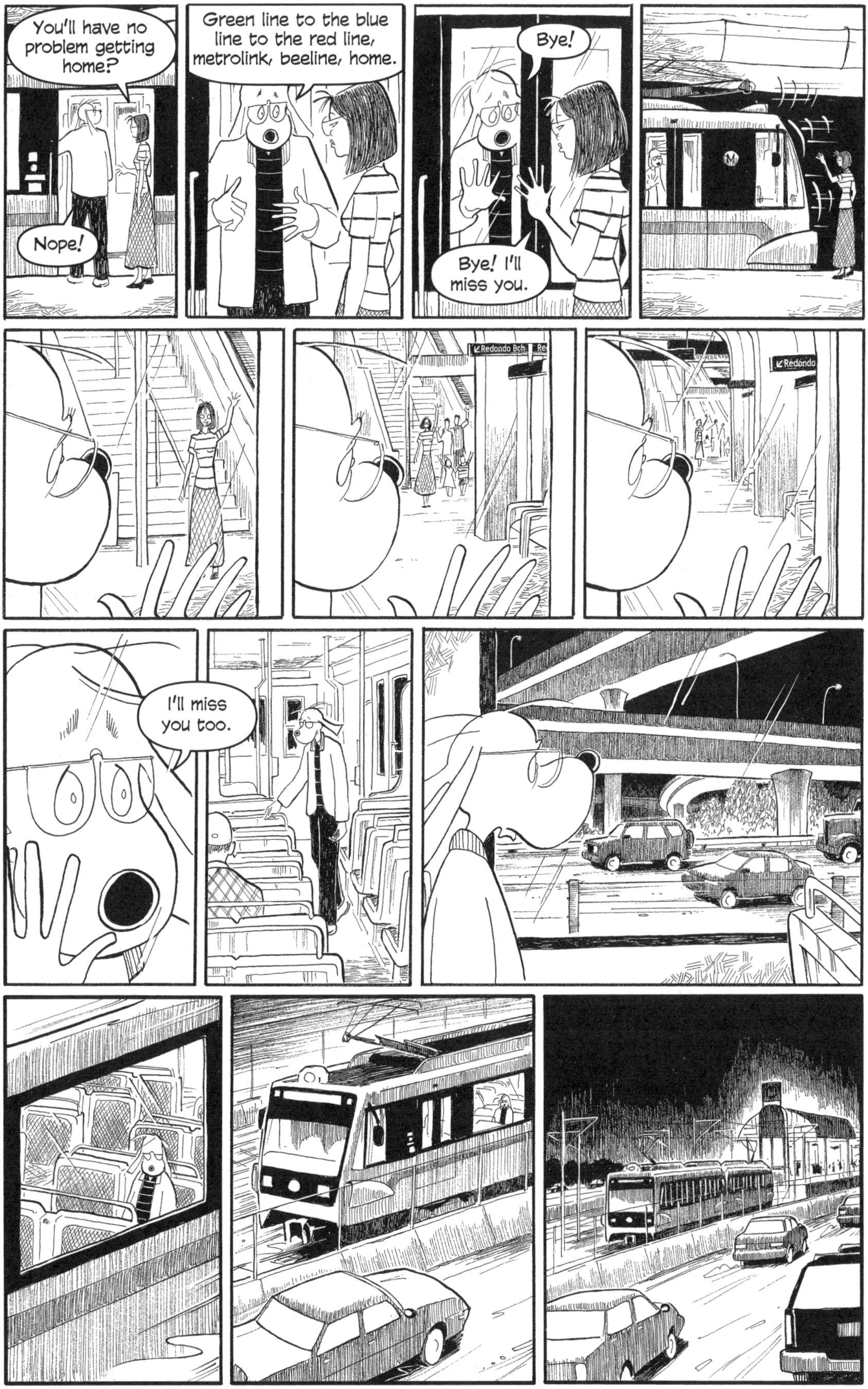
You'll have no problem getting home?
Nope!
Green line to the blue line to the red line, metrolink, beeline, home.
Bye!
Bye! I'll miss you.
↙Redondo Bch
↙Redondo
I'll miss you too.

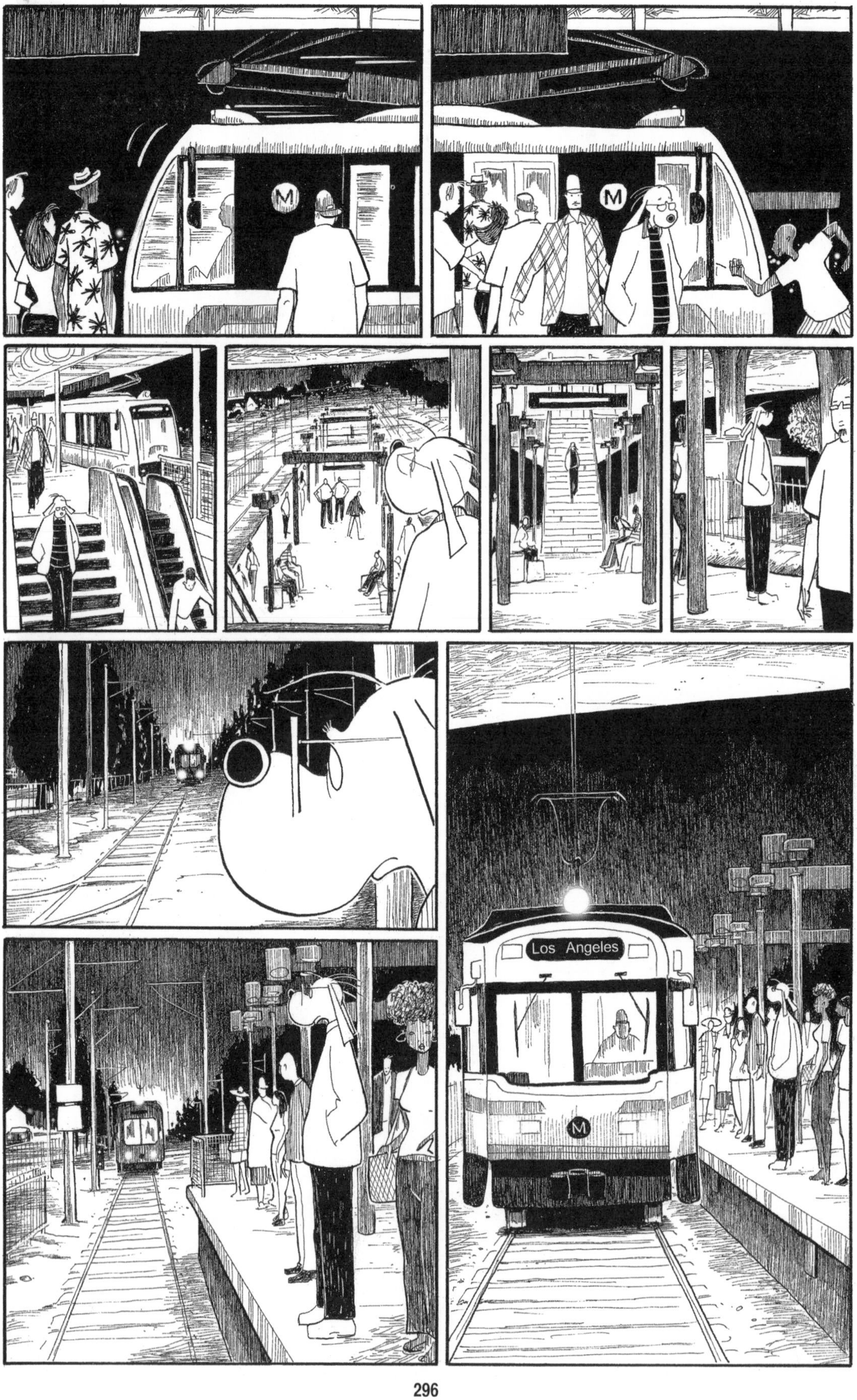
Los Angeles

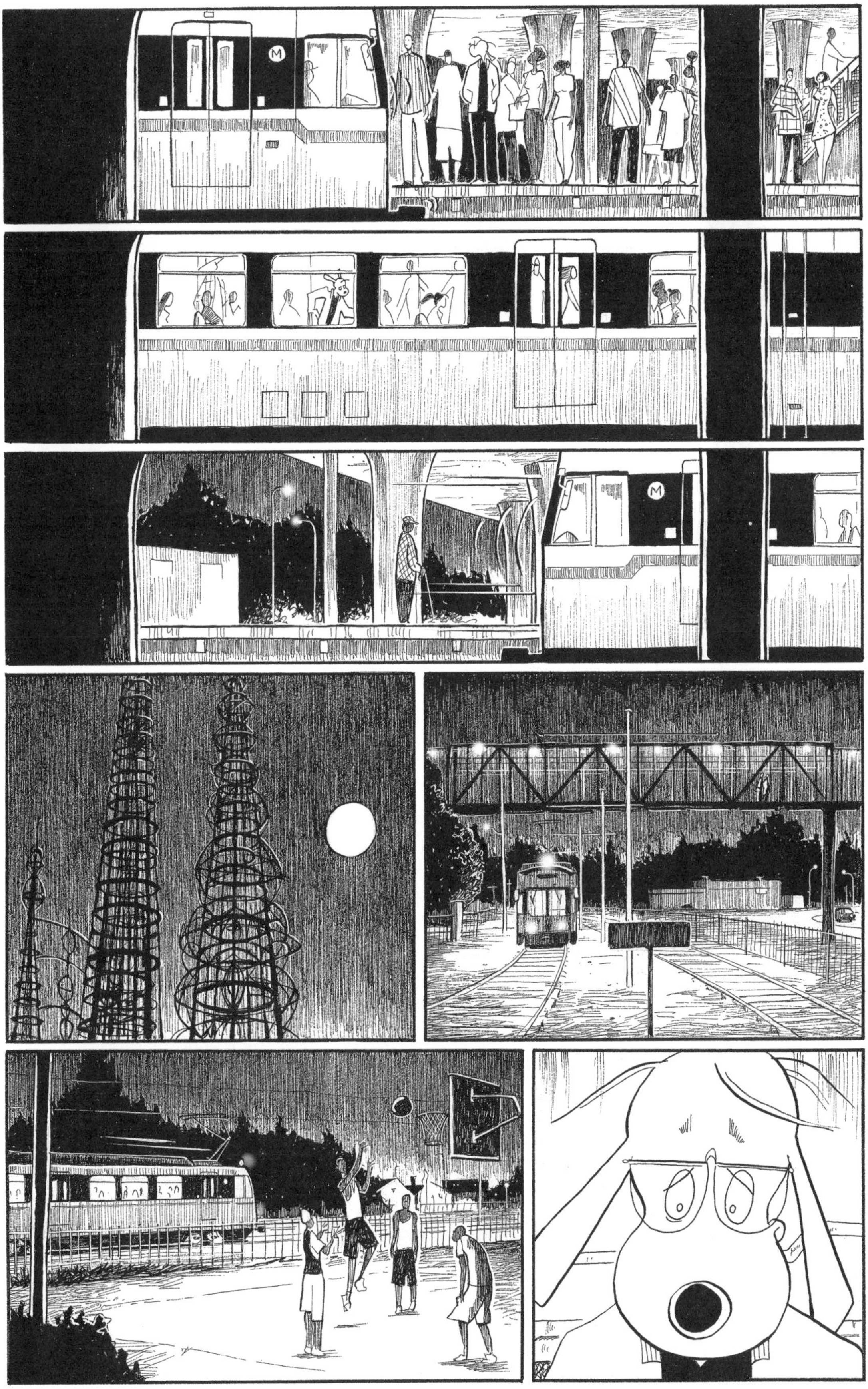

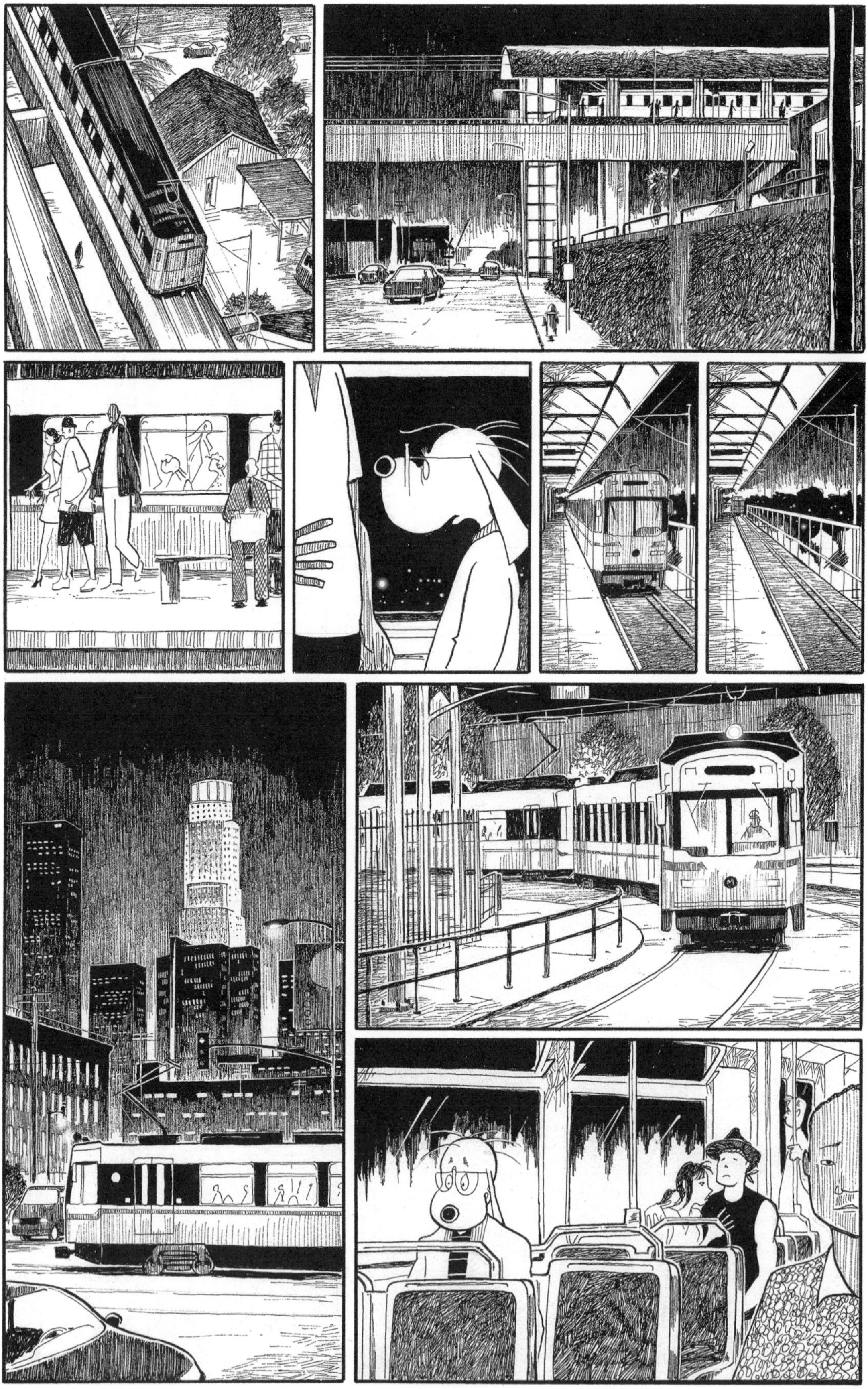

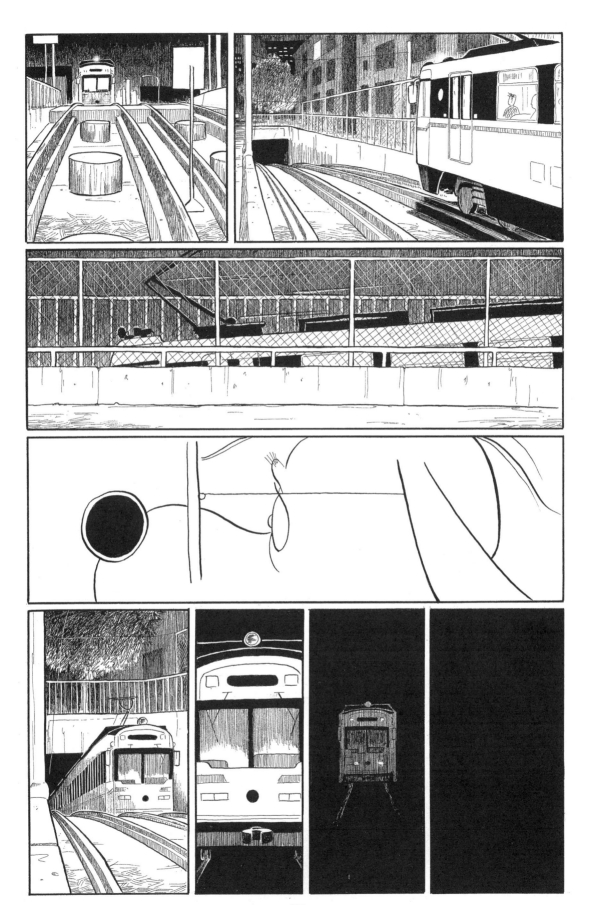

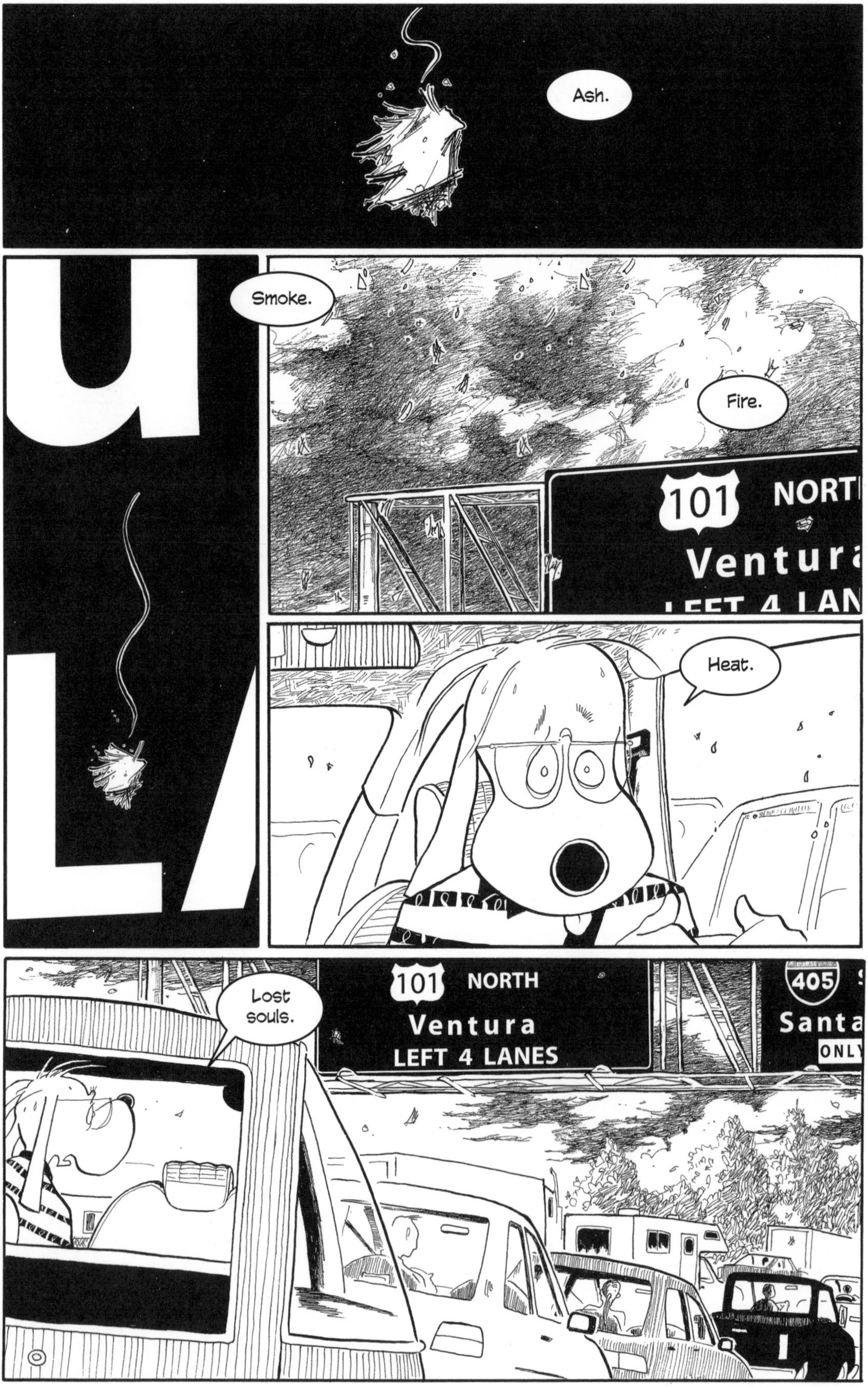
Ash.
Smoke.
Fire.
101 NORTH
Ventura
Heat.
Lost souls.
101 NORTH
Ventura
LEFT 4 LANES
405
Santa
ONLY

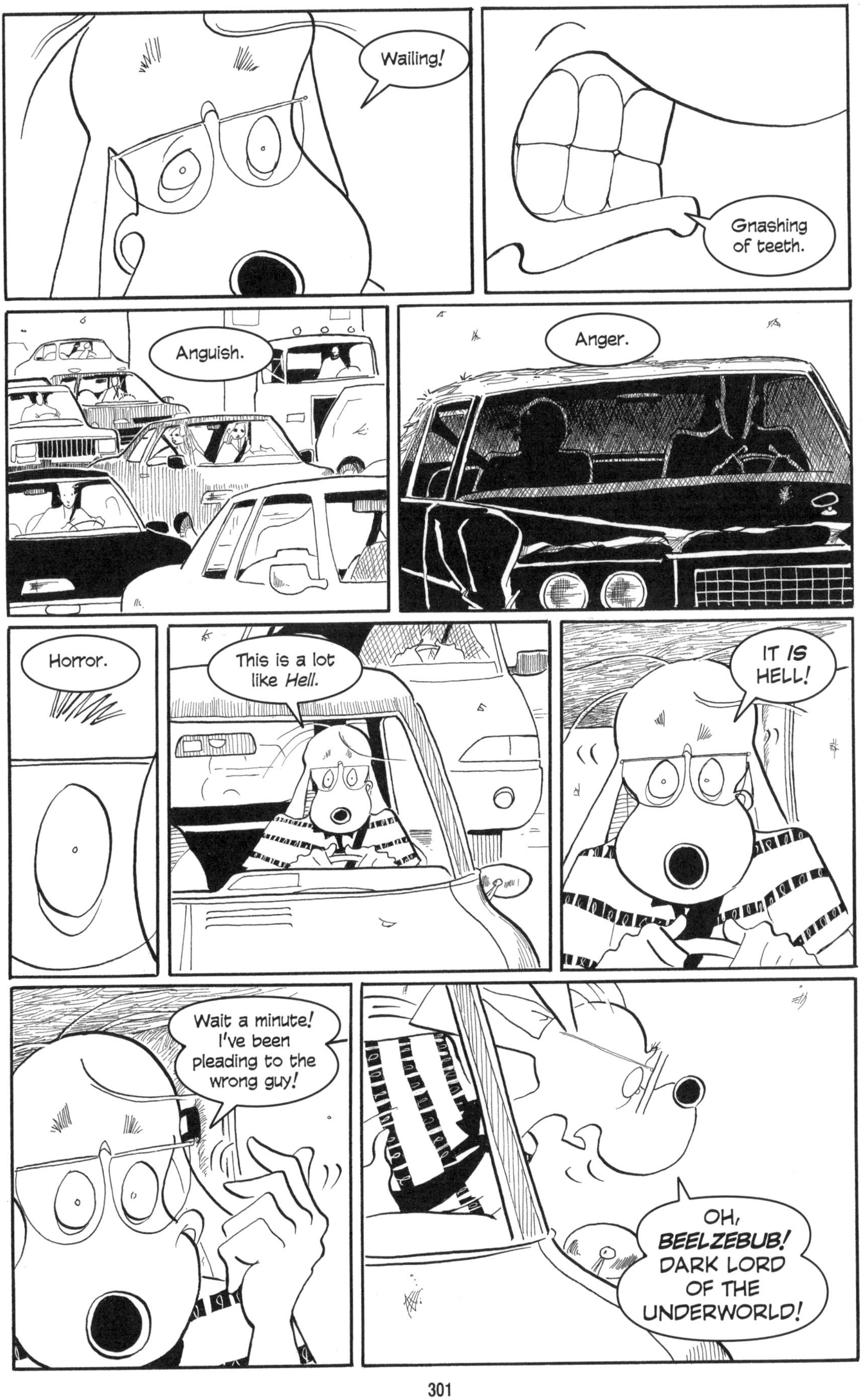
Wailing!
Gnashing of teeth.
Anguish.
Anger.
Horror.
This is a lot like *Hell.*
IT *IS* HELL!
Wait a minute! I've been pleading to the wrong guy!
OH, ***BEELZEBUB!*** DARK LORD OF THE UNDERWORLD!

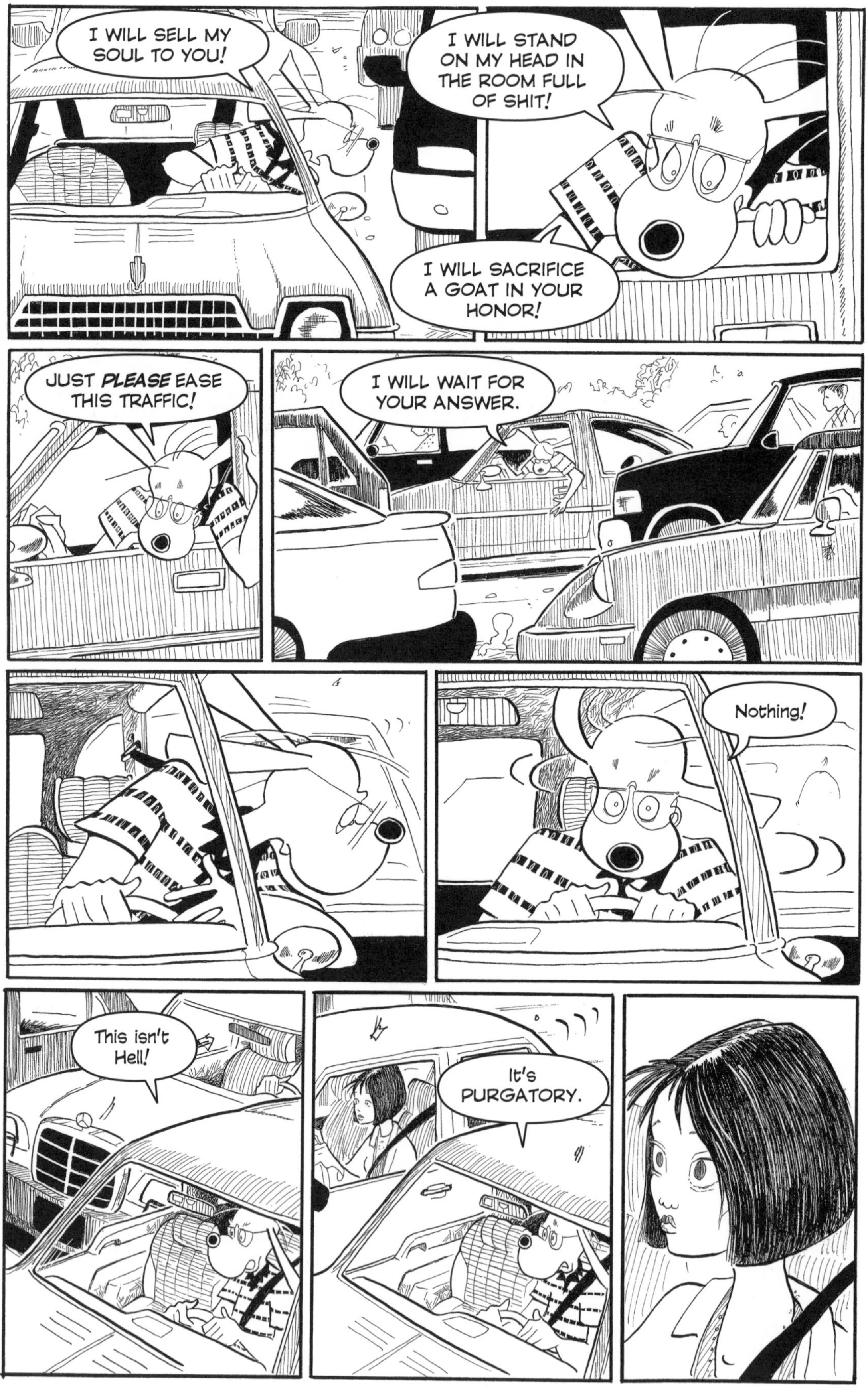
I WILL SELL MY SOUL TO YOU!
I WILL STAND ON MY HEAD IN THE ROOM FULL OF SHIT!
I WILL SACRIFICE A GOAT IN YOUR HONOR!
JUST PLEASE EASE THIS TRAFFIC!
I WILL WAIT FOR YOUR ANSWER.
Nothing!
This isn't Hell!
It's PURGATORY.

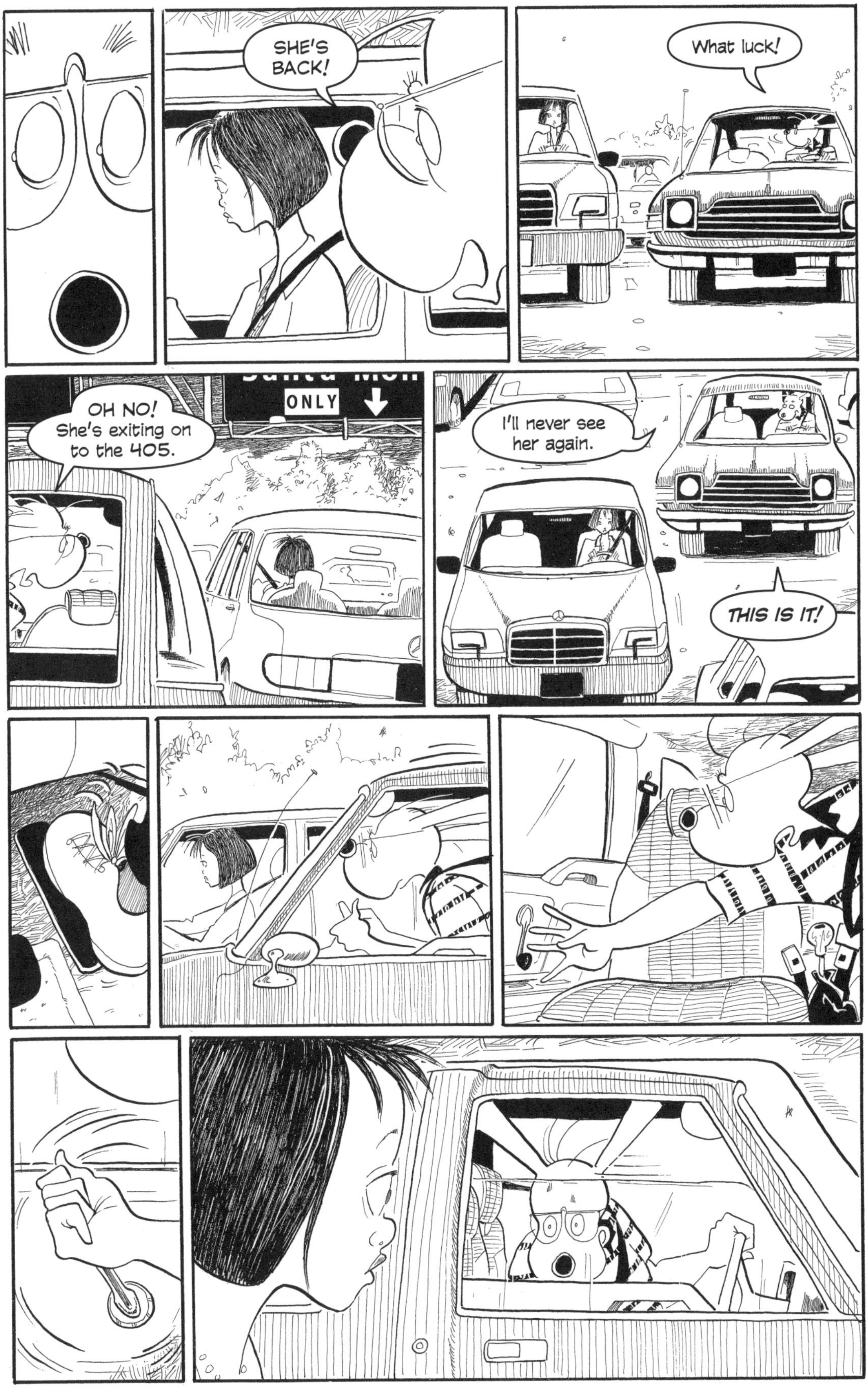
SHE'S BACK!
What luck!
ONLY
OH NO! She's exiting on to the 405.
I'll never see her again.
THIS IS IT!

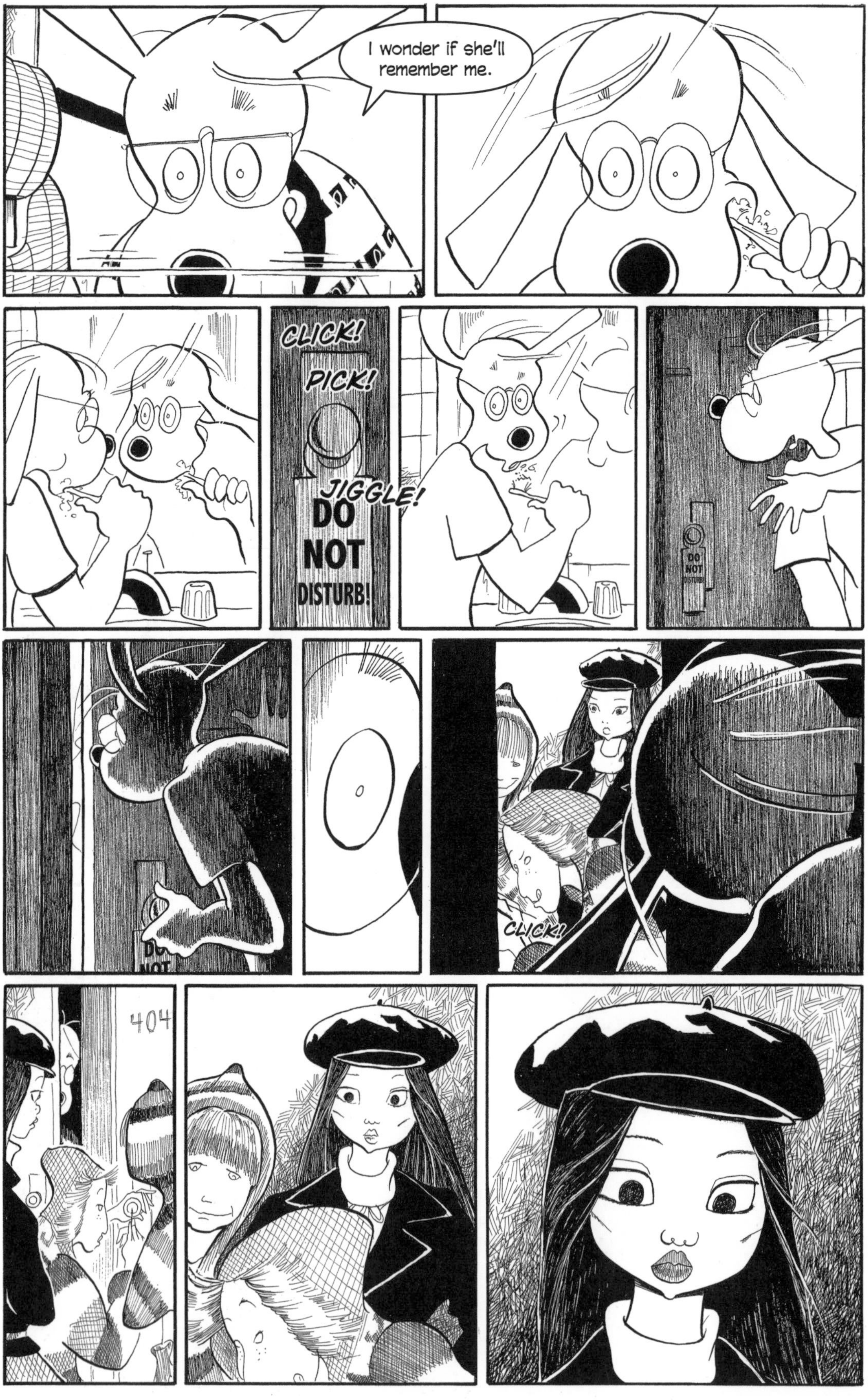

I wonder if she'll remember me.
CLICK!
PICK!
JIGGLE!
DO NOT DISTURB!
DO NOT DISTURB
CLICK!
404

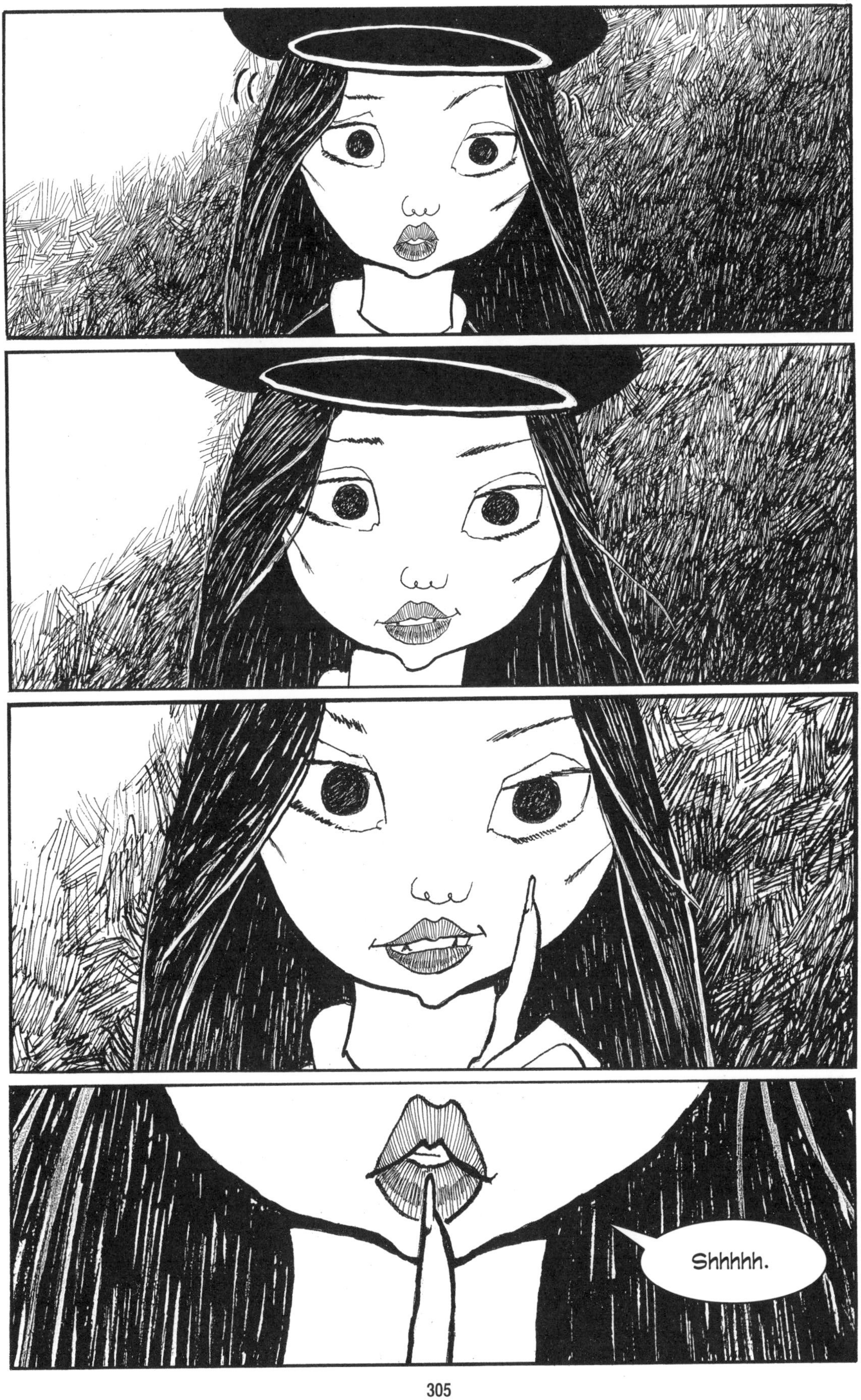
Shhhhh.

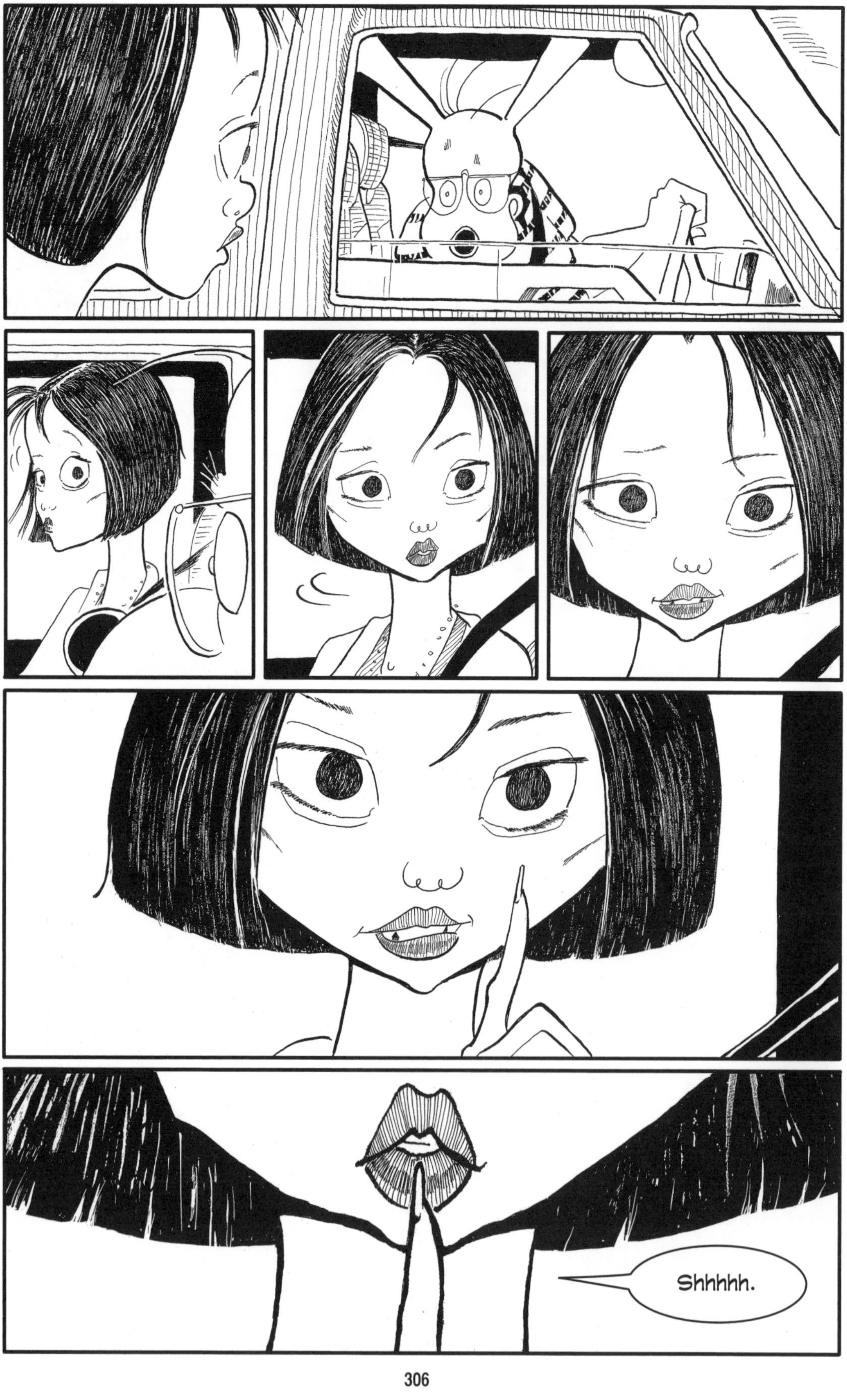
Shhhhh.

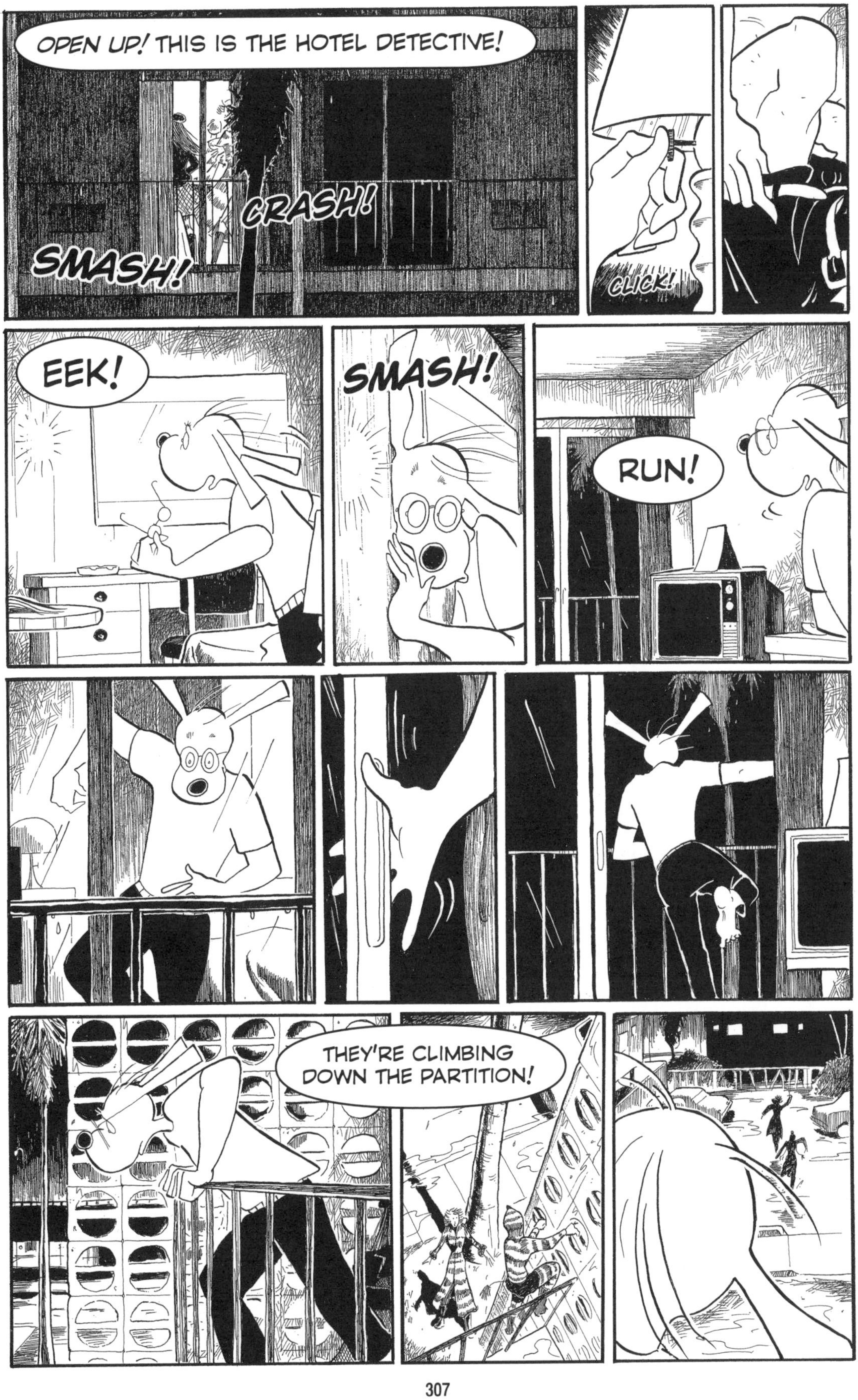
OPEN UP! THIS IS THE HOTEL DETECTIVE!
CRASH!
SMASH!
CLICK!
EEK!
SMASH!
RUN!
THEY'RE CLIMBING DOWN THE PARTITION!

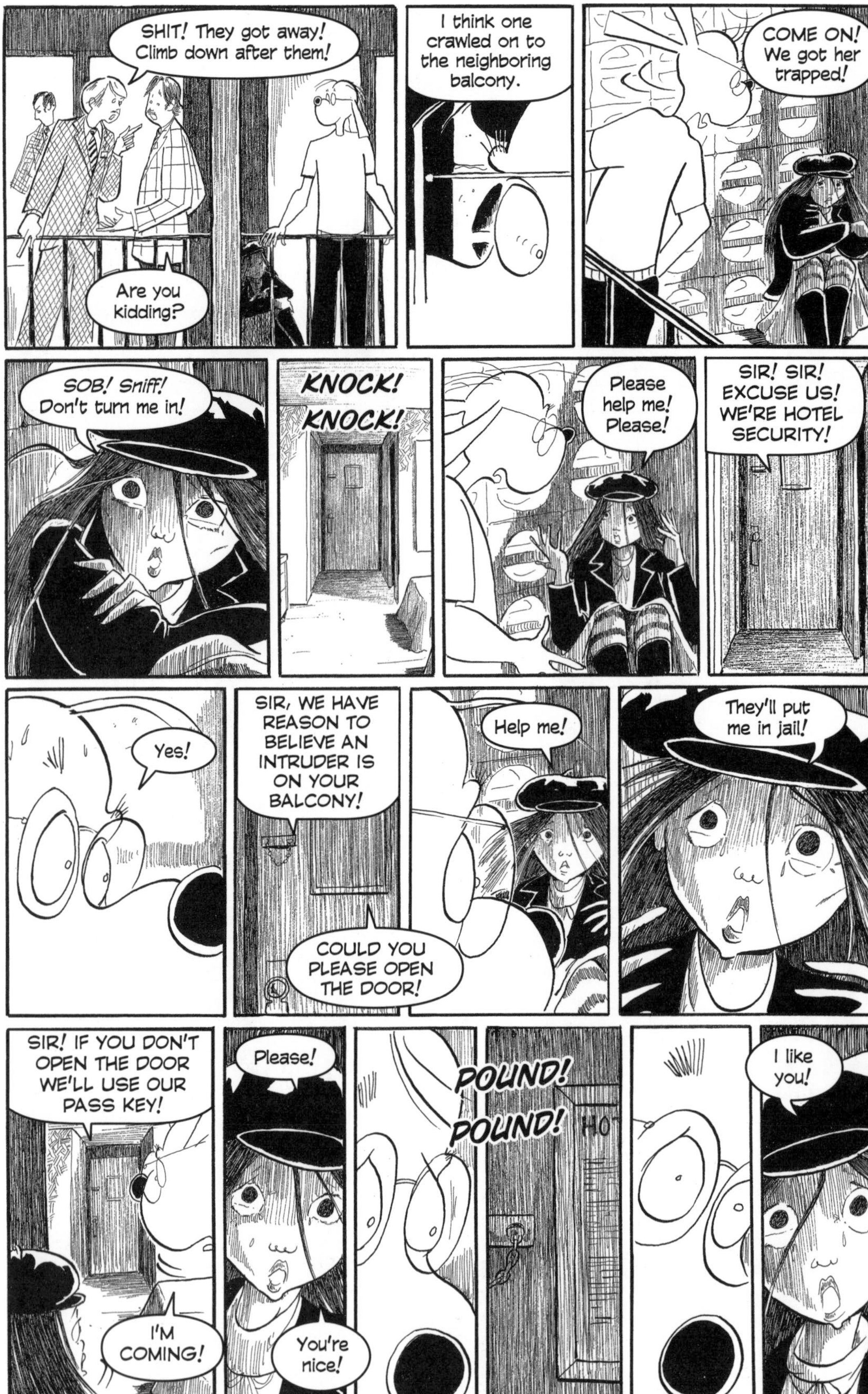
SHIT! They got away! Climb down after them!
Are you kidding?
I think one crawled on to the neighboring balcony.
COME ON! We got her trapped!
SOB! Sniff! Don't turn me in!
KNOCK! KNOCK!
Please help me! Please!
SIR! SIR! EXCUSE US! WE'RE HOTEL SECURITY!
Yes!
SIR, WE HAVE REASON TO BELIEVE AN INTRUDER IS ON YOUR BALCONY!
COULD YOU PLEASE OPEN THE DOOR!
Help me!
They'll put me in jail!
SIR! IF YOU DON'T OPEN THE DOOR WE'LL USE OUR PASS KEY!
I'M COMING!
Please!
You're nice!
POUND! POUND!
HOT
I like you!

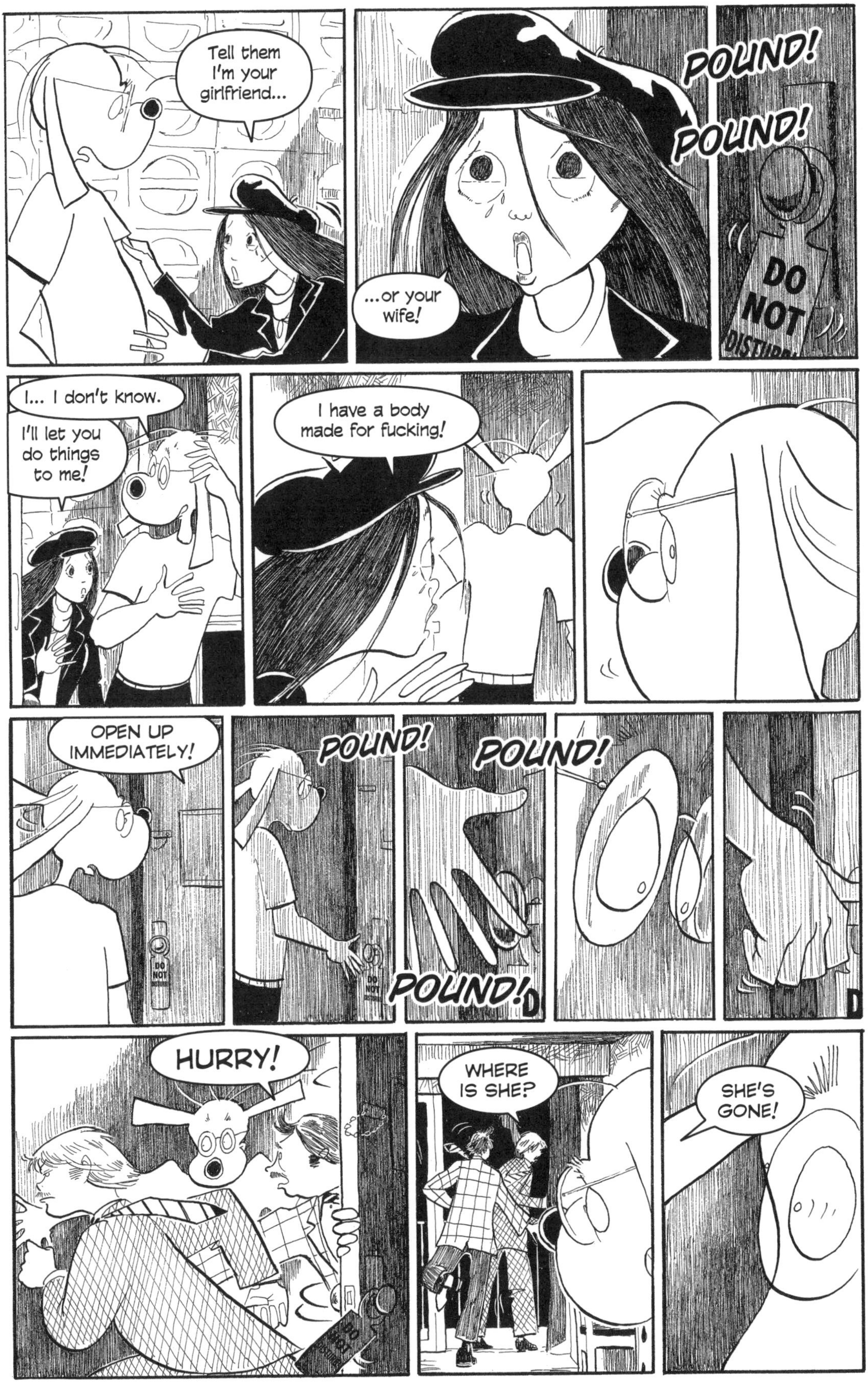

Tell them I'm your girlfriend...
...or your wife!
POUND!
POUND!
DO NOT DISTURB
I... I don't know.
I'll let you do things to me!
I have a body made for fucking!
OPEN UP IMMEDIATELY!
POUND!
POUND!
POUND!
HURRY!
WHERE IS SHE?
SHE'S GONE!

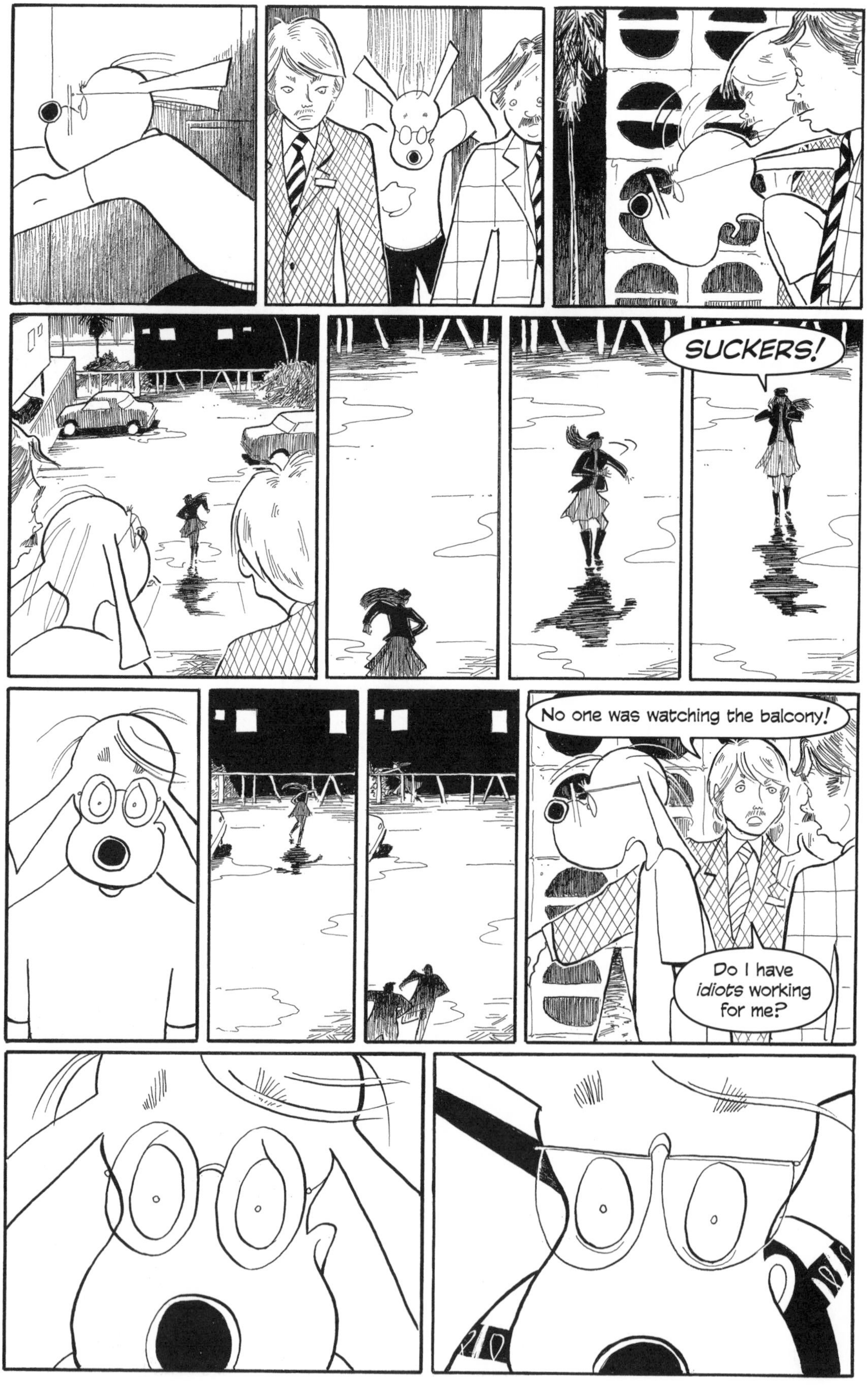
SUCKERS!
No one was watching the balcony!
Do I have *idiots* working for me?

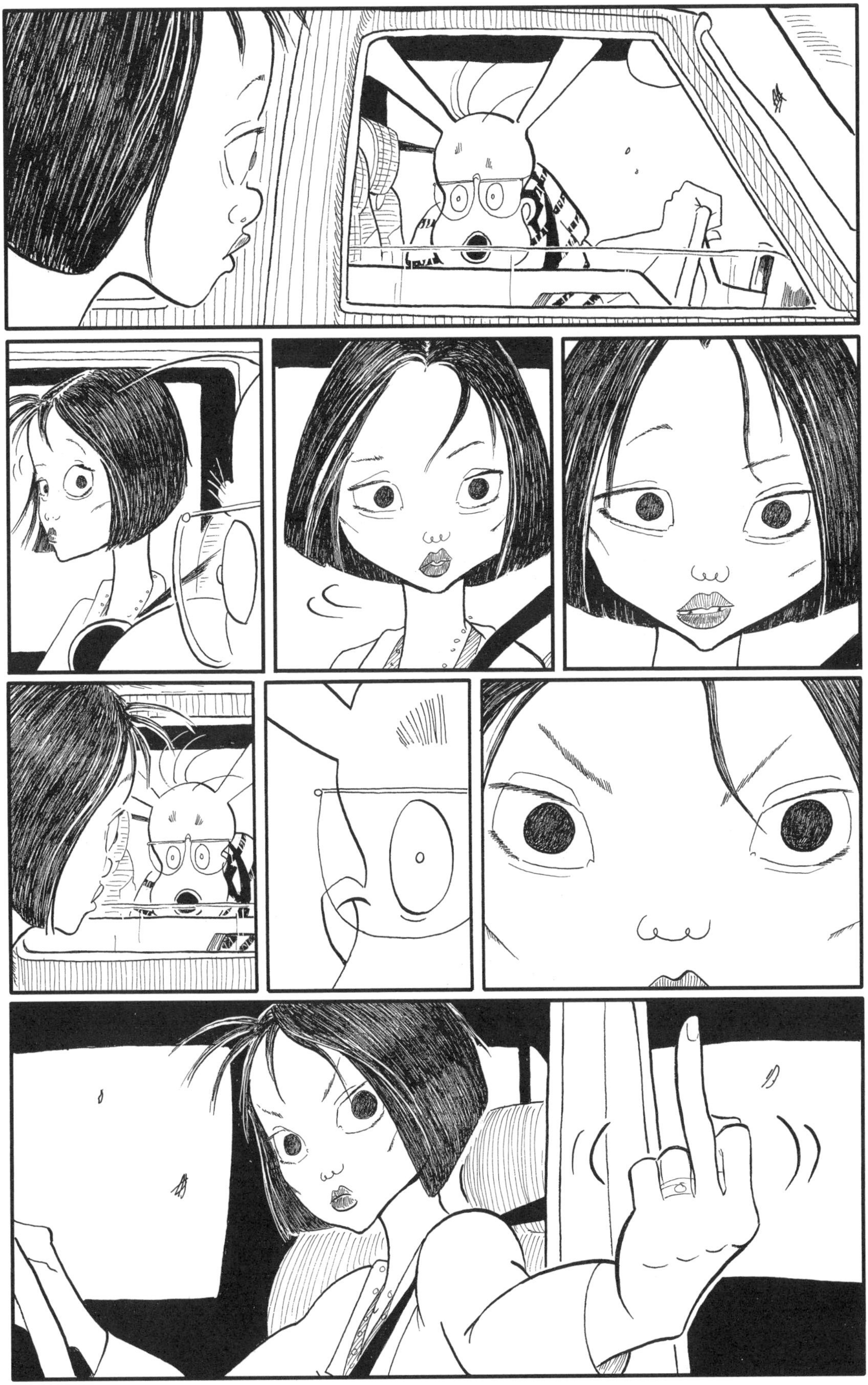

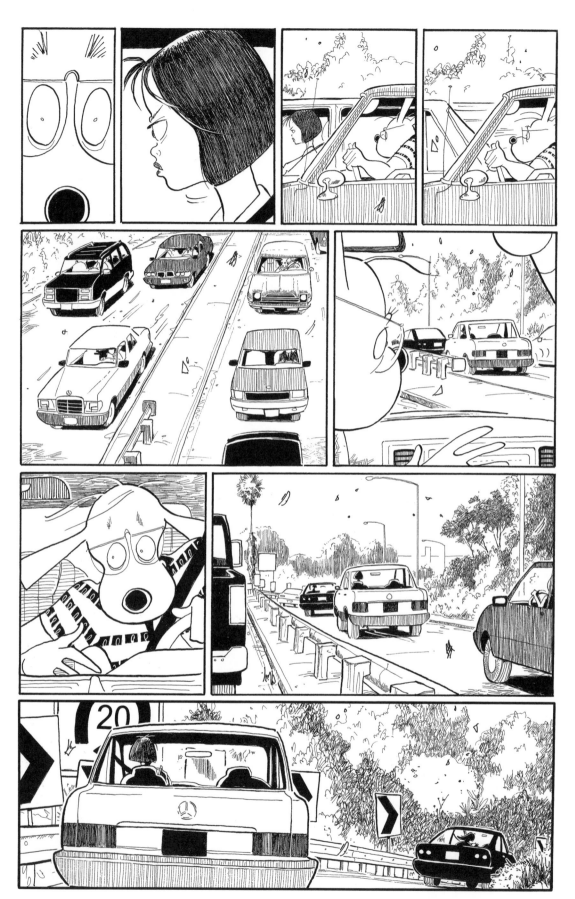

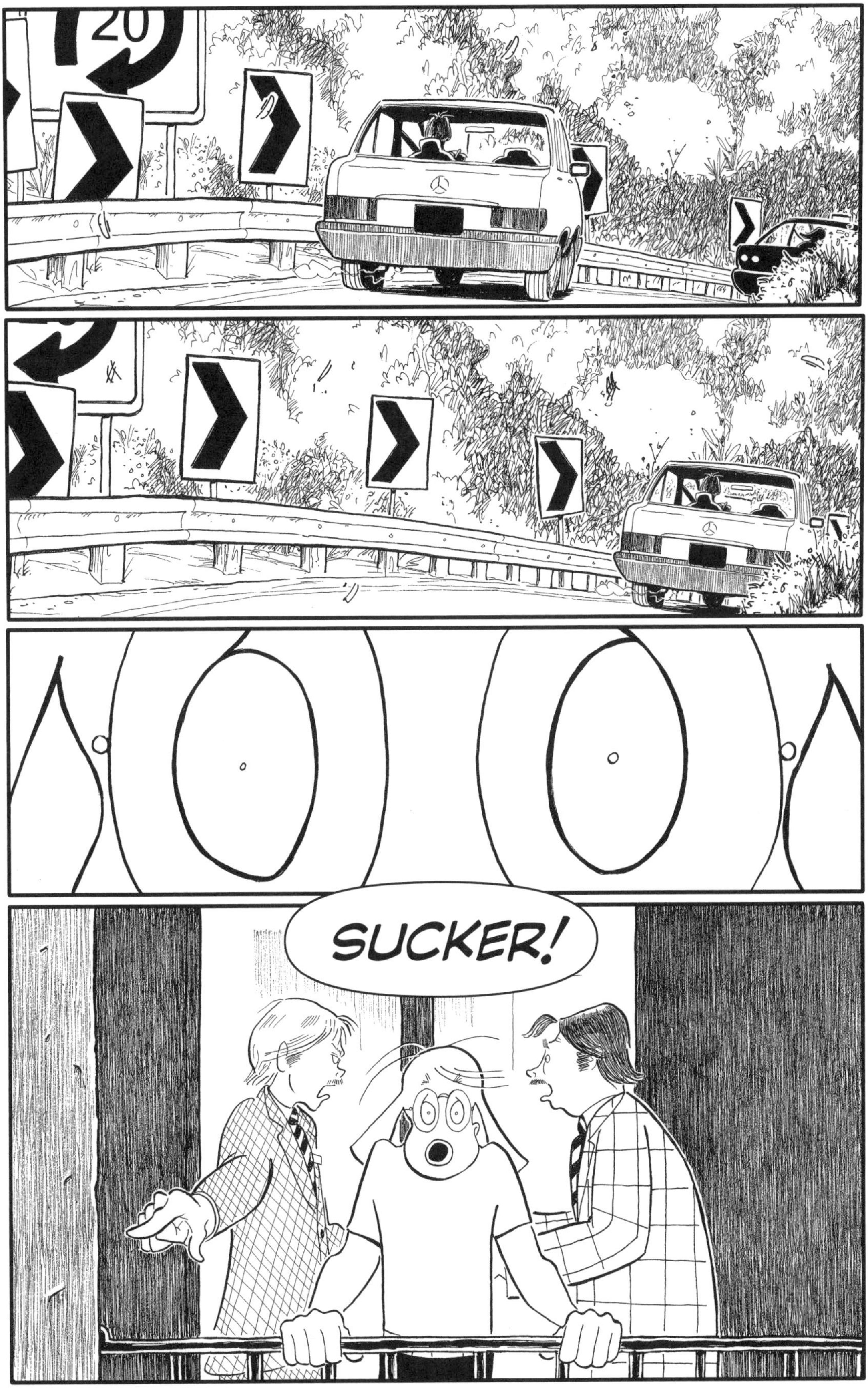
20
SUCKER!

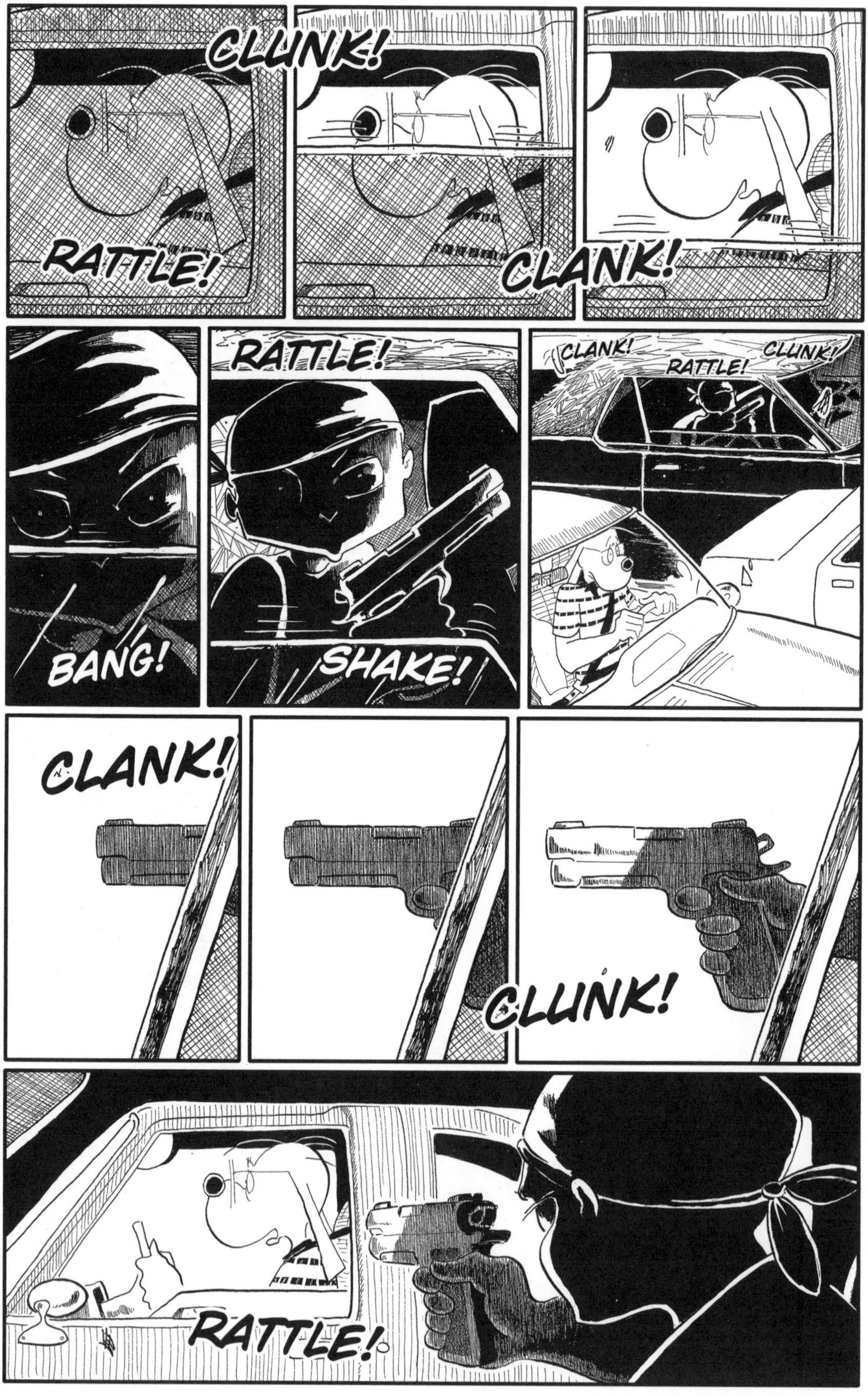
CLUNK!
RATTLE!
CLANK!
BANG!
RATTLE!
SHAKE!
CLANK!
RATTLE!
CLUNK!
CLANK!
CLUNK!
RATTLE!

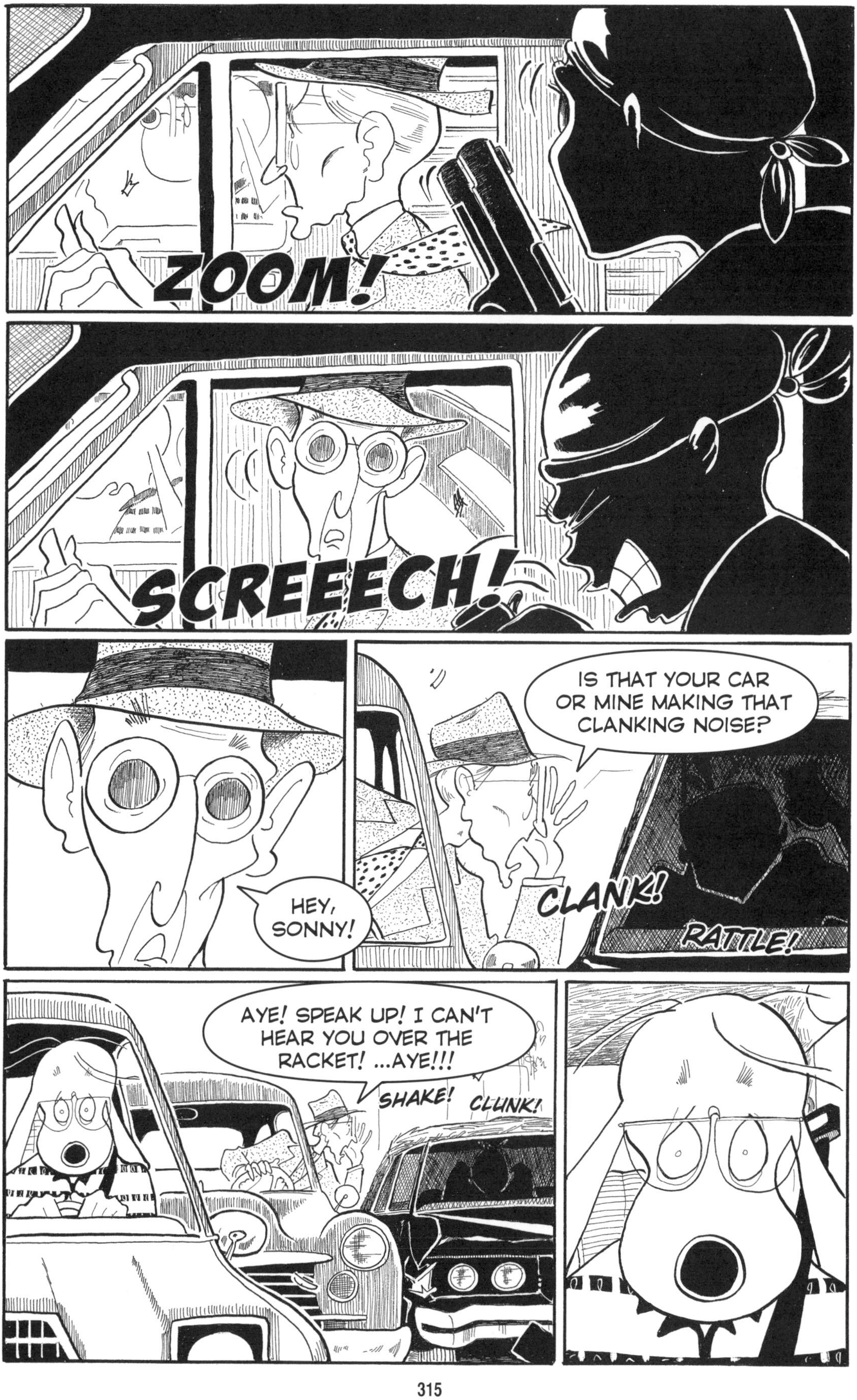
ZOOM!
SCREEECH!
HEY, SONNY!
IS THAT YOUR CAR OR MINE MAKING THAT CLANKING NOISE?
CLANK!
RATTLE!
AYE! SPEAK UP! I CAN'T HEAR YOU OVER THE RACKET! ...AYE!!!
SHAKE!
CLUNK!

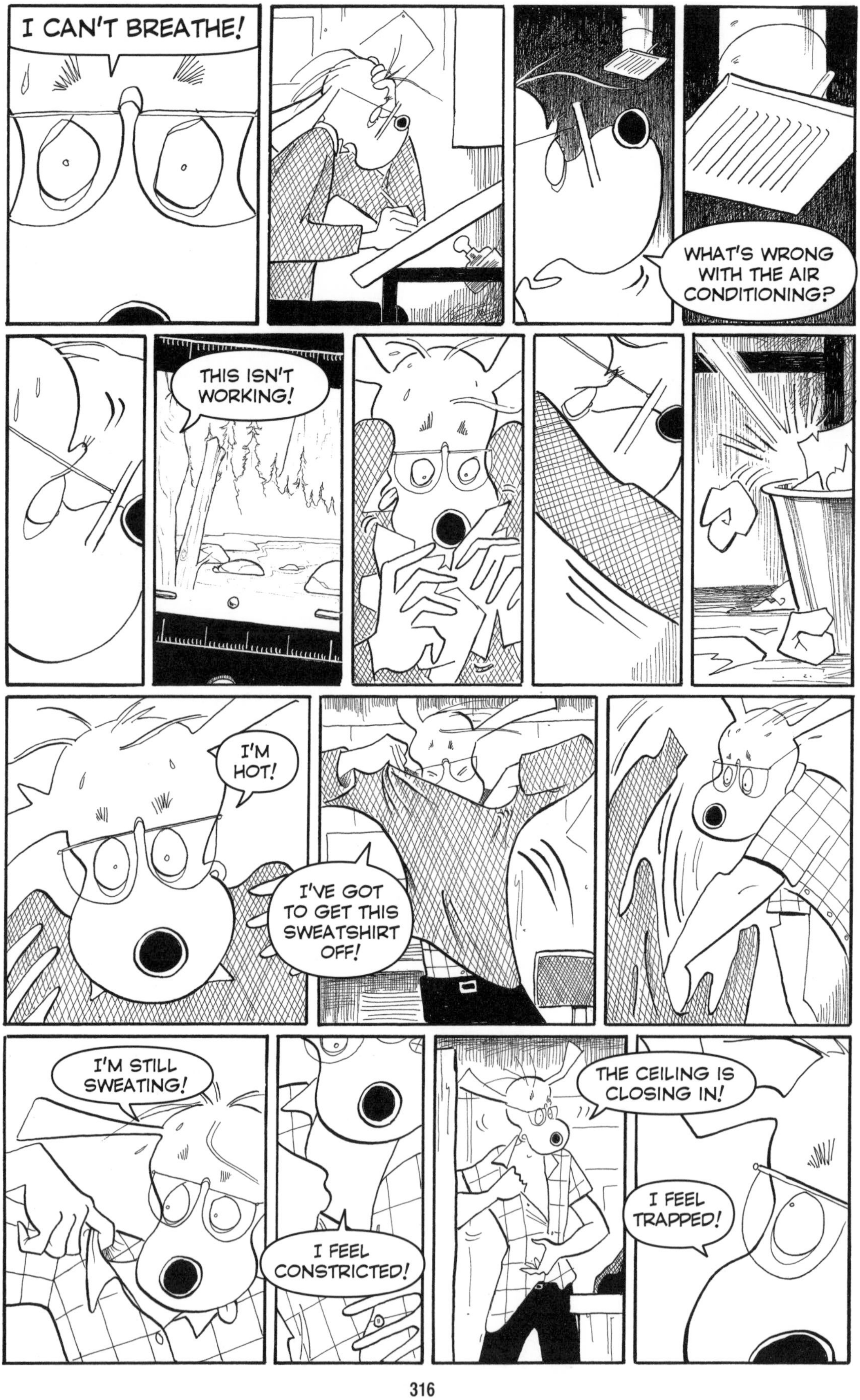
I CAN'T BREATHE!
WHAT'S WRONG WITH THE AIR CONDITIONING?
THIS ISN'T WORKING!
I'M HOT!
I'VE GOT TO GET THIS SWEATSHIRT OFF!
I'M STILL SWEATING!
I FEEL CONSTRICTED!
THE CEILING IS CLOSING IN!
I FEEL TRAPPED!

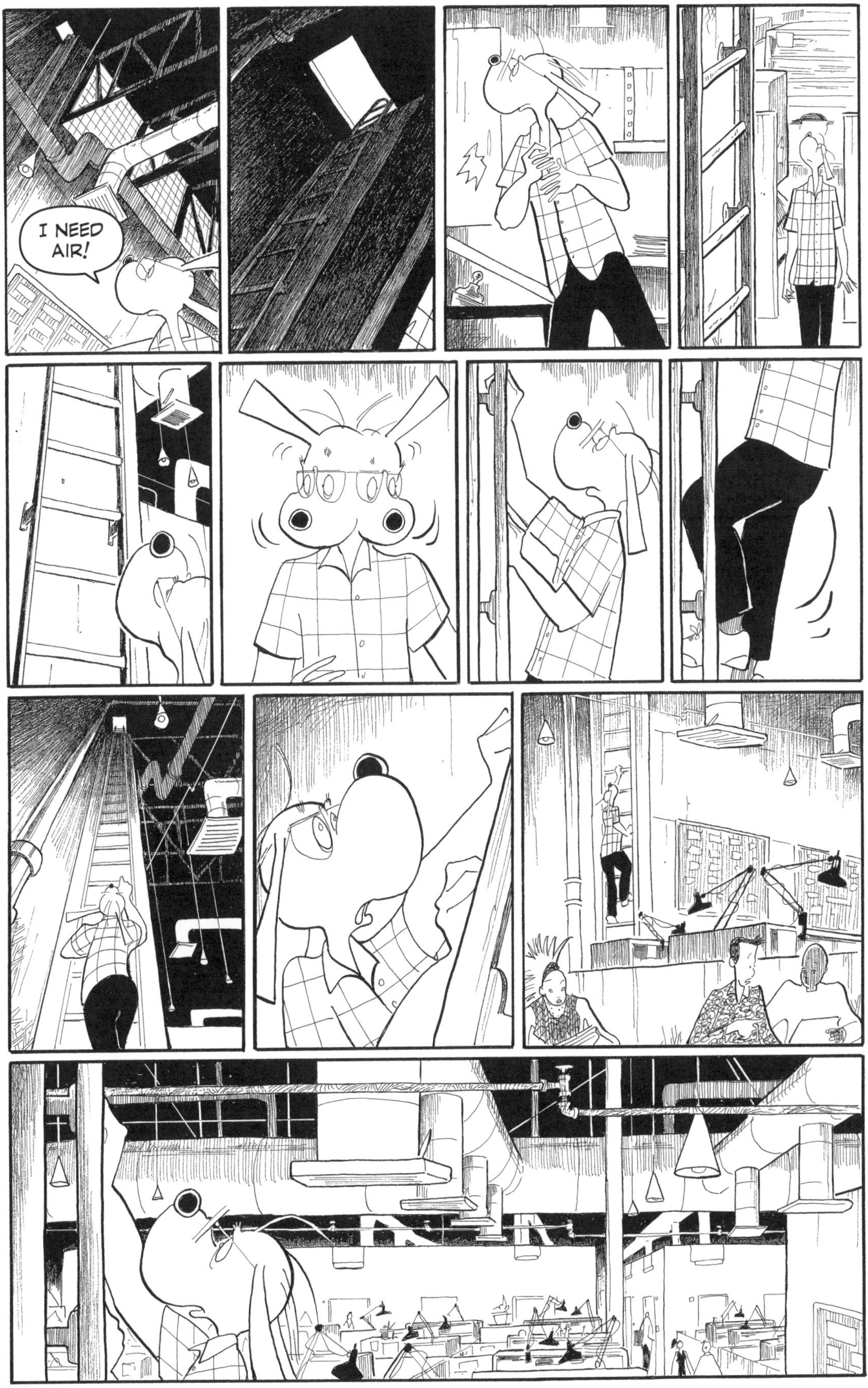
I NEED AIR!

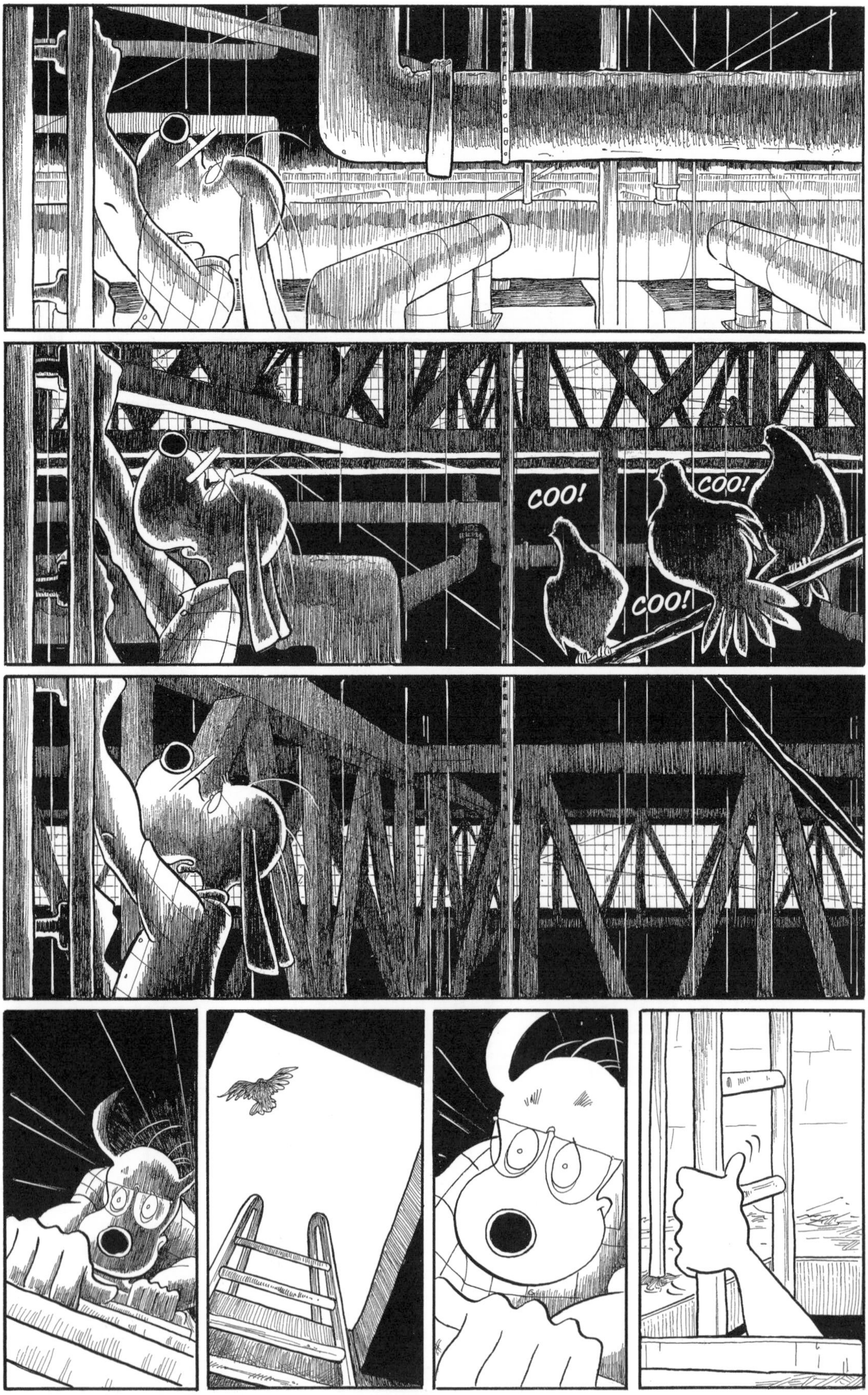
COO!
COO!
COO!

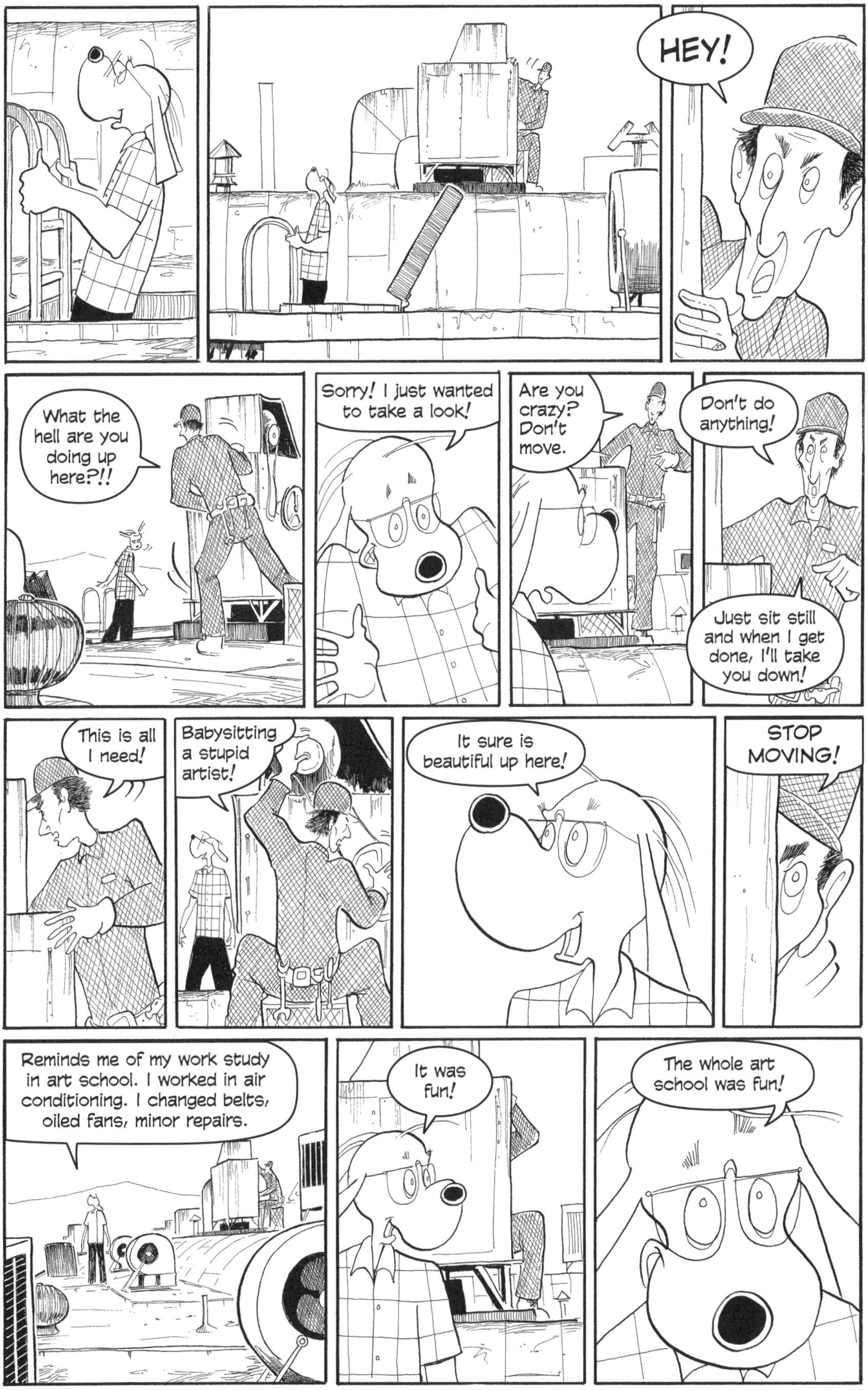

HEY!
What the hell are you doing up here?!!
Sorry! I just wanted to take a look!
Are you crazy? Don't move.
Don't do anything!
Just sit still and when I get done, I'll take you down!
This is all I need!
Babysitting a stupid artist!
It sure is beautiful up here!
STOP MOVING!
Reminds me of my work study in art school. I worked in air conditioning. I changed belts, oiled fans, minor repairs.
It was fun!
The whole art school was fun!

Once on the school roof, while working on a fan, I danced.

I DANCED FOR JOY!

THE JOY OF *ART!*

I was so excited.

Non stop ideas and creativity.

I was so happy.

GET AWAY FROM THE EDGE!

I wanted that joy again.

T.V. animation didn't do it.

STAY PUT!

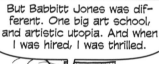

But Babbitt Jones was different. One big art school, and artistic utopia. And when I was hired, I was thrilled.

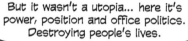

But it wasn't a utopia... here it's power, position and office politics. Destroying people's lives.

No art. No joy...

I'm done.

I'll guide you down.

...no more dancing on the roof.

320

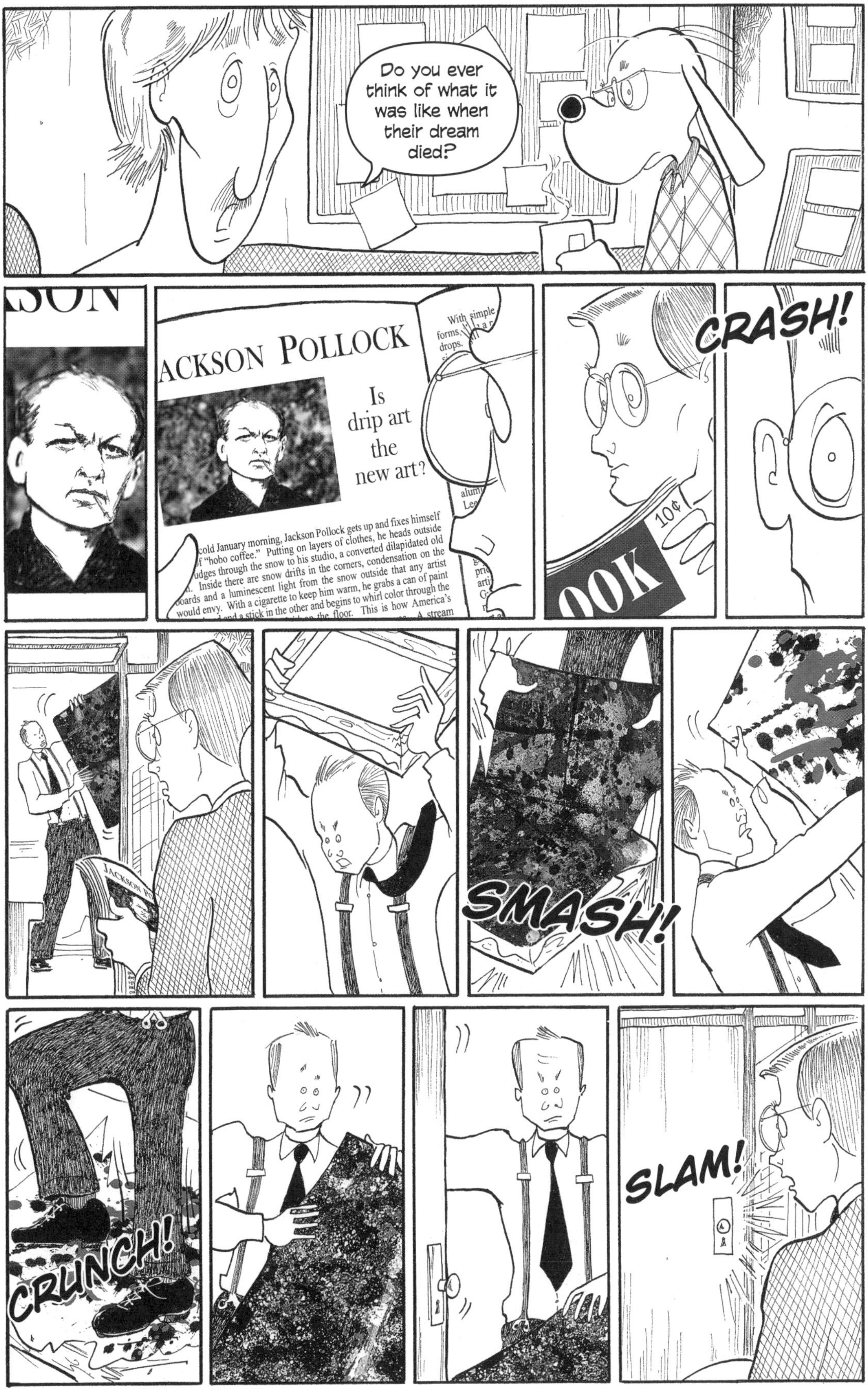
Do you ever think of what it was like when their dream died?
ACKSON POLLOCK
Is drip art the new art?
cold January morning, Jackson Pollock gets up and fixes himself
f "hobo coffee." Putting on layers of clothes, he heads outside
udges through the snow to his studio, a converted dilapidated old
. Inside there are snow drifts in the corners, condensation on the
oards and a luminescent light from the snow outside that any artist
would envy. With a cigarette to keep him warm, he grabs a can of paint
10¢
OOK
CRASH!
SMASH!
CRUNCH!
SLAM!

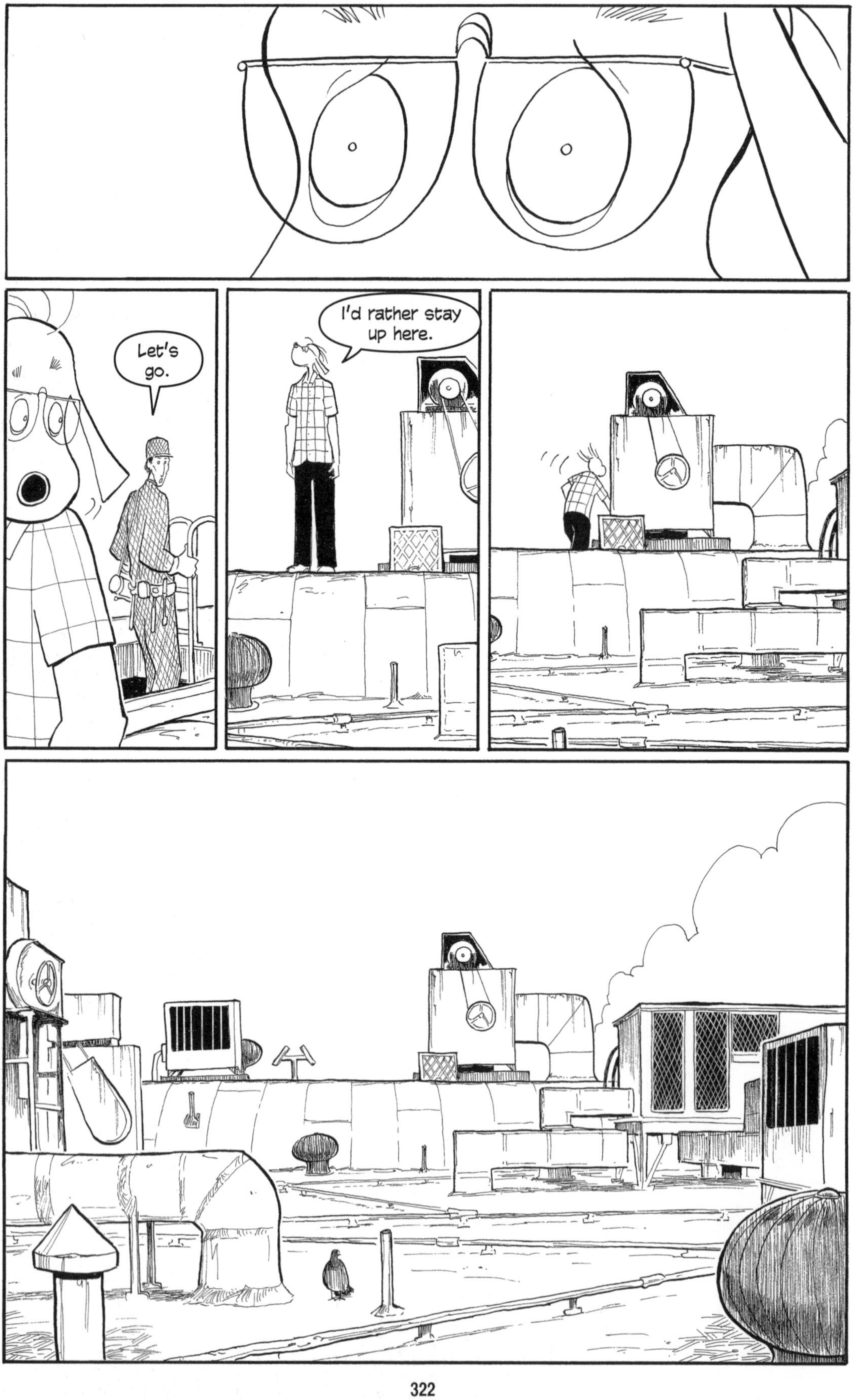
Let's go.
I'd rather stay up here.

CHAPTER 7

- -

ACCENTUATE THE POSITIVE

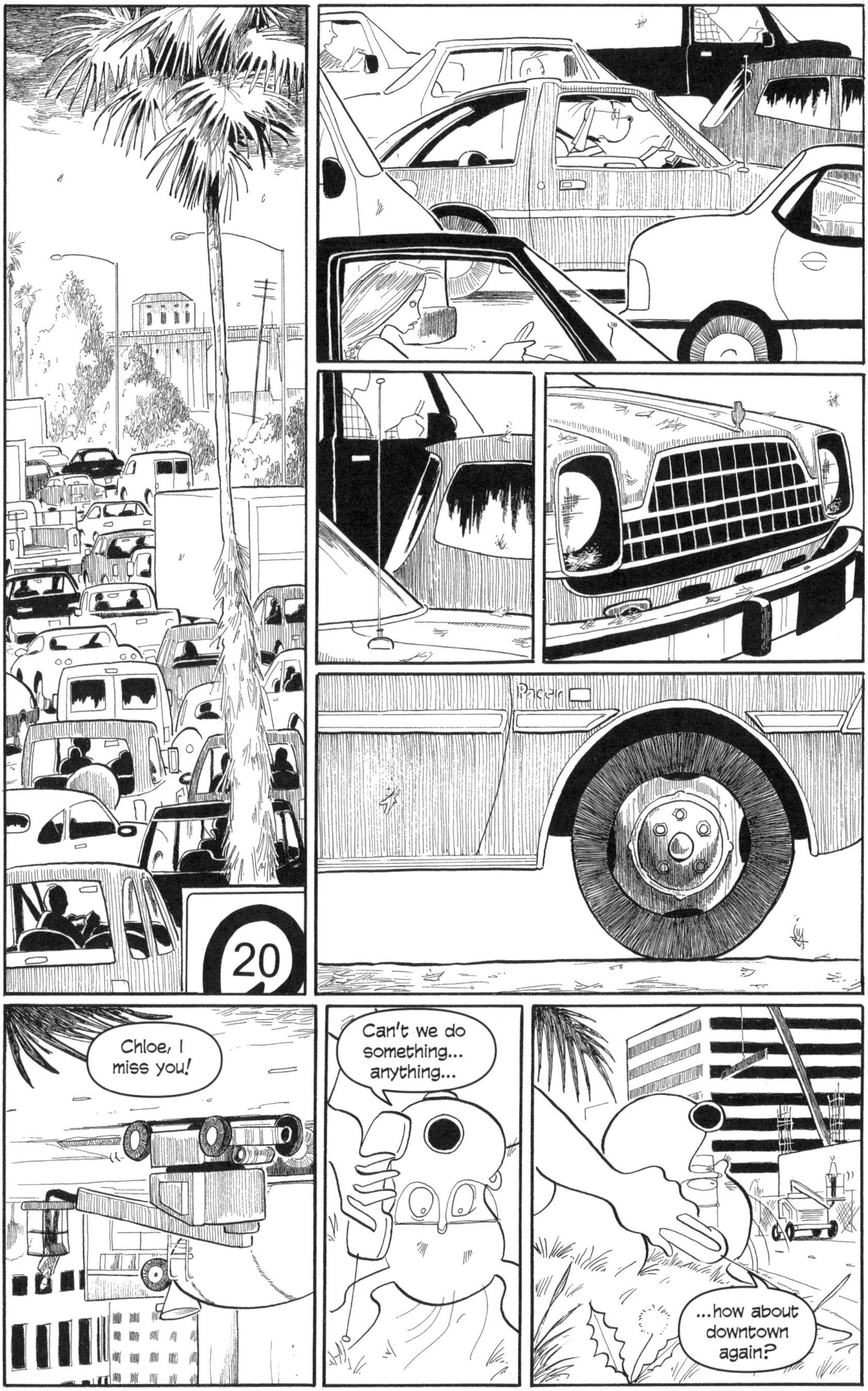
20
Chloe, I miss you!
Can't we do something... anything...
...how about downtown again?

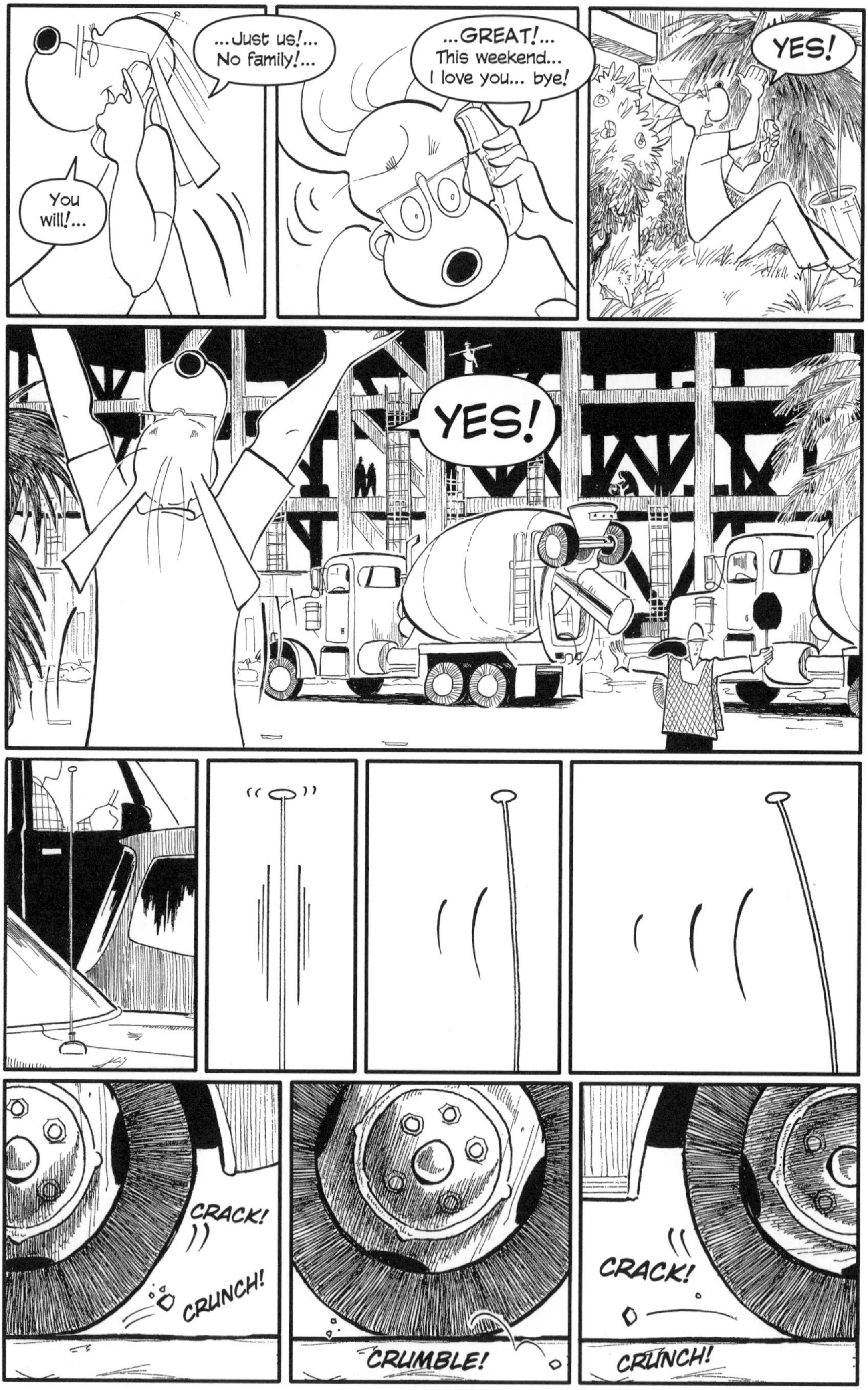
...Just us!...
No family!...
You will!...
...GREAT!...
This weekend...
I love you... bye!
YES!
YES!
CRACK!
CRUNCH!
CRUMBLE!
CRACK!
CRUNCH!

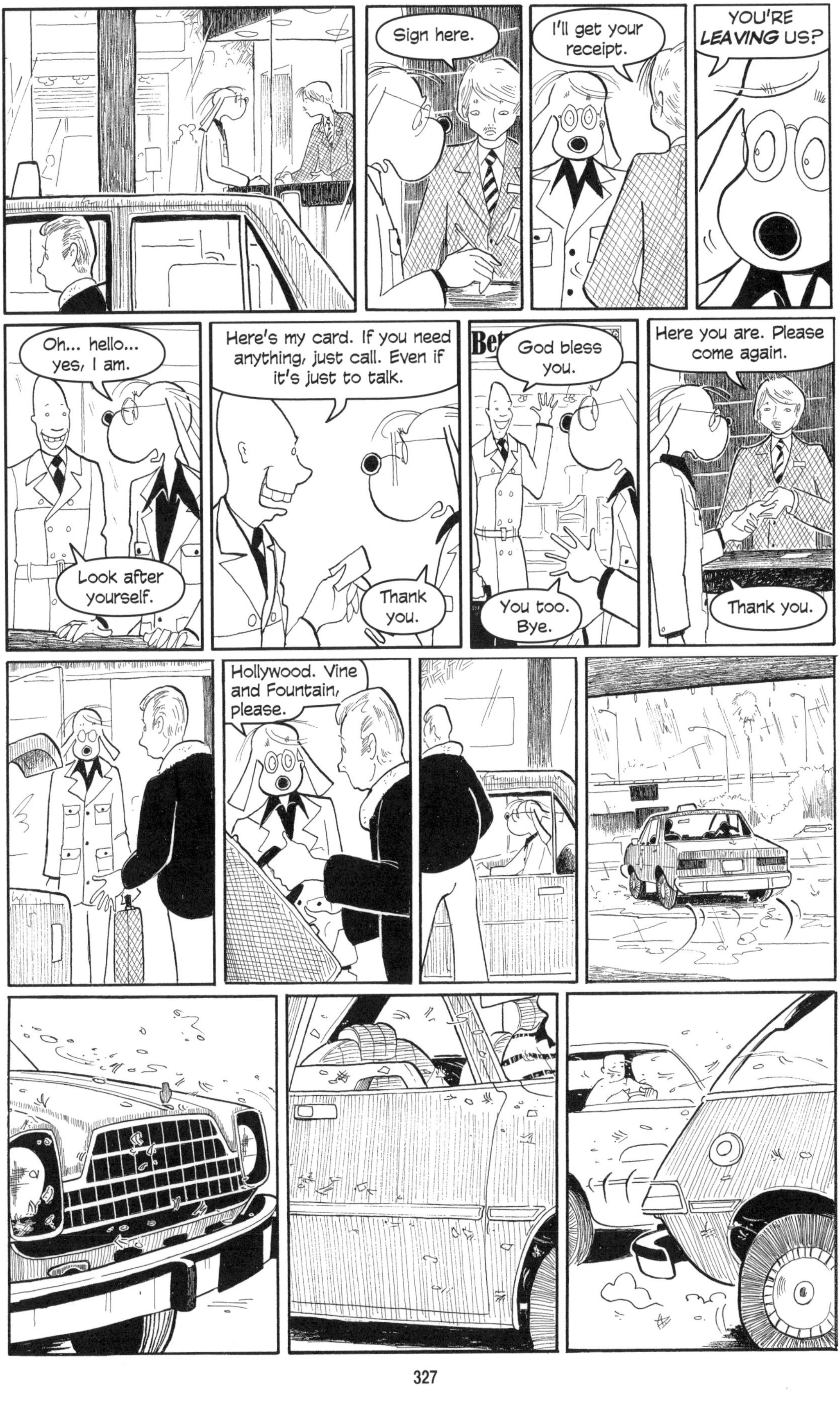
Sign here.
I'll get your receipt.
YOU'RE LEAVING US?
Oh... hello... yes, I am.
Look after yourself.
Here's my card. If you need anything, just call. Even if it's just to talk.
Thank you.
God bless you.
You too. Bye.
Here you are. Please come again.
Thank you.
Hollywood. Vine and Fountain, please.

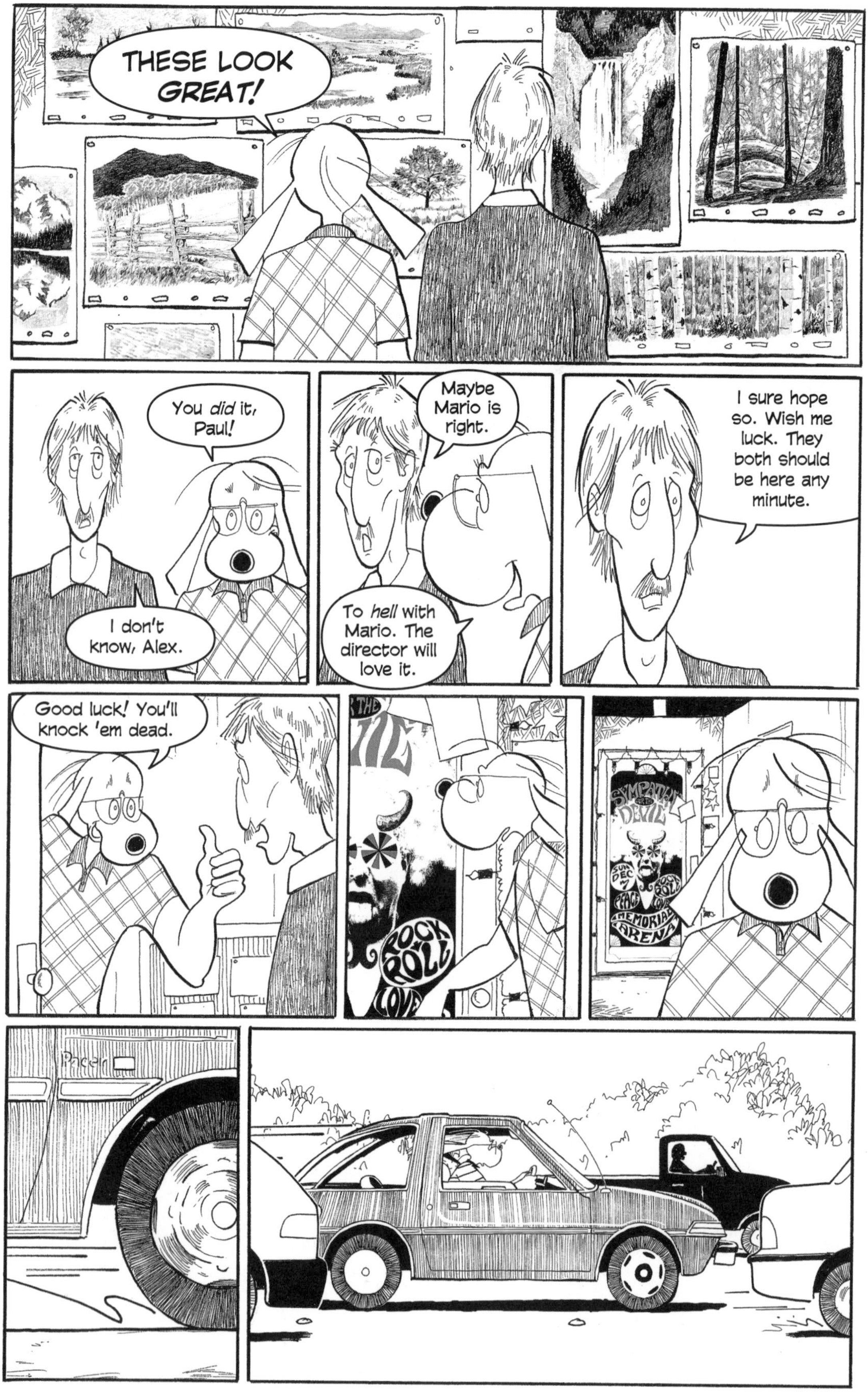
THESE LOOK *GREAT!*
You *did* it, Paul!
I don't know, Alex.
Maybe Mario is right.
To *hell* with Mario. The director will love it.
I sure hope so. Wish me luck. They both should be here any minute.
Good luck! You'll knock 'em dead.
Pacer

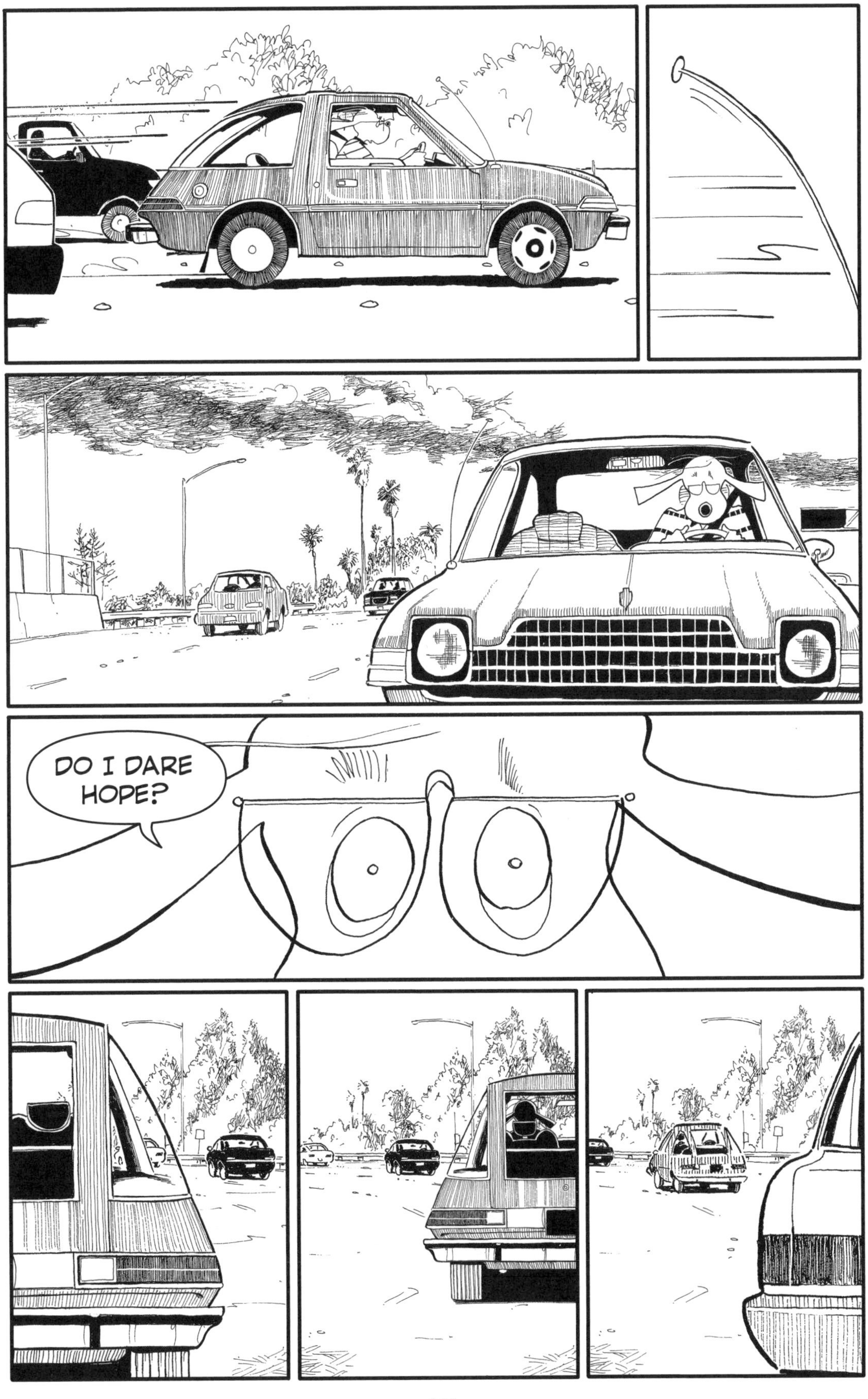
DO I DARE HOPE?

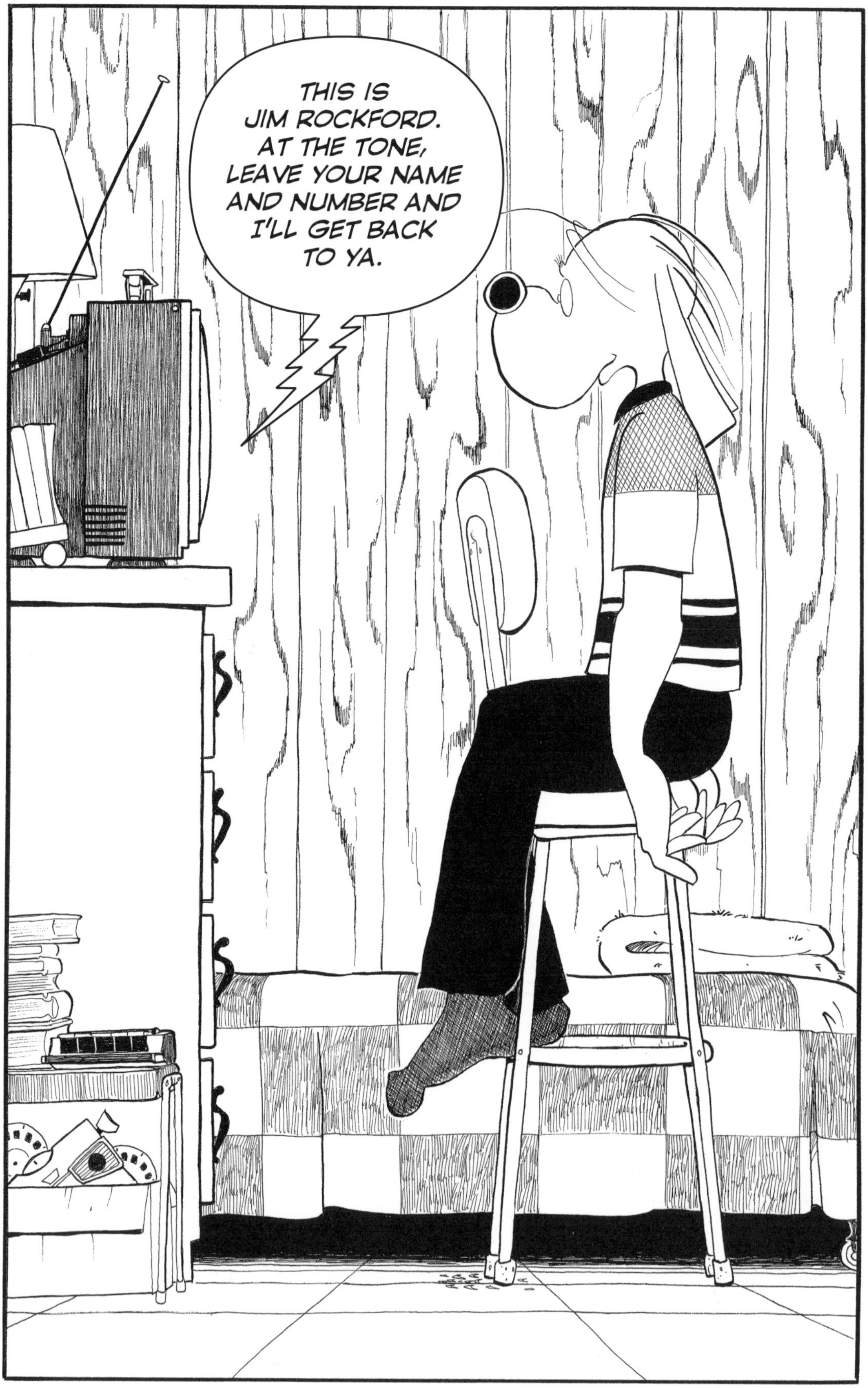
THIS IS JIM ROCKFORD. AT THE TONE, LEAVE YOUR NAME AND NUMBER AND I'LL GET BACK TO YA.

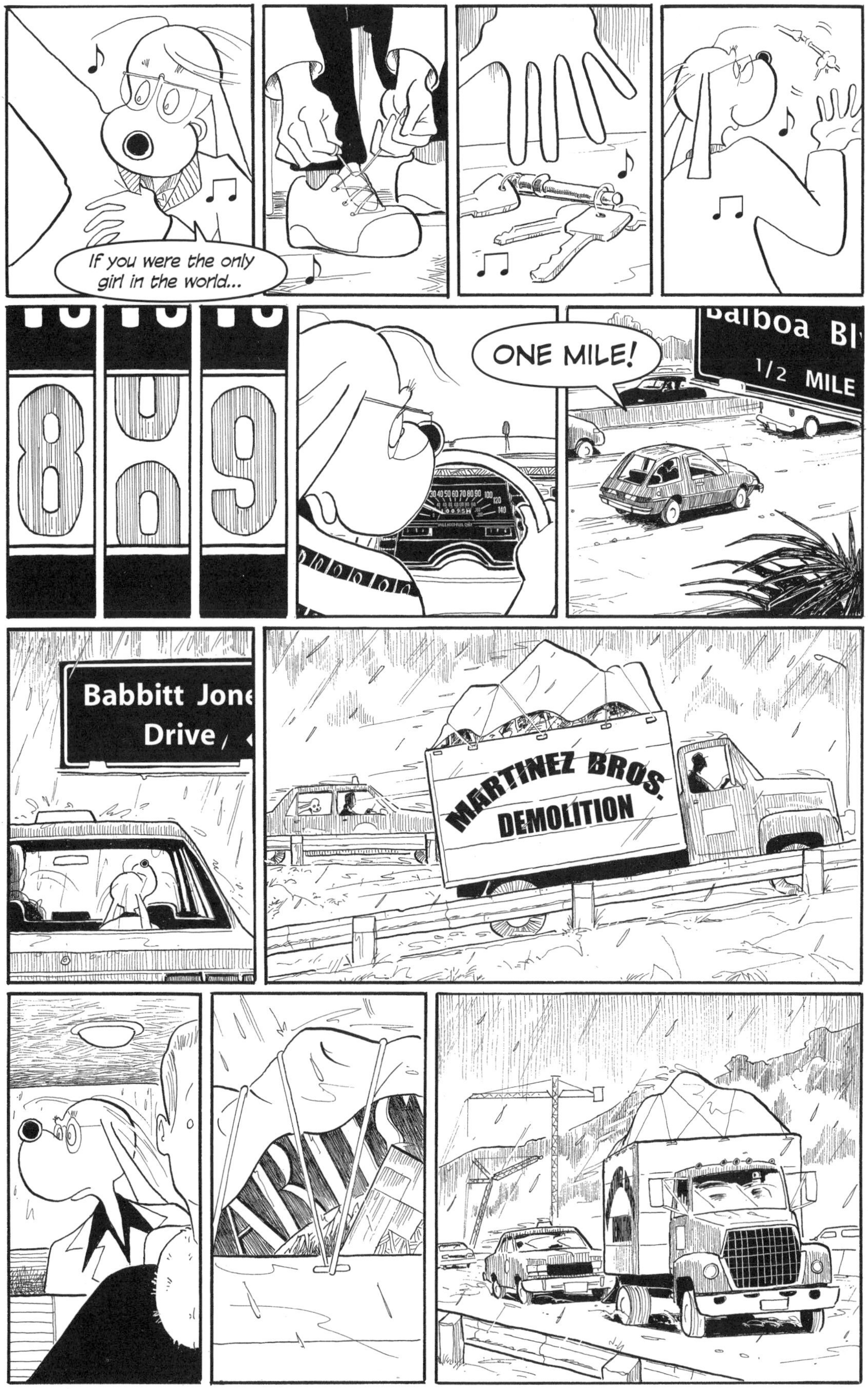
If you were the only girl in the world...
ONE MILE!
Balboa Bl
1/2 MILE
Babbitt Jone
Drive
MARTINEZ BROS.
DEMOLITION

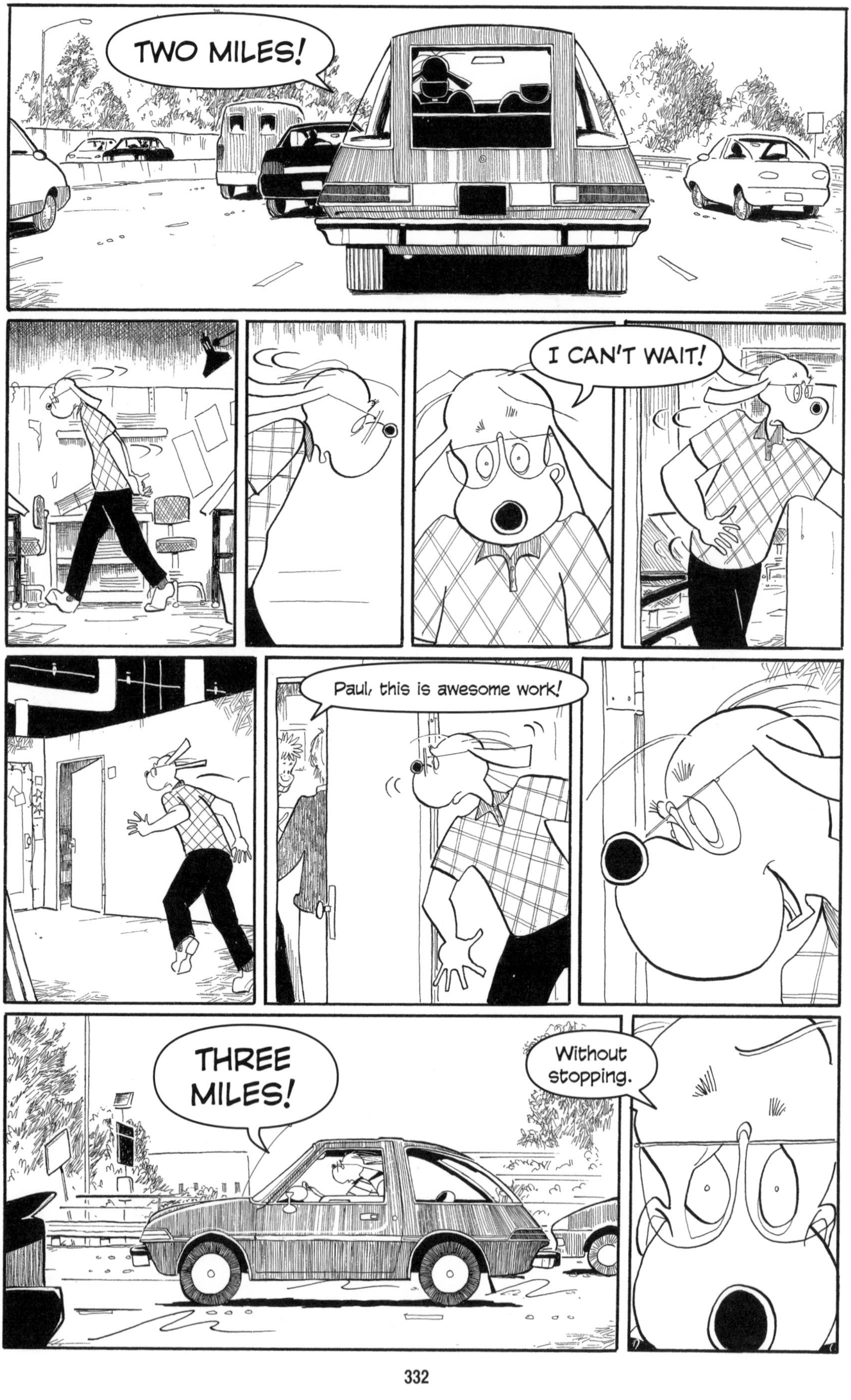
TWO MILES!
I CAN'T WAIT!
Paul, this is awesome work!
THREE MILES!
Without stopping.

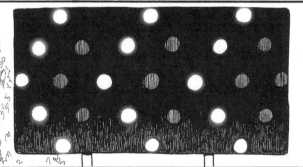

SMASH!

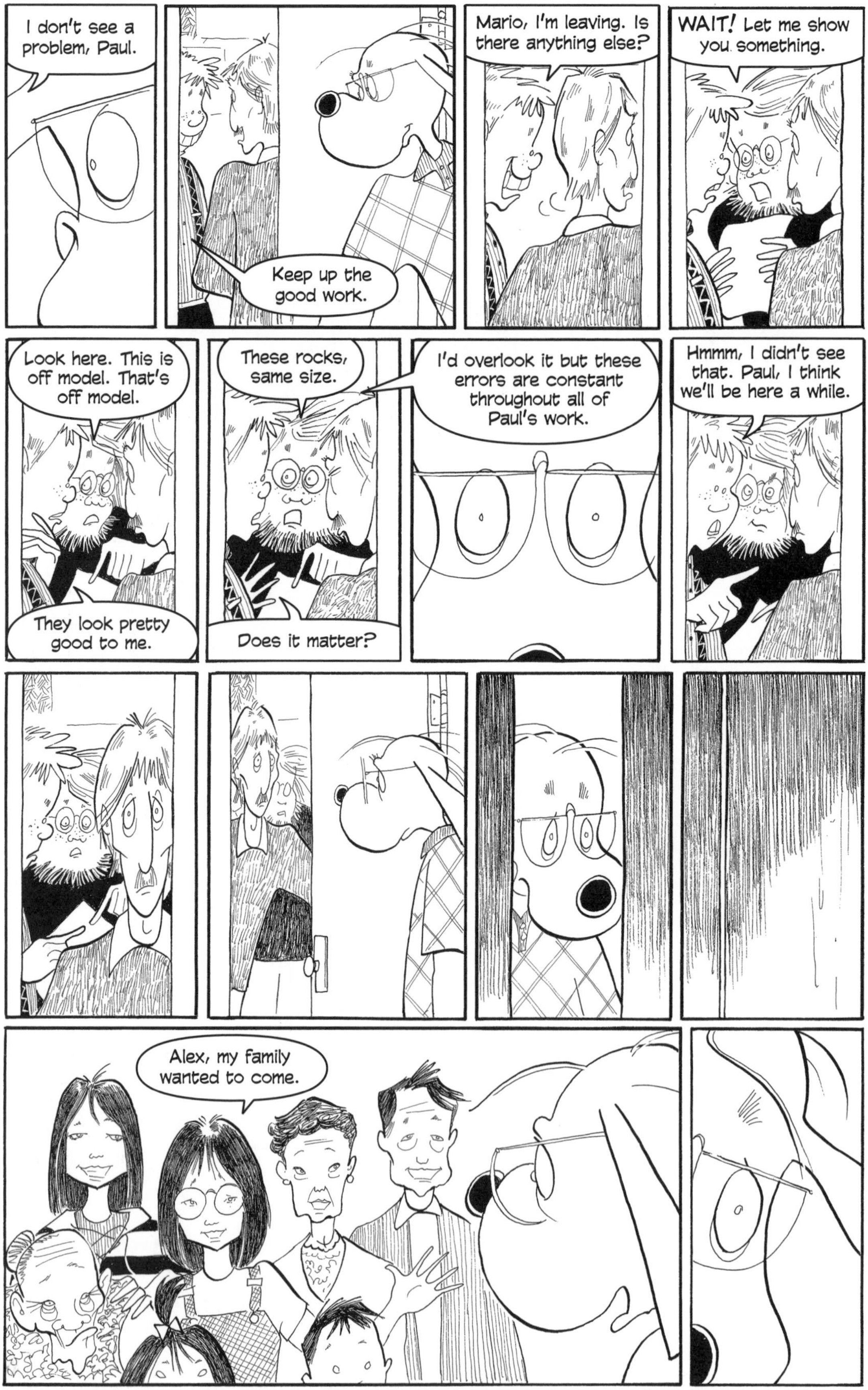
I don't see a problem, Paul.
Keep up the good work.
Mario, I'm leaving. Is there anything else?
WAIT! Let me show you something.
Look here. This is off model. That's off model.
They look pretty good to me.
These rocks, same size.
Does it matter?
I'd overlook it but these errors are constant throughout all of Paul's work.
Hmmm, I didn't see that. Paul, I think we'll be here a while.
Alex, my family wanted to come.

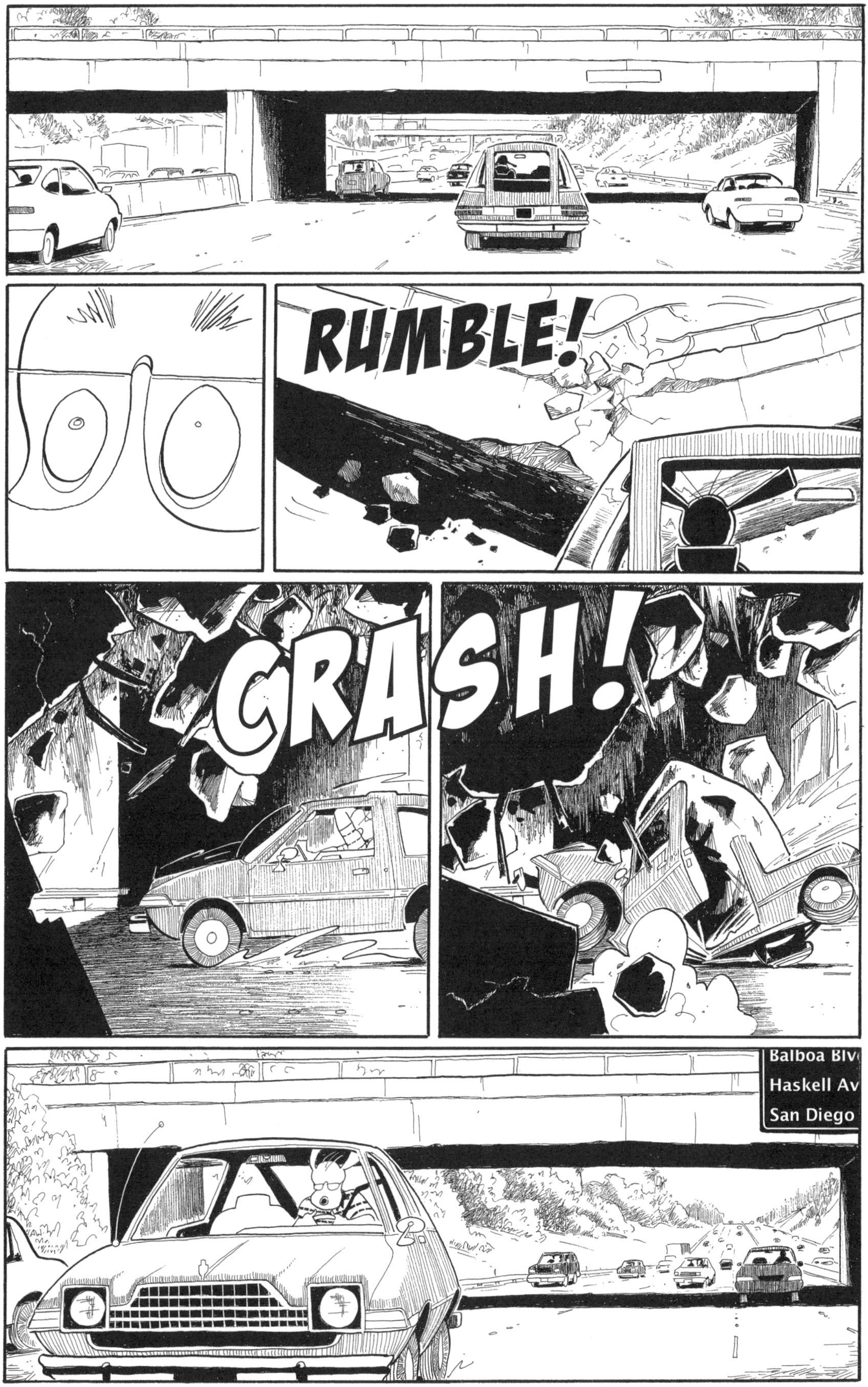
RUMBLE!
CRASH!
Balboa Blv
Haskell Av
San Diego

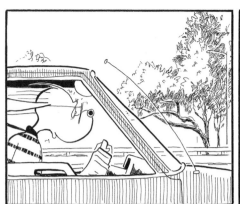
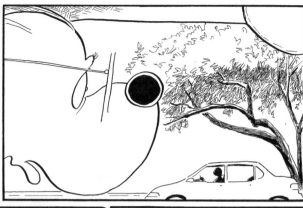

SNAP!
CRANG!
CRUNCH!
1207
1207
AAH
HH!

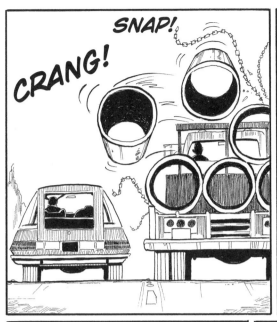

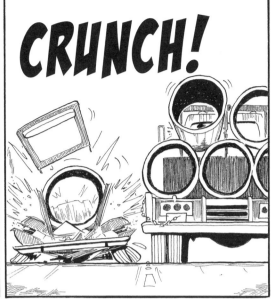

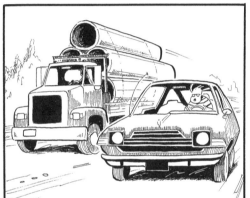

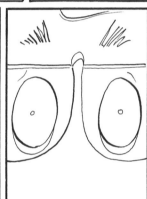

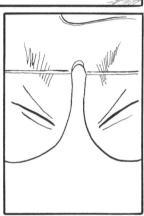

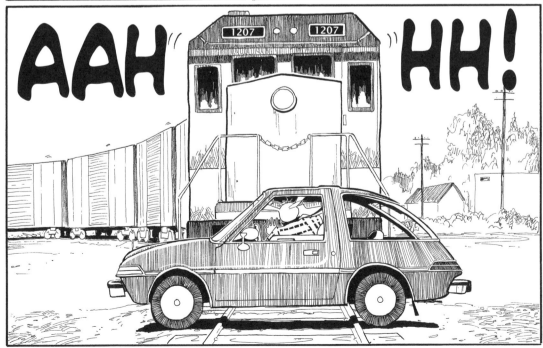

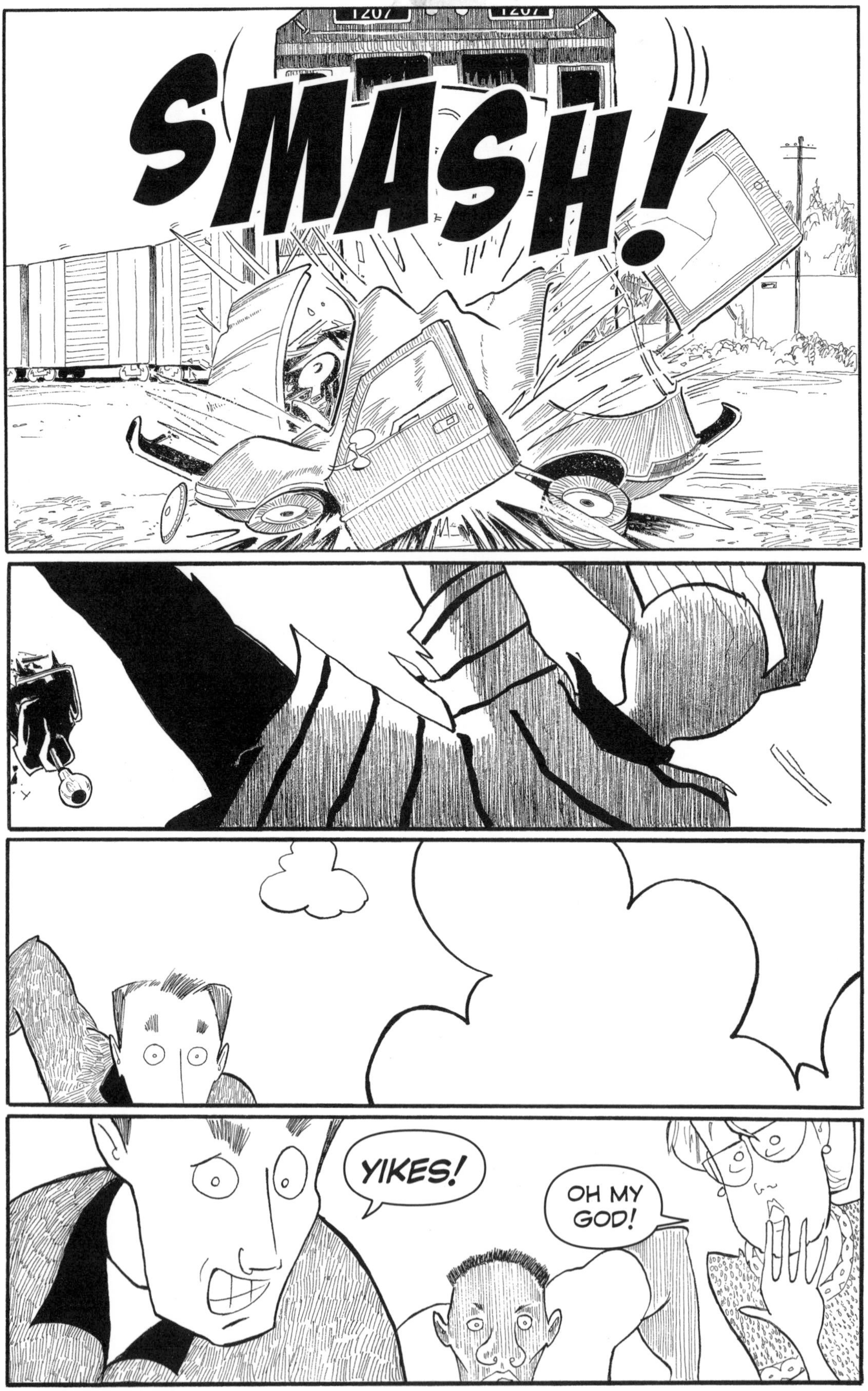
1207
1207
SMASH!
YIKES!
OH MY GOD!

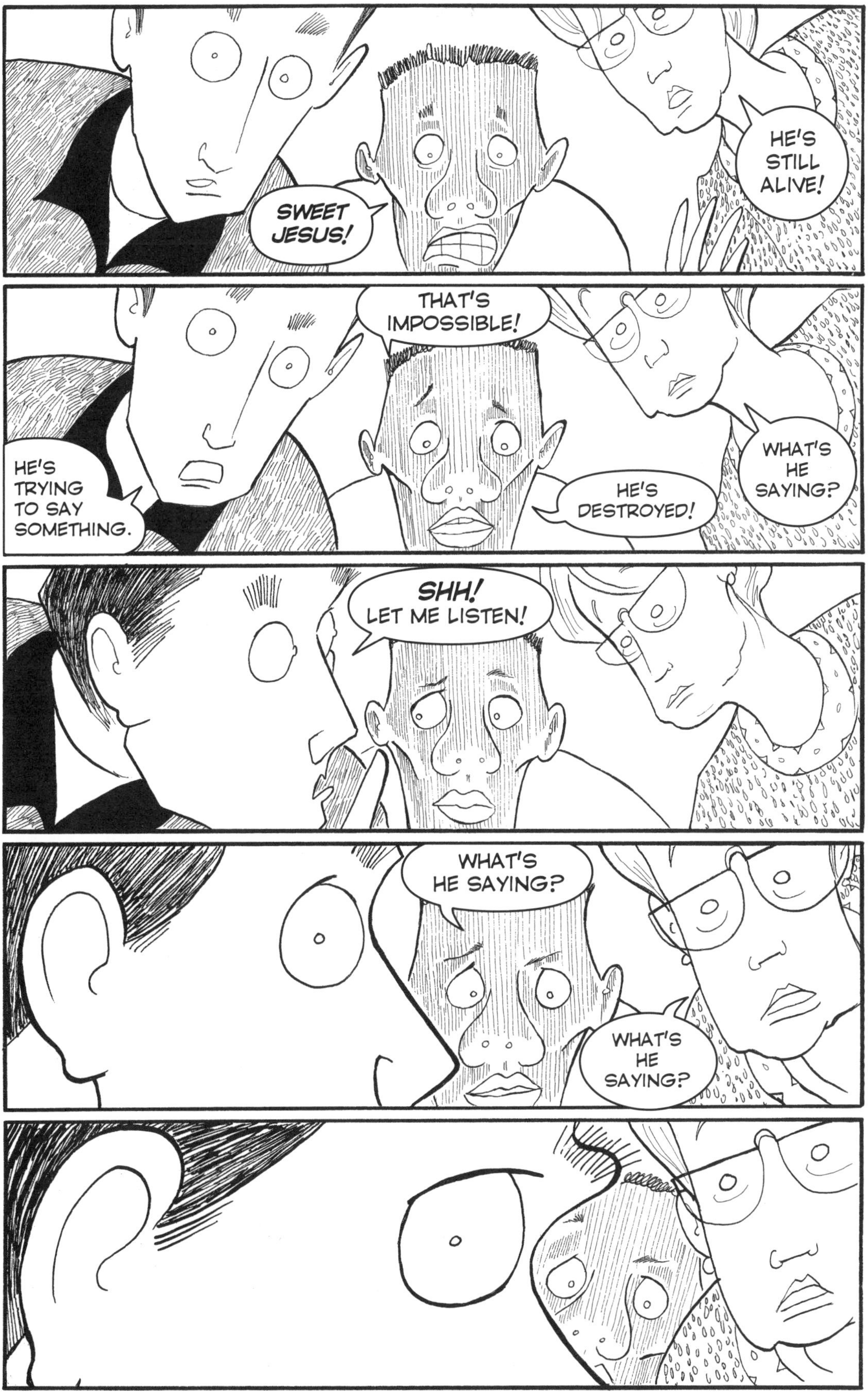
SWEET JESUS!
HE'S STILL ALIVE!
THAT'S IMPOSSIBLE!
HE'S TRYING TO SAY SOMETHING.
HE'S DESTROYED!
WHAT'S HE SAYING?
SHH! LET ME LISTEN!
WHAT'S HE SAYING?
WHAT'S HE SAYING?

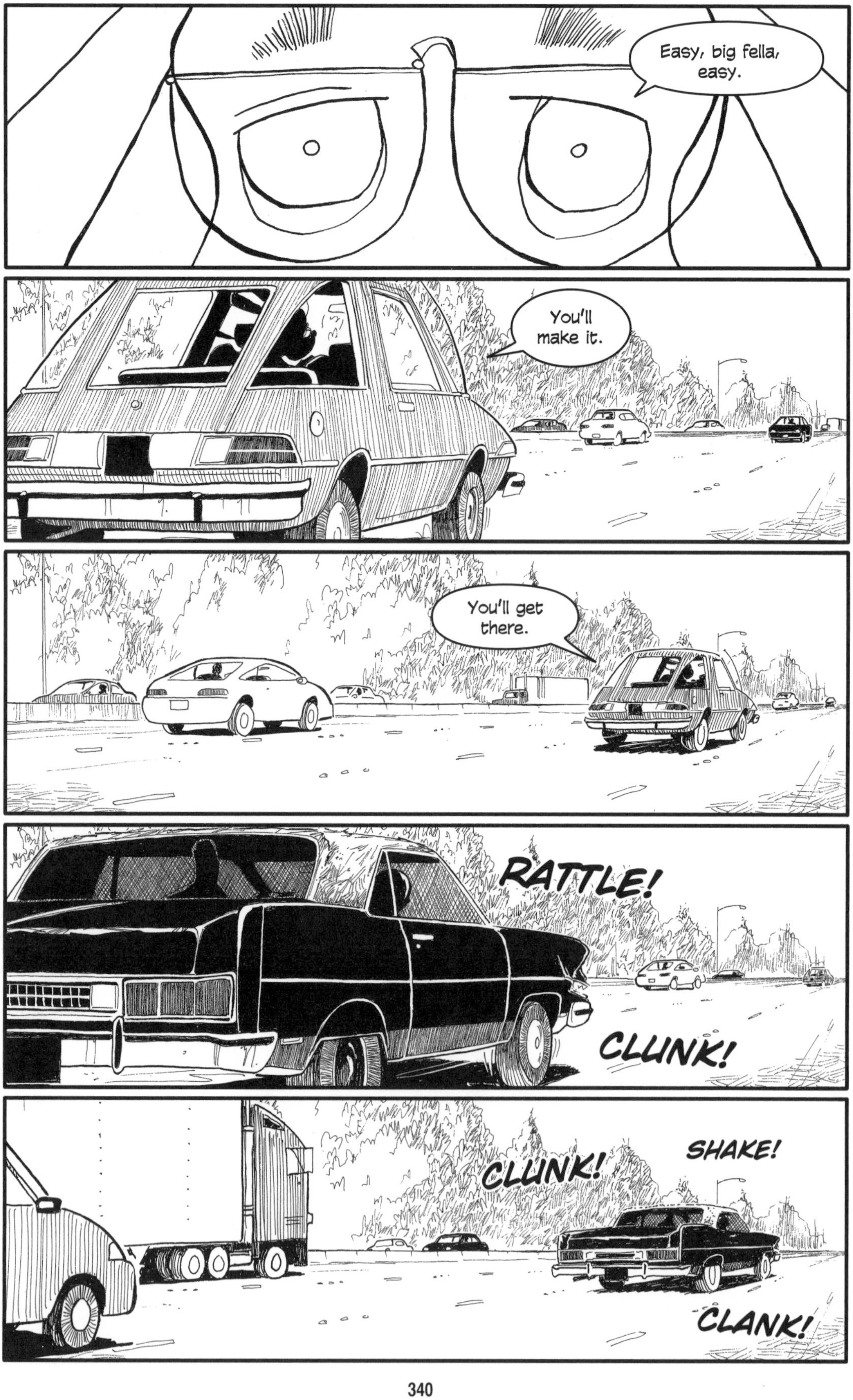
Easy, big fella, easy.
You'll make it.
You'll get there.
RATTLE!
CLUNK!
CLUNK!
SHAKE!
CLANK!

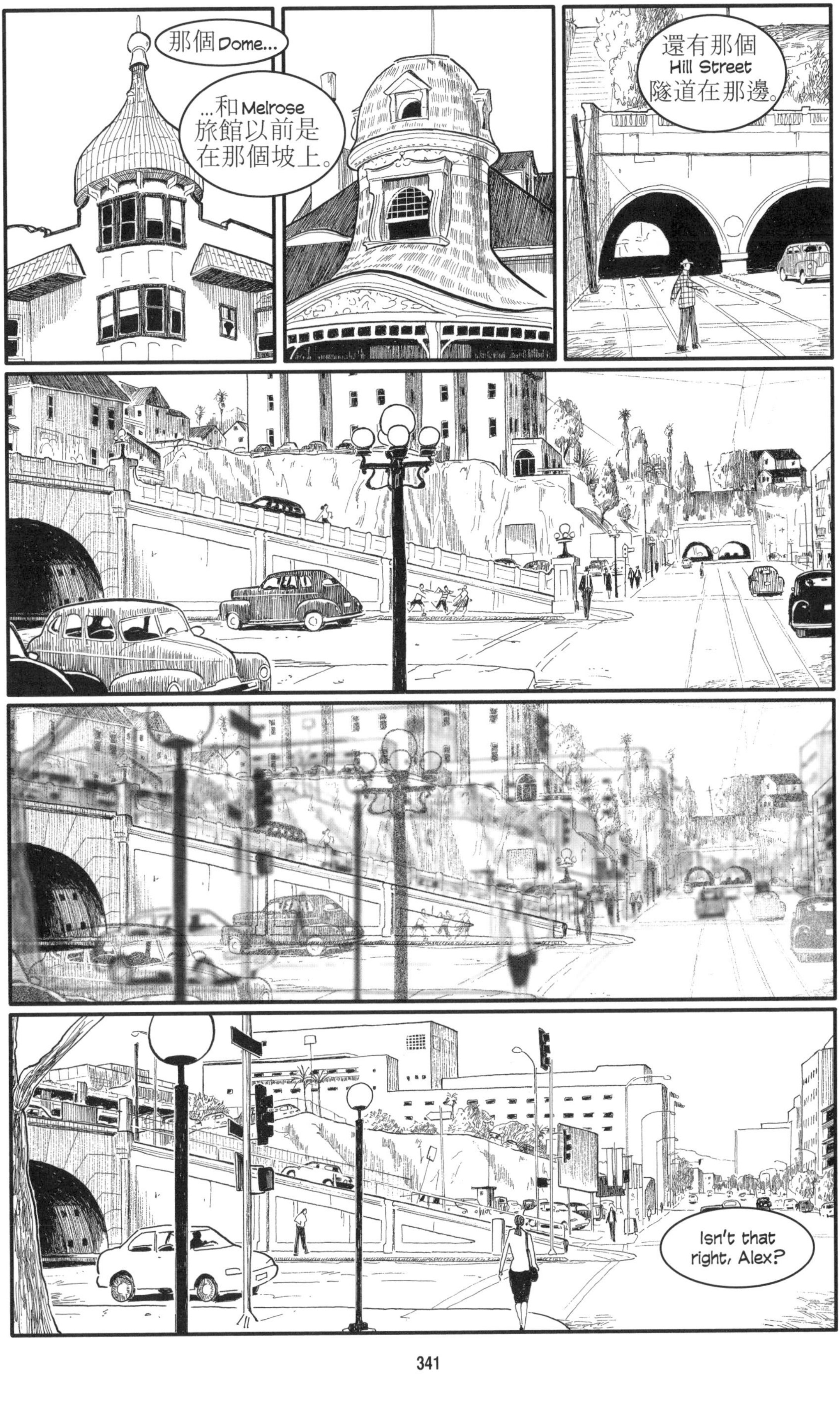
那個Dome...
...和Melrose
旅館以前是
在那個坡上。
還有那個
Hill Street
隧道在那邊。
Isn't that
right, Alex?

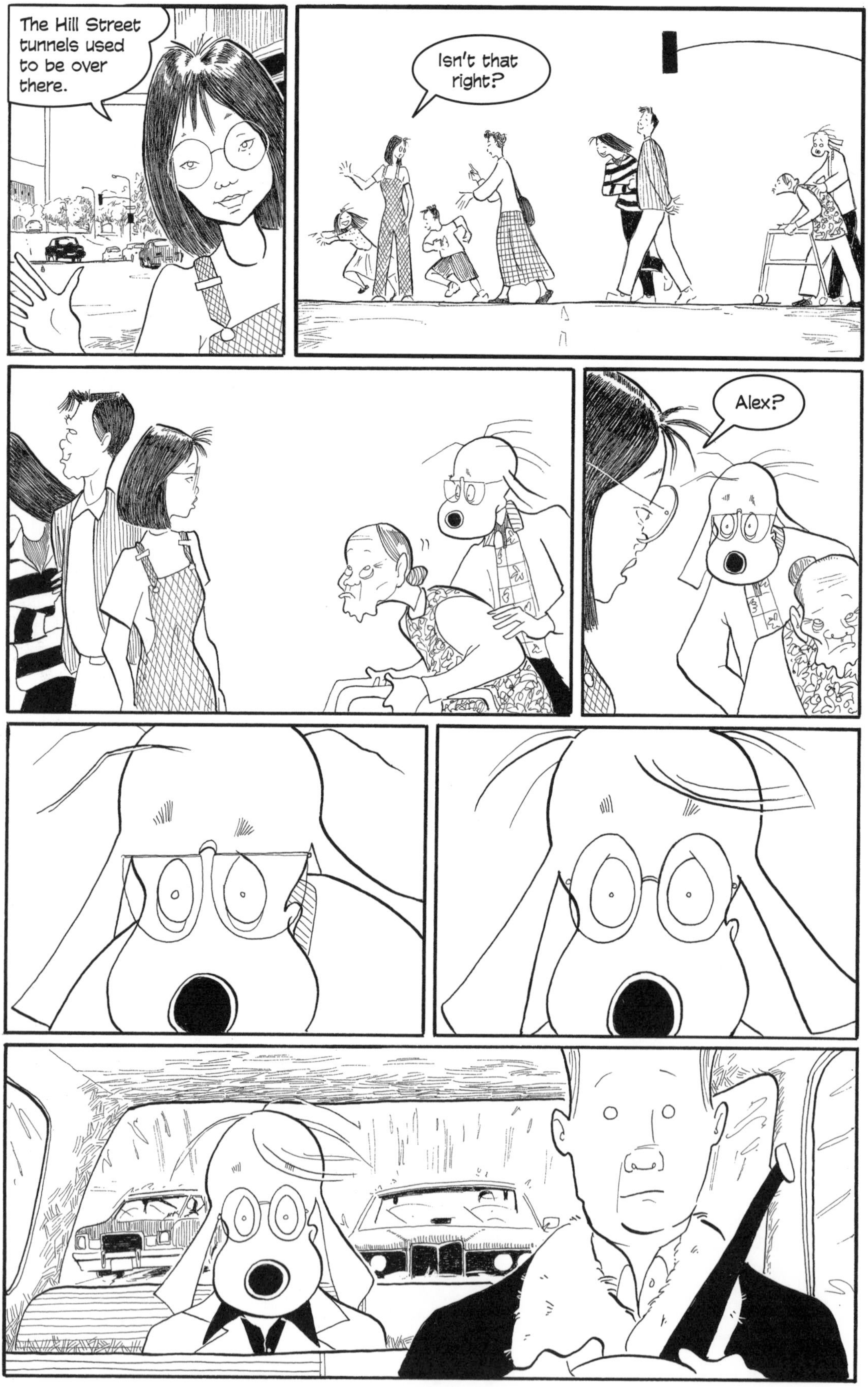
The Hill Street tunnels used to be over there.
Isn't that right?
Alex?

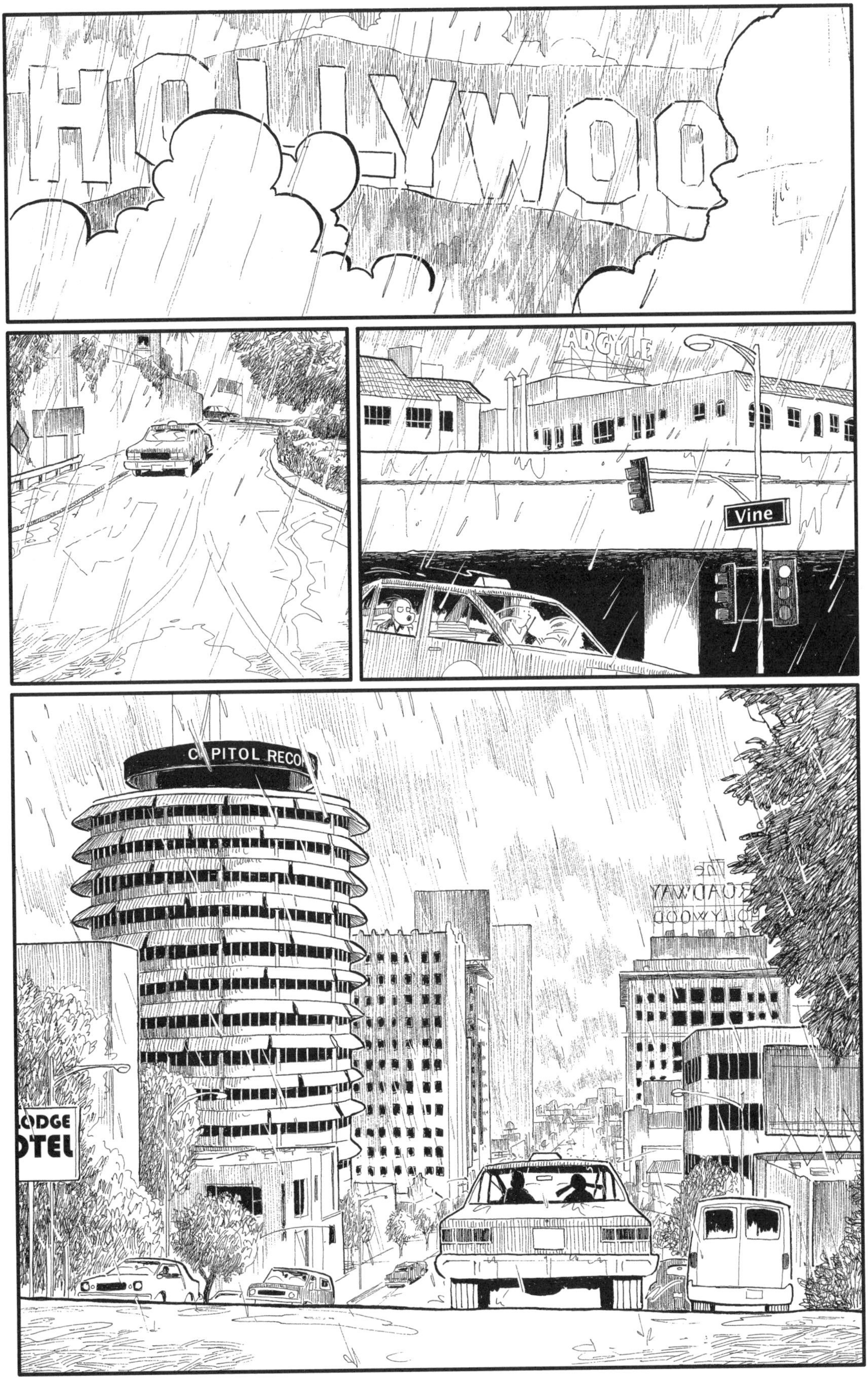
HOLLYWOO
ARGYLE
Vine
CAPITOL RECO
LODGE
OTEL

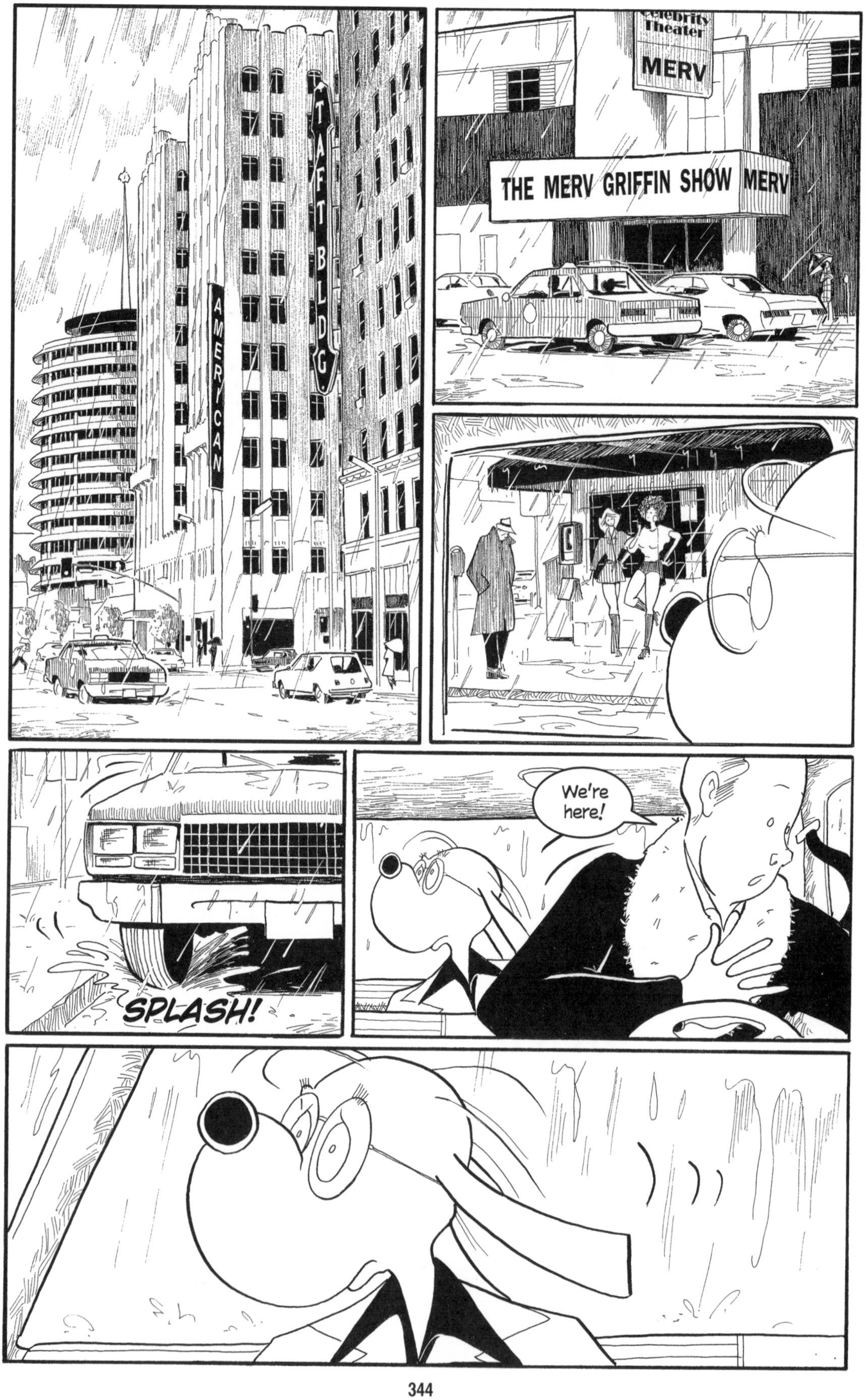
TAFT BLDG.
AMERICAN
Celebrity Theater
MERV
THE MERV GRIFFIN SHOW MERV
SPLASH!
We're here!

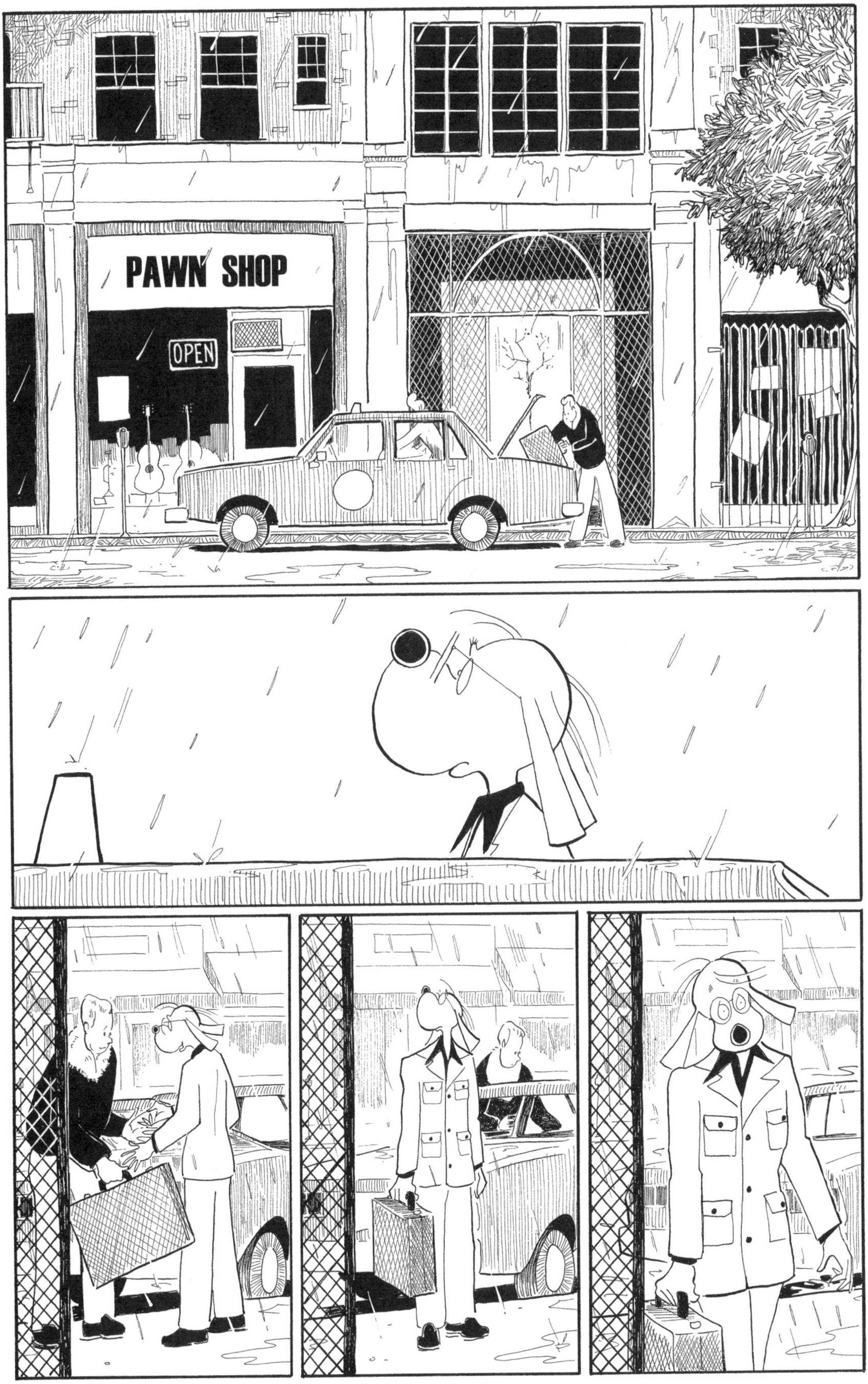
PAWN SHOP
OPEN

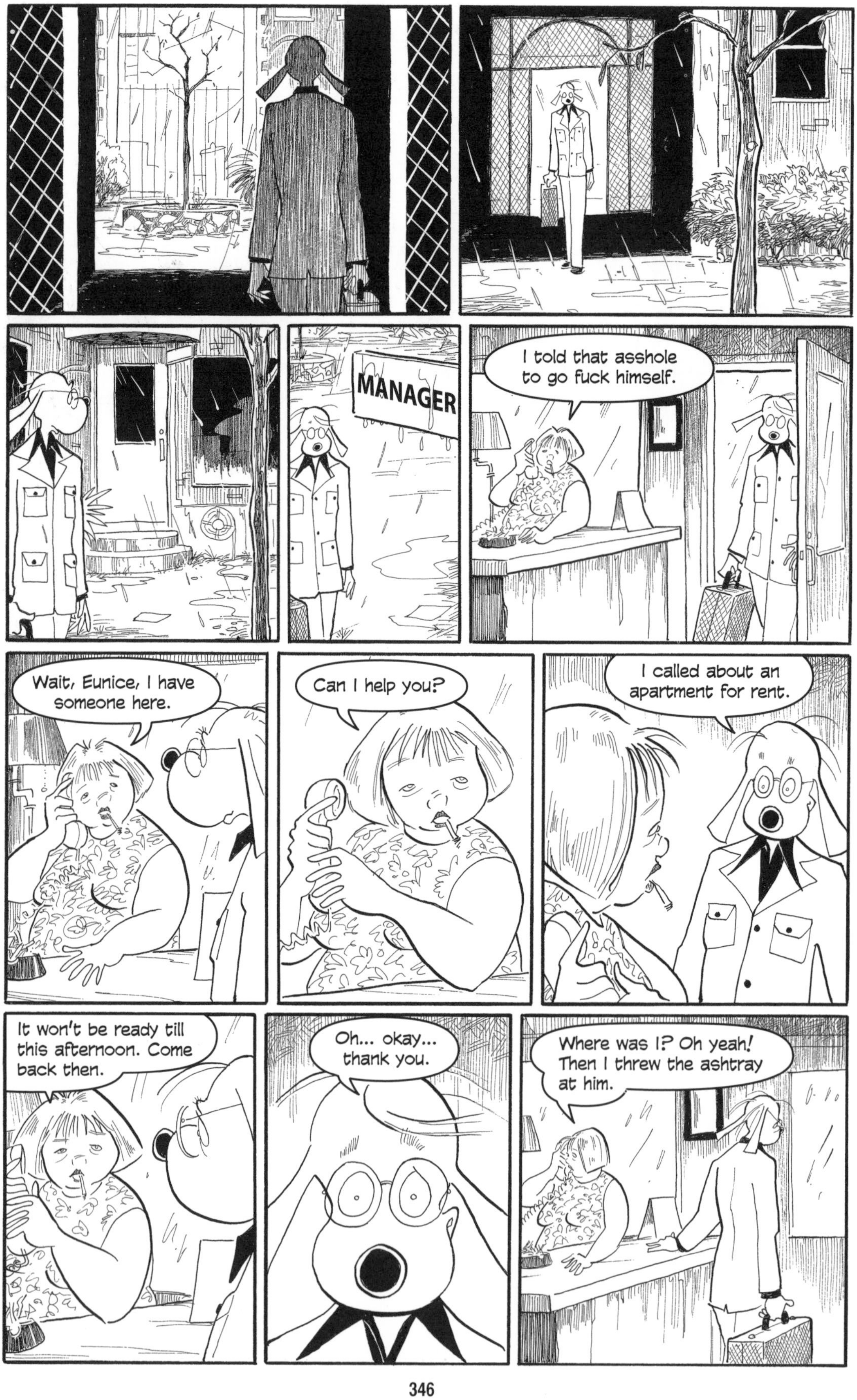
MANAGER
I told that asshole to go fuck himself.
Wait, Eunice, I have someone here.
Can I help you?
I called about an apartment for rent.
It won't be ready till this afternoon. Come back then.
Oh... okay... thank you.
Where was I? Oh yeah! Then I threw the ashtray at him.

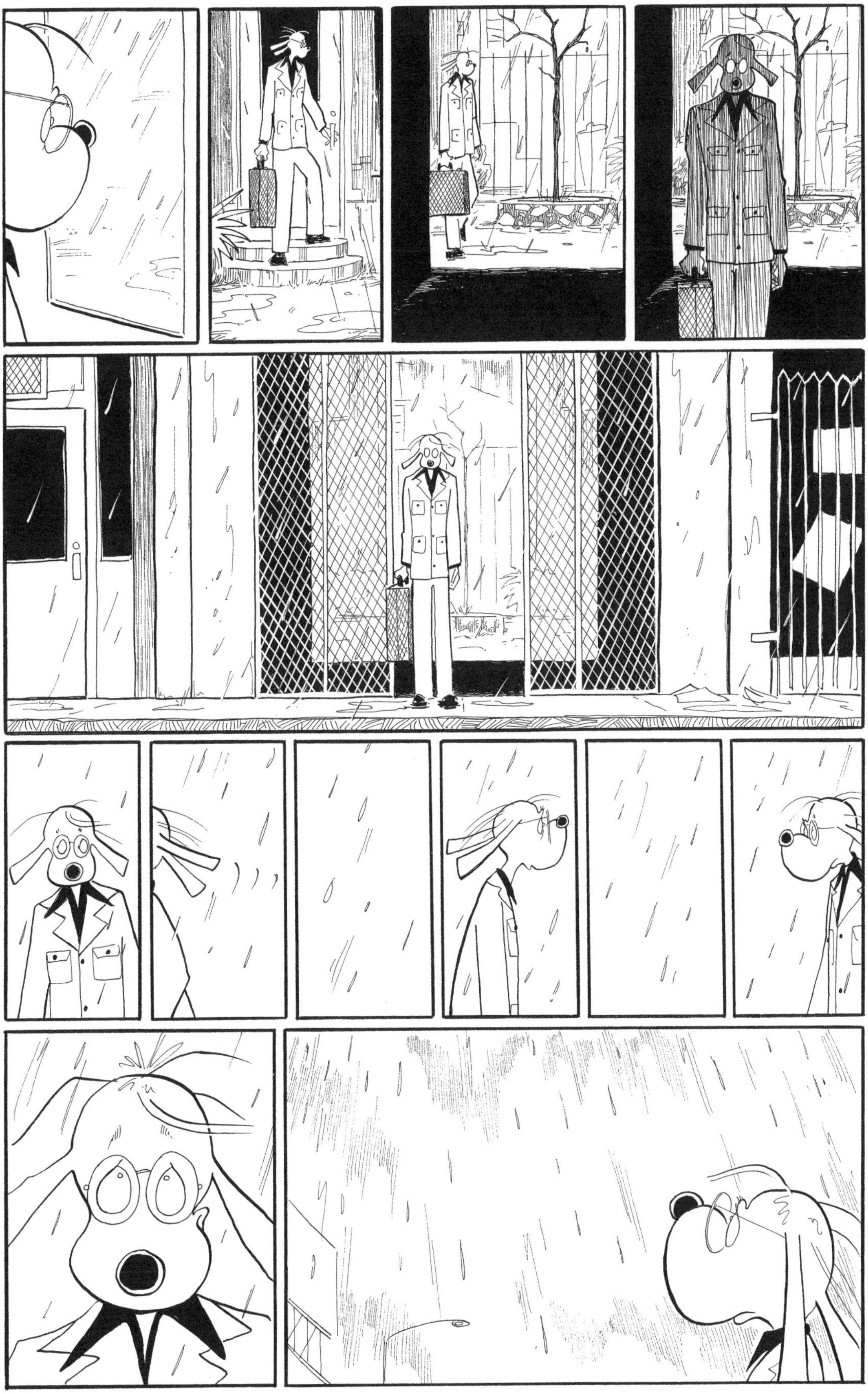

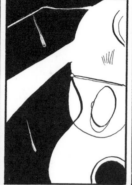

PAUL!

SHH! I'm listening to the radio.

Snow! Now I have to put chains on.

That's the problem living in a high altitude town like Acton.

But the wife wanted to live there.

PAUL!... WHAT HAPPENED IN THE MEETING?

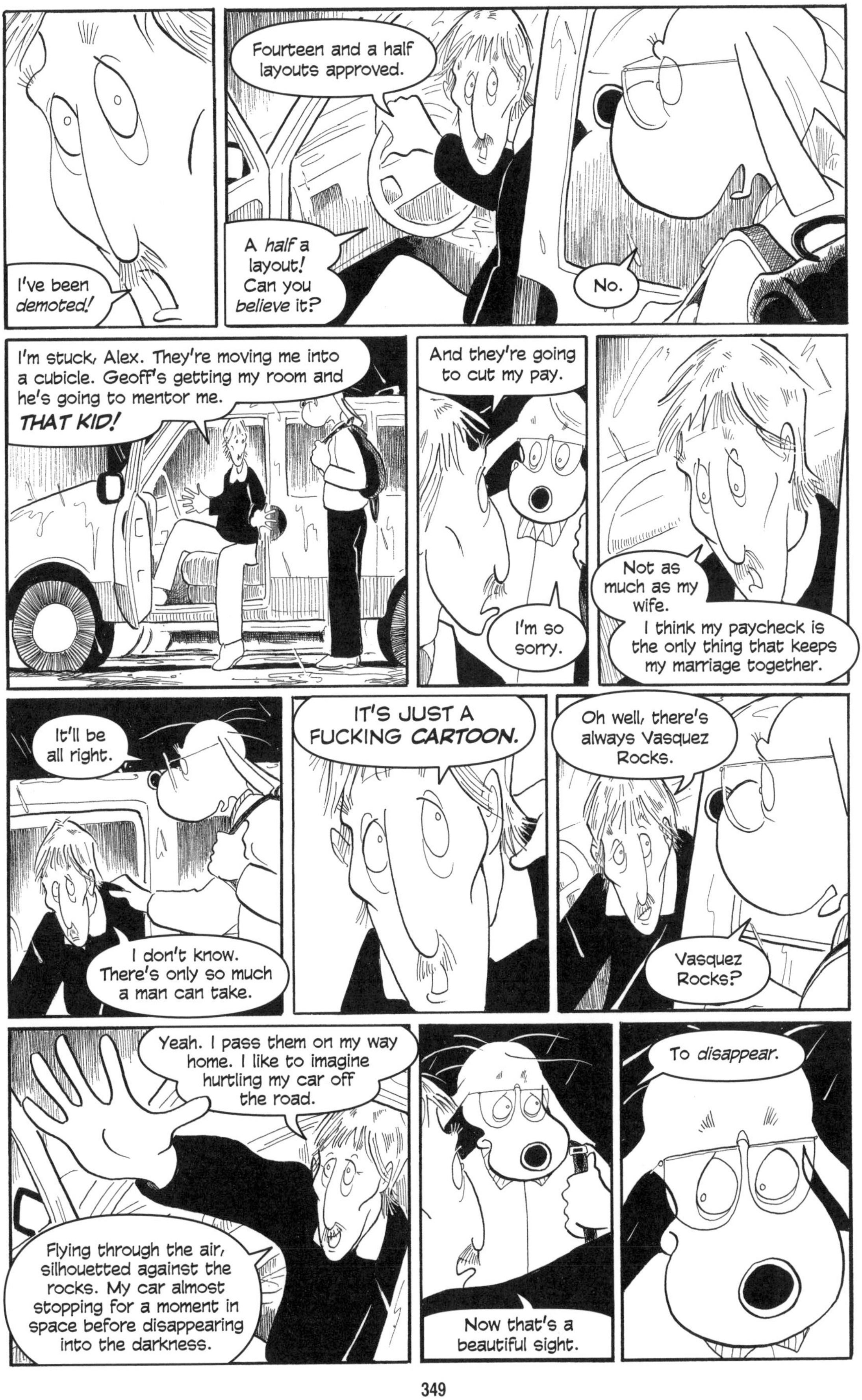

Fourteen and a half layouts approved.
I've been demoted!
A *half* a layout! Can you *believe* it?
No.
I'm stuck, Alex. They're moving me into a cubicle. Geoff's getting my room and he's going to mentor me. ***THAT KID!***
And they're going to cut my pay.
I'm so sorry.
Not as much as my wife.
I think my paycheck is the only thing that keeps my marriage together.
It'll be all right.
I don't know. There's only so much a man can take.
IT'S JUST A FUCKING ***CARTOON.***
Oh well, there's always Vasquez Rocks.
Vasquez Rocks?
Yeah. I pass them on my way home. I like to imagine hurtling my car off the road.
Flying through the air, silhouetted against the rocks. My car almost stopping for a moment in space before disappearing into the darkness.
Now that's a beautiful sight.
To *disappear.*

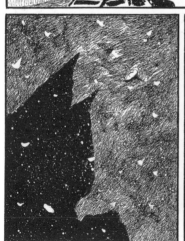

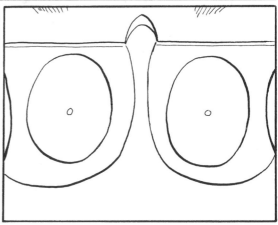

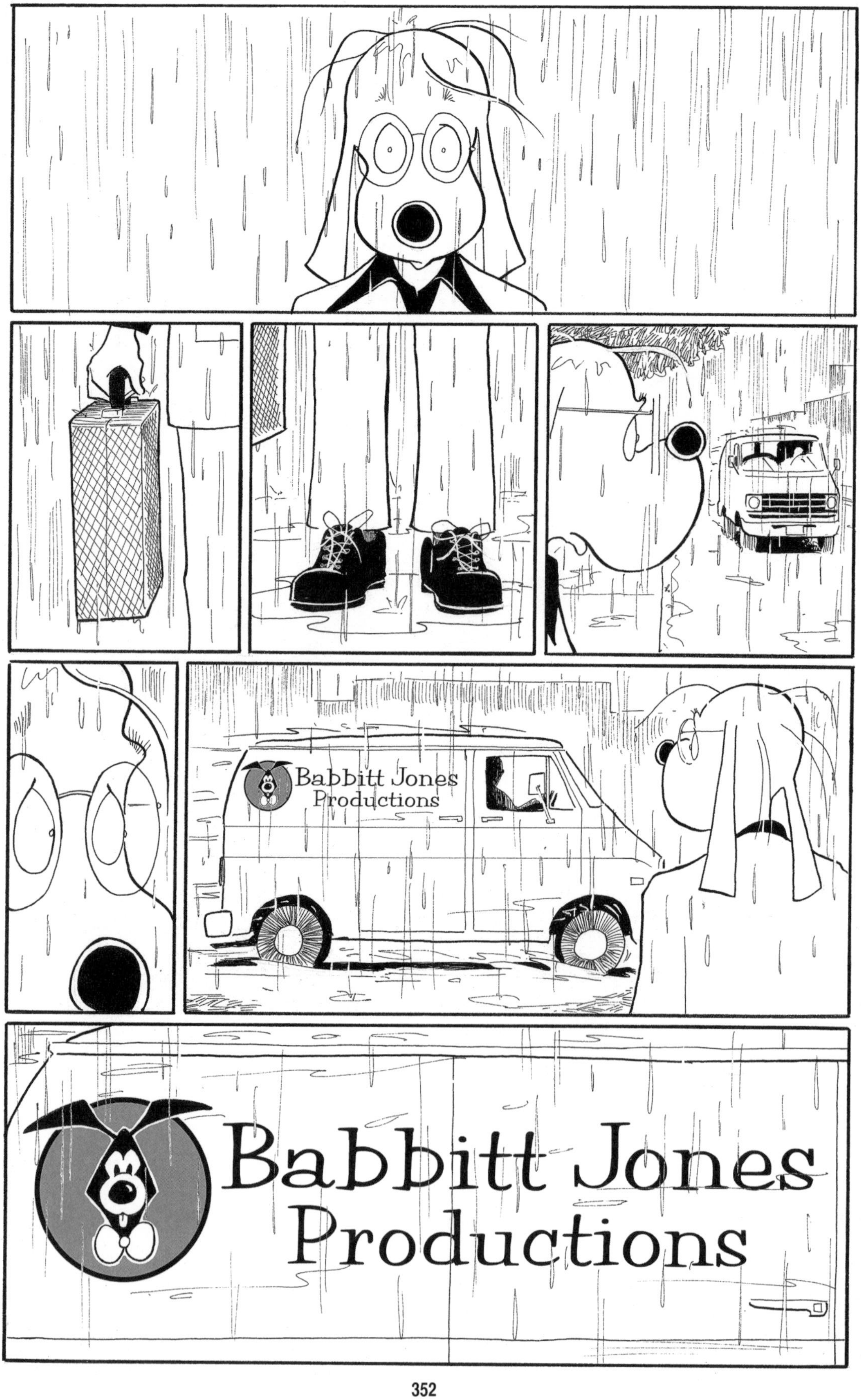
Babbitt Jones
Productions
Babbitt Jones
Productions

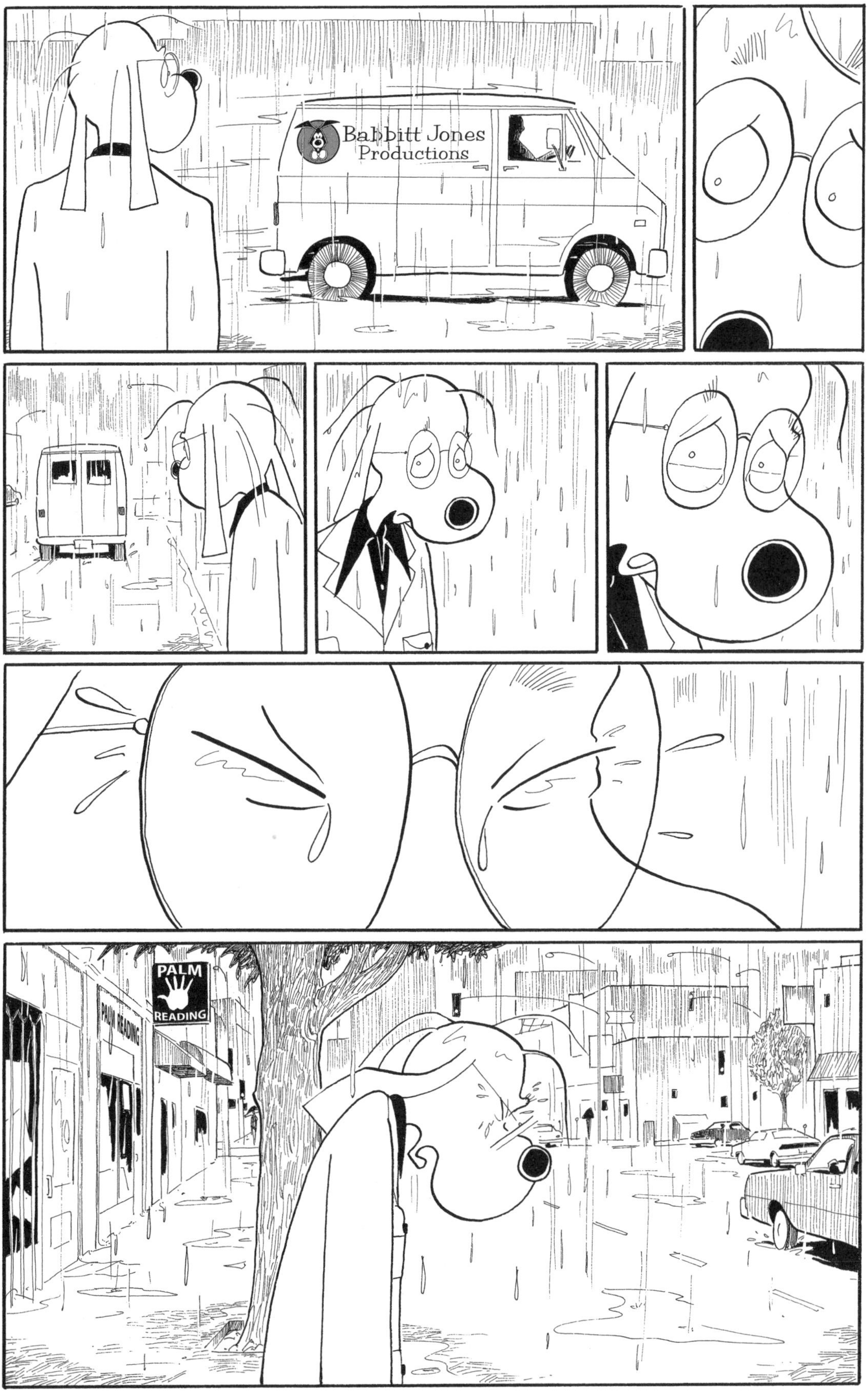
Babbitt Jones
Productions
PALM
READING
PALM READING

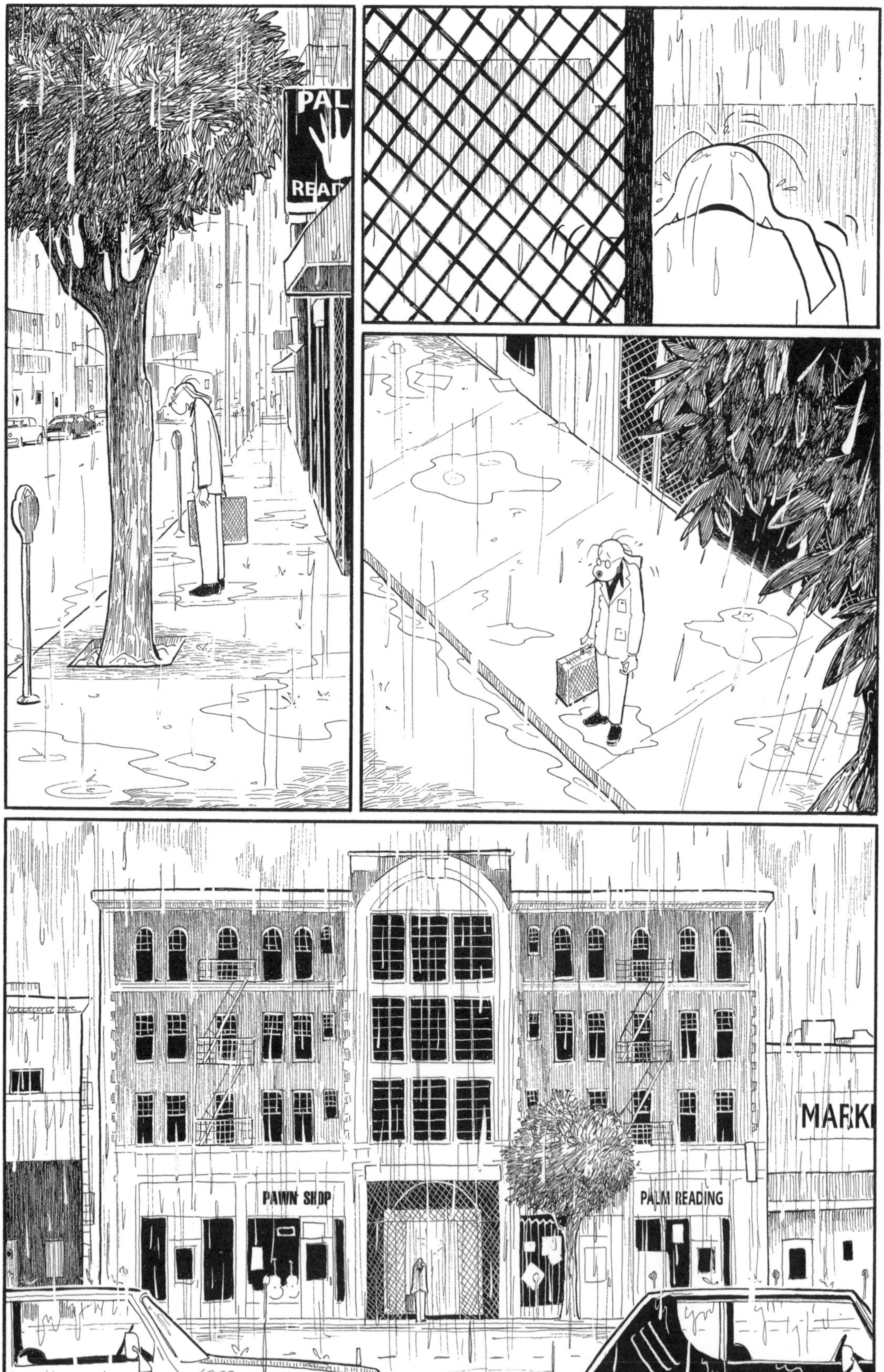
PAL
READ
PAWN SHOP
PALM READING
MARK

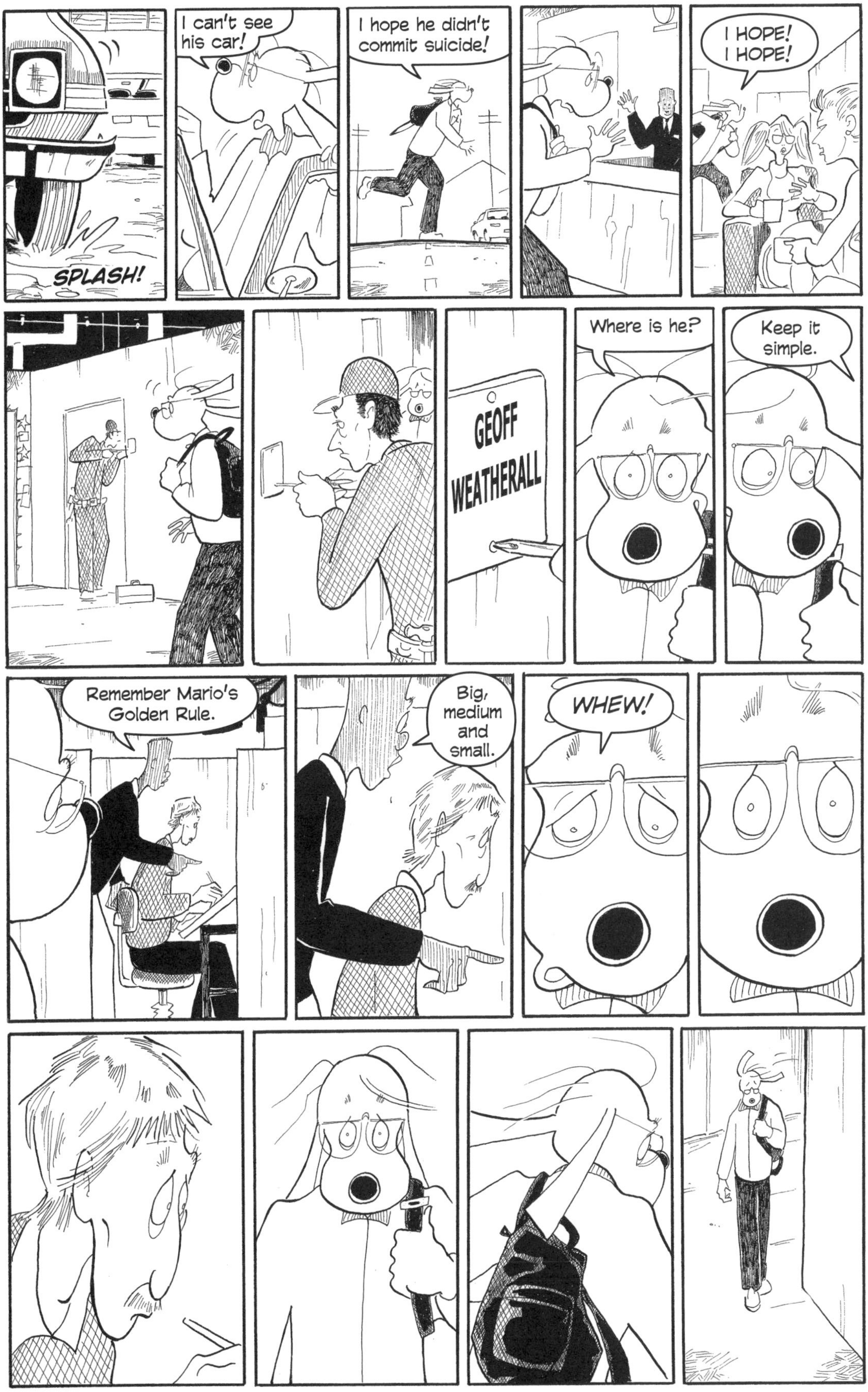
SPLASH!
I can't see his car!
I hope he didn't commit suicide!
I HOPE! I HOPE!
GEOFF WEATHERALL
Where is he?
Keep it simple.
Remember Mario's Golden Rule.
Big, medium and small.
WHEW!

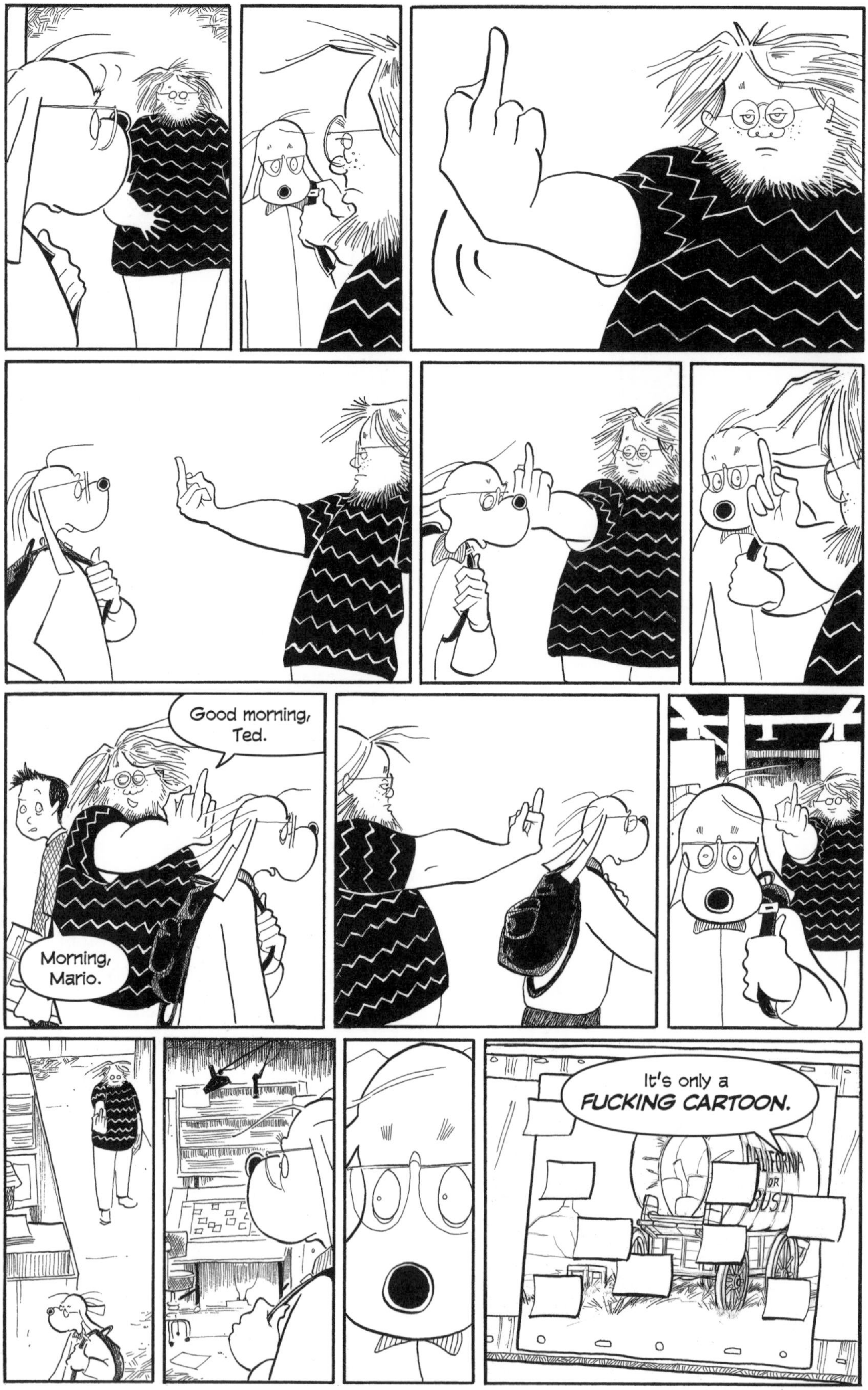
Good morning, Ted.
Morning, Mario.
It's only a FUCKING CARTOON.
CALIFORNIA OR BUST

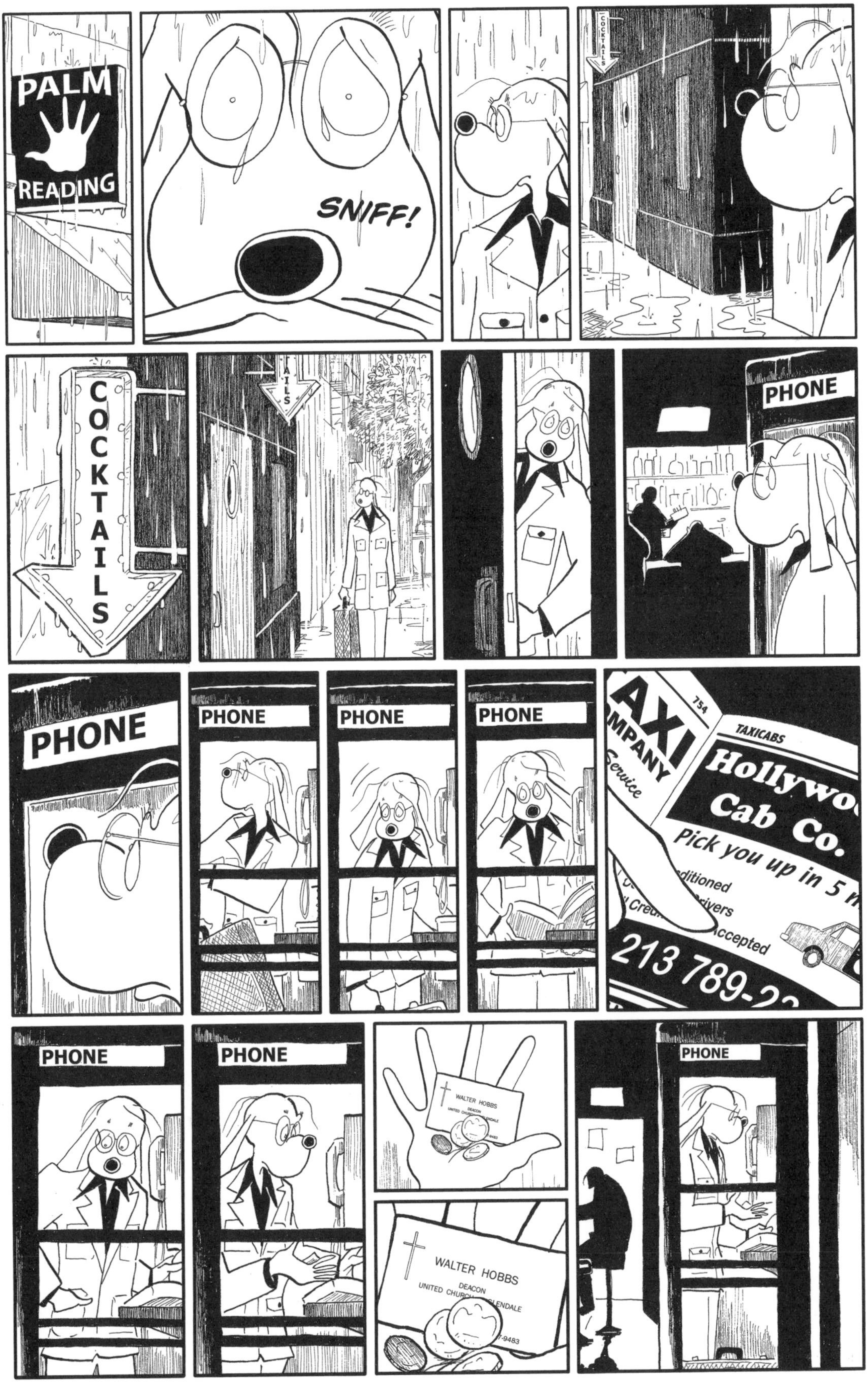
PALM
READING
SNIFF!
COCKTAILS
PHONE
754
TAXICABS
Service
Cab Co.
WALTER HOBBS
DEACON

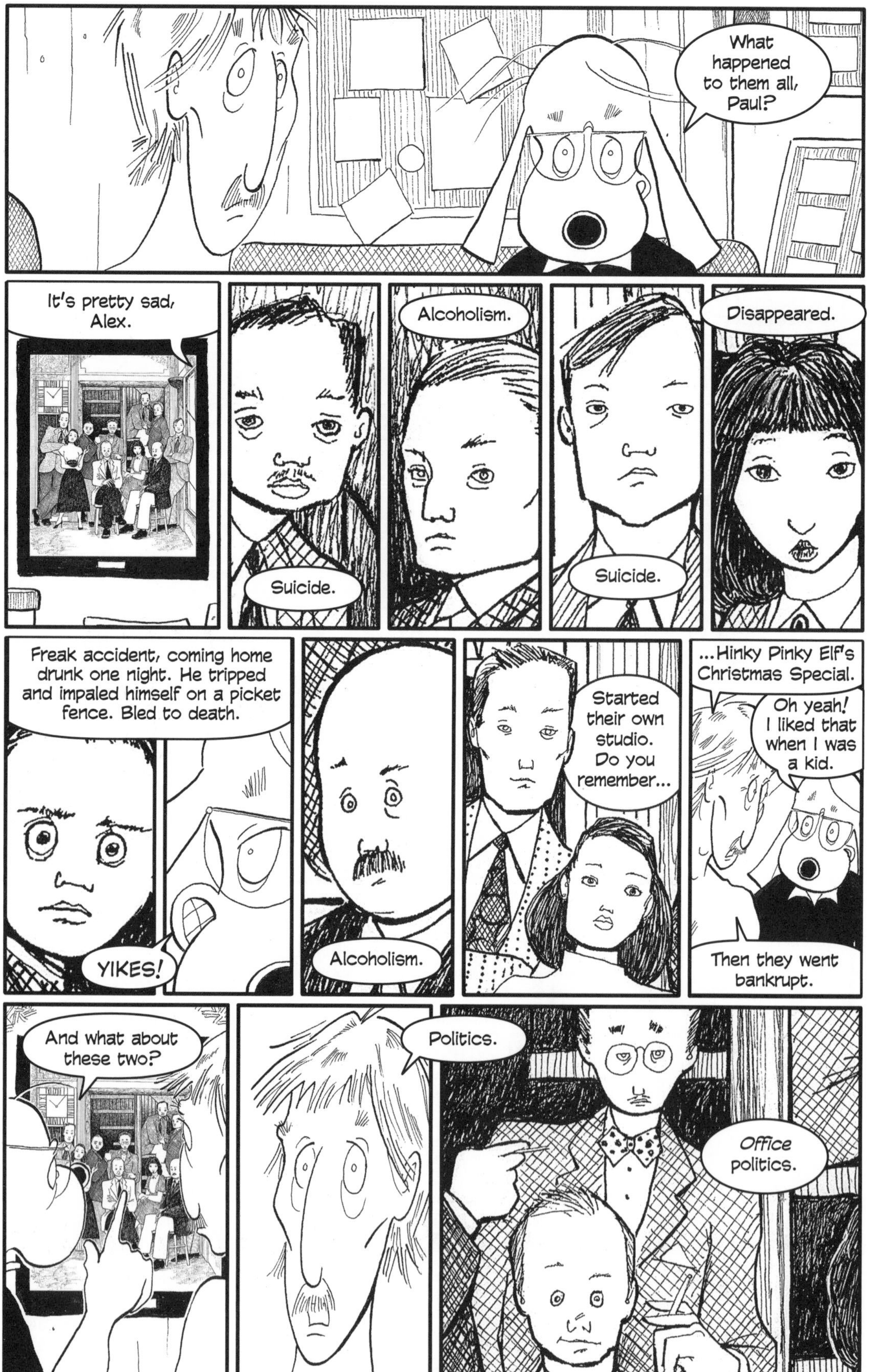

What happened to them all, Paul?
It's pretty sad, Alex.
Suicide.
Alcoholism.
Suicide.
Disappeared.
Freak accident, coming home drunk one night. He tripped and impaled himself on a picket fence. Bled to death.
YIKES!
Alcoholism.
Started their own studio. Do you remember...
...Hinky Pinky Elf's Christmas Special.
Oh yeah! I liked that when I was a kid.
Then they went bankrupt.
And what about these two?
Politics.
Office politics.

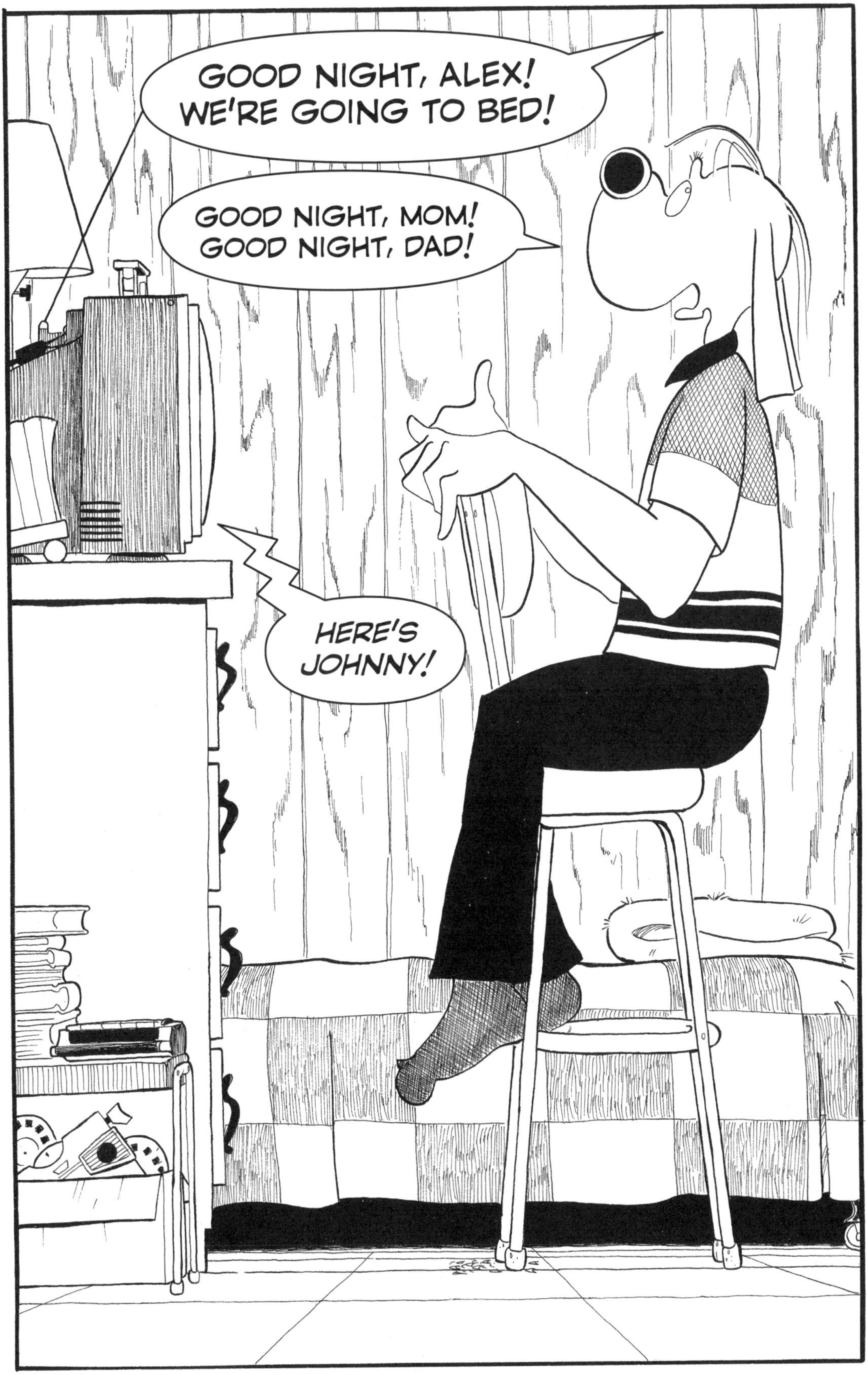
GOOD NIGHT, ALEX! WE'RE GOING TO BED!
GOOD NIGHT, MOM! GOOD NIGHT, DAD!
HERE'S JOHNNY!

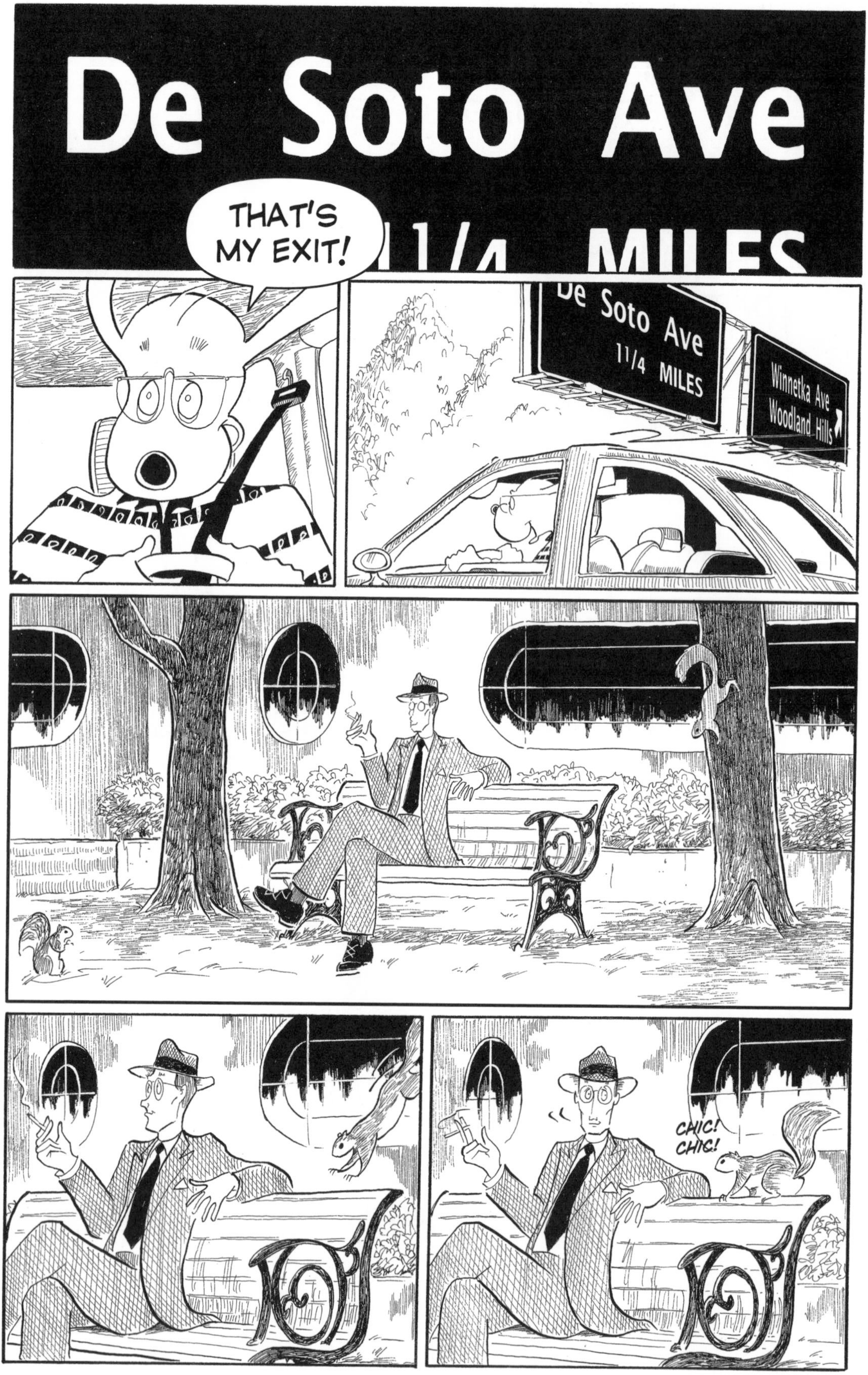
De Soto Ave
THAT'S MY EXIT!
De Soto Ave
1 1/4 MILES
Winnetka Ave
Woodland Hills
CHIC! CHIC!

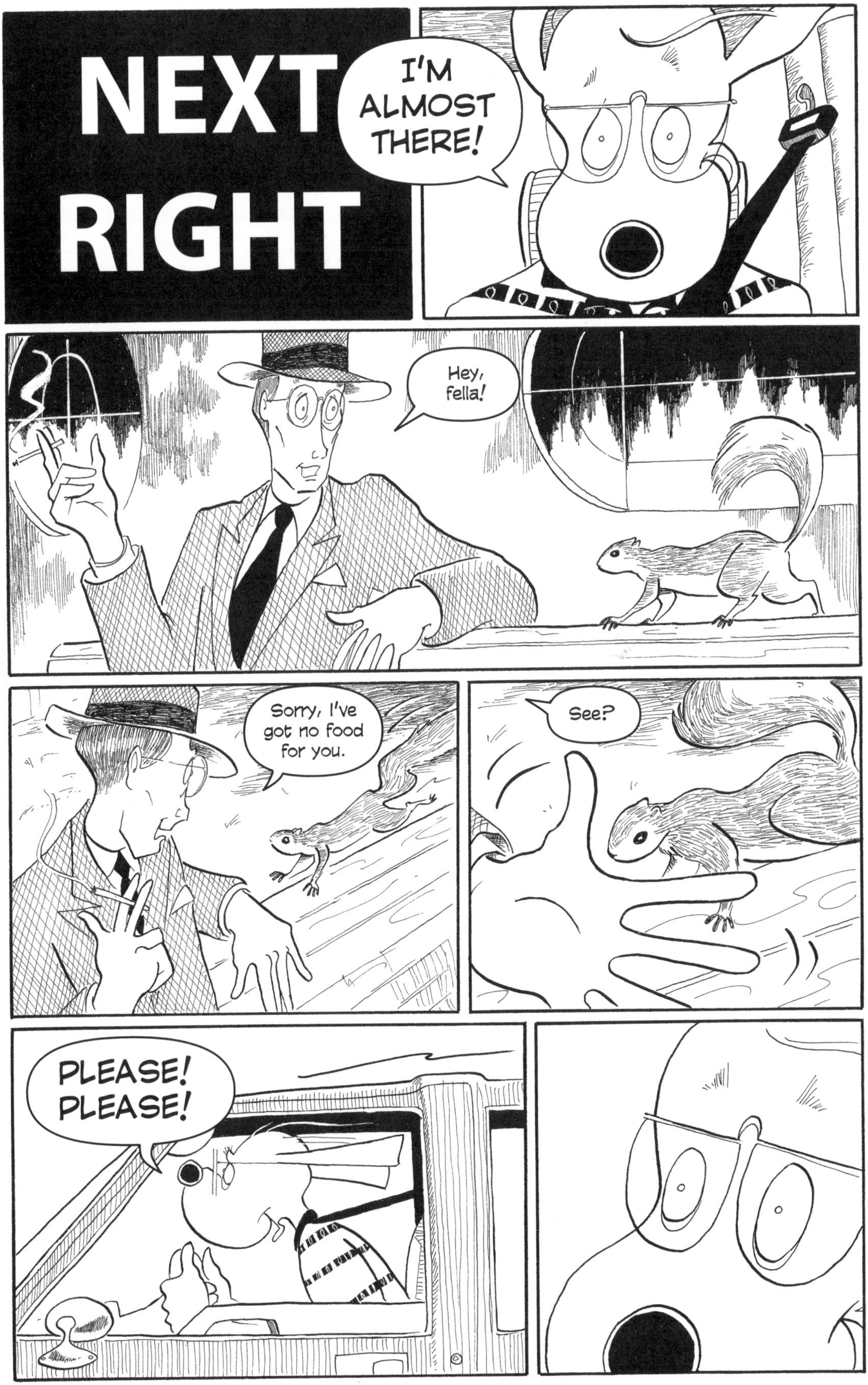
NEXT RIGHT
I'M ALMOST THERE!
Hey, fella!
Sorry, I've got no food for you.
See?
PLEASE! PLEASE!

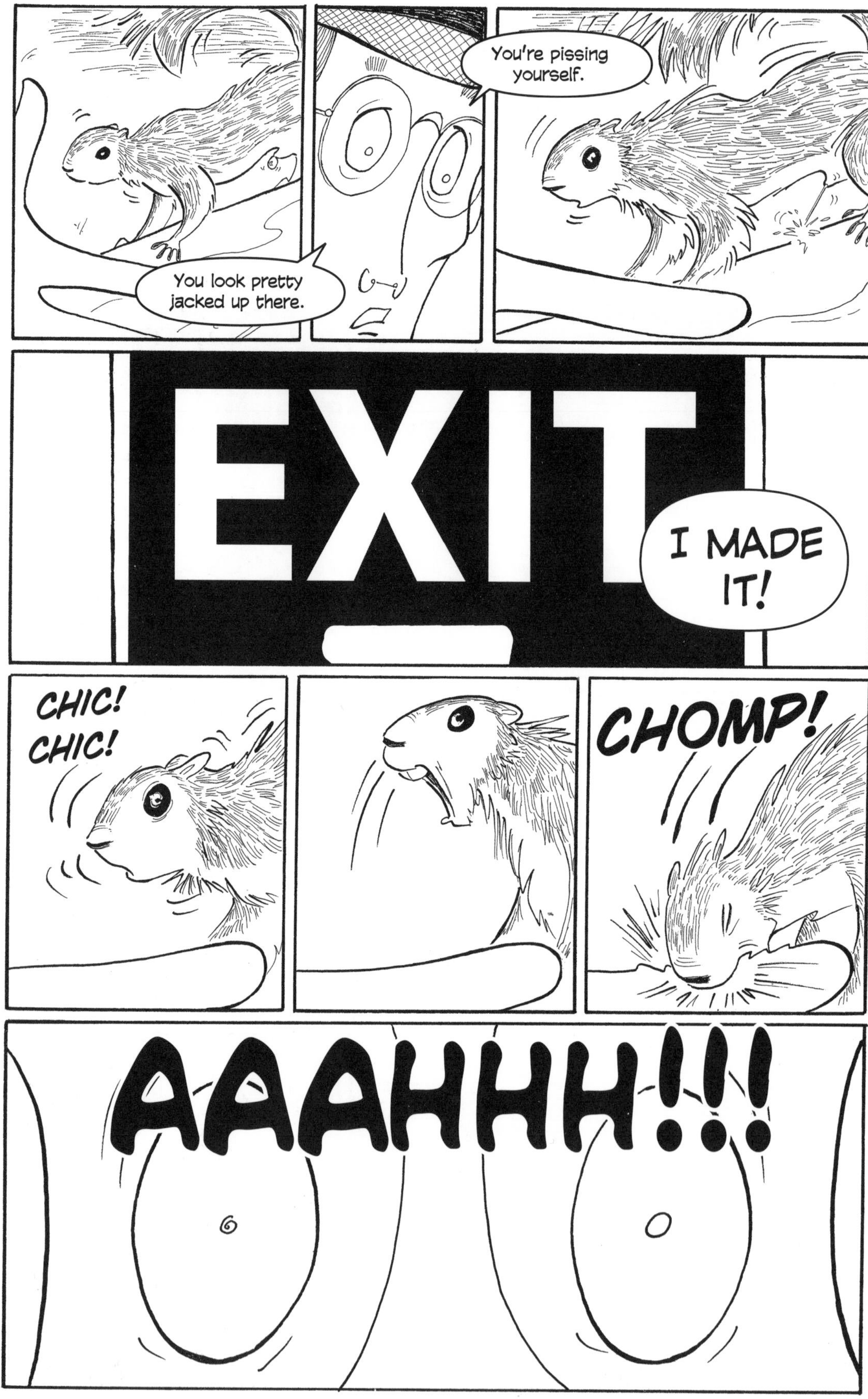
You look pretty jacked up there.
You're pissing yourself.
EXIT
I MADE IT!
CHIC! CHIC!
CHOMP!
AAAHHH!!!

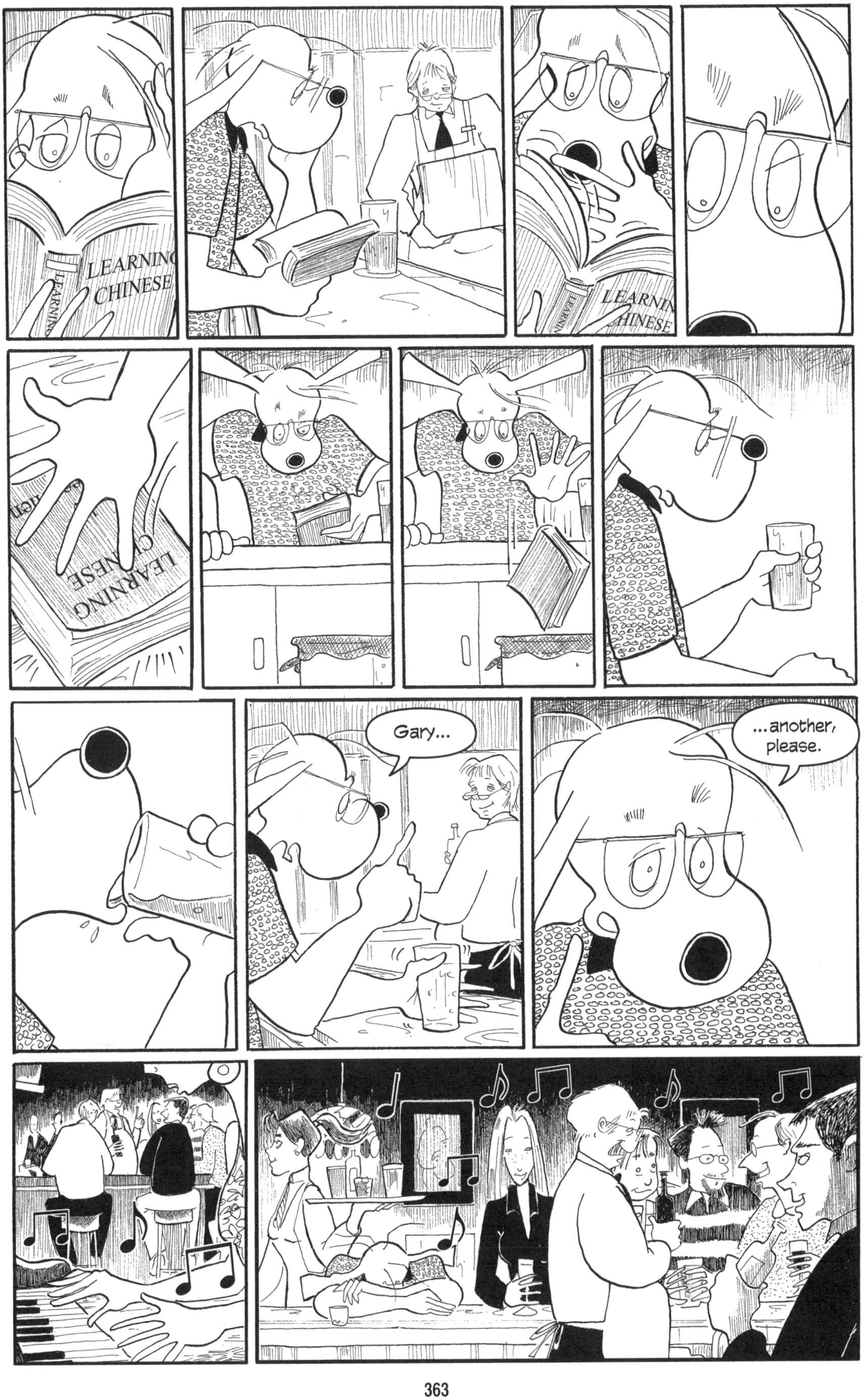
LEARNING CHINESE
Gary...
...another, please.

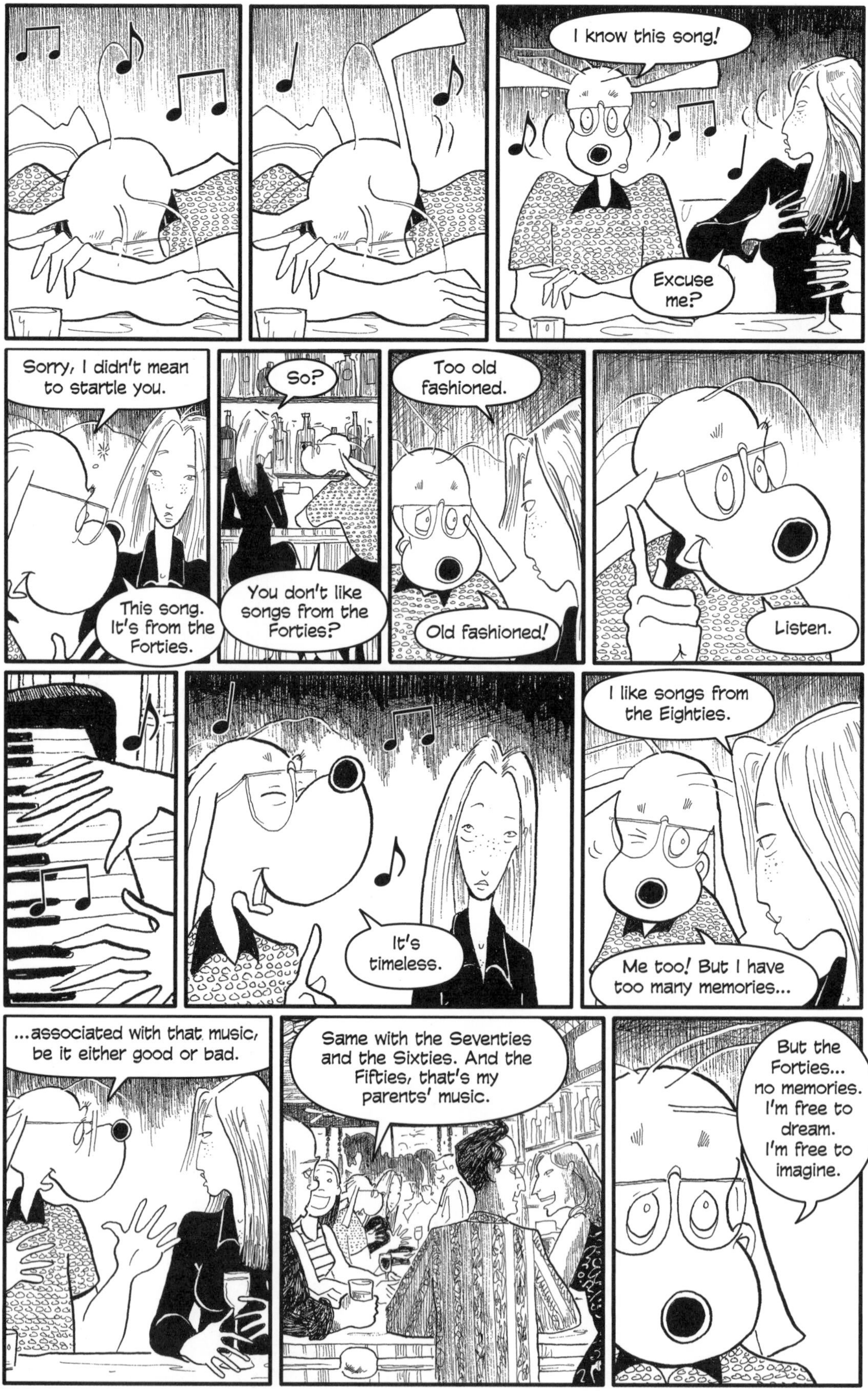
I know this song!
Excuse me?
Sorry, I didn't mean to startle you.
This song. It's from the Forties.
So?
You don't like songs from the Forties?
Too old fashioned.
Old fashioned!
Listen.
It's timeless.
I like songs from the Eighties.
Me too! But I have too many memories...
...associated with that music, be it either good or bad.
Same with the Seventies and the Sixties. And the Fifties, that's my parents' music.
But the Forties... no memories. I'm free to dream. I'm free to imagine.

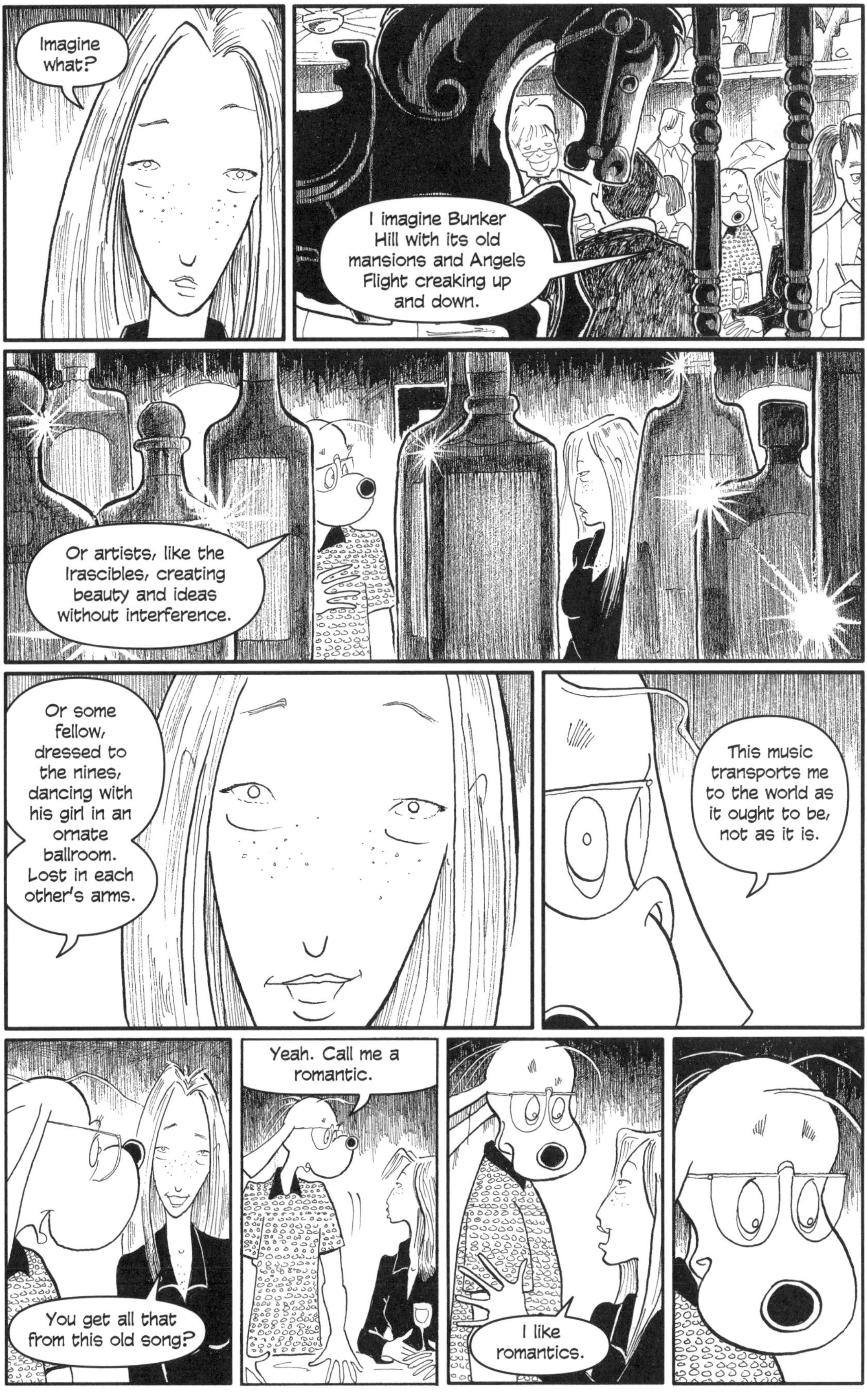
Imagine what?
I imagine Bunker Hill with its old mansions and Angels Flight creaking up and down.
Or artists, like the Irascibles, creating beauty and ideas without interference.
Or some fellow, dressed to the nines, dancing with his girl in an ornate ballroom. Lost in each other's arms.
This music transports me to the world as it ought to be, not as it is.
You get all that from this old song?
Yeah. Call me a romantic.
I like romantics.

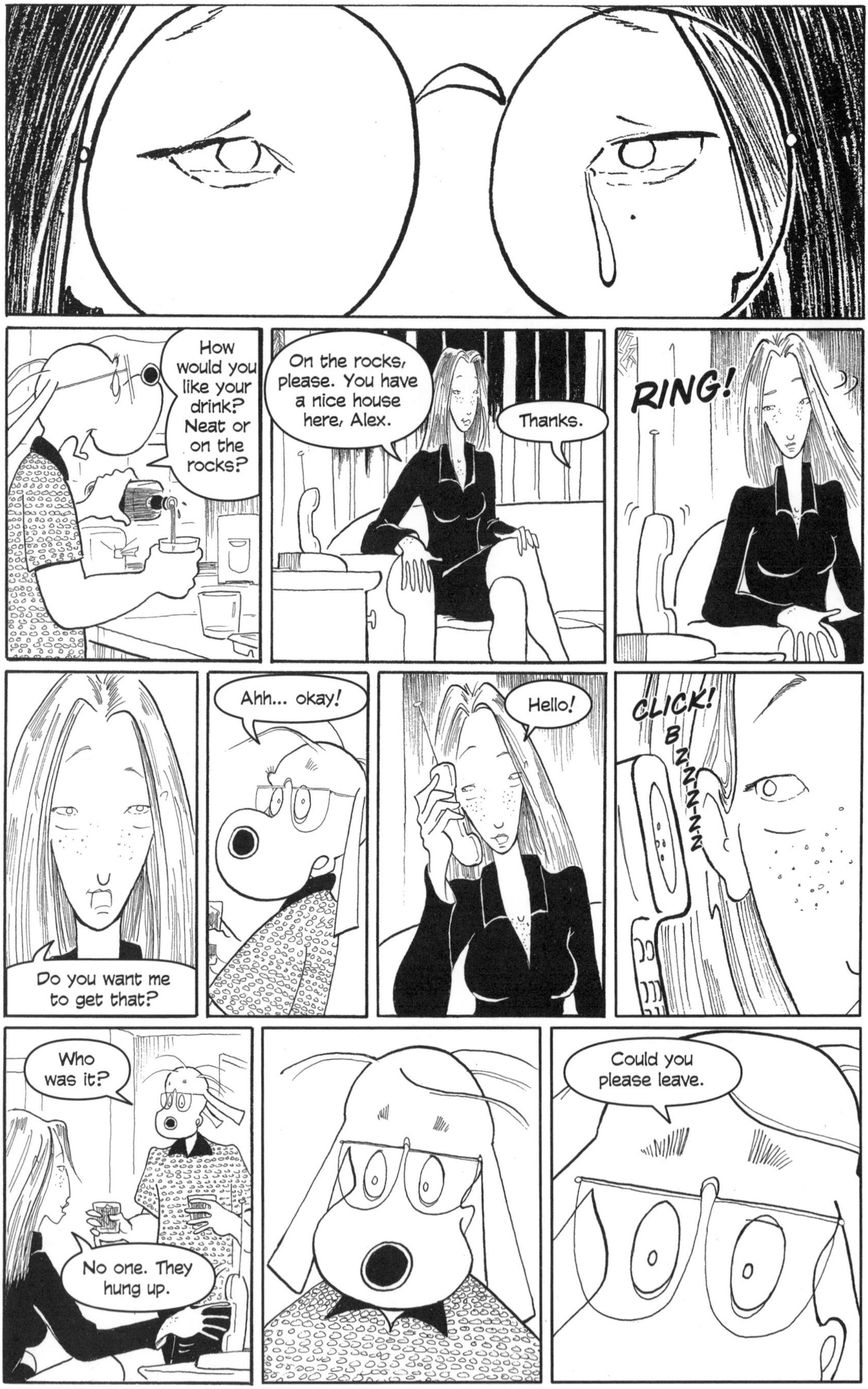
How would you like your drink? Neat or on the rocks?
On the rocks, please. You have a nice house here, Alex.
Thanks.
RING!
Do you want me to get that?
Ahh... okay!
Hello!
CLICK!
BZZZZZZ
Who was it?
No one. They hung up.
Could you please leave.

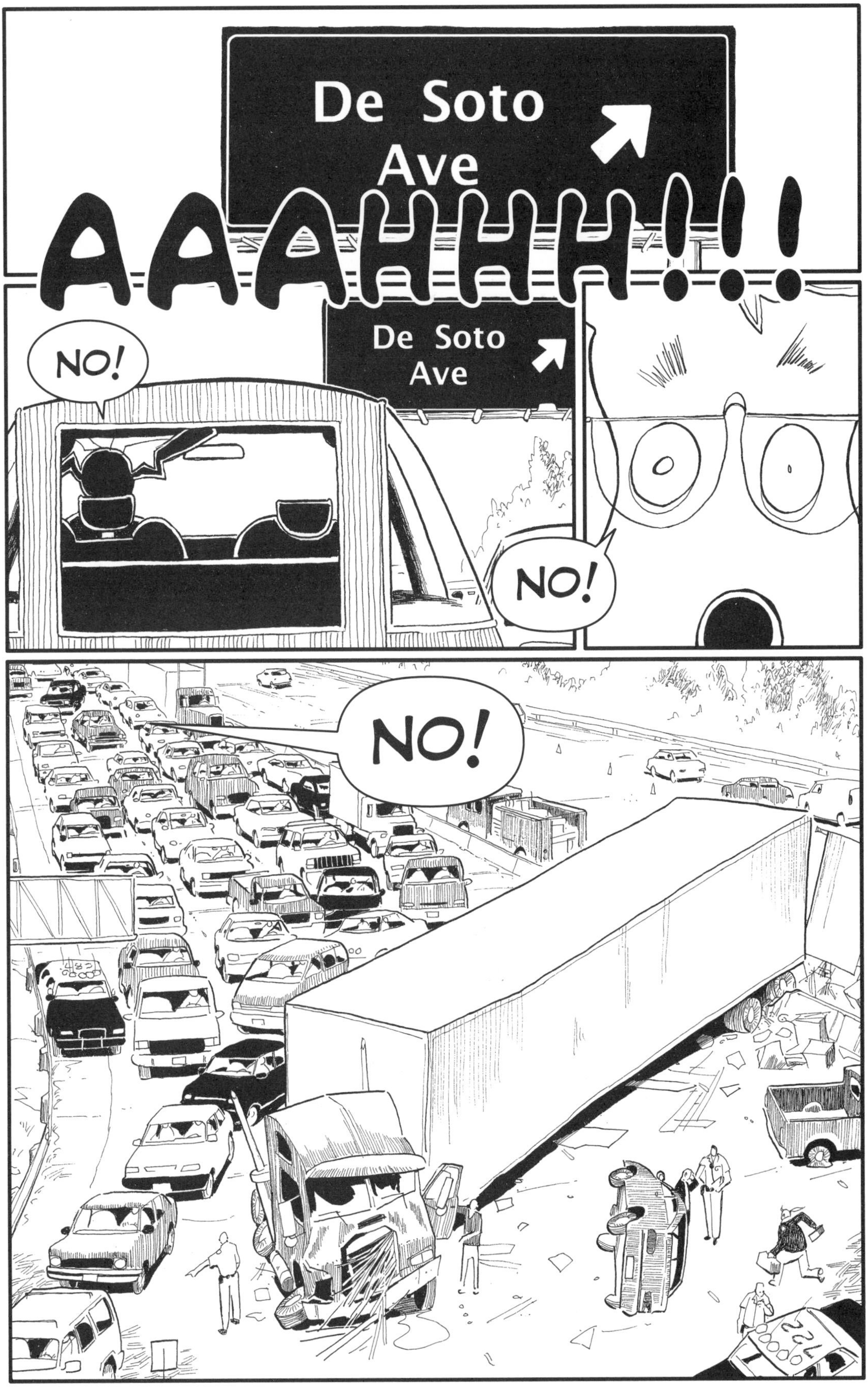
De Soto Ave
AAAHHH!!!
NO!
De Soto Ave
NO!
NO!

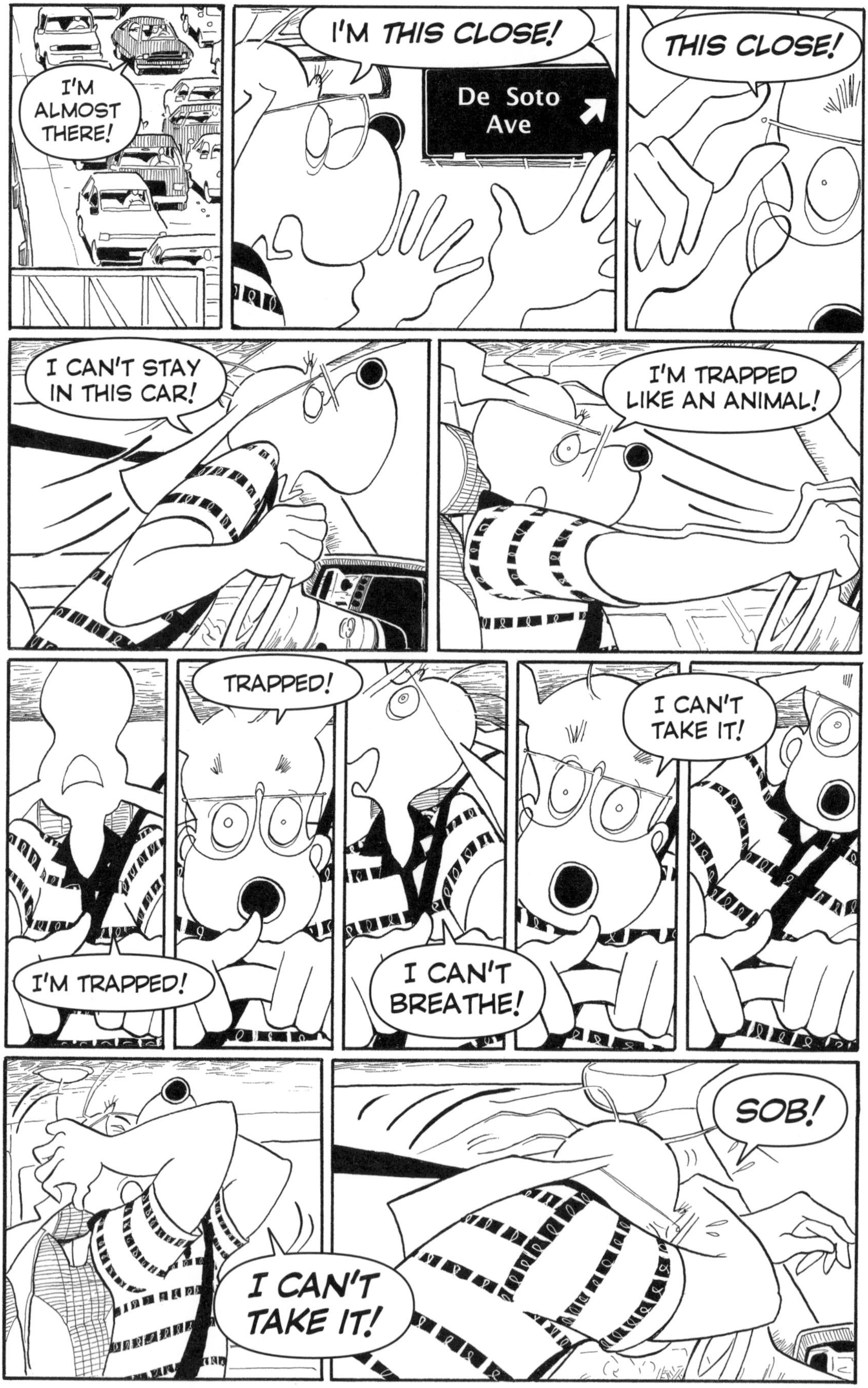
I'M ALMOST THERE!
I'M *THIS CLOSE!*
De Soto Ave
THIS CLOSE!
I CAN'T STAY IN THIS CAR!
I'M TRAPPED LIKE AN ANIMAL!
I'M TRAPPED!
TRAPPED!
I CAN'T BREATHE!
I CAN'T TAKE IT!
I CAN'T TAKE IT!
SOB!

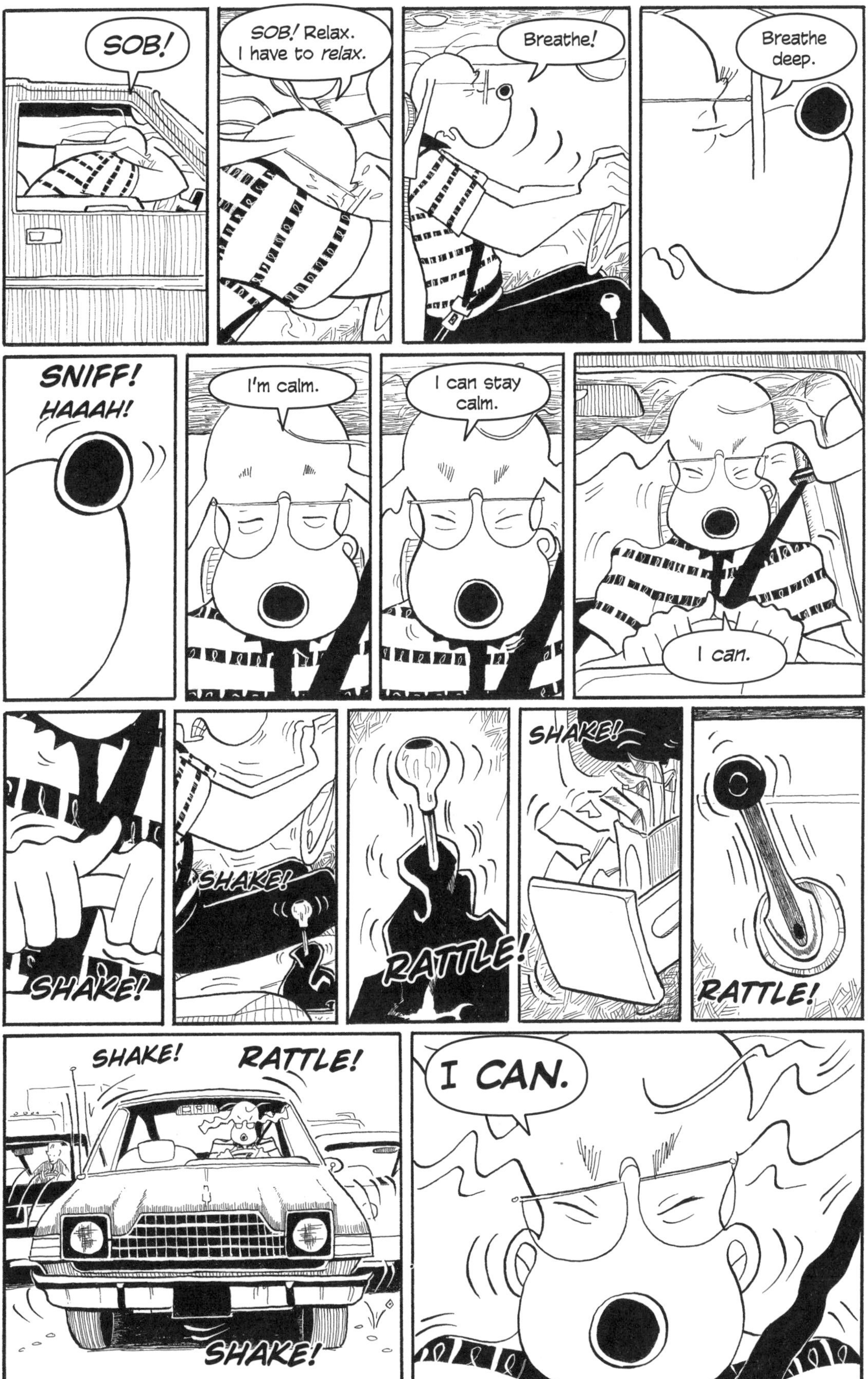
SOB!
SOB! Relax. I have to relax.
Breathe!
Breathe deep.
SNIFF! HAAAH!
I'm calm.
I can stay calm.
I can.
SHAKE!
SHAKE!
RATTLE!
SHAKE!
RATTLE!
SHAKE! RATTLE!
SHAKE!
I CAN.

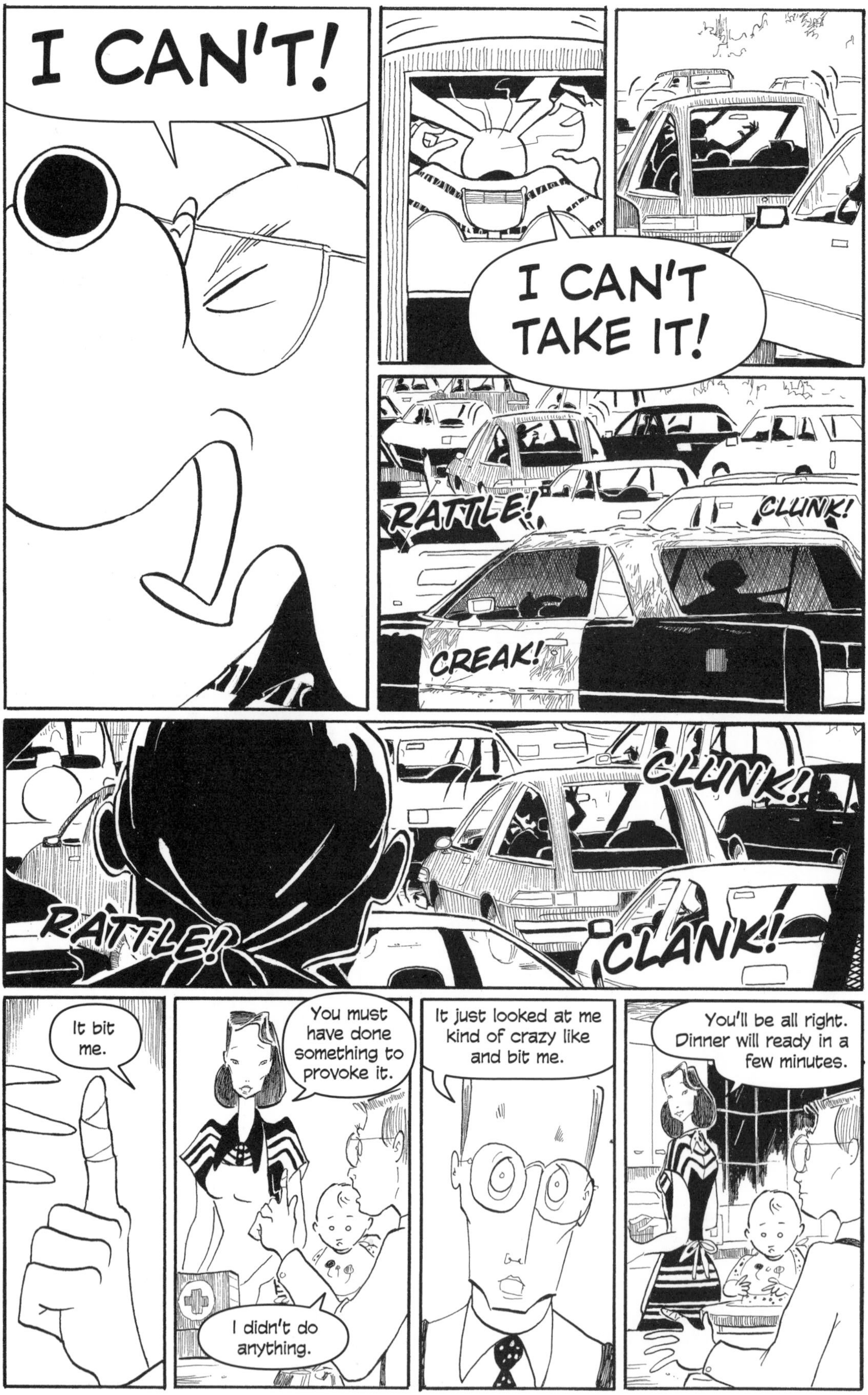
I CAN'T!
I CAN'T TAKE IT!
RATTLE!
CLUNK!
CREAK!
CLUNK!
RATTLE!
CLANK!
It bit me.
You must have done something to provoke it.
I didn't do anything.
It just looked at me kind of crazy like and bit me.
You'll be all right. Dinner will ready in a few minutes.

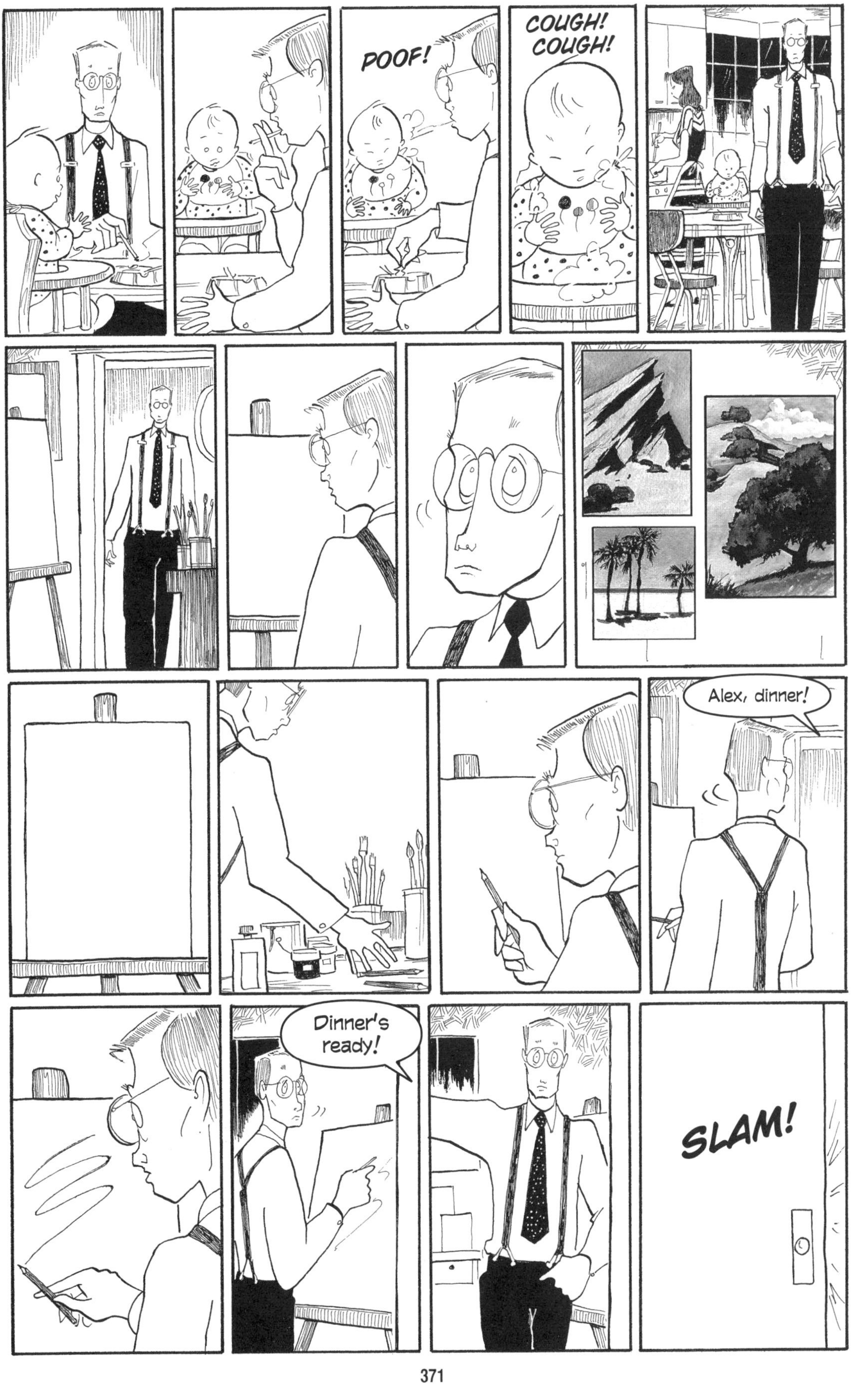
POOF!
COUGH! COUGH!
Alex, dinner!
Dinner's ready!
SLAM!

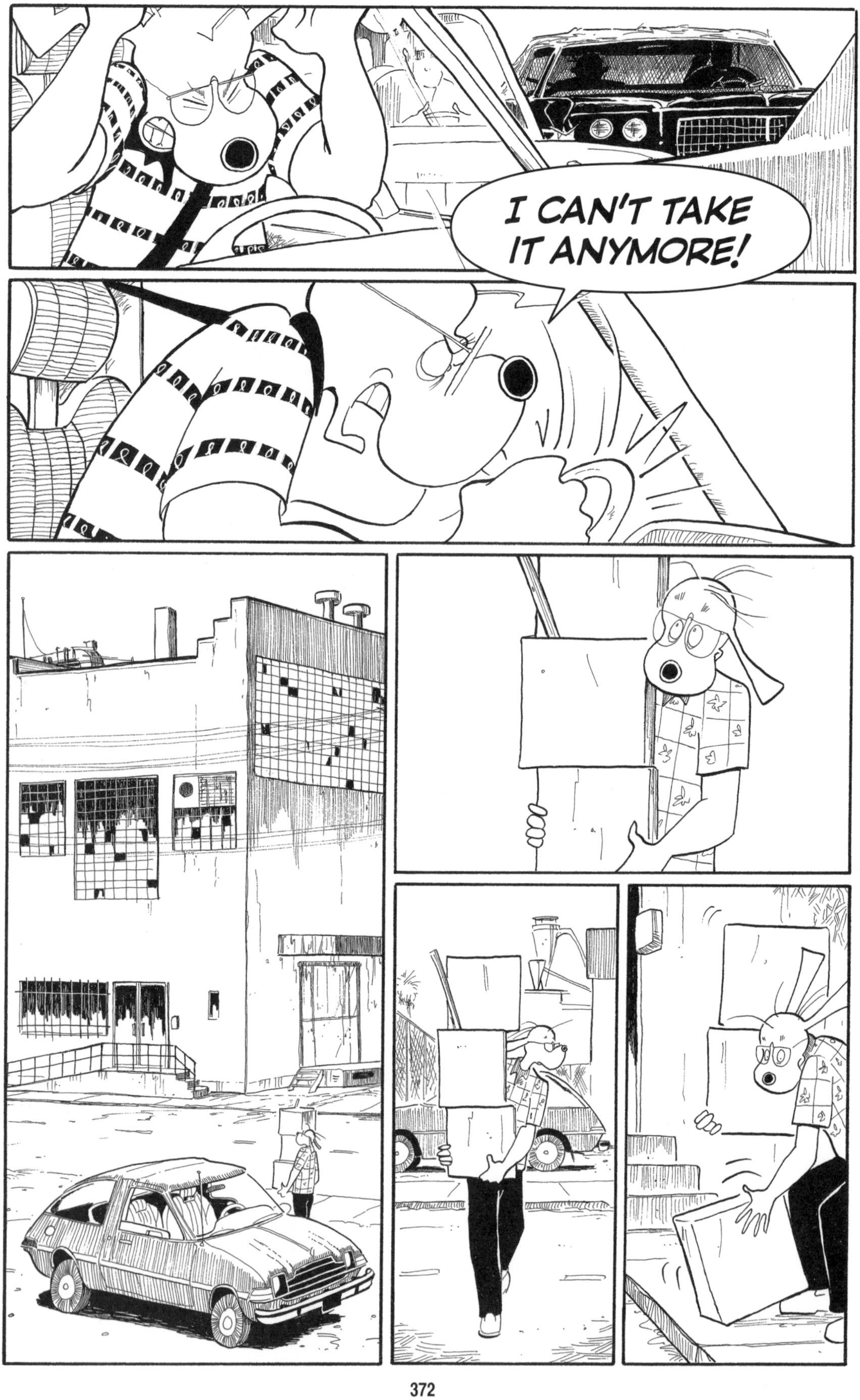
I CAN'T TAKE IT ANYMORE!

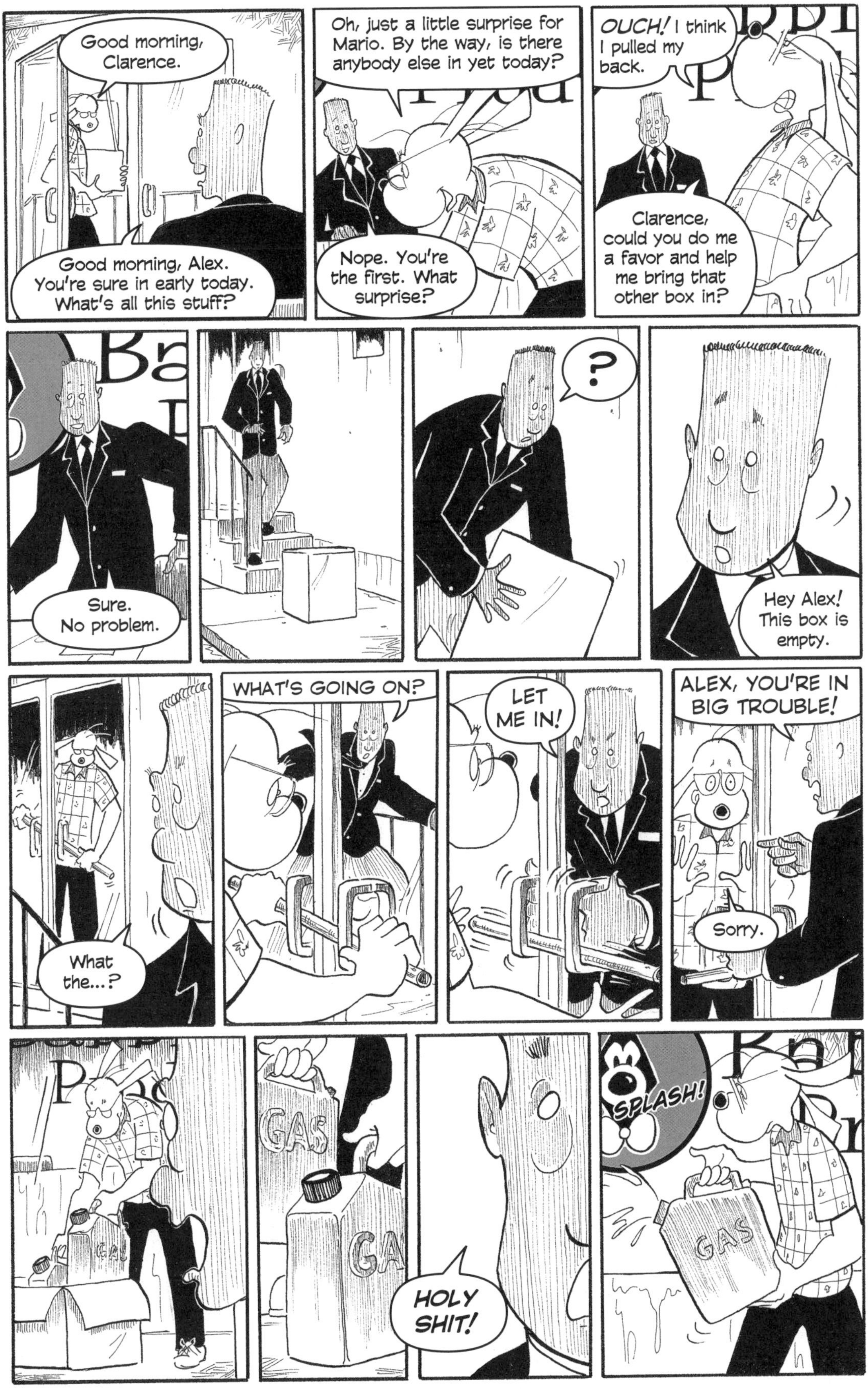
Good morning, Clarence.
Good morning, Alex. You're sure in early today. What's all this stuff?
Oh, just a little surprise for Mario. By the way, is there anybody else in yet today?
Nope. You're the first. What surprise?
OUCH! I think I pulled my back.
Clarence, could you do me a favor and help me bring that other box in?
Sure. No problem.
?
Hey Alex! This box is empty.
What the...?
WHAT'S GOING ON?
LET ME IN!
ALEX, YOU'RE IN BIG TROUBLE!
Sorry.
GAS
GAS
HOLY SHIT!
SPLASH!
GAS

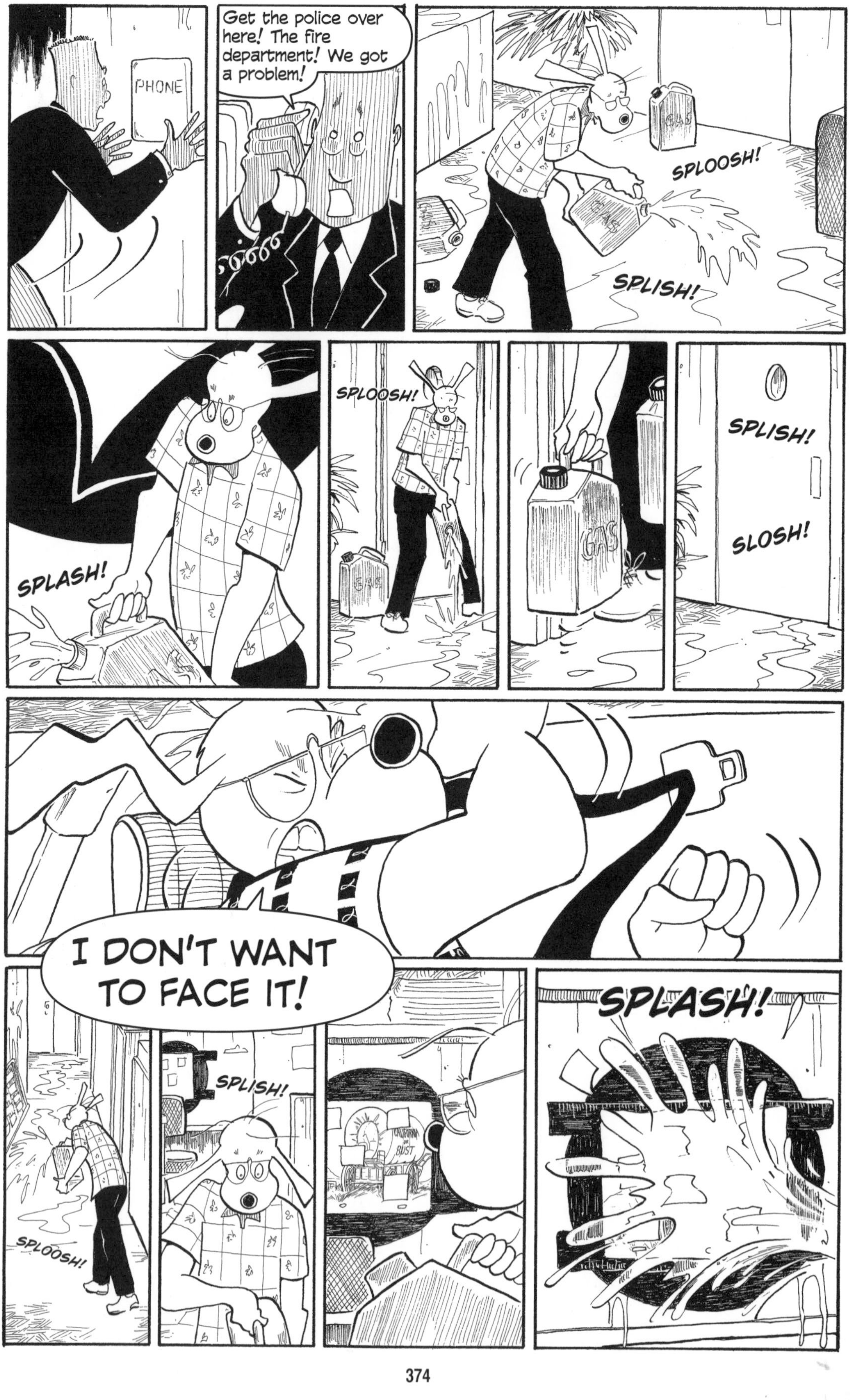
PHONE
Get the police over here! The fire department! We got a problem!
GAS
SPLOOSH!
GAS
SPLISH!
SPLASH!
SPLOOSH!
GAS
GAS
SPLISH!
SLOSH!
I DON'T WANT TO FACE IT!
SPLOOSH!
SPLISH!
CALIFORNIA OR BUST
SPLASH!

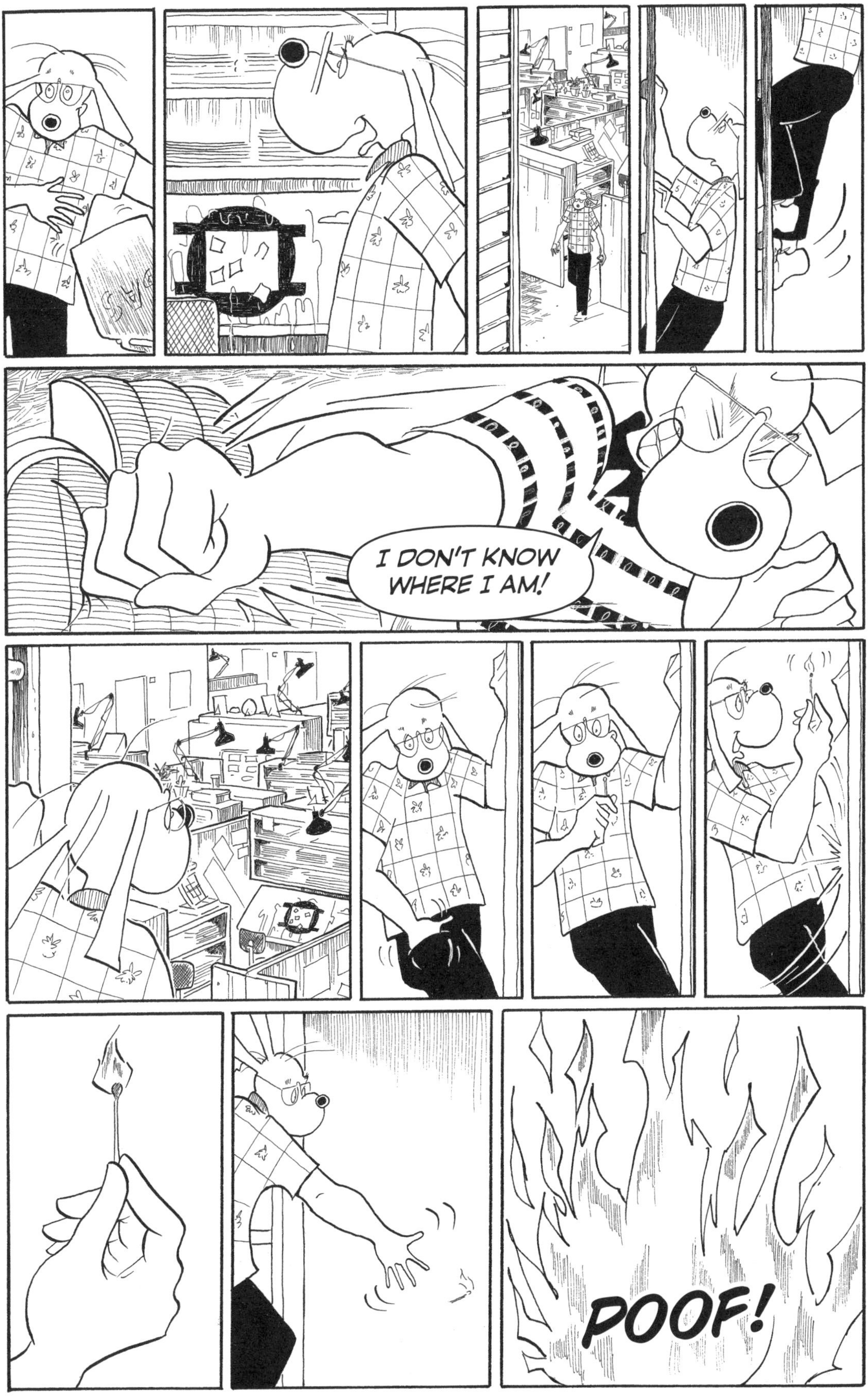
I DON'T KNOW
WHERE I AM!
POOF!

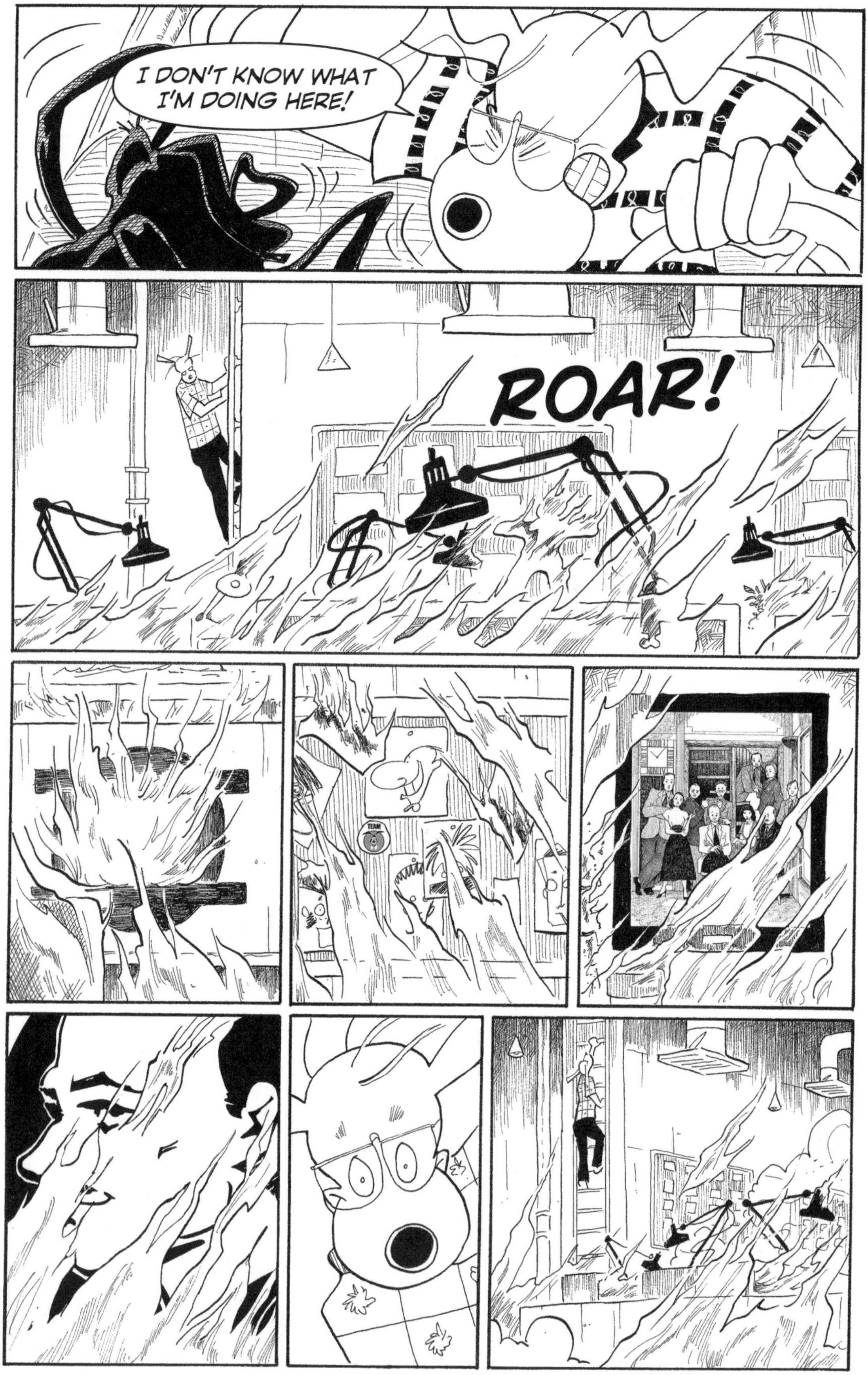
I DON'T KNOW WHAT I'M DOING HERE!
ROAR!
TEAM

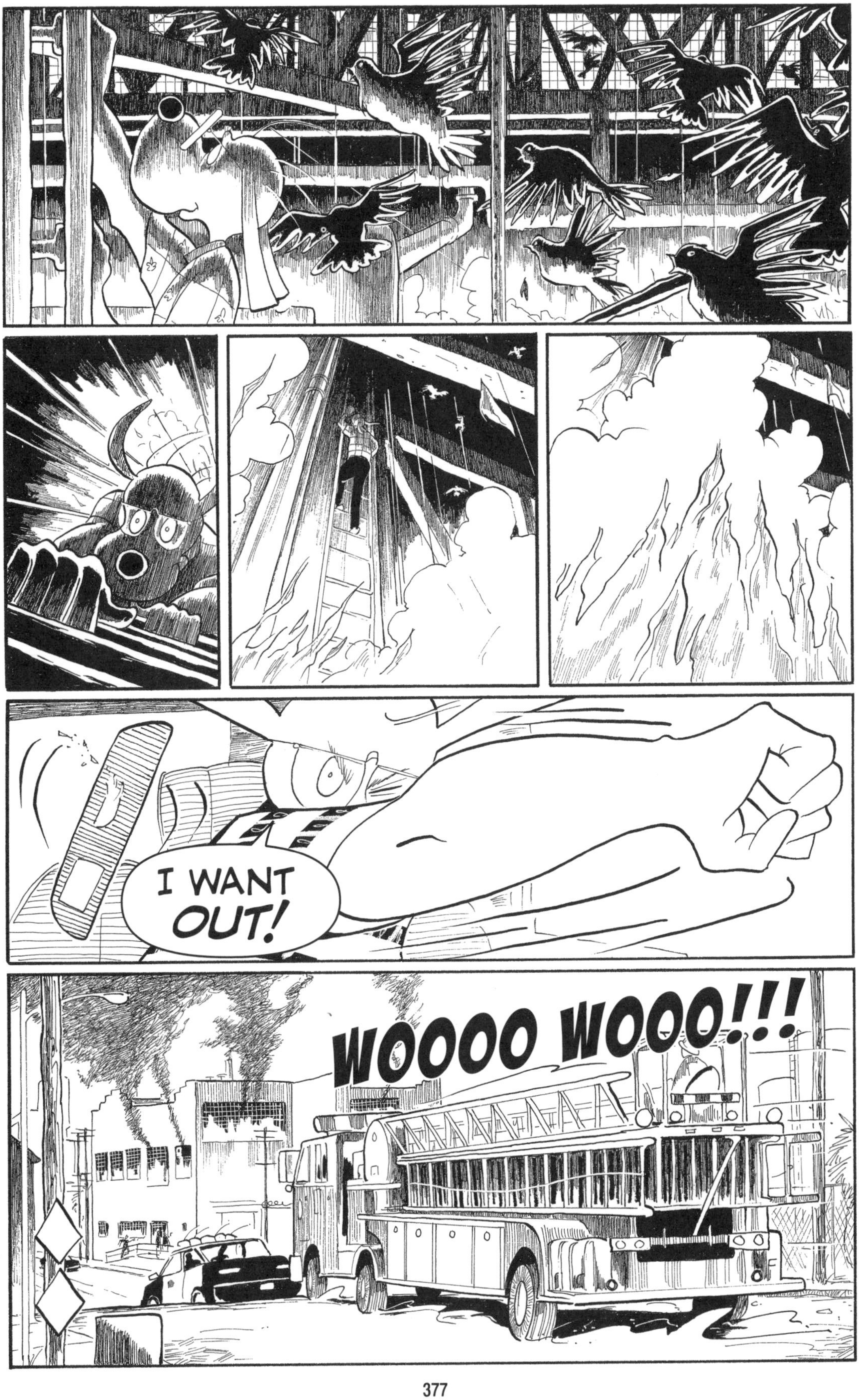
I WANT OUT!
WOOOO WOOO!!!

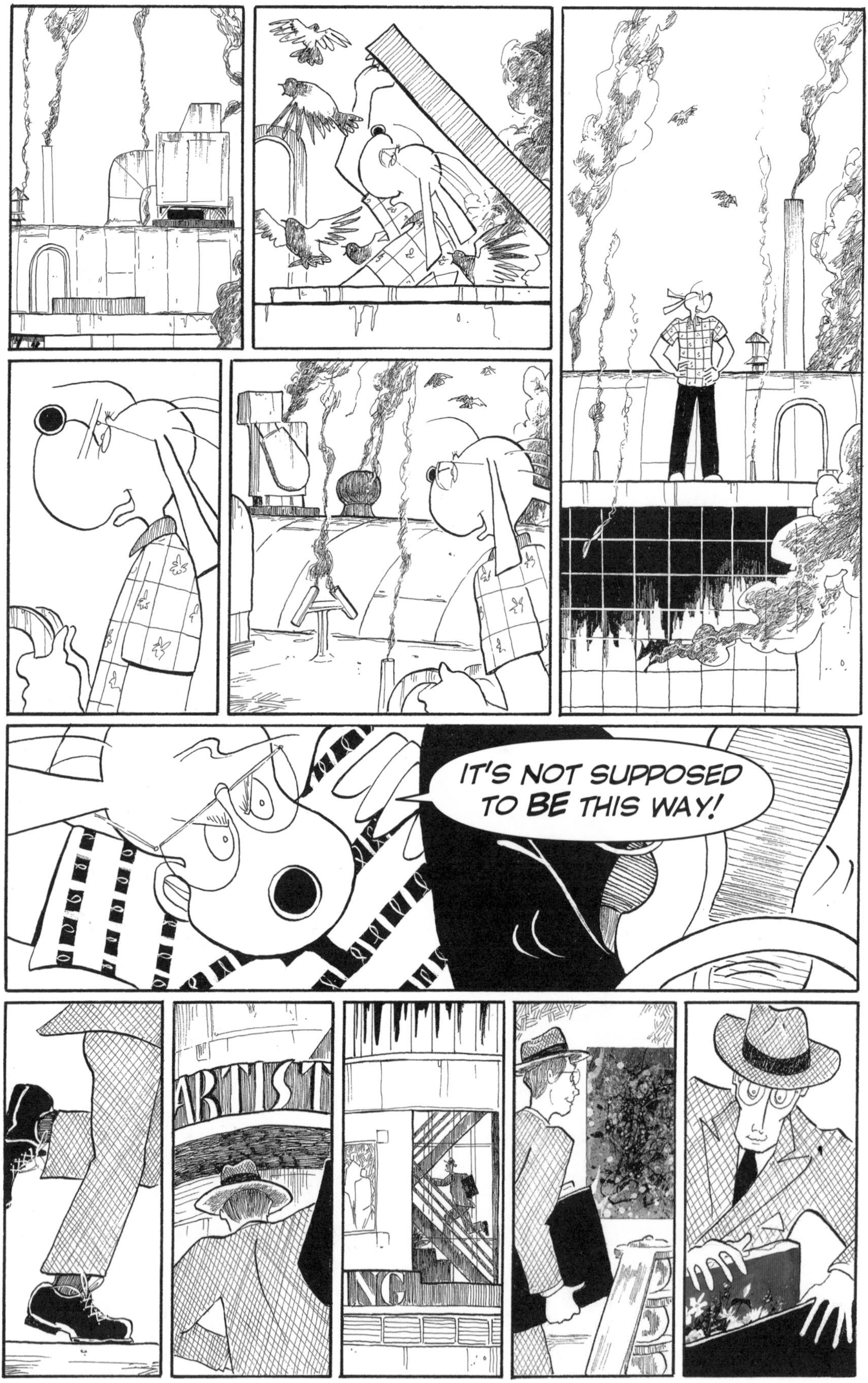
IT'S NOT SUPPOSED TO BE THIS WAY!

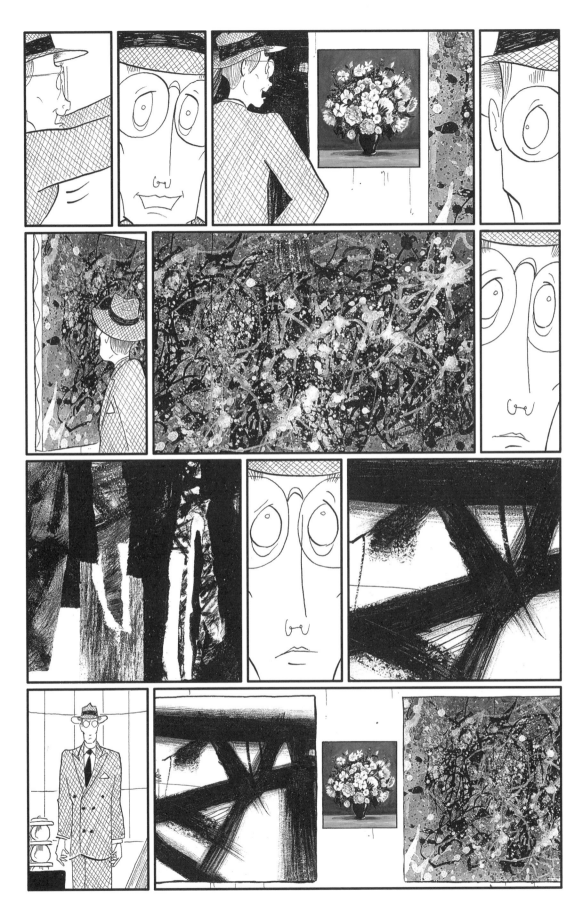

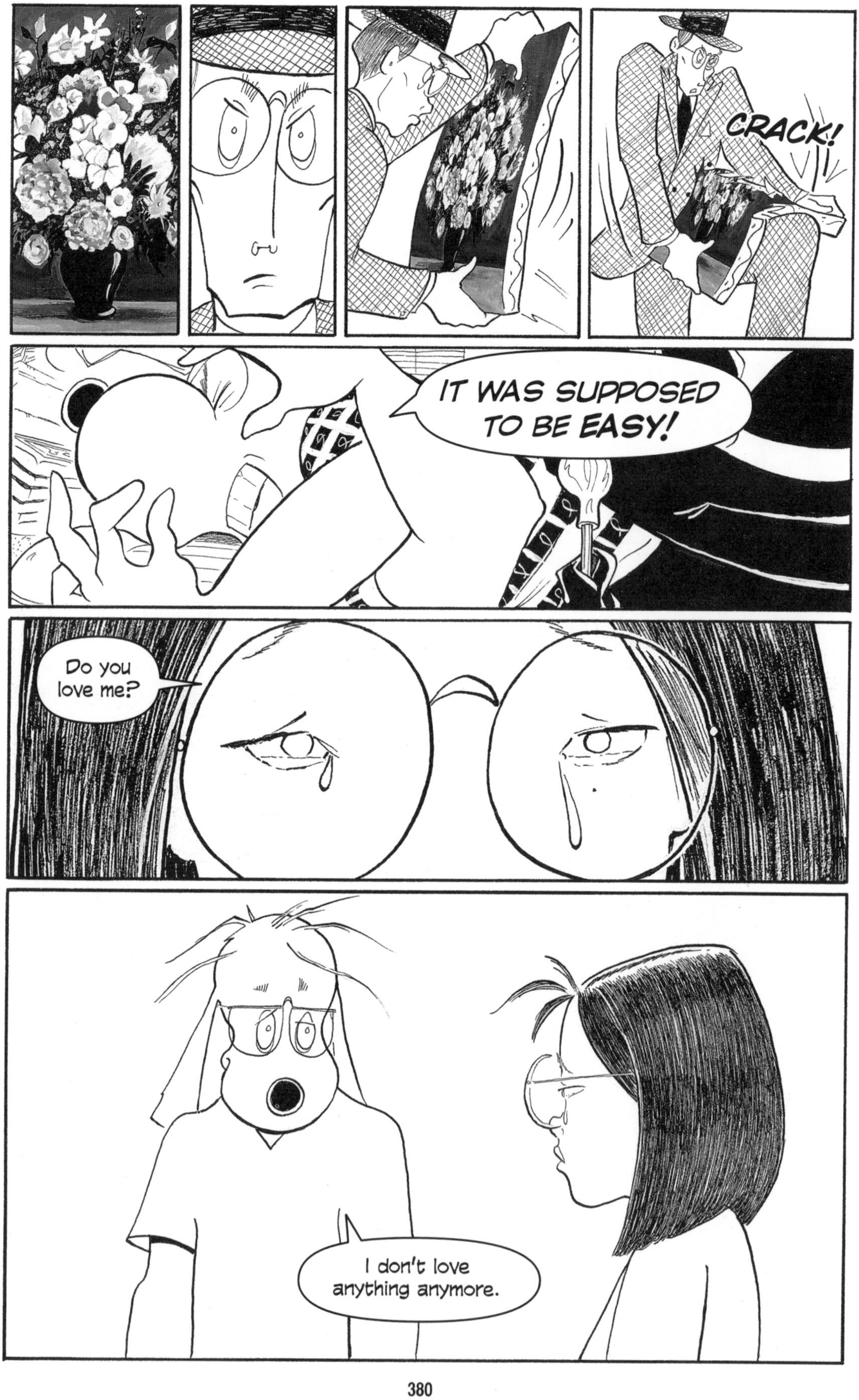
CRACK!
IT WAS SUPPOSED TO BE EASY!
Do you love me?
I don't love anything anymore.

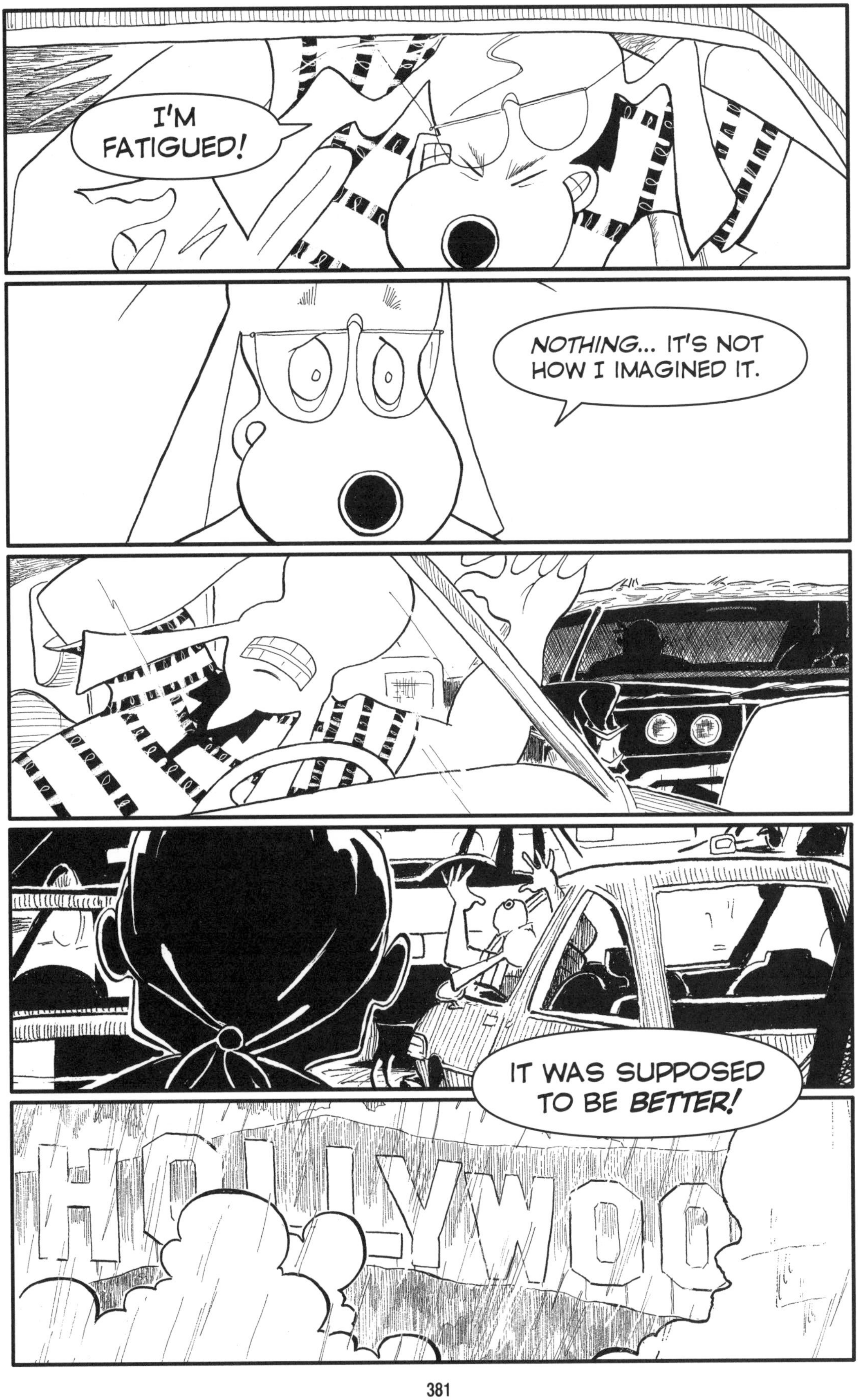
I'M FATIGUED!
NOTHING... IT'S NOT HOW I IMAGINED IT.
IT WAS SUPPOSED TO BE BETTER!

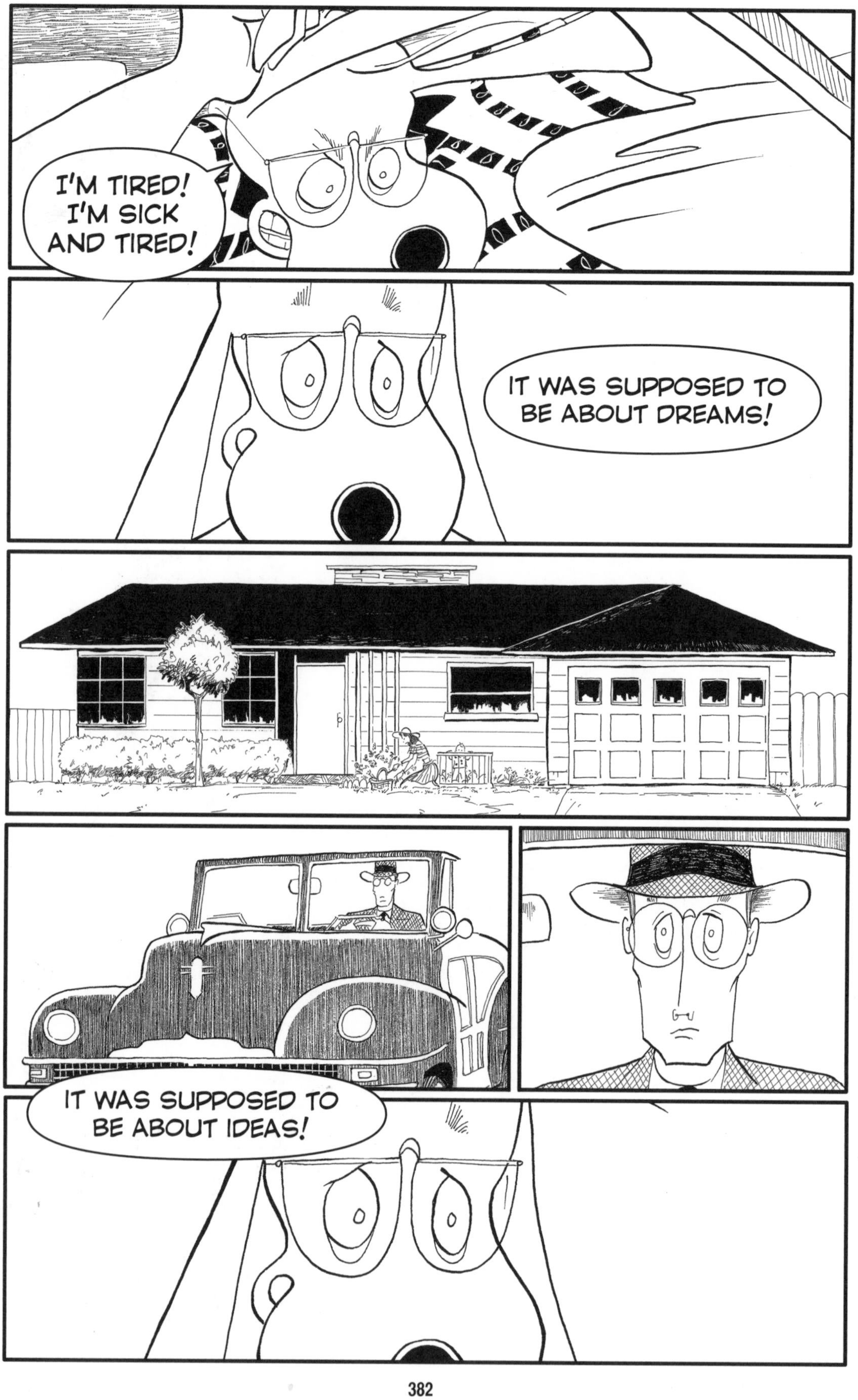
I'M TIRED! I'M SICK AND TIRED!
IT WAS SUPPOSED TO BE ABOUT DREAMS!
IT WAS SUPPOSED TO BE ABOUT IDEAS!

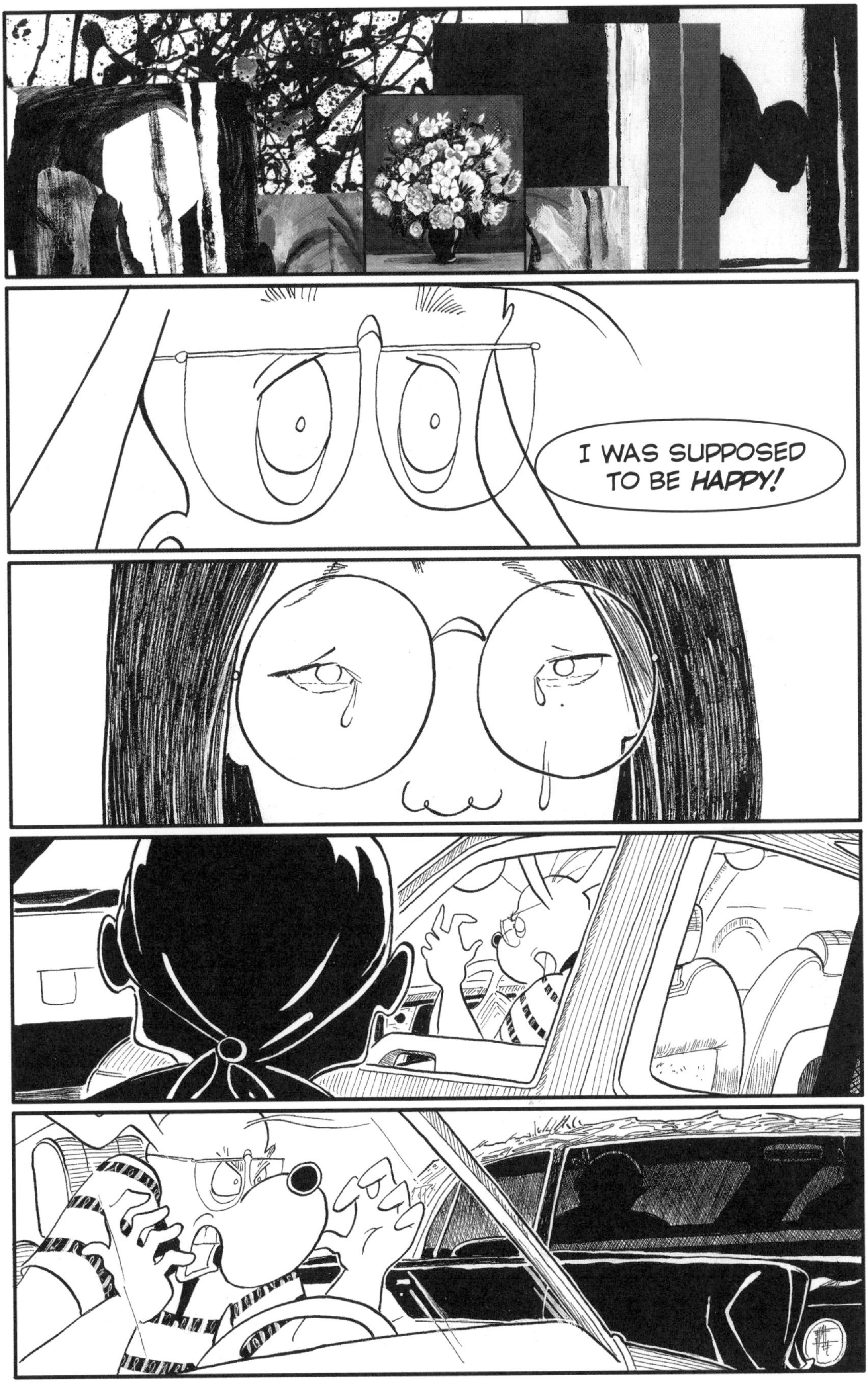
I WAS SUPPOSED TO BE *HAPPY!*

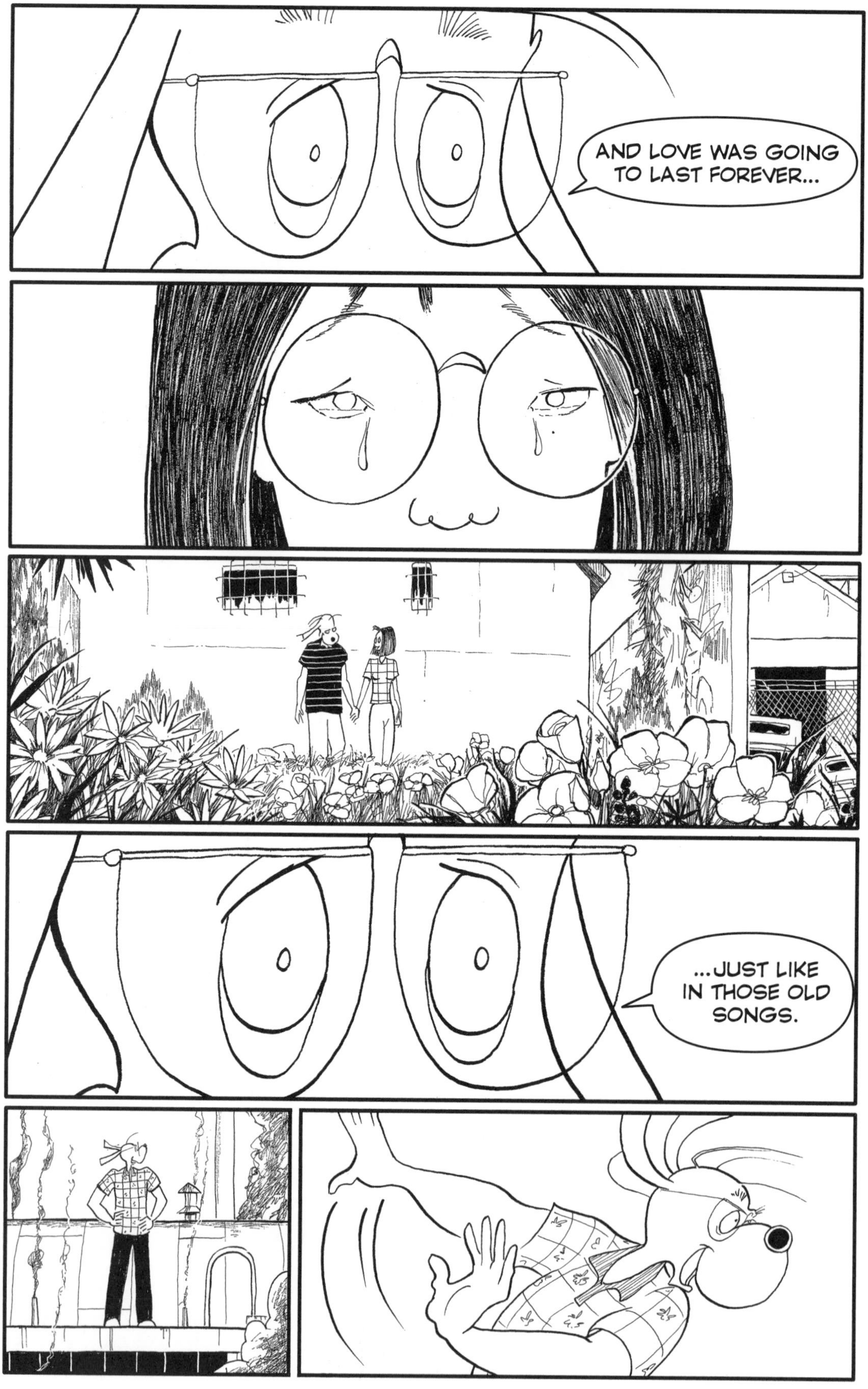
AND LOVE WAS GOING TO LAST FOREVER...
...JUST LIKE IN THOSE OLD SONGS.

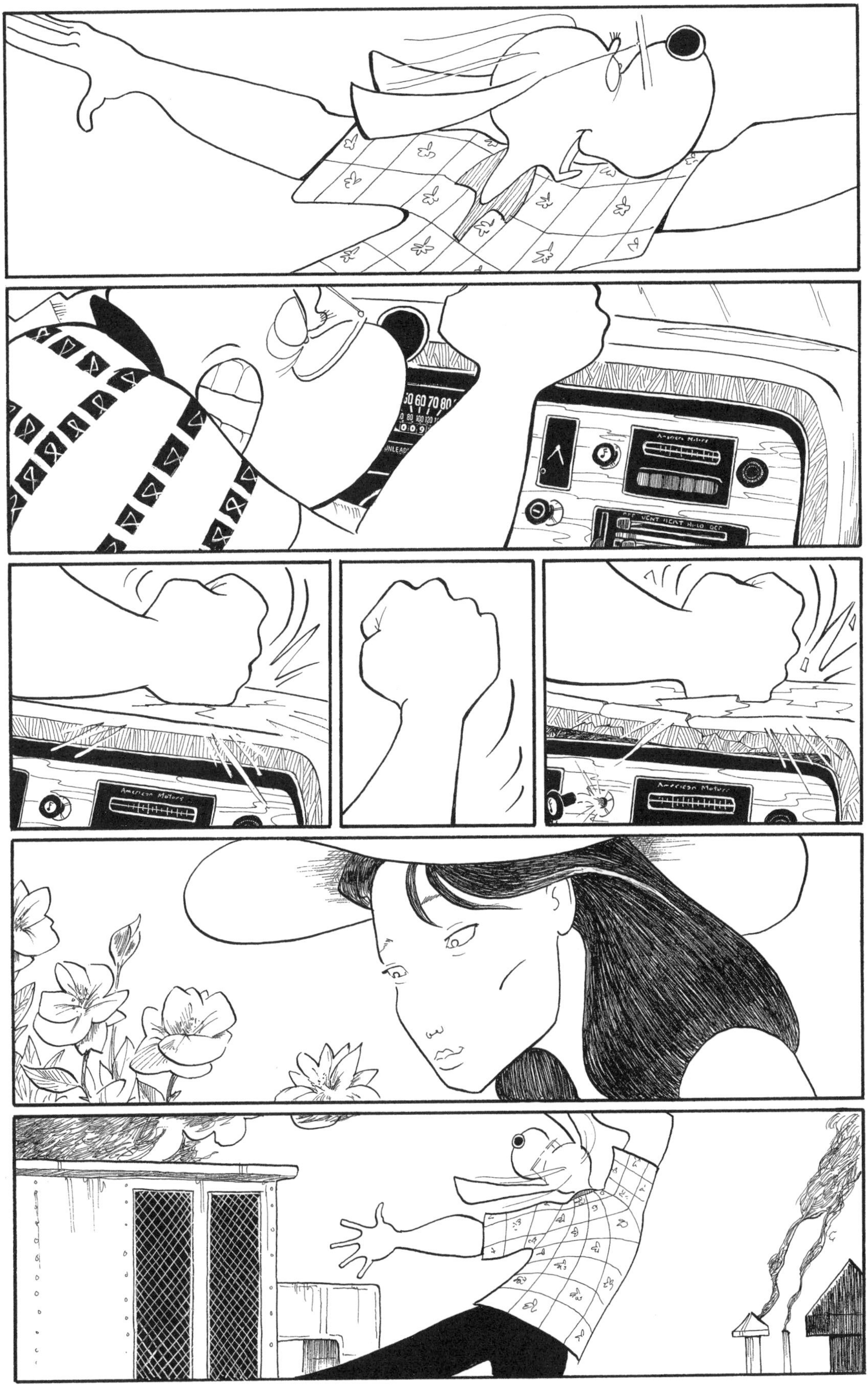
American Motors
American Motors
American Motors

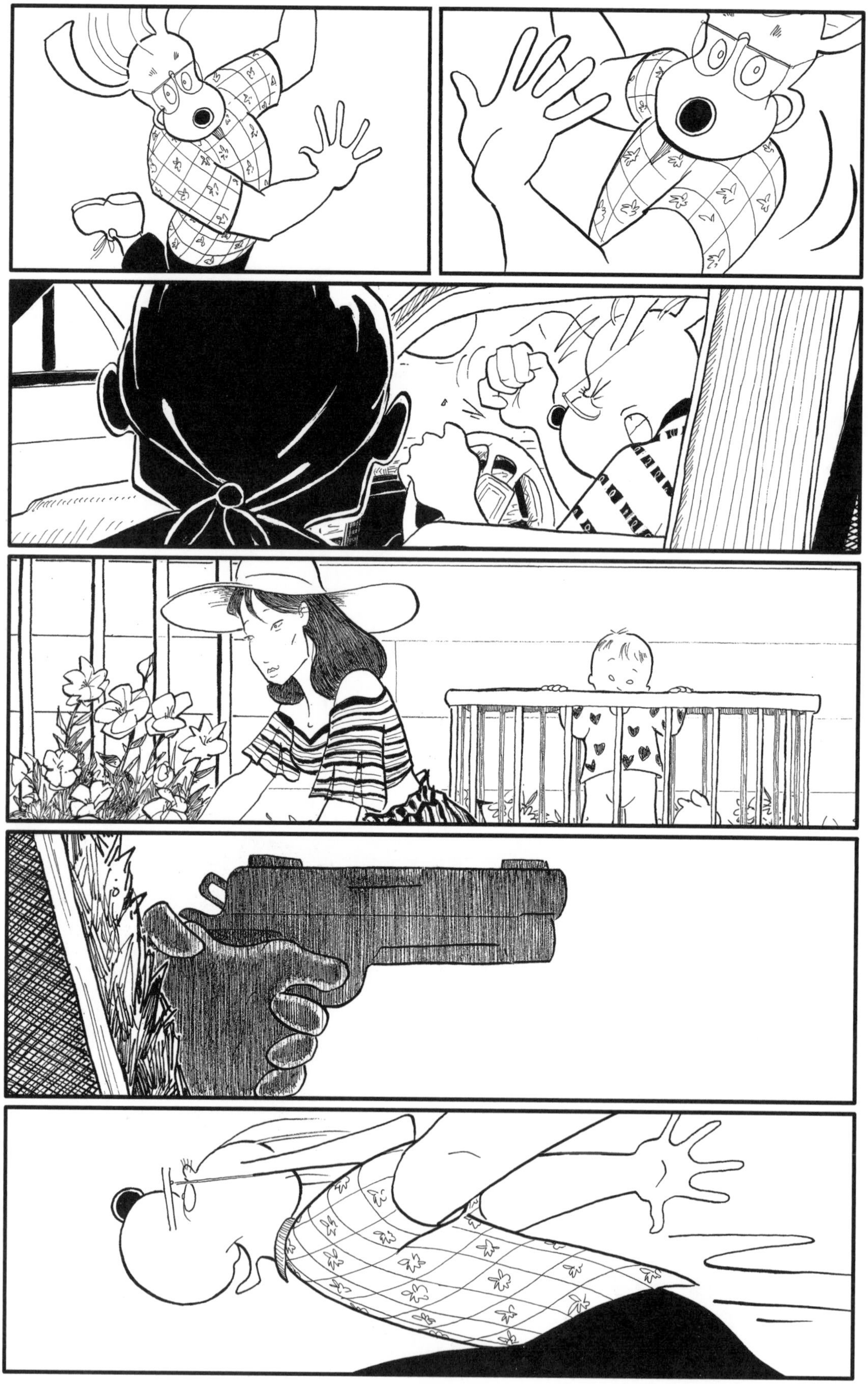

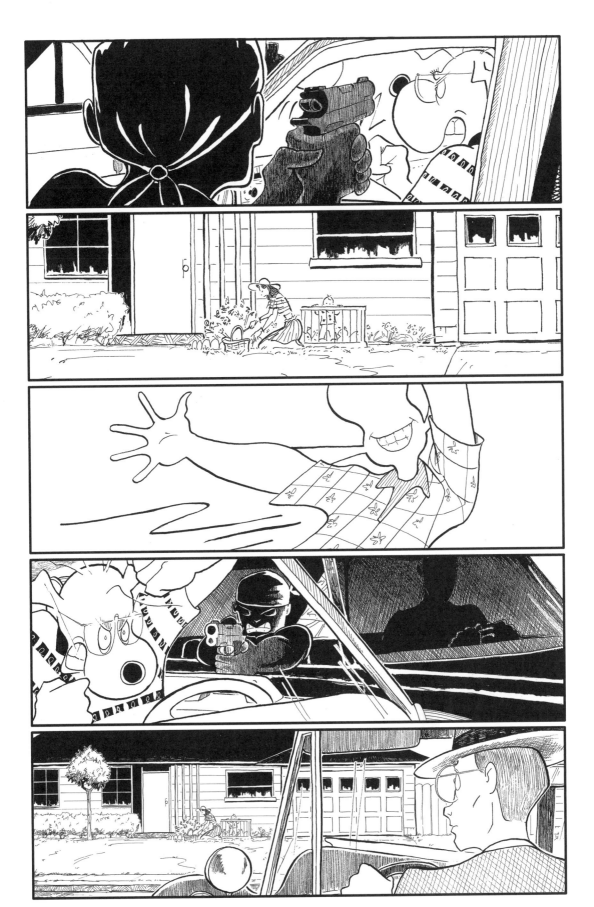

387

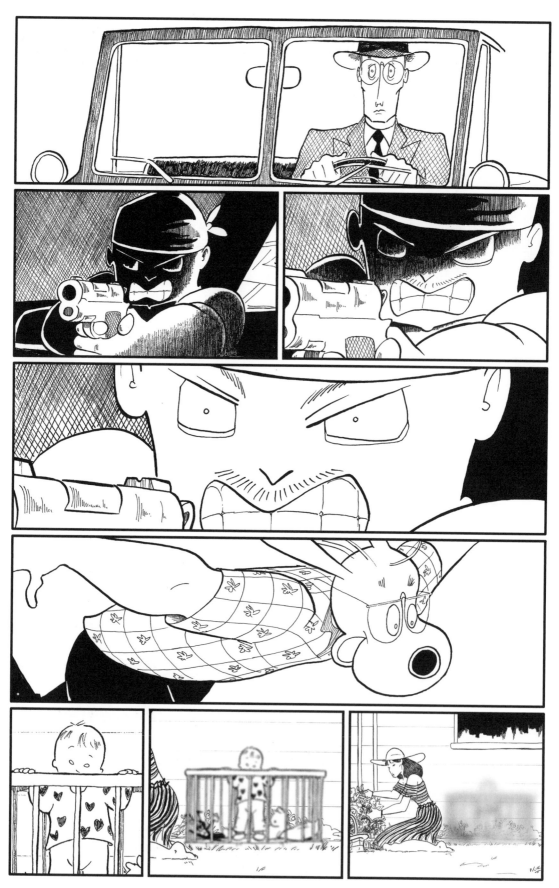

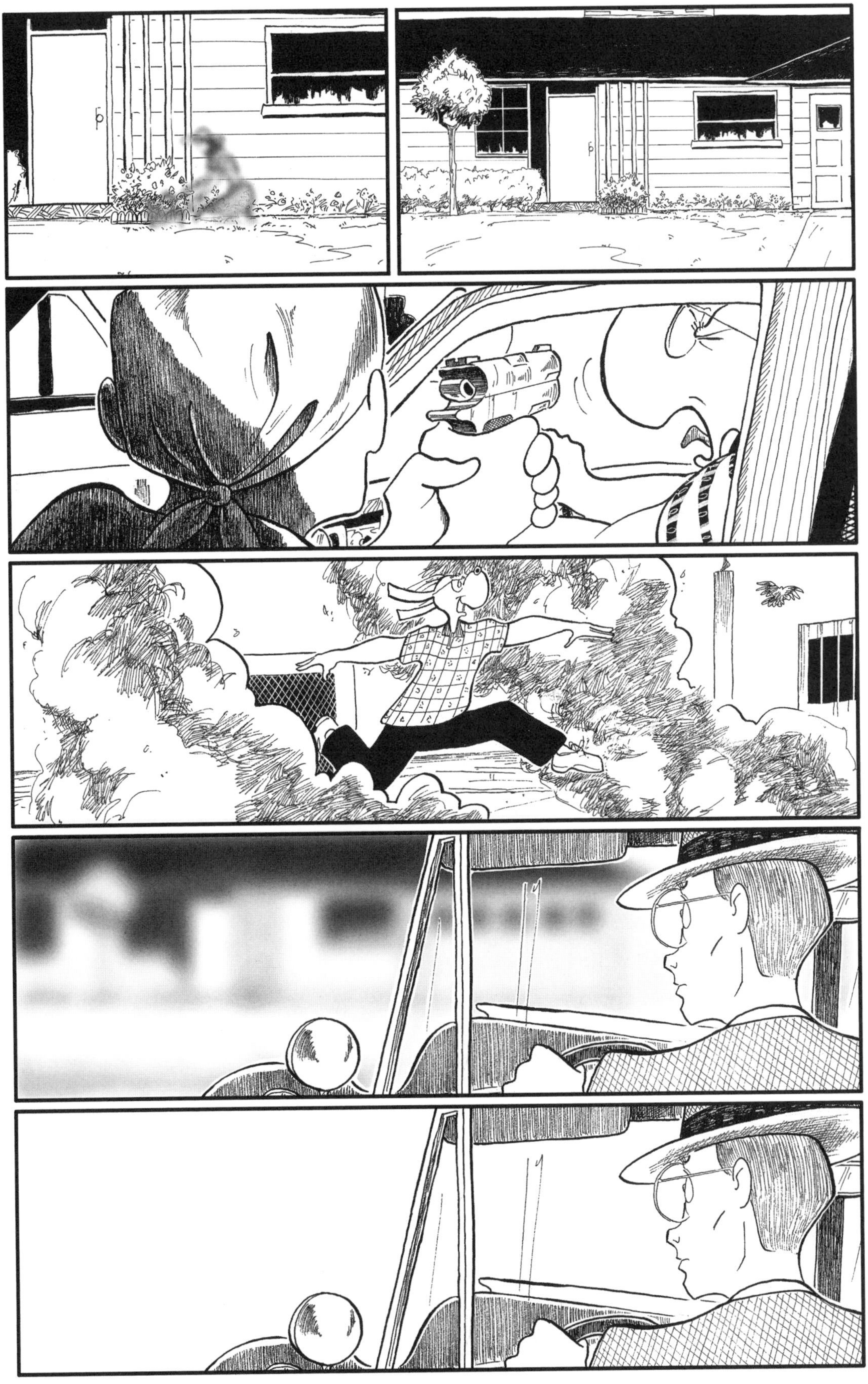

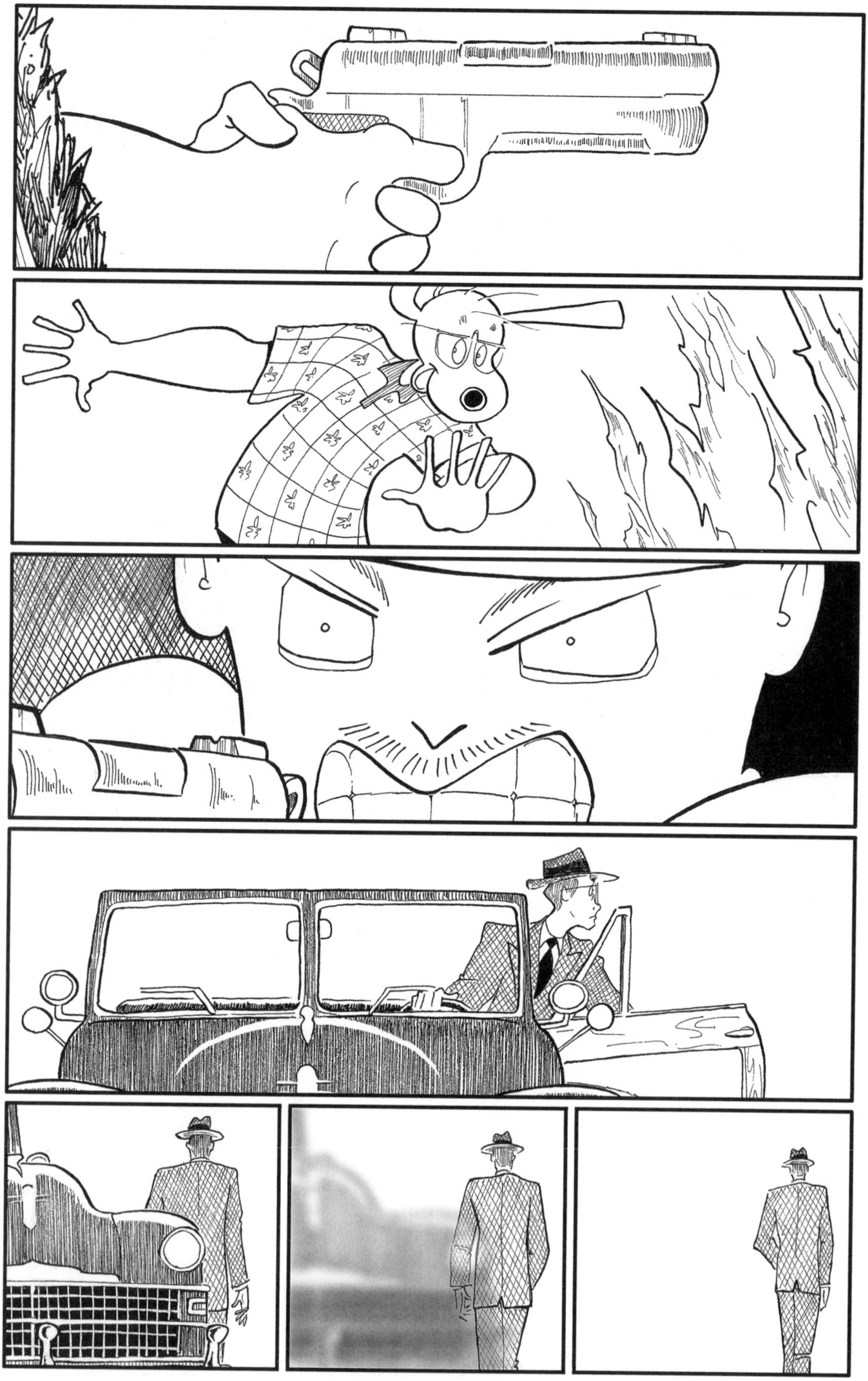

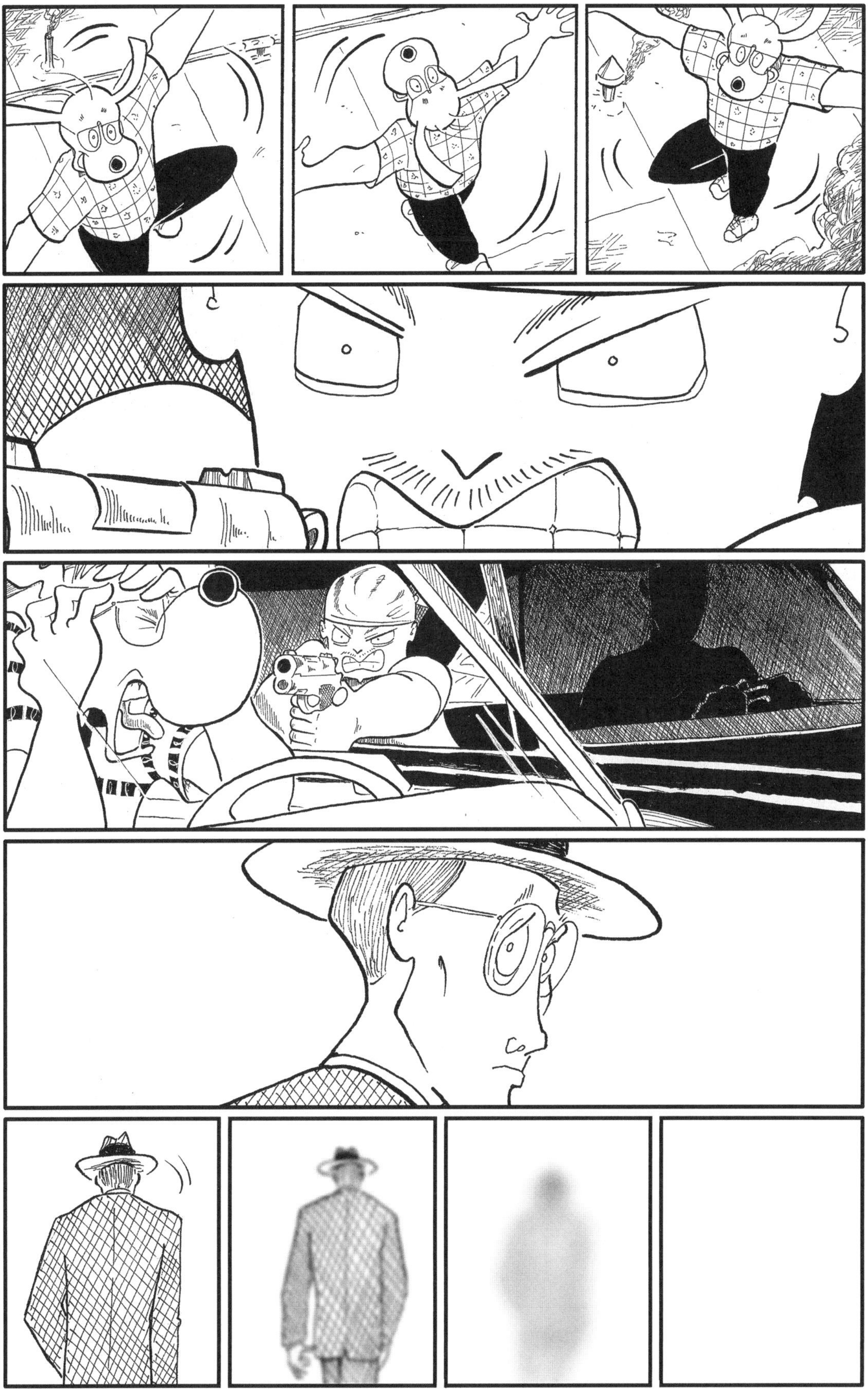

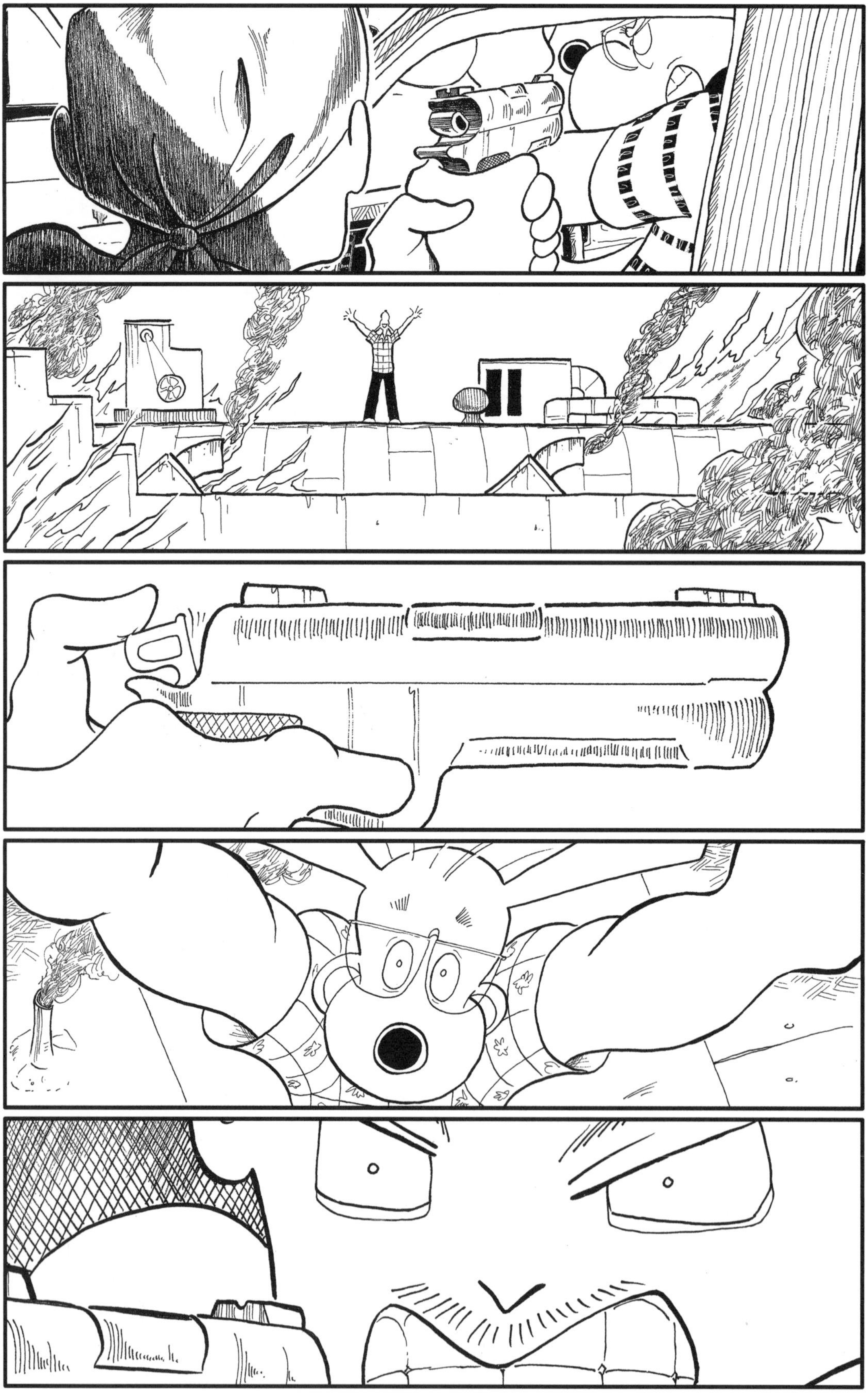

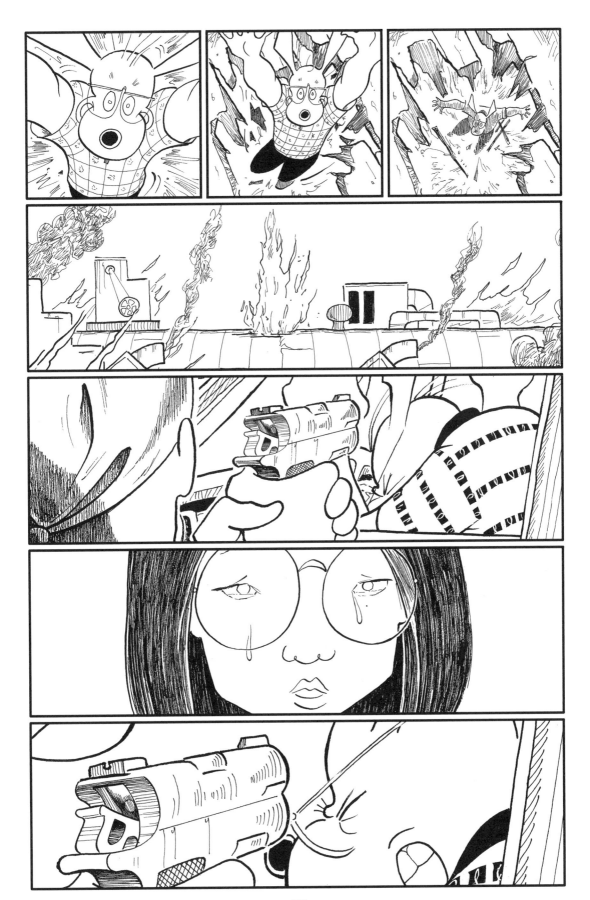

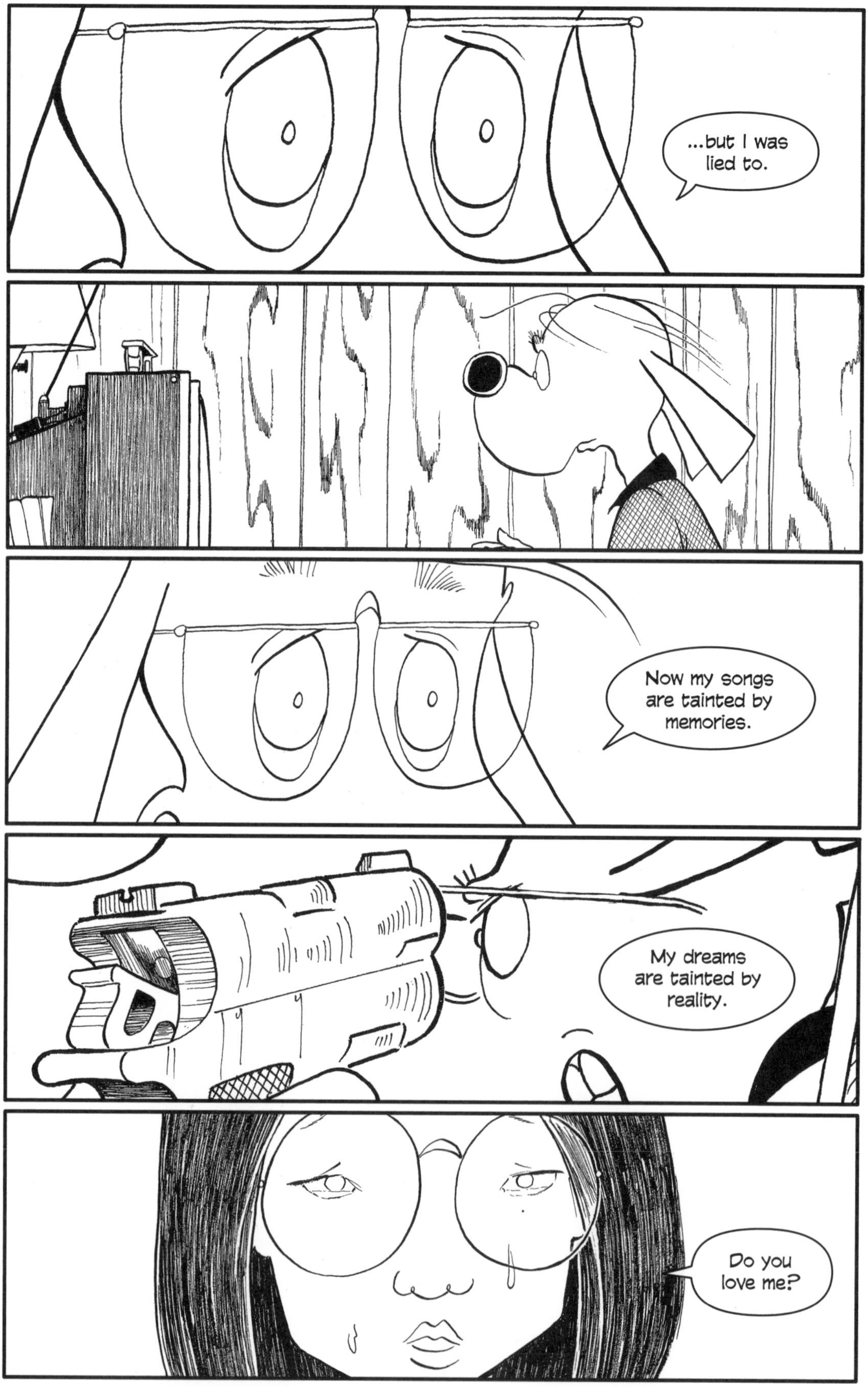
...but I was lied to.
Now my songs are tainted by memories.
My dreams are tainted by reality.
Do you love me?

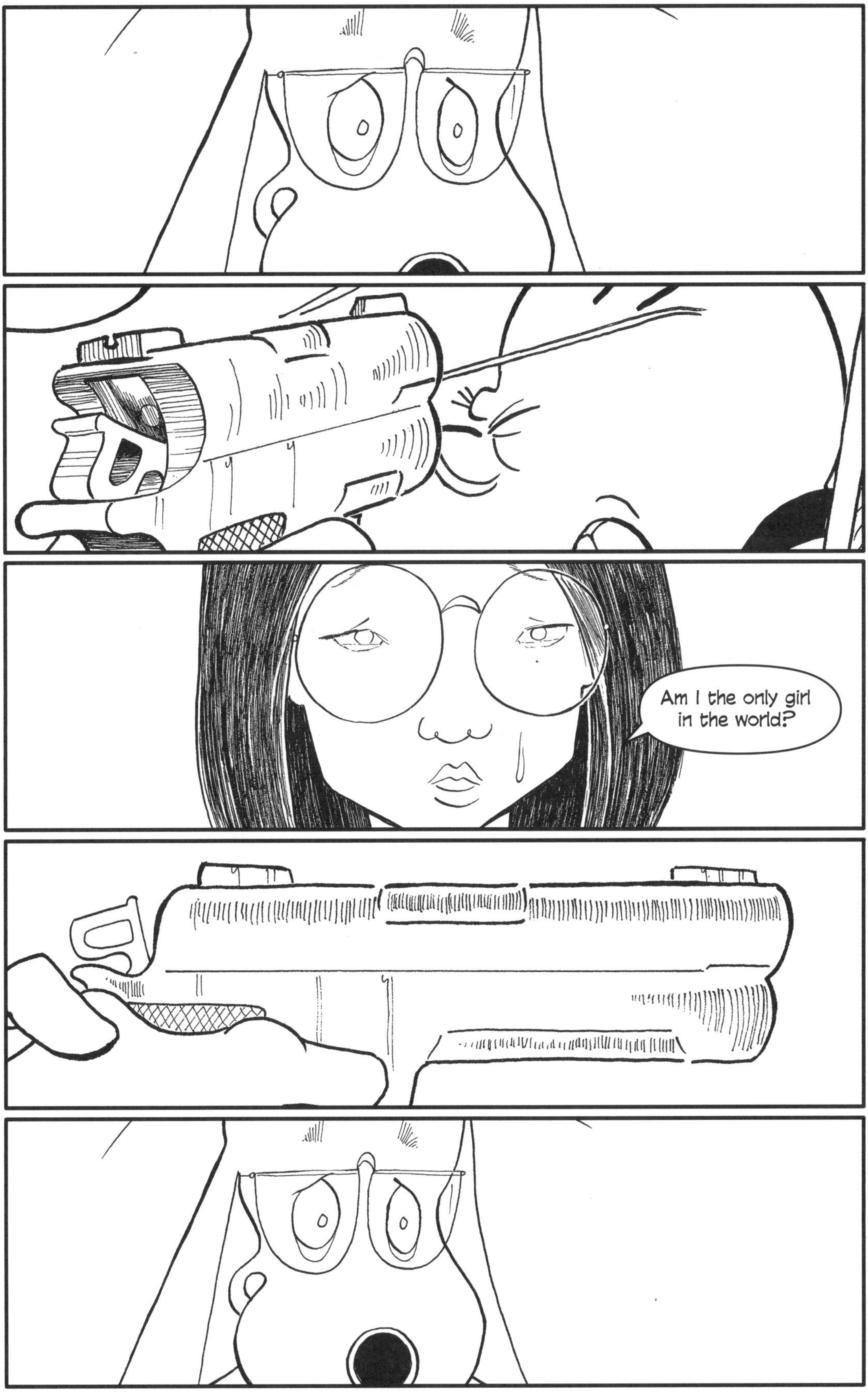
Am I the only girl
in the world?

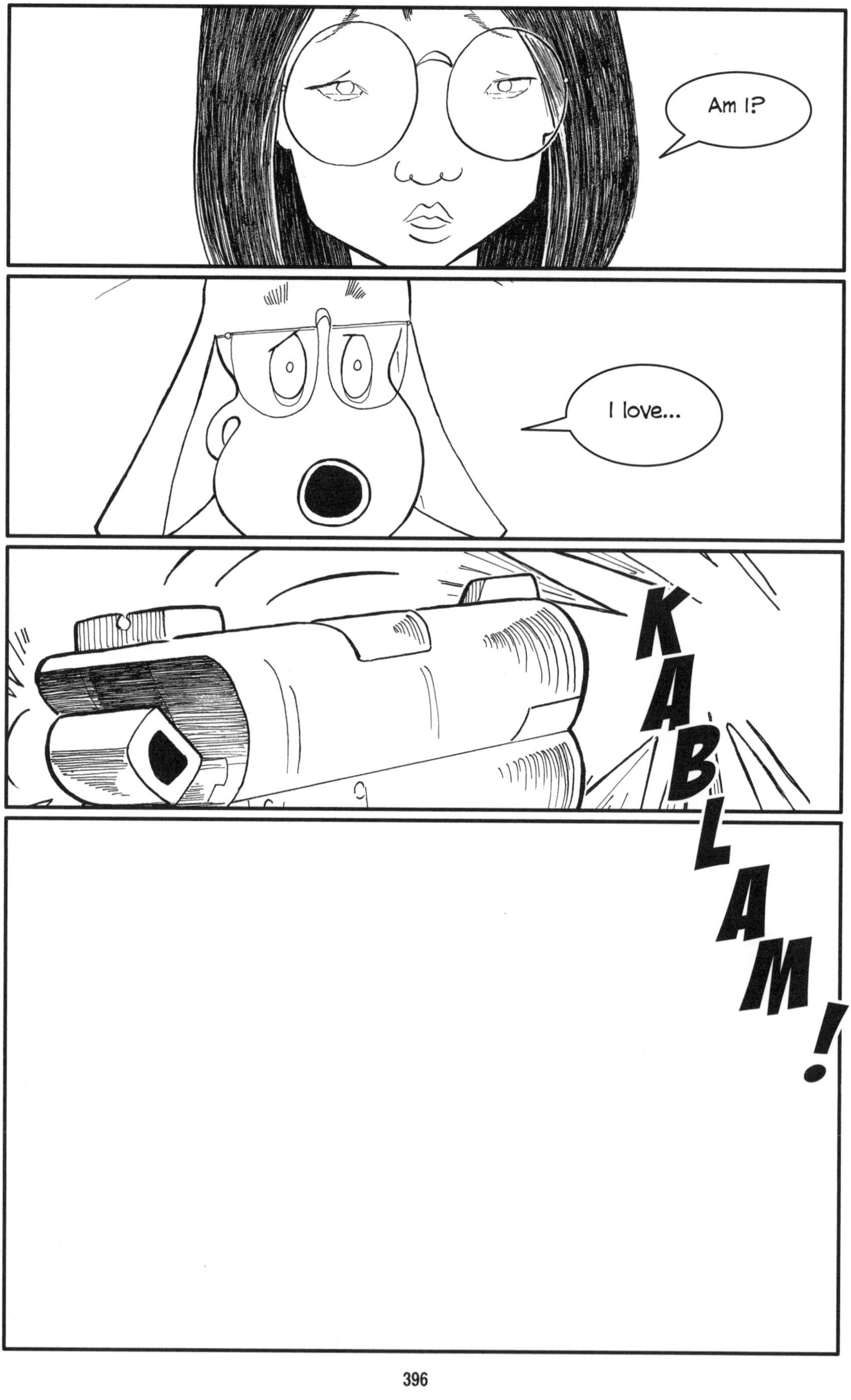
Am I?
I love...
KABLAM!

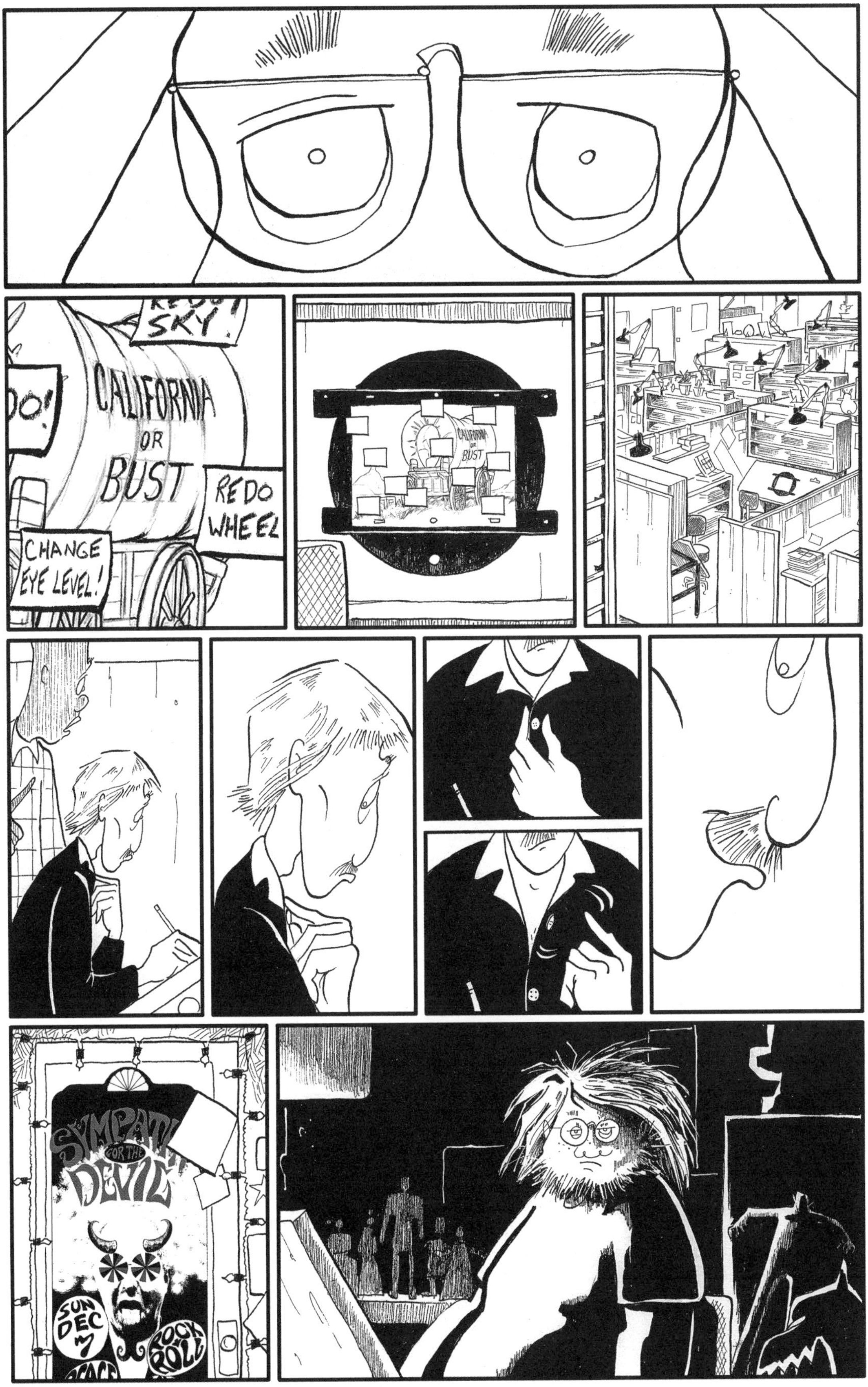
SKY!
DO!
CALIFORNIA OR BUST
RE DO WHEEL
CHANGE EYE LEVEL!
CALIFORNIA OR BUST
FOR THE
DEVIL
SUN DEC 7
ROCK ROLL

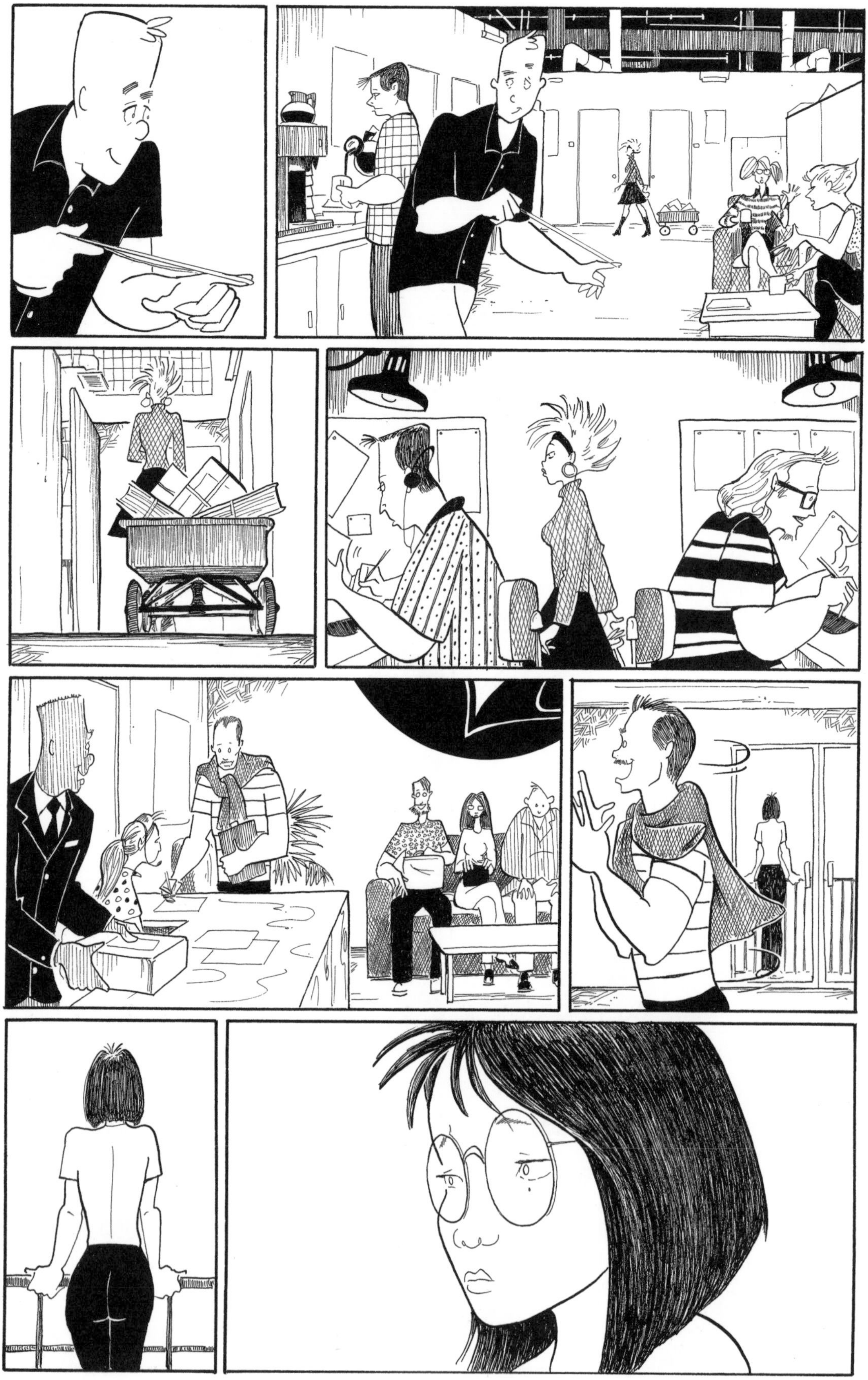

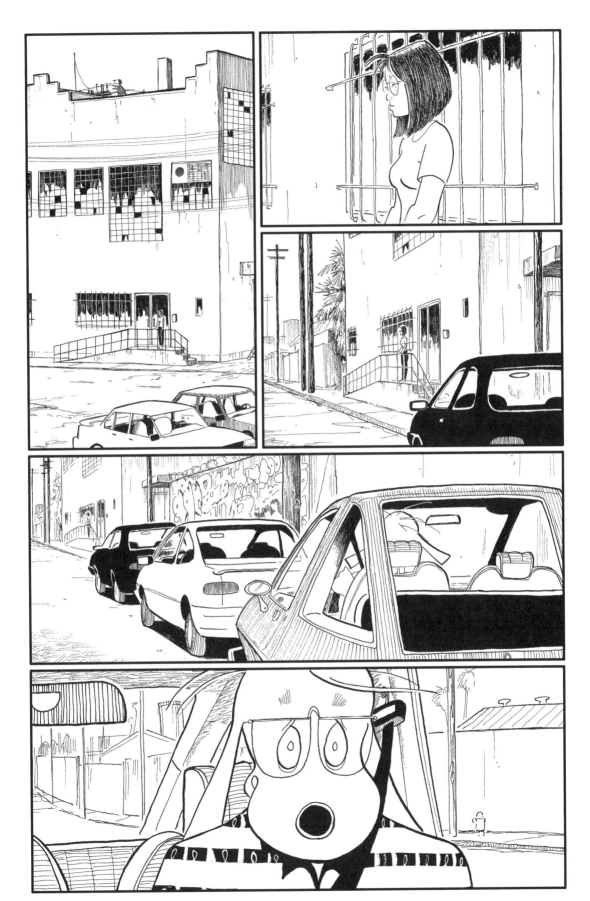

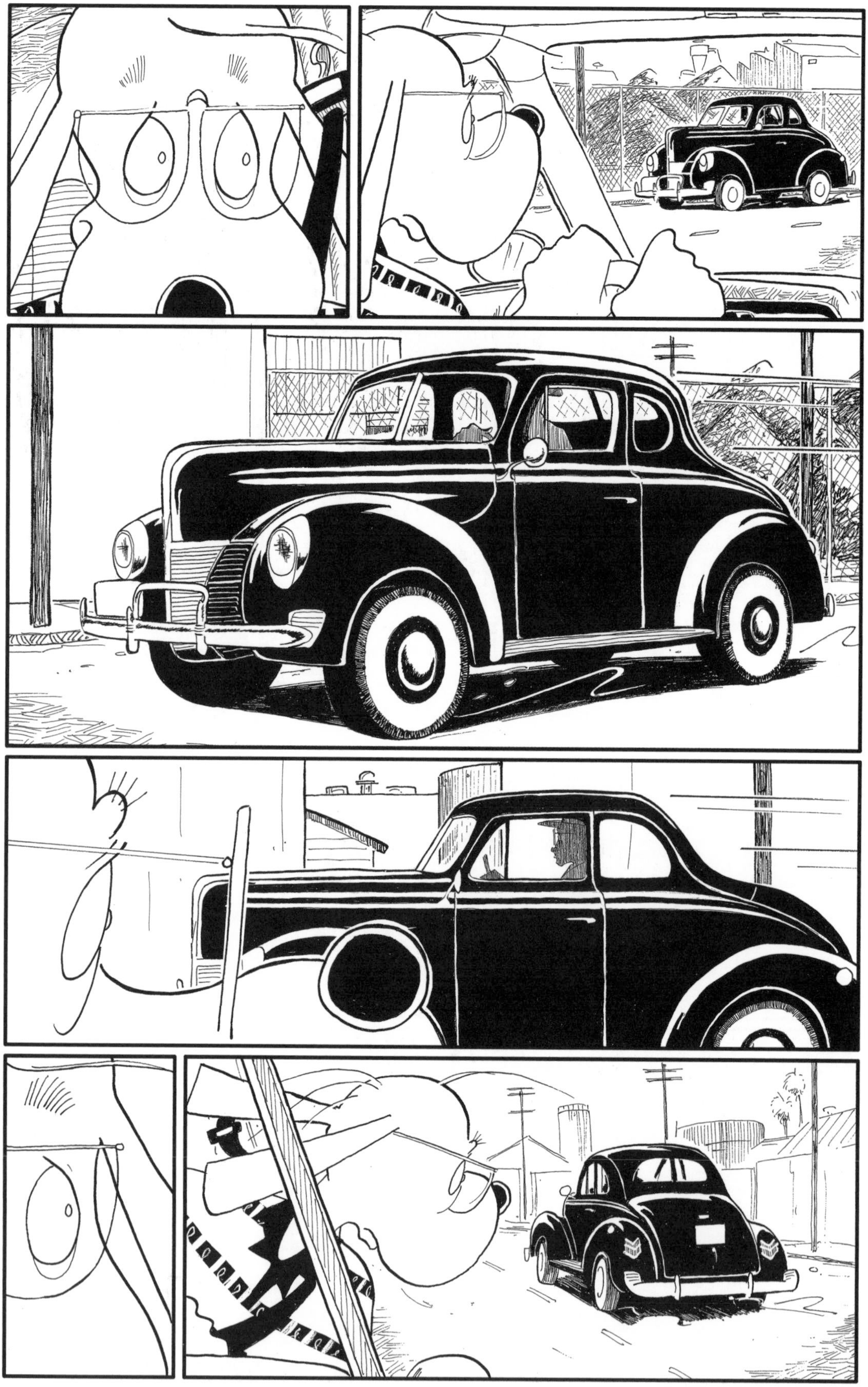

  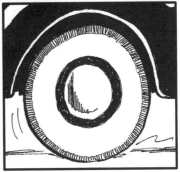

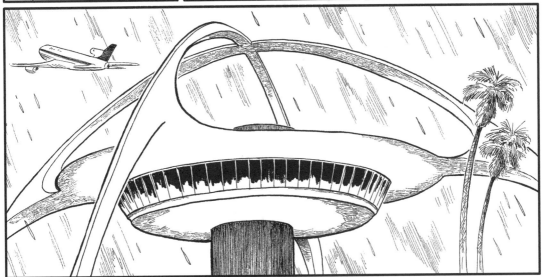

Flight 222 to Vancouver, Canada will be leaving at Gate 3B.

Thank you.

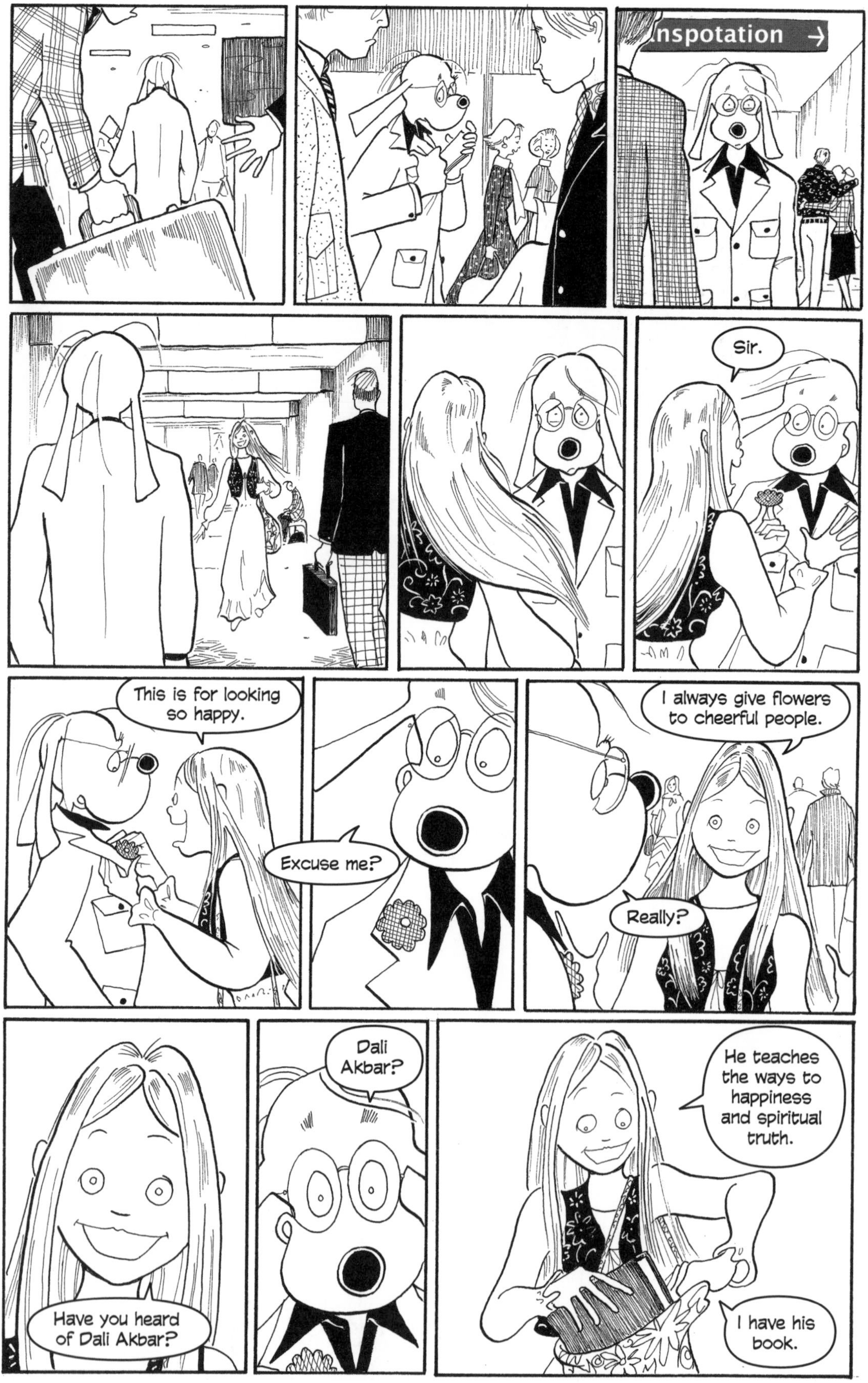
Inspotation →
Sir.
This is for looking so happy.
Excuse me?
I always give flowers to cheerful people.
Really?
Have you heard of Dali Akbar?
Dali Akbar?
He teaches the ways to happiness and spiritual truth.
I have his book.

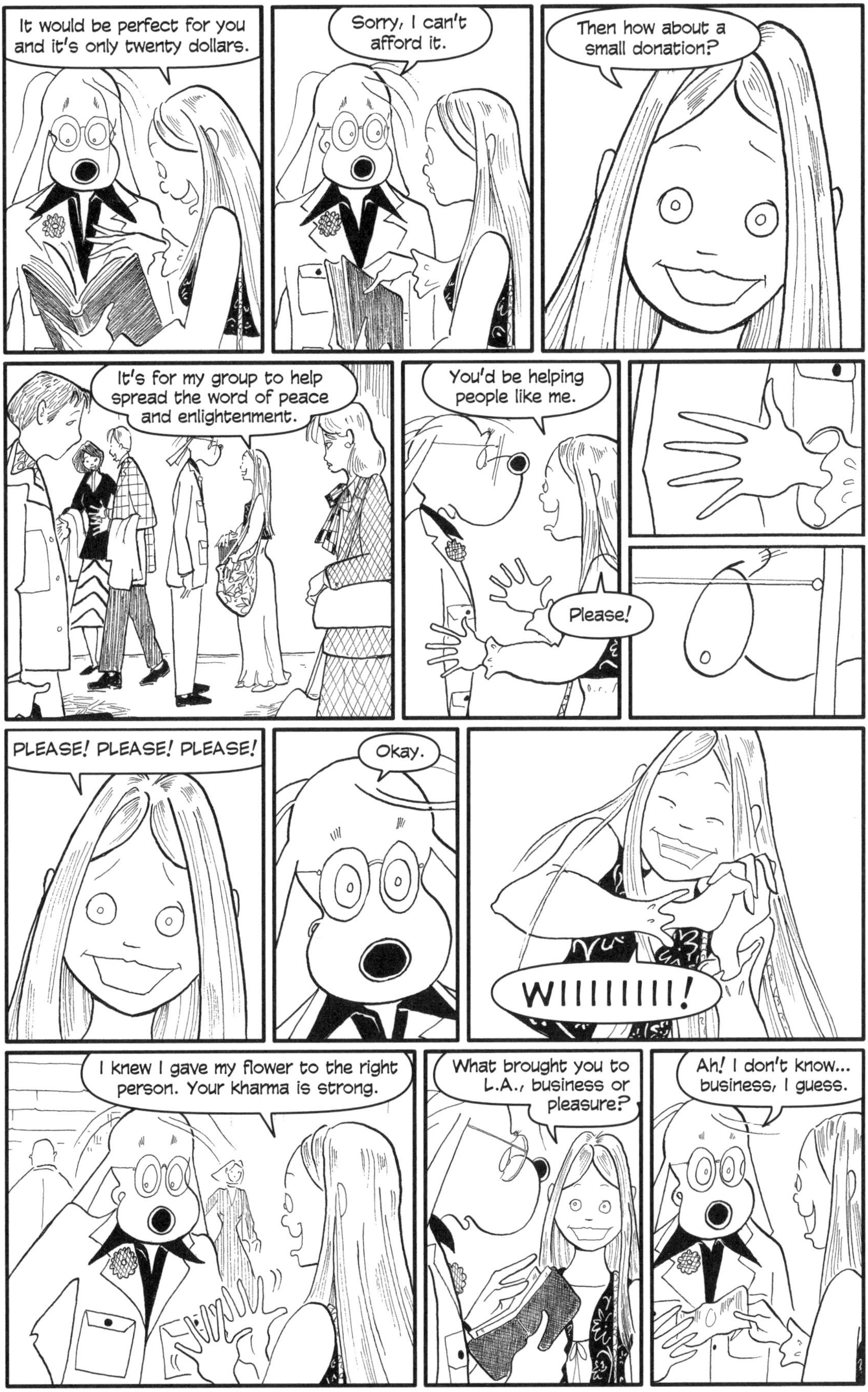
It would be perfect for you and it's only twenty dollars.
Sorry, I can't afford it.
Then how about a small donation?
It's for my group to help spread the word of peace and enlightenment.
You'd be helping people like me.
Please!
PLEASE! PLEASE! PLEASE!
Okay.
WIIIIIIII!
I knew I gave my flower to the right person. Your kharma is strong.
What brought you to L.A., business or pleasure?
Ah! I don't know... business, I guess.

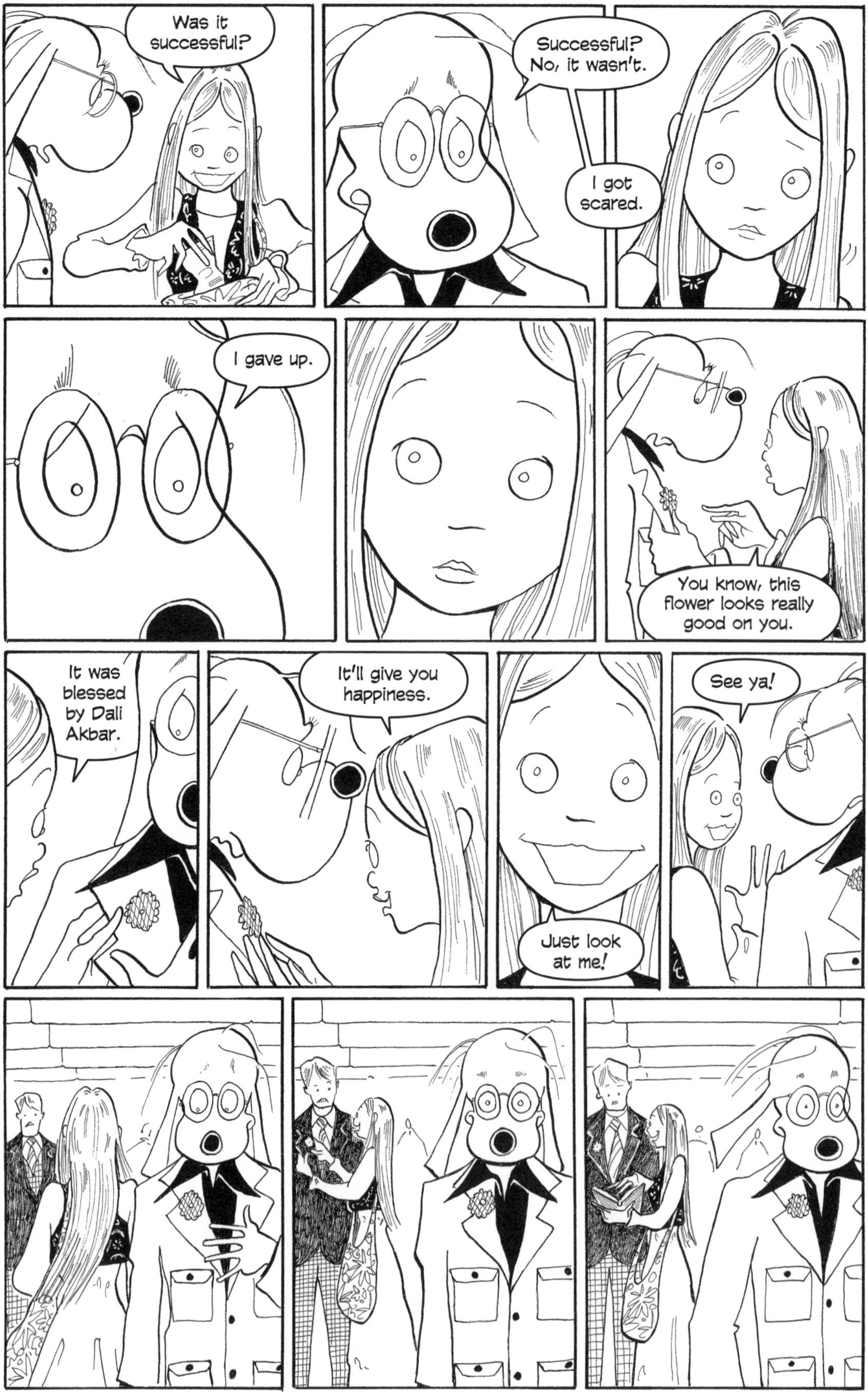
Was it successful?
Successful? No, it wasn't.
I got scared.
I gave up.
You know, this flower looks really good on you.
It was blessed by Dali Akbar.
It'll give you happiness.
Just look at me!
See ya!

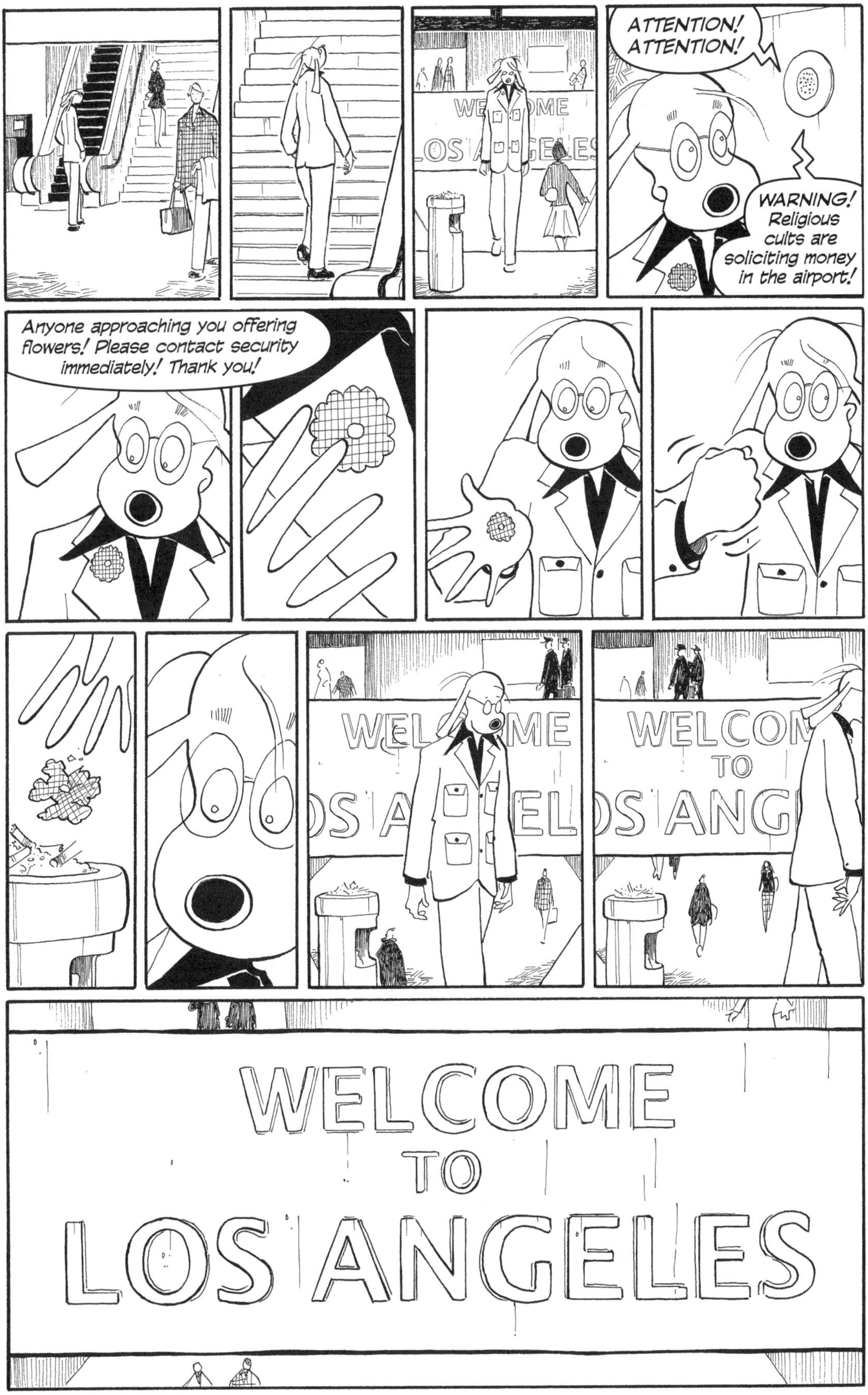
WELCOME
LOS ANGELES
ATTENTION! ATTENTION!
WARNING! Religious cults are soliciting money in the airport!
Anyone approaching you offering flowers! Please contact security immediately! Thank you!
WELCOME TO LOS ANGELES

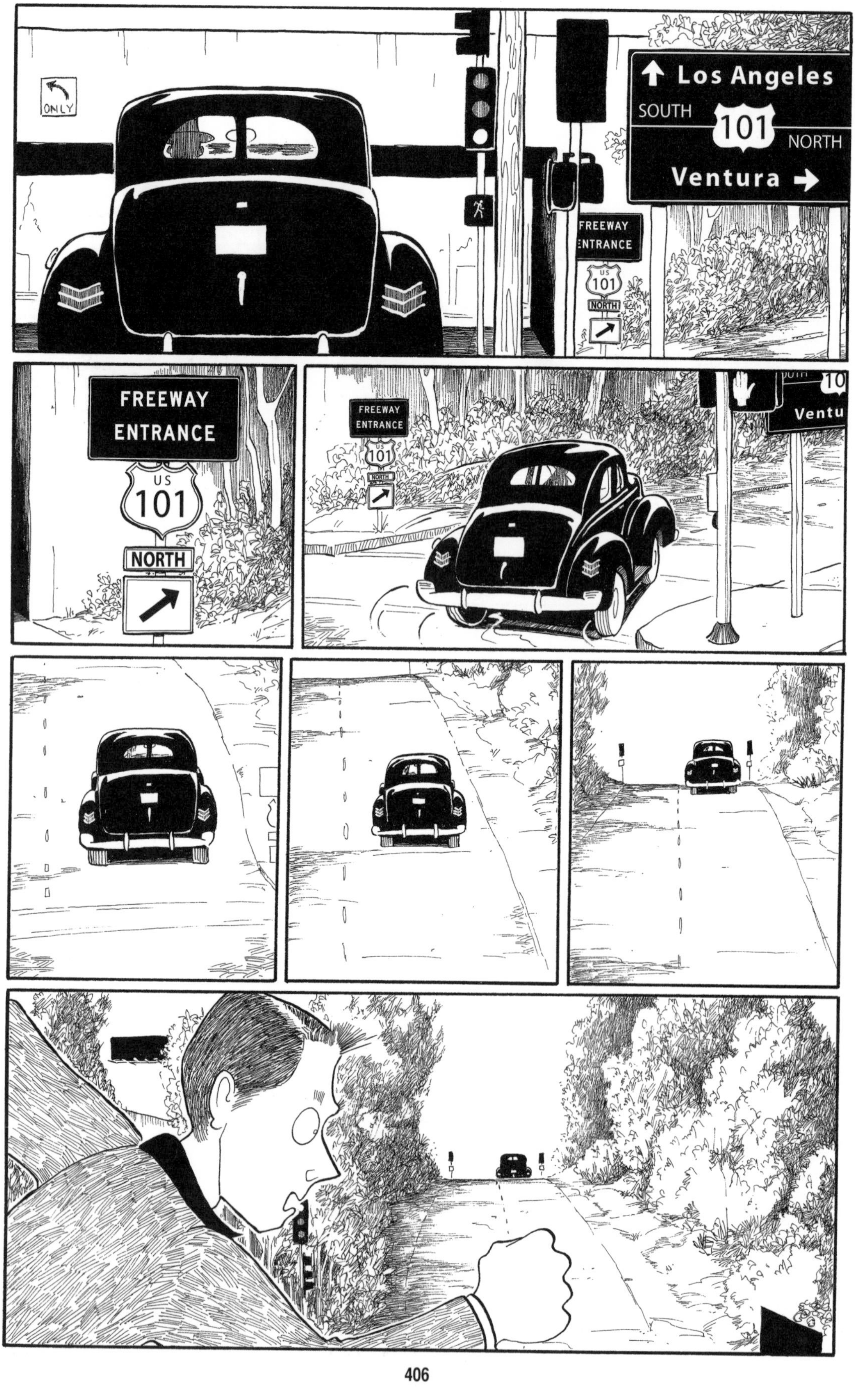
ONLY
Los Angeles
SOUTH
101
NORTH
Ventura
FREEWAY ENTRANCE
US 101
NORTH
FREEWAY ENTRANCE
US 101
NORTH
FREEWAY ENTRANCE
101
NORTH

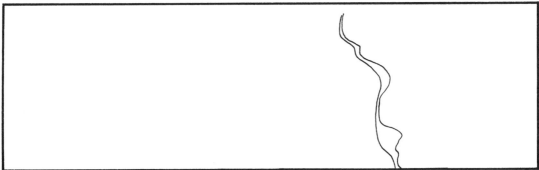

YIKES!

OH MY GOD!

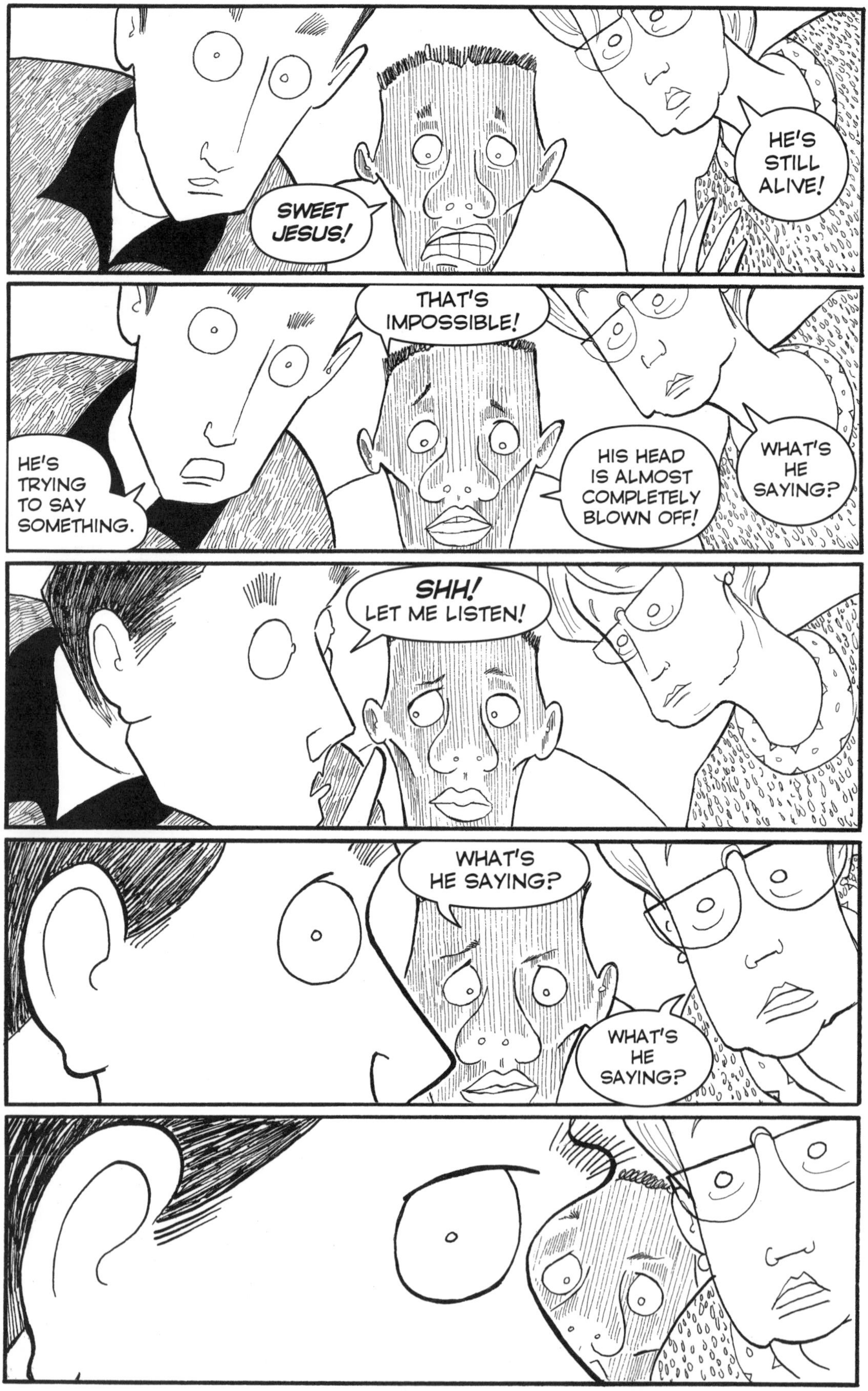
SWEET JESUS!
HE'S STILL ALIVE!
THAT'S IMPOSSIBLE!
HE'S TRYING TO SAY SOMETHING.
HIS HEAD IS ALMOST COMPLETELY BLOWN OFF!
WHAT'S HE SAYING?
SHH! LET ME LISTEN!
WHAT'S HE SAYING?
WHAT'S HE SAYING?

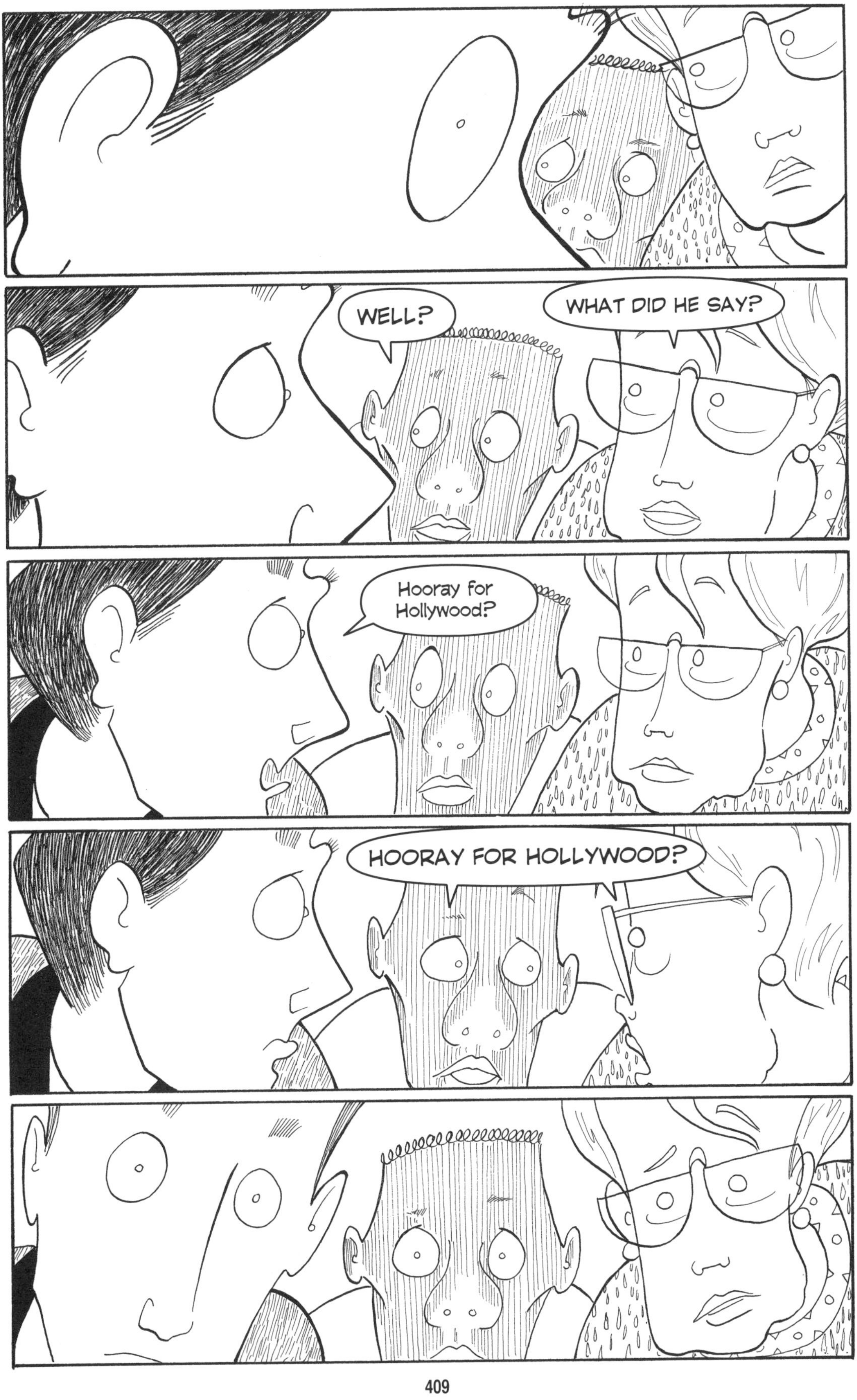
WELL?
WHAT DID HE SAY?
Hooray for Hollywood?
HOORAY FOR HOLLYWOOD?

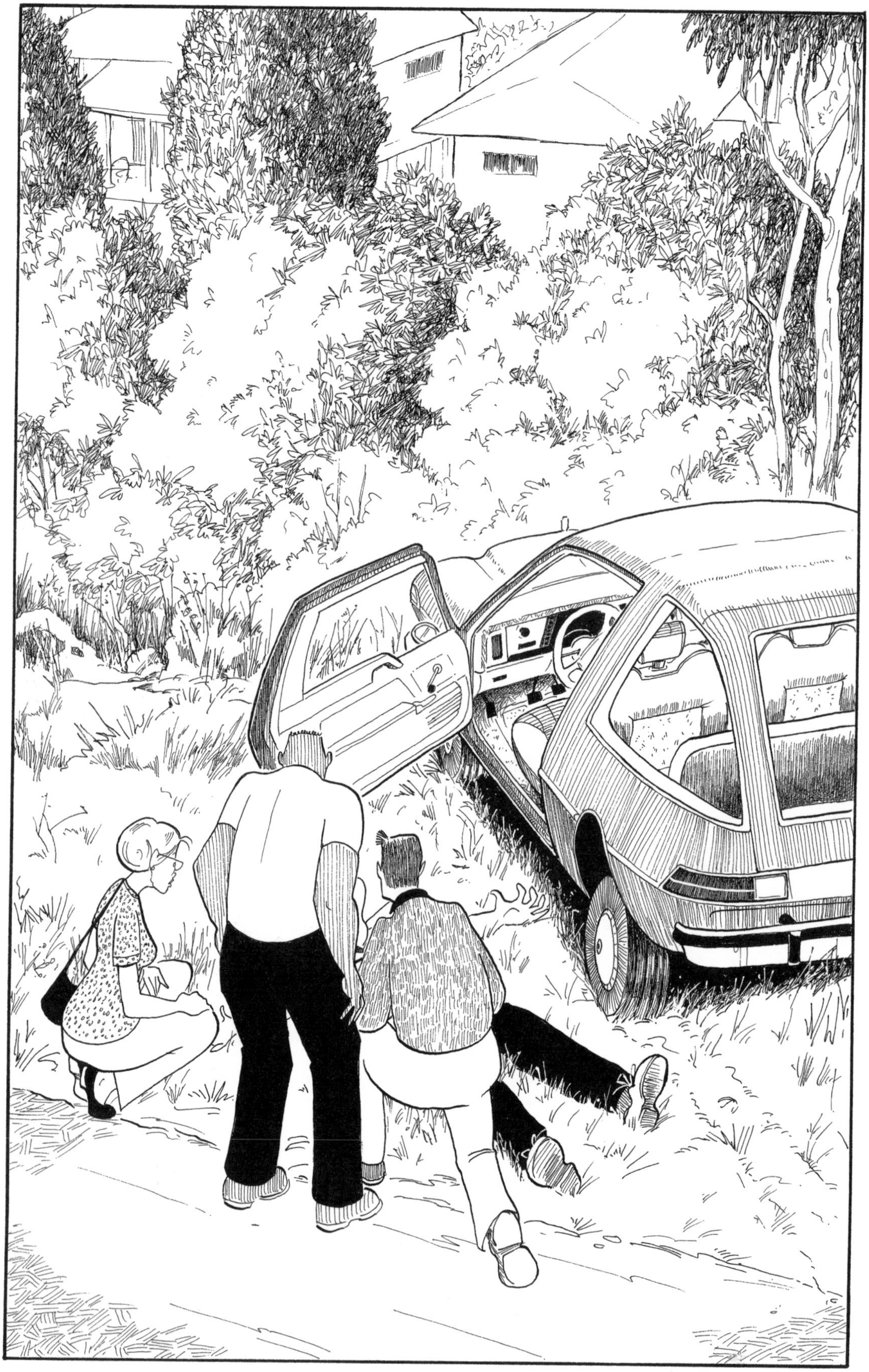

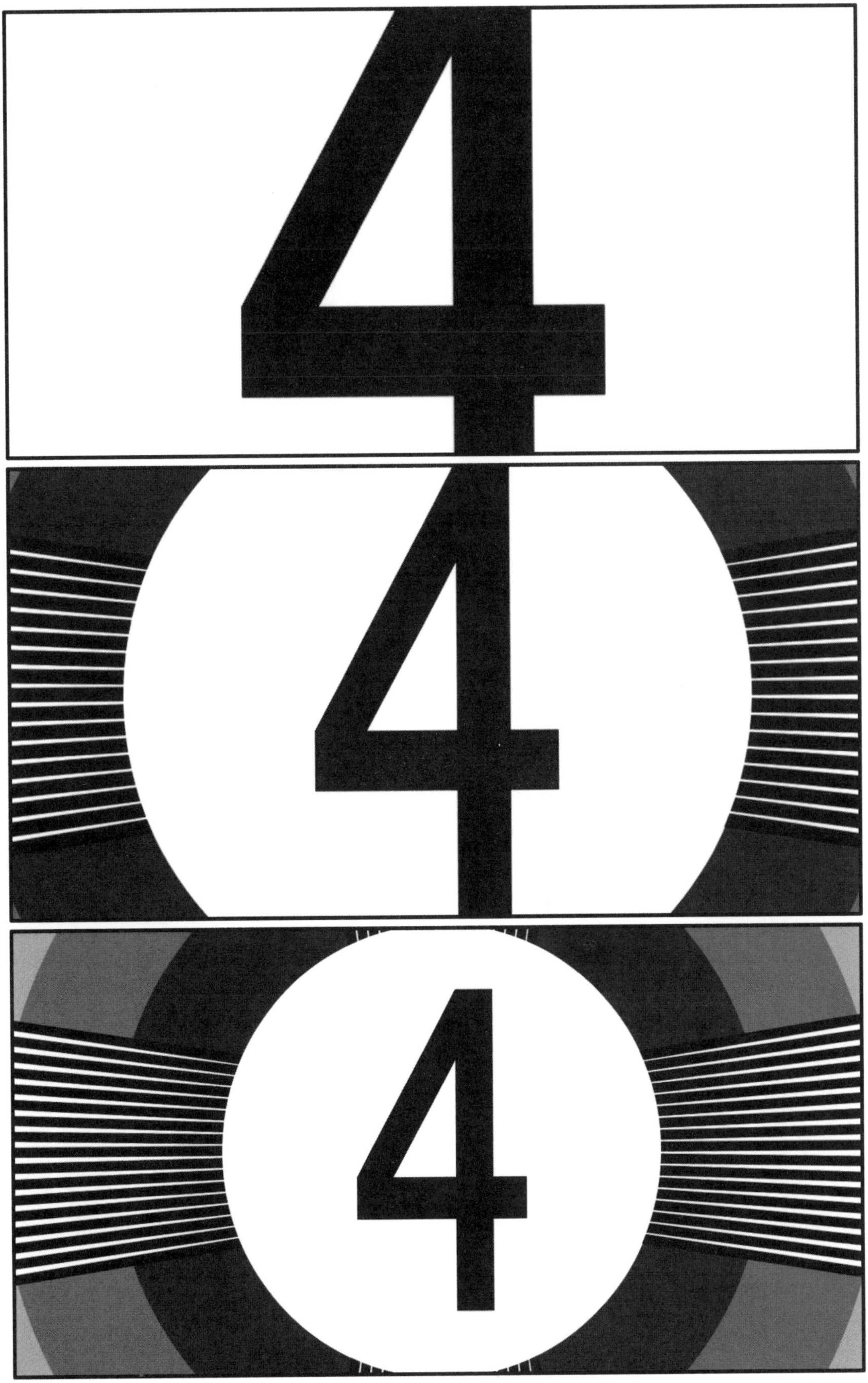
4
4
4

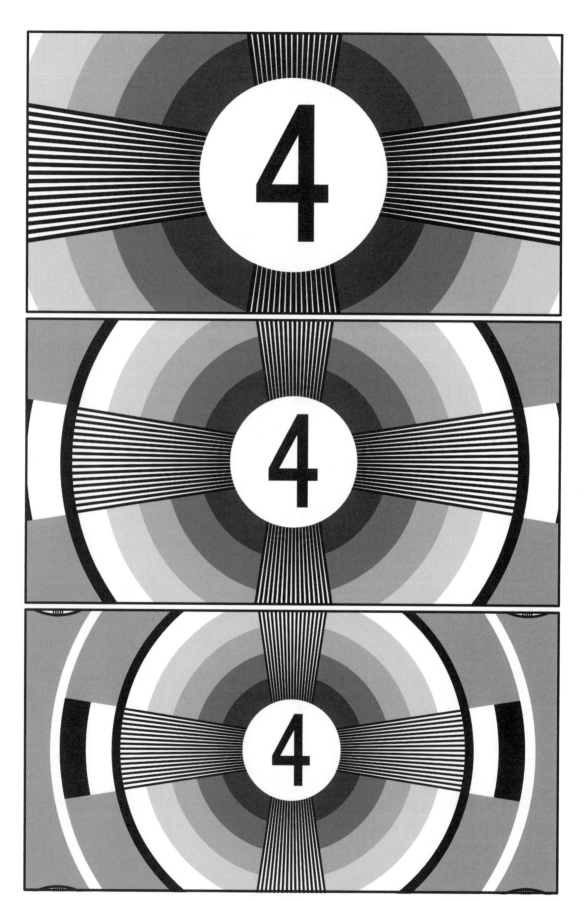

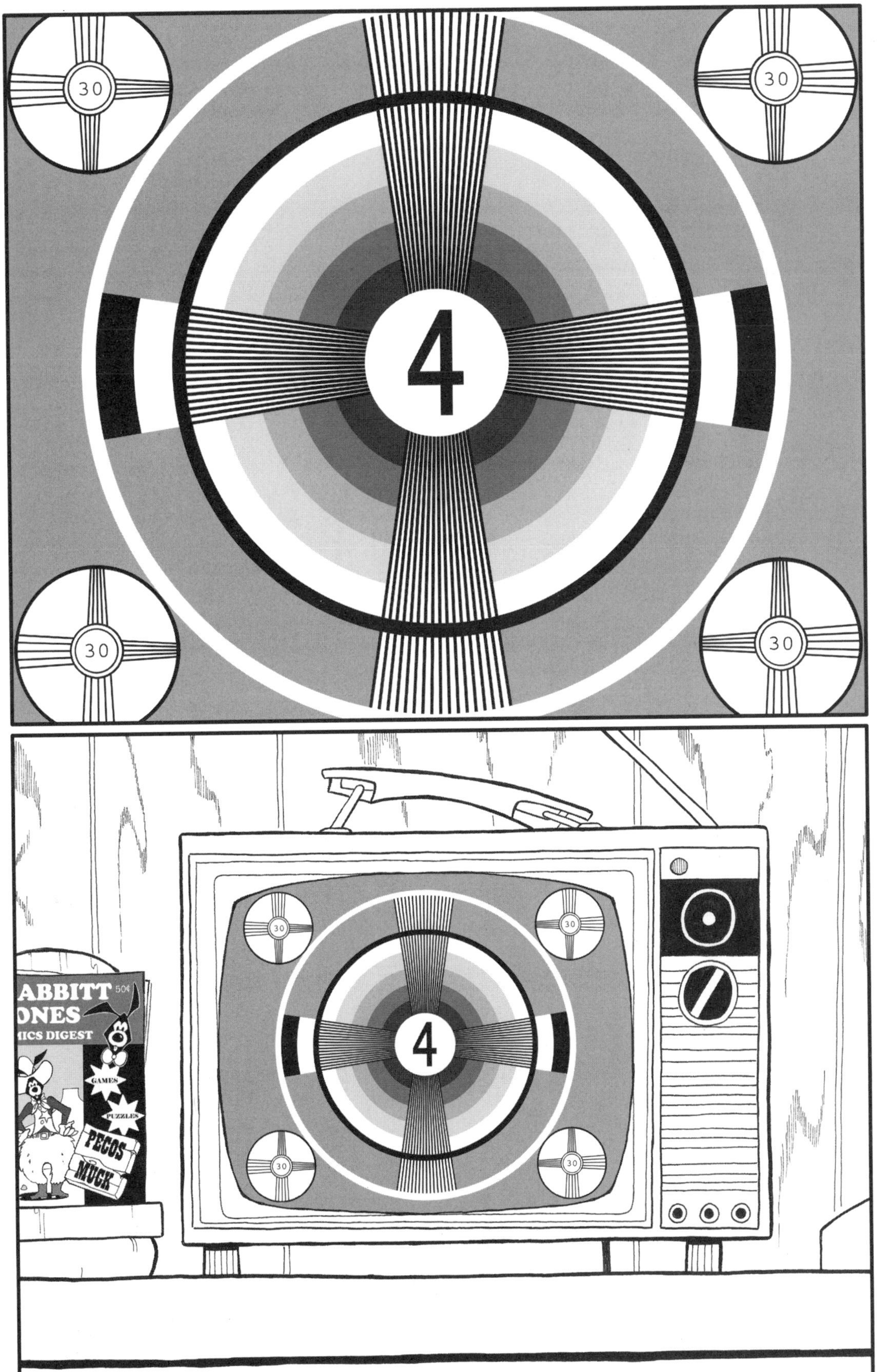
30
30
4
30
30
ABBITT
50¢
ONES
MICS DIGEST
GAMES
PUZZLES
PECOS
MUCK
30
30
4
30
30

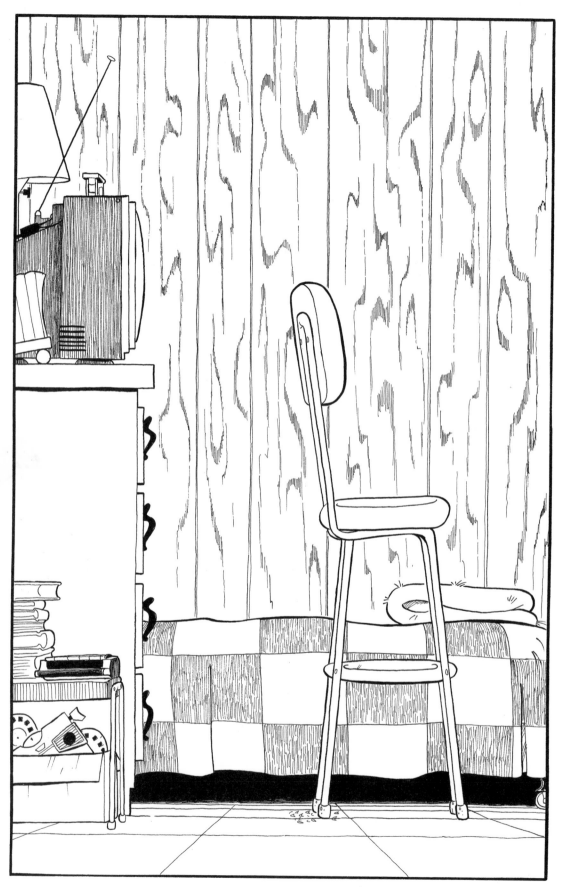

ACKNOWLEDGEMENTS

This book would not be possible without the help of so many people.

- -

I want to thank Carolyn Kozo Cole, Senior Librarian (Ret.),
Photograph Collections, History and Genealogy Department,
Central Library, Los Angeles Public Library, for whose
expertise, encouragement and enthusiasm for this book
I am deeply indebted.

Also I would like to thank John H. Welborne, President of the
Angels Flight Railway Company for giving me permission to use
the images of Angels Flight.

Gillian M. McCarthy, Director of Operations, Grand Performances /
Plaza Commons, Inc. for giving me permission to use the images of
the California Plaza and the Watercourt.

Also Francine Lipsman, General Manager at the Bradbury Building,
Filomena A. Eriman, General Manager at the Grand Central Square
and Robey Mueller, Director of Marketing at the Yellin Company
and the Los Angeles County Metropolitan Transportation Authority.

For legal advice Brandon A. Blake, Blake & Wang P.A.

I am also forever indebted to the great artists and mentors who
have personally inspired me over the years, specifically Ray
Aragon, Dave Dunnet and Frank Frezzo.

And finally, I have these memories of my wife and my family
during the creation of this book – holding hands on Mountain St.,
laughing until our sides ache, lending an ear on a Sunday morning
phone call; this book could not have been completed without the
love and encouragement of my wife Jennifer Yuan, my brothers
Michael Kalesniko and Glen Kalesniko and my parents, who this
book is dedicated to. Thank you all so much.